# OFFICE MANAGEMENT
# and
# CONTROL
The administrative managing of information

# OFFICE MANAGEMENT
## and
# CONTROL The administrative
## managing of information

**GEORGE R. TERRY, Ph.D.**
George A. Ball Distinguished Professor of Business
College of Business
Ball State University

SIXTH EDITION

1970

RICHARD D. IRWIN, INC., Homewood, Illinois
IRWIN-DORSEY LIMITED, Georgetown, Ontario

SIXTH EDITION

*First Printing, March, 1970*

*Second Printing, January, 1971*

Library of Congress Catalog Card No. 72–98252

*Printed in the United States of America*

*To the Memory of*
*My Mother*

# Preface

IN THE FIELD traditionally known as office management, change and evolution continue to make this area one of the most dynamic in our economy. Almost every day brings the announcement of a new office machine, the introduction of a different concept, or the unveiling of a heretofore unheard-of office technique. There appears no end to the already-long line of developments. These efforts continue primarily for one purpose: to enable managers to manage more effectively. Today's manager requires accurate and fresh information upon which to base his decisions, to know in which direction to go, how far, with what resources, and within what cost and time constraints.

The dynamics and the essentiality of the office justify this sixth edition of *Office Management and Control,* a thoroughly updated volume devoted completely to this vital management area. New patterns of thought, new and sharper tools with which to work, and a linking of the many specialized office activities into a coherent whole, feature this new edition. Thus, all major improvements and the most significant of mushrooming new developments are incorporated. In addition, the valuable suggestions and experiences shared by many users of the previous edition were taken into account in reworking, adding, deleting, and reshaping the contents. The result is an office management book thoroughly updated, comprehensive, and useful which (it is believed) meets the requirements of the teacher, student, and practitioner.

Information is a basic and universal need of a manager; it is an integral component of everything he does. To have the proper information, in the proper format, at the proper time and place, is a continuous challenge and in many instances poses problems not easily solved. Getting *what* information to *which* people is a fundamental task of office management. The computer and other office machines are revolutionizing our approaches to information handling. Likewise, innovations in the use of systems and procedures, automated equipment, microform, office work measuring, quality controlling, and employee motivating are sharpening our focus and efficiency in meeting these information requirements. A strong and steady forward-moving trend characterizes office management of today.

The dynamics of office management are stupendous and make this area one of the most exciting fields of managerial study. Several examples will be included here to reveal not only the nature of these changes, but also the type of new material in this edition. Unquestionably, the developments of the centralized computer are absolutely fantastic, but the advent of the "computer facility," with its network of terminal units—some even portable—its direct dialing to computer, and its almost unbelievable transmission of data, is destined to pioneer a new era in information handling. Also staggering the imagination of what the future will be like is the availability of machines that read information at speeds of over 300 book-lines a minute—the equivalent of this entire book in a matter of 80 minutes—without error. Along with this has come an upsurge in the use in optical character-recognition office forms. The day may not be far ahead when office papers as we now know them will be a thing of the past. In addition, the developments in records management are sensational and are contributing enormously to office progress. Illustrative are computer speed output direct to microform, providing almost instantaneous retrieval of information, and the automated microimage retrieving system whereby the contents of over a thousand printed book pages of standard size can be reproduced on two square inches of film. Further, the interesting developments of office landscaping in space planning, the techniques for resolving office organizational conflicts, the effective handling of organizational dysfunctions, and the latest ways of achieving effective motivation are indicative. Office management is on the move.

However, the emphasis in *Office Management and Control,* sixth edition, is not on these dynamics or new techniques, but on the management of information creating, processing, retaining, and distributing, whether manual or machine means are employed. The dynamics within this managerial area add to its challenge and stress the importance of keeping currently informed.

With all this panorama of change, the chief stabilizer of study in office management remains the same, namely, getting the necessary office work done in the best way. This was stated in the first edition, over 20 years ago, and is still true. Hence, the basic objective of this sixth edition remains the same: to present basic principles and successful practices used in getting needed office work accomplished. When new and better practices are developed, their superiority is quickly recognized. Adoptions spread, followed by modifications in the interpretation given the principle involved. But the principle endures, its application and importance varying with the particular situation being confronted.

The title *Office Management and Control* is retained for traditional and continuing purposes. However, *the subtitle The Administrative Managing of Information* has been added. Information is an inclusive term and identifies clearly the product or service with which the office manager deals. Hence, the terms office management and information management are used interchangeably in this book. It is believed the term information management is helpful. Yet the original and older identification, office management, is the generic term, and while perhaps not precisely connoting the managerial area being discussed, it is common and enjoys wide acceptance. Therefore, it is retained in the title.

The main structure on which the material is presented is based upon what a person practicing office management really does. These managerial activities or functions constitute a process commonly termed the management process. Experience with this approach in the past editions attests to its effectiveness and benefits. It provides a basic, complete, and readily comprehended arrangement for the study of this fascinating field of managerial study. Throughout the book are included examples of office operations pertinent to the immediate discussion. As before many helpful charts and illustrations are featured to assist the reader in comprehending the material and to add to its interest.

The presentation of the material is logical and easy to follow. Subjects follow sequentially in an orderly pattern. To begin, an introduction and general review of the office management area is offered. Following this, the work of conceptualizing or mentally determining how the office work will be done is presented. Included are the use, design, and improvement of systems and procedures, and the creating and use of office forms, letters, and reports. With the completion of these visualization concepts, the next consideration is planning the proper processing means to carry out the stated requirements. This entails knowledge of both manual and machine means, especially the proper use of the latest office machines—including the computer. In addition, planning is required in the area of records management, with emphasis given to the storing and retrieving of information and the managing of stored materials and records. Also, planning is required to select the most advantageous office location, space, and arrangement of facilities to provide an attractive appearance and an effective use of the physical facilities. Next, the area of office controlling is discussed. These managerial efforts are performed to ensure that what is planned for takes place. The employment of office standards, the efficient use of office time, and the achievement of desired office quality, quantity, and costs are among the important topics of this part. This is followed by a discussion of office organizing in which the means for getting the office employees to work together effectively are developed. Both the formal and informal organizing are presented in some depth. The special problems of organization as they apply in office management are fully covered. Lastly, the office manager's task of actuating his people to contribute their best efforts willingly is presented. The latest successful practices of office supervising, training, participating, performance appraising, and salary administering are included.

This sixth edition highlights 5 new chapters, a complete revising of 21 chapters, and updating of the remaining 7 chapters. In all, 33 chapters of concise, informative, and interesting office management material is presented. Included to facilitate study are nearly 400 review questions, over one half of which are new, and 83 case problems, 38 of which have never before appeared in print. Retained are only those former questions and case problems applicable to current office conditions or proven to be effective from usage of the previous edition. Thus, ample pertinent material is provided to insure purposeful participation in studying office management and to make it more meaningful and interesting.

Practicing office managers, teachers, and students have assisted me in preparing this edition by their thought-provoking questions, exchange of ideas, suggestions, and words of encouragement. To each of them I express my deep appreciation. Especially to Dr. Loren E. Waltz, School of Business, Indiana University, do I extend my sincere thanks for critically reviewing the previous edition and offering meaningful and important suggestions for its improvement.

*March, 1970*                                    George R. Terry

# Contents

xi

Means. Common Charts of Office Work Simplification. Process Chart. Movement Diagram. Procedure Flow Chart. The Left- and Right-Hand Chart. Production Study Chart. Operator-Machine Activity Chart.

# *part* III Planning for data processing

Terms. Programming. Common Business Oriented Language (COBOL). Coding the Work for Computer Processing. Typewritten or Printed Material on Paper. Binary Mode. Punched Card. Perforated Paper Tape. Magnetic Tape. Information Interchange. Magnetic Tape Ledger Record. Magnetic Ink Characters. The Anatomy of a Computer. Input-Output Units. Memory and Storage Units. Processing Units. Console Controlling Unit.

Attitude toward Work. Office Trade Unions. Organizing White-Collar Employees. Characteristics of Contracts. Labor Management Relations Act of 1947. Additional Important Provisions. Observations about Management-Labor Relations. Research in Actuating Office Employees. Suggestions for Effective Motivating.

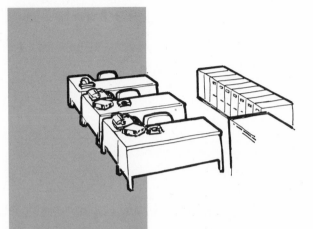

# PART I

# INTRODUCTION

We begin our study of office management with a discussion of what office work is, its reasons for being, and its essential features and characteristics. Following this, the meaning of management and its application to office work are presented. This introductory material consists of Chapter 1 "The role of information management."

# The role of information management

All that mankind has done, thought, gained, or been;
it is lying as in magic preservation in the pages of
books. They are the chosen possession of men.
—*Carlyle*

MAN's greatest tool today is *information*. To identify new markets, to design new products, to make decisions, to keep people informed, and to keep abreast of knowledge requires information. It is not only man's greatest tool, but it is also one of his greatest needs.

Information is required by all members of an enterprise and one of the problems in its management is to determine the nature of the information required, by whom, and in what format. Information is to help; it should assist its recipient in performing his assigned task. A second problem is providing the necessary information at the time and place needed and at a cost compatible with an accepted value criteria. In essence, the acts of collecting, processing, storing, retrieving, and distributing information comprise the function of the "office." In importance this ranks as a major activity, on par with all other essential functions of an enterprise. It is to the management of information that this book is directed. To accomplish this effectively, the professional manager must understand all the considerations that comprise the activity of information administration.[1]

---

[1] It will be helpful to point out here at the beginning of our discussion that the newer term, *information management* is gaining usage in preference to that of the older term, *office management*. The reason is that information management connotes more precisely the current activities of the managerial area being discussed. However, office management is the generic term and enjoys wide acceptance especially by the layman. Therefore, in the spirit of clarification, compromise, and progress, both terms are included in this book and can be considered interchangeable.

## IDENTITY AND NEED FOR INFORMATION

The understanding of information management is aided by adequately comprehending what is being managed, that is, information. Hence, before proceeding with the discussion of information management, we will discuss the vital aspects of information—why it is needed, its types, characteristics, and growth.

Information is meaningful data—words, figures, or symbols—that convey usable knowledge. Data are the raw materials of the office which by means of processing are converted into information. The processing, such as reading, writing, calculating, and sorting, puts the data in a form and relationship that reveals some significance pertinent to the event to which it applies. It is evident that not all data are information and, from the user's viewpoint, some information has far greater value than other information. Records can be considered synonymous with data. Actually there is no uniformity of terminology followed in the field, but the identities given here will serve our purpose satisfactorily.

Information is needed primarily for two major reasons (1) to serve as a discipline, and (2) to provide the basis for decisions. What an individual does depends in great measure upon the information that he receives and the information that he gives. This two-dimensional information flow is significant for its serves as an essential discipline. The flow of information to a person forms the basis for what action he takes; the flow of information from him includes the reporting of results achieved and the fulfilling of his responsibility as a competent member of the enterprise. These efforts stimulate the person to think and act in self-motivating terms. He gains understanding of what he is doing and why, and he develops personal initiative in the performance of his work. The challenge is to design and achieve these informational flows so that all members of a group or of an entire enterprise behave and act in keeping with the master plan. In this sense, complete integration of efforts is won and there is a common bond among all members via the information linkage. In other words, information serves as the essential medium through which various efforts of people of an enterprise are fused together. Thus, information can be called the "catalytic agent" of modern management.[2]

Regarding the second major reason, a manager's job is to achieve stated goals and the degree of his success in this regard is directly dependent upon his making the right decisions at the right time. The basis for right decisions is adequate, accurate, and timely information. Utilizing

---

[2] *Catalytic agent* is a term used in chemistry and means an element the presence of which is necessary to bring about a desired reaction between other elements but which does not itself enter into the reaction. In a similar manner, office work brings about a desired reaction of business elements but does not enter into the reaction itself.

poor information for decision making can lead to deep troubles. The task of meeting informational requirements for sound decisions boils down to determining what information the individual manager needs, when he can use it, where, and in what form. In the final analysis these efforts encompass a host of activities including designing systems, procedures, and office forms; utilizing various types of machines and equipment; and storing and transmitting information. Supplying the proper information is not an end in itself, but a device by which the decision makers get information to help solve their problems. By selecting, rejecting, and coordinating the information, the decision maker converts the information into intelligence and action. Hence, some aptly refer to a manager as an "information converter."

## CLASSES OF INFORMATION

Information is heterogeneous. Different types are employed for different uses and each must be viewed in light of its own peculiar properties. The classifications of information are helpful in understanding and applying information management. One dichotomy of information is *internal and external information,* the names referring to the source of the information generated. Payrolls and products sold are representative of internal information; production plans of a competitor and the status of an order placed with a vendor represent external information. A second classification is *repetitive and nonrepetitive information.* The former is generated at intervals of not less than once a year such as inventory information; the latter includes special studies made to assist managers. Another dichotomy is *active information* which requires its recipient to take some action, and *passive information* which does not, such as notification that a shipment has been made. A last and fourth classification is *past and future information.* Planning requires future information and projection based on past information.

From these classifications, the information manager normally employs generalizations helpful in analyzing the information requirements of an enterprise. To illustrate, the greater the number of management decisions at the higher levels, the greater is the importance of external and future information. Nonrepetitive information is a poor candidate for automation. In contrast, information that is repetitive and active usually offers good possibilities for automation. Further, the properties of timing and accuracy have high priority in active information.

Also suggested is that the information needed by managers is somewhat different in nature from that needed by members of the operating force. Figure 1–1 illustrates this concept. Levels of management are shown with corresponding information requirements.

FIGURE 1–1. Managers' Informational Needs Differ according to Management Levels.

| | Management Levels | | |
|---|---|---|---|
| | *Top* | *Middle* | *Operative* |
| Representative of information required | 1. Special requests<br>2. Substantiation for decisions<br>3. Trends | 1. Controls—cost, quality, and inventories<br>2. Plans to be followed<br>3. Reports on operations | 1. Schedules<br>2. Transactions<br>3. Work instructions |

## CHARACTERISTICS OF INFORMATION

Above all else, information is *facilitating* in that it contributes and aids in accomplishing work considered essential. Information assists in efforts to increase output, lower costs, stimulate employees, pay wages, purchase materials, and ship orders. The individual work of practically every department in an enterprise is implemented by information. For example, a credit department cannot operate successfully without current records of creditors, amounts and dates due, lists of delinquent accounts, credit histories of customers, and a quantity of correspondence.

Closely allied with this facilitating characteristic is the feature of information having a *service* attribute. In and of itself, information serves little purpose. It is, for example, a service to the top executives, to the production department, to the sales department, and to the finance department. Information helps top executives by providing them with data which are necessary in order to manage the enterprise. By means of information, the production department is helped to improve its service and to lower costs, the sales department is aided in its work of selling the product, and the finance department is assisted in maintaining written evidence of the financial status of the enterprise.

Information is *dispersed;* it exists in every department of an enterprise. The swing to office mechanization, and especially to computers, has resulted in much information being generated from a centralized area, but much still is created and used in other areas, for example, in the purchasing, engineering, or inspection department. Furthermore, a milling machine operator in a factory brings into being information in the normal course of his daily duty, and the amount may be considerable if incentive and production control are used. Likewise most salesmen handle sizable amounts of information; and the same is true of many employees of a personnel department.

Figure 1–2 indicates the dispersion of information in the form of papers and the basic functions of business. Selling gives rise to the order entry acknowledgment, and the subsequent paper work flow affects many

FIGURE 1–2. Information in the Form of Papers Permeates an Entire Enterprise.

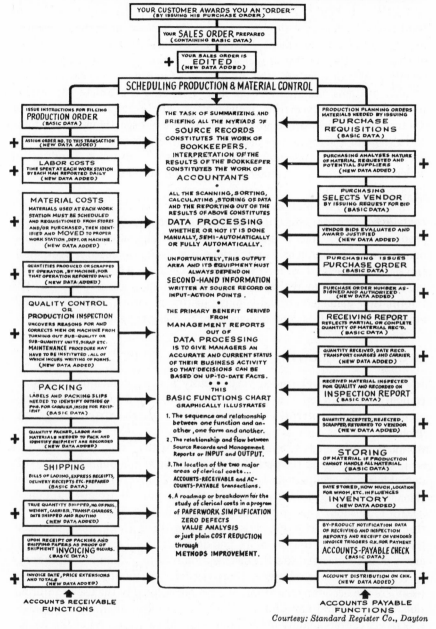

Courtesy: *Standard Register Co., Dayton*

departments, whether the goods are shipped or assembled from stock, or needed raw materials are obtained to take care of the customer's order. What we are saying is that information is dispersed because it is required by people throughout an entire organization, as well as by certain others outside the organization, in order for the enterprise to function effectively.

Further, it should be noted that to a significant degree the *volume* of information is determined by factors outside the control of those performing information management. Illustrative of these factors are the number of shipments, the amount of collections, the number of open accounts, the quantity of sales letters, the number of factory employees, and the number of items manufactured or sold. This unique characteristic makes for problems in information management. For example, provisions for fluctuations in the work load must be provided, even though the timing and extent of the variations usually cannot be accurately forecast. Also, decisions made by noninformation management members, and about which the information manager has little or nothing to say, affect the information volume.

In addition, information is generally characterized as being *an indirect contributor to profit,* since it acts through operative departments such as production, sales, and finance.³ This means that those in information management are frequently on the defensive insofar as justifying expenditures is concerned. It is, for example, unlike sales, where by spending so much it is hoped to realize a resultant gain in sales and profits. The information manager normally must justify his work and its cost and point out wherein it is good management to make the expenditure.

## INFORMATION GROWTH

Information has expanded very rapidly and a number of factors are responsible. High on the list are the growth and complexity of our economy and the enterprises within it. As companies expand, merge, and diversify, there is a greater need for formal information to keep personnel adequately informed. The industrial growth of the United States with its specialization, during the period 1900–1965, shows the number engaged in manufacturing occupations increased from 6 million to 17.8 million, and the number engaged in "service industries" spurted from 4 million to nearly 17 million. This growth brought with it large information expenditures. Another contributing cause is the growth in the number of executives. The trend is toward more management members over specialized areas, and this necessitates the distribution of information to a wide range of executives within relatively short periods. Furthermore, management members are becoming more and more sophisticated in the use of information. They demand more information. The problem of using information effectively centers mainly around questions of the type and of the format in which the information should come to managers. This is the reason for

³ *Profit,* as used here, is the residual income accruing to the owner of an enterprise after he has paid all the economic aids of production—that is, rent on all land used, interest on all capital used, and wages to all labor used.

much of the college student's and the management trainee's work being focused on training for information use, which includes such subjects as systems information, financial data, accounting data, and new analytical techniques.

Probably the most conclusive evidence of information growth is the increase in the number of people performing this type of work. Pertinent data are shown in Figure 1–3. Observe that from 1940 to 1968 the total population increased 52 percent, the total working force expanded 68

FIGURE 1–3. Total Population of the United States, Total Working Force, Number of Clerical Workers, and Percentage of Clerical Workers to Total Working Force for the Years 1870–1968.

| Year | Total Population of the United States | Total Working Force | Clerical Workers | Percentage— Clerical to Total Working Force |
|---|---|---|---|---|
| 1968 | 201,166,000 | 75,920,000 | 12,768,000 | 16.8 |
| 1965 | 194,700,000 | 70,169,242 | 10,963,761 | 15.6 |
| 1960 | 181,057,000 | 66,681,537 | 9,783,632 | 14.6 |
| 1950 | 151,230,000 | 55,835,340 | 6,866,374 | 12.3 |
| 1940 | 131,950,000 | 45,166,083 | 4,612,356 | 10.2 |
| 1930 | 123,080,000 | 48,829,920 | 4,025,324 | 8.2 |
| 1920 | 106,970,000 | 41,614,248 | 3,111,836 | 7.5 |
| 1910 | 92,410,000 | 38,167,336 | 1,718,458 | 4.5 |
| 1900 | 76,090,000 | 29,073,233 | 1,068,993 | 3.7 |
| 1890 | 63,056,438 | 22,735,661 | 801,505 | 3.5 |
| 1880 | 50,262,382 | 17,392,099 | 518,439 | 3.0 |
| 1870 | 39,904,593 | 12,505,923 | 305,502 | 2.4 |

Source: U.S. Government Printing Office publications authored by the following offices of the U.S· Department of Commerce.
Office of Business Economics, *Survey of Current Business* (May, 1969), pp. 5–13, 39; and, Bureau of the Census, *Statistical Abstract, 1965,* pp. 5, 216, 228. *1955 Annual Report on the Labor Force,* pp. 3–5. *1950 Census of Population,* vol. 1: *Population,* pp. 110–12. *Sixteenth Census of the United States, 1940,* vol. 3: *Population,* p. 76. *Fifteenth Census of the United States, 1930,* vol. 5: *Population,* pp. 10–22. *Twelfth Census of the United States, 1900,* Special Reports: "Occupations," pp. 1 and ii.

percent, and the number engaged in clerical occupations increased over 277 percent. In 1940, about one employee in ten was a clerical employee; in 1968, about one in six.

A further reason for the growth in information is the force of competition, both domestic and foreign. The managers of a company, for example, may have to decide where to locate a branch factory or warehouse for maximum marketing impact. The information requirements necessary to reach this decision are large and involve digestion of a considerable number of facts. In addition, the increasing expenditures for research and development, and the resulting new processes and new products, accelerate the need for accurate information on financial needs, production activities, and other phases of a business. In turn, these changes increase the complexity of the information and emphasize the need to schedule efforts economically. In addition, information of various types has been developed because it is required of enterprises by government. In this category are data relating to taxes, and compliance with regulations and numerous legal requirements. Without proper information, managers are unable to comply with the law. Numerous and far reaching, there were in 1968 over 5 million office employees in public administration. There are also many who believe the increasing emphasis upon quantitative techniques of management, the design of systems, and the increase in the number of computers are the basic causes for the growth of information. The term, *information technology movement,* identifies these changes. Further, some portion of the growth in information is undoubtedly due to inadequate efforts to control it. We have been lax in preparing essential information only, in adequate motivation of office employees, and in the development of proper systems, procedures, and methods.

There is an increasing number of organizations active in the area of information and its management. Among the more common are:

Administrative Management Society, 1927 Old York Rd., Willow Grove, Pa. 19090

American Accounting Association, College of Business Administration, University of Iowa, Iowa City, Ia. 52240

American Management Association, 135 W. 50th St. New York, N.Y. 10020

American Records Management Association, 738 Builders Exchange Minneapolis, Minn. 55402

American Society for Personnel Administration, 52 E. Bridge St. Berea, O. 44017

Business Equipment Manufacturers' Institute, 235 E. 42nd St. New York, N.Y. 10037

Conference of American Small Business Organizations, 407 S. Dearborn St. Chicago, Ill. 60605

Data Processing Management Association, 505 Busse Highway, Park Ridge, Ill. 60068

Financial Executives Institute, 50 W. 44th St. New York, N.Y. 10037

National Association of Small Business, 925 15th St. N.W. Washington, D.C. 20005

National Industrial Conference Board, 845 Third Ave. New York, N.Y. 10022

National Records Management Council, 555 Fifth Ave. New York, N.Y. 10017

National Secretaries Association, 1103 Grand Ave. Kansas City, Mo. 64106

Systems and Procedures Association, 24587 Bagley Rd. Cleveland, O. 44138

## THE MANAGEMENT OF INFORMATION

Any enterprise incapable of managing its information requirements is practically certain to find itself in difficulty. Managing information covers the creation, collection, processing, storage, retrieval, transmission, and ultimate destruction of information that appears in a variety of shapes including office forms, reports, directives, and correspondence. It involves the achievement of stated objectives and extends from the inception of

FIGURE 1–4. The Basic Elements Performed on Data.

| Basic Element Performed | Why Performed | Results in: |
|---|---|---|
| 1. Creating | To initiate and bring data into being | Data existence and availability |
| 2. Collecting | To bring together the data for processing or storing | Identity of data location and volume |
| 3. Reading | To interpret data by going over characters, words, and symbols | Awareness of data existence |
| 4. Writing, typing, card punching, or papertape perforating (frequently called *input*) | To facilitate processing by putting data on or in medium, i.e., alphabetical or numerical marks on paper, holes in paper, magnetic areas on tape, and magnetic ink on paper | Start of data processing |
| 5. Recording or printing (frequently called *output*) | To obtain results of processing, the data—in medium form for processing purposes—are converted to form easily read by a human being, if not already in that form | End of data processing |
| 6. Sorting | To classify the data | Data being related to one or more bases |
| 7. Transmitting | To disseminate, give or send out the data | Data availability for specific purpose and place |
| 8. Calculating | To manipulate the data mathematically | Numerical data being added, subtracted, multiplied, or divided |
| 9. Comparing | To check data for accuracy and completeness | Quantitative and qualitative inspection of data |
| 10. Storing | To retain or set aside the data for future use | Data being available when needed |

Note: The meaning of each of the following terms, frequently used in information management, is included in the above listing:

a) *Interpreting* (usually associated with No. 4 or No. 5) is imprinting the meaning of the punched holes in a punched card on that card.

b) *Reproducing* (usually associated with No. 4) is duplicating an exact copy of a punched card.

c) *Collating* (usually associated with No. 6) is merging sets of related data into a single set.

d) *Segregating* (usually associated with No. 6) is separating sets of related data into several sets.

e) *Verifying* (usually associated with No. 9) is determining the accuracy of data.

data or information at a remote point through its passage into the mainstream of the enterprises's processing and handling efforts to its final terminus.

Analysis shows that the supplying of information requires the performance of certain fundamental activities upon data. We will term these activities, basic elements. In any given individual case, a selected predetermined sequence or pattern of these elements is followed in order to obtain information in a form and at a time and place desired. Figure 1–4 shows the ten basic elements along with the corresponding reason each element is performed and the results obtained from it. For example, sorting (number 6) is performed to classify the data and results in the data being related to one or more bases. It would be difficult to overstate the importance of these basic elements. They serve as the nucleus around which all information work revolves.

Information management is, in essence, the application of management to the work associated with these basic elements. Management consists of four fundamental functions or activities including:

**1. Planning.**  To determine mentally a course of action, giving consideration to the factors influencing the particular situation and attempting to indicate future conditions in order to accomplish a desired objective.

**2. Controlling.**  To ascertain what is accomplished, evaluate it, determine the "feedback," and apply corrective measures, if needed, to insure results in keeping with the plan.

**3. Organizing.**  To establish the work environment, divide the work into amounts suitable for efficient performance, appoint personnel to specific positions, provide the necessary materials and machines to perform designated activities, and establish proper work relationships among both the organization units and the personnel.

**4. Actuating.**  To stimulate and maintain the desire of the members of the work group to perform their respective work enthusiastically in order to achieve the predetermined objective in accordance with the plan.

These four fundamental functions are the distinguishing characteristics of management. They apply universally to management, be it production management, sales management, finance management, or information management. They identify the information manager as a member of management. The student of information management will do well to fix these functions in mind for they not only assist in understanding, but also provide an all-inclusive viewpoint of information management activities.

Tying together the concept of the basic elements and the fundamental functions of management, we have the illustration shown by Figure 1–5. Within the area of information represented by the large rectangle are the basic elements. Data are created and collected, then subjected to any or all of the six elements of read, write, record, sort, calculate, and compare. Frequently these six elements are called "processing" the data. Further, the data are either transmitted or stored. If stored, they are ultimately either retrieved or destroyed. Retrieved data are transmitted or reprocessed. Also, some data created and collected are not processed, but transmitted or stored for future use.

The work represented by these various elements is subjected to or constrained by the management forces of planning, controlling, organizing, and actuating. This is illustrated in the figure by the headings listing the major managerial work performed. Controlling, for example, includes the manager taking actions of evaluate, approve, regulate, and correct.

FIGURE 1-5. Information Management In Diagrammatic Form.

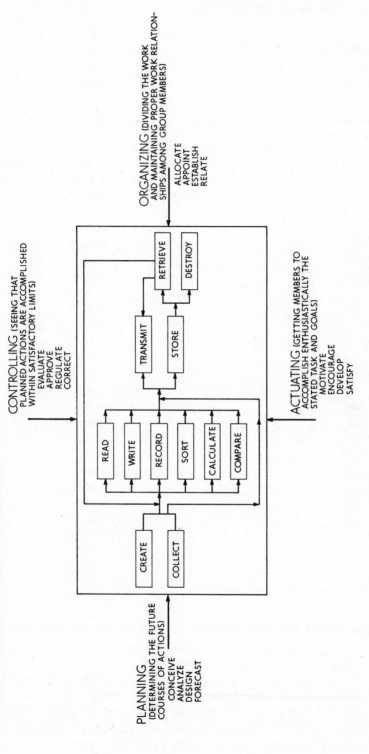

CONTROLLING (SEEING THAT PLANNED ACTIONS ARE ACCOMPLISHED WITHIN SATISFACTORY LIMITS)
EVALUATE
APPROVE
REGULATE
CORRECT

ORGANIZING (DIVIDING THE WORK AND MAINTAINING PROPER WORK RELATIONSHIPS AMONG GROUP MEMBERS)
ALLOCATE
APPOINT
ESTABLISH
RELATE

ACTUATING (GETTING MEMBERS TO ACCOMPLISH ENTHUSIASTICALLY THE STATED TASK AND GOALS)
MOTIVATE
ENCOURAGE
DEVELOP
SATISFY

PLANNING (DETERMINING THE FUTURE COURSES OF ACTIONS)
CONCEIVE
ANALYZE
DESIGN
FORECAST

CREATE
COLLECT

READ
WRITE
RECORD
SORT
CALCULATE
COMPARE

TRANSMIT
STORE

RETRIEVE
DESTROY

## OBJECTIVES

To clarify further the meaning of information management, it is help-ful to observe that management always concerns the achievement of certain desired goals or results. There is a mission to perform, a project to initiate, a service to supply. Examples of objectives include:

1. To furnish necessary and complete information when, where, and to whom it is required for the efficient operation of the enterprise.
2. To process data by the means most appropriate for the enterprise.
3. To provide adequate records and reports at lowest possible cost.
4. To supply accurate paper work and render maximum service to the customer.

Such statements may sound purely academic, but they serve a practical purpose in that they point out the sought-for goal. They define the target. Other objectives, subordinate but related to the overall goal, can be used to designate the aims for specific office groups or individuals.

Information objectives can be classified as pertaining primarily to (1) service, (2) social responsibilities, or (3) profit. Service is of great impor-tance because information work is done to assist others in doing their work more effectively. Also of significance is the objective dealing with social responsibilities which stresses the attainment of the goal in accord-ance with certain moral and ethical codes as set forth by the industry and society in which the enterprise operates. Lastly objectives emphasizing profit or gain assist in getting the work done effectively and for relatively low expenditures.[4]

Objectives should be specific, preferably in measurable terms for maxi-mum contribution in channeling efforts. "Reduce paper work costs by 10 percent this year" has more value than the simple, "Improve paper work efforts." Objectives may be specific or general, written or unwritten, long or short term, temporary or permanent, or applicable to certain segments of the enterprise or to the office only. Whatever their form or content, objectives are set and accepted, for without them the meaning of manage-ment becomes nebulous and there is no satisfactory basis for determining the effectiveness of the managerial efforts.

## ADDITIONAL CONSIDERATIONS OF INFORMATION MANAGEMENT

Information management is a distinct entity; it can be studied, and proficiency in it can be attained. Management is not a person or a group of people. One who performs the activity of management is a manager.

---

[4] The concept of profit as the objective of any enterprise or segment of an enterprise is actually quite limited. Profit, as such, can be the indirect or the direct aim, depending upon the thinking of the particular company involved. Profit is residual in nature, a by-product resulting from other direct goals.

Hence, those who perform planning, controlling, organizing, and actuating in the information work area are information managers. The use of these four fundamental functions of management marks the essential difference between a clerk and an information manager, or between an accountant and the manager of the accounting department. Knowing how to write letters, for example, is not sufficient to manage the correspondence department.

A schematic drawing of management is shown by Figure 1–6. The objectives are shown on the right. They are accomplished by utilizing the basic resources available to a manager, the so-called six M's, shown on the left of the figure. The information manager subjects the six M's to planning, controlling, and organizing. The men, or members of the work group, are actuated to want to achieve the objectives and help insure that the end results will be the stated objectives.

From what has been stated, it follows that information management can be defined as *the planning, controlling, and organizing of information work, and actuating those performing it so as to achieve predetermined objectives.* It deals with the life cycle of business data and information from their creation through their processing, distributing, and ultimate destroying, if obsolete. This concept of information is broad and inclusive; it includes managerial efforts over information work anywhere in an enterprise. Further, it suggests that decision making is imperative in information management. Planning, controlling, organizing, and actuating exist and have virile meaning only when adequate and effective decision making is practiced.

In this discussion we have followed what is known as the *management process approach,* in which management is viewed as an activity made up of four essential functions. Currently, this is the widely used approach to management study. However, there are other approaches that are making significant contributions and modifying our concepts about management. Some emphasize the behavior of the human being as the focal point of management thought. They constitute the *human behavior approach* to management thinking. The impact of what is achieved and why is viewed in relationship to people. The unit is considered a sociopsychological being and applications of behavioral sciences are stressed. There is also the *systems management approach* in which most activities are considered as components of systems. Related activities constitute a system and form a unity among the various parts. In essence a systematic framework for describing and working with interdisciplinary knowledge is provided and the conception of multitudinous activities with which a manager must work is expedited. Systems and systems management are very helpful in the study of information management as will be discussed in some detail in the next several chapters of this book. There is also the *scientific approach* to management thought which has greatly enriched our current practices in all management areas. In this school, management is based on

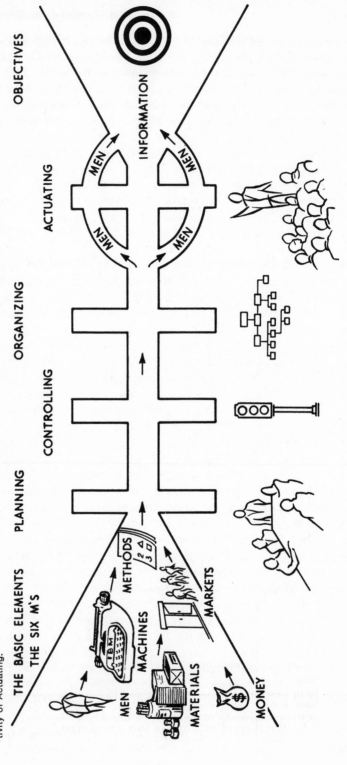

FIGURE 1–6. The Objectives of the Information Work Are Obtained by Subjecting the "Six M's"—Men, Materials, Machines, Methods, Money, and Markets—to the Application of the Managerial Functions of Planning, Controlling, and Organizing, and, in Addition, Subjecting the Basic Element of Men to the Activity of Actuating.

science, or an organized body of knowledge, derived by accumulation and acceptance of the understanding of truth by discovery utilizing the scientific method. The steps of this method are shown in Figure 1–7. In a sense, it can be summarized as controlled experimentation, since a tentative solution to a stated problem is tried out under specific and known conditions. Another approach in management is the *quantitative measurement* school of thought. Here management is looked upon as a logical entity expressible in terms of measurable units and mathematical relationships, i.e., in models or formulas. Operations research, linear program-

FIGURE 1–7. The Scientific Method Consists of Well-Defined Steps.

| BASIC ACTION | STEPS | |
|---|---|---|
| CREATE | 1. RECOGNIZE THE PROBLEM | |
| | 2. MAKE PRELIMINARY OBSERVATIONS AND ANALYSIS | |
| | 3. DRAW UP A HYPOTHESIS OR TENTATIVE SOLUTION TO THE PROBLEM | |
| PROVE | 4. MAKE A THOROUGH AND DETAILED ANALYSIS | |
| | 5. COLLECT ADEQUATE DATA | |
| | 6. CLASSIFY THE DATA COLLECTED | |
| | 7. MAKE A TENTATIVE ANSWER TO THE PROBLEM | |
| CONCLUDE | 8. TEST THIS SOLUTION OR ANSWER | |
| | 9. ADJUST IN LIGHT OF RESULTS UNDER STEP 8. | |
| | 10. STATE THE ANSWER TO THE PROBLEM | |

ming, and simulation are typical of the techniques used. The views of this management approach are followed in the utilization of computers. While currently somewhat limited in the total area of information management, applications of quantitative measurement thinking appear destined to continue their expansion in this area of management.

## INFORMATION MANAGEMENT ACTIVITIES

The activities included in information management are quite numerous; among them are the following:

1. Determining what information is to be made available, where, and to whom.
   a) Develop adequate systems, procedures, and methods.
   b) Apply work simplification to clerical work.
   c) Design information formats utilizing effective office forms, reports, and letters.
   d) Coordinate the work of the office with that of the nonoffice.
2. Deciding the type of processing to be used.
   a) Select and utilize information machines.
   b) Establish integrated data processing (IDP).
   c) Use source data automation (SDA).
   d) Distribute the information properly.
3. Following effective records management.
   a) File records and reports.
   b) Maintain information of permanent value, destroy obsolete material.
   c) Specify amount and place of copying information.
4. Supplying the office space and environment.
   a) Arrange the office layout—location of machines and equipment.
   b) Determine effective work environment—adequate lighting, elimination of noise, and proper ventilation.
   c) Select the office location.
5. Measuring and evaluating the information work.
   a) Establish office standards.
   b) Write office manuals.
   c) Time-study clerical operations.
   d) Maintain quality of information work.
   e) Schedule and dispatch information work.
   f) Keep information costs within acceptable limits.
   g) Prepare office budget.
6. Establishing and maintaining an effective office organization.
   a) Utilizing both the formal and the informal organization.
   b) Supplying proper organizational relationships.
   c) Providing organizational continuity and balance.

*c*) Motivate information employees.
7. Inspiring the information personnel to do the best of which they are capable.
   *a*) Give adequate supervision.
   *b*) Conduct information training programs.

## THE CHALLENGE OF INFORMATION MANAGEMENT

Abundant and attractive opportunities exist in the field of information management. The increasing importance and the rapid growth in this area emphasize the need for managers. And the work is extremely challenging. Among the more exciting challenges are (1) developing a greater appreciation for information among management members, (2) applying greater creativity to information management, (3) reducing the amount of unnecessary paper work performed, (4) improving information systems, (5) using effectively the "automated office," (6) establishing more and better information standards, (7) developing better means of motivating clerical employees, and (8) attracting and acquiring the better graduates from schools for information work.

New careers are appearing for those trained in information management. Indeed, the future is brilliant for the competent information manager who can contribute significantly to the successful operation of the entire enterprise. Information systems, computer programming, and records managing are further indications of areas where the demand for qualified personnel is high. There are also a wide variety of staff services dependent upon the individual enterprise's needs. Major qualifications include analytical ability, a thorough knowledge of general management, an appreciation of the work performed by various operating areas of an enterprise, and knowledge of systems and data processing.

A growing number of firms have established an executive position of "vice president of management services" or "manager—information center" or "administrative services manager" or "information manager" and under it have designated middle managers such as systems manager, data processing manager, archives manager, and office services manager. All of these deal with information requirements and development throughout the entire enterprise and coordinate their efforts into an effective unity of information services.

Justification for use of these titles is that they are more descriptive of the current managing of information and better denote the companywide range of activities dealing with information. Simply stated, they are another change in the current evolution taking place in information management. Demanded are new approaches and patterns of thought. Fresh viewpoints and contributions of information technologists, information administrators, and trained paper-work analysts are reshaping the concept of the information manager's role. He is proving himself to be an indispensable adjunct and meriting top management status by his gaining greater and greater recognition and occupying an increasingly vital role in the overall management of the enterprise.

## QUESTIONS

1. What is the meaning and the importance of information from the viewpoint of the modern office manager?
2. Select three common types of paper work found in an office with which you are familiar; and, for each type, name the basic elements of data processing required to prepare the paper work.
3. Briefly identify each of the following:
   *a*) Information management.
   *b*) Output of data.
   *c*) Specific objectives.
   *d*) Basic elements performed on data.
4. In your own words relate what Figure 1–5 shows.
5. Visit an office with which you are familiar and find out its major objectives. What do you deduce from the information obtained.
6. Can office work do a service job without being facilitating? Can it be facilitating without doing a service job? Explain.
7. Point out the essential difference between the management process approach and the systems management approach. Between the quantitative measurement school of management thought and the scientific approach to management thought.
8. What is meant by the statement, "Office work is a service work"? Of what importance is this in office management?
9. Do you agree with the following statement? "To achieve objectives requires action. This being true, planning can be considered nonproductive because nothing is achieved simply by planning." Elaborate on your answer.
10. What is your opinion regarding the future growth of office work?
11. Discuss five current major challenges of information management.
12. Relate an experience in some phase of business, preferably dealing with office work, which illustrates poor controlling.

## CASE PROBLEMS

### Case 1–1.  Solso-Hastings, Inc.

Business has not been good for Solso-Hastings, Inc. and three weeks ago, Mr. Allan Marshall, vice president in charge of sales in the New York district was promoted to president of the corporation. His record in New York was outstanding and it was generally believed that Mr. Marshall was the most competent manager the corporation had. Now ten days in his new job and office at the Chicago headquarters, he has found out that (1) net profits of the corporation were $107,000 a month a year ago and for the past month were $61,700, (2) sales have dropped $425,000 during the past year to a current level of $4,600,000 annually, (3) cost of purchased items have increased almost 11 percent during the past six months, and (4) labor costs are incomplete and no definite statement can be made about them. Current reports show favorable public reaction to the corporation's new products, advertising expenditures are up about 6 percent over last year, and accounts receivable reached an all-time high level of $1,043,000, roughly an increase of 8 percent over last year.

From his own personal experience and from conversations with the Chicago vice president of sales and the Los Angeles vice president of sales (via long distance telephone), Mr. Marshall concluded that deliveries are too slow, production promises mean very little for they are not kept, credit records of the corporation maintained by the Chicago central office do not reflect current data, and faulty material is being shipped—the present production quality control is inadequate. Mr. Otto Getzdanner, vice president of production at the Chicago main plant, points out that rush orders have become the rule, not the exception, and are accepted even though production facilities are taxed to capacity, sales personnel do not allow sufficient time to fulfill orders, and the cancellation of a customer's order takes excessively long to reach the factory, frequently being received several days after the order has been shipped.

From several lengthy talks with Mr. Daniel Heckmann, the director of information, Mr. Marshall is informed that the office is insufficiently staffed. Six months ago an order to economize was issued to him by the past president. Since then several office people have left the corporation claiming they secured higher paying jobs for the same work with other employers. No attempt was made to keep them by adjusting salaries or operating budgets. Mr. Heckmann states he has experienced great difficulty in acquiring competent help.

Mr. Marshall believed some long-range planning was needed, but before this could get underway, he asked Mr. Heckmann to take corrective actions immediately to help improve the company's present poor condition. Accordingly, Mr. Heckmann took these measures:

1. Hired an additional two male clerks and three female clerks.

2. Wrote a personal note to each office employee stating that both the quality and the quantity of the office work for each employee must be improved.

3. Stated that all office supervisors would become working supervisors in order to locate sources of mistakes in papers being prepared. Any employee caught preparing an incorrect billing or invoice would be given five demerits. A total of 15 demerits means automatic employment termination.

4. Indicated his greater involvement in the credit department to improve the work of credit extensions and collecting past due accounts.

## Questions:

1. What is the main problem in this case?
2. What is your opinion regarding the measures taken by Mr. Heckmann?
3. What action do you recommend the company take? Why?

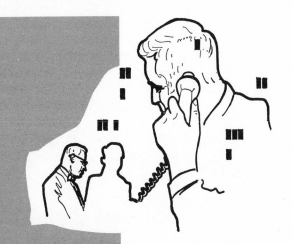

# PART II

# CONCEPTUALIZING THE WORK TO BE DONE

The initial step in office management is to visualize the manner in which the necessary work is to be accomplished. This requires considerable time, thought, and creativity. Extensive trial and error approaches are typical in these efforts. Logically the efforts start with the design and improvement of office systems and progress to procedures, methods, and finally to the media to carry the information such as office forms, letters, or reports.

Five chapters cover this important area and include "Systems design and integrating information," "Systems improvement and total systems concept," "Office work simplification—procedures and methods," "Information media—forms and records," and "Information media—letters and reports."

chapter **2**

# Systems design and integrating information

> There is no great achievement that is not the result of patient working and waiting.
>
> —*Josiah Holland*

INFORMATION management is strongly influenced by the use of systems. The so-called systems approach is popular for it is not only extremely helpful in meeting the need for fast and accurate information, but also has made possible the effective use of modern technological facilities to process data. Without systems, we would not be able to use the powerful information machines that are available.

The initial effort of the information manager is *to conceptualize* the work required in order to supply the information wanted. These conceptualizing efforts currently are made up of three different yet interrelated areas: (1) systems, (2) data processing, and (3) records management. The activities in these three areas comprise the *major planning efforts of information management.* That is, our study of managing information begins with planning, with deciding what information is given to whom and why (systems), with deciding what data is processed and how (data processing), and what information is made available to whom and when (records management). Some believe just two—systems and data processing—are adequate, but when this arrangement is followed, records management is considered under data processing. We prefer to show records management as a third area because it has a distinct identity and utilizes techniques quite apart from those commonly included and understood under data processing.[1]

---

[1] Part IV of this book deals with records management.

## SYSTEMS AND INFORMATION MANAGEMENT

There is nothing new about the concept of systems. It is as old as mankind. Early in life we become acquainted with the solar system and later discover that we ourselves have digestive, nervous, and circulatory systems. In business, reference is commonly made to the inventory control system, the sales-analysis system, the payroll system, and so forth. These systems are among the first applications handled by electronic data processing.

From the information management viewpoint, a system can be looked upon as a vehicle of thought and analysis. It is an attitude or way of viewing projects and problems. A system has been called a "think process tool." This identity stresses system as providing the medium of thought and conceptualization. Systems imply utilization of an encompassing approach, yet retention of and regard for the components making up the entirety employed.

The systems concept is part of man's need and desire to sharpen his conceptual tools for solving his informational problems. Information machines including computers with their capacity, versatility, and speed cannot in and of themselves supply the answers. They enable man to solve informational problems that heretofore were beyond his scope. Now he has the technical means available, but to utilize them, he must upgrade his conceptual horizons, identify critical informational problems, conceive the solutions to these problems, and evaluate their potential gain. In these efforts, systems are vital.

### SYSTEM IDENTIFIED

According to Webster a system is "a regularly interacting or interdependent group of items forming a unified whole." In information management the term, *system,* is widely used to designate a network of related procedures linked together in such a manner as to accomplish a specific activity. More specifically, *a system is a network of procedures which are integrated and designed to carry out a major activity.*

In many instances, an ordinary activity, commonly viewed as a single activity, is in reality made up of many different and relatively less important activities. Upon close examination we recognize the existence of an orderly relationship of some sort among these various lesser activities making up the entirety. And we discover that the interaction among the lesser actions or parts is necessary so that the entirety or end product performed is in keeping with accomplishing a given goal. Systems-minded people have been viewing problems in this light for many years.

Figure 2–1 illustrates graphically an activity common in business and

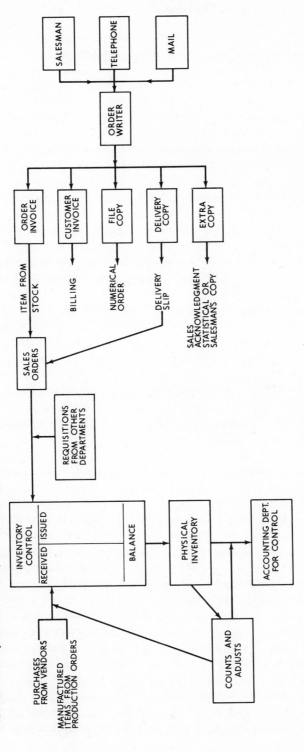

FIGURE 2-1. A System of Inventory Control and Sales.

one familiar to most of us. It shows the various activities making up a system of materials. In other words to ensure adequate amounts of the right types of materials being on hand, we follow a system designed to supply the proper information on certain activities to selected people who take action based on the information supplied. As indicated in the upper left portion of the figure, parts are either (1) purchased from outside suppliers or (2) made by ourselves. Either of these actions requires a number of activities such as determining and notifying the vendor, following up on deliveries, and checking prices or costs. The left central portion of the figure shows that the receipts of what is supplied are balanced with what is needed, as revealed by sales orders and requisitions from other departments. Shipments of sales orders are made from storeroom supply. A level of inventory is maintained to permit taking care of the sales orders in this manner. In addition, control of physical counts and the supplying of data to the accounting department are included in the system. Likewise, the various actions arising from sales orders are included on the chart (right portion).

This all appears simple enough, but note that a single entry on this chart, such as purchases from vendors, or sales orders, entail a whole series of actions involving paper work. We use a term to identify such a sequence of actions for achieving a definite type of information. It is *office procedure.*

Hence, this system of materials consists of three distinct procedures including (1) the procedure for purchasing from vendors or obtaining from our manufacturing facilities, (2) the procedure for determining the physical inventory on hand, and (3) the procedure for issuing for sales orders which are shipped from the storeroom supply. System supplies an orderly relationship among these procedures and the totality and also among the components of each procedure. The large overall picture is included, yet the interrelations of the various components making up this large picture are each given their proper attention both within the part itself and in its relation to the entirety. That is, the efficiency of each part, as well as the concern for the overall performance of the whole, is retained. The systems approach brings integration of related activities. Information which used to be considered and handled as separate entities is brought together. Fragmentation of information is minimized. Highlighted is the composite end result of many different informational activities working in many different ways. We consider the components as a dynamic totality or interaction of parts which is more important than the components themselves.

It is helpful to note that *a definite order* permeates every component of a system. By order is meant conformity to a predetermined mode and nothing can operate outside this particular sphere. This means adherence to predetermined schedules and explains why interruptions and special requests usually bring havoc to data processing. Adaption is also essential. Any factor incorporated into a system must be malleable so that it can, if necessary, be fused into the order or conformity required by the system. Further, collective existence of a system's components emphasizes adaption by them to the system's environment.

## ESSENTIAL MAKE-UP OF SYSTEMS DESIGN

The work of systems design can be conveniently divided into four major parts (1) performing major administrative tasks, (2) determining the requirements of the system, (3) performing the designing function, and (4) evaluating the system designed. Each of these parts include several important subheadings as shown by Figure 2–2. This figure suggests the approximate time frequently required to conduct each of the various major activities necessitated by systems design work. The length of the horizontal bar opposite each heading indicates the estimated length of time required to perform the respective work. For example, to establish objectives requires one month, to designate responsibilities takes one and one-half months. Some of these activities can overlap, others require

FIGURE 2–2. Major Activities in Systems Design.

| ACTIVITY | MONTHS |
|---|---|
| | 0  1  2  3  4  5  6  7  8  9  10  11  12 |
| 1. ADMINISTRATIVE TASKS | |
|    a. Establish objectives | |
|    b. Desginate responsibilities and policies | |
|    c. Define system constraints | |
| 2. REQUIREMENTS OF SYSTEM | |
|    a. Gather facts | |
|    b. Organize facts | |
|    c. Evaluate facts | |
|    d. Establish system premises | |
| 3. DESIGN OF SYSTEM | |
|    a. Consider various possibilities | |
|    b. Investigate tradeoffs | |
|    c. Decide on extent of mechanization | |
|    d. Weigh personnel preferences | |
| 4. EVALUATE THE SYSTEM | |
|    a. Review overall arrangement | |
|    b. Check company and manager requirements | |
|    c. Approve proposed system | |

completion of certain predecessor activities before starting. According to the illustration, it requires 12 months from the beginning of establishing objectives to the ending or agreement to system at the conclusion of "approve proposed system." The total time required will vary with the size, complexity, and urgency of the particular situation.

## ADMINISTRATIVE TASKS

Among the first administrative tasks is to establish the objectives. In most instances this is initially performed by a top management group of select members. A simple and general statement is: provide whatever information is required to the recipient in order to fulfill the facilitating and servicing informational needs. This resolves into what information is to be supplied to whom by the system. Further, is the goal also one of reducing present cost, is providing for future growth an important consideration, is more mechanization to be used, and is competition to be equaled or exceeded? At the start of system design, these identifications of objectives are necessarily couched in broad, inclusive, and general terms. However as the system design progresses, more finite objectives are developed. The exhaustive inquiry for needed information, by whom, when, and in what format uncovers specific goals of information that assist in the creative systems work. But the task of defining objectives must not be compounded. The true objective for an accounts receivable system is to collect money. Net results, costs, and machine availability tend to suffer when statements of objectives become too numerous and too sophisticated.

It is essential that proper designation of those responsible for the system design along with their responsibilities be established early in the program. A growing popular approach is for the top management group to appoint a committee composed of both operating and systems personnel. The former, or operating personnel, provide part-time study participation, assist in defining output requirements, and aid in training operative employees to meet the standards required. The systems personnel conduct the study, evolve the system, and provide the technical support required to maintain the integrity of the informational efforts expended. The committee is guided by and reports to the top management group. Justification for this arrangement is that systems work has become too complex and too important to concentrate it in the hands of one or two persons. Further, a person from each department or representing several departments formally designated to serve as a system liaison makes for system adequacy, acceptance, and affinity.

The committee also needs to establish policies to serve as a guide for decisions in creating the system. What is the policy concerning the continual employment of current personnel, the startup and conversion cost allocations, the extent of business machine usage, and whether to rent or to buy machines? The need for these policies will increase in importance when the proposed system is in operation. They merit careful consideration in the early stages of systems design.

## CONSTRAINTS OF SYSTEM

Another administrative task is the definition of the proposed system's constraints. Even though tentative, boundaries must be established to define the scope of the study and possible limits of the system. The boundaries serve to establish the framework within which the system

FIGURE 2–3. Chart for Assisting in Determining the Scope of a System.

| NAME OF DEPARTMENT | NO. OF EMPLOYEES | OBJECTIVES | FUNCTIONS PERFORMED | CONTROLS | ORGANIZATION | INPUT | OUTPUT | PROCESSING MEANS |
|---|---|---|---|---|---|---|---|---|
| Market Research | 8 | ✓ | ✓ | | | | | |
| Billing | 17 | | | ✓ | ✓ | | ✓ | |
| Sales | 26 | | ✓ | . ✓ | | | | |
| Purchasing | 9 | ✓ | ✓ | | | | ✓ | |
| | | | | | | | | |

evolved will operate. Any statement of system boundaries depends upon objectives sought and these, in turn, are dependent upon the definition of the proposed system and its content. This definition becomes the initial goal of the system designer. Such requirements can be classified as those which are (1) legal—required by law; (2) operational—required for profitable or serviceable operations; and (3) contractual—required by the customer or outsider to the enterprise.

In some instances, suggestions and specific wishes of top managers are supplied the systems designer. In effect, these serve as constraints for they restrict the scope of certain portions of the proposed system. For example, the chart of Figure 2–3 indicates certain areas for special attention of the designer. Departments are listed along with the respective number of employees. To the right, heading up the several columns are items which might warrant investigation and study. For example, opposite market research, the check mark under functions performed indicates some question about the clarity or feasibility of the activities of this department.

The check mark under organization opposite billing department means that the organization form or the relationship of the billing department to the total organization of the enterprise should be analyzed. A chart like this can be helpful, but admittedly is quite likely to be meager at the initial stage of the system design. In fact, both constraints and objectives are often incomplete at the beginning of systems design, but we make assumptions and the best decisions we can, realizing they can be questioned and revised as our design work progresses.

## REQUIREMENTS OF SYSTEM

Once the administrative tasks are completed, work can start in determining the requirements of the system. For example, to improve an existent system, we would want to know what departments are currently being used, what is the flow of information, how do users evaluate the present information means, and what improvements would they like to see made. An orderly methodology should be followed, otherwise the gathering of data will be chaotic and wasteful. It is possible to playact the part of a piece of paper being processed and trace every step in sequence from origination to its final processing. This is commonly called the "hound-dog" approach. In contrast, the start of getting facts can be made at the final processing stage and subsequently working backwards to the initiation of each document. Or it is sometimes convenient to begin at any point and work forward to the final step or backward to the first step. This is a common approach as exemplified by correcting a bottleneck or backlog in the information flow.

Facts are where you can find them, but care must be exercised in selecting the facts and the sources that are utilized. Experience helps the planner to be knowledgeable in facts selected, but even lacking experience he can proceed to gather many facts which will be helpful. The following fruitful sources are suggested:

*1. Organization Charts and Manuals.*   Organization charts give only sketchy details. However, with organization manuals, they indicate what activities are grouped together, probable authority of the respective members, and the tasks performed. Compiling a list of the tasks performed is especially recommended. From such a list, the identity of the work being done, where it is done, and possible duplications can be ascertained.

*2. Systems and Flows of Information.*   Every pertinent and available file on these subjects can be a source of pertinent information. They reveal the manner of work performance currently and in the past. More important, they indicate the managers' probable preferences. In addition, their general quality regarding accuracy, timeliness, and completeness gives clues as to the status of information handling in the particular enterprise. Usually they also provide valuable information on the paper forms being used; hence, helpful details are supplied.

**3. Observation of Work.** This source is always used and is reliable. Data collected by this means may be compared with data obtained from other sources for purposes of verification. Effective observation requires the knack of purposive watching and a concentration on meaningful actions. This takes some practice, as most laymen are not skilled in observing effectively.

**4. Study of Accounting Data.** Valuable material applying to existing cost and other financial controls is obtained from this source. Leads as to what information is considered important, how compiled, and how used are obtained. Sometimes partial, incomplete, or rejected accounting systems are found and for certain types of problems such information proves helpful.

**5. Talks with Supervisors and Operative Employees.** People who are involved currently in processing the data can be helpful. Conversations with personnel normally should be withheld until last because the system designer will then be more certain what questions to ask, better prepared for the interview—particularly important for noncooperative people—and can thus reduce the time required for the interview. Not all interviews proceed according to plan, however, and the designer may be forced to change his line of questioning or its sequence. Figure 2–4 gives some do's

FIGURE 2–4. Do's and Don't's of Interviewing to Obtain Information for System Design.

| *Do's* | *Don't's* |
|---|---|
| 1. Do make preparation for the interview; be familiar with and have with you organization charts, manuals, position descriptions, flow charts, and the like. | 1. Don't interrupt the respondent while he is answering your question or giving you information. |
| 2. Do radiate a friendly and genuinely helpful interest in the respondent and an appreciation of his helping you to obtain needed information. | 2. Don't let statements not understood go by; terminate the interview only after you have a clear understanding of the issue. |
| 3. Do keep the interview focused on securing data and facts pertinent to the system design. | 3. Don't ask questions that can be answered yes or no unless you want an opinion. |
| 4. Do take notes and be a good listener. | 4. Don't play the role of a consultant and suggest solutions to problems posed; this is not the purpose of your interview. |
| 5. Do ask questions designed to verify answers secured from this and other sources. | 5. Don't argue; if violent differences arise, change the subject area and avoid returning to the controversial area for awhile. |
| 6. Do leave the interview feeling you were the interviewer, not the interviewee. | 6. Don't ignore time; be ready to interview at the appointed time and terminate it promptly when the information is obtained or the allotted time expires. Arrange a second interview, if necessary. |

and don't's that apply to talking with supervisors and operative employees.

Attention is called to the fact that the use of questionnaires is not included in the above list. Why not use questionnaires? Primarily because they are very difficult to design and are probably never inclusive of all the information which it is found subsequently must be obtained. Also, the questionnaire method is slow, the total cost high, due mainly to the need for editing and interpreting the information, and many employees object to filling out questionnaires. However, questionnaires are acceptable when a relatively small amount of information is wanted from a large, dispersed group.

**6. Business Machine Manufacturers.** Today almost all data processing includes some mechanization. Even so-called manual operations include a typewriter, perhaps a device to assist in sorting cards, and frequently a filing cabinet. The machine utilization can extend in varying degrees all the way to an "automated system" employing the most sophisticated computers and peripheral machine units. Certainly the manner in which the data will be processed affects the system designed. Therefore, it is imperative that the systems designer be familiar with what is available and for what applications specific business machines and equipment are recommended. An effective source for this type of information is the business machine manufacturers who are very cooperative in supplying their assistance. Also, machine users may be interviewed or observation of their installed units may be conducted. When the machine is quite complicated, the systems designer may seek the help of the specialist in the particular business machine area.

## ORGANIZE AND EVALUATE FACTS

The data secured from the previous step will be, for the most part, a mass of pieces of information, forms, papers, reports, and ideas. They must be related or classified in order to be used effectively. Precisely how the accumulated information should be organized depends upon the makeup of the particular study. It should be emphasized, however, that at this point we are not trying to design the system; we are simply trying to get the information we have in an orderly and easily understood arrangement.

Graphic representation of data is usually easier to comprehend than that in written form. If the data and facts were not collected in graphic form, it is helpful to convert into this type of format. By this means the interrelationships of data will be revealed, duplicated data can be identified and discarded, and a composite picture of fairly large portions of information is gained. When detailed information is needed, the use of symbols on a graphic chart is advantageous. Flow charts of various types, process charts, operation charts, man-machine, and work distribution charts are popular.

A flow chart of bank credit cards is illustrated by Figure 2–5. In this case, the names of the interested parties are across the top. By following the arrow lines, the information work involved in handling bank card

FIGURE 2–5. Flow Diagram of Bank Credit Cards.

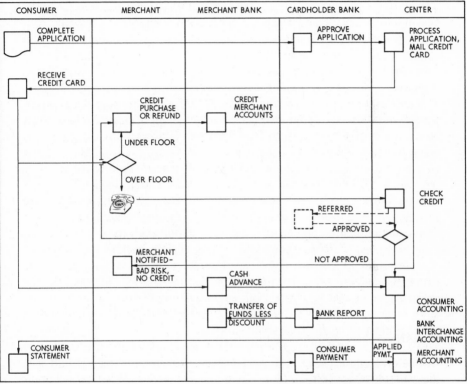

*Courtesy: Burroughs Corp., Detroit*

credit is depicted. It is helpful to add that participating banks are joined to the system's computer enabling a member bank to provide an almost immediate approval or rejection to a merchant inquiring about a cardholder's account. Also provided is an automated interchange of data and a daily net dollar exchange report for principal and associate institutions. This report shows the net amount due from or owed to each bank.[2]

Facts can be organized in many different ways. One common approach is by *the objectives to which they relate.* Generally this supplies broad classifications. The chief drawback is in identifying the objectives. They

---

[2] More is stated about the use of charts and symbols in subsequent chapters.

are not always easy to define clearly. Furthermore, they are commonly compounded so that this classification does not always give clear and distinct divisions to the information. A favorite means for classifying facts is by *organization*. Information is segregated by who decides what and upon what information a decision is reached. This means associating information—be it in the form of reports, records, or memos—as well as its distribution, to the organization units and their respective personnel. The purpose and use by whom, for each informational segment, serve as the classification. These relations, tied with management organization units, reveal the flow of data, at which level, who decides what issues, and the adequacy of the information structure. Consolidating these types of information into a single picture for the entire enterprise provides a blueprint for designing an inclusive and effective system.

There is also the organizing of facts by *input and output*. This approach is relatively simple and provides meaningful classifications when there are existent systems to be improved. However, to use this basis when there is no precedent from former or present systems, it is necessary to conceive vividly the proposed system and segregate data based on these conceptual notions. Another possibility is classification by the *processing means*. This is advantageous to reveal the current status of the data processing being followed. It is especially helpful in revealing the makeup of the nonautomated processes being utilized and the type of information being obtained. Further, some designers, in certain instances, recommend organizing the facts according to the *major problems or complaints discovered during the collecting stage*. These criteria will separate the information into large classes, but give meaningful related information. Care must be exercised to include only genuine problems and complaints which appear to be of major significance.

To assist in evaluating the facts, it is an excellent practice to assign quantitative values to general statements. If the systems man is told that an occurrence is exceptional, he should try to ascertain its frequency or percentage of the total represented. The statement that "certain facts are extremely beneficial" and knowledge of the designer is that they are expensive to provide, suggest an effort to access the value of the benefit. The system designed must eventually justify itself in terms of benefits so that a cost evaluation of the facts at this stage of the design work is appropriate. By the same reasoning the designer should try to evaluate savings and their effect upon need and convenience.

Generally quantitative evaluation is most helpful in the areas of cost, accuracy, and employee productivity. These possible areas for improvement make for proper consolidation of efforts to obtain desired optimization. Sampling techniques to determine the accuracy of source documents and the reliability of reports and records can be followed. Also, some indexes of employee productivity should be developed. When these are compared to levels of attainment in similar work elsewhere or to what level appears reasonable, the designer has tangible evidence of how efficient the present information work is.

However, some evaluation must remain the result of judgment and belief. There are nonmeasurable elements about information. For example, an executive needs certain information at his fingertips, he likes to play with it, amplify it, and manipulate it in different ways. No quantitative measure fully takes this intangible and service element of information into account. In addition, some facts supply operational information within an organized group or enterprise while other facts initiate action outside their organized totality, for example, facts which condition the trade or marketing forecasts. Evaluating such facts pose difficulties. However, now available are some interesting input-output matrices including one which includes pertinent data on 30,000 U.S. businesses. Where data processing facilities permit, such external information can be used for improving the evaluation of facts currently included in a system.

## ESTABLISH SYSTEM PREMISES

Actually the previous steps in system design provide excellent clues as to what premises should be established. For example, the system boundaries and the organized facts supply information on the quality standards and volume of work that have prevailed. It is a simple matter to project these and establish them as the levels upon which the system design will be made. But events of the future may prove far different than the projections so that the system must be modified. It is best, therefore, to keep the system flexible with built-in means for expanding or contracting as the future shows is necessary.

The process used is perhaps the major premise of any system. The assumption of the use of existing information machines of a company can condition the system design considerably. And the same effect results from the premise to acquire new machines or even a computer. Their means of doing the work shape the system's makeup, yet these means are subject to radical change, as demonstrated by the introduction of new machines and attachments almost daily on the market. Again, system flexibility is the answer.

No part of a system will remain absolutely the same over a period. Some change is inevitable. But for practical purposes, we need to assume some static concept in order to design the system. As conditions change sufficiently, we can adjust our system accordingly.

## DESIGN OF SYSTEM

This step necessitates considerable creativity which is vital for good systems design to be achieved. Design when used with *systems design* connotes two different meanings. The first is the application of accepted techniques to provide information that conforms to given specifications. The second is the generation of a new arrangement or network to express a particular idea or concept. The systems designer is normally expected to employ established means where they are appropriate to the need. However, he is expected to create a new approach either when he feels the existent means should be improved or he recognizes the situation demands a new concept to answer the existent problem. In any event, success comes in proportion to the amount of imagination and mental effort committed to the designing task.

Usually in any given case, there are many possible systems that can be designed to fit the requirements. They can differ widely in their suitability and cost. All factors pertaining to the problem must be understood, reflected upon, and considered in light of the facts gathered and evaluated. At every part of the system, emphasis must be given the necessity of the information supplied, to whom it is given, and for what purpose. This is fundamental and must not be ignored. Satisfaction of closing and of due dates for information, peak periods, and volume of work must be given ample consideration so that the needs are met. Any limitations of current equipment should be disclosed, along with recommendations as to how to process the required data. Above all else, the proposed system must be practical and economical.

There is no deep mystery of unknown powers in systems design. To a great extent, systems design consists of a lot of hard work, abiding by the "ground rules" or constraints set up, thoroughly knowing the facts, and keeping everlastingly at the designing until a suitable solution is reached. The creative requirement can be overstated.

Systems designing takes time; the work cannot be hurried. Various ideas are tried out, some are retained, many are discarded. The process is iterative. In some respects it is akin to putting the parts together to a jigsaw puzzle. It is tentative, gradually developing, and refining a series of operations. There is considerable working back and forth—from the desirable goal backward to what is required at the beginning, and from the beginning through various steps to a logical outcome.

Tradeoff studies compare the competitiveness as well as the weakness of the system resulting from substituting, adding, or subtracting possible alternatives for existing components of a tentative system. In other words, if by adding a certain portion to a system making it possible to modify or even eliminate another portion of the system, will the resultant system be an improvement? The tradeoff is commonly evaluated in terms of performance, cost, training, profit improvement, reliability, maintenance, or payout. Several tradeoffs are normally possible in every system design. Indeed, one cannot be certain the most satisfactory system for the stated objectives has been developed until the results from tradeoffs have been ascertained.

A major difficulty in utilizing tradeoffs is to make certain that fundamental problems not their symptoms are being cured by our actions. Changes in system design should not be made in order to satisfy or to get at symptoms. A careful thinking through of the objectives best orientates what final output is needed. This should be the ultimate criteria in whether a tradeoff is desirable or not. Further, the final selection, no matter what components make up the system, should reflect the systems designer's belief of what combination will prove superior in operating in the particular environment and in keeping with the expressed managerial needs and capabilities.

To help ensure that sufficient attention has been given tradeoffs, the designer can ask himself (1) what are the system limitations, (2) how are these limitations affected by the alteration of the initial constraints of the system, and (3) do I know what tradeoffs affect the sensitivity, operation, and adequacy of the system's components? His answers will suggest whether more study should be given to this phase of systems design.

## DECIDE ON EXTENT OF MECHANIZATION

Decisions must be firmed up regarding what types of business machines and equipment will be used.[3] This is actually a part of the considerations stated previously, but several additional comments are in order at this time. How automatic should the processing be is an important question that must be answered. Rarely is closed-loop automaticity a major objective as such. The question is more, to what extent should elements of the system control either the system as a whole or its individual components. The adaptability and flexibility of the machine to fulfill the system's requirement normally merit high priority.

To assume that if processing can be done electronically it must be the best way of doing it in every case defeats the real contribution of effective systems design. EDP is the best answer in many cases, but in some applications because, for example, of the volume, frequency, cost, managerial wishes, or type of service required, other means may be more appropriate. Fantastic information machines are available. How best to use them is the challenge and this, to reiterate, leads to systems design—better systems design perhaps than the current concept, with less emphasis on troubleshooting and figuring out how best to utilize a given piece of equipment and more attention to fundamental managerial problems, integration of the many informational efforts, and overall coordinating of efforts beyond the current constraining horizons.

Decision making regarding the degree of mechanization sometimes encounters "bench-mark problems," which while not common do seriously

---

[3] Business information machines are discussed fully in the chapters under Part III.

curtail design work when encountered. A bench-mark problem is the condition of a company having processing equipment dominated by several applications which require some two thirds of the company's data-processing capacity. When this condition restricts the choice of any additional equipment to that of a complement of the existing equipment, with respect to any new system, a bench-mark problem exists. Usually the term is confined to the situation where an alternate or different type of equipment might be better suited to the needs of a proposed system.

FIGURE 2–6. Questions to Assist in Designing the Best Possible System.

1. Are the stated objectives and requirements satisfied completely by the system?
2. Is every part of the information handled really necessary?
3. Does the system perform more efficiently, more accurately, and more quickly than the previous manner of work performance?
4. If organizational changes are required, are these acceptable, and if some are not, will modification seriously restrict the proposed benefits?
5. At what points are employees' judgments, interpretations, and decision making a part of the system? Are there adequate control mechanisms over employees at these points?
6. Are proposed savings to be gained by reducing manpower? If so, will requisitions for manpower be cancelled, present employees transferred, and normal attrition permitted to take care of the labor surplus?
7. Is any part of the system being accepted on the basis that "it has always been done this way"?
8. Are the inputs and the outputs of data identified as to form, content, method of transmission, time requirements, volume, and peak loads?
9. Are all workplaces well arranged for performing the work?
10. Does the space layout assist in getting the work to flow smoothly?
11. Does the system incorporate adequate feedback and controls?
12. Is the data processing specified regarding type, speed, volume, and other pertinent characteristics?
13. Is the recommended means of data processing completely justified on the basis of clearly stated premises?
14. Are any special purpose requirements included and if so, are they clearly stated and their probable impact upon the system set forth in terms of delivery, delay, maintenance, and cost?

Figure 2–6 lists pertinent questions to aid in system designing. Answers to these questions serve as a stimulus to devising the best possible system and to evaluating designing efforts.

## EVALUATE THE SYSTEM

A system evaluation is conducted to determine whether the proposed system is satisfactory. Commonly this consists of a careful review of the overall arrangement and a detailed check of its critical areas. Various approaches may be taken, but for our purpose we will confine the discussion to that of assuming the viewpoint of meeting the overall needs of the enterprise and of the managers. From the enterprise viewpoint, the system as conceived should fit in with the long-range plans of the enterprise. The volume of information on which the system is predicated should be ample to meet future requirements. Should work expansion or contraction take place, the future problem areas, as future objectives of the system, should be known; provisions to take care of these changes exist within the system. Further, a determination should be undertaken to assure that this system does not duplicate work performed elsewhere in the enterprise. If it does, the scope of the proposed system might be narrowed, or the possibility of using it as a check upon results, sometimes helpful in financial systems, can be considered. Also, the chances of the proposed system being used in another location, such as an affiliate or branch of the company, may be investigated. If so, the designer might ask if his system is attuned to other environments and whether the system can be transplanted easily. Finally, from the enterprise viewpoint there is the question of whether the system calls for responsibility by members of certain organizational units whose members are unwilling or unable to accept such responsibility. These requirements must be fully explored.

The needs of the managers closely parallel the needs of the company, but the former are more concerned with the information flow than the scope of the system. Not all managers manage exactly alike, so the individual managerial informational requirements must be considered and satisfied on an individual basis. This raises the question whether all managers interested in the input and output of the system have been interviewed and their information requirements of the system fully met. Also, agreement to commitments placed on them by the system should be fully understood and accepted. Lastly, if feasible, guarantees should be extended managers assuring accuracy and integrity of the information. Proper measures should be adopted to prevent unauthorized personnel from obtaining the information and to eliminate unauthorized changes being made in it.

## IMPLEMENTING THE SYSTEM

In this chapter we are concerned with the conceptualization of the information work to be done via the designing of the information system. We shall progress logically with this conceptualizing of the work idea in the next chapter. But before doing so, it will be helpful to state at this point that following the design is the implementation of the system. In many cases, implementation may require 12 months, equal in time to that of designing. Implementation consists of acquiring information machines and equipment, preparing manuals and detailing information about the system, hiring personnel needed, installing system and running trial tests, and final conversion to the proposed system. Most of these activities are discussed in subsequent chapters, but brief comments about several of these activities will now be given.

Acquiring the information machines and equipment is commonly performed by either the president, the vice president of purchasing, or other top executive. It is human nature to enjoy procurement especially when the purchase is new and a large item obtained at infrequent intervals. Usually assistance by the systems, data processing, and informational specialists are called for. Proper specifications, prices, and delivery dates are negotiated along with installation agreements, guarantees, and initial assistance in the use of the machines and equipment.

Trial tests are the rule and a number of runs should be made to ensure satisfactory operation as indicated by statistical validity. Pilot or test runs make it possible to detect and correct any shortcomings before permanent or large-scale commitments are made. Frequently the approach is to test portions of the system. Each portion is checked thoroughly. To the degree that successively they are independent they can be tested independently, but, in contrast, if they are dependent serially they must be tested serially. Testing portions helps to simplify the job and expedite understanding and handling the test. But compatibility of the portions is important. As the system begins to operate, what happens first must satisfy the requirements of those portions that follow.

Modifications may occur as greater insight is obtained from the testing. Some redesign of the system may be in order; usually this is confined to certain areas only. Generally a period is scheduled to permit operating personnel to become acquainted with the new plan of work and to gain the necessary proficiency in performing their assigned tasks. Usually there are some adjustments to be made to satisfy personnel opinions or complaints.

Eventually, after all sources of difficulty have been removed or corrected, the proposed system is put into full operation. Now there is a policing period to insure that what is designed and planned is being utilized properly and is functioning satisfactorily. Usually personnel problems dominate the policing period. Characteristic of the initial days during this period are efforts concerning the adaptation of the employees to their new work, adjustments to the working environment, and explanations regarding the equipment.

## QUESTIONS

1. Name and discuss four common sources of data and information that are used in system designing.
2. Discuss the relationship in information management between systems and conceptualizing the work to be done.
3. Do you favor quantitative measurement and evaluation of data used in system design? Justify your viewpoint.

4. Do you feel that business machine manufacturers are an effective source of information for a system designer? Why?
5. What is meant by "constraints of a system" and of what importance are they in information management?
6. Discuss the importance you attach to systems in information management. Justify your viewpoint.
7. Explain the meaning and significance of Figure 2–2 in your own words.
8. What are some important considerations to keep in mind while interviewing to obtain information for use in system designing? Elaborate on one consideration that you give.
9. Identify each of the following:
   *a*) A definite order of each component of a system.
   *b*) Bench-mark problem in system design.
   *c*) A premise of a system.
   *d*) Hound-dog approach.
10. Do you agree with this statement: "Mechanization is the key consideration in modern system designing. The logical beginning for conceptualizing the information work to be done is either the machine available or what can be made available." Why?
11. Name and discuss briefly three major means for organizing and evaluating factual data used in systems design.
12. Discuss the use of tradeoff studies in system design.

## CASE PROBLEMS

### Case 2–1.  St. Mary Hospital

A cooperative effort by personnel of St. Mary Hospital, representatives of a computer manufacturer, and personnel of a certified public accounting firm has designed and implemented information systems to handle accounts receivable, accounts payable, inventory, and payroll work. Analyses of the various hospital services are also provided. Actually, it can be stated that there are at present four major systems used by St. Mary Hospital including the patient accounting system, the inventory system, the payroll system, and the management reporting system. We are primarily concerned here with the first or patient accounting system.

For each incoming patient at the admittance office identifying data are typed on an admittance form, copies of which go to the business office and the service departments of the hospital. Two copies of the form are retained by the admittance office where one is filed alphabetically, the other numerically. In addition, an identifying plastic wristband showing name, number, and blood type is fastened onto the patient's wrist. From its copies, the admittance office transfers the information into punched cards, likewise the service departments make out service charge tickets depending upon the patient's needs. The information from these tickets is ultimately transferred to punched cards. These media (punched cards) are used to feed the information into a computer from which both a (1) charge master file and (2) a patient master file are updated and stored.

As required, various processed information from the computer in the form of reports is obtained. For example, the following are common: (1) daily summary of charges, (2) patient billing, and (3) census report. Inpatients and outpatients not yet discharged are included in the report covering daily summary of charges. The charges are by different categories and usually details miscellaneous charges not covered by insurance. The report shows balances due from insurance carrier and patient. It is used by the cashier at the time patients are discharged or as a means of informing the patient about the status of his account.

The patient billing report is produced automatically by the computer every seven days. For every patient in the hospital for 28 days, a balance forward bill is produced and used to bill insurance companies and patients for noncovered portions. Four days after discharge the computer produces the final bill showing what is due from insurance company and patient. At this time, a copy of the account is imprinted on a tubfile card for applying payments or making any adjustments. This file is maintained in the cashier's office, and between this file and the daily summary of charges the cashier has the status of all accounts, both in-house and discharged.

The census report lists each inpatient and outpatient admission, discharges, room transfers, and a midnight count by each hospital unit or wing. Copies of this report are used by personnel in each unit to show percentage of occupancy, patient condition reports, respiration reports, dietary, temperature, and pulse reports.

The hospital revenue from payments for services rendered represents accounts receivable. These are obtained from the charge master file under which are the daily and monthly revenue analysis report and the responsibility report. The former shows each service by inpatient and outpatient revenues. The report is distributed to each revenue producing department for statistical and work measurement purposes. The responsibility report is a tabulation prepared monthly showing for each account the amount and the identity (person or insurance carrier) responsible for the payment of accounts receivable.

Any cash or check payment from patients or insurance carriers is recorded in a receipt card journal with a copy sent to the accounting department. The information is transferred to a punched card form for feeding into the computer. In addition, the systems of accounts payable, inventory, and payroll are handled by the computer. However, different data from that discussed above are required to process information pertaining to these activities.

### Questions:

1. Draw the flow chart depicting the relationships of the various information activities dealing with the patient accounting system and accounts receivable of the hospital.
2. Would you describe these two systems as interdependent or dependent? Discuss.
3. What types of information other than that included in this case would you require in the hospital's payroll system? Are these types of information related to that of the patient accounting system? Discuss.

### Case 2–2.   Alexander and Ramsey, Inc.

A manufacturer of standard and custom-made picture frame mouldings in wood, plastic, and metal, Alexander and Ramsey, Inc., has enjoyed phenomenal growth since its inception some six years ago. Mr. Alexander, one of the owners, has charge of internal operations and has asked you to make improvements in the work of customer order handling and of purchasing.

The following describes the present manner of handling the work:

1. Orders are received by mail; a clerk in mail room sorts them by type of material—wood, plastic, or metal.

2. The orders are sent to the billing department for pricing. A listing is made of orders under standard and nonstandard, or custom, headings and under subheadings of (1) sales territory and (2) dollar amount. There is also major segregation by type of material as received from the mail room. Orders for standard items are priced and marked in green pencil, data being taken from a standard price list. Orders for custom items are sent to the factory manager for pricing, which is entered in red pencil.

3. Standard item orders and copy of listings are sent to the sales department. The orders are checked and marked for credit. Custom item orders from the factory manager are checked against listings for receipt of all custom orders, then checked and marked for credit. Listings are used for sales analysis. The orders are sent open account, "2% 10, net 30" where credit standing is satisfactory; otherwise the terms are c.o.d.

4. All orders are then sent to billing where a five-part order form is typed. Copies No. 2 and No. 3 are sent to the factory and used to fill the order. When shipped, copies are so marked, and Copy No. 2 is returned to billing where it is filed chronologically by date of receipt from the factory. Copy No. 3 is filed by the factory.

5. Upon receipt of Copy No. 2 from the factory, billing mails Copy No. 1 to the customer and retains Copies 4 and 5 for its records, one filed alphabetically by customer's name, and one filed numerically by order number.

6. The factory manager places purchase orders with vendors as indicated by his inventory control records or as required for special materials called for by custom orders. The purchase order is typed in duplicate in the factory office, with the original sent to the vendor and the copy for factory files. When the receiving and shipping unit gives notification that the material has arrived, the receiving report is compared to the factory copy of the purchase order, verified, and both papers are sent to accounting for payment.

## Questions:

1. Enumerate several areas in the above information handling that can give rise to difficulties. Why?
2. What specific recommendations would you offer to Mr. Alexander? Why?

## Case 2–3. Booth Company

About 60 percent of the Booth Company's sales are received from mail orders. Party supplies such as table decorations, inexpensive prizes, flages, novelties, and hobby items including model trains, puzzles, do-it-yourself paintings and ceramic art works are feature items. Because of the tremendous variety offered, it is not always possible to fill a mail order immediately upon its receipt. In these cases, a letter is written stating the reason for nondelivery. A sales correspondent dictates the letters and normally two typists are required to handle the typing of the letters. A copy of the letter is stapled to the customer's order and filed in the "pending sales" file by product type. Before mailing, the correspondent proofs each letter, corrects minor errors, and signs the letter. If mistakes are too serious, the letter is returned to the typist for retyping. Almost all the letters, however, are of satisfactory quality in the first typing.

It is the opinion of William Weston, the office manager, that valuable time is lost in notifying customers of delay in shipping their orders. This results in cancellations, complaints by customers, and poor business relations. He asked his assistant, Roy Samwell, to look into the situation and see what can be done. Accordingly, Mr. Samwell talked with the correspondent and typists, reviewed available company records, and made several investigative studies. From all this, he found that (1) each typist completes about 45 letters a day, but about 10 percent of these are for purposes other than nonshipment of orders; (2) the typists do not like their jobs because the letters are too repetitive and the work is not challenging; (3) salary of the correspondent is $92.50 a week, of one typist $67.50 a week, of the second typist $62.50 a week; (4) most frequent reasons for nondelivery of merchandise given in letters can be classified as (*a*) obsolete item—no longer available, (*b*) merchandise on order, will ship in *x* days; (*c*) partial shipment being made, remainder will follow shortly; (*d*) payment not included with order; and (*e*) insufficient payment sent with order.

With this information, Mr. Samwell proceeded to write his recommendation to Mr. Weston.

## Questions:

1. What alternatives of recommendations are available to Mr. Samwell?
2. What action do you recommend to Mr. Weston? Substantiate your views.
3. Outline the chief advantages of your recommended action.

# chapter 3

# Systems improvement and total systems concept

The great accomplishments of man have resulted
from the transmission of ideas and enthusiasm.
—*Thomas J. Watson*

YESTERDAY's information system can be a trap that creates tomorrow's crisis. Since information management is highly dynamic, it follows that the systems used in it must be updated and kept compatible with the latest requirements and demands of the information handling. Also, as new and better tools become available, it is mandatory that improvements be incorporated. Both the information supplied and the means by which it is made available are eternal candidates for improvement.

We strive to design the best possible systems in keeping with our current knowledge and experience deemed appropriate to the individual case. But we know the systems will require revision at some future date. It is simply a matter of time. With many new ideas popping up, managers' responsibilities and information needs changing, new machines appearing on the market, new applications of existent products being developed, and competitive actions increasing, the answer in part is to analyze systems currently in use and to seek improvement in them.

The tremendous growth of sophisticated systems in information management represents a truly fantastic story. The progressive manager has accelerated and aided this growth by insisting upon more effective systems. In these improvement efforts, however, four simple key questions must be answered. They are: (1) who needs the information (2) what kind of information does he need (3) in what format and how current should the information be and (4) within what constraint (especially cost) should the information be provided?

## KEYS TO IMPROVEMENT

There are a number of specific approaches that can be followed in improving systems. However, they all adopt the premise that improvement is obtained by either designing a new system or redesigning an existent system to conform to new objectives, constraints, premises, or facts. Hence, the designing format discussed in the previous chapter can be followed. But it is helpful to point out key considerations which help guide these improvement efforts. Included are the decision structure, the end-result concept, the improvement of the information itself, and the selection of a manageable area.

## THE DECISION STRUCTURE

Included in the meaning of the decision structure are the decisions that must be made by each manager, the extent of delegating decision making, and the relationship of information to action taken. We are concentrating upon information supplied by systems for decision making, although as pointed out in chapter 1, information also serves as a discipline. In essence, a guide toward improving information systems is to identify who decides what and strive to supply each decider with better information for his decision making.

Following this line of thought, we start at the top management level and work down identifying the decisions that must be made by each management member. To assist in these efforts, the questions listed in Figure 3–1 can be followed being sure to ask them in the sequence given.

After identifying the types of decisions, work is then directed to supply information specifically helpful for each manager. These efforts, however, are not solely rational. Every decision and its implementation are strongly conditioned by consideration for the human aspects involved and especially by what the manager believes to be his job, his authority, his responsibility, and his relationships with others in the enterprise. For example, a manager may see his primary job as one of processing papers on time. This being true, his decisions affecting scheduling are analyzed to reveal what factors are of most importance in meeting schedules. Perhaps controlling overtime and productivity per employee are found to have the maximum impact on achieving schedules. Hence, information on these factors would be supplied the manager who will probably utilize fully such information, since he tends to worry about schedules.

Some managers want to make all possible decisions themselves while others prefer to delegate portions of their decision making to subordinates. The former is found in a small enterprise where the manager is also the owner. In this instance, detailed information must flow to him at the top of the organization, since he makes all key decisions. In contrast, in larger, more complex enterprises, the top manager allows subordinates to make important decisions and he himself deals only with certain types of decision making including objective determination and the measuring of subordinate performance in terms of accomplishments. The manager who delegates decision making, even though he reaches certain decisions himself, requires a substantially different type of information system than the manager who decides all major decisions himself.

FIGURE 3–1. Questions to Ask to Determine Type of Decision Making Required by Each Management Member.

1. Specifically, what are your main work objectives?
2. For these work objectives, what are your principal responsibilities?
3. In keeping with these responsibilities, what types of decisions are you called upon to make?
4. What information do you feel you need to reach these decisions from the short-range viewpoint? From the long-range viewpoint? From within the enterprise? From outside the enterprise? From an idealistic viewpoint? From a practical viewpoint?
5. What are the key factors that throttle the work that you are supposed to do?
6. Classify the identified information given in answer to question 4 above into the following groups:
   a) Absolutely essential.
   b) Essential.
   c) Desirable.
   d) Helpful but really not needed.

The relationship of information to the action taken is another facet of the decision structure affecting the amount and type of information provided. The busy manager need not concern himself with those operations running smoothly or keeping within plans. He focuses attention on the exception or the deviates from their respective norm. This concept is expressed by the principle of "management by exception." From the viewpoint of improving an information system, the task may well be that of getting better information about or targeting available information to the exceptional cases—those that require managerial action. This results in shorter, action-geared information that assists the management member to use his time most effectively.

## THE END-RESULT CONCEPT

Many information systems could be improved by having them present information in keeping with the end-result concept. Simply stated, this concept is based on the economic fact that a small proportion of efforts produce a large proportion of results. To illustrate, 20 percent of the salesmen acquire 80 percent of the orders, or 18 percent of the products account for 75 percent of the profits. Commonly referred to as "the 20–80 ratio"—20 percent of efforts produce 80 percent of results, this phenomenon applies to the various areas of activities of an enterprise, areas where $20 of effort will yield $80 of results. It is on these influential areas that the information systems should focus and provide less depth and frequency of information on the numerous and less critical areas. A 5 percent decline in market share, for example, may be far more critical than a 15 percent decline in accounts payable. The challenge is to identify the really important areas and improve the systems to accomplish genuine information effectiveness in these key areas rather than following the traditional approach of spreading the information somewhat uniformly throughout all areas.

Applying the end-result concept or an adoption of it to achieve system improvement offers distinct advantages. Focusing on the really significant areas (always relatively few in number) has great impact on results. In turn, this necessitates considerable thought to decide what issues should be worked on and how much effort directed to each. Areas of critical value thus become known to employees and can be given attention in keeping with their relative worth. Second, deeper insight into major problems is encouraged. To illustrate, costing practices can be modified to reflect more accurately the cost incurred by various activities differing in importance. Thus, dividing a total expenditure by the number of activities to obtain the "average cost," which is questionable and in many cases inaccurate, could be eliminated so that large volume items would not be penalized by carrying an excess of cost which should be borne by certain small volume items. Further, the undercost burdened items lead to underpricing of them and possibly to the proliferation of small production runs and small sales orders. Third, applying the end-result concept to information systems assists in eliminating unnecessary paper work. As managers learn to rely more on information pertaining to essential areas, the preparation of voluminous data dealing with relatively insignificant operations will tend to minimize.

An interesting modification of the end-result concept is *systems contracting,* a technique for purchasing. Under this approach the traditional materials acquisition-retention cycle undergoes significant changes. Briefly a vendor is selected for a systems contract, the materials he is to supply are carefully identified as to price and specifications, catalogs of materials to be supplied by each vendor are prepared, materials are requisitioned using the catalogs as a guide, requisitions are approved by the purchasing authorization point (PAP), the order is placed with the approved vendor, and a "total payment" method of vouchering is followed whereby one payment check is issued periodically covering all of the completed transactions. A 60 percent improvement in service, better control, and the elimination of much needless purchasing paper work are claimed from utilizing this new system.[1]

## IMPROVEMENT OF INFORMATION ITSELF

To reduce the growing amount of paper work and to concentrate on the vital information, it is also essential to improve the information itself. This requires knowing the various activities and viewing the enterprise in a broad perspective to determine just what information is required. Enterprises differ widely in their information needs as reflected by their individual characteristics. For example, some enterprises are highly dependent upon style, others have large inventories subject to potential loss of obsolescence and price fluctuation, while others must exercise tight control to survive in their highly competitive market.

Most managers need to increase their skill in deciding what information they need and how they will use such information when they get it. The information system analyst can aid very materially in this respect, but frequently he is not in a position to comprehend or to suggest what specific information should be supplied. A great deal of the more common types of information now used by a manager is designed to meet statutory rather than managerial requirements. Much information describes the past without discriminating between essential and ordinary elements of the enterprise. Frequently lacking is information supplied regularly on adequacy of customer service, productivity, share and rate of growth of market, and competitors' activities—what they are doing, where, and how well. Yet these items would prove helpful to better management.

Some feel that the whole concept of information needs drastic revision. In their opinion much of the present information is incomplete, too late, unreliable, and poorly organized to have maximum value. Facts for today's decisions reach managers next week. Reams of detailed data are supplied, but helpful summaries and relationships are lacking. Distinction between the critical and the immaterial is not indicated. The need is for a complete reorientation of information. A large portion of what we now have is outmoded. In an economy such as ours, where manufacturing techniques, products, and markets change as rapidly as they do, we cannot operate an enterprise on fragmented and historical facts that are basically an extension of the past. The crying need is for improvement of the information itself.

## SELECTION OF A MANAGEABLE AREA

Revamping the information systems of an enterprise may prove too large a job to be handled at one time. At the start, it is usually advisable

---

[1] See Ralph A. Bolton "Systems Contracting—A New Purchasing Technique," New York: The American Management Association, 1966.

to choose a manageable area, that is, one which calls for a medium-size staff, average experience in office technology, and not distant geographic communication. If possible, the operations of the selected area should be primarily within itself so that the effect of interactions with other areas is minimized. Ideally the manageable area possesses nearly all of the functions and problems of the entire enterprise and has promise of a fast payout from a high probability of success. It should also represent a viable, growing segment which will most typify the problem of facilitating the managers in the totality of the enterprise.

These specifications are not easy to meet. Frequently, they must be approximated. In some instances, significant assumptions must be made in order to proceed with the system analysis and improvement. But the extent to which these specifications are met enhances the validity and the value of changes suggested for improvement.

## SYSTEMS SIMULATION

One technique rapidly gaining favor for redesigning and improving systems is systems simulation. As mentioned in chapter 1, simulation is an approach included in the quantitative measurement school of management thought. Systems simulation is a technique for determining by means of experiment the effect of varying the variables in the flow of information or material through the processes in a system. In other words, systems simulation permits the trying out of various ideas via the systems route to see what results are obtained. It answers "what if" questions. It is a means of obtaining experience with concepts that are beyond consideration in actual physical testing because of cost, risk, or time involved. The work is done on paper without having to try out the concept in practice. By accumulating and learning from this experience, better systems can be developed or each of several alternative systems can be evaluated.

Systems simulation enables the analyst to analyze not only a system independently, but also the interaction of systems of an enterprise so that the net result of all systems used is the best combination to achieve the stated objectives. Systems integration in keeping with definite goals is accomplished. Activities are expressed in quantitative values, but this is difficult to do for some actions. Quantification is used for as many factors and relationships as possible, thus highlighting the manager's attention to those activities that require managerial judgment.

The medium for simulation is a model which is a precise description, flow-diagram, or mathematical expression that can be manipulated to measure the effect of changing one or several variables in the system. The description may simply state the processes involved and how they vary and relate to each other, but for manipulability the written statement is usually expressed in the form of a flow-diagram or mathematical expression. The former indicates the relationships and their logical sequence of operation. The latter can be one or more mathematical formulas or equations. This mathematical model can be developed when there are sufficient data about the activities and their relationships along with how and why they vary as they do. The mathematical model adds precision to

FIGURE 3–2. Truck Maintenance Flow-Diagram.

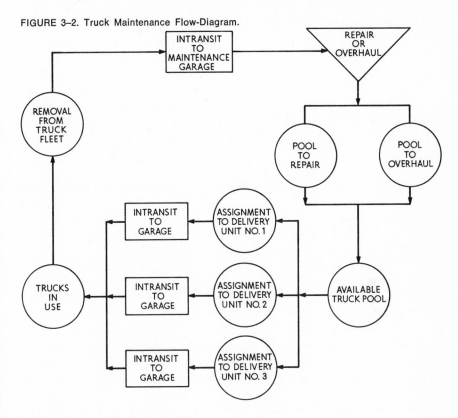

the technique and usually expedites the simulation work when a computer is employed. Figure 3–2 shows the beginning simple flow-diagram of a systems simulation study for the maintenance of trucks in a fleet. Eventually this was developed into quite a sophisticated diagram and ultimately converted into a mathematical expression.

To introduce change in the variables the model is subjected to input data. This input is processed through and by the relationships built into the flow-diagram or mathematical expression. After the processing, the results, or output data, are obtained and subjected to analysis and evaluation to note the changes obtained from varying the variables. When the diagram or mathematical expression is complex and is to be used many times, it is usually economical to perform the calculations rapidly by means of a computer. A large number of possible answers can then be obtained. The answer which best suits the specific needs of the particular situation can be selected and the system providing this answer adopted.

Systems simulation aids in evaluating new ideas and concepts which otherwise might remain dormant. Also, the training of personnel is expedited. Further, systems simulation provides a broad and inclusive understanding of systems and their basic nature. Complete analysis is promoted. The cycle from beginning to end, the processes involved, and the effect of change can be clearly identified. On the other hand, there are disadvantages of systems simulation. Accurate input data are difficult to obtain and are frequently underestimated. In addition, there are many assumptions in applying the technique and, in fact, the quality of these assumptions conditions greatly the value of the results. It is vital that all the assumptions made—the constraints, the relationship of one variable to another and to a constant—be clearly understood and results viewed in light of these assumptions. Further, it must be remembered that systems simulation is a tool, it permits evaluation of ideas which are the creation of the human mind. It is a technique to solve a problem and the emphasis should be on its problem-solving, i.e., obtaining an improved system. Sometimes the emphasis erroneously is shifted to the effectiveness of the technique itself.

## TOTAL SYSTEMS—A LOGICAL DEVELOPMENT

Attempts to make systems more effective have led logically to extending the systems concept to include all related systems to a totality. Why stop with one or two systems? The relationship of one system to another and to another eventually resolves into one overall inclusive system which it appears would be desirable from the viewpoint of high information service at minimum cost and effort.

Moving from a single system idea to that of several systems as the vehicle of thought informational efforts is a logical development. Historically, early information study focused attention on the task of an individual and how it was performed. Expanding this concept the related tasks of several individuals were considered, resulting in the development of a procedure. Later, related procedures were considered and the concept of a system became accepted. Continuing, from several related systems evolved the idea of a consolidated information system that would effectively provide the required information throughout an entire enterprise.

Slowly but surely, it is being recognized that information is crucially interdependent. What happens in one organizational unit influences what happens in other organizational units. No one bit of information is an island unto itself. It is related to and affects other bits of information.

With this fundamental in mind, the natural development was toward a more inclusive and all-encompassing concept about data gathering and processing.

## THE TOTAL SYSTEMS CONCEPT

With the total systems concept, a reservoir of information would be available to any management member in the enterprise any time it is needed. The probable impact of any contemplated action in any one segment upon the entire enterprise could be easily and quickly ascertained. Purchasing, marketing, and engineering data could be readily combined with material control, inventory, quality, and production flow information. Research and development progress could be tied in with forecasting; thus where and when to make engineering changes in a product line could be accurately calculated. In brief, complete legal, historical, fiscal, and operational data would be included and interrelated.

A graphic representation indicating the general idea of a total systems concept is shown by Figure 3–3. This is suggestive only and is not intended to be conclusive. Beginning at the top of the figure, top management members, either as individual department heads or as a group, perform basic operations which establish objectives and supply the necessary parameters within which these objectives will be sought. These resulting decisions are forwarded to an Information Service Center which cuts across all organization lines, is centralized, reports to top management members, receives feedback information on actions taken, and regulates information flow. As depicted, the Information Service Center is able to provide top managers with the broad scope of analytical and control data available and in use, plus the information flow related to forecasts, actual performances, feedback, evaluation, and coordination. Thus, effective implementation of information is enhanced and adequate control over it is provided. More specifically, and as shown in the figure, the Information Service Center designs and installs systems, processes data, and supervises information flow. This is done to establish fundamental practices shown on the figure, practices such as stock review, raw materials control, work in process control, product cost reports, and payroll accounting and variance. Feedback is obtained on all these practices by determining for each case the exception to what is wanted (management by exception) and taking the needed corrective action. The automatic feedback is indicated at the bottom of the illustration.

As illustrated, and in most cases, the total systems concept is based on forecasts of requirements over reasonable periods, together with establishment of the optimum manufacturing and selling plans based on the forecast. What is optimum can be from a cost, service, time, or capability viewpoint. Furthermore, implied in the total systems concept are determi-

FIGURE 3–3. A Concept of Total Systems for an Enterprise.

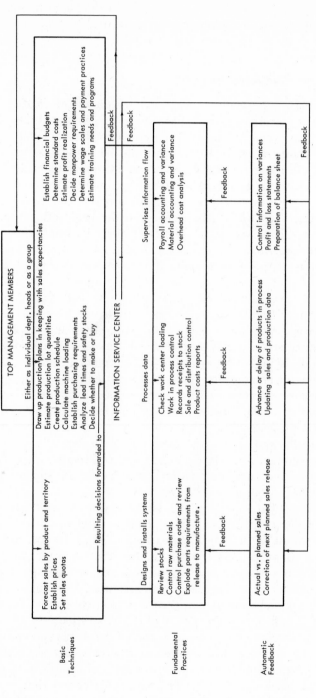

TOP MANAGEMENT MEMBERS

Either as individual dept. heads or as a group

Draw up production plans in keeping with sales expectancies
Estimate production lot quantities
Create production schedule
Calculate machine loading
Establish purchasing requirements
Analyze lead times and safety stocks
Decide whether to make or buy

Establish financial budgets
Determine standard costs
Estimate profit realization
Decide manpower requirements
Determine wage scales and payment practices
Estimate training needs and programs

Forecast sales by product and territory
Establish prices
Set sales quotas

Resulting decisions forwarded to

INFORMATION SERVICE CENTER

Processes data

Supervises information flow

Check work center loading
Work in process control
Records receipts to stock
Sale and distribution control
Product costs reports

Payroll accounting and variance
Material accounting and variance
Overhead cost analysis

Designs and installs systems

Review stocks
Control raw materials
Control purchase order and review
Explode parts requirements from
release to manufacture.

Feedback

Feedback

Advance or delay of products in process
Updating sales and production data

Control information on variances
Profit and loss statements
Preparation of balance sheet

Actual vs. planned sales
Correction of next planned sales release

Feedback

Feedback

Feedback

Practice management by exception

Basic
Techniques

Fundamental
Practices

Automatic
Feedback

nations for control limits within which the forecast will remain unchanged, feedbacks of actual requirements compared to the forecasts, and corrective actions either in the form of forecast adjustments or in operations. This is to say that manufacturing and selling efforts are based on the forecasts, not on actual requirements. The latter may vary sufficiently to suggest an adjustment in the forecast, and this is done when the forecast is obviously out of line. But fluctuations within established limits can occur without affecting the forecast.

Figure 3–4 outlines a total information system for banks offered by an information machine manufacturer. Managers concerned with financial

FIGURE 3–4. A Total Information System for Banks.

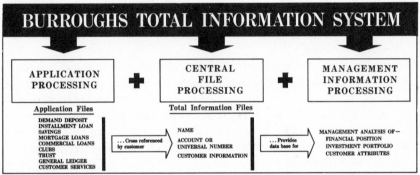

*Courtesy: Burroughs, Inc., Detroit*

data processing can utilize this centralized banking system to handle their information needs effectively. The system is bank oriented. As indicated by the illustration the system comprises three logical levels. First, the application processing whereby application files including the various types of bank papers are converted to computer data and put into a computer having large random access storage capabilities. Second is the central file processing which includes cross-referencing each application file to a customer-oriented total information file containing each customer's name and other personal data. Third, the management information processing by computer provides data required for key analyses helpful in reaching effective top management decisions.

## OBSERVATIONS ABOUT TOTAL SYSTEMS CONCEPT

The total systems concept is so logical that one wonders why we did not get to it sooner or why it is not universally adopted. Actually the reasons are many. During the initial adoption of office automation there was some tendency to automate the work that had always been done. The existent systems were given a sacred, do-not-alter status. Any new information needs were patched onto the old systems. Reports, records, data of all kinds were seldom culled, and if so, rarely in their entirety. Customarily any inspection was confined to a portion of the entirety. The result was that useless information was permitted to exist, even ignored, without purpose and without controls.

Objectives are always important in management, but in discussing the total systems concept, objectives warrant special emphasis. *What constitutes a system, or a total system, is determined by the objectives sought.* In every case, the objectives establish the limits and utilization of the systems making up the total systems concept. In fact, the total systems concept is meaningful to the degree that the objectives are identified. Furthermore, this means that a total systems is not a grandiose composite of all systems to do all things. Rather, it is an integration of systems designed for the purpose of achieving stated objectives. An illustration will clarify this fact.

With reference to an automobile, the question can be asked, "What is an ignition system?" We would answer in terms something like the following. It is a system actually made up of a combination of several systems designed to make certain activities take place which result in sparks or electric flashes igniting combustible fuel. Note that identification of the several lesser systems is couched in terms of what the total systems are intended to achieve, or in terms of the objectives. We could go into the details of the lesser systems making up the total ignition system, such as the timing system, the condenser system, the spark plug system, and so forth, but this is irrelevant for the point at hand. Next, suppose the question is asked, "What are the total systems that deliver brake horsepower on the wheels of an automobile?" We would answer, the ignition system, the combustion system, the cooling and ventilating system, and the transmission system. All these systems work together to achieve the objective—deliver brake horsepower on the wheels of an automobile. Suppose we change our objectives to include the potential supplying of transportation to a human being. Since our objectives have changed, we change the inclusion of the systems making up the total systems. Specifically, we would add the system of steering, the system of braking, and a human being, with all the systems he brings with him, behind the steering wheel. Again, if our objectives were to include transporting this human being, we get into additional systems such as a system of roads, traffic lights, highway instructions, and so forth.

The total systems concept expedites managerial planning. When a particular system is planned as a part of a total system for an enterprise, the system occupies a place compatible to the overall scheme of things and is properly related to the entirety. Furthermore, with the total systems concept, it is possible to make decisions that will maximize profits of an enterprise as a whole, minimize costs of the enterprise as a whole, or maximize benefits to the enterprise totality. In addition, information is maintained in a single data stream, a condition which normally insures greater accuracy and a better format of the information. Also special analyses or studies can be provided with minimum effort. In this connection, eliminated are delays due to decision making at various levels and departmentalized time-consuming clerical calculations. And it is not difficult to handle intricate information problems that extend into many facets of the enterprise.

At the same time there are shortcomings of the total systems concept. To illustrate, top management attention and backing are essential for its success and this support is not always present in adequate measure. A plausible explanation for this is the background of the top executives. Relatively few come up through accounting, personnel, or information areas and hence they may have neither a full appreciation of the nature of information problems nor the means to cope with them. They may also view total systems as helpful but not essential and prefer to direct their efforts to other areas. In addition, there is a tendency of the top executive to advocate the overall perspective, but practice that about which he knows or thinks he knows the most, either by training or experience. As a result, specialization creeps in and the broad, balanced viewpoint falls by the wayside. Finally, there is the hidden characteristic of systems improvements. Changes are not easily discerned and the benefits are mainly intangible. The improvement in service or the reduction in cost is frequently neither as meaningful nor as evident as an increase in sales orders or a new production level attained by a factory force.

Some have advanced the thought that the total systems concept is too extensive and too large to use effectively and that, at least for the present, satisfactory results are possible with something less than total systems. This appears to suggest that developing total systems for an enterprise poses hurdles and is more difficult and elusive than what might at first be suspected. But the acceptance and success of total systems concept appears to be one of degree more than of kind. If total systems cannot be used, some degree of it can. There is unanimity of opinion that within an enterprise a partial total systems is superior to several large but noncoordinated systems. As pointed out above, we specify the extensiveness of the coordination by the statement of the objectives. Literally we say that to accomplish these objectives we will use these integrated systems. Hence, what is a partial total systems may provide the needed results. Our problem may resolve into that of determining precisely and completely the total objectives of the enterprise. The day of total systems may not have arrived as yet, but it surely is on its way. As experience, greater skill, and better techniques are developed for systems, along with continued progress in processing equipment, the present hurdles to far-reaching and inclusive integrated systems will be surmounted.

## TOTAL MANAGEMENT INFORMATION SYSTEM

The ultimate of the total systems concept has been referred to by some as the Total Management Information System. An example of such a system is that developed by a machinery manufacturer, Farrel Corporation, for its overall information needs. The objective is to improve its profit possibilities and controls.[2] Figure 3–5 is a graphic representation of the system. The informational needs of planning, engineering, manufacturing, selling, and financing are integrated and designed to (1) give adequate and consistent planning and engineering documentation for each product line, (2) provide needed manufacturing information including purchasing data, schedules, and labor costs, (3) expedite sales forecasting, market penetration, and sales analyses, and (4) facilitate all fundamental finance information including accounts receivable, accounts payable, expenses, payroll checks, and standard cost data and control. With this unified arrangement, the managers of Farrel Corporation believe advantages well worthwhile are realized including a reduction of materials cost, better manpower utilization, improved flexibility in scheduling, shorter manufacturing cycles, shorter sales delivery periods, improved customer services, and better collection of accounts receivable. With all these gains, the ability to handle a greater volume of business with existent facilities seems likely. Also the new system supplies a broader and deeper knowledge of the enterprise and its behavior as a unit.

Excellent examples of what can be considered total management information systems are found in the U.S. Air Force. They are the Management Control System (MCS) and the Strategic Air Command (SAC). These are total systems encompassing total operations although they are operated by a subagency. If not truly all-encompassing in their scope, they come very close to it. They are inclusive in keeping with their stated objectives. Also worthy of mention is the total logistics system of the U.S. Air Force. It is worldwide, totally integrated, and covers supply and maintenance. By its operation, service has been upgraded, yet enormous dollar savings have been realized.

The other military services have also been active in developing total management information systems. Both the U.S. Army and the U.S. Navy have active offices of management information. The promulgation of DONMICS (Department of Navy Management Information and Control

---

[2] *What Farrel Corporation Is Doing To Maintain and Improve Its Competitive Position,* pamphlet published following annual stockholders meeting (Rochester, N.Y.: The Farrel Corporation, March 19, 1964).

FIGURE 3-5. One Concept of a Total Management Information System.

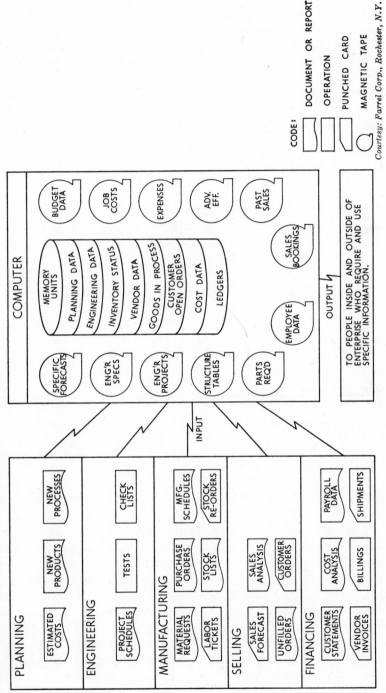

PLANNING

ESTIMATED COSTS
NEW PRODUCTS
NEW PROCESSES

ENGINEERING

PROJECT SCHEDULES
TESTS
CHECK LISTS

MANUFACTURING

MATERIAL REQUESTS
LABOR TICKETS
PURCHASE ORDERS
STOCK LISTS
MFG. SCHEDULES
STOCK RE-ORDERS

SELLING

SALES FORECAST
UNFILLED ORDERS
SALES ANALYSIS
CUSTOMER ORDERS

FINANCING

CUSTOMER STATEMENTS
VENDOR INVOICES
COST ANALYSIS
BILLINGS
PAYROLL DATA
SHIPMENTS

INPUT

COMPUTER

SPECIFIC FORECASTS
ENG'R SPECS
ENG'R PROJECTS
STRUCTURE TABLES
PARTS REQ'D

MEMORY UNITS
PLANNING DATA
ENGINEERING DATA
INVENTORY STATUS
VENDOR DATA
GOODS IN PROCESS
CUSTOMER OPEN ORDERS
COST DATA
LEDGERS

BUDGET DATA
JOB COSTS
EXPENSES
ADV. EFF.
PAST SALES

EMPLOYEE DATA
SALES BOOKINGS

OUTPUT

TO PEOPLE INSIDE AND OUTSIDE OF ENTERPRISE WHO REQUIRE AND USE SPECIFIC INFORMATION.

CODE:

DOCUMENT OR REPORT
OPERATION
PUNCHED CARD
MAGNETIC TAPE

*Courtesy: Farrel Corp., Rochester, N.Y.*

System) is a major management milestone for integrating and improving information flow across the whole spectrum of management. Hundreds of information systems in the Navy and Marine Corps are brought into a conceptual base. DONMICS has major subsystems including the master information systems of the Chief of Naval Operations (CNO), the Commandant of the Marine Corps (CMC), the Chief of Naval Research (CNR), the Controller of the Navy (NAVCOMPT), and the Director, Civilian Manpower Management (DCMM). It is intended to serve the

FIGURE 3–6. Diagram Showing Concept of Interrelationship of U.S. Navy and U.S. Marine Corps Major Information Systems.

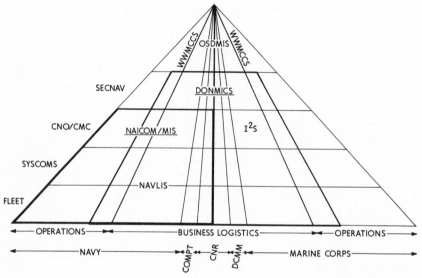

*Courtesy: U.S. Navy, Washington, D.C.*

needs of managers and commanders at all levels of the Department of Navy (DON) organization.

To visualize, a pyramid representing command level and functional areas of responsibilities, ranging over a spectrum from purely operational systems on the outside to business-oriented systems in the center can be used such as shown by Figure 3–6. DONMICS extends to the left and right and to the top of the SECNAV (Secretary of Navy) level, covers the entire business logistics segment, and extends into the operations areas. Also, as shown in the illustration, NAICOM/MIS (Navy-Integrated Command/Management Information System) covers the left side of the pyramid up to the bottom level of SECNAV whereas NAVLIS (Navy Logistic Information System) extends up to the lower level of the CNO/CMC (Chief of Naval Operations or Commandant of Marine Corps) on the left side and only the business logistic area of the Navy side, i.e., not into Navy operations. The area of activities for each of these three master information systems as well as their relationships to each other are shown by the illustration.

OSDMIS at the top of the chart stands for Office of the Secretary of Defense Management Information Systems, WWMCCS is World-Wide Military Command and Control System, and I²S (pronounced "eye-squared-ess") is Marine Corps Integrated Information System or shortened to the popular Integrated Information System. I²S, the Marine Corps' counterpart of the Navy's NAICOM/MIS, covers the right side of the

FIGURE 3–7. Makeup of Marine Corps Integrated Information System (I²S).

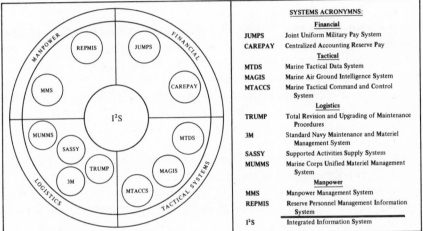

SYSTEMS ACRONYMNS:

**Financial**

| | |
|---|---|
| JUMPS | Joint Uniform Military Pay System |
| CAREPAY | Centralized Accounting Reserve Pay |

**Tactical**

| | |
|---|---|
| MTDS | Marine Tactical Data System |
| MAGIS | Marine Air Ground Intelligence System |
| MTACCS | Marine Tactical Command and Control System |

**Logistics**

| | |
|---|---|
| TRUMP | Total Revision and Upgrading of Maintenance Procedures |
| 3M | Standard Navy Maintenance and Materiel Management System |
| SASSY | Supported Activities Supply System |
| MUMMS | Marine Corps Unified Materiel Management System |

**Manpower**

| | |
|---|---|
| MMS | Manpower Management System |
| REPMIS | Reserve Personnel Management Information System |
| I²S | Integrated Information System |

illustration to the SECNAV lower level. I²S is made up of various systems. To demonstrate what they are, Figure 3–7 has been included.

## ADDITIONAL CONSIDERATIONS OF SYSTEMS

It is important to note that within an organization each unit not only receives information to guide it, but also produces information of importance to others. This receiving and giving of information by each unit makes for a chain of information which expedites system design. It also makes realistic the expression "flow of information."

Every system has a feedback of information which gives actual results being obtained. This characteristic follows naturally because a system is an entity within itself designed to accomplish certain work. The revealing of the degree to which this work is over- or underachieved is a natural outgrowth of the system's inherent properties.

Within their defined boundaries, systems are all-inclusive. They cut across common compartmentations recognized by organization, custom, and personal preferences. All essential component activities, regardless of their location or degree of contribution, are taken into account by a system. The guiding rule is to encompass all informational needs and contributions bearing on the objective of the system.

The use of systems in information management has numerous advantages among which the most important are:

**1. Encourages a Realistic and Totality Viewpoint.** An enterprise is an entirety. Appreciated is the total problem with its ramifications of various degrees of intensity in the different areas of the enterprise. And the application of management to broad concepts is encouraged. Planning and controlling are especially stimulated. Better coordination and less duplication of efforts and papers are won.

**2. Brings Order and Uniformity of Actions to Information Management Work.** The execution of work is reduced to a routine thus relieving the management members of many details and making it possible for them to devote most of their time to other work. Common clerical tasks are handled in an identical manner each time they occur. Work can be easily located and quick checks on progress can be made. Well-designed information formats, work habits, and controls can be utilized and the chances of error are reduced.

**3. Emphasizes Accurate and Reliable Controls.** Systems help show the need for checks in order to maintain accuracy, reliability, or other types of control. The overall picture utilized makes it possible to employ only those controls necessary for the whole system, thus lowering costs while retaining adequate control.

**4. Facilitates Automation of Data Processing.** Integrated data processing and the computer provide the practical means for handling large volumes of complicated data. To utilize these means, systems supply the needed medium to conceptualize how the data might be processed to satisfy stated goals.

**5. Simplifies Office Personnel Training.** The duties and operations of each job are clearly defined. Information is determined regarding what the employee must be capable of doing to perform the work satisfactorily. Selective training programs can be focused on the particular requirements needed by the employee.

**6. Brings Savings in the Supplying of Necessary Information.** The work is kept moving, delay is minimized, employees are guided in their respective tasks, and unnecessary steps are eliminated.


## SYSTEMS PERSONNEL

Before closing this chapter, a brief discussion on systems personnel will be included. The rise in demand for systems personnel over the last few years has been phenomenal. The main reason is that sound systems make possible the effective use of office automation. Common titles for systems personnel include "systems men," "systems engineers," "systems analysts" and "systems administrators." Illustrative of what can be considered typically their basic functions and duties are shown by Figure 3–8.

High on the list of desirable qualifications is conceptual ability, along with imagination and objectivity. He must be able to see future possibili-

FIGURE 3–8. A Systems Job Description.

Title:   Analyst—Systems and Procedures                    Div:   Allen Plant
Dept.:   Staff                                             Job No.:   33

Basic Functions:

Plans, develops, recommends, implements, and coordinates the systems and procedures activities within the Allen Plant. Advises vice president in charge of this plant on matters of systems and procedures to promote administrative efficiency and reduce clerical costs.

Duties:

Within the authority limits authorized by divisional policies, he has the following duties:

1. Advise and assist the vice president in regard to proposed systems and procedures.
2. Develop, recommend, and establish an effective cost and inventory system. This includes development of an effective manner for handling receipts and disbursements, handling vendors' and customers' claims, and taking and reporting physical inventories.
3. Review existing systems and procedures periodically in order to introduce improvements and controls to provide better service and lower cost.
4. Develop and maintain a Systems and Procedures Manual for the division to assure conformity to the pattern and format established by the corporation.
5. Coordinate the office mechanization program with all interested staff and operating personnel.

* * * * *

10. Keep informed on current developments in the area of systems and procedures, appraise their value for the division, and recommend adoption when advisable.

Approved James C. Clzin<br>Authorized Henry Pittibaugh<br>Date July 2, 196

ties in untried systems and anticipate possible trouble areas. Also, the ability to initiate and "dream practical dreams" are genuine assets. In addition, it is helpful to possess a general yet fundamental grasp of the background activities within which the system is designed and operated. Actually, he should have a keen interest in every aspect of the enterprise's operations and constantly be aware of top managers' present goals and plans for the future, as these may affect his systems design.

The systems man must update periodically his knowledge of techniques, tools, and equipment. New and better ways are constantly appearing in these areas. Definitely advantageous to the systems man are mental alertness, curiosity, and an understanding of human nature. He must have the ability to work with top managers, to understand their problems, and to push forward in his efforts despite complaints and disappointments. Finally, the art and skill of communication must be developed, for the systems man must be able to share his ideas, findings, and suggestions clearly and concisely. He must communicate easily with other people.

## QUESTIONS

1. Would you classify systems in information management as being static or dynamic? Why?
2. What is meant by the end-result concept in system improvement work? Relate an example illustrating the use of this concept.
3. What is systems simulation and how is it used to improve systems?
4. Select any type of information now used by a business with which you are familiar and suggest ways in which this information might be improved.
5. Other than those included in this chapter, relate an example showing the importance of objectives in the total systems concept.
6. Discuss the use of the decision structure in improving a system.
7. Explain Figure 3–3 in your own words.
8. Identify each of the following:
   *a*) A model for systems simulation.
   *b*) DONMICS of the U.S. Navy.
   *c*) Systems contracting.
   *d*) Total Management Information System.
9. Enumerate the main benefits offered by the use of the total systems concept.
10. Referring to Figure 3–6, answer the following:
    *a*) Is I²S a part of NAVLIS?
    *b*) Is I²S related with NAVLIS?
    *c*) What is the meaning of CNR?
    *d*) Does DONMICS cover business logistics only?
11. As you see it, is the total systems concept a theoretical idea or a practical reality? Why?
12. Relate and discuss the major desirable qualifications for systems personnel.

## CASE PROBLEMS

### Case 3–1.   Limpert Manufacturing Company

About three years ago a system to provide production cost information by different products or jobs was installed for the manufacturing work of this company. Commonly termed a "cost by job" system, labor time or charge is made against a specific job. Production control makes up in advance a job cost card which identifies the components of a job and accompanies the sequence of the work through the factory. At the top of the card is written (1) the part number, (2) the job number, (3) description, and (4) estimated time. Each employee who works on the job signs his company number and name on the card in the space provided, together with time registration at the start and at the finish of the time he spent on this job number. For example, an entry may read: "156 G. Lustig 4 May 8:00 8.90 0.90" indicating employee Lustig spent 0.90 hours, or 54 minutes, on job number 156.

In evaluating this present means, Dan Reeves, the assistant factory superintendent, observed that it provides a complete summation of time spent on the job as soon as the job is completed. The total of the times spent is compared to the estimated time. However, a daily posting is not provided since most jobs are in the factory longer than one day. The cost status on a job is not known until it is completed. Further, there is no control over nonproductive time. However, Mr. Reeves feels the company could live with the present arrangement, but if this is done, he suggests the card be modified to provide identification of all the operations to be done and their sequence on the total job. This would make the job card a routing card as well.

Prescott Carr, a systems analyst, suggests a cost by man per job or per day be used. Under this arrangement, a separate card is used by the employee to register his start and stop time on each different job on which he works. Nonproductive time is registered on a separate card. If the job lasts beyond the close of a working day, a new card is used the following day for registering time. Cards are sorted daily either by (1) labor distribution of employee time or (2) labor distribution to specific jobs. In Mr. Carr's opinion such a system should be adopted since it will supply needed control of labor time in production and can be applied to all types of operations. By using a punched card, the written data can be transferred on the same card to the punched hole median and sorting can be very rapid. Further, if an individual incentive plan is contemplated, the individual payments could be carried on the cards. It is also feasible to include additional helpful information on the card such as standard time, number of pieces made, number scrapped, standard rate, and incentive rate. From the single card, both labor cost of the item and payment due employee are calculated.

Timothy Tambone, assistant director of the accounting department, recommends a perforated daily job ticket be used. As each job is completed, a stub is removed by tearing along a perforated line, and as the work progresses the perforated sections are turned in to the foreman. Sometimes called a strip ticket or payroll attendance and cost by man and job system, it provides a continuous flow of time tickets or stubs to the costing department where labor can be distributed against both employee and job. On each ticket or stub are shown the employee's name, number, operation, job number, pieces, time in, time out, and elapsed time. In addition, the heading at the top of the ticket can provide payroll information such as employee name, number, time in, time out for the total working day.

"Eliminate all tickets that are or appear to be timeclock tickets," comments Ray A. Kreitzburg, popular personnel manager of the company. "Employees dislike having to punch in and punch out. Encourage and motivate them to get the work out and you don't need to record how each employee spends every tenth-of-a-minute of his workday."

## Questions:

1. Draw a sketch of the ticket suggested by Mr. Tambone.
2. What's your reaction to the suggestions of Mr. Carr? Of Mr. Kreitzburg?

3. Does this case illustrate the interdependence of systems in an enterprise? Discuss.
4. What is your recommendation to Limpert Manufacturing Company?

## Case 3–2.  Troast Wholesale Plumbers

The assistant sales manager tells Frank Reinhart, a systems analyst, that, upon receipt, a customer's order is time-stamped and checked for credit. If it is found satisfactory, a "Credit OK" stamp is placed on the order; if not, the customer is written a letter requesting payment on his past account or cash for the pending order. Order with credit approval are posted on customers' order cards, which are used for sales analysis work. Orders are then sent to the stockroom for filling and shipping. Subsequently, when merchandise is shipped and billed, the date and amount of shipment are posted on the customer's card. In response to his question of how the sales department knew that the order was shipped, Mr. Reinhart learned that this was by means of a "storeroom packing slip."

He then interviewed Hazel Mead, billing supervisor, who explained that her department receives a "packing slip form 07" which tells them the order is shipped. When they are so informed, this form 07 is checked with the customer's original purchase order and, if accurate, three billing copies are prepared. The first copy is sent to the customer, the second and third copies are filed respectively alphabetically and numerically in the files of the billing department. The original order is returned to sales, where it is filed, and the packing slip is filed chronologically by date billed.

The purchasing department buys upon requisition from the stockroom. The vendors are selected by looking in the vendor card file. Here the cards are arranged by part numbers and names showing the recommended supplier or suppliers. The purchasing agent can either write or telephone for quotations and base his selection of vendor on the answers received or he can simply select one of the approved vendors. Usually, on orders amounting to less than $100, he selects the vendor based on judgment only. Four copies of a purchase order are made out. Copy No. 1 goes to the vendor; Copy No. 2 goes to inventory control; Copy No. 3 goes to billing for payment, upon receipt of merchandise indicated by a receiving copy slip from the receiving and shipping department; and Copy No. 4 is the copy of purchasing filed by the purchase order number.

George Walker, the assistant manager of the stockroom, was interviewed next by Mr. Reinhart. An inventory card record is maintained for each item. When the amount of stock on hand reaches the replenishing point, an amount calculated for each item, a requisition is sent to purchasing to order a specific amount. Stockroom orders are stamped "PI" when they have been recorded in the daily tally sheet of orders for processing and also in inventory card records to reveal inventory depletion due to forthcoming shipping. PI orders are then picked, checked, packed, and shipped. Receiving and shipping, which is subordinate to the stockroom, makes out four copies of a packing slip 07, one of which is sent to billing; the second is a file copy of receiving and shipping; the third is sent to sales; and the fourth is the packing slip enclosed with the merchandise. Further questioning by Mr. Reinhart revealed that the stockroom receives the original customer's order from sales and that from this original a shop or stockroom order is made out. This latter order form highlights stockroom data, such as best sequence for picking items, location of stock, and approximate unit weights. After carefully checking the stockroom order, the stockroom sends the original customer's order to the billing department, as indicated previously.

## Questions:

1. Currently the processing of a customer's order is viewed as four separate operations. Do you agree with this viewpoint? Why?
2. Draw a diagram indicating the processing as described above to substantiate your answer to question 1.
3. Point out and discuss some areas for improvement in the current processing practices being followed.

### Case 3–3.   Jefferson Dairy Company

Currently collections are handled as follows: A file card is made out for each customer, showing name, address, monthly due date, and the amounts of credit, debit, and balance. These cards are filed alphabetically according to the customer's surname.

Each collection day, which is monthly, the office clerk goes through the file and makes out a list stipulating the name, address, and amount of accounts due. The collection sheets are given the drivers, who do the collecting. Upon payment, the customer is given a receipt, and the amount paid is written by the driver opposite the proper name on the collection list. From these sheets, the office clerk posts the collection date and amount on the proper file cards.

Office manager Russel Sayer feels that the present efforts require too much work and does not permit sufficient flexibility, for example, when only partial payments or advance payments are made. He believes improvement is possible. Mr. Sayer realizes that the common practice is for a dairy to sell the products to the driver, who collects on his own from his customers. However, top managers of Jefferson Dairy Company feel that the present credit arrangement to customers by the dairy gives better control and relieves the driver of much paper work. Market studies indicate that consumers like Jefferson Dairy's way of handling collections. Mr. Sayer states that the company has approximately 12,000 accounts, which is a large number, and that the average amount for each account is $7.18 monthly. Few owe for more than the amount of a month's bill. He believes that any proposed change must of necessity require little or no new office equipment.

## Questions:

1. Do you agree with Mr. Sayer, the office manager? Why?
2. Indicate the procedure you recommend for Jefferson Dairy Company. Substantiate your recommendation.

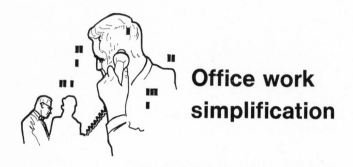

# chapter 4

# Office work simplification

If a man will begin with certainties, he shall end in doubts, but if he will be content to begin with doubts he shall end in certainties.

*—Francis Bacon*

CONTINUING our discussion of conceptualizing the information work to be done, we now focus our attention on smaller concepts, namely on office procedures and methods. An *office procedure* can be defined as *a series of selected clerical steps, usually performed by more than one person, which constitute an established and accepted way of carrying on an entire major phase of office activity.* Procedures are obtained by preplanning the various steps believed necessary to accomplish the work. They are applied to the handling of such things as incoming orders, accounts payable, purchase orders, making up payrolls, sending out statements, and handling mail. Frequently they extend throughout a large portion of the entire office.

The term *method* designates *the manner of work performance of a task consisting of one or more clerical acts by an individual employee.* To a degree, methods become quite routine under an automated arrangement. Methods planning is more important when manual means are followed. A series of methods which are cumulative and integrated make up a procedure. And, to repeat, several procedures which are related and integrated make up a system.

It is logical to discuss first systems as we have done, then the procedures making up this system, and finally the methods making up each procedure. In this way the broad activities are established, coordination is enhanced, the feasibility of automation effectively determined, and the end result of the total effort is clearly visualized. In practice, however, the information planner gives some consideration to procedures and methods while designing the system and to methods while designing the procedure. This is taking the bottom-to-top viewpoint and this is usually helpful in connection with the top-down viewpoint. The latter viewpoint, however, is dominant. To reverse this approach by starting with methods, tying them together for the procedure, and tying procedures together for the system is possible, but usually results in coordination difficulties and in excessive work scopes covered by the procedures and the systems.

## IMPROVING PROCEDURES AND METHODS

As in systems work, effort is made to devise the best possible way of performing the necessary work. What is presently being done may have resulted from previous planning, observing how others perform the same work, past experience, trial and error, or suggestions by others. Efforts to improve have been given much study. In fact, there exist principles to follow and a program of action to apply. Some call these efforts "office work simplification" which is formally defined as common sense organized to eliminate waste of material, equipment, time, energy, and space in the performance of office work. The possibilities for improvement are limited only by the ability, imagination, and aggressiveness of the analyst. There is no secret formula. Office work simplification is not confined to procedures and methods, but is employed to improve an office form, an arrangement, a layout, or equipment and machines.

The superior procedure or method includes only efforts to fulfill the work necessary to achieve the objective with a minimum of time and effort. Ill-directed and ineffective efforts constitute a great waste which is unnecessary and preventable. Work simplification is an available means to eliminate this waste. Laymen sometimes erroneously refer to work simplification applied to methods as speedup. Work simplification implies an increase in the rate of work production, not speeding up the movements of the employee. The latter means to hurry *all* the work steps, *both the necessary and the unnecessary ones.* In contrast, by work simplification the rate of work production is improved by *performing only the necessary steps in a normal manner.*

## GUIDES OF OFFICE WORK SIMPLIFICATION

Over a period, many lists of guides to office work simplification have been compiled. For our purposes the following five are discussed.

***1. Promote "Participation with Know-How" by Every Office Employee by Means of Training in and Encouragement of the Use of Work Simplification.*** An enthusiastic and strong desire by the operative employee for an improved way of doing the work satisfactorily and an understanding of the reasons for doing it the improved way are cardinal considerations. For the most part, these are won by encouraging employee participation in planning the improvement; for in this way employee interest, self-expression, acceptance, and cooperation are motivated and utilized. A person will usually accept what he himself proposes.

But participation alone is insufficient. Nothing is more frustrating to the employee than to be asked to take part in an activity about which he knows little or nothing. This means the know-how must be supplied. Short, effective training programs are in order. Information and examples must be made available to the office employee. Thus, the participation with know-how is supplied.

Most employees dislike being pushed around, not being informed of developments of changes which affect them, and have a fear of what might happen to them as a result of change. Factors such as these cause the employee to desire the *status quo* and to tend to reject a new means of work performance. To overcome this resistance, participation with know-how is recommended. If employees' enthusiastic participation for eliminating office waste cannot be won, it is almost a certainty that no really significant gains are going to be made. It is also vital to hold frank discussions pointing out the need for improvements to keep the enterprise competitive or to give greater security to the employee. Job loss need not result from work simplification. A policy of retraining and transferring to other jobs can be followed. In many cases, the normal labor turnover will take care of the number of employees needed; those leaving the company are not replaced. But these facts should be explained in simple language to the employees, so that they know what is going on and where they fit into the picture. Actually, the ideas of acquiring a real sense of accomplishment and of getting things done the simple way are strong appeals to many office employees.

**2. Make the Series of Activities Productive and Simple.**   The adopted series of work activities should represent the best possible combination for achieving the finished work, taking into account the available facilities and work conditions. Simply stated, justify each activity for its essentiality, and eliminate all the unnecessary ones. As far as possible, those contributing directly to the goal, or so-called productive elements of a procedure, should be maximized; and conversely, the nonproductive elements should be reduced to an absolute minimum. Normally, this provides for the greatest productivity.

**3. Combine Work Activities Wherever Possible to Avoid Recopying.** Frequently found is needless copying of data. In some offices this practice is part of the accepted manner of getting information processed. There is nothing uncommon, for example, in having the salesman write an order, his branch office recopy it, the factory recopy certain portions of the order, the billing department recopy on an invoice, and accounts receivable recopy on the proper ledger card. Most of these writing activities can and should be combined into a single operation.

**4. *Reduce Distances Traveled to the Shortest Amounts Feasible.*** Movement of papers or of people are costly and wasteful; most of them do not represent purposive effort. Therefore, movements should be closely scrutinized; if not essential, they should be eliminated. When travel is necessary, it is usually better to move the paper than the person. Sometimes, the machine can be brought to the work; or mechanical handling devices, such as conveyors, pneumatic tubes, and gravity feeds to deliver or to take away the papers, can be used. When messengers are employed, perhaps more items per trip are in order. Different arrangements of the office layout might also offer worthwhile improvements.

**5. *Arrange Activities to Provide a Smooth Flow from One Clerical Step to Another or a Rhythmic Pattern for an Employee at a Workplace.*** Excessive amounts or spurts of unduly heavy work loads tend to discourage the office employee. As a result, the feeling of never "getting on top of the work" or having a sense of accomplishment plagues the employee. In contrast, the situation of carefully throttling the work in order to keep busy is equally annoying. A steady, constant flow of work is normally desirable.

Delays and hesitations in the work flow should be minimized. Much time and energy are dissipated by tolerating the jumping around from one batch of work to another, then returning to the initial batch. This applies whether automated or manual means are used. It takes time to adjust to the different batches of work, not to mention the lost time in stopping one and starting another. For each employee, a rhythmic pattern of work actions with motions following curved, not straight lines, should be sought.

## APPLYING OFFICE WORK SIMPLIFICATION

Four basic steps are followed in applying office work simplification: (1) select work to be simplified, (2) obtain all the facts about this work, (3) devise improvement by analyzing these facts and using the questioning approach, and (4) apply the derived improved means.

The first step, select work to be simplified, may designate in the case of procedures a procedure that limits other information work or in which labor requirements appear unduly high. The procedure may be selected on the basis that the number of work activities is too large, the time taken to do the work is excessive, costs are unduly high, or the end result seems unjustifiable. For methods, repetitive tasks are favorites for work simplification. Generally they offer large savings possibilities. Even though the gain on each task performance might be small, the doing of this task over and over again results in sizable cumulative savings. Selecting repetitive tasks does not mean that other tasks do not warrant study. *Any task can be improved with sufficient effort.* Actually, the job selected and the extent and thoroughness of the study depend upon a number of things, such as the continuity of the work, the amount of processing required, the total cost or number of people engaged in the work, the value connected with the paper handled, and the interest of the operative employee, supervisor, or analyst.

Whatever work is selected, it must be defined. This helps to classify the objective and avoids the mistake of attempting to simplify office work without first gaining a clear concept of the work objective. Work definition assists in simplification because all efforts can be concentrated and directed toward this goal.

## OBTAIN ALL THE FACTS ABOUT THIS WORK

The second step is to find out how the selected work is currently being handled. For example, details of a present procedure are obtained from available record sources, i.e., job descriptions, charts, lists, outlines, and sample forms. Additional information can be obtained from study of the system of which the procedure is a part, talks with members of management, and inspection of the procedure in action, so that the type of work and the equipment used can be observed. The same general approach can be used for obtaining the facts on a method.

All the facts are needed to devise an effective improvement. To aid in this work and to gain a clear comprehension of them, graphic representations or charts have been developed. Many different types are available. Each chart has a particular purpose and value, and it is neither necessary nor practical to use every type of chart in a particular study. The major charts for procedure and for method improvements will be discussed in detail later in this chapter.

## DEVISE IMPROVEMENT

The third step is to devise improvement which is done by analyzing the facts and using the questioning approach. This phase can be described as one of challenging each detail of the present work. The facts are studied to reveal violations of the basic work simplification guides discussed previously. Correcting these weaknesses provides improvement. Creativity and experience are also helpful in suggesting areas for improvement.

Using the questioning approach is perhaps the most fruitful and widely adopted practice. Every work activity is subjected to questions pertaining to what is done, where, when, by whom, and how. To each of these, the big question of why is added making the first question, for example, what is done and why? and the second question, where should it be done and why? Answers to these questions help relate essentials, reveal unnecessary work, and provide clues for improvement. Figure 4–1 indicates these key questions along with their relationship to the major guides of work simplification utilized, and the resultant actions. To illustrate, answers to the question "What is being done and why?" following the principles of promote participation with know-how and make activities productive and simple, point out many unnecessary activities that can be eliminated. If

FIGURE 4–1. Key Questions, Major Principles, and Resultant Actions Used in Devising the Improvement of an Office Procedure.

| Key Questions | Major Principles* | Resultant Action | |
|---|---|---|---|
| What and why? | 1. Promote "participation with know-how." <br> 2. Make activities productive and simple. | Eliminate | |
| Where and why? <br> When and why? <br> Who and why? | 1. Promote "participation with know-how." <br> 3. Combine work activities—avoid recopying <br> 4. Reduce distances traveled. <br> 5. Provide a smooth flow from one step to another. | Combine <br> or <br> change | the place <br> the time <br> the person |
| How and why? | 1. Promote "participation with know-how." <br> 2. Make activities productive and simple. | Simplify | |

* Refer to pages 71–73.

so, eliminate them, for this is the zenith of work simplification. Questions of where and why, when and why, and who and why will suggest combining or changing procedural elements as to place, time, and person, respectively. An improved procedure will result. The question "How and why?" emphasizes simplifying the activity.

The sequence of the questioning and subsequent improvement action is logical and practical. Questions should be asked in the sequence shown. If the activity can be eliminated, there is no need to study it further for possible combination or change. Likewise, the "Who and why" question precedes the "How and why" question because the former might lead to improved labor utilization, and this should be determined before the manner of doing the work is improved.

Additional questions of a more specific nature can also be asked, but it is well to remember that good questions are required to get good answers. The questions should have a purposeful intent and lead to betterment, not just a conglomeration of responses to queries. Examples of specific questions for improvement of office procedures are shown by Figure 4–2, those applicable to office methods by Figure 4–3.

In the case of improving office methods, it is especially important to provide a suitable workplace. This includes pre-positioning papers, cards,

FIGURE 4–2. Suggested Questions for Improving Office Procedures.

1. Purpose of operation:
   *a*) What purpose is served by the office form? By the report?
   *b*) Could the information given be obtained from another source?
   *c*) Do numbers, ratios, or variations best answer and serve the needs of the procedure?
   *d*) Is the cost of preparing the form or report justified by the results it accomplishes?
2. Design:
   *a*) Is the size, format, and color of the form best suited to its use?
   *b*) Is the information on the form or report easy to interpret? Most convenient from a filing viewpoint?
   *c*) Is the work legible?
3. Process analysis:
   *a*) Is the operation duplicated at any point in the procedure?
   *b*) Should the information be filed permanently or temporarily, or be destroyed?
   *c*) Can the information be produced at one writing?
   *d*) Can the copying of information be eliminated by using original records?
   *e*) Is information compiled in the manner best suited for subsequent sorting, filing, or use?
4. Inspection:
   *a*) How is work checked for errors?
   *b*) Is it important that all parts of the work be letter-perfect?
   *c*) Would the use of mechanical devices improve the accuracy of the work to a desirable extent?
5. Material handling:
   *a*) Can the flow of information through the procedure be expedited by improved office layout?
   *b*) Can the amount of time papers are delayed while awaiting action be reduced?
   *c*) Is messenger service adequate?
   *d*) Can pneumatic tubes or other forms-conveying systems be used to advantage?

Source: Adapted from H. B. Maynard and G. J. Stegemerten, *Guide to Methods Improvement* (New York: McGraw-Hill Book Co., Inc., 1944), pp. 25, 28, 31, 35, 39, 40, 45, and 46.

and working tools so that they are handy and ready for use as required. For example, devices can be used to hold penciled notes while typing, locating frequently used supplies such as paper clips, stapler, and rubber stamps on a rotor where easy access is possible; and putting reference materials, including books, catalogs, and lists, on convenient racks within easy reach or vision of the operator.

The arrangement of unitizing can also be followed. Under this plan, each operating unit is considered a separate entity and is supplied individually with all the tools and supplies necessary for its work. The required papers, books, supplies, and the like are located on a wall rack or in a floor cabinet near the operator's desk. For the most part, this arrangement brings best results when a large portion of the office consists of widely dispersed and fairly independent units, although it is not limited to this particular type of setup.

Also, it is advisable to utilize the normal and the maximum working areas. The *normal* working area for the right hand on a desk top, for example, is the area determined by swinging the extended right hand and

FIGURE 4–3. Suggested Questions for Improving Office Methods.

1. Questions regarding setup or workplace layout:
   *a*) Is adequate storage space provided for required materials, supplies, and tools?
   *b*) Are desk tops and drawers kept in an orderly condition so that time spent looking for lost articles is reduced to a minimum?
   *c*) Is a desk necessary, or could the work be done as well on a flat-top table?
   *d*) Should a specially designed table be provided to facilitate the use of office machines?
2. Questions regarding tools and equipment:
   *a*) Should a machine replace hand methods?
   *b*) Can any foot-operated devices, such as a foot-operated stapler, be used?
   *c*) Can gathering or sorting aids be used?
   *d*) Are office machines properly maintained by qualified maintenance men?
3. Questions regarding working conditions:
   *a*) Are unnecessary noises and disturbances eliminated?
   *b*) Is privacy assured for telephone conversations of a confidential nature?
   *c*) Are suitable facilities provided for personal belongings?

Source: Adapted from H. B. Maynard and G. J. Stegemerten, *Guide to Methods Improvement* (New York: McGraw-Hill Book Co., Inc., 1944), pp. 51, 56, 60–61.

forearm only across the desk. The pivoting is at the elbow, with the upper arm being relaxed at the side of the body. The arm tends to swing out a little at the outer end of the arc. In a similar manner, the normal working area for the left hand is determined. These two normal areas overlap in front of the employee, and this overlapping area represents the location in which work requiring both hands can be performed most readily.

The *maximum* working areas are the areas determined by swinging the extended hand and entire arm, pivoting at the shoulder. Figure 4–4 shows graphically the normal and maximum working areas with dimensions for an average employee. Paper being worked on should be located within the arcs of the normal working areas common to both hands. Supplies should also be located within the normal and never outside the maximum working areas.

A comfortable workplace implies that the employee's chair, desk, table, or machine is of such dimensions that he can accomplish his work with

FIGURE 4–4. Illustration of Normal and of Maximum Working Areas.

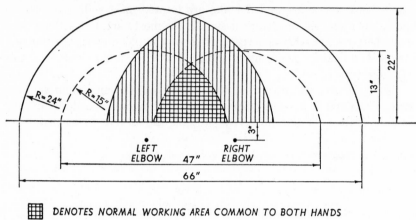

| | DENOTES NORMAL WORKING AREA COMMON TO BOTH HANDS |
| | DENOTES MAXIMUM WORKING AREA COMMON TO BOTH HANDS |

ease, that is, without excessive physical exertion or strain. When possible, it is usually desirable to have the employee sit part of the time and stand part of the time. Some change is apparently necessary for maximum comfort. The height of the workplace should be such that support is given the underside of the forearm at a point slightly below the elbows. Where the hands are self-supported, the workplace should be of such height that the hands work at a level slightly higher than that of the elbows.

Further, in the case of methods improvement, certain guides can be followed. These have been developed over a long period and represent short cuts which are effective. They are shown in Figure 4–5.

FIGURE 4–5. Guides for Improving Office Methods.

> 1. Do the work by machine, not manually, if possible. Develop the best motion for the operator with the machine being utilized.
> 2. Use both hands for doing work, avoiding the use of either hand as a holding device. Both hands should begin and complete their motions at the same time, moving simultaneously in opposite and symmetrical directions.
> 3. Employ a minimum of motions to complete the task. Use hand motions only or, if necessary, hands and eye motions only. Arm, leg, and body motions should be infrequently required.
> 4. Strive to have high-priced office help do high-priced office work only. Minimize, for example, the private secretary doing strictly typist work.
> 5. Avoid writing the same information twice.
> 6. Have source document and end result in the same format, if possible.
> 7. Use precomputed tables or graphic indicators.
> 8. Make only the number of copies that are needed and used.

## APPLY THE DERIVED IMPROVED MEANS

After the simplification has been worked out, it is a relatively simple matter to apply it, provided the employee has participated and understands why and how the new means is to be used. To accomplish procedures and methods improvement there is no adequate substitute for gaining and maintaining wholesome understanding between management and nonmanagement members. The purpose of the improvement should be clearly set forth, and the reasons for its importance in the enterprise made crystal clear to every employee affected by it.

It helps to show examples of what has been accomplished from work simplification in other offices, and to indicate that it is a key in achieving the combination of high wages and short hours. Everyone dealing with information should realize the importance of improving the way information work is performed. To realize this goal, training can be provided; meetings of department heads and supervisors are common. They can be conducted separately for each group or combined into one group, depending upon the individual circumstances.

## COMMON CHARTS OF OFFICE WORK SIMPLIFICATION

The remainder of this chapter will be devoted to work simplification charts. As mentioned above, these charts serve to provide the facts for a work simplification project in a clear and comprehensive manner. Specifically, work simplification charts serve the following purposes: (1) assist in securing, organizing, and visualizing the facts, (2) aid in analyzing and evaluating these facts, (3) help formulate an improved procedure, and (4) assist in convincing others of the value of the improved procedure. Unless the chart serves one or more of these purposes, it should not be drawn.

Frequently, more than one chart is used, and the right combination of several charts usually reveals information and clues for work simplification. In total three charts for procedures improvement—process, movement diagram, and procedural flow—and three charts for methods improvement—left- and right-hand chart, production study, and operator-machine activity—will be presented.

## PROCESS CHART

One of the most helpful charts in work simplification is the process chart which shows the successive detailed steps in a process. The steps are indicated by brief statements and symbols arranged vertically in chronological order, with the first step at the top of the sheet. Unfortunately, there is no standardized set of symbols used by analysts. Figure 4–6

FIGURE 4-6. Symbols for Process Charts.

| LIST A | | LIST B | | ILLUSTRATED BY |
|---|---|---|---|---|
| 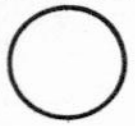 ◯ | OPERATION | 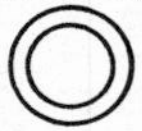 ◎ | OPERATION – ORIGIN OF RECORD | WRITING, POSTING, SORTING |
| — | |  ⊘ | OPERATION – ADDING TO RECORD | EXTENDING A BILLING |
| ○ | TRANSPORTATION |  ⇧ | TRAVEL OR MOVE | MOVEMENT OF PAPER OR WALKING BY EMPLOYEE |
| 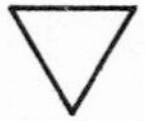 ▽ | DELAY OR STORAGE |  ▷ | DELAY – AVOIDABLE | PAPER AWAITING FURTHER ACTION |
| — | | 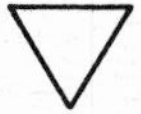 ▽ | FILE | PLACING IN FILE |
| — | |  ⧖ | COPY DISCARDED OR DESTROYED | TERMINATING PAPER |
| ▭ | INSPECTION | ▭ | INSPECTION | VERIFYING BUT NOT CHANGING DATA |

shows two sets of symbols that are widely employed. To illustrate, signing a memo constitutes an operation and would be represented by either a large circle or double large circles depending upon the set of symbols followed. Likewise, sending the memo to another office unit is transportation and is shown by a small circle or a small arrow. Filing the memo is represented by an inverted triangle. Checking the memo for errors constitutes inspection and is represented by a square. Many analysts have found that color is helpful in charting work. For example, operations constituting direct processing work and adding value to the product are distinguished by the use of a special color. In contrast, no special color is employed for operations used but not adding value such as operations done for preparatory or cleaning-up purposes.

The intended purpose of the process chart and the symbols is to give a clear picture of the office procedure and assist in analyzing and improving it. Any reasonable set of symbols can be used; the best is the set that assists the analyst most in his determination to eliminate paper work waste. In addition, it is customary to include on a process chart the time required, the distance covered if movement is involved, and a summary by type of action. This chart can either be drawn for an entire procedure covering many departments, or it may be confined to a part of a procedure.

Figure 4–7 illustrates a process chart. It shows the process of stopping an incorrect charge credit in a large department store. It is drawn for the credit form papers. This work is brought about by the following situation.

An article of merchandise is purchased by a customer, Mrs. John T. Smith, with a charge account. The merchandise is returned, but the clerk incorrectly writes Mrs. John F. Smith on the credit memorandum. Later, the customer telephones and informs the adjusting department of the store that the name is not Mrs. John F. Smith, but Mrs. John T. Smith. Meanwhile, the credit memorandum is in process in either the sales auditing department or the accounts receivable department, both located several floors away from the adjusting department. Hence, a "stop notice" is prepared and a duplicate copy sent to sales auditing or accounts receivable, telling them not to bill the credit memorandum made out to John F. Smith. This stop notice, along with the credit memorandum to John F. Smith, is returned to the adjustor who handled the telephone call.

The placing of the credit memorandum and stop notice on the desk constitutes step number 1 of the chart illustrated in Figure 4–7. Therefore, on line number 1, this action is briefly described in the column to the left. This action is an operation, in that something happens to the papers; hence, it is represented by a large-circle symbol and is indicated on the chart by filling in the large circle under "operation" on line number 1. Appropriate notes are made in the column to the right.

Next, the forms are picked up. Hence, on line number 2, this action is

## 82    Office management and control

FIGURE 4–7. A Fill-in Type of Process Chart Covering the Work of Stopping an Incorrect Charge Credit.

### MARSHALL FIELD & COMPANY
### FLOW PROCESS CHART

PAGE..............

JOB *Stopping any incorrect Charge Credit*

SUBJECT CHARTED *Credit form*

CHARTED BY *Ethel Marable*

DATE *November 19—*

DEPT *Customer's Service* SEC *Adjusting*

| SUMMARY | | | |
|---|---|---|---|
| METHOD | PRES. | PROPD. | SAVG. |
| NO. OF OPERATIONS | 17 | | |
| NO. OF TRANSPORTATIONS | 7 | | |
| NO. OF STORAGES | 5 | | |
| NO. OF INSPECTIONS | | | |
| MAN HOURS OR MINUTES | | | |
| DISTANCE TRAVELED | 92 ft. | | |

| | DETAILS (PRESENT / PROPOSED) METHOD | OPER. | TRANS. | STORAGE | INSPECT. | DIST. IN FEET | TIME IN MINUTES | WHAT? | WHERE? | WHEN? | WHO? | HOW? | NOTES |
|---|---|---|---|---|---|---|---|---|---|---|---|---|---|
| 1 | Placed on desk | O | O | ▽ | □ | | | | | | | | Credit and duplicate stop attached—sent from sales auditing or accounts receivable |
| 2 | Picked up | O | O | ▽ | □ | | | | | | | | |
| 3 | Placed in drawer | O | O | ▽ | □ | 2 | | | | | | | |
| 4 | Waits | O | O | ▽ | □ | | | | | | | | Time indefinite—may have other work of priority nature |
| 5 | Taken out of drawer | O | O | ▽ | □ | 2 | | | | | | | |
| 6 | Placed on desk | O | O | ▽ | □ | | | | | | | | |
| 7 | Waits | O | O | ▽ | □ | | | | | | | | Makes out request for claim which acts as out-of-file notice |
| 8 | Attached to request | O | O | ▽ | □ | | | | | | | | |
| 9 | Carried to central files | O | O | ▽ | □ | 15 | | | | | | | |
| 10 | Placed in basket | O | O | ▽ | □ | | | | | | | | |
| 11 | Waits | O | O | ▽ | □ | | | | | | | | For central file clerk |
| 12 | Picked up | O | O | ▽ | □ | | | | | | | | |
| 13 | Carried to file cabinet | O | O | ▽ | □ | 25 | | | | | | | |
| 14 | Waits | O | O | ▽ | □ | | | | | | | | Looking for claim under correct name |
| 15 | Attached to claim | O | O | ▽ | □ | | | | | | | | |
| 16 | Carried to out basket | O | O | ▽ | □ | 25 | | | | | | | |
| 17 | Placed in basket | O | O | ▽ | □ | | | | | | | | |
| 18 | Waits | O | O | ▽ | □ | | | | | | | | For pickup |
| 19 | Picked up | O | O | ▽ | □ | | | | | | | | |
| 20 | Carried to desk | O | O | ▽ | □ | 15 | | | | | | | |
| 21 | Placed on desk | O | O | ▽ | □ | | | | | | | | |
| 22 | Stop taken from claim | O | O | ▽ | □ | | | | | | | | Original stop now placed on claim |
| 23 | Credit voided | O | O | ▽ | □ | | | | | | | | Write "Void," claim number and initials |
| 24 | Picked up | O | O | ▽ | □ | | | | | | | | |
| 25 | Placed in house envelope | O | O | ▽ | □ | | | | | | | | |
| 26 | Picked up | O | O | ▽ | □ | | | | | | | | |
| 27 | Carried to house mailbox | O | O | ▽ | □ | 8 | | | | | | | |
| 28 | Placed in house mailbox | O | O | ▽ | □ | | | | | | | | |
| 29 | Wait for pickup | O | O | ▽ | □ | | | | | | | | |

24-01-01 Form 187

*Courtesy: Marshall Field & Co., Chicago*

expressed and represented by a large circle. In a similar manner, the entire process is described and charted. The totals of each action and of the distances traveled are then determined and recorded in the summary table at the top of the sheet. In this illustration, the figures are:

Operations........................17
Transportations................... 7
Storage........................... 5
Distance traveled.................92 feet

A study of the chart shows that this procedure can be simplified. To do this, the work simplification principles and the questioning attitude, as already discussed, were applied. For example, when step number 3—placing paper in drawer—is subjected to the question "What is done and why?" it is found to be unproductive and hence can be eliminated. In similar manner, every operation, transportation, storage, and inspection not proved necessary is eliminated; and actions found necessary are combined wherever feasible or changed to provide better accomplishment of the work. Finally, each necessary step is simplified as much as possible.

Figure 4–8 shows an improved procedure over the one shown in Figure 4–7. In the light of what has been written, it is suggested that a careful

FIGURE 4–8. An Improved Procedure over That Shown in Figure 4–7.

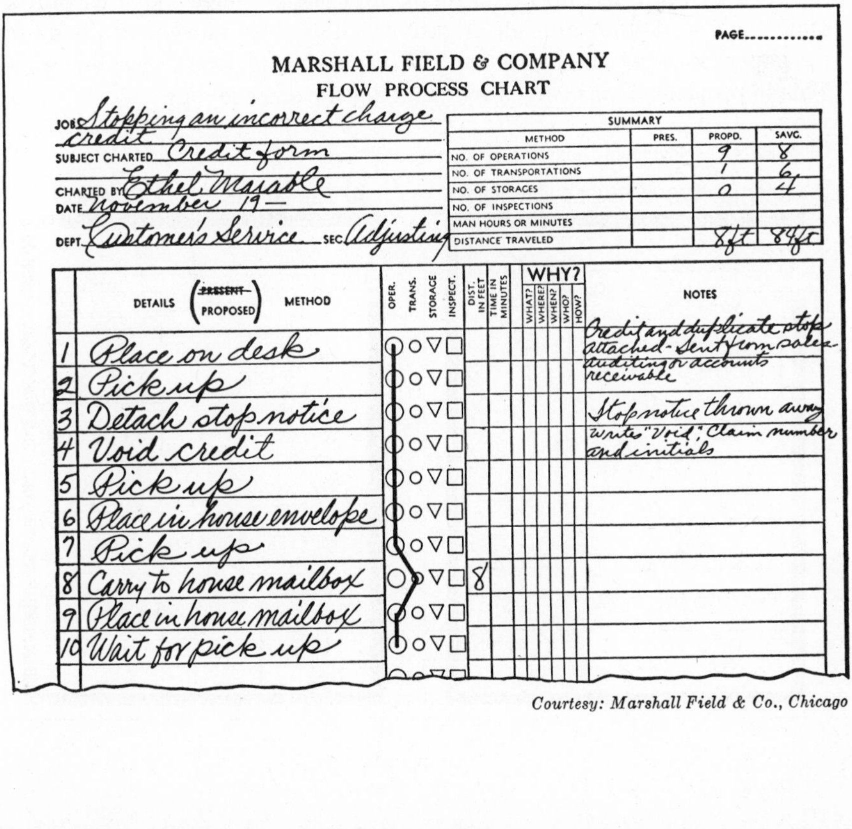

*Courtesy: Marshall Field & Co., Chicago*

comparison of these two charts be made in order to gain an insight as to how a procedure can be improved. Under the new procedure, credits are voided with a claim number on them and sent to sales auditing or accounts receivable. The stop notice can be discarded, since its duplicate is already on the claim. The elimination of requests to pull claims out of the central file accounts for getting rid of steps 7 through 21 of the original procedure. Also, steps 3 through 6 have been eliminated; they were simply delaying actions brought about by the makeup of the original procedure. The improved procedure requires eight less operations, six less transportations, four less storages, and less than 10 percent of the former distance traveled.

## MOVEMENT DIAGRAM

A movement diagram portrays motion through space. It is drawn on a scaled layout of the office floor plan so that the movement can be measured and viewed in proper relationship with the physical factors. These charts are helpful in spotting backtracking, visualizing the physical motion involved, and locating congestion and bottlenecks.

Movement diagrams are of two types: those showing paper movement and those showing employee movement. The entire chart should be of one type of the other. Attempting to follow first one and then the other on the same chart leads to confusion. Figure 4–9 illustrates movement diagrams for paper, showing the movements before and after work simplification. This improvement was gained by changing the office layout.

FIGURE 4–9. Movement Diagrams for Paper.

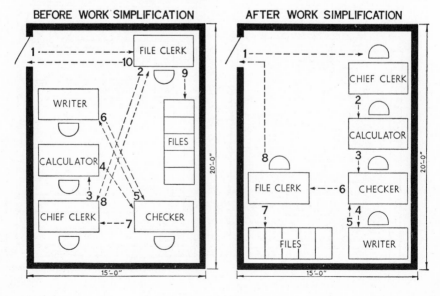

In many instances, however, the paper is not moved by simply handing it to the person at the adjacent desk or by messenger service; it is carried by the person last working on it to the next successive station. This is part of the procedure. It is therefore apparent that an analysis of employee movement is equally as important as an analysis of paper movement. Charts showing employee movement are especially helpful where the work is nonrepetitive and where the employees operate over a large area. The employee movement chart is similar in appearance to the paper movement chart.

## PROCEDURE FLOW CHART

This type of chart is very effective where multiple-copy forms are used. It depicts graphically the distribution and subsequent steps for each form from physical inception to permanent storage or destruction. Generally, this type of chart is not difficult to construct.

Figure 4–10 shows a procedure flow chart of work performed for handling uniform express receipt-collect shipments. Four separate writings are required for each package. These include separate typings for each of two labels, a packing slip and duplicate, and the copies of the uniform express receipt-collect. As indicated in the chart, the labels are put on the package. One copy of the packing slip is sent to the billing department for filing, the other copy placed in the package. Other operations can be determined from the chart.

A procedure to accomplish the same objective, but with much waste eliminated, is shown in Figure 4–11. As illustrated, a seven-part form is written at one time from the sales order. The writing is checked, and then the copies are sent to the shipping department, where they are distributed and used as indicated on the chart. The total number of operations has been reduced from 30 to 17, a saving of nearly 45 percent. Waste elimination, achieved by planning, has resulted in making activities productive, combining operations, eliminating others, and increasing the accuracy.

## THE LEFT- AND RIGHT-HAND CHART

Turning our attention now to methods improvement, the first chart discussed is the left- and right-hand chart. In this chart the detailed motions of each hand are shown. Some believe it is best to observe the actions of both hands to indicate these data on the chart as the work progresses. Others prefer to prepare the chart by following the actions on the right hand only, the actions of the left hand only, then combining the two charts in order to show the relationships existing according to time of execution. Attention must be given to details. A few seconds saved on an action or the elimination of a short movement, perhaps 3 or 4

FIGURE 4-10. A Procedure Flow Chart before Work Simplification.

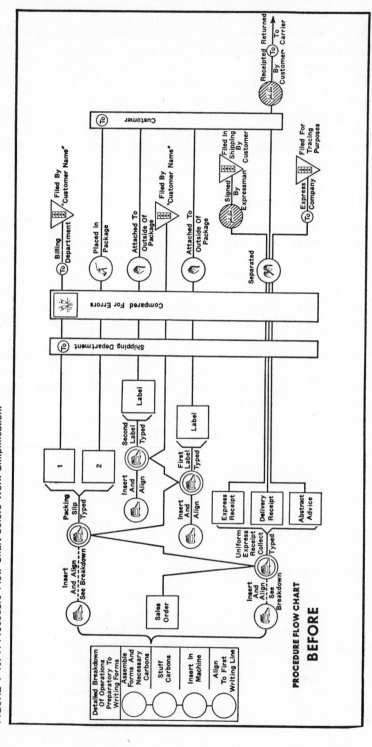

*Courtesy: Standard Register Co., Dayton*

FIGURE 4–11. The Improved Procedure over That Shown in Figure 4–10, after Work Simplification.

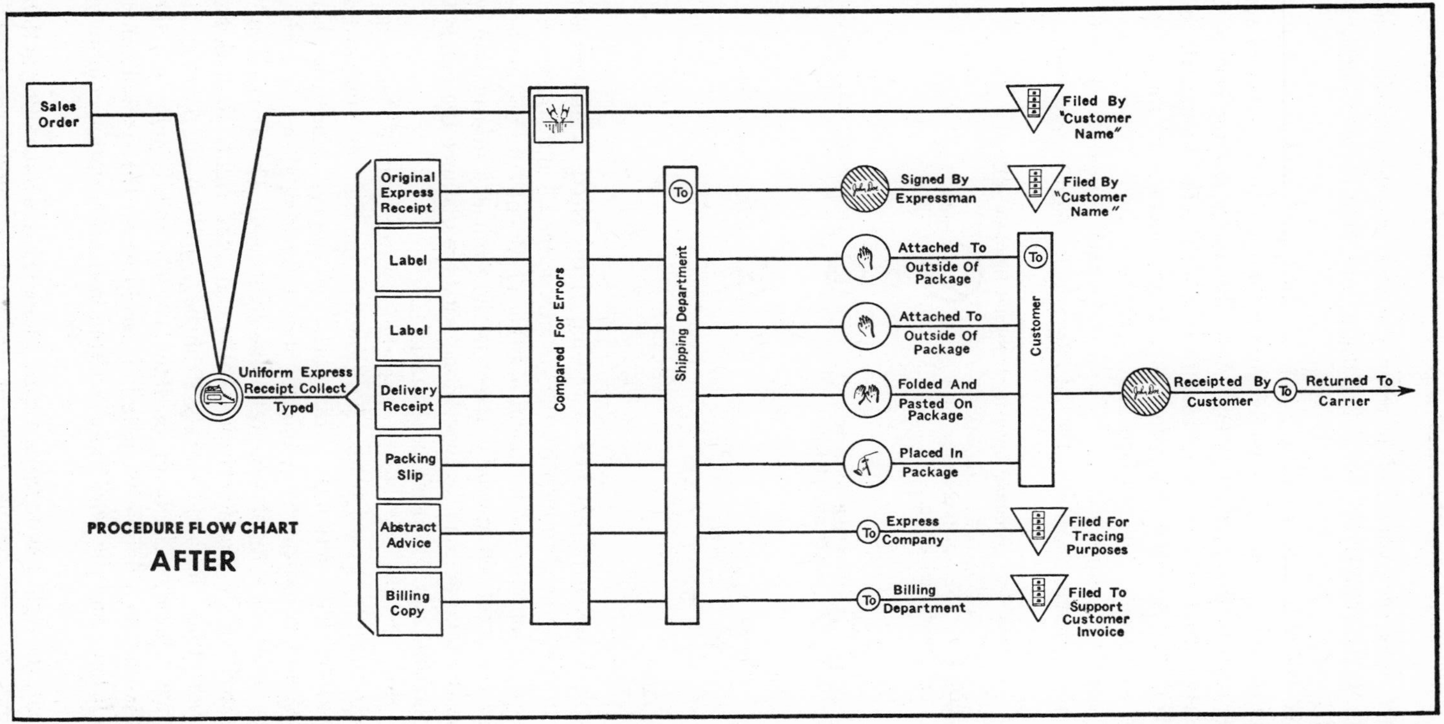

PROCEDURE FLOW CHART

AFTER

Courtesy: Standard Register Co., Dayton

inches, may seem small; but when the task is repeated over and over again, the cumulative savings in fatigue and time become highly significant.

Six symbols are generally used as illustrated in Figure 4–12. Here again there is no universal agreement on the type and number of symbols to be used in this charting work. Actually this is not too serious as the important concept is to make certain that all the facts about the method are collected and the conceptualizing of the method of the work to be done is complete. The symbols are merely to assist in these endeavors.

Figure 4–13 illustrates a left- and right-hand operation chart for typing, in duplicate, original sales data sent in by field representatives. The

FIGURE 4–12. Symbols Used for Left- and Right-Hand Chart.

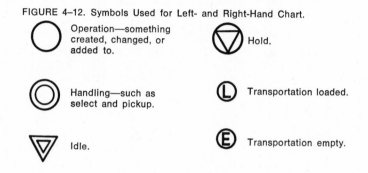

Operation—something created, changed, or added to.

Hold.

Handling—such as select and pickup.

Transportation loaded.

Idle.

Transportation empty.

workplace layout is sketched at the top of the chart. A number or code system can be used to identify the various materials and equipment used. Also, provisions for the inclusion of other pertinent data are made at the top of the sheet. Of special interest is the summary information, which shows the total actions by type, along with the distance the hands travel and the time taken to perform the task.

In this case, the task begins with the operator reaching with the right hand to the pile of copy blanks positioned to the right and forward of the typewriter. This action is "transportation empty," since the hand is empty, and is indicated on line number 1 by a small circle with an $E$ inside under the symbol column for the right hand. The description "to # 2" is written in the description column on the right. In making this transportation, the hand travels 20 inches; and this is recorded in the distance column, right hand, on line 1. While this is going on, the left hand is idle, so a double triangle is inserted under the symbol column of the left hand and the word "idle" written in the description column on the left.

Next, the right hand grasps a copy blank. This is a handling action and is shown by large double circles on line number 2 under the right hand.

FIGURE 4–13.

| LEFT HAND–RIGHT HAND OPERATION CHART |
| --- |

Subject_____   Project No._____
Operator_____   Date_____
Location_____

1 = ORIGINAL BLANK
2 = COPY BLANK
3 = ORIGINAL DATA
4 = PAPER CLIPS
F = FINISHED WORK
C = CARBON
T = TYPEWRITER

| F | | 1 |
| --- | --- | --- |
| | 4 | 2 |
| 3 | T | C |

| CHARTED BY | SHEET _1_ OF _1_ | METHOD BEFORE _X_ AFTER____ | OPERATION | HANDLING | IDLE | HOLD | TRANSPORTATION | | TIME |
| --- | --- | --- | --- | --- | --- | --- | --- | --- | --- |
| *IRT* | | | 6 | 23 | 4 | 3 | LOADED (10) 131" | EMPTY (12) 136" | 1.25(x) |

(X) NO TYPING

| | LEFT HAND | SYMBOL | IN. | MIN. | MIN. | IN. | SYMBOL | RIGHT HAND | |
| --- | --- | --- | --- | --- | --- | --- | --- | --- | --- |
| 1 | idle | ▽ | | | 0.05 | 20 | Ⓔ | to #2 | 1 |
| 2 | | | | | 0.02 | | Ⓞ | grasp #2 | 2 |
| 3 | | | | | 0.05 | 16 | Ⓛ | to top of T | 3 |
| 4 | | | | | 0.01 | | Ⓞ | release #2 | 4 |
| 5 | | | | | 0.04 | 9 | Ⓔ | to C, carbon paper | 5 |
| 6 | | | | | 0.02 | | Ⓞ | grasp C. | 6 |
| 7 | | | | | 0.04 | 13 | Ⓛ | to top of T | 7 |
| 8 | | | | | 0.01 | | Ⓞ | release C | 8 |
| 9 | | | | | 0.06 | 25 | Ⓔ | to # 1 | 9 |
| 10 | | | | | 0.02 | | Ⓞ | grasp #1 | 10 |
| 11 | | | | | 0.06 | 25 | Ⓛ | to top of T | 11 |
| 12 | | | | | 0.02 | | Ⓞ | release # 1 | 12 |
| 13 | grasp #1-C-#2 | Ⓞ | | 0.01 | 0.01 | | Ⓞ | grasp #1-C-#2 | 13 |
| 14 | to platen of T | Ⓛ | 3 | 0.03 | 0.03 | 3 | Ⓛ | to platen of T | 14 |
| 15 | hold | ▽ | | | 0.02 | | Ⓞ | release #1-C-#2 | 15 |
| 16 | | | | | 0.02 | 4 | Ⓔ | to platen knob | 16 |
| 17 | | | | | 0.07 | | ◯ | twist platen knob | 17 |
| 18 | release #1-C-#2 | Ⓞ | | 0.02 | 0.02 | | Ⓞ | release platen knob | 18 |
| 19 | to keyboard | Ⓔ | 6 | 0.03 | 0.03 | 5 | Ⓔ | to keyboard | 19 |
| 20 | type | ◯ | | — | — | | ◯ | type | 20 |
| 21 | to #1-C-#2 | Ⓔ | 6 | 0.03 | 0.03 | 5 | Ⓔ | to T platen knob | 21 |
| 22 | grasp #1-C-#2 | Ⓞ | | 0.02 | 0.02 | | Ⓞ | grasp platen knob | 22 |
| 23 | remove #1-C-#2 | ◯ | | 0.05 | 0.05 | | ◯ | twist platen knob | 23 |
| 24 | to top of T | Ⓛ | 3 | 0.03 | 0.02 | | Ⓞ | release platen knob | 24 |
| 25 | hold | ▽ | | | 0.03 | 3 | Ⓔ | to top of T | 25 |
| 26 | | | | | 0.03 | | Ⓞ | grasp C | 26 |
| 27 | | | | | 0.05 | 13 | Ⓛ | to "C" on desk | 27 |
| 28 | release #1-C-#2 | Ⓞ | | | 0.02 | | Ⓞ | release C | 28 |
| 29 | to paper clips, #4 | Ⓔ | 15 | 0.06 | 0.05 | 13 | Ⓔ | to top of T | 29 |
| 30 | grasp paper clip | Ⓞ | | 0.02 | | | ▽ | idle | 30 |
| 31 | to #3, original data | Ⓛ | 10 | 0.04 | | | | | 31 |
| 32 | grasp #3, original data | Ⓞ | | 0.03 | | | | | 32 |
| 33 | to top of T | Ⓛ | 20 | 0.05 | | | | | 33 |
| 34 | release original data card on #1-#2 | Ⓞ | | 0.02 | 0.02 | | Ⓞ | grasp #1-#2 | 34 |
| 35 | attach clip | ◯ | | 0.04 | | | ▽ | hold #1-#2 | 35 |
| 36 | to "F" on desk | Ⓛ | 25 | 0.06 | | | Ⓞ | release | 36 |
| 37 | release | Ⓞ | | 0.02 | | | ▽ | idle | 37 |
| 38 | to T | Ⓔ | 25 | 0.06 | | | ▽ | | 38 |

"Grasp # 2" is written on the same line in the description column. During this particular operation, the left hand was idle. Since this is the same as the previous entry for the left hand, no new symbol is necessary on the chart.

In a similar manner, each step of the operation is observed and noted on the form. It is important that all details be included and that extreme care be exercised to insure accuracy in this work.

A study of Figure 4–13 shows that the method can be improved. In this figure, it should be observed that the right hand moves first to number 2, the copy blank pile. The analyst will question the necessity and purpose

FIGURE 4–14.

| LEFT HAND | | SYMBOL | IN. | MIN. | MIN. | IN. | SYMBOL | RIGHT HAND | |
|---|---|---|---|---|---|---|---|---|---|
| 1 | grasp #1 | ◎ | | 0.04 | 0.04 | | ◎ | grasp C and #2 | 1 |
| 2 | to top of T | ϙ | 19 | 0.02 | 0.02 | 16 | ϙ | to top of T | 2 |
| 3 | grasp C and #2 | ◎ | | 0.01 | 0.01 | | ◎ | grasp #1 | 3 |
| 4 | to platen of T | ϙ | 3 | 0.03 | 0.03 | 3 | ϙ | to platen of T | 4 |
| 5 | hold | ▽ | | | 0.02 | | ◎ | release #1–C–#2 | 5 |
| 6 | | | | | 0.02 | 4 | ⊙ | to platen knob | 6 |
| 7 | | | | | 0.07 | | ◯ | twist platen knob | 7 |
| 8 | release # 1–C–#2 | ◎ | | 0.02 | 0.02 | | ◎ | release platen knob | 8 |
| 9 | to keyboard | ϙ | 6 | 0.03 | 0.03 | 5 | ϙ | to keyboard | 9 |
| 10 | type | ◯ | | — | — | | ◯ | type | 10 |
| 11 | to #4, paper clips | ϙ | 10 | 0.04 | 0.02 | 6 | ϙ | to # 1–C–#2 | 11 |
| 12 | grasp paper clip | ◎ | | 0.02 | 0.01 | | ◎ | grasp #1–C–#2 | 12 |
| 13 | to #3, original data | ϙ | 8 | 0.03 | 0.02 | | ◯ | pull # 1–C–#2 from T | 13 |
| 14 | grasp #3, original data | ◎ | | 0.03 | 0.02 | 2 | ϙ | to top of T | 14 |
| 15 | to top of T | ϙ | 18 | 0.04 | 0.01 | | ◎ | release #1–C–#2 | 15 |
| 16 | release on top #1–C–#2 | ◎ | | 0.02 | 0.03 | | ◎ | grasp c | 16 |
| 17 | grasp #3 and #1–C–#2 | ◎ | | 0.04 | 0.05 | 12 | ϙ | to "2" on desk | 17 |
| 18 | hold | ▽ | | 0.02 | 0.02 | | ◎ | release | 18 |
| 19 | | | | | 0.03 | 16 | ⊙ | to left hand | 19 |
| 20 | | | | | 0.02 | | ◎ | grasp clips | 20 |
| 21 | | | | | 0.04 | | ◯ | attach to #3, #1–#2 | 21 |
| 22 | to "F" on desk | ϙ | 25 | 0.06 | 0.02 | | ◎ | release | 22 |
| 23 | to # 1 on desk | ⊙ | 10 | 0.04 | 0.03 | 16 | ⊙ | to "2" on desk | 23 |
| | | | | | | | | | |
| | | | | | | | | | |

of this action. He will ask the question, "What is being done, and why?" He will strive to eliminate this motion and also to get the operator interested and active in this work simplification effort. Participation in simplification is sought.

Also, he will observe that the right hand successively makes six transportations—three empty and three loaded—all to the same general area. Are these necessary? Can they be eliminated, combined, or simplified? Can they be made productive? Further, it will be observed that, in the beginning, the right hand is occupied, while the left hand is idle. As already pointed out in Figure 4–5 motion economy results from both hands moving simultaneously in opposite directions. Therefore, arrangements should be made to have both hands moving at the same time, and in opposite directions if possible. By following this minute and careful consideration of each action, the work is simplified and wasted motions are eliminated.

Figure 4–14 shows improvements for accomplishing the same work. The new work layout is sketched at the top of the sheet. Idle time has been eliminated, and simultaneous hand motions have been made a part of the method. The two transportations—empty and loaded—to the copy blanks and the two transportations to the carbon paper have been combined. A comparison study between the two charts will reveal other work simplification accomplishments. The tabular comparison shows:

|  | *Present Method* | | *Proposed Method* | |
|---|---|---|---|---|
| Operations | 6 | | 5 | |
| Handling | 23 | | 17 | |
| Idle | 4 | | 0 | |
| Hold | 3 | | 2 | |
| Transportation loaded | 10 | (131 inches) | 9 | (106 inches) |
| Transportation empty | 12 | (136 inches) | 8 | (73 inches) |
| Time | 1.25 minutes | | 0.71 minutes | |

Worthwhile savings have been accomplished.

## PRODUCTION STUDY CHART

The production study chart shows how an employee spends his working time and the major functions performed. Either the employee can record his activities, or the supervisor or the planner can obtain the data by means of observation. In any event, the employee should be informed of the study and its purpose and told why and how the recordings are made. For meaningful results, the job content should be fairly consistent from day to day, and the observed employee should neither hasten nor retard his normal efforts. The data should be collected for several consecutive days, preferably a week, in order to arrive at what would seem to be a normal pattern.

There are several ways in which the information of a production study chart can be recorded. One method consists of using graph paper with sections representing time units throughout the working day. These sections are filled in with colored pencil according to a color-identification key for the various functions performed. Another method consists of simply marking down in tabular form the various types of work done and the time each job is started and finished. The latter is illustrated by Figure 4–15. The usual identification data—employee name, date, and the

FIGURE 4–15. Chart Showing How an Employee Spends Her Working Time. Data Are Secured by Observing the Employee.

PRODUCTION STUDY CHART

Sheet 1 of 5 Sheets

Date 3/21  Employee's Name Nancy Taussig
Study By CRH  Division or Unit Transcription - 32
Computations By CRH  Job Title Transcriber

| TIME | TRAN-SCRIBING | COM-PUTING | FILING | SUPER-VISION Rcvd. | SUPER-VISION GIVEN | TELE-PHONE | HAND-LING MAIL | PERSON-AL TIME | MISC. | COMMENTS |
|---|---|---|---|---|---|---|---|---|---|---|
| MON. 9:00 / 9:20 | | | | | | | | | | |
| 9:50 | √30 | | | | | | | | √20 | Cleaning typewriter |
| 10:05 | | | | | | √15 | | | | Business Call |
| 10:18 | √13 | | | | | | | | | |
| 10:25 | | | | √7 | | | | | | |
| 10:50 | | | | | | | | | √25 | Rest period - Idle |
| 10:59 | | | √9 | | | | | | | |
| 11:08 | | | | | | √9 | | | | Business Call |
| 11:10 | | | √2 | | | | | | | |
| 11:22 | | | | | | √12 | | | | Personal Call |
| 11:30 | | | | | | | | √8 | | |
| 11:35 | | | | √5 | | | | | | |
| 11:50 | | | | | | | | | √15 | Idle |
| 12:00 | | | | | | | | √10 | | |
| LUNCH 1:00 / 1:07 | | | | | | | | | √7 | Tardy |
| 1:10 | | | | √3 | | | | | | |
| 1:40 | √30 | | | | | | | | | |
| 1:55 | | | | | | | | | √15 | |
| 3:05 | √70 | | | | | | | | | |
| 3:42 | | | | | | | | | √37 | Rest period - Idle |
| 4:05 | | | | | | | √23 | | | |
| 4:15 | | | | | | | | √10 | | |
| 4:25 | | | | | | √10 | | | | Business Call |
| 4:45 | | | √20 | | | | | | | |
| 4:58 | | | | | | | | √13 | | Idle |
| 5:00 | | | | | | | | √2 | | Cleaning Desk |
| | | | | | | | | | | |
| TOTALS | 143 | — | 31 | 15 | — | 46 | 23 | 43 | 119 | 420 |
| PERCENT | 34.1 | — | 7.4 | 3.6 | — | 11.0 | 5.4 | 10.1 | 28.4 | 100.0% |

like—are shown at the top. A series of vertical columns are used for the various functions, with the extreme left column utilized for time and the extreme right for comments. Since the study begins at 9:00 A.M. Monday, the insertion "Mon. 9.00" is written on the first line under the Time column. The employee is observed cleaning her typewriter, so a check mark (✔) is made on the first line under Miscellaneous and "cleaning typewriter" is written under Comments. She finishes this task at 9:20 A.M and begins transcribing. Hence, "9.20" is written on the first line under Time, and a check mark is made under Transcribing on line 2. She stops transcribing at 10:05 A.M. to telephone. Hence, on line 3, a check mark is made under Telephone, and the entry "10.05" is made in the Time column. In a similar manner, entries are made throughout the entire day.

The calculations for figuring the elapsed time per function can be made as the study progresses or at the completion of all observations. In the illustration, the ordinary 60-minute watch has been used. For the first line, the elapsed time between 9.00 and 9.20 is 20 minutes, which is recorded in the same square as the check mark under Miscellaneous. For the second line, the elapsed time is 9.50 minus 9.20, or 30 minutes. The itemized totals are shown at the bottom of the form along with the percentage figures. For example, the total time spent on transcribing is 143 minutes. This constitutes 34.1 percent of the total day's working time, calculated by dividing the transcribing time, 143 minutes, by the total day's working time, 420 minutes.

These types of data are helpful because they tell what the status of the jobs is at present and give, per employee, a picture of the overall work pattern which might form the basis for methods improvement, better supervision, and equalization of the work load. They can also be used to supply basic information for the construction of a work distribution chart.[2]

For example, a production study chart may reveal that a typist, with a typing speed of 50 words per minute, spends only 50 percent of her time typing. The remaining 50 percent is spent on other activities, most of which are nonessential, including positioning papers in typewriter, checking work, removing papers from typewriter, separating copies, cleaning typewriter, answering telephone, filing papers, and getting information from the supervisor. In this case, the effective typing production is at a rate of only 25 (50 percent of 50) words per minute. In too many offices, the sole emphasis is upon the speed of the operator. True, this has value, but when the methods improvement efforts reveal only 50 percent of the employee's particular skill being utilized, it is a challenge to the manager to eliminate such waste. The production study chart reveals such situations and assists in correcting them.

---

[2] See chapter 25 for discussion of work distribution chart.

## OPERATOR-MACHINE ACTIVITY CHART

This last chart to be discussed shows the relation between the operator and the machine. Its use is somewhat limited in office methods, owing to the general nature of most office activities. It is chiefly employed to determine idle machine time and the number of machines which one operator can reasonably handle, thus in effect determining the superior method.

Figure 4–16 shows an operator-machine activity chart. Pertinent data and a sketch of the workplace layout are included at the top. Time is

FIGURE 4–16. An Operator-Machine Activity Chart.

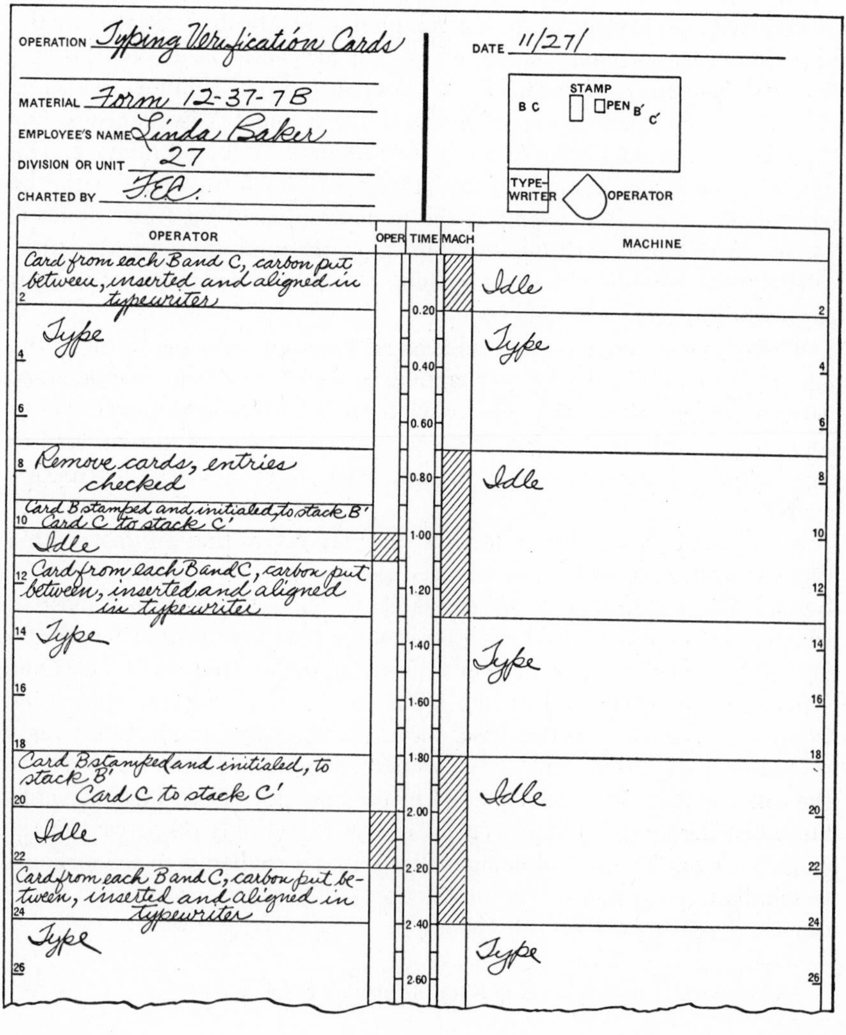

represented by vertical distance on the scale shown in the center column of the sheet. For example, two scale units represent two minutes, four scale units four minutes, and so forth. The activities of the operator are listed in the left column, those of the machine on the right.

The vertical height of each spacing in these respective columns is determined by the time devoted to the particular activity. For example, in the illustration, the first action by the operator was to take a card from each *B* and *C,* put a carbon between, insert and align in typewriter. This required two tenths (0.2) of a minute, so a horizontal line was drawn two units down from the beginning horizontal line. During this time, the typewriter was idle; hence, a horizontal line was drawn across the right column under Machine, two units from the same beginning line, and "idle" written in the space so formed.

Next, the operator typed. This action continued five tenths (0.5) of a minute, so a horizontal line was drawn across the Operator column five units below the last horizontal line, or in this case opposite the 7 mark on the time scale. The space so formed was marked "type." Since the typewriter action stopped at the same time, a horizontal line was also drawn across the Machine column opposite 7 on the time scale, and the space above was marked "type." In a similar manner, the entire chart was constructed.

This method can be improved easily. Multicopy form sets with interleaved carbon offer one possibility. This would reduce the labor time per unit and increase the operating time of the machine—both contributing to greater efficiency. However, a more significant improvement would be the use of continuous-strip office forms with carbon interleaved, thus permitting the operator to type continuously until a quantity of work is finished. The checking and separating of the forms could subsequently be handled on this quantity. This method would provide a smooth and rhythmic flow of work, permit specialization upon the immediate task, and eliminate unnecessary reaching, as well as excessive finger and arm motions. Elimination of much waste would be achieved.

## QUESTIONS

1. Describe your understanding of the "questioning approach" in the efforts of devising a work improvement.
2. List four guides of office work simplification, and briefly discuss the one you feel is most important.
3. What are the four major purposes of charts as used in office work simplification?
4. For each of the following pairs, carefully point out the difference between the two identities:
   *a*) Movement diagram and the "What and Why" questions.
   *b*) Normal working area and maximum working area.

    *c*) Speedup and motion study.

    *d*) A "handling" and a "transportation loaded."

5. Discuss five guides for improving office methods, using illustrations to demonstrate your answers.

6. Analyze your motions in typing a letter, or taking notes from a reference book, or sorting and then filing cards in a file. What do you conclude from your study? Discuss.

7. Explain Figure 4–13 in your own words.

8. Comment fully on the following: "For a given quantity of work, it is entirely possible for methods improvements to reduce employee fatigue in performing that quantity. But methods improvements usually result in increasing the amount of work performed; and as a result, the employee spends the same amount of energy or more than before the improvement. Hence, the employee is quite likely to be just as fatigued under the improved method as before the improvement."

9. Identify each of the following by a simple statement:

    *a*) A method

    *b*) A process chart.

    *c*) Office work simplification.

    *d*) A "make-ready" operation.

10. As an office manager, would you agree to the suggestion that the employees fill out the data on their respective production study charts and turn these data in to you for analysis and interpretation? What would be the advantages under such an arrangement? The disadvantages?

11. Draw up a tabular listing by including vertically the left- and right-hand chart, the production study chart, and the operator-machine chart. Across the top, list column headings (1) what data are shown, (2) best means to obtain these data, and (3) use or purpose of chart. Fill in the information for each column as it applies to each chart. What conclusions do you draw from your completed tabular listing?

12. In your opinion will office methods improvement become more or less important in the future? What effect will the increasing use of office automation have upon office methods improvements? Give reasons for your answers.

## CASE PROBLEMS

### Case 4–1.  Weaver-Grundig Corporation

    A great deal of sales promotion material is prepared and mailed by the company's sales service department. One big mailer is a 20-page booklet which is assembled, plastic bound, and inserted into a mailing envelope. Volume on this item now is 1,000 per month and is expected to reach 1,400 per month by the middle of next year.

    The time in minutes now for 100 booklets include: assembly 28.5, inspecting 5.0, plastic binding 18.0, inserting in envelope 31.0, stack finished items on dolly 2.0, replenish pages 1.5, and replenish envelopes 1.0. Cost of labor is $2.80 an hour.

    Bill McCullough, an office methods man, is investigating the present manner of performing the work to see if it can be improved. After study, he estimates that by using a special fixture costing $100, he can save 0.13 minutes per booklet of the assembly. Also, including a simple $125 device for the operation of inserting in the envelope will make possible the performing of this work at a rate of 25.0 minutes per 100 booklets.

## Questions:

1. What is the yearly current labor cost for performing this work?
2. How much time per month will be required to do this work with present methods based on the estimated future volume?
3. What is the estimated cost for the future volume under the improved methods suggested by Bill McCullough?
4. Has Bill McCullough exhausted the possibilities to simplify this work? Explain your answer.

## Case 4–2.   Sharon Palmer

Sharon Palmer is a general clerk and is being observed for the purpose of making a production study chart. She has been informed of the study and has agreed to follow her normal work manner. The data recorded include the following: Starting at 8:30 A.M., the official office starting time, Miss Palmer checks her typewriter and arranges work on the desk; at 8:35, files a broken finger nail; at 8:42, types; at 9:03 answers a business telephone call; at 9:11, types; at 9:29, idle; at 9:40, sorts requisitions; at 10:15, rest period; at 10:30, idle; at 10:33, files; at 11:05, talks with supervisor; at 11:15, runs errand for supervisor; at 11:35, makes business telephone call; at 11:46 plans work; at 11:53, makes personal telephone call; at 11:59, idle; at 12:00 lunch; at 1:00, idle; at 1:07, sorts requisitions; at 2:12, idle; at 2:20, makes personal telephone call; at 2:25, idle; at 2:30, posts on inventory records; at 2:45, rest period; at 3:00, idle; at 3:10, posts on inventory records; at 3:32, files; at 4:01, talks with supervisor; at 4:09, makes business telephone call; at 4:15, talks with supervisor; at 4:24, puts work away; at 4:28, idle; at 4:30, official quitting time, leaves desk.

## Questions:

1. Draw the production study chart.
2. Calculate the itemized totals of the activities of Sharon Palmer.
3. What interpretations do you make from these data? Discuss.
4. What actions do you recommend as a result of the factual data assembled? Why?

## Case 4–3.   Owens Direct Mail Sales, Inc.

For purposes of sales analysis and taxes, customer orders are sorted by state. A seventh copy of the invoice prepared by the company is used. The volume fluctuates from week to week, but an average weekly volume is 15,000 orders. To do the sorting job, a rack, laid out in a straight line with eight sections horizontally and five sections vertically, is being used. The rack, which is 10 feet long and 4 feet high, sits on a long table. The 40-way sort is used because several of the states are grouped.

The operator, a tall girl, holds a batch of orders in her left hand, reads the state on the order at the top of the batch, picks the order up with her right hand, and inserts it into the bin of the rack for the particular state. The operator walks back and forth to cover the distance of the rack. She is expected to accomplish a rate of 20 orders sorted a minute, and succeeds in doing so.

Because of the volume, all the orders cannot be sorted by the operator using the rack. The overflow is sorted by another girl, who spreads the work out in little piles over several tabletops. Although the second girl works all day at this job of sorting orders, she does not accomplish as much as the girl working with the rack. From this, the office manager concludes that the rack idea is better than sorting tabletops. He is about to order another rack for use by the second girl; but before doing this, he has requested you to study the work method and see if any improvements for this order sorting can be developed.

## Questions:

1. What are some tentative methods you feel should be investigated to find a possible improvement?
2. What is your recommendation to the office manager?

chapter **5**

# Information media— forms and records

There are two ways of meeting difficulties: you alter
the difficulties, or you alter yourself to meet them.
—*Phyllis Bottome*

FORMS AND RECORDS retain and convey much of the information that is
utilized in all phases of operations including purchasing, manufacturing,
selling, expediting, and controlling. The heart of the office system or
procedure is the office form and record and their importance has increased
with our era of automatic data processing. Some refer to office forms and
records as the raw materials of the office. They are the essential components for processing the information.

The work of analyzing and improving the role of office forms and
records is so important that the term, *forms management,* is sometimes
used to identify these efforts. Forms and records reach into every corner of
an enterprise; they make contact with every employee, customer, and
prospect. In essence, they form a busy network relaying information,
issuing instructions and directions, and supplying data for decision making covering every function within an enterprise. It is vital, therefore, that
forms and records be properly designed and constructed to provide a
proper flow of required data at reasonable cost consistent with the individually prescribed performance and quality.

*An office form is a printed piece of paper which provides space for
entering records, information, or instructions which are to be conveyed to
other individuals, departments, or enterprises.* Common examples include
cost tickets, expense accounts, factory orders, requisitions, sales data,
purchase orders, invoices, and credit memorandums. *A record is any*

*written data that is made for possible future use.* Records include various papers. The meaning of record is more inclusive and connotes far more coverage than does office form. For purposes here, we will confine our discussion to office forms, but to a significant degree, what we state about office forms applies equally to records.

## OPTICAL CHARACTER RECOGNITION FORMS

With the development of reading machines has come specially designed forms to take full advantage of these mechanical readers. Data from an entire sheet is read in a matter of seconds.[1] Use of so-called OCR (Optical Character Recognition) forms ends the search for a means of eliminating costly and time-consuming data preparation prior to computer processing. *OCR forms serve as a source document for computer input.* Keypunching is eliminated.

An OCR form requires high precision and quality control in order to function properly in the reading machine. Ink too dark, paper too reflective, or the printing matter of the form a fraction out of line can render the form useless, and the information is lost. Except for registration marks and items to be seen by the reading machine, many OCR forms are preprinted in a drop-out blue ink. These horizontal and vertical blue rules help guide the typist in lining up the form in preparation for typing the material. The typist must have full instructions so she can edit and make decisions about the content while typing. The copy made is final and the need to supply accurate, clean work must be emphasized.

Figure 5–1 illustrates several OCR forms. In the top illustration the form is designed for machine-entry of the information. The form printing is in ink that the reader will not pick up except for location registrations to guide the input work into the proper spaces of the form. The entry material is imprinted in OCR type font suitable for the reader. In the bottom illustration the form is a hand-entry form. Note a handwriting guide is included on the form. This tells what style digit to use in writing in the data so that the machine reader can read it.

It should be observed that the use of OCR forms makes it possible to generate documents at various recording stations, shipping docks, truck stations, and mobile locations of salesmen. And these source documents are accurate, legible, and uniform. A receiving clerk or a shipping clerk can fill out the required information about his operation at his workplace. Likewise, a traveling salesman can make his writing of an order serve several functions including preparing the invoice, notifying warehouse, and taking care of back orders. In this way, transcription work is avoided, mistakes are minimized, and the order-service is streamlined.

---

[1] Reading machines are discussed in chapter 10, pp. 228–30.

FIGURE 5-1. Optical Character Recognition (OCR) Forms.

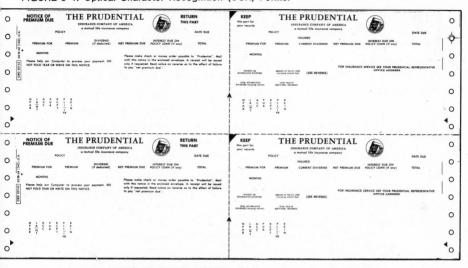

Courtesy: Acme Datagraphic Business Systems, Inc.,
South Hackensack, N.J.

# FORM DESIGN

In designing an office form it is wise to enlist the help of forms-design engineers for they are trained and experienced in this type of work. They usually are able to suggest improvements. Most manufacturers of office forms offer the services of design engineers. Commonly, the author of a form is not its designer. The user or the systems and procedures man frequently has ideas about what the form should be, what information it should convey, and who adds what information where, when, and how. Normally the designer questions the necessity for each item. Then he determines which items should be grouped, what areas of the form are given to what items, and what is the most convenient sequences for entries. Finally, the type of form is decided. More will be discussed about this work in the following pages.

Effective form design aids in processing the data and assists in the utilization of the information. An excellent illustration, revealed by the "before and after" comparison, is shown by Figures 5–2 and 5–3. The op-

FIGURE 5–2. Original Form before Redesign.

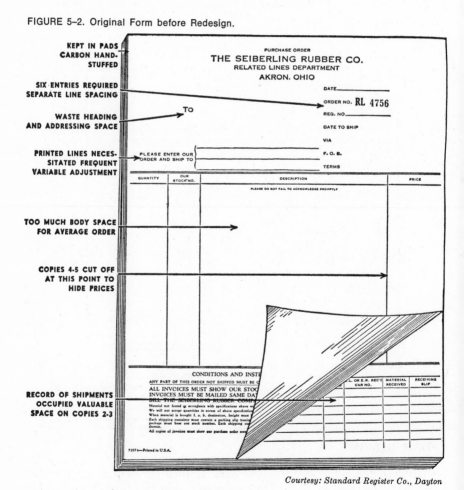

*Courtesy: Standard Register Co., Dayton*

portunities for better design and the improvements accomplished are noted on these figures. Note the holes along the vertical margins of the form. These are for pin-feeding which permits the form to advance in a machine in desired alignment and holds the form in place while entry is being made. The standard spacing for pin-feed holes is two holes every inch.

Usually the best form design is the simple design. It should include the amount and kind of information that is required—no more, no less. The design should also make it easy to enter and to use the information of the form, for it can be thought of as both a recipient of data and a conveyor of data to a receiver who has a definite need for the data provided. In

FIGURE 5–3. Form after Redesign.

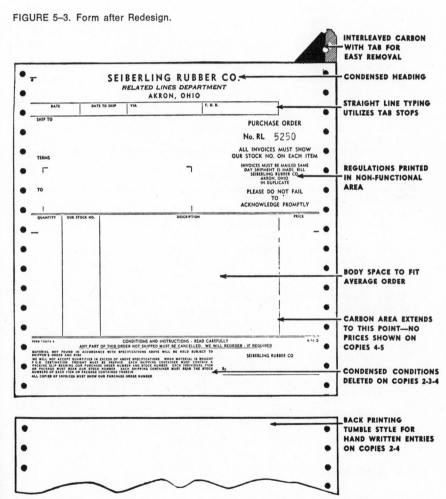

*Courtesy: Standard Register Co., Dayton*

addition, the form should assist in maintaining high quality by reducing the chances for errors. Likewise, it is desirable to keep the cost of the form and of using it to a minimum.

To provide a more specific and better comprehension of the many considerations included in office form design, Figure 5–4 has been included. Some of these checks may seem obvious such as identifying form with name and number, but in reality too often this consideration is violated. Others, such as making self-instructing the filling out of the form and having the best arrangement for the data, pose more difficult design problems.

FIGURE 5–4. Form Design Check List.

1. Is the form identified with name and number?
2. Are type faces clear and readable?
3. Are all captions easily understood?
4. Does the information supplied by the form tie in with the stated requirements of the adopted systems, procedures, and methods?
5. If machine-entry, are machine specifications such as maximum size of paper, size of printing characters, and length of line taken into account?
6. Are the supplied space requirements adequate for each individual item?
7. Is fill-in writing reduced to a minimum and is repetitive information printed?
8. Is information grouped logically and, if source document, are data in sequence that they will be transcribed?
9. Are box and columnar arrangements featured?
10. Are vertical and horizontal spacing in conformity with the writing method to be used?
11. Is the need for tabular stops held to a minimum?
12. Are bold types, markings, numbers, shaded areas, and color used to facilitate handling, routing, and checking?
13. Are varying thickness of rulings used to set off sections of the form?
14. Is form self-instructing—are instructions clear, brief, and located either at the top of the form or close to the section to which they apply?
15. Is the routing of the form clearly identified?
16. Is information for filing placed advantageously on the form?
17. Will the form fit standard binders and file folders?
18. Is adequate gripper space included in the form design?
19. Are the proper weight, grade, and color of paper being used?
20. Are the combinations of paper and carbon acceptable for desired carbonization?
21. Are carbonless papers preferable for this form?
22. Are perforations, die-cuts, and narrow plies of paper and of carbon used for positive selection of data on certain copies?
23. Is the form suitable for window envelopes if it is mailed?

## FORM DIAGNOSIS

Every office form consists of three major sections: (1) introductory, (2) working area, and (3) conclusion. The introductory section is normally at the top and includes the title and number of the form, the routing, the ship to, customer's name and address, and the major instructions on how to fill out the form. Some prefer to locate the instructions at the bottom of the form, but in this location they may not be seen until after at least a part of the form is filled out. The same is true when instructions are put on the reverse side of the sheet. The preference of some designers is to place instructions adjacent to the applicable material. This is effective, but may require an excess of space. In all cases, the instructions should be outlined with a separate paragraph for each statement. To print the instructions in a large single paragraph makes it difficult to read.

The working area, or what is sometimes called the main body, is normally the largest part of the form. Adequate space and proper arrangement are the keys here. The space should provide ample room for all the information needed and be designed to facilitate entries and to reduce errors. Proper use of rulings, columns, data alignment, spacings, and box entries are essential in this section.

The conclusion, at the bottom of the form, includes information relating what happens to the form next. Authorization, signature, and statement of conditions under which data are valid typify the content of this section of the form. Usually the conclusion occupies the smallest space of the three major sections of a form.

It is helpful to consider the designing of office forms in terms of functional considerations and physical considerations. The former deal with factors such as the way the form is used, its purpose, the information supplied on it, and the number of copies required. Physical considerations include the ink, print type, paper, and size.

## FUNCTIONAL CONSIDERATIONS

There are seven major functional considerations that merit discussion here, including:

*1. Purpose of the Form.* The foremost consideration is the job for which the form is to be used. An office form is actually a road map of the work. It shows the flow and sequence to be followed. The form directs employees from the beginning to the end of work.

Office forms are used not only because they serve as work guides, but also because their use reduces copying, insures uniformity, gives official sanction to the written work, and implements office mechanization. All or any one of these may be the foremost consideration in any given case. But the major purpose or purposes influence the design that is used.

Usually the purpose is fairly well defined from the system and procedure design. If this is not the case, the usual practice is to follow the form in use and observe precisely the form's normal cycle of operations from point of origin to ultimate disposal. No gaps should be permitted for this is where design inefficiencies frequently exist. Sometimes a sluggish work flow is found among highly skilled personnel. It may be that a procedure is faulty or that personnel hold up the forms or that a poorly designed form is being used. Sufficient observation, questioning, and analyzing of the facts will reveal the apparent cause. The application of work simplification will assist in bringing about the needed correction.

**2. Information to Include.**  Knowing the purpose of the form and observing its application, if now in use, leads to deciding what information should be included in the form. It is difficult to keep such data in mind, so it is best to write it down with the intent being to gather more data than probably will be needed. Actual form design efforts frequently reveal the need for more data than initially anticipated. Help along this line can be secured by answering such questions as:

*a*) What information is needed to accomplish the stated purpose?

*b*) Who uses the form, for what purpose, and in what manner?

*c*) Who handles the form before the employee being observed?

*d*) What does the observed employee do with the form?

*e*) What happens to the form after the observed employee finishes with it?

*f*) Is there consultation with other forms in order to prepare the one at hand?

*g*) Is the observed employee the last person to enter data on the form?

*h*) If the observed employee works with one copy, where are the other copies?

*i*) Can any of the information be simplified or eliminated?

*j*) If the form is simplified or eliminated, what problems would result?

*k*) What suggestions do the present or proposed users of the form offer? The list will vary somewhat with the particular study. A careful review of the task at hand helps in selecting the questions and areas believed essential for investigation.

**3. Adequate Identification.**  The form name should suggest its purpose. For example, the title "Sales Records" is not complete; "Weekly Sales Records by Territories" is more descriptive. Usually, the identification is in the introductory section. The center or the upper left corner is preferable for the location of the name of the company. Numbering all forms helps identify them and serves as a quick reference. The identification number should be in a convenient location, preferably near the title. In the case of multiple forms, it is usually advisable to number each copy for handy reference. Quick identification can also be gained by using different colors of papers.

**4. Sequence of Items.**  The order should be mainly that of the normal flow of the work, and related items should be grouped. When items are transcribed from one form to another, the items should be arranged in the same sequence on both forms. This means that related items are placed in a sequence which eliminates unnecessary writing motions and makes it easy to transcribe information from one form to another. Search and

FIGURE 5–5. Proper Sequence of Items on Form Expedites Processing.

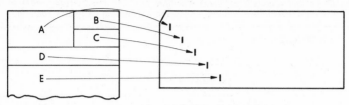

backtracking are eliminated. The numbering of items makes reference easier and faster. Figure 5–5 shows an effective sequence of items when data from form are transferred to a punched card.

**5. General Pattern of the Form.** The method of completion is important. If the work is to be done manually, ample writing space is necessary, and horizontal rulings on the form are desirable. A heavier horizontal line about every third line across the form helps the eye to move from left to right. In contrast, if the work is to be done by machine, the form should be spaced in accordance with the demands of the machine. The data should be arranged to utilize a tabular alignment, and horizontal lines on the form should be omitted. In general, for hand entries the horizontal spacing should be about eight characters to an inch, vertical spacing not less than four lines per inch. For machine entries, horizontal spacing is one twelfth of an inch per character for elite type, one tenth of an inch for pica, and vertical spacing is one sixth of an inch or multiple thereof. Certain type characters and machines vary from these dimensions and it is best to check the characteristics of the machine to be used.

So-called box captions should be used wherever possible as they assist in both the entry and use of the information, conserve space, give more room for data, and add to the appearance of the form. Figure 5–6 shows effective use of box captions.

Also the use of check boxes, sometimes termed "boxed style" is effective and should be employed wherever appropriate. Their use saves filling-in time, conserves space, and improves legibility. It is helpful to provide a reference number for each space to be filled in. By this means, tabulation, comparison, and interpretation of data are expedited. Where long sentences are necessary, it is desirable to have them printed in columnar form

FIGURE 5–6. Box Captions Provide Effective Means of Identification on Items of a Form.

| TO | | FROM | |
|---|---|---|---|
| DATE | CLASS | | AREA |

FIGURE 5–7. A Printed Form Using the Checked Boxes for Recording Answers, Numbers to Expedite Machine Tabulation, and Columnar Arrangement of Material. This form saves time in writing, conserves space, and expedites reading.

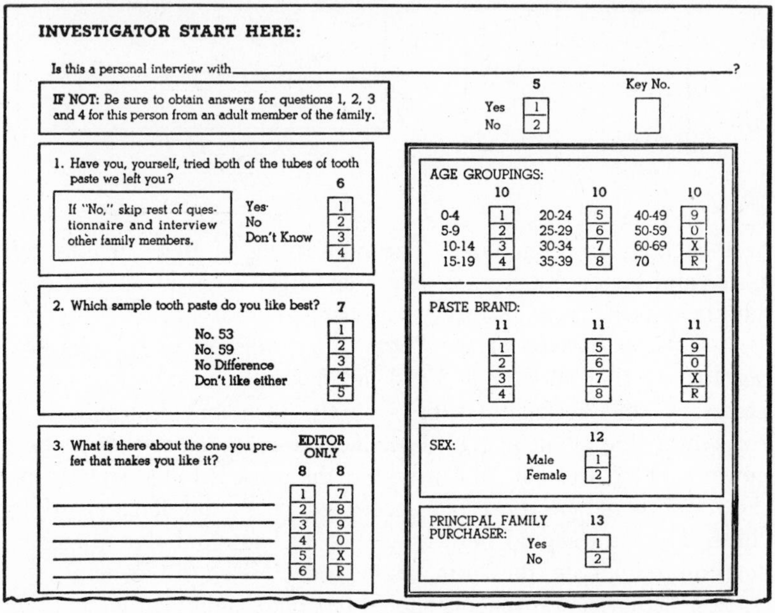

instead of across the full width of the sheet, as this expedites reading and makes for better appearance. However, when the information to be filled in is lengthy, the boxed style is usually inappropriate; the regular or "open" style is better. An illustration of a form featuring the boxed style for answers and numbers to expedite machine tabulation is shown in Figure 5–7.

Shading can also be used to advantage. Emphasis is provided by a heavy shaded border around a particular item. Also, shaded areas effectively indicate areas and spaces not to be used. This is especially helpful for somewhat complicated data shown in tabular form.

Even right-end alignment of items is also recommended. This arrangement utilizes the tabular stops of a machine and makes for an easier to read and neater form. It should be followed for all forms—machine and hand entry. This design arrangement is probably the most common of all violations. The correct and incorrect arrangements are:

| Correct | Incorrect |
|---|---|
| Name: | Name _____ |
| Address: | Address _____ |
| S.S. Number: | S.S. Number _____ |
| Age: | Age _____ |

If a form is filed, it should include captions to expedite the filing. Normally this should be a part of the introductory section. It is helpful to show the file reference material vertically, if the form is filed on a vertical edge. If frequent filing reference is required, a tab at the top of the form may expedite this retrieving work. Collation of forms within a folder provide clues as to the combining of separate forms into one, with resultant less handling required. Commonly the data on the separate forms are presented differently, but slight design changes overcome these hurdles.

**6. Number of Copies.** Whether a single or multiple copy form should be used depends mainly upon two considerations: (1) who requires a copy and (2) when the copy is needed. Multiple forms afford a quick means of supplying many copies. However, it is best to keep the number of copies at a minimum. Only the required number of copies should be made; and extreme prudence and care in this respect is recommended, as excess papers tend to clutter up an office and contribute to inefficiency.

**7. Type of Form.** There are several different types or arrangements of office forms. One is the single type which is used where the original copy only is required, as, for example, in the case of an employment application form. When necessary, copies can be obtained. Many single-unit forms are used in an office. Other arrangements are multiple forms. These are illustrated in Figure 5–8.

Multiple forms require only one writing, minimize mistakes, help attain uniformity, improve departmental coordination, and save time. The equipment used for multiple forms is either ordinary office equipment or the same type of equipment with simple attachments, for example, a special roller on the typewriter platen or a holder. Figure 5–9 illustrates units of this sort.

## PHYSICAL CONSIDERATIONS

The following considerations, although technical in nature, are involved in forms planning:

**1. Ink.** The ink selected should provide proper contrast to the paper and should give a clear, uniform, and smooth imprint. Certain printing processes require a certain type of ink. Use of more than one color of ink adds to the cost of the form. Special type inks are also used to meet processing machine requirements. For example, magnetic ink containing iron oxide is now common for bank check identification data. Typing or printing with this type of ink makes impressions on the paper which can be read by electronic means used to put various counting and sorting mechanisms into action.[2]

---

[2] See chapter 10, p. 237.

FIGURE 5–8. The Main Types or Arrangements of Multiple Office Forms

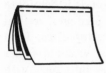

STUB TYPE UNIT

Can be made with stub at top, bottom, or either side. Carbon is fastened to stub, is used once, and can be of same or different widths and lengths to permit selective copying. Form is in proper alignment. Widely used when a number of stations initiating the form are employed.

These are provided in continuous strips with perforated accordion folds at left and right edges. The arrangement is available in either packs or rolls. Being joined at alternate sides, the forms can be separated from the strip but still retained in sets. The fan arrangement is available with or without interleaved carbon.

FAN OR Z

CONTINUOUS FORM
MARGINALLY PUNCHED

Provides continuous flow of sets through a machine. Features accurate registration in machine from form to form. Side-tie perforation holds form together without staples or gummed edges.

CONTINUOUS FORM
NOT MARGINALLY PUNCHED

Provides continuous flow and permits movement from one typewriter to another for writing forms. Can be without carbon interleaved, but in this event the writing machine is equipped with a carbon shifter device.

CARBONLESS PAPER FORM

Usually of a stub type utilizing carbonless paper, thus eliminating smudged hands or clothing and the disposal of carbon sheets.

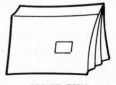

POCKET FORM

Available in several basic styles, but major feature is a pocket of the form to hold punched cards or tape which holds data used in connection with the form.

FIGURE 5–9. A Pack Holding Refold Tray Used for Continuous Multiple Form.

This attachment, called a "dual feed," makes it possible to produce two records in one operation. Common information is typed on two forms of different size, with independent spacing as the work requires.

*Courtesy: Standard Register Co., Dayton*

**2. Print Type.** Readability and distinctiveness should govern the selection of print type. For any one form, it is best to keep the type sizes and type styles to a minimum. Items of equal importance should be printed in the same type throughout the entire form. Normally, italic and boldface type should be used for emphasis but confined to words where special stress is required. Again, certain font types may be required if certain machine reading and processing are followed.

**3. Paper.** The five important physical properties of paper are weight, grade, grain, color, and size.

*a*) Weight. Paper is usually sold by weight. Normally, the mill supplies paper in standard sizes according to the different grades and the intended purposes for which the paper is to be used. To illustrate, the purposes and corresponding sizes are shown in this table:

| Use of Paper | Size |
|---|---|
| Bonds, ledgers, general writing | 17″ x 22″ |
| Book papers and offset pages | 25″ x 38″ |
| Cover stock | 20″ x 26″ |
| Newsprint | 24″ x 36″ |
| Bristol board | 22½″ x 28½″ |

A ream is the common measurement for quantity of paper and is approximately 500 sheets. For example, bond paper listed as 17″ x 22″—20 means that 20 pounds of this grade and size of paper includes approximately 500 sheets. Likewise, bond paper 17″ x 22″—13 means that 13 pounds of this grade and size of paper contain approximately 500 sheets. Comparing these two, the latter sheets would be thinner, since, based on the same size and approximate quantity, their weight is less (13 pounds) compared to the former (20 pounds).

The lightest paper which will give satisfactory results should be used. Among the factors which determine the proper weight of paper are number of copies, amount of handling, purpose of the form, how filed—on edge or side, length of time retained, and whether printed on one or two sides. The following weights are usually recommended:

| Application | Weight of Paper Recommended |
|---|---|
| Legal documents | 28 pound |
| Ledgers | 24 pound |
| Letterheads | 20 pound |
| When 1–4 copies are made | 16 pound |
| When 5–8 copies are made | 13 pound |
| When over 9 copies are made | Tissue |

*b*) Grade. The grade of paper means the quality and is chiefly based on the kinds of materials used in the manufacturing process. Paper is made from rags, mechanical wood pulp, sulfite wood pulp, soda wood pulp, and sulfate wood pulp, which are used in varying amounts, depending upon the kind of paper. The grade selected for a form depends upon such things as the life of the form, the amount of handling, and the appearance. The following table is helpful.

| Life of Form | Grade of Paper |
|---|---|
| 1–5 years | 100 percent sulfite |
| 6–12 years | 50 percent sulfite and 50 percent rag |
| Over 12 years | 100 percent rag |

*c*) Grain. Like wood, paper has a grain characteristic. The direction of the grain is determined by the alignment of the fibers making up the paper. The expression "with the grain" signifies the longitudinal direction of most fibers. Grain direction is the result of the manufacturing process. The grain of paper determines its rigidity. Some processes require that the grain of the paper run with the length of the printing roll. The grain should be parallel to the typewriter platen, because the paper then rolls around the platen better and there is less tendency for the sheets to slip. Paper folds more easily and quickly when it is parallel with the grain. On the other hand, the graining should run vertically on forms posted by machine or filed on the bottom edge, since in this manner there is a tendency for the forms to buckle and curl.

*d*) Color. Colored paper for office forms frequently affords an effective medium for securing a strong appeal, a unique identification, and a simple means of facilitating the handling of forms. However, colored paper usually costs more than white.

*e*) Size. The size of the form is determined by the amount of information, the economical paper size, the size and types of office equipment and machines, and the mechanical requirements. The limitations of the printing process must, of course, be considered in determining the dimensions of a form. Wherever possible forms should be cut from stock sizes of paper. It is advisable to discuss the subject of economical stock sizes with the prospective supplier.

**4. Means of Carbonizing Copies.** The providing of carbon paper for use with the forms can be achieved in several ways: (*a*) inserting carbon by hand, (*b*) one-use carbon interleaved into the form, (*c*) carbon in the machine—using a simple "floating carbon" device, and (*d*) spots of wax carbon applied to the back of the form during the manufacturing process.

As indicated in Figure 5–8, some multiple forms provide one-use carbon paper interleaved into position. Other arrangements do not use carbon interleaving, but a floating carbon device. In this case, the forms slip over the carbon sheets which remain in the machine, and these sheets are used many times over until the impressions indicate the need for a carbon change. The fourth method, application of spots of wax carbon, makes it possible to apply the carbon to certain parts of a form, thus permitting only certain portions of the original writing to appear on the copies. Frequently, price information or specification data do not appear on all copies, since this information has little value for the purpose of some copies. A similar result can be achieved in the other carbon methods by cutting off certain carbon sheets or portions of them or blacking out, with a solid mass of dots or other marks, that portion of the form which is not to receive an impression. The carbon mark is not visible on the blackened area.

Observe that "carbonless paper" forms are included in Figure 5–8.

These forms are printed on paper chemically treated on one or both sides. Copies are obtained simultaneously with the original writing, the same as with carbon paper. The labor cost of inserting carbon between sheets, jogging, aligning, straightening, and extracting carbon after writing is eliminated by the use of carbonless paper. Its proponents claim that for a two-copy form, and a salary rate of $55 per week, this savings amount to $5.33 per thousand forms, at $75 per week, the savings are $7.26 per thousand forms. For a 12-copy form and a weekly salary of $75, the savings jump to $53.47 per thousand forms. In addition to possible labor savings, carbonless paper is clean and convenient to use.

## SPECIAL FORM SITUATIONS

Numerous special designs of forms to expedite the information work are in daily use. The list of such designs is quite long and no attempt will be made to include them here. But representative of these forms are (1) unit analysis comparative forms used for reports, and (2) paper strips used in pegboard accounting. Much data can be summarized in a neat and concise arrangement by unit analysis comparative forms. Figure 5–10 illustrates their use. The data are written on the specially designed forms held in place by binder rings through holes at the top of each form. At the close of each period, such as a month, the data for the current month are posted in the left-hand column of a strip and the year-to-date figures in the right-hand column; the center of the strip is used for identifying information. By properly positioning the newly completed monthly strip in the binder, comparisons between figures for the current month and those of previous periods are supplied. In the illustration, for example, comparisons are expedited between (1) April this year and previous months of this year and (2) April this year and April last year. If desired, additional data can be included by adding columns to the right. The unit analysis method assists in presenting calculated data in a convenient and usable pattern, in determining trends, measuring the efficiency of the operations, and highlighting the status of different components making up the entire activity.

## PAPER STRIPS AND PEGBOARD

Pegboard accounting, also known as shingle-strip and summary-strip accounting, is another type of strip arrangement for accumulating or summarizing a large number of items with minimum time, maximum accuracy, and convenience. The equipment consists of a special board and ready-made paper strips, about 2 to 3 inches wide and 16 inches long, fastened to the board. Original data are written on the strips. These strips

FIGURE 5–10. Comparative and Accumulative Operating and Financial Information Presented in an Effective Arrangement.

| PERIOD JANUARY THIS YEAR | PERIOD FEBRUARY THIS YEAR | PERIOD MARCH THIS YEAR | PERIOD APRIL LAST YEAR | PERIOD APRIL THIS YEAR | OPERATING REPORT | % OF SALES | TO DATE APRIL THIS YEAR |
|---|---|---|---|---|---|---|---|
| | | | | | SALES | | |
| 0,125 | 62,411 | 63,147 | 51,675 | 57,355 | PRODUCT A | 55.2 | 243,038 |
| 1,312 | 61,387 | 62,298 | 44,375 | 55,467 | PRODUCT B | 44.8 | 230,464 |
| 1,437 | 123,798 | 125,445 | 96,050 | 112,822 | TOTAL | 100.0 | 473,502 |
| | | | | | COST OF SALES | | |
| 2,086 | 42,439 | 43,571 | 35,643 | 41,296 | PRODUCT A | 69.9 | 169,371 |
| 6,462 | 43,279 | 43,921 | 30,234 | 38,272 | PRODUCT B | 70.0 | 160,934 |
| 7,528 | 85,718 | 87,492 | 65,877 | 79,567 | TOTAL | 70.0 | 330,305 |
| | | | | | GROSS PROFIT | | |
| 8,059 | 19,972 | 19,576 | 16,032 | 16,060 | PRODUCT A | 30.1 | 73,667 |
| 5,850 | 18,108 | 18,377 | 14,141 | 17,195 | PRODUCT B | 30.0 | 69,530 |
| 3,909 | 39,080 | 37,953 | 30,173 | 33,255 | TOTAL | 30.0 | 143,197 |
| | | | | | COST OF SALES ADJUSTMENTS | | |
| 1,211 | 657 | 752 | 418 | 456 | INVENTORY ADJUSTMENTS | | 3,076 |
| 2,075 | 1,947 | 1,846 | 1,157 | 1,411 | OVER OR UNDER ABSORBED BURDEN | | 7,279 |
| 3,286 | 2,604 | 2,598 | 1,575 | 1,867 | TOTAL | 1.9 | 10,355 |
| 0,623 | 35,476 | 35,355 | 28,598 | 31,388 | GROSS PROFIT AFTER ADJ. | 28.1 | 132,842 |
| | | | | | GENERAL EXPENSES | | |
| 6,317 | 7,185 | 7,321 | 5,732 | 6,930 | ADMINISTRATIVE - SCHEDULE A | | 27,753 |
| 8,245 | 9,345 | 8,560 | 7,048 | 6,742 | SELLING - SCHEDULE B | | 32,892 |
| 3,612 | 4,782 | 5,121 | 3,848 | 4,637 | SHIPPING - SCHEDULE C | | 18,132 |
| 2,098 | 2,417 | 2,860 | 2,461 | 2,420 | BRANCH - SCHEDULE D | | 9,795 |
| 0,272 | 23,709 | 23,862 | 19,089 | 20,729 | TOTAL EXPENSES | 18.7 | 88,572 |
| 0,351 | 11,767 | 11,493 | 9,509 | 10,659 | NET PROFIT FROM OPERATIONS | 9.4 | 44,270 |
| | | | | | OTHER INCOME | | |
| 251 | 187 | 252 | 142 | 210 | INTEREST EARNED | | 900 |
| 516 | 518 | 675 | 587 | 572 | DISCOUNT ON PURCHASES | | 2,281 |
| 122 | 158 | 145 | | 112 | DIVIDENDS RECEIVED | | 537 |
| | | | 250 | | PROFIT ON SALE OF ASSETS | | 250 |
| 218 | | | | | PROFIT ON SALE OF INVESTMENTS | | 218 |
| 1,107 | 863 | 1,322 | 709 | 894 | TOTAL OTHER INCOME | .9 | 4,186 |
| | | | | | OTHER DEDUCTIONS | | |
| 378 | 112 | 87 | 123 | 75 | INTEREST PAID | | 650 |
| 676 | 458 | 567 | 482 | 420 | DISCOUNT ON SALES | | 2,123 |
| | | 100 | | | LOSS ON SALE OF ASSETS | | 100 |
| | | | | | LOSS ON SALE OF INVESTMENTS | | |
| 1,054 | 670 | 654 | 605 | 495 | TOTAL OTHER DEDUCTIONS | .6 | 2,873 |
| 53 | 193 | 668 | 104 | 399 | NET | .3 | 1,313 |
| 0,404 | 11,960 | 12,161 | 9,613 | 11,058 | NET PROFIT BEFORE TAXES | 9.7 | 45,583 |
| | | | | | TAXES | | |
| 55 | 55 | 55 | 45 | 55 | CAPITAL STOCK | | 220 |
| 146 | 152 | 159 | 127 | 121 | STATE INCOME | | 577 |
| 3,675 | 3,742 | 3,815 | 2,655 | 3,420 | FEDERAL INCOME | | 14,652 |
| 3,875 | 3,949 | 4,029 | 2,827 | 3,596 | TOTAL TAXES | 3.1 | 15,449 |
| 6,529 | 8,011 | 8,132 | 6,786 | 7, | NET PROFIT FROM ALL SOURCES | 6.6 | 30,134 |

JUST LIFT UP

*Courtesy: Royal-McBee Co., New York*

are held in alignment by means of holes across the top which fit into a peg strip at the top of the board. The arrangement of the paper strips is offset so that a vertical margin of each strip is exposed, thus disclosing a column of figures. Quick summaries and "recaps" can be run off. A movable horizontal bar is used to guide the eye to the proper line across the forms.

This arrangement of data is particularly effective in making distribution analyses of various kinds, including cost, payroll, stock control, and sales, and it can be designed to serve almost every type of business. The boards are made in various sizes, ranging from approximately 20 x 18 inches to 36 x 18 inches. The advantages of the use of peg strips include the following: Copying of the data is eliminated—the original forms are used to obtain final results; accurate information can be provided; flexibility is permitted, since variations in the number and kind of distributions are possible; and the cost is economical—there is a minimum of handling, and the equipment required is simple.

## QUESTIONS

1. What types of information are usually contained in the introductory section of an office form?
2. Select six questions from Figure 5–4 and relate how they would be helpful in office form designing.
3. Relate four reasons why office forms are utilized.
4. What is meant by each of the following:
   *a)* "Floating carbon" device.
   *b)* Grain of paper.
   *c)* Pin-feed holes.
   *d)* Box captions of an office form.
5. Discuss the form designer's major considerations in determining the general pattern of an office form.
6. Referring to Figures 5–2 and 5–3, point out and discuss four improvements that you deem of special importance in designing a more effective office form.
7. Discuss the why, what, and where of optical character recognition forms in the accomplishment of office work.
8. Relate four different considerations normally included under the physical characteristics of an office form. Discuss the one that in your opinion is probably most important.
9. Discuss the various means of carbonizing copies of office forms.
10. Give a complete and concise definition for each of the following:
    *a)* Office form.
    *b)* Unit analysis comparative form.
    *c)* Pocket form.
    *d)* Forms management.
11. The sequence of the items on a form is important. Why is this? Illustrate your answer.
12. Discuss the meaning and use of pegboard accounting.

## CASE PROBLEMS

### Case 5–1.  Tiger Company

Many different items of summer clothes for boys and girls are sold by Tiger
Company. Sales are made directly to retail stores. Terms vary depending upon the
buyer's credit and past experience with the company. In general relationships with
buyers are excellent.

Currently the invoice form being used is shown by the accompanying illustra-

EXHIBIT 5–1A.

**Tiger Co.**

MANUFACTURERS OF TOUGH, LONG-LASTING
SUMMER APPAREL FOR BOYS AND GIRLS

ORIGINAL INVOICE

| No merchandise may be returned for credit without our written consent. All claims for shortages and damages in shipment must be filled out with carrier within 72 hours after delivery. Any claims for errors in filling orders must be made to us within 7 days after receipt of goods. | Shipped | | |
|---|---|---|---|
| | Date: | Via: | From: |
| | Terms: | Invoice Date: | |
| | Invoice No. | Reference No. Customers Order No: | Customers Account No: |
| SOLD TO | SHIP TO | | |

| Dept./Div. No: | Store No: | No. of Cartons: |
|---|---|---|

| | | Description | | Price | |
|---|---|---|---|---|---|
| Quantity | Unit | Style and Model | Unit | | Extended |
| | | | | | |
| Total | | | | | |

| Make check payable to | | Total | |
|---|---|---|---|
| TIGER CO. 100 Northbrook Road Halifax, New York 13625 | | Itemized Additional Charges | |
| Salesman: | Special Dating: | | |
| Indicate whether complete or partial shipment: | Our Reference No: | GRAND TOTAL | |

THANK YOU FOR THIS BUSINESS

tion. Recent study has revealed that this present six-copy form being used can be reduced to a four-copy form. Tiger executives also feel that the format can be improved, although the present form includes all the necessary information.

### Questions:

1. Design an improved invoice form which represents a better format than the present one.
2. Point out the specific improvements of your recommended invoice form and indicate why users should favor your suggested changes.

### Case 5–2.   Kessinger Quality Products Company

The assistant office manager has designed a new purchase order and receiving form. He asks you what you think of it. You observe the size is 6½ x 10½ inches; total number of copies is six (including original); different colors of paper will be used for each copy; six type styles are used in the composition of the form; and all the printing is in black ink except the company's name, which is in light blue. The column heading for price and the inserts, "total price" and "shipping route," are in red, so that they will stand out. The spacing of lines on the form is five to the inch. In answer to your specific questions, the assistant office manager tells you he intends to get reactions to the form from various vendors now supplying the company. A good price from the printer can be secured in quantities of 60,000 which is about a two-year supply. A standard typewriter billing machine, pica type, is used for writing purchase orders, and in about 30 percent of those written, two extra copies are needed (seven copies total) and are inserted in the five-copy pack as required.

### Questions:

1. Outline your reply to the assistant office manager.
2. Discuss the specific recommendations you would make to the assistant office manager.
3. Explain the probable reasons for the weaknesses, if any, of the proposed form.

### Case 5–3.   Pryor Company

Currently, requests for salary increases are typed in duplicate on Form 2297 by each department and the original is sent to the personnel department. This form shows in tabular form the following: $(a)$ employee name, $(b)$ employee number, $(c)$ job, $(d)$ current salary, and $(e)$ recommended increase. On the right margin is space for comments. Ordinarily these papers are made out every two weeks, if needed. The personnel department compiles a tabular master list every two weeks from the Form 2297s received. In addition, the department adds for each employee listed $(a)$ the salary range for the present job and $(b)$ date of last increase. These entries are on the right portion of the master list. There are also four blank columns headed $(a)$ increase granted, $(b)$ increase refused, $(c)$ effective date, and (*d*) comments. Copies of these master sheets are distributed to members of the salary committee. Subsequently, at their meeting salary decisions on each listed employee are made and recorded in the proper blank columns of the master list. From this completed list, the personnel department fills out a Form 3229, "Advice of Salary Increase," for each listed employee and Form 3710, which is a tabular listing of the data of personnel department's master list *for employees granted increases only*. Copies of Form 3710 are sent to the payroll department and to the Group Insurance Agency. Form 3229 is sent to the proper department manager, who gives it to the employee.

## Questions:

1. Devise an improved procedure and form which will combine all the necessary information and eliminate duplicate typing and unnecessary work.
2. Briefly describe your recommended procedure and sketch the improved form or forms you recommend.

chapter **6**

# Information media—
# letters and reports

> You have not converted a man because you have silenced him.
> —*Viscount John Morley*

ESSENTIAL in the creating and supplying of necessary information are letters and reports. Even in its most limited concept, information management includes consideration for letters and reports for they are the common media for keeping persons both within and without an enterprise informed on important matters.

Letters are not only conveyors of information, they are also one of the main carriers of the corporate image. Public relations and good will are developed tremendously by the use of effective letters. Many stories attest to the fact that a friendly, well-written letter paved the way for a million dollar sale with a previously unknown party. Such a letter obviously is important, but so are all letters. Each one alone may seem trivial, but cumulatively they have enormous potential. Similarly, reports are vital information media. They assist in keeping designated personnel informed on past, present, and future managerial actions. Reports supply the needed information or suggest possible avenues of approach which might reveal potent information.

## TYPES OF LETTERS

Letters have been classified into many different types to expedite study and improvement of them. The various types form a very long list and no attempt to include it will be made here. For our purpose, we can view letter classification based on either (1) function or (2) format. Under the first are letters dealing with such major activities as complaints, employment, purchasing, sales, and credit. In turn, each of these types can be analyzed further into subtypes. For example, under complaints, the subtypes are usually (a) acknowledgement of complaint and promise to investigate and report, (b) adjustment of complaint, giving date and amount and thanking addressee, (c) refusal to adjust complaint, with reasons explaining why, and (d) request that the goods be returned for inspection and advisement that further consideration will be given. Further, for employment, three types of replies are generally given (a) acknowledgment of application, stating that there is no opening at present, (b) acknowledgment of application and request to report for work, and (c) welcome to newly hired worker of the company and explanation of company policies.

The major classifications of letter format concern arrangement, appearance, or makeup of a letter. A business letter should convey the necessary information and make a favorable first impression. Information well placed on the page, margins as even as possible, and uniformity of type are universal standbys. The arrangement itself can follow any of several patterns, depending upon the preference of the writer. But certain arrangements dominate because writers conform; a reader becomes accustomed to look for information in certain locations of the letter. Figure 6–1 shows the format of several different arrangements including (1) indented paragraphs, (2) block paragraphs, and (3) simplified letter. Slight variations from these three forms of letters are employed.

The so-called speed letter has won favor for transmitting information effectively. In this type a printed format is used with space provided for listing recipients making up a mailing route and for checking other appropriate information. Individual information can be added as required. See Figure 6–2.

Formally stated: *A speed letter is a preprinted form designating certain spaces for filling in desired information.* Commonly, three copies are

FIGURE 6–1. The Respective Forms of Three Different Letters Used in Business.

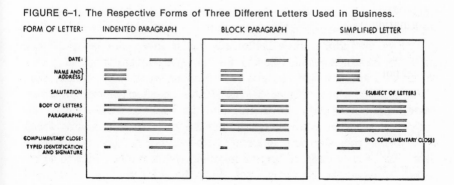

FORM OF LETTER:    INDENTED PARAGRAPH    BLOCK PARAGRAPH    SIMPLIFIED LETTER

FIGURE 6–2. A Well-Planned Printed Form to Expedite Written
Information Transmission.

| DEMPSTER CORP.<br>CHICAGO, ILL.<br>SPEED LETTER | | DATE | | |
|---|---|---|---|---|
| TO:<br>1 | LOCATION | | INITIALS | DATE |
| 2 | | | | |
| 3 | | | | |
| 4 | | | | |
| 5 | | | | |
| APPROVAL | | NOTE AND FORWARD | | |
| AS REQUESTED | | NOTE AND RETURN | | |
| COMMENT | | NOTE ENDORS'T OF ACTION TAKEN | | |
| FOR YOUR INFORMATION | | PER CONVERSATION | | |
| INITIAL FOR CLEARANCE | | PREPARE REPLY | | |
| NECESSARY ACTION | | SIGNATURE | | |
| MESSAGE | | | | |
| | | | | |
| SIGNATURE | | TITLE | | |

made. The original is retained by the sender; copies 2 and 3 are sent to
the receiver, who writes in his reply, returns copy 2, and retains copy 3.

The memorandum, while technically not a letter, can be mentioned
here. The memorandum is effective for conveying information when simple criteria are followed. It tells the recipient what, why, where, how,
when, and by whom. Figure 6–3 illustrates an effective memorandum.
Terse headings simplify the writing and the reading. While it may initially impress as being too abrupt, it does the job of communicating which
is the prime consideration. A memo is to remind, to confirm, to make
clear. Placed on a desk, it keeps reminding and it reaches hard-to-locate
people. However, in too many cases the memo is incomplete, wordy, and

FIGURE 6–3. Example of an Effective Short Memorandum.

| | |
|---|---|
| April 25, 19— | |
| To: | T. E. Miller |
| SUBJECT: | Storing purchased parts in our stores. |
| OBJECTIVE: | To reduce damage to parts while in transit or in stores. |
| SCOPE OF PROJECT: | Try to attain: |
| | 1. Better package design and material. |
| | 2. Improved physical inventory taking. |
| | 3. Better utilization of stores space. |
| | 4. Efficient housekeeping in stores. |
| TIME REQUIRED: | Approximately six weeks. |
| SUBMITTED BY: | J. D. Black |

its claim to fame is in helping people make jobs for themselves. There is no better way for two managers to get out of touch with each other quickly than by retiring to the seclusion of their offices and writing memos to each other.

Another classification of letter format is form letters and paragraphs. Since, as stated above, most letters deal with a limited number of subjects, it is possible to use the same or similar answers to common requests and inquiries. In other words, standardized information is used to answer letters on a similar or recurring subject or to give the same information to many addressees as, for example, in a large direct-mail campaign. A form letter may be used for accounts past due. Such a letter, keyed "Delinquent Collection Letter No. 1," is sent to all accounts in arrears, with the appropriate name and address added at the top. After a certain amount of time, a "Delinquent Collection Letter No. 2" may be sent to those accounts which remain unpaid.

Form paragraphs are similar in idea to form letters but apply to standardized paragraphs only. Under this practice, letters are composed of form paragraphs plus individual ones. Several variants of a form paragraph are used, thus gaining some diversity. The approved form paragraphs are listed, keyed, and indexed, and are made available to all correspondents.

Form letters and form paragraphs can be "armchaired" from handy references, or they can be obtained by actual practice. The latter is recommended and consists of collecting for a period of several weeks a copy of every letter written, sorting these by major subject, selecting the best reply for each subject, modifying as circumstances suggest, and standardizing on these superior replies. For this work, the services of all letterwriting people in the office should be enlisted. Participation will not only help win acceptance for improving letter writing, but also for acceptance of form letters and paragraphs, in addition to improving morale and increasing efficiency.

Generally speaking, form letters and paragraphs serve a very useful purpose. They are tailored to fit certain conditions and are usually worked over by several correspondents to create the best possible results. They need not be impersonal, and it is not necessary to send the same letter again and again to the same customer. When they are properly handled, there should be no objection to form letters and paragraphs. They provide a uniform operation, conserve time and effort, and reduce correspondence cost. On the other hand, they may not fit a particular case, lack a personal touch, and follow a stilted manner.

## DESIGNING THE LETTER

Recognizing the need to communicate factually and effectively is a prime consideration in designing a letter. Customers want information, employees want answers to their questions, and the public wants to know certain specifics about an enterprise. How do they receive this information? In large measure by means of letters. Here is a vital and common medium that enables the writer to establish credibility, win confidence of customers and employees, and cultivate a climate helpful to sound motivation. But more than this, letters are media to identify a company's trouble spots, and for suggesting modification in policies and practices to meet better current conditions and update activities in light of current social and economic changes.

With this as a background, attention can be directed toward three essential elements required for meaningful writing of letters. First, is getting the facts. To write meaningfully, the writer must have all the facts. To write a sales letter, for example, one must have information on what the product will do, its good points, its price, and the like. If filed material is required, make certain it is made available before the writing starts. Strive to know the subject at hand. Second, analyze these facts and organize your message. Put yourself in the reader's position and focus your thoughts on what you feel the letter should convey. In most instances, a letter is an effort to have its recipient believe and act toward a subject as the writer does. Following this line of thinking, the opening statement of a letter should be designed to get the reader's attention. Following this, develop the reader's interest. Then, lead this interest into a desire and finally culminate the entire letter with action—to order the service, to accept the adjustment, to pay the bill, or whatever the case might be.

The writing style can be varied to the specific task. The "sell" approach characterizes many letters and consists of presenting the product or service favorably and pointing out the benefits to the reader. But other approaches are popular including the "firm-but-fair" approach consisting of studying the facts, being objective, taking account of precedent, and protecting the company's position. Likewise, the "persuasive" approach is common. Its pattern is usually that of attracting interest, giving the facts, anticipating objections, and summarizing the pertinent advantages to the individual recipient.

## TYPES OF REPORTS

Like letters, reports can be classified into many types, including private, public, company, departmental, restricted, nonrestricted, technical, and nontechnical. However, for purposes of office usage, the three groups of executive, periodic, and special are quite satisfactory. Under each of these classifications are the following:

*Executive reports* stress broad concepts and results rather than details, usually covering a three-, six-, or twelve-month time period. For the most part, they are prepared for members of top and intermediate management levels. They include (1) balance sheet, (2) statement of cost of goods sold, (3) statement of profit and loss, (4) budgetary statement, (5) annual departmental report, and (6) report to stockholders.

FIGURE 6–4. A Portion of a Special Report.

---

| 35—E | X Research Company | N 58 |
|---|---|---|

### SUMMARY OF FINDINGS

OBJECTIVE:

To obtain a measure of consumer acceptance of Product Y.

RESULTS:

1. Product Y is not as well liked as Product No. 17.
2. The market potential of Product Y is somewhat between 50% and 80% of the market for Product No. 17. These are the limits indicated by consumers' stated preferences and test-package consumption.
3. The preference for Product No. 17 over Product Y prevails in all geographical areas and among all types of consumers. The greatest liking for Product Y was found among women.
4. Product No. 17 is preferred chiefly because it is crisp, easy to eat, and has a sweet, mild flavor.
5. Product Y is preferred by those who like a harder and heavier cereal than Product No. 17. Most cold cereal users, however, thought Product Y too hard to chew.
6. While food value is not a dominant factor in consumers' preferences between cereals, Product Y was the choice of consumers who emphasize this point.

CONCLUSION:

There is a limited market for an expanded cereal that is harder and heavier than Product No. 17. The potential volume of one such cereal—Product Y—is between 50% and 80% of the Product No. 17 market.

*Periodic reports* deal mainly with departmental activities and typically cover weekly, monthly, or quarterly periods. Usually some detailed infor- mation pertinent to the operation of the particular department is in- cluded. Periodic reports include (1) monthly reports on operation, (2) departmental records of performance, (3) monthly credit reports, (4) purchasing reports, (5) material-handling reports, (6) salesmen's reports, (7) advertising and sales promotion reports, and (8) personnel manage- ment reports.

*Special reports* cover activities not covered by other reports. They are published at frequent intervals and include subjects such as product development, marketing research, plant location, company insurance and pension revisions, and various projects of a nonrecurring nature. A portion of a special report dealing with the findings of a market research study is shown in Figure 6–4 on page 125.

## DESIGNING THE REPORT

There is no one best way to arrange the information of a report. In some instances, a standardized format is well established and accepted; but in many cases, the writer is free to choose the makeup. Material should be presented logically. Aids which will help in the reading should be provided—for example, simple statements, sectional headings, summa- ries at the beginning, and a table of contents. A reader often glances through a report, noting the various headings and reading a sentence here and there. For this reason, it is advisable to make it possible to obtain a "quickie" on what the report is all about and what it includes. This approach will maintain the reader's interest and lead him to correct conclusions and proper actions.

The so-called playscript procedure is an effective format for certain types of report writing. It clearly spells out who does what in a sequential order. Its use is rapidly spreading. Figure 6–5 shows this arrangement.

Every report should follow a carefully developed general outline. The first step in preparing such an outline is to select the information to be included in the report. This is ordinarily dictated by the purpose of the report, what information is available, or what can be uncovered. Next, the items of information should be classified under headings which normally are grouped as major and minor, or as many groups as judgment suggests.

There are a number of general outlines for reports; the following is preferred by many: (1) summary of findings, (2) methodology, (3) detailed results, and (4) appendix. Another outline which is effective and adaptable for many subjects, especially those of a technical nature, in- cludes: (1) summary, (2) objective and scope, (3) equipment used, (4) methodology, (5) data obtained, (6) conclusions, and (7) recommenda- tions. The following has also won favor: (1) introduction and definition

FIGURE 6–5. Writing by the "Playscript Procedure" is Winning Wide Acceptance.

## PROCEDURE NO. 2

Subject: Retrieving Records from the Center

| *Performed by* | *Action* |
|---|---|
| Department records clerk | 1. When information is needed from an inactive record, phones records center. |
| | 2. Refers to the returned copy of form PSC-418, TRANSMITTAL LIST —INACTIVE RECORDS. Gives the records center location carton number, folder, and document wanted. |
| Records center clerk | 3. Asks inquirer if this information can be given by telephone. |
| | 3a. If phone answer is OK, goes to shelf location, retrieves record, and gives information wanted. |

*Variations*

4. If information cannot be given by telephone, and requester wants entire record, asks if a copy will do.

## PROCEDURE NO. 3

Subject: Destroying Inactive Records

| *Performed by* | *Action* |
|---|---|
| Records center clerk | 1. Checks destruction tickler file each month. Pulls out cards indicating the records which are scheduled for destruction. |
| | 2. For each group (same form No. etc.) Fills out form PSC-435, DESTRUCTION NOTICE in 2 copies. |
| | 3. Sends one copy to the department records clerk of the department of "basic interest." |
| Department manager | 3a. If, upon notice of scheduled destruction, decides the group of records should be retained longer, fills out form PSC-445 RETENTION SCHEDULE REVISION. |
| Department records clerk | 3b. Sends or takes form PSC-445 to records center clerk. |
| Records center clerk | 3c. Retains records for an additional 30 to 90 days. |

*Courtesy: Systemation, Inc., Colorado Springs*

of problem, (2) conclusions and recommendations, (3) discussion of procedure and results obtained, and (4) summary. Another is: (1) digest of findings and recommendations, (2) background of study, (3) savings and other benefits to be gained, (4) possible drawbacks, (5) alternatives and why choice of the one recommended, and (6) proposed implementation plan.

It should be observed that in each of these outlines, either the summary, conclusion, or recommendation is included near the beginning of the report. This may seem illogical; but actually it is not. The sequence of items need not be chronologic; however, there should be *some order* in presenting the material. The great majority of report readers want the gist of the findings or the conclusions right away, so it is effective to put this information at the beginning.

Charts, drawings, pictures, and maps help to convey the meaning to the reader, but they must be carefully selected and employed in "reasonable" amounts for maximum effectiveness. In many cases, the chart or drawing must be explained and significant relations pointed out to the reader, because the exact meaning may not be gained simply by looking at the illustrative material. Pictures are especially helpful in dealing with technical subjects.

## WRITING EFFECTIVELY

Writing presents a tremendous challenge. One of the most powerful factors in the world is the presentation of helpful ideas and facts in writing that can be clearly understood. Skill in effective writing can be developed. It is not an ability with which some are blessed and which others can never hope to achieve. Writing can be stimulating and it is a powerful tool. It can win men's hearts to a stated cause; it can distribute knowledge; it can implement effective action. However, too often the challenge of writing is not even recognized, let alone mastered.

What can be done to improve our business writing? Considerable help is given by following pertinent guides which include the following.

*1. Make the Writing Serve a Known and Definite Purpose.* In the case of letters, for example, know exactly what is to be accomplished by the letter. Settle on one main issue and concentrate on it. Letters pertaining to a single subject are easy to understand, and they expedite filing.

Reports are written to help the recipient and should be appropriate to the plan, decision, or directive about which he is concerned. It is essential that the aim of the letter or the report be known to the person preparing it because this knowledge guides the writer and helps him point the communication toward its intended uses.

*2. Keep the Recipient in Mind.* The aim of a letter or of a report stands a much better chance of accomplishment if its text is understood. To expedite this understanding, the needs, wants, and interests of the recipient should be given prime consideration. Put the reader in the center of what is written. Look at the subject from his viewpoint; visualize the reader while writing, and tailor the material and expressions to him.

In letter writing, for example, the technique of the "you viewpoint" can be followed. To illustrate:

Write:

You may have quick service if you'll just telephone ORchard 1–7777.

Do not write:

We wish to call attention to the fact that we are in the dry-cleaning business and have a 15-year record of excellent service. Our telephone number is ORchard 1–7777.

**3. Be Factual and Unbiased.**  Accuracy is essential to good writing regardless of the scope, subject, medium, or level for which it is intended. The facts should be relevant to the subject; opinions should be identified as such. Irrelevant details should be excluded. What is basic to the stated purpose should be included. Information which is incomplete and not essential to the purpose should be avoided. Remember the writing is being done to inform the reader of the situation or subject as it is. A letter or a report can be colorful, yet not filled with emotional statements.

**4. Use Short Familiar Words and Simple Sentences.**  Word choice is vital; simple words are bold and clear and usually convey the intended meaning. Employing words in common usage is a good rule to follow. Words having a vague or difficult meaning to different people should be avoided, i.e., "high" salary or "good" job. And simple sentences are perhaps the most helpful ingredient of clear writing. Although variety in sentence length is desirable, short sentences are normally preferred. But too many short sentences make the writing monotonous. Some say that no sentence should be longer than 25 words. However, a sentence should be long enough to convey the thought. A practical suggestion is to fit the sentence to the reader's span of attention. Omit involved phrases and weed out the extra words. Tabulate lists for greater clarity. Correct punctuation also helps.

**5. Employ Active Verbs.**  Present-tense verbs create more interest and convey activity better than past-tense or subjunctive-tense verbs. "He understands" has more vigor than "It is understood by him" or "He should have understood." While some variation is desirable, try to use a good portion of active verbs in your writing.

**6. Use Conversational Style.**  Letters and reports are communicative media and are more readily understood when written in a style to which we are accustomed. We are familiar with the conversational style and from it quickly grasp the meaning. Ordinarily we do not use exotic words and long sentences with qualifying phrases in our normal speech. Why insist on using these communication blocks in our written work?

**7. Establish an Acceptable Mood.**  When writing use a tone that wins cooperation or puts the reader in a mood to read the communication and give thought to it. Positive expressions help to accomplish this goal. For example, in a letter, write: "We can send you tickets for the November 27 performance," instead of "We cannot send tickets for any performance prior to that of November 27."

Be friendly and let your writing reflect your own natural self. Letters and reports are written to human beings, not merely to names. Write naturally and humanly. Stilted, highly formalized statements are taboo. Avoid "whisker" expressions, examples of which, along with improvements, include:

| *Do not use* | *Use* |
|---|---|
| I am not in a position | I cannot |
| My attention has been called | I notice |
| Enclosed please find | We enclose |
| Acquaint me with the facts | Tell me |
| Contents duly noted | I have read |
| We have reviewed our records | We find |
| It is our opinion | I believe |
| At all times | Always |

**8. Make the Writing Clear.** This requires knowing what must be included and in what sequence it should be presented. The writer should express each thought so clearly that the reader is certain to understand it. Normally, the transcriber helps in acquiring clarity by straightening out improper sentence structure and switching words. It is well to have a competent person edit a report to insure that the meaning is clear.

Have your writing say exactly what you intend it to say, and mean what the writing says. These eight words form the basis of all great writing: "Write so that you cannot possibly be misunderstood."

**9. Interpret Findings Adequately.** Avoid exaggeration or the inclusion of unqualified interpretations which cannot be reasonably derived from the available information. It is usually best to understate rather than to overstate conclusions. Also, recommendations must be practical and sound.

**10. Summarize Briefly and Make Writing Conclusive.** Normally, it is best to state the results in a summary statement. Convey the essentials to the reader easily; under no circumstances should the receiver be required to dig through quantities of words and figures to find out what the writing discloses or is all about. Include what action, if any, is desired of the reader and what the writer will do. Be decisive. Avoid double meanings and long, qualified explanations. Strive to set forth the recommendations so clearly and effectively that they will be followed.

## MANAGEMENT OF LETTERS AND REPORTS

Making sure that only necessary letters and reports are prepared is a key area in the management of letters and reports. In the typical enter-

FIGURE 6–6. Estimate of Time and Cost to Write a One-Page Letter (Original and Three Carbon Copies).

|  | *Personal Basis* | *Machine Basis* | *Form Letter* |
|---|---|---|---|
| Planning the letter | 13 min. | 13 min. | 0 min. |
| Dictating the letter | 13 " | 8 " | 0 " |
| Transcribing and typing | 7 " | 9 " | 3 " |
| Checking and signing | 3 " | 3 " | 2 " |
| Total time | 36 min. | 33 min. | 5 min. |
| Labor cost @ $2.90/hr | $1.74 | $1.38 | $0.21 |
| Supplies and office overhead | 0.90 | 0.50 | 0.07 |
| Total cost | $2.64 | $1.88 | $0.28 |

prise, too many letters and reports are written. Replies are written when no reply is required and the habit of preparing certain documents remains long after the original need has ceased. Periodic reevaluation of the necessity for all writing should be followed. It is usually enlightening to calculate the percentage of payroll cost represented by letter and report writing and note if the trend is up or down. Also view this percentage in relation to the written work being done. Does it appear reasonable? Does it satisfy the purpose for which intended? In what areas can this work be improved? What is being done today to accomplish these improvements?

Cost analysis is effective in managing letter and report writing. Figure 6–6 shows an estimate of time and cost factors in writing a typical one-page letter. Note under the personal basis the cost per letter is $2.64. Even a form letter costs 28 cents. The cost varies, of course, depending on the length, difficulty of material, method of transcription, and nonproductive time. When the volume is large and an automatic typewriter or a duplicating process is used, the cost is considerably decreased.[1]

Some believe that using the "reply at bottom" type of letter lessens correspondence work and makes controlling efforts easier. In this type of letter, the answer or comment is written in the margin or at the bottom of an incoming letter. A copy is then made and sent to the interested party, the original being retained for the files. This practice may not be suited for all correspondence, but when satisfactory it does save considerable typing and filing space.

In the case of weekly reports, for example, it may be found that a complete report every week is unnecessary. All that is required is the statement that activities are proceeding according to plans or that they are within acceptable limits. This is called a "tolerance report." If plans are not being fulfilled, the recipient wants to know what is out of line and how best to correct it. Such a report is termed an "exception report." In

---

[1] See discussion on page 136.

neither case is it necessary to write a complete report with all the minute details. And, of course, the idea of changing the report to a monthly or quarterly writing merits study.

Another management area to watch carefully is the distribution of the information media, especially in the case of reports. Too often the distribution list includes names of persons who neither need nor read the report. An approach that brings excellent results is to remove the names of nonessential receivers and give no notice of this action. Subsequently, in most instances, the absence of the report is not noticed by the new nonreceiver, complaints or inquiries about the report being rare. Some argue that the cost of copies is low in view of the copying machines available today. This is true, but evades the real issue which is that "surplus" recipients look at the report, become interested in the content which may not be their concern, waste their time on these "foreign" activities, and use filing space to retain the report for some doubtful future reference.

In the case of a report, the cost depends upon many factors. Expense of gathering data and the time of the writer are key costs. Studies show that what appears to be a simple 20-page report may cost upward of $1,500 to prepare. Most executives underestimate what a report costs. Computer-prepared reports also usually mean a considerable expenditure.

A practice commonly used is to inform the recipient of a report what it costs to prepare it and indicate in the future that his unit or department will be charged for this work. If the costs do not justify the use made of the reports, the recipient will request his name to be withdrawn from the distribution list. Discretion and judgment must be exercised in this approach, but it is effective.

Part of the problem in managing letter and report writing is that the writing is done by different employees located in many different departments. Many top executives prefer to handle their correspondence work in their own unit, i.e., by their secretaries and themselves. And report writing can be found in almost any organizational unit—it is not confined to "the office." For example, the assistant sales manager may have the responsibility of writing the monthly sales report; the technician, a research report; and the personnel manager, a report on the company's industrial relations. On the other hand, a large amount of letter writing is usually performed by correspondents who either have transcribers permanently located in the various departments performing letter writing or have transcribers in a centralized transcribing department or "pool."

Whatever the organizational arrangement, the producing of letters requires coordination among various personnel. For example, the dictator must correct or redictate if the transcriber's work is in error, the dictator cannot be effective if the file clerk supplies the wrong materials, and the transcriber cannot be efficient if the dictator does his work poorly. The organizational relationship should foster the needed cooperation and coordination among those engaged in letter-writing work. And reliance on effective actuating efforts to improve writing is normally required.

These actuating efforts take the form of establishing the importance of writing and pride in this type of work, and instruction in effective writing practices. The importance of writing adds prestige to the writer as a doer of work that is needed and is beneficial to all members of the enterprise. Writing provides the means to desirable ends—to get certain action started, others curtailed, and controversial issues settled. Pride in writing is aided by keeping writing personnel busy at the level of skill for which he or she is hired. Stenographers should not be tied down to typists' jobs. Correspondents should not spend a great deal of their time filing. High-salaried executives should not dictate letters in those cases where a correspondent will do an equally effective job. Full utilization of all correspondence facilities is the goal.

Regular meetings to discuss the principles of good business writing should be held. Material written by employees can be evaluated and possible ways for improvement noted. Frequently it is found that conferences with individual employees are most effective. Samples of the employee's work can be inspected and personalized help given. The belief is growing that a writer needing help has perhaps only two or three weaknesses, not all of them. Intensive corrective work, individually applied, is the best way to correct these faults. But no single training program can guarantee perfect writing. It has been said, one never learns to write, one is always learning to write. Samples to illustrate writing fundamentals and improvements help tremendously.

Mutual of New York undertook a comprehensive correspondence simplification program and, among other things, drafted a series of "guide letters" for its correspondents. Figure 6–7 shows an example. These letters were meticulously prepared to give customers the answers they wanted in understandable terms and in a friendly, helpful manner.

In addition, the management of writing efforts includes the adoption of standards to measure both quantity and quality output. Usually the output must be sorted according to type of work, counting the number of each classification that is written during a period of a week or two. This period is suggested in order to obtain a "package of typewritten work"—a requirement brought about by the fact that the work with respect to difficulty of writing varies widely and the work within too small a period may not be representative. Quality can be based on freedom from errors, clearness, conciseness, and completeness of the writing. Further, an accounting of such things as the machine assigned to each correspondent, the amount of work turned out by each machine, the extent of machine idleness, and the amount and frequency of repairs can also be employed. These data, plus proper follow-up, will help to improve the work output.

FIGURE 6–7. A Guide Letter Furnished Company Correspondents to Assist Them In Writing More Effectively.

```
Example of The "Long" and "Short" of It


              DEATH CLAIM - EXPLAINING AGE ADJUSTMENT

                           Original


         We are enclosing a letter addressed to the payee under
         the above numbered policy, explaining the adjustment
         which we made because of a difference in the Insured's
         age.

         Will you see that we are furnished with the best
         evidence available as to the correct date of birth?  A
         copy made by a notary of a family or public record,
         made at or near the time of birth, of the date of birth
         together with a statement by the notary as to the date
         of publication of the book from which the record is
         obtained, and by whom the record was made and when, is
         the most satisfactory evidence.  Form 3593 covers such
         information.  If no such record is obtainable, an
         affidavit to that effect should be furnished together
         with the best information available with a full
         statement as to its source and why it is believed to
         be correct.

         Please forward the above information to us at your
         earliest convenience.

                               Yours very truly,


                           Revised
                         To Manager

 DCA-14   We will gladly make adjustments on this claim, if
          necessary, when correct birthdate is established.  If
          (name) is unable to complete Form 3593, please get an
          affidavit stating why the date is believed correct and
          return with the best evidence available.

          Also, kindly give the enclosed  letter* of explanation.

                               Thank you.

          *  Key No. DCA-15

          Original 160 Words:  Revised 53 Words:  Saving 67 Per cent

            Note:  The Original is a splendid example of a letter
                   that goes to great unnecessary length in stating
                   the obvious.  Notice that the Revised states all
                   that a manager need be told to know how to proceed.
```

*Courtesy: Mutual of New York*

Finally, the use of an office manual should be considered. Manuals provide the employee with standard practices and instructions in a form that is convenient and easy to use. They help the employee to help himself and assist in eliminating many needless errors.[2]

---

[2] See chapter 23 for discussion of office manuals.

## TYPEWRITERS

The basic machine for letter and report writing is the typewriter. In common use, it speeds the handling of most written work. It should be added, however, that in this day and age many outputs are printed by computers. A convenient classification of office typewriters is standard and electric. The former is operated by human energy, i.e., by the depression of a key. While typing, the carriage is moved to the left by action of a spring. In contrast, the electric typewriter is motivated mainly by electricity. Manual energy is still used to touch the keys, but the energy input is about one fifth of that required for manual machines. Work done on an electric typewriter is of uniform type impression, and a greater number of copies can be obtained without any increase in manual energy. An electric machine costs more and has fewer moving parts than a standard machine.

Figure 6–8 shows a "Selectric" typewriter which is electric and features "balls of type" for selective typing elements, thus making it possible to use the style of type best fitted for the particular writing application.

FIGURE 6–8. An IBM "Selectric" Typewriter.

This is an electric machine adaptable for various "balls of type" supplying various type styles in keeping with different writing demands. The ball of type or selective element can be quickly interchanged with other elements. A wide variety of elements is offered.

Regular correspondence can be a distinctive type, invoicing of a large type, and personal notes of a script style. In general, almost all typewriters available are equipped with a standard keyboard. Special keyboards or parts of keyboards, such as engineering, mathematical, chemical, or foreign language signs and marks, are available at an additional cost.

Most typewriters on the market today are excellent machines and have many common features including "set" and "clear" tabulators, either of a single- or decimal-key type. Tabulators are very helpful for the rapid movement and alignment of the carriage which is required in reports and other written work that have frequent indentations. Typewriter platens are available in different degrees of hardness. Use of a soft platen is recommended where the number of copies are few and quietness is desired. Conversely, a hard platen is recommended when a large number of copies is required. It causes more noise, however, than does the soft platen.

## AUTOMATIC TYPING MACHINES

The automatic typing machine has won wide adoption for the typing of similar letters when they are either in large quantities or similar format having slight changes only. It consists of a regular typewriter to which a special mechanism has been attached. The paper is inserted in the machine in the same manner as in a regular typewriter; and the date, name, and address are typed in by hand. At the touch of a button, the machine takes over and automatically types the letter, stopping at the first place where a special fill-in is required. This is typed in by hand, and then, after another touch of the button, the machine continues typing the letter to the next stop. Figure 6–9 shows a letter typed in this manner. All paragraphing, spacing, and the like are handled by the machine. If possible, the location of each fill-in should be at the end of a line or paragraph, to provide the required elasticity in space. Words or numbers of varying lengths can be inserted without difficulty. The entire letter has been typed automatically by machine, with the exception of the individualized parts as noted on the illustration.

As many as 200 short letters a day can be typed with this machine. Multiple combinations of machines, requiring one operator, can produce approximately 500 short letters a day. For this volume and using a five-year depreciation basis for a battery of four machines, direct labor cost of $20 a day, the cost figures about 6 cents a letter—an extremely low expense.

Form letters or paragraphs are originally cut on either a paper roll or a tape. This perforating work is done in the individual office or at the local service office. The holes are punched according to a code that conveys the

FIGURE 6–9. A Letter Typed by an Automatic Typewriter.

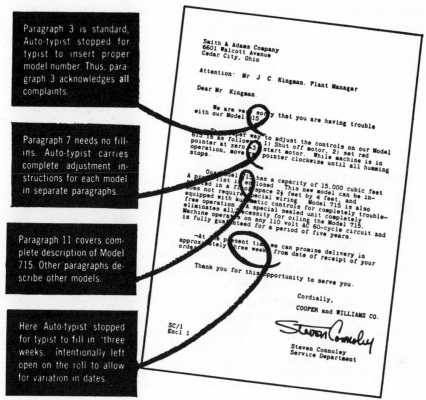

Paragraph 3 is standard. Auto-typist stopped for typist to insert proper model number. Thus, paragraph 3 acknowledges all complaints.

Paragraph 7 needs no fill-ins. Auto-typist carries complete adjustment instructions for each model in separate paragraphs.

Paragraph 11 covers complete description of Model 715. Other paragraphs describe other models.

Here Auto-typist stopped for typist to fill in 'three weeks,' intentionally left open on the roll to allow for variation in dates.

Paragraph Selection and Individual Fill-in Material Are Easily Handled As Described in the Illustration.

information. Mounted in the machine, this roll passes over a trucker bar in which a vacuum is maintained. Any opening in the roll causes a change in pressure, which operates the type, thus causing the machine to write. The capacities and details of operation vary with the machine and the manufacturer. About 20 different letters or an equivalent of form paragraphs can be placed on one record roll. The operator selects the material to be machine-typed by means of simple controls.

When a perforated tape is used, the operation of the automatic typewriter is quite similar to that described above. The holes in the tape cause the mechanism to operate specific typewriter keys which result in the desired writing. Perforated tape is being used more and more to operate office machines automatically. Its growth has been stimulated by the application of source data automation (SDA) which is described in chapter 8.

A modification of this is electronically edited automatic typing. In this arrangement, while a rough draft is typed, a small deskdrawer control unit stores copy of typing. The typist calls for an "instant-replay." After checking the replay hard copy, edit and correction footnotes are typed at the bottom of this copy. The machine automatically edits the copy per the footnotes entered. By calling for another instant-replay, a perfect hard copy on fresh paper is obtained. This typing means is especially helpful in editing a manuscript where corrections, deletions, and additions can be easily handled. The memory units holds 100 letters for instant recall. No special typing skill is required and extra typewriters share the same control unit.

## PRODUCING LETTERS BY DUPLICATION PROCESS

When the requirement is for a substantial quantity of letters with written material exactly alike, the use of a duplicating means is fast and economical. The name and address are omitted, and simply "Dear Sir" is put on each letterhead, with the name and address on the envelope only. As an alternative, the name and address can be typed carefully on the letter, but it will not match precisely the duplicated part of the letter. However, with typing skill and experience, satisfactory results are possible. The cost for identical letters produced by a duplicating process is far less than those individually typed with or without an automatic machine.

FIGURE 6–10. A "Window Letter" Which Features the Use of a Preaddressed Card to Individualize a Form Letter.

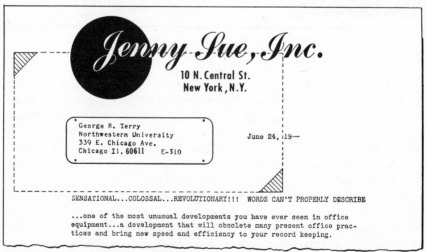

The card, also used as a business reply card, is held in place either by a pocket in the back or by slots into which opposite card corners are inserted (as illustrated). The name and address appear through a window opening in the letter. The mailing can also utilize window envelopes.

The cost differential depends upon the duplicating process used and the quantity involved.

Another possibility for volume mailings is to use a "window letter." A preaddressed card is attached to the back and top of the duplicated letter, so that the name and address appear at the normal location and can be read through a window opening in the letterhead. The card also serves as a business reply card with necessary postage and name and address of the sender on the reverse side. This arrangement is illustrated in Figure 6–10.

For correspondence, a machine is available that in a single run will write a complete letter from blank paper to finished letter—including the individual name and address, salutation, letterhead in color, date, text, and facsimile ink signature. Since the same basic process is used at the same time, all the typing is perfectly matched. The machine will print and personally identify a reply card. The machine operates at a speed of 100 complete letters per minute.

## DICTATING MACHINES

A dictating machine consists of a recorder unit used by the dictator, and a transcriber unit used by the typist to play back the recorded dictation; or a combination unit featuring both recording and transcribing. The latter is practical when the dictator and transcriber can plan their day for separate periods of dictation and transcription. Most recorders are equipped with a hand microphone for ordinary dictation and a desk microphone for recording over-the-desk conference discussions. By means of a foot-control device, the transcriber is started and stopped as desired in order for the operator to listen and transcribe what has been dictated. Usually a signaling device is included whereby the amount of dictation and places of correction can be indicated. There is usually a backspacer for repeating dictation and voice-control adjustments to regulate speed, volume, and tone. The recording medium is usually a plastic belt, disk, or roll. A plastic belt medium is an endless belt of thin, tough plastic, 3½ inches wide and 12 inches in circumference. It withstands rough handling, accommodates about 15 minutes of dictation, and serves as a permanent, one-time recording medium. As many as five belts, nested one within the other, will fit into a small business envelope and can be mailed for a few cents. Figure 6–11 shows a dictating machine using a plastic belt.

Different models stress different features. For example, one is completely portable (weight 27 ounces) and operates on either a.c. current or batteries. It fits snugly in the palm of your hand and uses a magnetic tape having 50 minutes of recording time. Precision corrections are possible and connection for remote foot control and earset are provided. Another

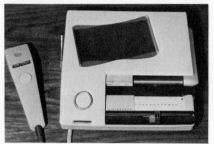

FIGURE 6–11. Taking Up Less Space Than a Letter and Weighing about Eight Pounds, This Fully Automatic Dictating Machine Is a Recorder-Transcriber Unit and Employs a Plastic Belt as the Medium.

*Courtesy: Dictaphone Corp., New York*

dictating machine employs "dictate and cut" whereby the roll of magnetic film, serving as the medium, is cut after completion of dictation and written on either to identify or instruct what disposition to make of the material. In some applications, this cut film is attached to a copy of the transcribed material for future reference, if needed. The machine holds enough film for six hours of dictation. Dictated material can be released with only one letter on it; a unit of the dictating medium need not be held until it is fully used.

Of course a dictating machine is not mandatory for writing letters and reports. Preferred by many is the personal basis whereby the dictator talks to a stenographer who manually takes down the statements in shorthand and later transmits these notes. This basis permeates a feeling of mutual understanding of the type of letter or report to be written. Also, it employs written notes which usually are easier to comprehend than audible data. Furthermore, the dictation can take place anywhere—a machine is not required and the cost of it need not be incurred. However, a machine for recording dictation by the stenographer can be used. The notes are printed in letters on a tape in accordance with a special code. The machine looks like a small typewriter and requires special training for proficient operation. These are attractive advantages, but the machine advocates are not lacking in claims of superiority. They are quick to observe that dictation can take place when it is on the dictator's mind; he can record his thoughts as they occur to him. The transcriber's presence is not required while the dictation is being recorded, thus saving time. In addition, the dictator can work at his convenience; he need not wait for his stenographer. Further, being alone, the dictator can concentrate and think more clearly. Finally, the dictating machine makes it feasible to allocate the work fairly among the transcribers.

## QUESTIONS

1. What is the purpose of a memorandum? Relate briefly what guides can be followed to write an effective memorandum?

2. Discuss the most common types of letters under the classification of letter format.
3. Identify clearly each of the following:
   *a*) Speed letter.
   *b*) Guide letters for correspondents.
   *c*) "Whisker" expressions.
   *d*) A tolerance report.
4. As an information manager, what measures would you take to make sure that only necessary letters and reports are prepared?
5. In your opinion, what is the best way to get report writers to want to improve their writing?
6. Discuss the form or arrangement of material of a business letter. Of a report.
7. Cost data supplied you as head of a sales research unit shows an average expenditure of $2.08 to write and mail a one-page letter in your office. What significance would you attach to this information and what, if any, action would you take? Be specific.
8. Discuss the use of standards, quality control, and office manuals for controlling business writing activity in an office.
9. Do you favor the use of the "reply at bottom" type of letter? Why?
10. Claude Rice, a process engineer, is enthusiastic about having the dictating machine that he was provided three months ago. He uses it to record data and information when it is on his mind and for ideas that he feels might be helpful in the future. But he finds it extremely difficult to dictate a finished letter or memorandum on the machine. He prefers to write these out manually and make needed corrections and additions. What are your reactions to Mr. Rice's experience and conclusion?
11. Explain Figure 6–9, indicating how the automatic typewriter is used in writing letters.
12. Secure a report written for an executive. Study its contents and determine the main purpose it is intended to serve. Assuming that the purpose is a valid one, explain in what specific ways you feel this report can be improved.

## CASE PROBLEMS

### Case 6–1.  Dillon Corporation

A fund raising dinner at $100 a plate is scheduled at the largest hotel for the incumbent U.S. senator. President of Dillon Corporation, Mr. Carl M. Dillon, is chairman of the sponsoring committee. The senator will be the featured speaker and other local elected public officials of the same political party will also appear on the program. At his private club, Mr. Dillon spoke with Mr. Jack Lee, owner of a local prominent manufacturing company urging him to attend. Mr. Dillon pointed out that they hoped to raise considerable money for campaign purposes. Mr. Lee had attended political meetings before with Mr. Dillon. Usually at these dinners, Mr. Lee brought along several of his friends.

The following day Mr. Lee mailed a letter on his own stationery to some 100 of his business executive friends. He selected the names carefully to help ensure a good response. The letter was sent out without Mr. Dillon's knowledge and read as follows:

Dear Friend:

Carl Dillon, who is known and respected by all of us, requests your presence at the forthcoming "Senator's Night" at Hotel Grand, May 24, at 6:30 P.M. You will enjoy an outstanding and informative program and have the opportunity to meet many of our selected public officials.

Carl informs me that the quota and limit is 800 tickets. He is striving to make this "Senator's Night" the best ever. Plan now to attend and enjoy a delightful get-together with friends. Wives are invited.

Write your check for $100 (each plate) to Senator's Night Committee, Room 504, Butler Building, Megapolis, U.S.A.

Cordially yours,

Jack Lee

cc Mr. Carl Dillon

One recipient, Mr. Howard Stevens, vice president of the local Chamber of Commerce, destroyed his copy of the letter and telephoned several prominent members of the chamber to inquire if they had received a copy. If so, he informed them what he had done with his copy and urged them to do likewise. He termed the entire affair, "a brazen, unethical, imposition for funds upon local businessmen."

The following day when Mr. Dillon learned of the letter and some of the reaction to it, he immediately got in touch with Mr. Lee who assured him not to worry about it. He would handle the whole affair. Accordingly he issued a second letter in which he stated:

As a private citizen of our great nation I acted in the best interests of all the people in our community. I do not seek any personal favors. It did not occur to me that my forthright motive might be misinterpreted. If I even thought it might be, I would certainly not have written you.

My invitation, extended honestly and sincerely, is for a very worthy cause. I assure you I have no ulterior motive.

Again I urge you to attend. Won't you come?

Thank you.

## Questions:

1. What is the source of the problem in this case?
2. Why did some recipients feel the Lee letter was "unfortunate?"
3. Evaluate the letters mailed by Mr. Lee. Be specific.
4. What is your recommendation to Mr. Dillon? Why?

## Case 6–2.   Hamlin-Hawley, Inc.

Gregory Pierson, president of Hamlin-Hawley, Inc., has jotted down the following notes covering items to be included in his report to shareholders for the year just ended.

1. Sales are up—$51,652,000 this year compared to $48,430,000 last year.

Certain operations were eliminated during the year. The general products line accounted for 60 percent of our total volume. Sales to chains represented 19 percent of our volume—lower than year before last. Reason: sale of Reston Division in June. Foreign sales up—now 14 percent of our total sales.

2. Earnings before taxes this year—$4,075,000; last year, $4,218,000.

3. Paid four quarterly dividends of 12½ cents a share; total for year, 50 cents.

4. Federal income tax, $1,825,000 this year.

5. Inventory increased $3,700,000 during the year. Present level is $26,500,000. Probably too high and efforts to reduce will be made. Yet with sales outlook bright, present level may be OK.

6. New plant in Richmond began operation in March. Good location and will work out very well, I am sure. Also purchased 20 acres in southern California in anticipation of new facilities for our specialty products line. In Newark, New Jersey, we acquired three acres to expand warehouse and marketing facilities.

7. Earnings down in part due to our building decisions and land acquisitions. Plant and equipment value this year $15,400,000; last year, $11,800,000. Interest rate on long-term debt is also higher. Plus, new investments in marketing and distribution must be taken into account.

8. Year not as good as anticipated. Looking back, a number of things we should have done but did not. Had to conserve cash and try to improve earnings. Believe we are on our way and long-term results should be satisfactory. Several discussions with other companies interested in merger, but feel best decision is to remain independent and continue to concentrate on our own growth.

## Questions:

1. Prepare the report to shareholders that you feel appropriate for Mr. Pierson to have distributed.

2. What are the major features of your report? Elaborate.

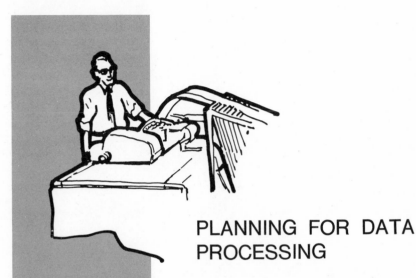

# PART III

# PLANNING FOR DATA PROCESSING

We now direct our attention to the way in which the data will be processed in keeping with our conceptualizing efforts and the objectives we seek. Manual or machine means can be followed. A different degree of any selected means can be used.

This area is foremost in reflecting the tremendous dynamics of office management. Here new machines, new technology, and new processes are the rule, not the exception. It is these activities that have thrust office management into the spotlight on the management stage. New developments bringing various selections to the office manager appear to be endless.

The six chapters of this part are "Information machines and equipment," "Source data automation," "The computer and information management," "Computers—technical considerations," "Computer processing —current developments," and "Information distribution."

# chapter 7

# Information machines
# and equipment

If a little knowledge is dangerous, where is the man
who has so much as to be out of danger?
—*Thomas H. Huxley*

HAVING COMPLETED our conceptualizing of the work to be done from the
overall systems to the individual papers to be used, we are now ready to
determine how or by what means these data are to be processed. A quick
answer to the question, "What means should be followed?" is "By machine or by computer." With a moment's reflection, however, we realize
that much information work is performed manually and a considerable
amount with quite unsophisticated machines. We have the spectrum then
from manual means on the one end—through various combinations of
man and machine—to the other end of complete mechanization, or office
automation as it is commonly termed.

## IMPORTANCE OF MANUAL MEANS

Manual effort still represents a goodly portion of our total information
work. In some cases, work simplification has improved the means sufficiently to eliminate the present need for mechanization. Usually the
volume, type, and occurrence of the work are decisive in justifying a
nonmechanized means. Further, the human being has appropriate data-
processing capability representing human-powered processing which is
brought to bear when appropriate. In fact, human participation is present
in some degree in all data processing. This may be obvious, but it is
appropriate to state since, too often, the human endeavor is overlooked
and the immediate urge is to use automated data processing.

This is neither questioning the tremendous influence of modern machines on information processing nor their unlimited, almost unbelievable potential. It is saying that not all manual operations are less efficient and more expensive than machine means, that not all information problems are solved by simply installing sophisticated processing units, and that not all enterprises have information requirements that justify highly mechanized data-processing machines. However, in this day and age, some degree of mechanization is usually worthwhile, the extent depends upon the individual requirements.

## SELECTION OF INFORMATION MACHINES AND EQUIPMENT

Selection of what machine, if any, necessitates having knowledge of available facilities on the market and deciding the best units in keeping with the particular requirements set forth by the conceptualizing of the system, procedure, method, and form to be utilized. More specifically, the information manager needs to know the types of machines and equipment

FIGURE 7–1. Each Office Production Unit Performs Specific Basic Elements of Data Processing.

| OFFICE PRODUCTION UNIT EMPLOYED | READING 1 | WRITING, TYPING, ETC. 2 | RECORDING, PRINTING 3 | SORTING 4 | TRANSMITTING 5 | CALCULATING 6 | COMPARING 7 | STORING 8 |
|---|---|---|---|---|---|---|---|---|
| ACCOUNTING MACHINE | | V | V | V | | V | V | |
| ADDING AND CALCULATING MACHINES | | V | V | | | V | | |
| ADDRESSING MACHINE | | | V | V | | | | |
| COMPUTER WITHOUT SPECIAL ATTACHMENT | | | V | V | V | V | V | V |
| COPYING MACHINE | | | V | | | | | |
| ELECTRONIC READER | V | V | | | | | | |
| HUMAN BEING | V | V | V | V | V | V | V | V |
| MICROFILM UNITS | | | V | | | | | V |
| PNEUMATIC TUBE | | | | | V | | | |
| PUNCHING MACHINE | | V | | | | | | |
| SORTER | | | | V | | | | |
| TABULATOR | | | V | | | V | V | V |
| TELAUTOGRAPH | | V | V | | V | | | |
| TELEGRAPH | | V | V | | V | | | |
| TELETYPEWRITER | | V | V | | V | | | |
| TYPEWRITER | | V | V | | | | | |

available, the characteristics of each, the unit cost of output, the initial outlay, and the maintenance cost.

Although not an easy task, this selection work is one of the most interesting aspects of information management. Suitable facilities have contributed tremendously to the advance and status of information management. Sales of the business machine industry for 1970 reached $15 billion and are predicted to reach $25 billion within the following five years. A somewhat surprising realization is that much of the present-day devices were nonexistent ten years ago. An efficient information machine is now available for performing nearly every type of office work. Figure 7–1 relates various office production units employed to some of the basic elements of data processing performed referred to in chapter 1. For example, as indicated by the check marks, an accounting machine performs the basic elements of writing, recording, sorting, calculating, and comparing. In contrast, a copying machine performs just one basic element of processing—recording. A human being performs all the basic elements of data processing.

## THE SELECTION COMMITTEE

It is a common practice to create a committee for purposes of study and recommendations as to which machine should be used along with the reasons why. The information manager is a key person on such a committee. Knowledge about various machines and equipment must be acquired by the committee members, and this is best done by attending schools offered by the machine manufacturers, reading available literature on the subject, and conferring with executives of companies having the machines in operation. Also, consultants can be retained to give assistance. Their wide and varied experience can save much time and spark the action to move ahead. But participation by company personnel is essential, for it provides them with practical insight as to what is going on and why. Furthermore, familiarity with the proposed processing is gained, and the background needed for successful installation and operation is obtained.

The committee can assist in attaining a desired program of preparation and installation. Employees from various departments such as systems, personnel, and those in which changes will occur can be represented on such a committee. Planning pertaining to the feasibility of the machine and the means for handling changes—especially with reference to personnel—can be handled quite successfully by a committee.

## SELECTION FACTORS

Usually careful evaluation of eight key factors are required to select wisely. The decision should never be made hastily or impulsively. These factors include:

***1. The Required Work and the Manner of Accomplishing It.***   The purpose of the work should be clearly defined and critically examined, to assure that it is absolutely essential. The individual requirements of the work should be given high priority. Use by others is not sufficient grounds for adoption. It is unwise to mechanize an office operation whenever it is possible to do so; it is far better to consider the available machines in the light of the way each one will assist in getting the individual work accomplished. However, there is emerging a universality of data processing adaptable for most enterprises. Adoption of these universal concepts may prove quite adequate for in certain cases it could well be that individual requirements are stressed too much, necessitating some work that is unnecessary. Knowledge of what is probably the best way of doing the work, along with alternative effective ways, should be determined. If this is omitted, an ineffective means of processing data is preserved and, in the case of computers, the inefficiency can continue for a long time, since computer processing does not readily lend itself to modifications once the program is installed. The design of the system and the use of work simplification employed in the conceptualization of the work should aid in answering these requirements.

***2. Adequacy of Present Information.***   By adequacy is meant a satisfactory volume, speed, and standard of service. The volume of transactions is commonly a deciding attribute. Machines handle very large work volumes within extremely short periods. When an enterprise is faced with an increasing volume of accounts to be processed, the signal for computer utilization may be at hand. This is especially true when the current noncomputer equipment has limited capacity and prohibits refinement and expansion to more mechanization.

Speed of processing is another important consideration. Reference is commonly made to speed as an outstanding gain in the use of machines. It may be vital, but usually speed of processing should be considered in relation to service required. To know that with a given machine, information for a report can be completed in two hours, in contrast to four days under the present setup, is convincing, provided the report will be used in two hours and will not be ignored or filed away for four days before any use is made of it. The challenge here is to get management members to improve their usage of the material made available. Perhaps this starts with more rapid processing to make information available more quickly and hence more up to the minute.

In addition, speed of processing may directly influence the company's standard of service in comparison with that of its competitors. When an advantage in service is keenly sought, the proposed machine should be evaluated to determine how much its contribution in speed and service will mean in sales and in customer relations.

***3. Machine Economics.***   Price is always an important managerial consideration, but it should be considered in terms of what is received as well as what is paid out. In many instances, purchases of equipment are made on the basis that expected savings will recoup the initial investment within about one-fourth the life of the unit. Savings in clerical payroll of 15 to 25 percent are not uncommon. A word of caution, however, is in order. Steer clear of wild claims for possible savings. Expecting a benefit of $200,000 from better management reports to come from a proposed computer installation is open to question.

However, the factors which determine how quickly an office machine should pay for itself vary somewhat with the policies of the individual purchaser and with the importance attached to each factor. Usually, the

FIGURE 7–2. A Quick and Convenient Means of Determining Whether an Office Machine Will Pay for Itself within a Reasonable Period.

| Salary per Year (1) | Approximate Salary per Minute (2) | Cost per Day for $10,000 Accounting Machine (3) | Personnel Time Required to Save (in Minutes) (4) |
|---|---|---|---|
| $ 5,000............. 5.0¢ | | $4.00 | 80.0 |
| 7,500............. 7.5 | | 4.00 | 53.4 |
| 10,000.............10.0 | | 4.00 | 40.0 |
| 12,500.............12.5 | | 4.00 | 32.0 |
| 15,000.............15.0 | | 4.00 | 26.6 |

Note: The approach is based on determining the time required to be saved by the employee who will use the machine.
Column 2 is based on 250 working days a year, 8-hour day, and 83 percent efficiency.
Column 3 is based on 250 working days a year, 10-year life span.
Column 4 is column 3 divided by column 2.

decision is based on an evaluation of such things as (*a*) the current complete price, including installation and delivery; (*b*) if a replacement, the make, model, type, and condition of the replaced unit and its probable current market value; (*c*) the percentage of working time the unit will be used; and (*d*) the investment percentage return to the company (the effect of income taxes and overhead expenses in reducing the gross earnings should be included in this calculation).[1]

Figure 7–2 shows a quick rule-of-thumb approach to decide whether to purchase a particular piece of office machine or equipment. It is based on timesaving by personnel, as illustrated by a ratio of personnel to machine or equipment. For example, the salary cost per minute for an employee receiving $5,000 a year is approximately 5 cents. The number of thousands of dollars per year is approximately the equivalent number of cents per minute. For a $10,000 accounting machine, the cost per working day is $4. Hence, $4 divided by 5 cents per minute gives 80 minutes as the time

---

[1] Depreciation and the influence of trade-ins are discussed later in this chapter.

required to be saved by a $5,000 employee to pay for the accounting machine.

Generally speaking, the greater the capacity, speed, and versatility of the machine the lower the unit cost of work processed. For example, a large computer with high usage rate will do for less than $1 what it would cost $10 to do on a small computer or perhaps $8,000 with an ordinary desk calculator. Volume and type of work are the key factors.

Four choices are available to the user of a machine: he can (1) buy, (2) rent, (3) lease, or (4) use a machine service. The cost differs for each of these conditions. With purchase there is a capital expenditure plus an annual expenditure for operation and maintenance. Rental entails a smaller initial expenditure, with standard expenses for operation. Commonly the rental represents 3 percent of purchase price per month. For a $1,000 machine, the rental would be $30 per month. A lease usually is for a minimum of 75 percent of the useful life of the machine, rates vary, and some provide for purchase for a small percentage of original cost. The terms must abide by the Internal Revenue Service conditional sales regulations. There is also the sales-leaseback arrangement whereby a company purchases the machine, sells it to a lessor who leases it back to the company. By this arrangement the company receives nearly all its fixed assets in the form of immediate cash which, if needed, provides a satisfactory arrangement.

The determination of whether to buy or lease information machines is made by the federal government on the basis of a *cost advantage point*. This is the point when purchase price plus accrued maintenance equals cumulative rentals for a particular machine. When this point is reached in six years or less, purchase is warranted. Limited research indicates that in the case of computers it usually takes around six years for the investment to be recovered. Low point in recovery is the end of two or three years, due primarily to the effect of start-up costs, changeover, and adjustments.

Information machine service, especially that of a computer, is offered by nearly 200 U.S. companies who are specialists in this area. Some are independent companies; others are service bureaus owned or operated by office machine manufacturers. Their charges vary according to factors such as type of machine and the amount of work, but generally charges are considered nominal and in line with the services rendered. The services offered are ideal for excess work loads.

It can be seen that many considerations can enter into the decision on which of the four alternatives should be chosen. The total cost can vary widely. A helpful comparison among the choices is obtained by forecasting the annual total expenses for the most suitable arrangement for each choice. This can be projected over a reasonable number of years. Such data, along with attention to nontangible considerations, assist in arriving at a decision.

**4. Flexibility and Capacity.** The extent to which the machine can be used for various types of work in the office governs the economies gained. If the machine being considered can be used effectively for many types of office work, its adoption usually can be justified. Likewise, the feature of expansion and contraction in order to accomodate varying amounts of paper work is normally advantageous.

It is imperative that the machine capacity be sufficient to permit efficient operations. Nothing is gained by getting a smaller machine than the reasonable expectancy of work volume indicates is necessary. The expected output can be judged from experience of actual users, data from the manufacturer, and actual test runs in the office. When feasible, this latter source is recommended; in fact, it is always advisable to obtain a demonstration of an office machine. Free trials, however, should be carefully qualified as to purpose, use, and extent of time; for unless this is done, a machine originally brought in for trial tends to remain, and eventual purchase may be required, regardless of selection efforts.

**5. Effect upon Personnel Requirements.** In many cases, the installation of office machines and equipment changes the requirements, regarding both the number of employees and the level of their skill; and the problems of transferring, reducing, and training the work force must be considered. The availability of trainable operators commonly is a foremost consideration. Furthermore, when machines are adopted to perform monotonous work, the effect upon personnel is also important, because usually a happier and more satisfied work force is the result.

**6. Future Work Load.** As in all planning, not only must the current volume and type of work be considered, but also the probable future requirements and the adequacy of the unit to fulfill these future needs. Future requirements should be estimated for about five years, and such forecasts are sometimes quite difficult. Good management requires, however, that the unit neither become inadequate to handle the work volume several months after its installation nor stand idle a large portion of the time because of a decline in work volume which could have been predetermined.

**7. Aesthetic Values.** The appearance of the office—a desire to impress by having the latest or the finest in office machines and equipment—is an important, although sometimes subdued or concealed, consideration. Aesthetic values are highly subjective; justification for certain selections is based on personal likes. Such values have a place, for office machines and equipment are not only a *physical* means of assisting employees to accomplish their work but also serve as a *mental* stimuli. Supplying the proper unit makes for a positive and cooperative attitude and helps place the employee in the right frame of mind to work efficiently.

**8. Employee Preference.** This consideration is of great significance because the human element is vital in determining whether the equipment is properly utilized or operated. A strong bias against a particular unit prevents maximum benefits from being realized, regardless of the suitability of the unit to the work. The highly successful office manager will seldom force the use of a particular unit against a prejudice which the employee may have concerning that unit. Most office employees will turn out consistently the maximum work of acceptable quality when they are supplied with the equipment and machines *they feel* are the best available. This is particularly important when the employee has a personal feeling about the unit such as a stenographer and her typewriter or the junior executive and his desk.

## TREND TOWARD COMPUTER USAGE

The computer industry is one of the fastest growing in the United States. Each year since 1955, the computing power within our country has increased. Currently it is expanding at a rate of nearly 20 percent annually. Most information processing units today utilize all or at least some features of electronic data-processing principles. The trend is definitely toward computer usage.

Since 1951, when the U.S. Bureau of the Census installed the first large electronic data-processing system for business data, over 65,000 computers systems have been put into operation. This estimate is for general-purpose systems; it does not reflect specialized installations, as in banks, except in the case of the larger banks where large general-purpose systems are in use. Included in this estimate are the miniature or desk-sized computers which have opened up a number of users with relatively limited amounts of data processing to be handled. Governmental sources reveal that the number of computers in federal government use as of June, 1970, was nearly 1,000.

New improvements and developments appear almost daily. There is little question that the computer will continue to dominate the information processing field. It is destined to influence more and more the efforts of information work and to occupy a vital position in information management.

## DEPRECIATION AND TRADE-IN

There is no one set of answers to the questions of how to figure depreciation and when it is economically sound to purchase a machine or to make a trade-in. The planner must refer to the accounting practices followed. Most companies consider office machines and equipment as assets; and over a period, they write them off because of depreciation. The period will depend upon the kind of product. For example, the following are common:

Desks......................20 years
Files......................15  ”
Accounting machines.........10  ”
Rugs and carpets............10  ”
Typewriters................. 5  ”

The rate used over the period can be calculated by various methods. Straight line and sum-of-digits are common, but the new "guideline form," permitted by present tax laws and designed to encourage new purchases, is gaining favor. Some companies follow the practice of charging to expenses any equipment purchase of less than a stated amount, for example, $100; and any equipment purchase over this amount is put into an assets account. Other practices are also followed, but they must be reasonable and within the meaning and intent of income tax laws.

Some general overall guiding policy for trade-ins should be followed, tempered with certain adjustments based upon the individual circumstances. Several considerations influence a trade-in. The availability of the cash and capital resources of the enterprise is always present in any trade-in discussion. Also important is the expected cash savings to be derived from the new unit's use. A trade-in is usually in order if, as stated earlier, savings will pay for the net outlay within one-fourth the life of the unit or within a rule-of-thumb period of 24 months. Another consideration is the difference between the accrued net depreciation and the expense necessary to keep the unit operating. If the net (present book value minus trade-in) is less than the cost of repair, a trade-in is probably best.

## MAINTENANCE

All office machines and equipment require attention periodically in order to keep them in satisfactory condition. Ordinary use results in wear and tear, making cleaning, oiling, adjusting, and installing new parts the rule rather than the exception. Preventive maintenance, rather than remedial maintenance, should be stressed. The former seeks to catch trouble before it happens; this is accomplished by scheduling inspections at carefully determined intervals. The latter, or remedial maintenance, deals with trouble after it occurs. Preventive maintenance provides greater employee satisfaction and efficient product performance. Uninterrupted service at the lowest cost should be the chief objective. Maintenance can be handled in any of the following ways: maintenance contracts, individual service calls, company-operated service, and combined leasing-maintenance contracts.

Many manufacturers, or their sales distributors, prefer to service their products in order to insure complete satisfaction; and to this end, they offer maintenance contracts which call for regular inspection, cleaning, adjusting, and oiling. Charges are made on a predetermined basis, and the rates and conditions for special service calls are usually stated. Advocates of this type of maintenance service claim that the regularity of service, the use of genuine parts, the employment of skilled, factory-trained mechanics, and the overall, long-range low cost warrant its use. This means is probably the most popular for offices of all sizes.

Individual service calls are a "when required" type of service. This is sometimes called "no service contract" maintenance. It is of a remedial nature. The age and number of units are the chief factors which influence the choice of this policy. If most of the units are new, it is reasonable to expect that they will not require repair service; likewise, when a large number are in use, it is logical that not all will require maintenance service. However, a service call on an individual basis usually costs more than one under a maintenance contract. Also, the regular cleaning and oiling of most equipment and machines are usually advisable, and these must be provided on an individual service basis when this plan of maintenance is used.

A company-operated service is followed primarily because of considerations of cost, control, or availability of service. Maintenance costs may be lower under this plan, provided there is a sufficient volume to warrant full-time maintenance employees. With a company-operated service, it is possible to exercise close control over the progress of the work, the expenses, and the regularity of inspections. In some instances, available outside services are inconvenient, owing to the remoteness of the office, and in such cases the company-operated plan may be desirable.

When a facility is leased, the leasor usually provides for the maintenance. Terms for such service are included in the lease. Both periodic and on-call maintenance are provided. Also, as a part of the agreement any design improvements in the unit or its attachments are usually supplied as quickly as available.

## ACCOUNTING MACHINES

To reiterate, planning for data processing necessitates having knowledge of what machines and equipment are available so that the most appropriate unit can be adopted. We will now discuss briefly a few selected types to provide some idea of the range and variation among these units. The list here is limited. Other types of information machines and equipment are included in other chapters under discussion of the specific work or the function that the unit performs. This includes units such as copying machine, typewriter, and intercommunicating device.

We will start with accounting machines and include in this category billing machines, posting machines, and bookkeeping machines. These machines are basically mechanical aids which simplify and expedite paper work. Many are equipped with "bars," "panels," or "cartridges" which make it possible to change the work program, to process, and to distribute accounts, that is, features which are valuable in records dealing with cost, sales, and payroll. Accounting machines can be classified in a number of ways. Figure 7–3 shows some common bases for classifying machines, along with comments on each type of machine.

These machines are not wholly automatic, but many feature miniature computer units or processors that automate certain or nearly all functions of the processing. Usually the proper keys or buttons must be depressed to start each cycle of machine operation. Some feature checking or proofing devices the designs of which differ with different manufacturers. In some, they consist of showing a number which is compared with an original, such as "old balance," or with an entry number, for proof of accuracy. For each horizontal line of figures, the proof-line figure must be

FIGURE 7–3. Common Classifications of Accounting Machines.

| Basis of Classification | Types | |
|---|---|---|
| Processor.....*Electronic Machine.* Features units to automate data processing, is actually a mini-computer. Permits low cost, versatile processing. | *Nonelectronic Machine.* Employs machine but nonautomatic data processing. Low cost, flexible, and dependable. Many units in operation are of this type. | |
| Keyboard.....*Descriptive Machine.* Equipped with both typewriter and numerical keyboards. | *Nondescriptive Machine.* Has numerical keyboard only. | |
| Bed.........*Flat Bed Machine.* The printing surface and the papers are placed horizontally onto this flat bed. Advocates claim it simplifies insertion of papers. | *Platen or Carriage Machine.* The papers are inserted in the carriage, and platen is turned similar to that of a typewriter. | |
| Print.........*Single-Print Machine.* Prints two or more copies simultaneously. Papers are inserted into machine as a pack with carbon interleaved. | *Multiprint Machine.* Papers are placed side by side into the machine, which prints one paper and then moves over and prints the same data or portions of them on the other paper. | |
| Style.........*Window Machine.* Papers are placed in an opening or window; machine entries are printed while papers are held in this position. Easily handles entries in booklets, as in a bank, and expedites visual checking by operator and customers. | *Nonwindow Machine.* Papers are placed in the carriage or on the flat bed—there is no window opening of the machine. | |

equal to that of the old balance; otherwise, an error is in that horizontal line. In some cases, the machine locks and will not print if old entries have been picked up incorrectly.

Figure 7–4 illustrates the manner in which an electronic accounting machine may be used for processing business information. Here the application is automated payroll accounting. The machine accepts alphabetic and numeric data, performs arithmetic operations by its electronic processor, prints, punches, or stores computer results. Various media can be used for output data. The employee master payroll is retained and updated, including deductions, straight and overtime rates, and current information for governmental reports. Observe that the raw payroll data are sorted and then fed into the machine where such things as the hours worked are indexed and accumulated, verified, and straight and overtime are checked. These data are then run through the same machine with a different program for processing being used, a check with the master file is made, the paycheck is written, and by-products of punched cards and punched tape are made. Subsequently the cards are used to print job order or departmental expense data (shown at upper right) and deduction listings (shown at lower right). The punched tape by-product is used to prepare the payroll registers.

Different features are stressed by many different machines. However, current accounting machines are adaptable for various types of work including general ledger, accounts payable, accounts receivable, payroll, sales analysis, and profit analysis. Featured by the electronic billing machine illustrated in Figure 7–5 is a snap-on cartridge containing the complete program. When changing applications, one cartridge is simply replaced by another. It is a modern machine, desk-size, controlled by one typist. An example of the work is also shown in the illustration. This machine's electronic processor is actually a limited, small computer. Over 200 sell-cost invoices per day can be prepared with it. It will handle almost any accounting, billing, and statistical problem in an enterprise.

The top view of another electronic basic accounting machine is shown by Figure 7–6. As is the case with several other types, this particular machine can be expanded into a desk-type general-purpose computer. Economy and compactness are stressed as its built-in expansivity permits it to grow as needs require, that is, from a basic billing machine to a quite sophisticated data-processing system simply by expanding the capacity, not replacing the components. Shown in the upper left of the illustration, the sectional seat-like units are the central processor which utilizes integrated circuitry to provide maximum processing productivity.

The nonelectronic nondescriptive (numerical) accounting machine is still very popular. Offered by a number of the information machine manufacturers, it is highly practical, flexible, dependable, and features

FIGURE 7–4. The Procedure Flow Chart Followed by an Electronic Accounting Machine in Performing Automated Payroll Accounting.

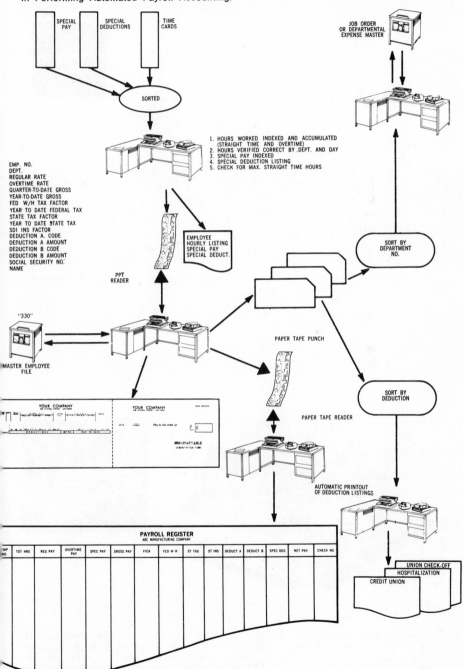

1. HOURS WORKED INDEXED AND ACCUMULATED (STRAIGHT TIME AND OVERTIME)
2. HOURS VERIFIED CORRECT BY DEPT. AND DAY
3. SPECIAL PAY INDEXED
4. SPECIAL DEDUCTION LISTING
5. CHECK FOR MAX. STRAIGHT TIME HOURS

FIGURE 7–5. This COMPUTYPER Electronic Billing Machine Features Punched Tape Programs in Snap-on Tape Cartridges.

SOLD TO ┌HOWE ELECTRIC COMPANY
328 COMMERCIAL STREET
AKRON, OHIO

SHIP TO ┌SAME

**Friden**

| INVOICE NO. | INVOICE DATE | CUSTOMER ORDER NO. | CUST. NO. | TERMS | SHIPPING INSTRUCTIONS |
|---|---|---|---|---|---|
| 10005 | 3/19/68 | X-1098 | 3289 | NET 30 | EXPRESS |

| DESCRIPTION | QUANTITY | PRICE | NET AMOUNT | COST | COST EXTENSION |
|---|---|---|---|---|---|
| CLOCK AND TIMER NO. 8743 | 125 U | 12.50 | 1562.50 | 10.34 | 1292.50 |
| DIODE NO. 5567 | 300 C | 22.00 | 66.00 | 20.00 | 60.00 |
| SOLDERLESS TERMINAL NO. 18 | 1000 M | 24.50 | 24.50 | 23.75 | 23.75 |
| | | | 1653.00S | | 1376.25S |
| TRADE DISCOUNT | | 4% | 66.12- | | |
| SPECIAL PACKAGING | | | 45.00 | | 25.00 |
| CONTAINER CREDIT | | | 15.00- | | 5.00- |
| FREIGHT | | | 20.00 | | |

| TAXABLE TOTAL | TAX STATE 4% | NON-TAXABLE TOTAL | QTY. TOTAL | 2% DISCOUNT IF PAID IN 10 DAYS | TOTAL | PROFIT MARGIN | COST TOTAL |
|---|---|---|---|---|---|---|---|
| 1636.88 | 65.48 | .00 | 1425 | 32.74 | 1702.36 | 240.63 | 1396.25 |

*Courtesy: Friden Division, The Singer Co., San Leandro, Calif.*

Observe detail shown at bottom right. To change application the operator snaps on a new cartridge and touches a key. Variable data are entered by means of the familiar typewriter keyboard. In the work illustration at top, the operator entered the name, address, description, quantity, price, and cost. All the remaining data and calculations were performed automatically by the machine.

FIGURE 7-6. A Modern Desk-Type Computer Featuring Built-in Expansivity.

*Courtesy: Victor Comptometer Corp., Chicago*

low cost. Figure 7-7 shows the machine and typical work done by it, in this case the preparation of the ledger, statement, and proof-tape journals.

## ADDRESSING AND LISTING MACHINES

Affixing addresses or other information in applications where the same information is used periodically typifies one of the popular uses for addressing and listing machines. A popular application is in addressing envelopes or advertising literature. The use of these machines is beneficial wherever a small quantity of identical information must be written repeatedly. In addition to mailing lists, the following are typical applications: names of employees along with standardized payroll information, i.e., check number and social security number; addresses on shipping labels and tags; headings on invoices and ledger cards; listing of customers; items ordered; items of storekeeping; lists of tools; tax roll; names and addresses of stockholders; and the list of dividend recipients.

The information is embossed on a plate made of either metal, plastic, or tissue. Metal plates give very long service; they practically never wear

FIGURE 7-7. A Modern Nondescriptive Accounting Machine (Insert) and Illustration of Accounts Receivable Work Done by It. The Work consists of processing the original ledger, statement, and proof-tape journal.

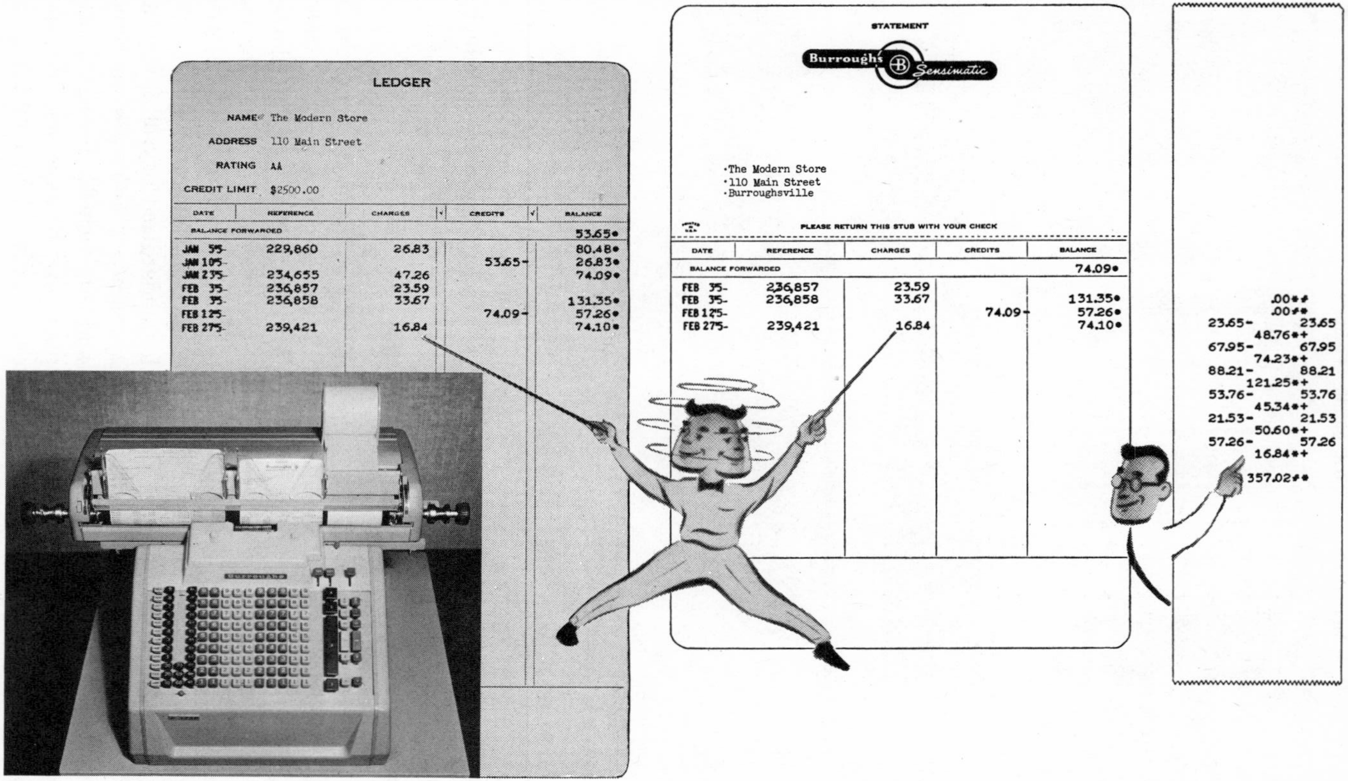

LEDGER

NAME The Modern Store
ADDRESS 110 Main Street
RATING AA
CREDIT LIMIT $2500.00

| DATE | REFERENCE | CHARGES | | CREDITS | √ | BALANCE |
|---|---|---|---|---|---|---|
| BALANCE FORWARDED | | | | | | 53.65• |
| JAN 5- | 229,860 | 26.83 | | | | 80.48• |
| JAN 19- | | | | 53.65- | | 26.83• |
| JAN 23- | 234,655 | 47.26 | | | | 74.09• |
| FEB 5- | 236,857 | 23.59 | | | | |
| FEB 5- | 236,858 | 33.67 | | | | 131.35• |
| FEB 12- | | | | 74.09- | | 57.26• |
| FEB 27- | 239,421 | 16.84 | | | | 74.10• |

STATEMENT

Burroughs Sensimatic

·The Modern Store
·110 Main Street
·Burroughsville

PLEASE RETURN THIS STUB WITH YOUR CHECK

| DATE | REFERENCE | CHARGES | CREDITS | BALANCE |
|---|---|---|---|---|
| BALANCE FORWARDED | | | | 74.09• |
| FEB 5- | 236,857 | 23.59 | | |
| FEB 5- | 236,858 | 33.67 | | 131.35• |
| FEB 12- | | | 74.09- | 57.26• |
| FEB 27- | 239,421 | 16.84 | | 74.10• |

```
            .00•*
            .00•*
 23.55-    23.65
 67.95-    67.95
           48.76+*
           74.23+*
 88.21-    88.21
           121.25+*
 53.76     53.76
           453.4+*
 21.53-    21.53
           50.60+*
 57.26     57.26
 16.84•*
          357.02•*
```

Courtesy: Burroughs Corp., Detroit

out. Plastic plates are lightweight, thin, inexpensive, and easy to emboss. They print clean and make maintenance of the list easy. Plates made of tissue stencils can be prepared on a typewriter equipped with a special platen, last a long time, but should be handled carefully. It is also possible to type or cut a punched tape which, when fed through an automatic machine for making plates, will produce them at a high rate of speed.

Most machines using metal plates permit attachments which add considerably to their value for specific operations. Included are:

*1. A Cutoff Device.* This permits only part of the plate to print at one time. It is useful where a portion of the information on the plate is printed in the first column of a spread sheet, another part in the second column, a third part in a third column, and so on.

*2. A Selector.* By its use certain plates pass through the machine without writing. This feature is desirable, for example, when certain plates are wanted for a particular mailing. The sequence of the plates remains unchanged.

*3. A Repeater.* Duplicate impressions are made from each plate before advancing to the next plate. To illustrate, the name and address might be required on the check stub and on the check, or on the statement and on the envelope. Settings for triplicate impressions are also available.

*4. A Dating Device.* This enters the date simultaneously with the printing of other data. It is used in connection with statements and letters.

*5. Tabbing Sockets.* By inserting small metal projections into selected tabs of the plate, selective sorting of the plates is accomplished. The sockets are located along the top edge of the plate and tabs are inserted according to a code.

## PUNCHED-CARD MACHINES

Among the most important, versatile, and still widely used office machines are punched-card machines which put information in such a form that it can be easily handled for any of a number of subsequent operations. The "punched card" is the key physical unit about which the whole process revolves. The common language supplied by this card provides the real significance to these machines.[2] They provide flexibility, accuracy, and rapidity to data processing and are employed for many different uses, including the analyzing and summarizing of statistical data, the writing of invoices, payrolls, inventory control, labor distribution, market research, sales reports, and accounts payable. They are also used to obtain correlated data. In market research studies, for example, the number of respondents who answered yes to a given question, broken down according

[2] Punched cards as a medium for data processing are discussed in chapter 10.

FIGURE 7–8. The Space on the Punched Card is Allocated according to the Needs of the Particular Study.

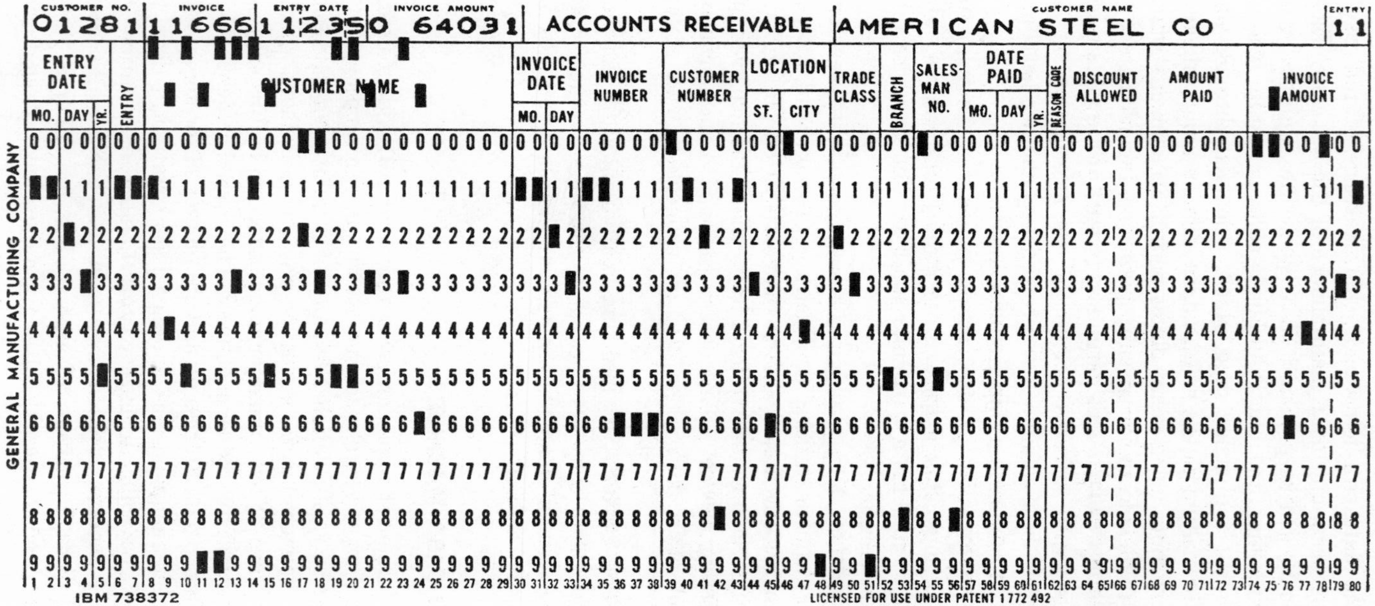

Courtesy: International Business Machines Corp., White Plains, N.Y.

to age, income, and occupation, can be quickly obtained. Likewise, sales analyses by units, dollars, territories, and months, or manufacturing costs by various types of labor operations, can be easily determined.

## ARRANGEMENT OF DATA ON CARD

Holes are coded to represent either alphabetical or numerical information. For example, vertical columns of the card are allocated to different items. Information on months is given two columns so that a 1 in the first column and a 0 in the second are punched to indicate 10, or the month of October. Figure 7–8 shows the allocation of space on a punched card covering accounts receivable.[3]

Laying out the punched card or deciding what information to punch in the card warrants careful thought. This emphasizes the planning function. Only information which is valuable to management, which will reveal pertinent major relationships, and which will provide the basis for meaningful subanalyses should be included.

## BASIC PUNCHED-CARD MACHINES

There are three basic punched-card machines, including a punching machine, a sorter, and a tabulator. A punching machine punches small holes in the card, representing the numerical and alphabetical information desired. The machines have many automatic features, depending upon the model and the manufacture. Figure 7–9 shows a card-punching machine.

The sorter arranges the cards according to any desired classification and in alphabetical or numerical sequence. The sorting is really a box sort. Cards are passed through the machine; and the punched hole causes a mechanism to operate, resulting in the card being directed into a specific box or pocket of the machine. Sorting at any one time is done according to one vertical column, i.e., a unit number or a letter. For example, consider the numbers in the left column of Figure 7–10 as the data to be placed in proper numerical sequence. The first sort arranges the data in sequence according to the unit column. Then, the second sort rearranges this sequence according to the 10's column. In like manner, the third sort rearranges the 100's column, thus placing the cards in proper numerical sequence. Sorting machines are capable of handling 1,000 cards per minute, or 60,000 per hour.

The tabulator prepares printed reports from the data contained on the punched and sorted cards. These machines can print individually or in summary; a great variety of reports is possible. The number of reports that can be printed is almost limitless but depends mainly upon the

---

[3] The code for punched holes is given in chapter 10, p. 233.

FIGURE 7–9. A Card-Punching Machine Which Features an Automatic Card Control of Skipping and Duplicating, a Fast Method of Duplication When Desired, and a Design Which Permits Efficient and Rapid Operation.

*Courtesy: International Business Machines Corp., White Plains, N.Y.*

information to be "read" by the machine, the forms on which the reports are prepared, and the arrangement and rearrangement of the cards. A tabulator—or as it is sometimes called, a punched-card accounting machine—is illustrated in Figure 7–11.

FIGURE 7–10.

| Unsorted Data | Arrangement after First Sort | Arrangement after Second Sort | Arrangement after Third Sort |
|---|---|---|---|
| | ↓ | ↓ | ↓ |
| 828 | 750 | 904 | 107 |
| 107 | 460 | 107 | 191 |
| 542 | 191 | 212 | 212 |
| 904 | 542 | 828 | 375 |
| 212 | 212 | 542 | 388 |
| 375 | 904 | 750 | 460 |
| 191 | 375 | 460 | 542 |
| 750 | 107 | 375 | 750 |
| 388 | 828 | 388 | 828 |
| 460 | 388 | 191 | 904 |

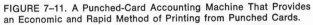

FIGURE 7–11. A Punched-Card Accounting Machine That Provides
an Economic and Rapid Method of Printing from Punched Cards.

*Courtesy: International Business Machines Corp., White Plains, N.Y.*

## SPECIAL PUNCHED-CARD MACHINES

Special machines for specific operations are also available. A complete
listing of these is beyond the scope of this discussion, but the more
common ones will be included. A machine called an "interpreter" prints at
the top of the card the data represented by the punched holes. This
information is sometimes desired for quick identification and reference.
However, many experienced and skilled operators can read the punched
cards as easily as the average person reads normal print. A "verifier" can
be used to check the accuracy of the holes punched in the cards. See
Figure 7–12. Another machine, called a reproducer or "gang punch," is
designed to punch standardized information on cards. For example, data
such as date and location of customer, which are repetitive for a batch of
cards, can be punched at one time and not performed individually for each
card. There is also a calculator, or "multiplying punch," which senses, for
example, two factors prepunched in the card, computes the product.

punches it into the card, and records the factors and the product on a paper.

Variable information such as meter readings, job data, and stores requisitions can be pencil-marked in appropriate spaces on a punched-card area. Then, by means of a machine called an "optical scanning punch," the variable information is read and automatically punched into the card, thus making it ready for processing.

With the developments in office automation and especially source data

FIGURE 7–12. A Modern Designed Verifying Machine.

*Courtesy: International Business Machines Corp.,*
*White Plains, N.Y.*

automation, many punched cards are now produced simultaneously with the typing of the information on a typewriter equipped with special attachments or units "connected with" the typewriter. Such machines will be discussed in chapter 8.

## USAGE OF PUNCHED-CARD MACHINES

The most common uses for punched-card machines are (1) correlating, analyzing, and summarizing data, such as sales by customer, and net revenue by salesman, as illustrated by Figure 7–13; (2) preparing bills or invoices—the data on cards can be easily grouped and totaled; (3) handling accounts payable—each payment to a creditor is processed via a punched card; (4) keeping inventory records—purchases and usages by items are simple operations with punched cards; (5) preparing payrolls and distributing labor costs—checks are prepared from information on the card for each employee, and tabular lists can be quickly run as well as

labor cost allocated to predetermined groups; and (6) production control
—for each production operation, pertinent data and its relationship to
other operations are put on separate punched cards, from which production routing and dispatching information are easily prepared.

Key considerations in the usage of punched cards include the cost and
time of getting the raw data punched into the cards, the extent to which

FIGURE 7–13. Samples of the Work Prepared by a Tabulator of Punched Cards.

### SALES AND GROSS PROFIT BY CUSTOMER

| CUSTOMER | | COMMODITY | | QUANTITY | UNIT | COST OF GOODS SOLD | SALES AMOUNT |
|---|---|---|---|---|---|---|---|
| BR. | NO. | CODE | DESCRIPTION | | | | |
| 1 3 | 6 7 | | ACE DRUG CO | | | | |
| 1 3 | 6 7 | 0 3 0 1 | BEAUTY SOAP REGULAR | 1 2 | D Z | 1 9 8 0 | 2 4 0 0 |
| 1 3 | 6 7 | 0 3 0 2 | BEAUTY SOAP GUEST | 1 2 | D Z | 2 0 4 0 | 2 5 2 0 |
| 1 3 | 6 7 | 0 3 0 3 | BEAUTY SOAP BATH | 1 2 | D Z | 2 1 6 0 | 2 7 0 0 |
| 1 3 | 6 7 | 1 3 1 4 | SHAVE SOAP LARGE | 2 4 | D Z | 4 8 0 0 | 6 9 6 0 |
| 1 3 | 6 7 | 1 3 5 2 | BRUSHLESS CREAM LRG | 2 4 | D Z | 3 1 2 0 | 4 3 2 0 |
| | | | (FOR THE PURPOSE OF THIS EXHIBIT, ONLY / A FEW COMMODITIES ARE ILLUSTRATED) | | | 2 7 5 0 0 ✻ | 3 7 5 0 0 |
| 1 3 | 1 0 5 | | ADAMS DRYGOODS CO | | | | |
| 1 3 | 1 0 5 | 0 3 0 1 | BEAUTY SOAP REGULAR | 2 4 | D Z | 3 9 6 0 | 4 8 0 0 |

### NET REVENUE ANALYSIS BY SALESMAN

| BRANCH | SALESMAN | | GROSS SALES | RETURNS AND ALLOWANCES | NET SALES | COST SALES | TRAVEL AND EXPENSE | COM |
|---|---|---|---|---|---|---|---|---|
| | NO. | NAME | | | | | | |
| 1 3 | 2 9 | A ANDREWS | 5 4 0 3 0 0 | 3 7 5 0 0 | 5 0 2 8 0 0 | 2 9 6 0 0 0 | 2 5 7 0 | |
| 1 3 | 3 2 | G DRISCOLL | 6 1 1 9 0 0 | 4 3 5 0 0 | 5 6 8 4 0 0 | 3 8 2 5 0 0 | 2 6 4 0 | |
| 1 3 | 4 5 | R M EDWARDS | 3 9 0 5 0 0 | 3 4 0 0 0 | 3 5 6 5 0 0 | 2 2 4 0 0 0 | 2 9 0 0 | |
| 1 3 | 4 7 | A H FRANKLIN | 7 5 1 3 0 0 | 4 5 0 0 0 | 7 0 6 3 0 0 | 5 1 3 5 0 0 | 2 8 0 0 | |
| 1 3 | 5 1 | J A HOLLAND | 6 2 5 7 0 0 | 4 4 1 0 0 | 5 8 1 6 0 0 | 3 8 5 5 0 0 | 2 6 2 5 | |
| 1 3 | 5 5 | L B LAWSON | 6 1 2 0 0 0 | 4 2 9 0 0 | 5 6 9 1 0 0 | 3 8 5 0 0 0 | 2 5 7 5 | |

*Courtesy: International Business Machines Corp., White Plains, N.Y.*

correlated or listed information will be helpful, and the value of additional facts gained from being able to interpret the data in a more feasible
form. The use of punched cards is not necessarily confined to large
companies. In most instances, punched cards are feasible when the data
(1) are fairly repetitious, permitting prepunching for much of the data,
and (2) require analysis to show pertinent relationships.

## MARGINAL NOTCHED-CARD MACHINES

These machines are used to notch precoded holes *along the edge* of a
card so that sorting of the data by key classifications can be accomplished
quickly and accurately. After sorting, data referring to a similar attribute,

such as sales, inventories, or indirect labor costs, can be totaled and used in management reports. The process is versatile; it is applicable to many transactions, including sales orders, stock requisitions, purchase and expense vouchers, payroll records, and production control data.

The cards are available in varying sizes; for example, there are 2 x 3½-inch and 7½ x 8½-inch cards. Pertinent information is written in the center position of the card. Holes along the margins are assigned definite values depending upon their location. Identification with a particular classification is made by notching away the portion of the card between the hole and the edge. For example, in Figure 7–14, the operation number

FIGURE 7–14. Card Punched with Holes and Notches to Indicate Definite Information.

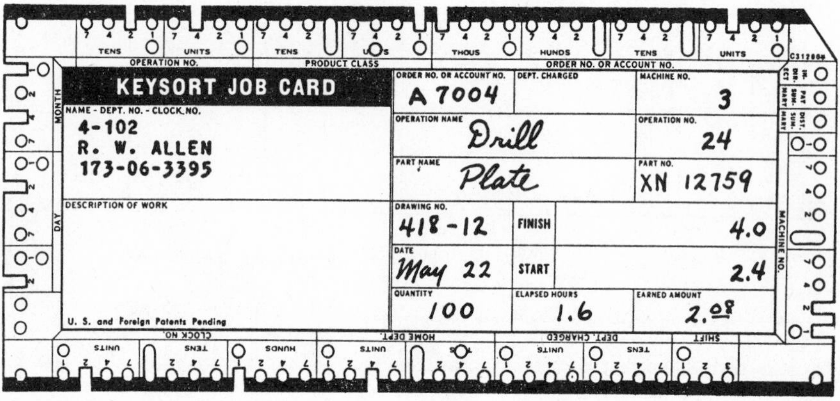

*Courtesy: Royal-McBee Corp., New York*

24 can be identified by the notches in the upper left margin of the card where the 2 under the 10's and the 4 under the units have been notched. Likewise, the date, May 22, is coded in the left margin, indicating that the month is 5 and the day is 22. Observe that for any one segment, the holes of values 7, 4, 2, and 1 make possible any value from 1 through 9. Zero is indicated by no notches.

To sort cards, either a special machine or a manual means can be used. The former is recommended for large volumes of cards. The latter utilizes a single or a multiprong fork which is positioned so that it slides through a designated hole or holes in a stack of cards. By shaking the pack, the operator causes the cards with notched holes at the prong location to fall clear of the other cards. In this way a fast, accurate sort is provided.

## ADDING MACHINES

Modern adding machines have reduced adding to a very simple task. Lengthy columns of figures can be added in a matter of seconds; and, if wanted, a written record is available for checking the accuracy or for future reference. Errors due to handwriting figures incorrectly, carelessly or out of column are eliminated by use of these machines.

Adding machines are basically of two types: key-driven and crank-driven. In the former case, the machine mechanism is actuated by depressing a key; in the latter case, the number is put in the machine by depressing the key, and the mechanism is actuated by pulling a lever or pressing a motor bar. These two basic types are subject to important variations, including full keyboard or ten-keyboard, listing or nonlisting, and manual or electric.

FIGURE 7–15. Adding Machines. *Left:* Listing Ten-Key Model. *Right:* Listing Full-Keyboard, Ten-Column-Capacity Machine.

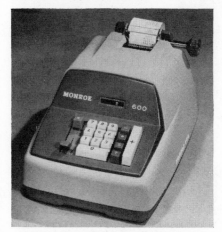 

*Courtesy: Monroe Calculating Machine Co., Inc., Orange, N.J.*

*Courtesy: Burroughs Corp., Detroit*

A full-keyboard machine provides a column of keys from 1 to 9 for each digit position. Thus, a five-row machine can handle a number like 628.47. The full keyboard permits high speeds where numbers of four or less digits are involved, because the keys can be depressed simultaneously. A ten-keyboard type has, as the name suggests, ten keys from 0 to 9. Within the machine capacity, all numbers are recorded by means of these ten keys. The number 629.43 would be handled by first pressing the key 6, then 2, and then 9, and so on until the number is completed. The ten-key machine is usually very satisfactory for large numbers. The hand travel is small, since it is confined to ten keys. Numbers with five or more digits are quickly handled on this machine. Illustrations of these different types of adding machines are shown by Figure 7–15.

A listing machine lists or produces a written record of the figures on a tape. This can serve as a machine record, for visual comparison or as

FIGURE 7-16. An Electronic Calculator and Card Programmer for Accurate, Incredibly Fast Work That Can Require Complex and Involved Calculations.

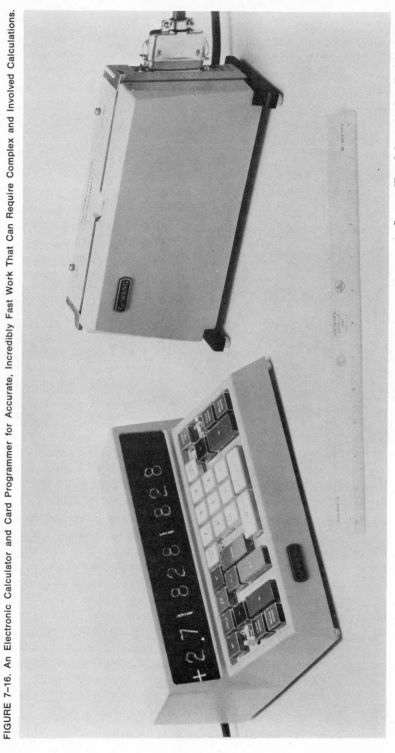

proof of work. Where a long column of numbers, over a hundred, for example, is involved, a listing is usually desired. However, when a nonlisting machine is used and proof of work is required, the work can be checked by going through the addition twice and comparing answers. In some instances, this method is as quick as checking a tape record.

The names *manual* and *electric* are self-explanatory, but in both cases the keys are depressed by hand. The manual usually has lower maintenance cost, is lighter, and no electric cords are necessary; the machine can be operated anywhere. In contrast, the electric machine is faster and saves the operator's energy; however, its initial cost is usually greater. Most adding machines can also be used for subtracting, and a number are adaptable for work involving multiplying and dividing.

## CALCULATING MACHINES

Commonly called calculators, these machines are specially built for multiplication and division work, which is really repetitive addition and subtraction, respectively; that is, 3 times 3 is the same as 3 plus 3 plus 3, and 9 divided by 3 is equal to the number of times 3 can be subtracted from 9, i.e., 9 less 3, less 3, less 3. The same considerations apply to calculators as discussed above under adding machines.

Among the latest calculating machines is the electronic unit that displays the results on an illuminated display screen. Featured are simplicity of machine operations, noiseless and automatic accumulator switches for products and multipliers or entries. Units are available for special work such as square root and squaring. Extra memory registers are available. Accessory card programmers that accept punched cards provide a convenient method for solving repetitive calculations. Figure 7–16 illustrates a calculating machine and card programmer.

There is also available an electronic printing calculator which performs seven operations automatically in milliseconds. In addition to the four basics of multiplication, division, addition, and subtraction, this machine handles percentages, square roots, and raising to the power by simple depression of the proper key. Complete decimal control is included and answers are printed from 0 to 15 decimal places as required. Six registers are featured, three for retention of factors and results, and three for accumulations of constants. An illustration of this calculator along with examples of the work it can perform are shown by Figure 7–17.

## QUESTIONS

1. Discuss several advantages in employing a selection committee to study and recommend which office machine to obtain.
2. Rank the following factors—effect upon personnel requirements, adequacy of information, flexibility and capacity—used in the selection of office machines in the order of their importance as you see it. Justify your answer.

FIGURE 7–17. Illustrations of Work Performed by Electronic Printing Calculator. The Machine, Shown at Bottom, Is Fast, Versatile, and Easy to Operate.

Invoicing:

| Pounds | Price per pound | | |
|---|---|---|---|
| 22 × | 2.857 | = | 62.85 |
| 43.5 × | 1.86 | = | 80.91 |
| 29.75 × | 5.00 | = | 148.75 |
| | | | 292.51 |
| | −5% | | 14.63 − |
| | | | 277.88 |
| | +3% | | 8.34 |
| | | | 286.22 |

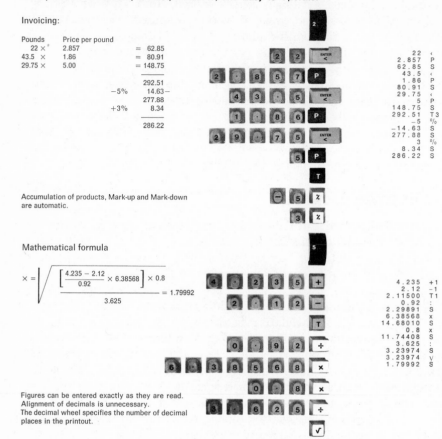

```
        22    <
     2.857    P
    62.85     S
      43.5    <
      1.86    P
     80.91    S
     29.75    <
         5    P
   148.75     S
   292.51     T3
        -5    %
   -14.63     S
   277.88     S
         3    %
      8.34    S
   286.22     S
```

Accumulation of products, Mark-up and Mark-down are automatic.

Mathematical formula

$$x = \sqrt{\dfrac{\left[\dfrac{4.235 - 2.12}{0.92} \times 6.38568\right] \times 0.8}{3.625}} = 1.79992$$

```
    4.235    +1
     2.12    -1
  2.11500    T1
     0.92    :
  6.38568    x
 14.68010    S
      0.8    x
 11.74408    S
    3.625    :
  3.23974    S
  3.23974    √
  1.79992    S
```

Figures can be entered exactly as they are read. Alignment of decimals is unnecessary. The decimal wheel specifies the number of decimal places in the printout.

3. What arrangement do you favor to provide for the proper maintenance of a new accounting machine in a small office employing nine people? Justify your answer.
4. For what types of applications are addressing and listing machines used?
5. Explain the meaning of Figure 7–4 in your own words.
6. Carefully distinguish between each in the following pairs:
   *a)* Full keyboard adding machine and ten-keyboard machine.
   *b)* Trade-in of office machine and leasing of office machine.
   *c)* Marginal notched cards and punched cards.
   *d)* A listing machine and a gang punch.
7. What are marginal notched-card machines and for what purposes, in general, are notched cards used?
8. Discuss the advantages of renting office machines rather than buying them. Do you favor renting or buying? Why?
9. Assume an office manager is considering the purchase of a calculating machine costing $750 for use by an employee receiving $4,800 a year. Explain how Figure 7–2 might assist the office manager to reach a decision regarding the purchase of the calculating machine.
10. Name the common punched card machines, briefly relating what basic work each machine performs. In general, the usage of punched card machines can be classified into six different groups. Name four of these groups.
11. Discuss the latest features of the modern calculating machine.
12. You are contemplating the purchase of seven electric typewriters for a centralized stenographic department. Three different manufacturers' makes are being considered. Basing your decision on the following data, which make of machine would you purchase?

| | *Electric Typewriter* | | |
| --- | --- | --- | --- |
| | A | B | C |
| Unit cost............................ | $565 | $490 | $520 |
| Done business with manufacturer in past. | Yes | No | No |
| Employees' preference................. | Third | Second | First |
| Quality of work done by machine........ | Satisfactory | Satisfactory | Satisfactory |
| Aggressiveness and competency of sales representative.................... | Average | Average | Very Satisfactory |

Justify your decision.

## CASE PROBLEMS

### Case 7–1. Naylor Company

The "Naylor" name is well known for quality paint products. The Naylor Company manufactures and distributes a complete line including regular, all-purpose aluminum, rust preventative, and paint thinner. Much of the company's production is sold through chain stores. Although only nine years old, several important innovations in paint manufacturing have been developed and the sales growth of the company has been especially rapid. With this growth has come a corresponding increase in the number of invoices generated each day.

The present means for writing invoices is an expansion of the initial arrangement using an electric typewriter and calculator. Jerry Nowak, in charge of the billing department, is convinced that good productivity is being achieved, errors are very few, and the morale of the personnel in this department is excellent. The main problem is that the volume is becoming too large. Competent billers cannot be found and many who apply for employment will not accept the job of billing with the "typewriter-calculator" setup.

The present work load averages about 175 to 200 invoices per day. The length and type of information included on the invoice permits about seven invoices to be written an hour. This includes verification, which is followed in all cases as incorrect invoicing can cause serious and expensive difficulties with customers. In addition, analyses of sales by type of paint and by market outlet are prepared monthly. As both the number of accounts and products have increased, the analysis work has become quite a chore. Some officials question its completeness and accuracy, but Mr. Nowak claims it is a true picture of the monthly sales. The feeling among several managers, other than Mr. Nowak, is that a machine should be used for the invoicing work.

## Questions:

1. Calculate for the present arrangement (*a*) the required number of invoice writers, and (*b*) the average labor-time expenditure for an invoice writing.
2. Discuss the probable effect a machine would have on the work of sales analysis.
3. If a machine is used, what type would you recommend? Explain how this recommended machine would be used to handle the invoice writing.
4. What is your recommendation to the Naylor Company? Why?

## Case 7–2. Dunaway and Heaton Company

Purchase of an office machine is being considered for work now performed manually. Either machine "A" or machine "B" will process the work satisfactorily, but the cost of the former is $4,500 installed while that of the latter is $4,800 installed. Labor cost to operate machine A will be $2.75 an hour, supplies, $100 a year, power, $5 a month. In contrast, for machine B, the labor cost will be $2.60 an hour, supplies, $125 a year, and power, $5 a month. Currently, the labor cost is $2.50 an hour for the one employee required. She devotes full time to the work, which can be considered 2,000 hours a year (50 weeks x 40 hours a week). Supplies now cost $192 a year.

It is estimated that to accomplish the work machine A will be used about 70 percent of a normal work year (2,000 hours) or machine B about 50 percent. Practices followed by the company are to charge 6 percent interest on money invested in an office machine, use 10 percent annual allowance for depreciation, and 12 percent annually for taxes and machine maintenance.

## Questions:

1. Calculate the total annual costs for the first year using (1) manual, (2) machine A, or (3) machine B.
2. How long will it take for machine A to pay for itself out of savings? Machine B?
3. What is your recommendation for this company? Justify your viewpoint.

### Case 7–3.   The Underhill Company

A current problem in the office of the Underhill Company is keeping notes receivable accounts up to date. The majority of these notes are monthly, although some are weekly. Currently, a general ledger and a supplementary ledger in the form of a visible card index are used. When a payment is received, a receipt, in duplicate, is made out; the original is sent to the customer, and the copy is retained by the company for its records. From this copy, payments are posted to the customer or account card, all of which make up the visible card file. When posting, the balances due, discounts earned, and total paid to date are calculated and entered upon the card. Because of the volume and urgency of other work, the posting to the cards is performed about every sixth day and to the general ledger about every three weeks.

Under the present arrangement, it is difficult to be aware of all delinquent accounts immediately. Also, from time to time, serious errors have occurred in the posting of the information to the cards and to the general ledger. Finding such mistakes is a problem in itself, but more serious is rectifying the error with the customer. In addition, during the past three years, there has been a constant growth in the number of accounts, and there is good reason to believe that this growth will continue.

The office manager is considering several actions that might be taken. He is of the opinion that an office machine should be used for this work.

## Questions:

1. What are the major actions that the office manager should take?
2. Assuming that you agree with the office manager that a machine should be used, what type of office machine would you recommend? Why?
3. Describe in necessary detail how the work would be handled, utilizing the machine recommended in the answer to question No. 2, above.

chapter **8**

# Source data
# automation

The highest service we can perform for others is to
help them to help themselves.
—*Horace Mann*

In the processing of business data, it is common to find certain data
copied, frequently repeated over and over again, and rearranged according
to different formats. Sometimes the repetition takes place within the use
of one machine; sometimes it takes place in each one or most of a series
of machine operations. Observation of this fact led to efforts to simplify
such data processing. The idea was to put the data subsequently to be
repeated into a form permitting reuse of the data as needed, thus eliminating the writing of such data each time they were used. Further, if this
form could be such that it would be common or acceptable to all common
and standard information machines, it would be possible to process the
data utilizing the type of machine needed without rewriting or reentering
the information for each machine. In addition, the data processing would
be integrated and once the information was captured in the common form
it could be processed by a variety of machines. Additional benefits were
envisioned including large savings as well as greater accuracy.

Success in these early efforts led to the identification of Source Data
Automation (SDA) of which the name is self-explanatory. It is automation of source data—where information begins. Initially it included the
use of repetitive data expressed by a common media acceptable to various
types of information machines for the processing of data, thereby integrating the various machine operations and forming a unity of processing.

178

With time and the development of many new information machines, the concept of SDA has been modified. A recent definition is *the capturing of data in machine-readable form at any point where the information originates without need for media conversions.* In this sense a general purpose computer can be included as an SDA data-processing system. While this terminology is not in common usage, the concept emphasizes the use of common media to expedite machine processing. Actually in some SDA applications, the medium is changed, for example, from card to tape at some points in the processing. But with modern machines this proves to be an advantage and does not detract from the benefits of SDA. Specifically, constant and semiconstant data, in the case of billing, for example, customer's name, address, terms, and so forth, are obtained from a medium of perforated tape. Variable data such as date, quantity, and so forth, are obtained from the machine's keyboard, thus supplying a finished paper or "hardcopy" with carbon copies for distribution and filing. We will discuss this further in subsequent chapters.[1]

## THE EVOLUTION OF SDA

SDA was introduced in 1954 by executives of the U.S. Steel Corporation. They used it for various portions of their paper work operations. Employing the medium of punched cards and perforated tapes, the original data were transferred to one of these media and subsequently processed on any of several common machines. Those work portions which were different for each processing were performed manually, but a large percentage of the total work was automated. In effect, mechanization was used and common machines which were basically dissimilar in their processing work were integrated into a purposeful, coordinated mechanized group.

The idea was quickly exploited by many other companies. Some viewed it as a means for utilizing common office machines more effectively, others as an economical way to integrate data. Within a short period, "common language" machines or attachments to common machines became readily available. The vast array of machines, including card-reading machines, paper-tape reading machines, and optical-character recognition machines, made it feasible to keep alive data without the need for direct manual rehandling.

It was logical to attempt to simplify and integrate the work of filling out various forms required for a procedure. As alternatives to gaining the benefits of SDA, carbon copies were used and, in some instances, only a portion of the data was copied, but these approaches were primarily separate individual processes and were not interchangeable among various

---

[1] See especially chapter 11, pp. 256–60.

processes. In addition, it was rediscovered that business data are interrelated. Data showing price figures alone mean little. Required in addition to price for one set of data are vendor's name, address, and terms of sale; whereas for another set of data, date of delivery, means of transportation, and shipping cost are needed. Some flexibility in order to obtain the processed results are mandatory and this again points to the advantage of SDA.

## THE COMMON LANGUAGE LINK

To implement SDA, conventional office machines such as the typewriter, adding machine, calculator, and nonelectronic accounting machine, must be adapted to speak the same language; that is, a basic and direct compatibility, so to speak, between different types of machines and between machines of different manufacturers, must be achieved. In this manner, data originating on one type of machine can be used later on other types, without human reading, interpreting, and writing.

The common language medium joining all machines utilized is the key to the mechanization aspect of source data automation. The medium is acceptable to all the machines, permits each to perform its particular task, passes the result on to the next machine, which utilizes this information and passes on the accumulated data. To reiterate, the group of conventional machines is connected into a harmonious entirety. When the machines are widely dispersed geographically, appropriate media are available for the necessary communication. The idea of the common language link in SDA is shown graphically by Figure 8–1.

There are three common language media for SDA in use today: (1) perforated tape, (2) punched card, and (3) edge-punched card. Whatever the medium, it is prepared simultaneously with the initial writing of the data. For example, when a sales order is initially typed, a mechanism attached to the typewriter automatically prepares the medium. As stated above, this medium is then used to operate all subsequent machines required. Normally, each machine is equipped either to prepare the medium or to read it or both. Figure 8–2 illustrates a nondescriptive accounting machine connected to a tape perforator. In this application, the following is performed in one operation: A voucher is posted, the voucher check is computed and printed, and a voucher register is prepared. Integrated with this operation, a perforated tape is made for subsequent preparation of punched cards used in the processing and the analyzing of the data. The source data has been put in a medium suitable for subsequent processing. No further writing of these source data are necessary.

Punched cards as the medium for conveying data in an SDA arrangement were historically the first medium used. Also employed is the

FIGURE 8–1. The Key to SDA Is the Common Language Medium Integrating the Common Office Machines.

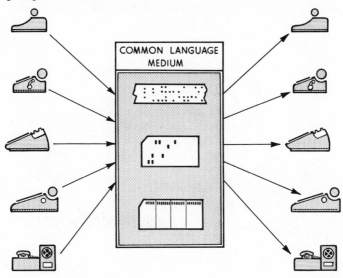

edge-punched card which is, as the name suggests, punched along the edge of the card. Many prefer cards as they are easy to handle and file; however, the information on one card is limited by its length, generally about seven inches. This is sufficient, however, for many purposes. Figure 8–3 shows an office machine equipped to utilize edge-punched cards.

FIGURE 8–2. Installation of an Accounting Machine Connected to Tape Perforator Providing Perforated Tape for Subsequent Integrated Data Processing.

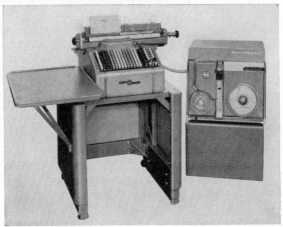

*Courtesy: Burroughs Corp., Detroit*

FIGURE 8–3. The FLEXOWRITER Automatic Writing Machine Prepares Edge-Punched Cards or Perforated Tape Simultaneously with the Typing of the Document, or in Reverse, the Document from the Media—Automatically.

*Courtesy: Friden Division, The Singer Co., San Leandro, Calif.*

## DISTINGUISHING FEATURES OF SDA

It is important to note that all SDA studies should first be systems-oriented and then machine-oriented. SDA demonstrates the need for using the systems approach in order to acquire the overall picture of what work is to be done where and how the total effort is coordinated toward achieving a given goal. This precedes the decisions pertaining to the mechanization of the data processing.

Further, a detailed analysis of the work requirements and how they will be accomplished must be made. Every step of the system and procedure followed requires study to insure that the language prepared at one point is exactly as required at another point of use. The selection of the machines and the media also warrant careful analysis.

The preservation of source data, determined by thorough systems analysis to be necessary, in a mechanical and reusable form at the time of origination, is another distinguishing feature of SDA. All subsequent processing of the data is performed and preserved in this reusable form. The original data are (1) recorded at the point of origin in a mechanized form, (2) processed exclusively in a mechanized form, and (3) utilized in all subsequent operations, where needed, resulting in the integration of the processing work.

SDA is flexible. Machines can be added or subtracted, and the sequence of operations can be. changed as requirements of data processing change. With its building block approach, SDA can be engineered to fit a variety of individual needs. Furthermore, nonrepetitive and special entries can be made manually without disrupting the normal progress of the work.

Although economic considerations are not always governing, quite frequently SDA must be justified on that basis. Usually some additional equipment is required to make an SDA installation, redesign of office forms may be needed, and retraining of office personnel is required. A detailed cost and time analysis comparing the present to the proposed means of performing the work is essential.

From what has been stated it follows that SDA is especially effective where a large part of the data is constant and is continually reproduced from day to day and from paper to paper. There are many such applications in the typical enterprise. This arrangement lends itself to handling large volumes of data. The machine operations are fast and constant, and machine downtime is held to a minimum. A volume almost impossible to handle within a given period by manual means can be processed efficiently by SDA. Furthermore, deadlines can be met. The processed data are kept current and can be used while they are fresh and in keeping with present requirements.

## ACHIEVING SDA

The applications of SDA are practically limitless. Every major system, either by itself or along with other systems, offers possibilities. The gains to be realized are usually substantial. For best results, a definite program should be followed, patterned along these steps:

*1. Review Areas for Study.* This can be started by preparing check lists revealing pertinent facts about present paper work or the proposed information activities in the manufacturing, procuring, and distributing areas. Information on the present methods of preparing papers, and their route or travel in the normal operation of the business, is the type to be obtained. By studying and evaluating this information, specific goals will emerge, such as improving production control communication, reducing processing time for purchase orders, providing quick shipping information, sending out invoices promptly, and eliminating copying errors.

*2. Secure Top Management Approval.* Being integrated, SDA will cross departmental lines, involve many employees from different organizational units, and affect what they do. Hence, authorization of and support for the SDA effort must be given by top management; otherwise, the program will be seriously hampered, and little, if anything, will come of it.

*3. Appoint Director to Head All SDA Activity.* With its blessing, top management should appoint an individual to manage the activity, giving him the necessary authority and help to direct the study to a successful installation. Designated groups, carefully selected, should be appointed to assist the director in finding and evaluating all the necessary facts. These, groups will include members from the departments affected by proposed changes, systems and procedures personnel, and possibly specialists from a management consultant firm.

**4. Establish Target Dates.** SDA programs have a tendency to bog down or to extend over long periods unless they are controlled and adherence to a definite schedule is maintained. Target dates for completion of work should be established for each major element in the program. Activities such as finding the facts, charting and analyzing present systems and procedures, and determining recommendations seem to go on and on unless specific dates for their completion are established and enforced.

**5. Gather and Analyze Pertinent Information.** Many details are required, and suitable forms should be used for securing them in order to expedite identification, comparison, and evaluation. All participating members must be supplied proper instruction, so that they observe and understand what information to obtain and how to record it. The analysis should seek to disclose the major advantages and the disadvantages of the present manner of performing the work.

**6. Make Recommendation and Install.** As study and analysis proceed, possibilities for improvement are disclosed and verified. Substantiation of all gains should be made. Decisions must be made regarding what office machines are to be used and what arrangement of the information on the paper forms will be followed. Finally, the proposal of what to do and why is presented to all interested management members, followed by a discussion to modify the proposal if necessary, but primarily to secure full agreement and approval. As soon as practical thereafter, the installation of the program should commence.

In applying the above steps, certain guides are helpful. These include the following: (1) Permit no restricted areas; instead, make the program comprehensive and truly integrated; (2) code first-hand material as much as possible in order to reduce future looking-up time; (3) use an adequate number of control totals between transmissions of data to insure accuracy; and (4) relate data from various sources and for various purposes to the greatest possible extent.

## OFFICE ILLUSTRATIONS OF SDA

Large department stores have the problem of inventory control so that the proper quantity and quality of each item are on hand in order to maximize sales and gross margins. To help solve this problem economically, SDA is being used. At the time a customer transaction is originally entered into a National Cash Register, a perforated tape recording is made. The recording shows cash or credit sale; salesperson's number;

customer's number; description of merchandise, including material, size, style, and retail price; and the vendor's number. A prepunched price ticket—actually a small card about 2½ inches wide and 1 inch long—attached to the product is removed upon sale and inserted in a unit called a Media Reader which automatically starts the tape recorder and produces a detailed record of the item sold. Complete information on inventory control, by units, is thus accurately and economically provided. Figure 8–4 illustrates the price ticket, tape, and machine used for this purpose.

Figure 8–5 illustrates an interesting application of SDA for a national manufacturer having four widely separated plants. All production scheduling, stock control, receiving and billing of customers' orders, releases to manufacture, and routing of shipments are made from the centralized

FIGURE 8–4. Price Ticket Tape and Machine Used for Effective Unit Inventory Control by Large Retail Outlets.

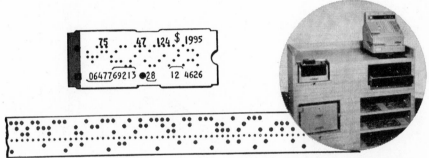

*Courtesy: National Cash Register Co., Dayton*

office located in a large city, different from that of any of the plants. All customers' orders sent direct to one of the plants by customers are immediately forwarded to the central office. Referring to Figure 8–5, and beginning at the left, the sequence is as follows. Customers' orders are received; edge-punched cards are pulled for customer name and for products ordered and are sent to the FLEXOWRITER machine with auxiliary tape perforator. Insertion of the edge-punched cards into the Flexowriter reader causes a six-part invoice and two perforated tapes of the transaction to be typed automatically. Tape number one is sent to a Teletype machine, which, using the tape, transmits the order to the proper plant. The tape made at the receiving unit of the plant is used to write a five-part bill of lading and packing slip. Tape number two from the FLEXOWRITER machine is used in a tape-to-punched card converter. Two sets of punched cards are prepared, one set being used by general accounting accounts receivable, the other set being used for statistical analysis purposes

FIGURE 8–5. Integrated Data Processing of Order Entry, Shipping, and Billing by a National Manufacturer with a Centralized Office and Four Widely Separated Plants.

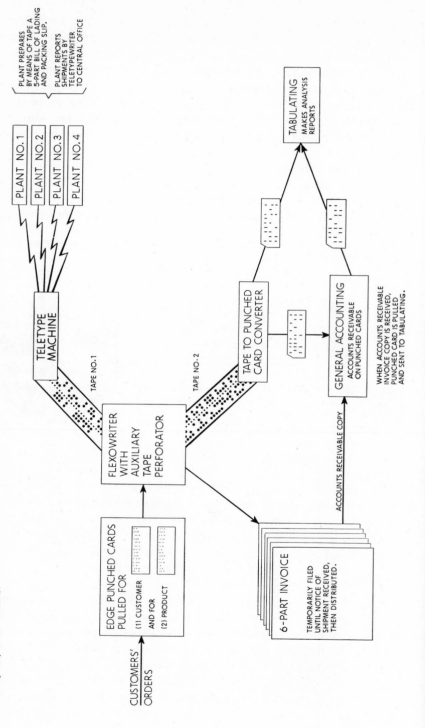

and tabulated open orders file. Plant shipments are teletyped daily to the central office. Upon notice of shipment, the invoice copies are distributed, the accounts receivable copy being sent to general accounting, upon receipt of which the punched card of the transaction in their possession is pulled and sent to tabulating, where costs and other reports are prepared.

Mention should also be made of public utility bills submitted in the form of "turn-around documents." These are machine-produced, sent to customers, and returned for further processing—typical of SDA. The initial data do not have to be rewritten in order to perform the additional processing. The use of turn-around documents normally draws quick response in returning documents, and they can be processed immediately upon receipt and without costly preparation for processing.

## SDA AND MANUFACTURING APPLICATIONS

Some interesting uses of SDA have been made possible by the availability of a machine called a Source Record Punch, which is illustrated in Figure 8–6. It is a desk-top electric data collection machine which, at one writing, records simultaneously a typed man-readable document and a punched machine-readable document. The former information is immediately ready for human use, the latter for machine or computer processing without further manual handling or transcribing. Merged are three kinds of numeric information (1) constant (alphabetic and numeric)—cus-

FIGURE 8–6. A Source Record Punch.

*Courtesy: Standard Register Co., Dayton*

tomer, order, part number (obtained from a prepunched card), (2) semi-constant (numeric only)—date, department, location (obtained from me-chanical slides within the machine, and (3) variable (numeric only)—quantity, color, size (obtained from machine keyboard). The newest models provide the capability to read information (numeric) from a plastic identification badge. There are also modifications allowing for direct automatic input from scales or time clocks. In essence, the machine gathers all the needed information at the point of origin and in just one operation captures it for input data for machine processing. It can be adopted for many different types of reports and information, fits into the normal workflow, is simple to operate, and the cost is low.

Figure 8–7 shows how information dealing with material control can be integrated and easily processed by the use of the Source Record Punch. By this approach the records of purchasing, receiving, inspecting, and stores issuing are tied together. Beginning in the lower left, a request for purchase listing is used by the buyer. Each purchase request is reviewed against the stock status report (bottom center of illustration). If OK, the appropriate master item and vendor cards are removed from purchasing files and along with semicontrol and variable information, the four-copy purchasing order is prepared by means of the Source Record Punch. The identification and distribution of these four copies are shown in the left portion of the illustration. Copy C, or receiving master card, is used to write by the Source Record Punch the receiving documents, the use of which is illustrated in the left upper portion. Copy E of these receiving documents has a dry gum backing and is pasted to the lead carton to indicate authorized movement and identification. Again one copy, or G, is used to write the necessary three documents for inspection quality as shown in upper right of illustration. In some cases, when the material is moved to stores no master card is sent with the stock since it is unneces-sary to identify vendor or purchase order number after it has been inspected. As shown in lower right, stores use punched card to relieve inventory employing a deck of master cards punched with a part number in each card. Stores writes three cards for move ticket, audit card, and data-processing card.

The stock status report is maintained by data-processing cards sent to it, one from each of four functions. The type of information contained in this report is shown by the illustration. Additional reports can be pre-pared including data on vendor performance, cost of allocated stock, and purchase order payment checks. The information processes can be indi-vidually selected as the Source Record Punch provides this needed flexibil-ity. While the arrangement discussed here is representative and illustra-tive, it is not intended to be complete for every application.

Another expanding application of SDA in manufacturing areas is Nu-merical Control (NC). Some prefer to call it symbolic control. NC is an

FIGURE 8–7. Basic Flow of Information Providing the Input-Output Data Necessary to Accurate Material Control.

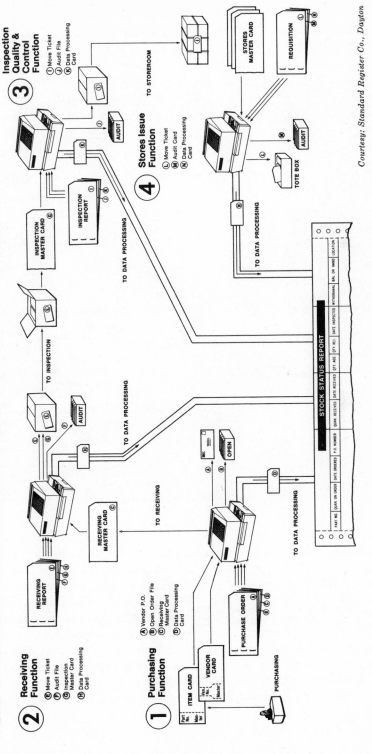

Courtesy: Standard Register Co., Dayton

FIGURE 8–8. A Vertical-Spindle Machine Equipped with Giddings and Lewis Numeridrill Featuring Five-Second Automatic Tool Changer and Program Combinations of Spindle Motions for Drilling, Tapping, Boring, Milling, and Jump Feeds. A three-axis control is standard equipment but special controls can be furnished.

*Courtesy: Giddings & Lewis Machine Tool Co., Fond du Lac, Wis.*

automatic means of operating a factory machine by feeding a previously prepared punched tape or card with all instructions in numerical form into a mechanism that directs the machine. A computer can also be used, but it is not essential in many NC applications. Computers are more likely to be employed for controlling complete processes such as metal-rolling mills and chemical production than for discrete parts manufacturing.[2] NC instructions are detailed and include every step required to operate the machine in order to obtain a machined part exactly according to blueprint specifications. The old concept of the operator's "running" the machine is eliminated. Basically there are two fundamental types of

---

[2] See chapter 11, pp. 271–72.

numerical controlling: (1) positioning and (2) contouring. The former deals with getting the tool and the material in the desired relationship, after which the tool is advanced either automatically or manually to perform the required work. The second type, or contouring, requires that the path of the tool be controlled continuously. In fact, this type is commonly referred to as the "continuous-path" method. There is constant synchronization of the movement of the tool in several axes. Among the advantages of NC are (1) more machine utilization time, less machine setup time, and lower lead times; (2) elimination of fixtures and templates used as guides in manual means; (3) less inspection and fewer rejects; and (4) feasibility of machining otherwise "impossible" parts.

NC has wide application in metalworking, including use with machines for drilling, milling, planning, routing, welding, riveting, tube bending, and coil winding. Figure 8–8 shows a vertical-spindle machine equipped with a Giddings and Lewis Numeridrill (numerical control), made up as shown in the figure of the pedestal-mounted control unit which is immediately back of the operator, and the cabinet housing the electrical control circuits which is located to the operator's right and to the rear of the illustration. This vertical-spindle machine with Numeridrill features an automatic tool changer, removing one tool from the spindle and replacing it with another within a time of five seconds.

## QUESTIONS

1. Discuss your understanding of what is meant by Source Data Automation.
2. Discuss "turn-around documents," pointing out their importance and usage in present-day business activities.
3. Enumerate three helpful guides to follow in developing a program for an SDA application.
4. Discuss the evolution of Source Data Automation.
5. Discuss the important considerations which influence the choice of medium for conveying data in a SDA arrangement.
6. Identify clearly each of the following:
   *a*) Media Reader.
   *b*) Numerical Control.
   *c*) Contouring numerical controlling.
   *d*) Common language link.
7. What is a Source Record Punch and how is it used in modern information management?
8. In your own words, describe the meaning of Figure 8–5.
9. How do you justify Numerical Control's being considered a part of SDA? Discuss.
10. Name and discuss each of the common language media used in SDA.
11. In your opinion is the future of Source Data Automation bright or will it be absorbed by computer developments? Justify your viewpoint.
12. Discuss the possibilities and a manner of using SDA for any series of office

tasks with which you are familiar, such as (a) processing the purchase orders by a bookstore and its sales to students; (b) maintaining students' records in a large university; (c) handling the requisitions, purchases, and inventory records of a manufacturer; or (d) any selection of office work you care to make. Indicate the means now followed and also the suggested SDA way, and why you feel SDA would prove beneficial in the particular application.

## CASE PROBLEMS

### Case 8–1.  Bruce Beard Company

Millions of dollars worth of finished products are shipped annually from a large five-story complex in Minneapolis. To have information about the movement of products from production to storage and from there to shipping, a five-copy form is currently being used. When a pallet load is ready for transfer to storage, information is entered on this form, copy No. 1 is sent to the warehouse office, copy No. 5 is retained by production, and the remaining three copies are placed with the merchandise. For each move, that is, from materials handling to storage, from storage to shipping, and from shipping to public carrier, information is added and a copy of the form removed. These copies are sent to an information center where they are numerically sorted manually. Subsequently, the data are keypunched, verified, and computer processed to provide daily reports.

Difficulties are being experienced in completing the daily reports in time for important decisions to be made. Also, it is believed that errors exist in the data, a major cause of which is the sometimes illegible, inaccurate information that is entered on the form. If possible, it is desired to relieve the foremen of the job of laboriously handwriting data on the forms and to simplify and to speed the processing of the data.

The managers believe some type of Source Data Automation can be used advantageously. What they want is an accurate and speedy continuous audit trail from the production line to final shipment. They want to know at all times where and how much finished goods are located in the warehouse and how much are shipped.

Questions:

1. Draw a flow diagram showing the work done and use made of the different copies of the present form.
2. Discuss the improvements you envision over what is now being done.
3. What is your recommendation to this company? Explain.

### Case 8–2.  Reeger Manufacturing Company

The main office and factory of Reeger Manufacturing Company in Minneapolis, Minn., employs 677 people. Branch plants are maintained at Wichita, Kans., with 252 employees; Dallas, Tex., with 110 employees; Piqua, O., with 61 employees; and Richmond, Ind., with 88 employees. Most of the office and accounting work of the company is done in the main office in Minneapolis. The outstanding exceptions are the payroll and the direct labor distribution, which are currently prepared manually at the respective plant offices for each plant. It had been assumed that local preparation would be expedient and convenient, but the vice president of finance states that necessary control is lacking, poor methods are being used by the branch offices, and the cost of performing the work is excessive. The Minneapolis office uses a modern accounting machine which is a part of a modern processing center featuring punched card, tape, and equipment for SDA. At the present time, employees are paid every two weeks, with one week waiting time. That is, on Friday, October 21, an employee is paid for the two weeks ending Friday, October 14. Preliminary inquiry shows that the two-week pay period should be retained, but each plant need not necessarily pay on Friday.

## Questions:

1. Devise a suitable SDA arrangement utilizing the Minneapolis office for preparing all payroll checks and direct labor distribution data. Describe the procedure followed and type of equipment and office forms to be used.
2. What do you envision as the outstanding advantages of your recommended SDA arrangement? Disadvantages? Discuss.

chapter **9**

# The computer and information management

> More trouble is caused by doing nothing than by doing too much.
> —*Italian Proverb*

DATA processing in this day and age is greatly influenced by the use of the computer. Scientific breakthroughs are speeding the accomplishments of information automation and it is now possible to automate nearly every task dealing with information. We are living in an age of computers. They prepare and calculate all types of data for documents, assist engineers in designing, and guide astronauts in orbit. Many conveniences and advancements we know today have been made possible by use of computers.

The computer is king and the center about which a great deal of our current data processing revolves. We turn our attention now to this dominant and fantastic machine that is rapidly changing the entire information management picture by its sensational data-processing accomplishments. Computers and their applications are a vital, modern, and exciting area of information management. Our discussion in this chapter will concentrate on the managerial consideration of the computer and in the following chapter on the technological aspects of the computer.

## INTERESTING ILLUSTRATIONS

Significant office technological advances have been won, yet even greater things to come are predicted. Routine jobs in the office are being

194

eliminated, information work is being accomplished at fantastic speeds, and the whole makeup of information work is undergoing unbelievable changes. For example, much sorting and copying work is now done by machine, complete reports are prepared entirely automatically, and multiplications are performed at a speed of 31 millionth second for two 13-digit numbers, or at a rate of 32,000 such multiplications in one second. It is predicted that the file of the future will retain plastic media on which data are photographed or marked at the amazing reduction of 200,000 to 1, so that the contents of an entire library could be kept in an ordinary card file from which any bit of information can be retrieved automatically in a fraction of a second.[1]

Computerized information work is also prevalent in the factory, in sales, in research, in medicine, in the military, and in transportation. For example, airplanes can be guided in "blind" takeoffs and landings, movement of trains controlled, and railroad cars located by means of computers. Further, the course of storms can be charted and weather maps quickly sent to stations across the nation by a computer arrangement. Managers of retail stores can find which items are selling satisfactorily, which poorly, which items to discontinue, which to promote, which to purchase, and where to display (shelf and location in store), all by means of a point-of-purchase analysis rapidly calculated by a computer. In another application, voluminous data on the buying habits of soft drink purchasers in a given sales territory are fed into a computer, in addition to data on the composition of newspaper and television audiences in this same territory. Within minutes the most efficient combination of media for a given advertising budget is calculated by the computer.

## WHY COMPUTER UTILIZATION

These accomplishments are impressive, but the question can still be asked, "Why does an information manager use a computer?" The general answer: To solve a problem. More specifically, the number one reason is to supply quickly the information needed to facilitate enterprise operations including data for decision making and for service to customers. Modern managers need considerable data to help them make effective decisions. In the fast pace of today, events affecting enterprises seem to occur with increasing rapidity, and many managerial decisions must take into account at least part of these events. Under such conditions, the gathering, processing, and distributing of information must be done rapidly. In certain areas, the tremendous amounts of information work required can be handled within a reasonable period only by machine. In the case of supplying scientific and research data calculated from mathematical formulas, a machine accomplishes in several hours what would require years of manual calculation.

---

[1] See chapter 13, pp. 314–20.

A second major reason for computer utilization is to reduce office costs. Actually this is more fancy than fact. In some instances, cost reduction is achieved but in many it is not. One is inclined to believe that in any installation, because of the speed and versatility of the computer, paper work costs are reduced. Unfortunately, it is difficult to make accurate comparisons of a "before and after," and further, many innovations are effected by automation. For example, the report requirements may change, the total volume of information work may increase, primarily because "we have the necessary machine." Also, some departmental operations may undergo significant transitions of one type or another. The condition that commonly develops is more data processing and more information with approximately the same dollar expenditure.

Yet the computer investment is attractive; otherwise, managers would not utilize it. Based on the utility and volume, a well-managed installation will return a saving of approximately 30 to 40 percent on the total investment each year. This requires 5 days a week, 16 hours a day operation. However, individual circumstances govern and must be taken into account for the particular conditions present.

The search for competent and adequate help plagues the information manager. Ways of getting out the work with a limited number of people have been eagerly sought, or an arrangement requiring employment of only the more competent employees has won favor. Both these conditions are met by automating office work. In many cases, the capacity of the computerized arrangement is sufficient or can be modified to increase as the work load increases so that it will not be necessary to add people, who are difficult to acquire.

There are also several minor reasons for adopting a computer. One is a reduction of errors. The computer tends to integrate data processing, thus minimizing the handling of data by human beings who usually but certainly do not always commit what mistakes are made. It appears that higher-quality information work should be viewed as a by-product of computer usage, although errorless work is important. Another minor reason, sometimes not admitted to, but having some significance, is the desire for a status symbol which the computer supplies. Having a computer signifies progress, favorably affects public relations, and may supply a competitive edge.

## THE DEGREE OF AUTOMATION

No office is completely automated. Even though technologically possible, at least in the conceptual stage, the fully automated office is not *economically* feasible. And it is the economics of each situation that is a strong determinant of the degree to which automation proceeds. The best current estimates are that some 15 to 20 percent of the total information work is performed with computers, and an additional 25 percent by some type of mechanization. But certainly the automation of information work is not a 100 percent robot operation.

Some work is best done by a willing hand and a pencil, especially when the cost of operating the machine is taken into account. In contrast, excessive work may be done by means of a computer, if available. This results from a policy of charging arbitrarily each department for machine time of a centralized computer unit. Net result: Some work which should not be handled by computer is sent to it for processing. The remedy lies in educating every management member to the economic considerations and limitations of the computer and to the idea of total information integration.

Akin to this excessive work is the danger of having a computer of either over- or undercapacity for the information needs of the enterprise. From the lack of carefully determining information needs and matching these with the computer's capacity stem many automation difficulties. If the computer capacity is excessive, the investment is excessive. Or frequent and expensive breakdowns may occur primarily because too much work or too many different types of work are being attempted for the computer available.

On the other hand, some processing of information work suffers because a computer is not used or the unit available is too small or of the wrong type for the work to be done. This state of affairs arises from indifference, fear, ignorance, and lack of direction by managers. Seldom do nonmanagers demand a computer. Their common reaction is not to make any changes. Management failure to perceive the broad implications of automation is the major reason for lack of proper computer usage.

## THE COMPUTER AND MANAGEMENT

The basic issues pertaining to data processing are the reflection of basic issues of management. The computer is an adjunct to management; one of its roles is to supply information to managers so that they can do their jobs better. But managers have to know their requirements, achieve a clarity of thought, and develop precise plans in order to obtain satisfactory results from a computer. The modern computer emphasizes the importance of management. Success with computerized information efforts depends mainly upon the understanding which managers can and do bring in communicating with processors. The computer, for example, cannot be viewed as an autonomous "black box" that will solve in some ingenious manner the headaches of managers. Computers enhance the functions of management; they do not replace it. Computers call for better utilization of the managerial mind, better managerial actions, and better managerial accomplishments. Significant improvements in management are possible by use of the computer, but managers must be truly objective and honest with themselves if they are to gain the benefits which the computer can bring about. It is erroneous to think that depositing a modern computer in the midst of inept management policies, outmoded practices, and an archaic organization will somehow or other cause corrective miracles to take place.

Properly used, computers increase the power and influence of the human mind, not minimize its importance. They provide help never before believed possible or even conceived. Instead of being overburdened with the processing of data, the human mind can be relieved of such mental drudgery and concentrate its efforts and attention to create, to plan, to ponder and reflect about information, and to decide what should be done and whom to inspire. Managerial judgment, insight, coverage, and values are still paramount. Computers should stimulate managers to think, to create, to perform those vital activities which human intelligence can provide.

Computers increase the responsibility of managers. With the assistance given by computers, the human mind can soar to new heights of accomplishment and acquire knowledge and judgment not yet imagined. The computer can show the way to greater progress, but the accomplishment of hoped-for outputs and gains are regulated by the person issuing the instructions to the computer or figuring out how the computer can be utilized to do what he wants it to do. The potential lies with the manager, not with the computer. In essence, computers are tools to be exploited by managers. The challenge is not to be satisfied with the processing of data as such, but to initiate new and revolutionary applications and concepts which are made possible by the use of computers. This necessitates management thinking of the highest order.

## COMPUTER MANAGERIAL ASSISTANCE

The computer offers many genuine aids to the information manager. The rapid and accurate processing of data is, of course, highly significant. With the tremendous current volume of information work in every enterprise, it is doubtful that this work can be handled satisfactorily without the computer in some direct or indirect manner. Usually there must be a relatively large volume of work requiring considerable calculating, sorting, and comparing. Otherwise, the miniature computer and nonelectronic machines designed especially to perform the particular work will provide entirely satisfactory results at lower cost.

Managerial decision making can be considered to mean the selecting of a solution from possible solutions or courses of action, with due consideration given to the objectives and available information. This broad concept includes both strategic and operating information and whether actions will be taken on a continuous or periodic basis. When computers are utilized, the decision making can be either (1) a programmed and routine type, usually featuring measurable quantities; or (2) a programmed but nonroutine type, where the information is restricting and interpretation is emphasized. For the former, typical decision-making examples are those dealing with such things as the quantity of a product to produce next month or an operating budget for a forthcoming fiscal period. For the latter, representative are decisions concerning the products to be included in a product line, and those relating to level of customer service to be provided to compete successfully. To decide these latter types of questions, information is needed and the computer will supply it. But the information must be studied and interpreted by the manager in order to arrive at the decision.

Simulating made available to the information manager by the computer is the testing of numerous operating plans to determine the most productive plan. In other types of analyses, the plans are expressed by models commonly in mathematical form. However, in all instances, the data must be of a measurable type. In aircraft research, for example, computers are used to supply needed information by simulating different flights for jets. Data on such factors as allowable pay load, fuel consumption, and speed can be determined accurately without even putting the plane in the air. Likewise by means of a computer, advertising agencies can determine the best combination of media for a particular advertising campaign. The computer is used to try out hundreds of different media combinations and thus reveal the one which maximizes the particular qualities that are being sought. To duplicate manually the information of many combinations would be extremely costly and time consuming. In one such experiment, it required a four-man crew three months to duplicate what the computer provided in six minutes.

Another category of computer assistance to the manager is designing. By this is meant the confirmation or rejection of an intelligent guess or hypothesis by the data obtained from carefully directed experimentation usually in a technical subject area. The characteristics of each guess are calculated and checked against specifications. The computer performs these calculations very rapidly. A wide range of possibilities can be processed and from them the best possible design is identified and used.

We will now look at the computer's effect upon the various functions of management and see how the manager can benefit by the opportunities made available by the computer and how best he can meet the challenges provided by the computer. First is the function of management planning.

## THE COMPUTER AND MANAGEMENT PLANNING

The computer changes ways of doing things and it has considerable impact upon planning activities. Important is that the scope of planning can be broadened by the use of a computer. More activities can be included, the parameters can be pushed back, and a far more inclusive picture of what makes up the totality of the information work can be included.

The trend of computer influence appears to be toward the reaction by an entire enterprise to any given stimulus. The enterprise is being viewed more and more as a responsive body instead of a cluster of individual and, to some extent, isolated departments. Further, information management is being viewed as an activity affecting not only all components of an enterprise, but areas outside the enterprise as well. Actually there should be no restricted areas in the initial development stages of computer usage. Compromises can always be made later, but beginning with circumscribed areas inevitably means ending with restricted areas. The usual pattern in the application of a computer is to a smaller range of activities than was initially considered. Seldom can the best results be achieved by confining it to predetermined limits of activities or to certain organizational limits. Computer work commonly cuts across conventional lines originally established for nonautomated purposes.

Computer utilization is almost certain to alter systems and procedures followed under nonautomated conditions. As pointed out in previous chapters, in this transition, existent means of performing information work should be carefully analyzed to eliminate any unnecessary information work and to process what is necessary in the best possible way. It is folly to put into a computer work that you know is unnecessary. Much of this improvement can be made by company personnel, but outside help— consultant services or the computer manufacturer's representative—may be used. Excessive reliance upon outside assistance, however, may prove unwise, for frequently such assistance is neither fully familiar with the detailed needs of the company nor aware of the human problems confronting the company personnel.

In addition, some policies will require adjusting, and in some instances modification in objectives will be made. Computers can open the door to improved management and service opportunities, but to gain them it is necessary and desirable to adjust, delete, and add planning efforts so that these benefits can be won. Almost always needed are statements specifying who is responsible for what decision, who exercises prescribed control, and what the "good rules" are.

The planning should also include the type of decisions for which the computer will be used. A common practice is to have computer participation in all decisions. This is not only unnecessary but it is also unwise. Too many technicians and specialists get into the act. A simple decision is expanded all out of proportion to its importance. The manager becomes more confused and frustrated. Computers are to assist managers in making better *big* decisions. And our approaches and practices to computer usage should allow the manager and the computer to work together closely.

Furthermore, adjustments in long-standing practices assist in acquiring harmonious relationships. Included in the types of popular changes made are (1) elimination of many special files; (2) greater degree of centralized filing; (3) use of "centless accounting"; (4) uniform "days in period" for comparable reports; (5) more data retained on previous functions, such as sales, costs, and collections, to provide helpful trends or comparisons with current data; and (6) greater availability of pertinent data to lower levels of management. In addition, periodic reviews of current computer applications help to uncover other helpful uses and take advantage of available computer time.

## THE COMPUTER AND MANAGEMENT CONTROLLING

Computer utilization is commonly of a multiproject nature, and this fact emphasizes the importance of establishing effective progress-reporting techniques and carefully monitoring them in order to maintain proper control over each project. Effective reporting techniques are simple, comprehensive, and easy for either the technical or the nontechnical employee to understand. To maintain the support of top management members, it is a good practice to provide them with clear, concise, and up-to-date reports which reveal how each project is progressing and to what extent established goals are being attained.

Job completion dates must be realistic and adhered to; otherwise, control efforts become dissipated. Failure to provide sufficient lead time and allowances for unexpected contingencies is a common cause of establishing completion dates that cannot be fulfilled. The delay of one project aggravates the entire program because work scheduling for a computer closely interrelates all projects within the system. As a result, certain projects may be subjected to completion on a "crash basis," which usually means higher costs and extra follow-up efforts.

A computer usually increases relatively the machine cost and decreases the labor cost. In turn, the greater machine expenditure spotlights attention upon questions of depreciation; scheduling and maintaining even work flows, and keeping the mechanized units in top working condition; utilization of records; and format of reports.

## THE COMPUTER AND MANAGEMENT ORGANIZING

For genuine success, the various accomplishments of a computer must be integrated with the operational activities of the company. The computer should not be regarded as a new, mysterious entity separated from the main body of the company or as an interesting, captive consulting facility. To achieve the needed integration between information and action functions, it is essential that those working directly with the computer have a clear understanding of their relationships with members in other units of the company and that the authority of the computer personnel be clearly defined. This brings up questions of organization.

Initially, a common practice was to place the computer in the controller's office. Reasons for this varied, but it was thought that this provided a logical organizational location and was an ideal spot for the computer to prove itself a valuable asset. If not in the controller's office, the computer was quite likely to be located somewhere in the finance department. Recent surveys reveal that currently two out of three computers are the responsibility of the financial executive. In some instances data processing has been moved up in the organization; in others it has been relocated. Quite a number feel that the computer should occupy a separate organizational unit and that the manager in charge should report to the president. This arrangement not only accords great importance to information automation, but it also permits a broad scope of operation and a cutting across traditional organizational boundaries, considerations which probably are necessary for a truly integrated information-processing system to exist.[2]

The computer can be a source of controversy between the technician, who knows precisely what the computer can do, and the manager, who can put what it can do to work. It frequently happens that the technician isn't familiar with the manager's needs and, in turn, the manager doesn't understand the technician and is suspicious of the computer because of its far-reaching and revolutionary potential. These divergent viewpoints can be brought together or at least minimized to an appreciable degree. It is a matter mainly of effective planning and actuating. Essential is giving the manager basic facts concerning computers and their operation and, likewise, the technician should acquire knowledge of the enterprise and its management. In a sense this is a plea for empathy and, once accomplished, will assist amazingly in acquiring better manager-technician relationships. Mastery of the other's specialty is neither needed nor recommended, but an appreciation and understanding by each of what the other is trying to do, and how he is trying to do it, is mandatory.

Organization and the computer give rise to the question: "Should centralization or decentralization be followed?" The situation is primarily whether to have (1) a single large installation to serve the office needs of the various operating units of a big enterprise or (2) a number of smaller facilities, each designed and located to serve the needs of one or several of the company's various operating units. The availability of a large computer facility made up of a centralized computer joined to widely dispersed in-out terminal units offers the advantage of centralized processing with decentralized conveniences.[3] The decision reached regarding this

---

[2] The location of the computer in an organization is discussed in detail in chapter 24, "The office organization." See especially pp. 584–86.

[3] See also chapter 11, pp. 256.

organization issue depends upon many factors, including the physical size of the enterprise, the total volume of work, the uniformity of work, and the investment required for the equipment.

From the organizational viewpoint, there is also the task of determining clearly the authority and responsibility assigned to those in charge of the computer. Likewise, each subgroup of the computer unit needs to know how it is to work with other groups and the particular duties that it is expected to carry out. In too many companies this organizational relationship has been permitted to become established mainly on an empirical basis, without proper definition of the authority and responsibility of those in charge of this specialized work.

## THE COMPUTER AND MANAGEMENT ACTUATING

With all the glamour now being associated with the new computer, it is easy to forget that people are still vital to information management and will continue to be so. It requires people to operate and maintain computers, and it requires people to interpret and utilize the information made available to them. Successful computer usage requires effective managerial actuating.

Computers should mean less preparation of records and reports by supervisors and operative personnel, thus enabling them to devote more time to their primary functions. They are relieved of much monotonous work and have more freedom to exercise their individual talents and contribute to the total enterprise efforts in their own unique way. Properly handled, the computer system becomes a means of office work that is easier and more practical than any other way. Generally employees will, in time, like the computer way. Like any other means, the computer means is dependent upon the good will, understanding, and cooperation of the employees. To ignore the personnel considerations is certain to invite disaster.

When a computer system is first introduced, there is the problem of manpower displacement. To cope with this difficulty, it is generally advisable to (1) tell the office automation story as it is developed, so that all employees will know what is going on, (2) terminate the employment of no employee because of the computer—normal attrition commonly takes care of any excess, (3) reduce the salary of no employee because of the computer, and (4) change job content with reassignment and provide retraining. Employees to be affected by the change should be encouraged to participate in designing the change in its beginning stages. Not only are excellent suggestions offered, but by this practice a needed sense of belonging and importance is enjoyed by the employee. High employee participation usually means high employee cooperation.

It must be remembered that with the passage of time people tend to become more ready to accept change. The attitude toward changes in data processing almost always becomes more favorable several months after completion of the planning and installation periods than it had been during these periods. People tend to adjust to their surroundings. Experience with computers usually demonstrates that many of the fears and unpleasantnesses believed associated with the change actually do not exist or are of much less importance than originally conceived.

## SOCIAL ASPECTS OF COMPUTERS

From the broad sociological viewpoint, change stimulated by computers emphasizes employment modifications which can be viewed as offering either (1) greater opportunities or (2) fewer opportunities, even to the point of mass unemployment. The former stresses the view: "What will automation help us do better, or assist us to achieve that has never been achieved?" There is a problem, however, in adapting to this greater opportunity. Over a period, much human effort will shift from manual to mental work and from menial to more challenging tasks. Automation puts at our disposal the means to a materially more abundant life. The belief of fewer work opportunities being available because of office automation highlights a dominant force of fear. It appears to lack long-term justification. Past experience indicates that technological advancements have increased the overall level of employment. New demands have developed, the machines themselves creating a large labor force required for their construction and maintenance. However, many people are *displaced*, not *replaced* to other areas of duty. For example, a large computer installation in a Chicago office required the displacing of several hundred employees to other jobs. Not a one lost his job; each was trained and placed in new work. This called for real management ability and, of course, necessitated an adjustment on the part of each employee.

One may ask: "What is the alternative to office automation?" The answer appears to be to maintain the status quo and to refrain from utilizing technological progress and faster and better ways of performing information work. Such action would place limits on improving our information efforts, our economy, and our society in general. We would be saying to hundreds of thousands of scientists and engineers striving to advance our office technology that we don't want and will not use this additional knowledge. We must ever be mindful that progress means change and places before us broad challenges and threats which we must meet and conquer; otherwise we shall stagnate.

Undoubtedly, the number of irksome, monotonous tasks is reduced by automation. Much laborious and time-consuming information work is done by the machine. This is desirable from the social point of view and is a benefit to mankind. Many feel that we are at the beginning of what might be described as a second Industrial Revolution, which will substitute machines for human beings in performing mental drudgery, just as the first Industrial Revolution substituted machines for carrying out most backbreaking physical drudgery.

Opinions differ with respect to the changes in skill requirements as a result of computer usage. For many new jobs created by the computer, the skill requirements have increased, yet many relatively low skill jobs remain. Certainly training and the need for proficiency in specific skills are emphasized by information automation. Both the person with no skill and the senior employee, whose total experience consists of performing work requiring little judgment, are hard put to find employment. They are the two classes presenting the majority of troublesome dislocation difficulties.

## FEASIBILITY OF AUTOMATION

Before deciding on the use of a computer or not, it is customary to conduct a study to determine if automation is desirable, economically justified, and totally acceptable. Two aspects of data processing are involved (1) the makeup of the paper work itself, and (2) the processing of the data as such. The first was discussed under conceptualizing of the work, chapters 2 to 6 inclusive. It includes the information design of the entire cycle but not to a detailed degree. The second point, processing of the data, includes the selection and actual operation of the machines and computer. Again, it warrants repeating that these two aspects of automation feasibility—conceptualizing and processing—are interrelated. The experts in each area should work together as a team, with each aware of the other's problems.

What is included in a thorough and sound feasibility study? A number of considerations, including the objectives of the enterprise and the contributions expected of each functional area or organizational unit to the achievement of these objectives. The decision-making activity vested in each management member is clearly stated so that the information needs of each member can be identified. Familiarity with the organization structure assists in answering who decides what, who is expected to inform whom, and what information is needed. Generally, it is also helpful to know the relative importance of the various basic functions of the enterprise—manufacturing, marketing, financing, engineering, and personnel—in order to obtain some impression of the probable characteristics of the data to be handled. Also, any future increased work loads and contemplated changes should be taken into account, as well as the existing means of performing the work, no matter how primitive, because such facts can have an important bearing upon the recommendations.

The question to be answered is not whether a computer can be used. It can; the computer is a reality. The issue is: will the resultant costs, time in process, flexibility of usage, and ability to meet future requirements be to the enterprise's best interests and in keeping with the management members' needs and desires? Discretion in emphasizing the features of any particular type of computer is suggested; too much attention directed on such things as machine capacities, engineering features, speeds, and peak loads may cloud the essential considerations and purposes which is to process the proper data in order to help somebody do his job better because of the processed data supplied him. Discussing too many technical details is chaotic; the average layman wants to know what the computer will do for him rather than how it does it. Some people must know all the details, but most people who are involved in the "computer age" are neither technicians nor do they want to be. Of course, some technical data are essential and should be provided. But too much regard for how the data are processed can result in too little regard for what kinds of data are being provided. The data processing becomes an end in itself rather than a means to an end.

## BATCH OR REAL-TIME?

An important managerial decision regarding computers is whether batch or real-time process scheduling will be used. Under the former means, all incoming computer data are batched or allowed to accumulate and then processed on a scheduled basis, perhaps once a eeek. In contrast, for the real-time means data are entered into the computer as soon as available and processed immediately. When real-time is used and the computer is "on-line" with the activity being performed, the expression "on-line real-time" is used.

There is no uniformity of opinion as to when a computer arrangement is precisely real-time. Some contend only control applications are real-time because in these applications processing takes place while the related physical manufacturing operations take place. Others give the term broader meaning and include many types of application where the stored information can be removed at random—called "random access"—in contrast to "serial" types of stored data, which must be removed from the computer in the order of their input. The decision on this issue rests with the individual company. How quickly are the processed data wanted? Letting a customer know within five days of order placement when shipment will be made may be entirely satisfactory, and a batch arrangement would be used. On the other hand, information for a seat reservation on an airplane usually requires a real-time arrangement. At the present stage of progress, most payroll, accounts payable and receivable, cost, and sales analyses are on a batch arrangement, but with the development of systems and the movement toward integrating them, the real-time arrangement is increasing significantly in adoption.

## ADDITIONAL MANAGERIAL CONSIDERATIONS

Arbitrary classifications by size of computer are sometimes followed, including (1) large, (2) medium, and (3) small. Such classifications are actually very broad and rough. The classification large includes computer systems renting for over $30,000 monthly. These represent the sophisticated systems with top speeds and special features. "Program interrupt," for example, will usually be included in the abilities of this group. This is the ability of the computer to accept instructions simultaneously by selecting an input or output device ready to join the processing and start this processing at the same time other input and output devices are completing their functions. This raises the "throughput" and assists in conserving valuable processing time. The second group, medium, constitutes those with rental costs averaging between $5,000–$10,000 monthly. They make up the popular computer systems, widely used and perhaps best known of all computers. Most in this group have mass memory hardware and effective input and output devices. The last group, small, represents machines renting for around $1,000–$2,000 per month. These have relatively limited capacity but perform satisfactorily within their limits. Many have very limited mass memory, a condition which poses problems in processing if, for example, the processing includes referencing of indicative data.

To the newcomer, computers have given rise to its own jargon, comprising a strange terminology unlike anything previously encountered. Words like bit, binary number, access time, real-time, buffer, program, and storage take on special meanings quite different from those previously associated with them.[4] Furthermore, there is some variation and confusion about the meaning of certain basic words. Hence, the same word doesn't always have the same meaning. Obviously, this state of affairs makes for common difficulties and poses adjustment problems. A sales manager may attempt to learn the intricacies of computer processing but become discouraged by the specialized and somewhat stilted language of the technical books recommended to him. Or, as inferred above, he may find it a real chore to communicate with the executive in charge of computer activities. In contrast, data-processing personnel encounter difficulty in presenting ideas to sales management personnel. A common complaint of the processor is that he "just can't get through to top and middle managers."

---

[4] A glossary of computer terms is included in chapter 10, pp. 222–23.

Computers require nonvarying, disturbance-free electrical power and office space that is regulated as to temperature, dust, and humidity. The layout of the office may have to be changed to place the heavy machine where ample structural support is provided and the flow of information work can most efficiently be handled. Channels under the floor in which to run electrical cables connecting the various units sometimes pose a technical problem, especially when a controlling factor is the maximum lengths of cable specified by the computer manufacturer.

Converting to a computer can represent a Herculean task and too often is brushed off as a minor consideration. Much work is involved and it is not uncommon to require eight to ten months or more. Conversion difficulties include inaccuracy and lack of uniformity in existing records, missing papers, unexpected deviations of records from a supposed format, errors in reading or in putting information into a computer medium, the maintenance of an adequate work force to accomplish the conversion work, and the accomplishment of the work within reasonable budget limitations.

The conversion process includes what is known as "application in parallel." This means the practice of continuing both the processing of information in the normal way and also through the computer, then comparing the results in order to check the accuracy of the computer. Normally, the work is run in parallel for several complete cycles, or until the new process is completely "debugged." This can be a very frustrating period. Consistent results are obtained; and then, without warning, inconsistencies occur. Finding and correcting the sources of errors frequently pose major tasks. In some installations, conversion problems are minimized by beginning with areas that are already using punched cards or have been subjected to a certain amount of office mechanization, but there is no guarantee that this approach will eliminate conversion difficulties.

## SUGGESTIONS FOR COMPUTER USERS

Many problems of computers must be solved in managers' offices rather than in the laboratories of the designing engineers. Certain general practices by managers usually aid in achieving satisfaction on assignments dealing with computers. Among these practices are:

1. View the computer as a data-processing system, not as a single machine. See it as a means for supplying information to an enterprise, not as a replacement for a single or particular office machine.

2. Learn as much as possible about the various uses of computers. This knowledge will broaden your viewpoint and assist in maximizing utilization of the computer.

3. Have top managers or a top group decide what work should be done

with a computer. Do not permit one involved department head to make this decision.

4. Never consider a computer the cure-all for all current information ills. A computer assists in attaining improvements, but employees must improve the system. The computer does what it is told to do.

5. In planning a data-processing system, take into consideration the probable needs for the future five to ten years.

6. Always relate computer capability to the specific requirements of the installation being considered. Capacities and special types of work performed which are not needed by the computer system at hand are superfluous.

7. With sufficient training, use present personnel for computer operation, as they usually operate a computer very satisfactorily.

8. Work closely with the computer manufacturer who is anxious to assist and meet every reasonable request.

## QUESTIONS

1. Discuss the meaning and the importance of "the degree of office automation."
2. Do you agree with the following statement: "Although there is much glamour about automation in the office, the real reason for its development is the reduction in office costs that it brings about." Why?
3. Justify the viewpoint that computers increase the responsibility of managers.
4. Identify each of the following:
    *a*) Application in parallel.
    *b*) "Program interrupt" of a computer.
    *c*) Programmed and routine type of decision.
    *d*) "Throughput" of computer processing.
5. What do you believe are and will continue in increasing measure to be the major effects of computer usage upon management planning? Why?
6. What are the major considerations included in an up-to-date feasibility study of office automation for an enterprise? Discuss the one you believe is highly important.
7. Point out several factors essential to good relationships between the manager and the computer technician within a given enterprise.
8. What is your reaction to the following statement: "Eventually and in the not too distant future—possibly by the year 2000, computers will have taken over the work of most managers as we think of managers today. Hence, in the future I envision an important concentration of study known as "Computer Administration." Justify your answer.
9. Are the social aspects of office automation of major concern to the office manager? Elaborate on your answer.
10. Do you agree with the following statement: "The biggest challenge to successful computer usage is in the technical abilities and capacities to build computers to meet the truly sophisticated requirements of modern information management. Based on the tremendous progress made during the past several

decades, it can be stated that we are well on our way toward meeting this challenge quite successfully." Why?

11. Discuss possible major considerations in managerial decision making to determine batch or real-time scheduling in connection with computer usage.

12. As you see it, will office managerial actuating become less important as office automation increases? Justify your viewpoint.

## CASE PROBLEMS

### Case 9–1. National Administrative Academy

The executive committee of the National Administrative Academy, an organization whose members are recognized leading managers from business, education, government, and military, invited Dr. Albert R. Wanetik to address them at their annual meeting on the subject, "The Great Expediter of Information—The Computer." Among the comments of Dr. Wanetik in his speech were the following:

It is not easy to be neutral about office automation. The computer age has stirred up office operations with a whirlwind of new ideas and change. Most of us are wrapped up with solutions to our immediate problems and we neglect to sit back and assess what is going on around us. We view the past to find and correct our mistakes. We look ahead to determine where new opportunities are greatest. But taking place during the present is the formation of what historians will call the "Age of Information." And the computer will play an even more important role in this age than perhaps any of us can envision. I assure you that what we have seen to date is only the first of a vast new information technology that will alter the very foundations of administration.

Let us look at three different fields of endeavor—education, medicine, and the sciences, both physical and social. The greatest enemy any nation faces is ignorance. To reduce ignorance is an objective of education. And educational facilities are being refined, thanks in large measure to computers. Already computer-aided instruction is growing rapidly. Scientific and engineering studies of all types are becoming feasible by the use of central computation centers. Computerized libraries will place the world's knowledge at the fingertips of the researcher. The learning process is being hastened by the computer.

In the fascinating field of medicine, the unconquered knowledge of what causes certain diseases and pertinent correlation of data between treatment and results face a powerful new tool to overcome them. The techniques of X ray are being enhanced and the laboratories, dietetic, and other hospital departments are using the computer to improve the care of the sick.

In the sciences, great progress has been won, aided by the application of the computer which has provided us with a tool to help solve the problems associated with the required broad technological and social adjustments of today. The past mechanisms that have sufficed during the past are currently inadequate. Restructuring and revision to adopt them to present society needs are aided by the computer as, for example, its use in the more efficient handling of the law processes including the speeding of hearings, assembly of evidence, apprehension of criminals, and in fact, improved action of the entire legal work load.

With all the data available to me, I predict, by 1978, an increase in the number of clerical employees of 35 percent. This increase is greater than the growth to be experienced by the number of factory employees and also by those in the sales group. In short, we are to become a nation of clerical workers. Information will be our most important product. The increasing volume of paper work and communication will far more than offset any success to win savings in our office management endeavors.

Few enterprises are realizing the full potential of their computer system. Many employ the computer only for two or three specific applications such as payroll, inventory and purchasing, and sales analysis. Full benefits will not be realized until office automation is used for all office operations. The entire spectrum of information is the ultimate application of the computer. However, this will not be obtained until we, as managers, comprehend and apply the concepts of information automation and resolve to take full advantage of it.

Let me add, and I'm going to state it very frankly, in this connection, managers have not made it known what information is needed and in what form the information should be so that they can make the best use of it. By and large, the problem of what information and where have been left to the technician. The result is that managers receive too many facts that do not pertain to their real needs.

## Questions:

1. Would you say, based on Dr. Wanetik's comments, that a teacher or a medical doctor will be expected to master the computer that will serve him? Why?
2. In general, are you inclined to agree or disagree with Dr. Wanetik's comments? Discuss.
3. What additional comments do you feel would have been proper for him to make?

### Case 9–2.  Beattie, Edgil, and Thurman, Inc.

The majority of the executive committee members of Beattie, Edgil, and Thurman, Inc., an advertising agency commonly referred to as BET, believe strongly that the agency should acquire a computer. With headquarters in New York City and branch offices in Detroit and Chicago, BET employs 607 people, and its clients number over 75.

Mr. Karl Beck, chairman of the executive committee, reasons that with the amount of paper work they now have, a computer would certainly be advantageous. In his opinion, the number of accounts payable to different TV stations, publishers, and suppliers, as well as the accounts receivable, payroll, cost reports, and research studies presently conducted, make a computer economically feasible. However, several members of the executive committee dissent, pointing out that processing paper work is really not a major problem of the agency and a continuation of "farming out" much of their specialized processing demands, such as research studies, would appear to be the better decision.

After reviewing the various operations in the agency's main office, Herman Noble, representative of a large computer manufacturer, informed Mr. Beck that much of the paper work now being done manually should be automated and that improved systems and procedures should be installed. In his opinion, some of the research work could be put on a computer, but most of this work was special and did not lend itself to computer processing. He offered to make a survey of the agency's work and submit it to Mr. Beck for his consideration. However, it would be several weeks until such a survey could be started. To Mr. Beck's direct question, "Do you believe a computer is feasible, advantageous, and practical for us?" Mr. Noble replied, "Yes, sir. I certainly do." Mr. Beck then indicated that any survey would show the same general conclusion and since the majority of the executive committee agreed, the agency should proceed with the computer acquisition. He added that some agency business demanded his being out of his office a great deal; he was turning the entire project over to Mr. Levinson, the agency's controller.

After several weeks, Mr. Levinson introduced Mr. Noble to the accounts receivable and the accounts payable supervisors, the payroll supervisor, and the assistant director of research and explained his purpose at the agency. To each of these supervisors and their employees a brief letter was given:

> This is to advise you that as soon as possible manual handling of work in your unit will be discontinued and a computer will be installed. This move will necessitate some transferring of employees, but rest assured that this will be worked out to the mutual advantage of all concerned.
>
> Signed   Harry Levinson
>            Controller

The accounts receivable supervisor was unfavorable toward the change. She believed it would make the work monotonous and reduce her importance within the company. She spoke with the payroll supervisor, who also was negative about the contemplated change. Both favored use of late-model accounting machines which, in their opinion, were ideally suited for the accounts receivable and payroll work.

About five months later, on a Tuesday morning, various units of a computer arrived and were located within the accounts receivable area. On the same morning, the controller held a meeting in his office with two representatives of the computer company and the accounts receivable supervisor at which time each step of the new process was explained. Many questions were asked, and the representatives answered each one of them. The meeting took all morning. After lunch, the controller introduced the representatives to the employees of the accounts receivable department, informed them of the meeting held during the morning, and requested that any questions they might have should be directed to their immediate supervisor, who would either answer the question directly or find out the answer and give it to them. The changeover date was set for three weeks hence; and the names of six employees, with the respective departments to which they were being transferred, were announced.

Two weeks after the changeover date, Mr. Beck, along with Mr. Levinson, visited the accounts receivable department. He spoke with the supervisor, who said: "Well, it is a mess right now. My desk is piled high with work. We're working overtime but not making much headway. We have a manual that appears to give all the details about the operation. It reads OK, and the representatives are very willing to help in every way possible."

## Questions:

1. Evaluate the actions of Mr. Beck.
2. Do you feel that, given a reasonable amount of time, the present difficulties in the accounts receivable department will take care of themselves? Why?
3. Would you expect the same conditions as now exist in accounts receivable to exist in the other units where the computer will first be used? Why?
4. What action, if any, do you suggest Mr. Beck take? The controller? Substantiate your viewpoint.

# chapter 10

# Computers—technical considerations

The concern for man and his destiny must always
be the chief interest of all technical effort. Never
forget it among your diagrams and equations.

—*Albert Einstein*

To ACQUIRE a background for understanding the operation and contribution of a computer, we will discuss its main technical facets. The content of this chapter is minimal for basic computer comprehension. It is intended to provide technical computer facts believed essential for the information manager today.

A computer is actually a group of mechanical and electronic devices connected into a unit or system to process data. Since it is made up of several units, interrelated and operating as a totality, it is more accurately designated as a computer system. It is a tool for solving problems. In simplest terms it reads, writes, and performs arithmetic. The system takes a bundle of data, processes them according to the necessary string of operations, including any or all ten of the basic elements of data processing discussed in chapter 1, turns out the answers with fabulous rapidity and without error, and proceeds automatically to the next bundle of data and processes them.

## BASIC TYPES OF COMPUTERS

The basic types of computers are (1) digital, (2) analog, and (3) hybrid digital-analog. Digital computers, or arithmetic machines as they

214

are sometimes described, deal with actual numbers, and their answer is a set of numbers or letters, which can be made as accurate as desired. These computers perform according to a set of instructions, or a program, and if required, will perform hundreds and hundreds of repetitive calculations. A digital computer performs the work immediately after it is given a problem. It is a common type of machine for processing business data and represents by far the greatest number of computers in operation today.

An analog computer operates on the basis of using a formula or system to represent that which is being investigated or by duplicating mathematical behavior. It can instantaneously solve a mathematical equation with ten variables. It is actually based on approximations, and both input and output of an analog computer are approximate positions on a continuous scale rather than absolute numbers. Results from the analog computer are never precisely accurate, but they are commonly within $\frac{1}{20}$ of 1 percent, which is entirely satisfactory for most applications. Calculating flows and pressures in pipelines and the position of a moving target are accomplished by an analog computer in only a split second, whereas for the same application the digital computer would calculate enormous quantities of data for an hour or so. Many analog computers are used for research and scientific investigation.

A hybrid digital-analog computer is a combination of the first two, digital and analog, utilized to obtain a computer capable of more work than the two can accomplish working separately. This hybrid type is a more recent development. It has been used advantageously for outer space projects and satellite programs. To date there are relatively few hybrid digital-analog computers in use.

## THE FOUR BASIC CONSIDERATIONS

To simplify this discussion we will organize our thoughts around four basic subject areas. These are: (1) the converting from a system or procedure to the computer programming, (2) the programming work for computer processing, (3) the coding work for computer utilization, and (4) the anatomy of a computer. The first includes transferring the conceptualization of the work to be done, as recorded by the system or procedure, to a form required for computer programming. The second includes preparing the work for computer handling. The third, or coding, deals with putting the work into a form or language that the computer can handle. The term, *software*, is commonly used to identify these three areas, that is, converting, programming, and coding. The fourth subject area, anatomy of a computer, deals with the physical makeup of a computer. The term, *hardware*, is commonly used to identify this area.

Frequently, the usage of the term, *software*, includes the development and implementation of systems and procedures, but this work is essential whether manual, machine, or computer processing is followed. Further, systems personnel concentrate on systems work; they perform a different function from that of the programmer. This distinction will be readily recognized in the immediate following pages.

## CONVERTING FROM SYSTEM TO COMPUTER PROGRAMMING

In chapters 2 through 6, the conceptualizing of the information work to be done was discussed. These efforts provide a blueprint, expressed in written and chart form, of what information we want where, in what format, to whom, and at what time. To carry out these plans poses no new techniques in the case of manually or nonautomated processing. The guides and instructions are studied, and the implementation takes place in accordance with the indicated sequence and relationship of operations.

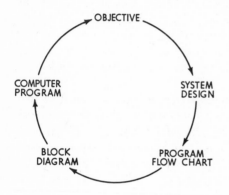

FIGURE 10–1. Steps between Objective Statements and Attainments When Computer Processing Is Employed.

In contrast, when processing by computer we encounter a different situation. The system requirements must be converted into a form which the computer can handle. Specifically, the relationship is between the system design and the computer programming function which includes the detailing of the work in the form of a package of instructions for a computer to follow.

To get from the system design to the computer program, a program flow chart and a block diagram are used. Figure 10–1 shows the arrangement. An objective is to be accomplished. To this end, a system is designed. The system is expressed in a program flow chart which, in turn, is converted to the block diagram and then to the computer program.

The development of the program flow chart and the block diagram identifies this converting step. A detailed breakdown of the step-by-step activity requirements of the system are mandatory. Symbols are used in the preparation of program flow charts. The most widely adopted and recommended symbols and their description are shown in Figure 10–2.

FIGURE 10–2. Program Flow Chart Symbols and Their Descriptions.

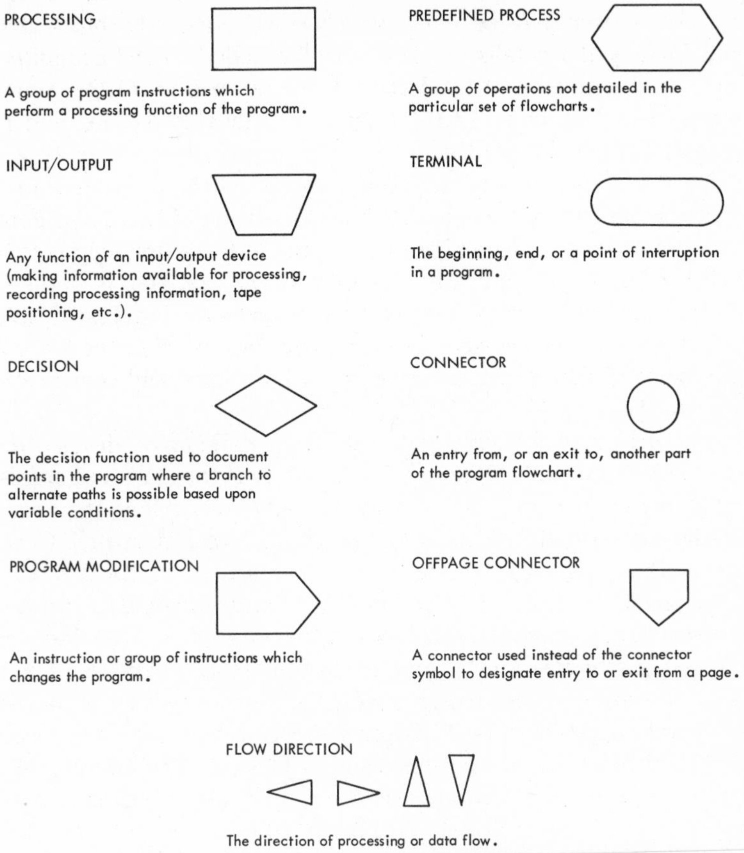

PROCESSING

A group of program instructions which
perform a processing function of the program.

PREDEFINED PROCESS

A group of operations not detailed in the
particular set of flowcharts.

INPUT/OUTPUT

Any function of an input/output device
(making information available for processing,
recording processing information, tape
positioning, etc.).

TERMINAL

The beginning, end, or a point of interruption
in a program.

DECISION

The decision function used to document
points in the program where a branch to
alternate paths is possible based upon
variable conditions.

CONNECTOR

An entry from, or an exit to, another part
of the program flowchart.

PROGRAM MODIFICATION

An instruction or group of instructions which
changes the program.

OFFPAGE CONNECTOR

A connector used instead of the connector
symbol to designate entry to or exit from a page.

FLOW DIRECTION

The direction of processing or data flow.

*Courtesy: International Business Machines Corp.,
White Plains, N.Y.*

Although at fantastic speed, the computer processes just one minute
step at a time and, if a choice exists, either of two ways must be indicated, such as either "yes" or "no," "stop" or "go" to another operation.
When necessary details are missing, the processing by computer is not
feasible, and meaningless and incorrect results are obtained.

To illustrate the degree of detail, let us assume the system deals with
payroll processing and we have progressed through steps (1) gross pay
from straight salary, (2) gross pay from overtime, and (3) gross pay from
incentive. The next steps are (4) develop deductions, and (5) get new
up-to-date balance. Is step number 4 in sufficient detail? To process it, we
must (4.1) determine withholding tax, (4.2) determine F.I.C.A. and (4.3)
calculate other approved deductions, i.e., for group insurance, union dues,
and purchase of U.S. bonds. Unless these details are inserted in the
computer program, the processing will fail. Carried further, we can ask,

"Is step number 4.1, 'determine withholding tax,' in sufficient detail?"
Again the answer may be no in which event either the block diagram
should include the details or they must be added to the computer program. For step number 4.1, additional details such as (4.11) exemption
amount, (4.12) tax class, (4.13) existence of taxable income, and (4.14)
tax amount might be needed.

From the system design has been constructed the program flow chart
shown in Figure 10–3. It deals with the calculation of thermal differential
means and variances. Beginning in the upper left, the first step is to test if
switch B is on. If yes, indicated by letter Y, the next step is to the right;
if no, indicated by letter N, the next step is downward to Test C, to see if
switch C is on. The successive steps progress downward in the left column
of the figure to the bottom where point A is reached and continue in the
column to the right.

From this program flow chart, the block diagram is developed. The
start of this is shown by Figure 10–4. Block A is the start and consists of
"Test if switch B is on." Moving to the right, block B is the next step,
consisting of Test C, which is composed of "Test if switch C is on."
Progressing to the right, the next step is indicated in Block C. To the
right of each block are two columns for insertion of data needed for
conversion to the computer. In block A, for example, in the first column
are Y and N standing for yes and no. In the second column and opposite
Y is 2L, meaning if the answer is yes, the successive step is 2L; in the
same column opposite N is B, meaning if the answer is no, the successive
step is B, or block B, shown to the right of block A. The meaning of 2L is
a code for a program modification which in this case is "set time switch to
transfer setting" as indicated in Figure 10–3, upper left, as the step
following a yes answer to the question, "Is switch B on?" By studying
Figure 10–3 in conjunction with the block diagram of Figure 10–4, the
identity and need for each block of Figure 10–4 is revealed, along with the
coded operations which the computer must perform.

In actual practice the systems man can stop at the system design and
let the computer programmer develop from the system the program flow
chart, the block diagram, and the computer program. In contrast, the
systems man may extend his efforts all the way through computer programming, and turn over the complete package to the computer operator.
Neither of these extremes is recommended. The best arrangement is an
overlap in efforts in the area of reasonable details of the program flow
chart. In this way the systems man gains an understanding of the programming and the programmer gains an understanding of the system
design work. By this approach cooperation is enhanced between the
system designer and the programmer, ambiguity of data is minimized,
training is facilitated, and interdepartmental flexibility is encouraged.

## GLOSSARY OF COMPUTER TERMS

Before proceeding with the second point, programming, a glossary of selected terms used with computers will be inserted. See Figure 10–5 on pages 222–23. This serves as a convenient reference for the special terminology used. Scanning the terms and their meanings will assist in grasping quickly the technical significance of computer operations. Later a more intense review of the glossary may be undertaken.

## PROGRAMMING

The complete package of instructions for a computer to process specific data is known as a *program*. It is developed by "programming." This work consists of breaking down in most complete detail the operations to be performed by the computer. A programmer performs this work.

To illustrate the necessary detail and sequential accuracy of programming, consider processing requiring multiplication. In this case, the computer must be directed not only to multiply, but to perform (1) the operation that precedes the multiplying, (2) the operation that follows the multiplying, (3) the identity and location of the multiplicand, and (4) likewise that of the multiplier. In addition, after the multiplication is completed, the program must indicate where the result is to be delivered —to the storage device or to an output device of the computer. There are certain exceptions to this, however, as for example when magnetic tape ledger records are used as the input medium, in which case part of the stored data are on the tape or strips of the ledgers. Also, in the case of magnetic ink characters being used as the input medium, little of the data is stored in a storage unit of the computer.[1]

Hence, by means of computer programming, the machine progresses by moving from one minute element of work to the next in a prescribed sequence. The first operation may be locating specific data in the storage device of the computer, followed by transferring it to the processing device, multiplying these data by a given number, returning it to the storage device along with the separate initial data, and finally outputing the multiplication (processing) result by means of the output device of the computer. Again in some instances the sequential operation can be either of two possibilities, but no more, represented by yes or no, go or no go, on or off, and so forth. When the program designates the answer is yes, for example, the computer follows the element of this designation. In contrast, if the answer is no, the alternate element is followed. This means that minute, detailed, sequential steps in the work to be done must be set

---

[1] Magnetic tape ledger records and magnetic ink characters are discussed later in this chapter, pp. 236–37.

FIGURE 10–3. A Program Flow Chart.

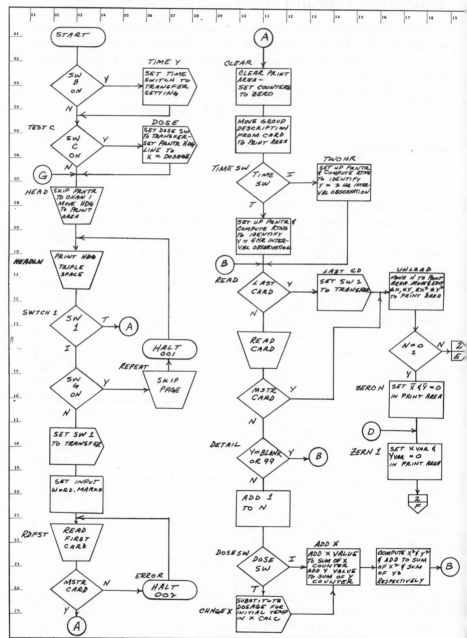

Courtesy: Johnson and Johnson Co,.
New Brunswick, N.J.

FIGURE 10–4. A Block Diagram for Conversion Work to Computer.

**A START** Y 2L
TEST IF SWITCH B IS ON — N B

**B TESTC** Y 2M
TEST IF SWITCH C IS ON — M C

**C HEAD**
SKIP PRINTER TO CHANNEL I AND MOVE HEADING TO PRINTER OUTPUT AREA

**D HEADLN**
PRINT HEADING + TRIPLE SPACE

**E SWTCH I** I F
LOGIC SWITCH I — T K

**F** Y 2F
TEST IF SWITCH G IS ON — N G

**G**
SET SWITCH I TO TRANSFER SETTING

**H**
SET INPUT WORD MARKS

**J RDFST** Y K
READ FIRST CARD + TEST IF MASTER CARD — N 2G

**K CLEAR**
CLEAR PRINT AREA + SET COUNTERS TO ZERO MOVE GROUP DESCR. FROM CARD TO PRINTER AREA

**I TIMESW** I 2H
LOGIC SWITCH TIME — T M

**M**
SET UP PRINTER + COMPUTE ROUTINES TO IDENTIFY Y = 4 HOUR INTERVAL OBSERVATION

**N READ** Y U
TEST IF LAST CARD READ — N O

**O** Y V
READ CARD + TEST IF MASTER CARD — N P

**P DETAIL** Y N
TEST IF Y VALUE IS BLANK OR 99 — N Q

**Q**
ADD I TO N

**R DOSESW** I S
LOGIC SWITCH DOSE — T 2N

**S ADD X**
ADD X VALUE TO SUM OF X COUNTER ADD Y VALUE TO SUM OF Y COUNTER

**T** N
COMPUTE X² AND Y² AND ADD TO SUM OF X² AND SUM OF Y² RESPECTIVELY

**U LASTCD**
SET SWITCH 2 TO TRANSFER SETTING

**V UNLOAD**
MOVE N TO PRINT AREA. MOVE + EDIT ΣX, ΣY, ΣX²+ΣY² TO PRINT AREA

**W**
TEST IF N = 0 — Y 2J / N X

**X**
COMPUTE $\bar{x} = \frac{\Sigma x}{N}$ + $\bar{y} = \frac{\Sigma y}{N}$ + MOVE TO PRINT AREA

**Y** Y 2K
SUBTRACT I FROM N AND TEST IF = 0 — N Z

**Z**
COMPUTE X + Y VARIANCES + MOVE TO PRINT AREA
$$X_{VAR} = \frac{\Sigma x^2 - \frac{(\Sigma x)^2}{N}}{N-1}$$

**2A PRINT**
PRINT LINE + DOUBLE SPACE

**2B SWTCH 2** I C
LOGIC SWITCH 2 — T D

**2C**
TEST IF PAGE OVERFLOW — Y 2C / M 2K

**2D END JOB**
SKIP TWO PAGES AND HALT 000,999

**2E** 2A
SET SWITCHES I + 2 AND DOSE + TIME SWITCHS TO N-TIAL SETTING SET PRINTER HEADING LINE TO X = TEMP.

**2F REPEAT** 2D
SKIP PAGE AND HALT 000,001

**2G ERROR** 2J
HALT 000,002

**2H TWCHR** 2N
SET UP PRINTER + COMPUTE ROUTINES TO IDENTIFY Y = 2 HOUR INTERVAL OBSERVATION

**2J ZERON**
SET $\bar{X} + \bar{Y} = C$ IN PRINT AREA

**2K ZERN I** 2A
SET X VAR + Y VAR = 0 IN PRINT AREA

**2L TIME Y** 2B
SET TIME SWITCH TO TRANSFER SETTING

**2M DOSE** 2C
SET DOSE SWITCH TO TRANSFER SETTING + SET PRINTER HEADING LINE TO X = DOSAGE

**2N CHNGEX** 2S
SUBSTITUTE DOSAGE FOR INITIAL TEMPERATURE IN X CALCULATIONS

**2O**

**2P**

**2Q**

**2R**

**2S**

**2T**

**2U**

**2V**

**2W**

**2X**

**2Y**

**2Z**

*Courtesy: Johnson and Johnson Co., New Brunswick, N.J.*

FIGURE 10–5. Glossary of Common Terms Used In Computer Technology.

---

*Access time*—time required for computer to move a piece of data or an instruction from a memory unit to a processing unit.

*Accumulator*—a storage register where results are accumulated.

*Alphameric characters*—letters of the alphabet, numerical digits, or symbols used for communicative purposes.

*Analog computer*—one representing variables by physical analogies in continuous form. An analog computer is said to measure, not count.

*Batch processing*—the means by which a number of similar input items are grouped for processing during the same machine run.

*Bit*—a unit of information content.

*Buffer storage*—the temporary storing of information during a transfer of that information. Buffer storage is used to permit simultaneous computation and input or output of data.

*Bug*—a malfunction or mistake.

*Cathode ray tube* (CRT)—a picture tube used in visual display terminal.

*Character*—a letter, digit, or symbol used for representation of data.

*Checkout*—the determination of the correctness of the computer routine, locating errors in it, and correcting them.

*Compile*—to produce a machine-language routine by translating from ordinary or non-machine program. Concerns programming.

*Compiler*—a program that compiles, i.e., prepares a machine-language program from a program written in another programming language by making use of the overall logic structure of the program.

*Data bank*—a comprehensive collection of organized information used for study and reference.

*Data processing*—the performance of a systematic sequence of operations performed upon data.

*Data transmission*—the sending of data from one part of a system to another part.

*Decision table*—a table of all possibilities to be considered in describing a problem and the actions to be taken. Commonly used in place of flow charts for problems documentation.

*Digital computer*—a computer in which information is processed and represented in discrete form. A digital computer counts; it does not measure.

*Display unit*—a device supplying a visual representation of data.

*Eight line code*—a code utilizing not more than eight impulses for describing a character.

*First generation computer*—a computer utilizing vacuum tube components.

*Hard copy*—written or printed copy of input or output data in human visually readable form.

*Hardware*—the mechanical and electrical devices making up a computer.

*Information retrieval*—the recovery of specific information from stored data.

*Interface*—a shared boundary usually applying either to linkage of two devices or to accessibility to stored data by two or more programs.

*Library*—an organized collection of proven and standard routines which can be incorporated into larger routines.

*Line printing*—the printing of an entire line of characters as a unit.

*Location*—a place in a storage unit where a unit of data or an instruction may be stored.

*Loop*—a technique of coding in programming whereby a group of instructions is repeated with alterations of some of the instructions and usually with modification of the data being processed.

*Macro instruction*—instruction in a source language equivalent to a specified sequence of machine instructions.

*Micro instruction*—a basic machine instruction.

*Microsecond*—one-millionth of a second.

*Millisecond*—one-thousandth of a second.

*Multiprogramming*—the concurrent execution of two or more programs by a single computer.

*Nanosecond*—one-thousand-millionth of a second.

*Network*—a series of points interconnected by communication channels.

*OCR*—optical character recognition used by machines for identifying printed characters by means of light-sensitive devices.

*Off-line*—the operation of input or output devices are not under direct control of the central processing unit.

*On demand system*—a system for which data are available at time of request.

*On-line*—the operation of input or output devices are under direct control of the central processing unit.

*Openended*—refers to a process that can be augmented.

*Parameter*—a quantity to which arbitrary values may be assigned for such things as decimal point location, record format, and size.

*Parity bit*—a binary bit added to an array of bits to make the sum of all the bits always odd or always even.

*Parity check*—a checking means based on making a total number of "on" or "off" in some grouping of binary digits.

*Peripheral equipment*—any unit of equipment distinct from the central computer group which provides the group with outside communication.

*Problem program*—any program not a part of the operating system.

*Random access*—the finding and getting of data in storage is relatively independent of the location of the information most recently obtained.

*Real time computation*—data processing by which the computer supplies information to a business activity whenever the information is demanded.

*Real-time output*—output data removed at time of need.

*Regeneration*—restoration of stored data.

*Register*—a device that holds information while or until it is used.

*Second generation computer*—a computer utilizing solid state components.

*Sequencing*—ordering and performing in a series in accordance with rank or time.

*Software*—the determining of systems, programming, and coding work required for effective computer data processing.

*Tape relay*—a method of relaying messages between the transmitting and receiving stations when perforated paper tape is used.

*Telecommunication*—either transmission of telegraph, radio, and TV signals over long distances, or data transmission between a computer system and remotely located devices.

*Terminal*—an input-output device at a point at which information can leave or enter communication network.

*Third generation computer*—a computer utilizing solid logic technology.

*Time sharing*—participation by multiple users in available computer time by means of terminals.

*Turnaround time*—interval between submitting a program to a computer and receiving output from that program.

*Zero suppression*—elimination of zeros which are nonsignificant in a numeral.

forth, and where choices arise, the decision must be one of two alternatives set forth in the program. The computer having the information of the precise element determines if yes or no is to be followed. In this sense computers can be considered to reach simple decisions. The program shown by Figure 10–6 illustrates this concept in a humorous but helpful way.

Since the programmer normally designs and evolves the program in the

FIGURE 10–6. This Diagram Illustrates How Programmers Have to Instruct the Electronic System to Work.

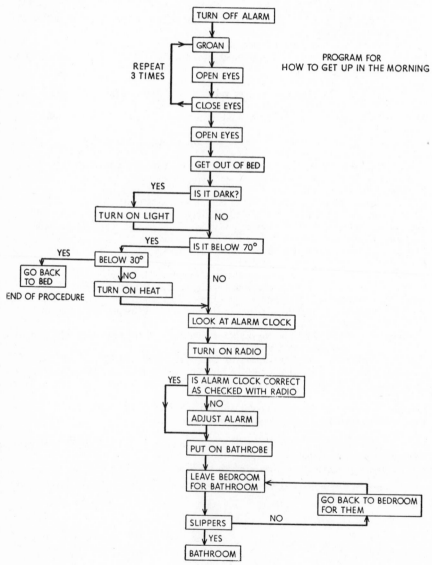

form of a flow chart listing the precise step-by-step action to be taken, it is extremely helpful to have an intimate knowledge of the systems, procedures, and methods being employed. In addition, a complete understanding of the purpose for which the finished data are used appears paramount in programming work. To perceive the detail of programming, consider that it is common for the preparation of customers' invoices to require 1,500 or more steps. Typically, many steps or minute operations covering relatively small amounts of processing to large quantities of data characterize business data processing. The simple recording, recalling, and arithmetic work necessitate much programming. In contrast, for much research and scientific data processing, the work entails relatively small quantities of data processed many, many times. Commonly the processing task is to substitute various values in mathematical formulas in order to determine critical values. Handling such repetitive processing using different numerical values necessitates relatively simple programming. Historically this is a major reason for the computer being used extensively first for scientific work. As the restricting influence of programming was lifted, computer processing for ordinary business data became feasible.

When program or instructions are placed in the storage device of a computer, they are commonly termed *stored programs*. A computer can be supplied with a number of different programs for different work by simply putting in, or loading, the programs into its storage device. When a number of stored programs are thus accessible to a computer, it in essence has the ability to alter its own program in response to conditions revealed as the processing takes place. Some like to think of this as "computer judgment" which in a sense, it is, but note that the "judgment" is constrained by the man-created programs within which the computer operates.

## COMMON BUSINESS ORIENTED LANGUAGE (COBOL)

For computer usage, it is necessary to have a network of preprogrammed packages which range from simple service routines to highly complex compilers. A compiler accepts a special code or a natural language, interprets it for the computer, selects the proper routine from a library retained by the computer, supervises the coding, allocates data, assembles a complete program, and gives a report on this program. The first compilers were all algebraic or mathematical, because the language of mathematics is concise and definite. With time, however, attempts were made to orientate the input language of a compiler to the natural language of the user. Subsequently MATH-MATIC, FORTRAN, and UNICODE were developed.

With the great interest developing in computers for processing business data, efforts were stimulated toward developing more suitable programming languages. Different computer manufacturers developed different languages, a condition that was costly. In 1960, however, a plan for perfecting and advancing a common and simplified English language for business system programming was launched. This simplified language, called COBOL, stands for Common Business Oriented Language and is shown in Figure 10-7.

FIGURE 10-7. COBOL Permits Instructions to Computers with Simple English Words of Everyday Business Language.

---

This language is COBOL:
SUBTRACT QUANTITY-SOLD FROM BALANCE-ON-HAND. IF BALANCE-ON-HAND IS NOT LESS THAN REORDER-LEVEL THEN GO TO BALANCE-OK ELSE COMPUTE QUANTITY-TO-BUY. . . .

COBOL eliminates the use of detailed and difficult computer language instructions such as:

| 06011 | ' | 12040 | 12047 |
| 06028 | C | 12048 | |
| 06074 | ? | 12046 | 12014 |
| 06145 | S | 12012 | 12010 |

---

This advance toward a common computer language suitable for all computers, regardless of their manufacture, is the most significant advance in programming. Once a program is written in COBOL, it need not be rewritten if a switch from one data-processing system to another takes place. Further, the burden of programming is eased. As an indirect result of the COBOL influence, many business-oriented "canned" or subroutine programs have been created for each type of computer. Also, automatic compilers and translators have appeared on the market.

## CODING THE WORK FOR COMPUTER PROCESSING

The third subject area in technical considerations of computers is coding the work for computer processing. All information is conveyed by symbols. In the English language, there are familiar letters of the alphabet, numbers, and punctuation marks. For everyday correspondence, these symbols are recorded on paper according to a prescribed sequence and grouping. When transported to another person reading and writing English, these symbols convey a particular message.

In the same manner, to communicate with a computer system necessitates that the information be expressed in symbols and in a form that can be read and interpreted by data-processing devices. In the case of the computer, this language has been called "computerese." It is language the machine can understand and act upon, in keeping with the desired processing. Man invented computerese to utilize the machines. It represents symbols making up a mutual language to provide communication between people and machines. In other words, every detail which the machine is to follow must be put into language that the machine can handle. This includes the use of special codes and numbers which, put on or into the data-transmitting medium, will cause the machine to perform the operation desired.

There are a number of different media that can be used. For input data, the following are included: (1) typewritten or printed material on paper, (2) punched card, (3) perforated paper tape, (4) magnetic tape, (5) magnetic tape ledger record, and (6) magnetic ink characters. The processing of output data, being basically the reverse of that for input data, means that the same media can be used for output data as for input data. However, since output data are either for human use or for subsequent machine use of a relatively limited sort, not all the communication input media are used for output. For the latter purpose, the communication media include: (1) print on paper, (2) punched card, (3) perforated paper tape, (4) magnetic tape, (5) magnetic tape ledger record, and (6) print on film. The concept of input data, output data, and data processing by a computer is shown by Figure 10–8.

FIGURE 10–8. Media of Input Data, Processing, and Media of Output Data of a Computer System.

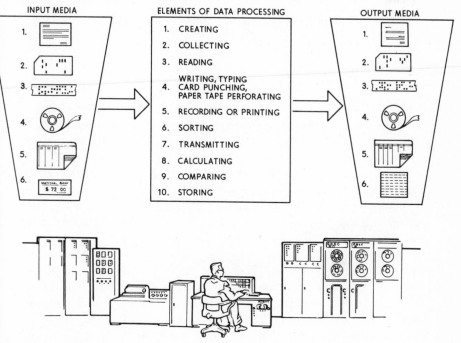

## TYPEWRITTEN OR PRINTED MATERIAL ON PAPER

Data can be transmitted into the computer by a machine that is capable of doing what you are doing right now—reading. All letters of the alphabet, numeral 0 through 9, standard punctuation, and special symbols are read. Various size documents, even continuous-length fanfold sheets are handled. Up to about 90,000 documents per hour can be read and recorded on the system's own magnetic tape deck. Expressing the speed differently, a reading rate of 370 characters per second or a line-reading speed of about 37 inches per second is attained. The reading speed is attained in part because only that portion of a line that it is instructed to read is read, and time is not wasted scanning blank lines and unwanted data. The font or type style of the information fed into the reader is similar to conventional fonts as illustrated by Figure 10–9.

FIGURE 10–9. Each Character in the Font Has a Distinctive Shape in Order That the Page Reader Performs Accurate Reader Performance.

THE PAGE READER READS ONLY UPPER CASE LETTERS AND A TYPEWRITER

USED EXCLUSIVELY FOR PAGE READER DOCUMENTATION NEED HAVE ONLY

AN UPPER CASE FONT. IT IS, HOWEVER, POSSIBLE AND PRACTICAL

TO EQUIP SUCH A TYPEWRITER WITH A LOWER CASE FONT OF SIMILAR

APPEARANCE WHICH ENABLES ITS USE FOR GENERAL BUSINESS PURPOSES

AS WELL AS FOR PAGE READER DOCUMENT PREPARATION.

*Courtesy: Control Data Corp., Minneapolis*

The machine operates in conjunction with a computer that directs its reading operations, that is, the computer governs the document position, reading, and sorting of the reading machine. Optical-electronic means are followed. Software is available for use with this system either for simple document reading or for editing, proving, sorting, and listing the reading machines output. Actually the machine reads and translates what it reads into computer language. Figure 10–10 shows the machine with the insert highlighting the adjustable loading hopper for feeding documents automatically to the machine.

A page reader system, now widely used, has a very efficient throughput rate combining accuracy and flexibility. Basic to this system is a page reader. In its input hopper are placed documents to be read. The characters are read left to right, line by line, and converted into electronic signals which are transmitted to the electronic unit of a computer which controls the entire system. The operation is exceptionally fast—as great

FIGURE 10–10. The 915 Page Reader Performs Direct Conversion of Typewritten or Printed Form Information into Computer Language by Optical-Electronic Means.

*Courtesy: Control Data Corp., Minneapolis*

as 400 characters per second reading speed. A typewriter console permits communication with the system. Program changes are possible. Up to ten characters can be displayed on a video screen, checked, and corrections keyed in so that the rejection rate will be zero. Rescan is possible whereby the reader reads the lines again if poorly printed data are not recognized the first time. A variety of output media is available including punched cards, punched tape, and magnetic tape. Figure 10–11 illustrates the units included in this modern page reader system.

In addition, the system features the reading of either white-paper (free format) or preprinted forms, and the utilizing of a built-in system of controls so that dependable and precise operation is achieved. A large magazine publisher uses this system to enter all new subscriptions and changes; a railroad employs it in the processing of waybill accounting, switching data, and maintenance reports; and governmental agencies employ this system for handling inventory and motor vehicle registration data.

Machine readers are also available that read data within a relatively small area of a document in keeping with the processing requirements. It may be an account number, an account to be paid, a name and address, a Zip Code number, or a varying number of lines from a printed listing. If desired, punched cards or perforated tapes are prepared as a part of the system. It is claimed that when three or more operators are continuously employed in reading and punching cards or tapes, the machine reader is to

FIGURE 10–11. Machines Making Up a Widely Used and Versatile Page Reader System.

*Courtesy: Farrington Manufacturing Co.,*
*Springfield, Va.*

be preferred. Credit invoices, checks, order cards, and bill stubs of public utility companies are among the more common uses. Its main areas of application can be classified under two groups: (1) where the input information consists of a long number of separate units recorded in a great number of places and must be processed quickly and economically, and (2) where the output data of today becomes the input data of tomorrow. To illustrate, if a statement with a stub consisting of printed material only is sent to a customer who subsequently returns payment and the stub, it is feasible to put critical portions of the printed matter of the stub in a form that the machine reader can easily handle when the stub is returned and becomes input data.

## BINARY MODE

Before proceeding with the discussion of the remaining media, some fundamentals employed in the coding of data should be pointed out. To be processed by the computer, data are converted into electric impulses in keeping with the binary code, whereby all numbers and letters are represented by two symbols in various combinations. These electric impulses following one another billions of times per minute magnetize very small areas in the computer enabling the machine to process the data. The two basic symbols, for example, include a hole in a card or no hole in a card, a magnetic impulse on a tape or no impulse, electric current is in one direction or in an opposite direction, and a switch is either closed or open.

In other words, the base is two, just as decimals refer to a base of ten. Tubes or transitors or cores can exist in only two states—"off" or "on," emitting or not, magnetized in one or the other electric charge.

One binary digit is called a *bit,* the contraction for "binary digit." For the decimal digits from 0 through 9, four binary positions are required and represent from left to right the decimal digits, 8, 4, 2, and 1. That is, different values are placed on the four positions and the value represented is the sum of these positions. See Figure 10–12.

The handling of zero in a computer is usually noted as ten, i.e., an eight and a two. In the binary position this avoids registering all blanks for zero, for if we did this it would be difficult to determine whether the register is supposed to be zero or the machine has failed to transfer data.

FIGURE 10–12. Illustrating the Four Bit Position and Values to Represent Decimal Numbers. For decimal 5, the "bits" of "4" and "1" are "on," "8" and "2" are "off."

BINARY CODE

| DECIMAL | 8 | 4 | 2 | 1 IS REPRESENTED BY | TOTAL VALUE (READ ACROSS) |
|---|---|---|---|---|---|
| 0 | 0 | 0 | 0 | 0 | 0 |
| 1 | 0 | 0 | 0 | ✳ | 1 |
| 2 | 0 | 0 | ✳ | 0 | 2 |
| 3 | 0 | 0 | ✳ | ✳ | 3 |
| 4 | 0 | ✳ | 0 | 0 | 4 |
| 5 | 0 | ✳ | 0 | ✳ | 5 |
| 6 | 0 | ✳ | ✳ | 0 | 6 |
| 7 | 0 | ✳ | ✳ | ✳ | 7 |
| 8 | ✳ | 0 | 0 | 0 | 8 |
| 9 | ✳ | 0 | 0 | ✳ | 9 |

To express in binary code larger decimal digits and letters of the alphabet additional binary digits would be required. Illustrative is adding to the 1, 2, 4, and 8 columns 16, 32, 64 so that the columns headings would read 64, 32, 16, 8, 4, 2, and 1. Decimal 10 would be binary 1010, and decimal 29 would be binary 11101. Some computers use four binary columns for each decimal digit. To illustrate, the number 24 would be shown as 0010–0100. To show 124, we would need another four binary columns. Letters of the alphabet can also be shown binarily; it's a matter of using more bits to show letters.

Returning to the statement made previously that there are only two states—off or on, emitting or not for each position, we can show the decimal numbers and their respective binary numbers as indicated at the left position of Figure 10–13. Examples of addition, subtraction, multiplication, and division are indicated at the right of this figure. For example, the decimal 4 + 3 = 7, expressed binarily is 100 + 011 = 111.

FIGURE 10–13. Relationships between Decimal and Binary Codes.

| Decimal | Binary | Decimal | Binary |
|---------|--------|---------|--------|
| 1 | 0001 | 6 | 0110 |
| 2 | 0010 | 7 | 0111 |
| 3 | 0011 | 8 | 1000 |
| 4 | 0100 | 9 | 1001 |
| 5 | 0101 | 10 | 1010 |

Examples:

| Decimal | Binary |
|---------|--------|
| 4 + 3 = 7 | 0100 + 0011 = 0111 |
| 6 − 2 = 4 | 0110 − 0010 = 0100 |
| 2 × 4 = 8 | 0010 × 0100 = 1000 |
| 10 ÷ 2 = 5 | 1010 ÷ 0010 = 0101 |

Codes other than binary are used by some computers including a numerical coding to the base eight, known as octal notation, a seven-bit alphameric, a six-bit numerical, and a biquinary system indicating numbers to the base five. The number system followed is a technical consideration, and assistance in its understanding is offered by the computer manufacturer both before and after machine installation.

## PUNCHED CARD

The typical punched card is about $7\frac{3}{8}$ inches long by $3\frac{1}{4}$ inches high. In the IBM type, the card is divided into 80 vertical columns, each one containing 12 units which, read from the top down, are: 12, 11, 0, 1, 2, 3, 4, 5, 6, 7, 8, 9. The 12 and the 11 zones are frequently called $R$ and $X$, respectively. Data from original records are put on the cards by means of punched holes; that is, when certain holes are punched in the card, these holes represent definite information. High-speed machines are used for this purpose. The letters of the alphabet number 26, and there are 10 digits (0–9), making a total of 36 characters, each of which must be assigned to coded representation by a positioned hole in the card. Since there are 12 units in a vertical column on the card, it requires three different vertical arrangements totaling 36 ($3 \times 12$) characters to represent all possibilities. This is clearly illustrated by Figure 10–14.

Information represented or coded by means of the presence or absence of holes in specific and exact locations is read as the card travels through a card-reading mechanism. The reading is automatically converted to an electronic language utilized by the computer in its data processing.

It is also possible to record binary information by the use of row binary, in which the data are arranged serially across each row beginning at the lower left, moving across from left to right for each horizontal row, and progressively upward on the card. A punched hole in the card represents yes, no punch indicates no. It is also possible to arrange the

FIGURE 10–14. A Code Used for Punched Holes Which Represent Letter and Figure Data.

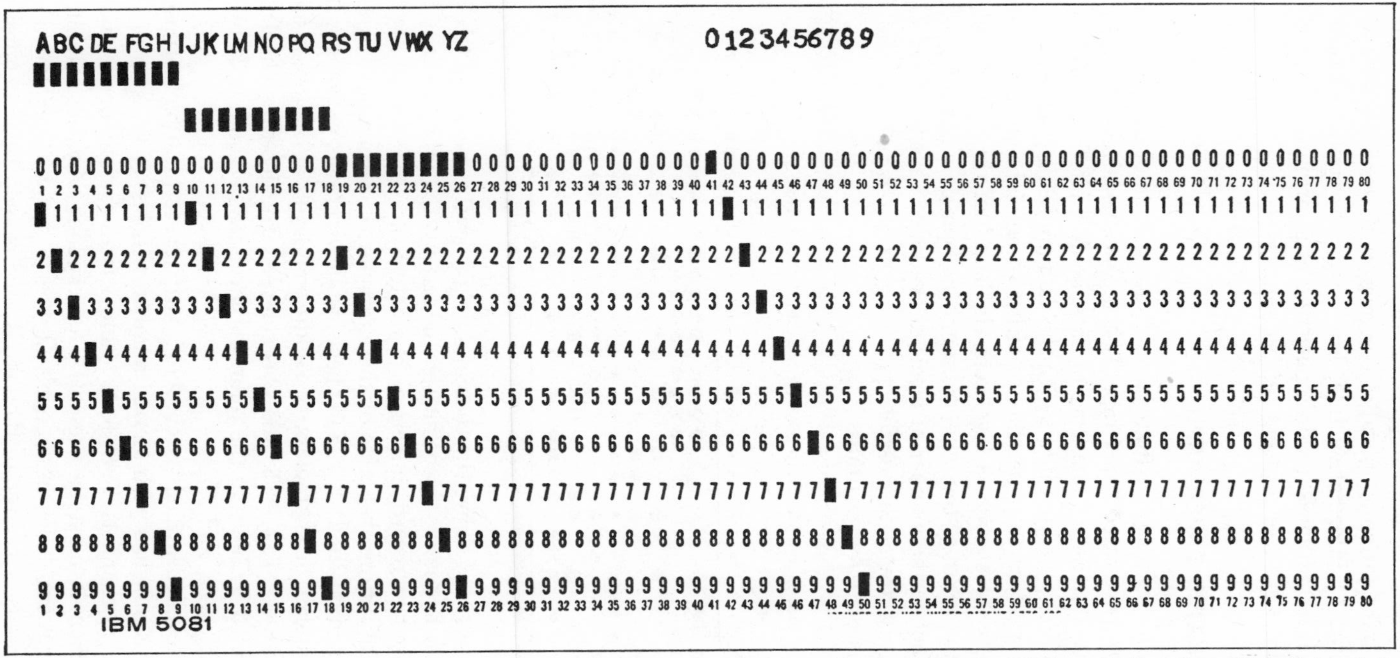

*Courtesy: International Business Machines Corp., White Plains, N. Y.*

binary information in parallel columns, with each column of the card containing 12 information bits. For certain computers, where the basic unit of information is a word consisting of a maximum of 36 consecutive bits, a total of three adjacent card columns is used.

## PERFORATED PAPER TAPE

Another common medium for the transmission of data into a computer system is perforated paper tape. It is a continuous recording medium and can be used to record long runs of data, being limited only by the capacity of the storage medium into which the data are being placed.

Most perforated paper tape is either of an eight-level or channel code or of a five-level code. A level runs the length of the tape. In any column across the width of the tape, the number of possible punching positions is equivalent to the number of levels of the tape. That is, in the eight-level tape, there are eight possible punching positions; and in the five-level tape, there are five positions.

FIGURE 10–15. Code for Eight-Level Perforated Paper Tape.

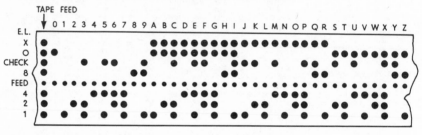

Figure 10–15 shows the code of an eight-level paper tape. Observe that the lower five levels, identified on the left by 1, 2, 4, and 8, and "check," when used to record numerical characters, are the sum of the position values indicating the value of the character. For example, 3 is expressed by holes in positions 1, 2, and check, while 7 consists of holes in 1, 2, and 4. For alphabetic characters, two additional levels at the top, $X$ and $O$, are used with the 1, 2, 4, 8, and check levels. To illustrate, the letter $A$ is represented by holes in the following levels: $X$, $O$, and 1; $K$ by holes in levels $X$, check, and 2.

The level identified as check is used for verification purposes. Each column is punched with an odd number of holes. If the sum of the holes punched in channels $X$, $O$, 8, 4, 2, and 1 is an even number, a hole in the check channel must be present. This explains why the column for the letter $V$ shows holes in channels $O$, check, and 8. The "end of line" or "El" channel at the top of the tape is used to indicate the end of a record or the tape.

## MAGNETIC TAPE

The principal input medium for computer systems is magnetic tape. It is one-half inch wide, made of plastic, and coated on one side with a metallic oxide. Information recorded on magnetic tape is permanent, but previous recordings are destroyed as new information is put on the tape. It is possible to utilize the same tape many times, thus saving in recording costs. Magnetic tape is supplied on plastic reels containing approximately 2,400 feet of tape.

The data are recorded on the tape in the form of magnetic dots or impulses. The code employed is illustrated by Figure 10–16. Starting at

FIGURE 10–16. Coding of Magnetic Spots on Tape to Transmit Information. This is the seven-bit alphameric code. Translation of the spots is shown at top of sketch.

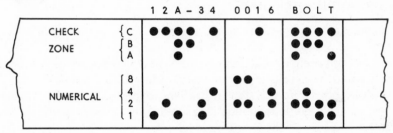

the top is level $C$, for checking, followed in order by $B$ and $A$, commonly called zone tracks, and 8, 4, 2, and 1, the numerical tracks or levels. In similar manner to that described under binary mode and perforated tape, numbers are coded, using the numerical channels. The decimal number 3 is coded as binary 2 and 1; and 6 as 4 and 2. The zone tracks are used in combination with the numerical tracks to indicate letters. In this code, for every column, the total spots add to an even number. If for a column the total of the spots in the zone and numerical tracks is an odd number, a spot is added at track $C$.

It is appropriate to state at this point that an electronic system is not infallible. Therefore, it checks itself to find any error. The impulses on channel $C$, or check, of the tape are used for this purpose. For example, every transfer of information from the computer memory units might be tested on an odd-even basis. If the sum of the group of digits is an odd number when it is supposed to be even, the machine indicates the error and stops. This is all done automatically by the machine.

The use of magnetic tape as an input medium is further demonstrated by the availability of a hand-operated, portable, magnetic tape digital recorder. Use of this recording machine eliminates the need for punched cards and paper tape for data acquisition and processing. In the case of inventory taking, for example, the bin number, quantity, and material or reference number are recorded on the magnetic tape. Subsequently this tape is fed into the computer, the data processed, and inventory reports printed. The unit has found favor with public utility companies for meter reading. The account or meter number and the reading are recorded by the door to door meter reader. When the tape is filled, it is sent to the computer center where statements to customers, account lists, and reports are prepared. The recording unit is battery powered and handles different sizes of tape cartridges. The maximum cartridge holds about 400 feet of tape. The unit records serially 15-decimal digits per block, a feature which is helpful in attaining error free data collecting.

### INFORMATION INTERCHANGE

There are strong efforts being made to adopt a permutation code whereby all coded irformation could be interchanged between business machines and computers. To this end the American Standards Association has assisted in developing a standard code which is all-inclusive and provides room for future standardization programs. Figure 10–17 shows this standard code. Its adoption is voluntary by business machine manufacturers, but no doubt it will gradually and surely be utilized. At the same time, the older codes will continue, due to their existence in present machines and to preferences by certain customers for no change.

### MAGNETIC TAPE LEDGER RECORD

This medium consists of a magnetic strip imbedded in the margin of either or both sides of a regular hard-copy ledger record. It serves as a dual-purpose record that is readable by machine and by people. Ordinary typing of information is translated into computer language on the magnetic strips of the same ledger record. The strip is capable of storing a large variety of information. Normally, some of the data on the strip is used for positioning purposes prior to an entry being made on the ledger record.

The advantages of this medium are unique. They include unlimited access to external memory and to familiar, hard-copy accounting data. Also, simultaneous access to both electronic and human language is provided, thus eliminating separate searching operations. Instructions to the machine can be stored on the magnetic tape ledger records along with human language instructions on the front side, thus expediting the handling and processing work. Changes in instructions are easy to make. In

FIGURE 10–17. The Standard Code for Information Interchange among Information-Processing and Communications Systems.

| b7 | | | | 0 | 0 | 0 | 0 | I | I | I | I |
|---|---|---|---|---|---|---|---|---|---|---|---|
| | b6 | | | 0 | 0 | I | I | 0 | 0 | I | I |
| | | b5 | | 0 | I | 0 | I | 0 | I | 0 | I |
| b4 | b3 | b2 | b1 | | | | | | | | |
| 0 | 0 | 0 | 0 | NULL | DC0 | ƀ | 0 | @ | P | ↑ | ↑ |
| 0 | 0 | 0 | I | SOM | DC1 | ! | I | A | Q | | |
| 0 | 0 | I | 0 | EOA | DC2 | " | 2 | B | R | | U |
| 0 | 0 | I | I | EOM | DC3 | # | 3 | C | S | | N |
| 0 | I | 0 | 0 | EOT | DC4 (STOP) | $ | 4 | D | T | U | A S |
| 0 | I | 0 | I | WRU | ERR | % | 5 | E | U | N | S |
| 0 | I | I | 0 | RU | SYNC | & | 6 | F | V | A | I |
| 0 | I | I | I | BELL | LEM | (APOS) | 7 | G | W | S | G |
| I | 0 | 0 | 0 | FE0 | S0 | ( | 8 | H | X | I | N E |
| I | 0 | 0 | I | HT/SK | S1 | ) | 9 | I | Y | G | D |
| I | 0 | I | 0 | LF | S2 | * | : | J | Z | N | |
| I | 0 | I | I | VTAB | S3 | + | ; | K | [ | E | |
| I | I | 0 | 0 | FF | S4 | (COMMA) | < | L | \ | D | ACK |
| I | I | 0 | I | CR | S5 | – | = | M | ] | | ⊙ |
| I | I | I | 0 | SO | S6 | . | > | N | ↑ | | ESC |
| I | I | I | I | SI | S7 | / | ? | O | ← | ↓ | DEL |

*Courtesy: American Standards Association, Inc. New York*

It consists of eight columns of 16 characters each. Control characters occupy the first two columns, punctuation the third, numbers the fourth, alphabet the fifth and sixth. The last two columns are unassigned, being reserved for future standardization. This material is reproduced from the American Standard Code for Information Interchange, X3,4—1963, copyright 1963 by ASA, copies of which may be purchased from the American Standards Association at 10 East 40th Street, New York, N.Y., 10016.

addition, the stored information on the magnetic tape is introduced into the machine as needed, or on a random access basis, thus permitting greater processing flexibility and more utility of the internal memory of the computer for processing.

## MAGNETIC INK CHARACTERS

Information can be printed with magnetic ink on ordinary paper. This serves as a medium that can be read by either man or machine. This medium is best known for its use in connection with bank checks and deposit slips. As yet it has not been extensively adopted for other types of business paper work, but extensive research is being made in this direction.

Many are of the opinion that in the future, magnetic ink characters will provide the most reliable and most feasible means yet devised for automating single documents. Current thinking is to use an Encoder, which imprints the proper digits, at each point where a charge form, internal debit or credit, and the like are created. Thus, the documents themselves are made the input data, and the need for other medium such as punch cards or tape is eliminated. The imprinting is such that transit, routing, account number, and amount can be included. Estimates indicate the cost would be only about 25 percent that of other appropriate means.

FIGURE 10–18. Type Font Selected for Magnetic Ink Characters.

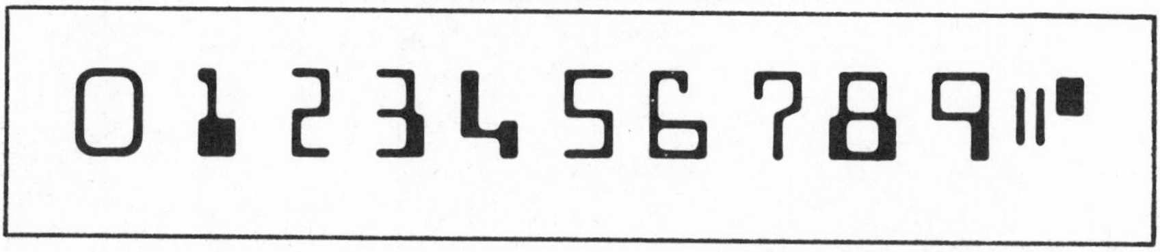

*Courtesy: Moore Business Forms, Inc.,*
*Niagara, N.Y.*

With reference to bank checks the magnetic ink character numerals and characters are the same style and size for all checks. The information conveyed by these imprints is utilized in processing the check in its journey back to its maker, with the proper bank and individual account being debited or credited. The printing is done with an ink containing iron oxides which are electronically charged and read by magnetic ink character-reading equipment. A special type of design is used in order that the characters can be read visually, and maximum machine readability is provided. The printing type employed is of a style called "Font E-13B," illustrated by Figure 10–18. The characters are located on the bank documents in specific areas, such as definite distances from the bottom and right edge, in order that the machines may perform automatically and not have to search for the data.

## THE ANATOMY OF A COMPUTER

The fourth and last area to be discussed in technical considerations of computers is the anatomy of a computer. The top portion of Figure 10–19 diagrams the essential makeup of a computer; the bottom portion, the general appearance of actual units. Different models will vary somewhat in detail and specific purposes, but the fundamentals outlined here are common to all computers.

FIGURE 10–19. Basic Components of an Electronic Computer.

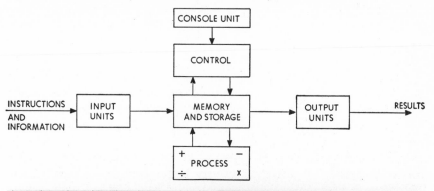

*Courtesy: International Business Machines Corp.,*
*White Plains, N.Y.*

For processing, a series of planned operations are applied to the data. Utilizing an *input unit,* the data in a suitable medium are fed into the computer system. They are stored or retained in a *memory unit* which also stores the programmed instructions. When needed, the data are released to a *process unit* which processes the data. The end result of the processing is obtained from the computer by means of an *output unit.* Directing the entire operation is a control section which is regulated by a *console unit.* By its means, the program, or chain of instructions, are given to the system for each new group of data, required data are sent from the memory unit to the process unit, any step is examined to select the following one, entry of required data by a human operator is made possible, and the processing is started for the next group of data.

From what has just been stated, it follows that a computer is a group of interrelated units forming a totality as stated in the beginning of this chapter. Hence, the term *computer system* is appropriate to identify it.

The units include: (1) input-output, (2) memory and storage, (3) processing, and (4) console. Discussion of each in more detail follows.

## INPUT-OUTPUT UNITS

Input units supply data to the computer. They read data from typed or printed paper, punched cards, perforated tape, magnetic tape, or magnetic ink characters and make them available to memory and storage units of the computer. Output units convert the processed data from the computer by transferring the "computer language" to a suitable form, such as printed records, punched cards, perforated paper tape, or magnetic tape. In the processing of business data very large quantities of input and of output must be handled. Some output units have a speed equivalent to printing the amount of print on one page of this book in about two seconds.

FIGURE 10–20. Illustrating the Use of Buffering in Computer Operation.

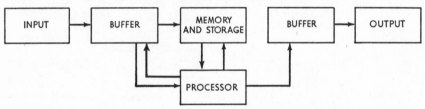

While this is a terrific rate, it is less than the speed of processing the data by a modern computer. This means that input-output operating speeds commonly limit the total computer operations. To alleviate this condition, the computer is used to perform other internal operations on available data while the input data are being fed in, or other devices are employed to perform relatively simple handling and transcribing work. A buffer type of device is also utilized to minimize interruption to the computer processing unit. A buffer is actually an auxiliary storage device which receives data at high speed from the input unit or the processor, returns control to the processor, and then either feeds the data at high speeds to the processor or accepts data at high speeds from the processor. One arrangement is shown in Figure 10–20.

As previously indicated, the term *throughput* and its efficiency are used to explain this same idea of acquiring a maximum of data flow, not in, not out of the computer, but through the computer. In most data processing it is throughout that governs the performance. That is, the quantity of data taken in, processed, and put out as completed results should be maximized for best computer operation.

## MEMORY AND STORAGE UNITS

These units make up the components of the computer capable of storing information which is subject to recall or reference. Varying in type, size, design, and capacity, the memory and storage units also serve to store programmed instructions and to provide work area for editing. All data to be processed must pass through what is commonly referred to as "main storage." This storage is supplemented by secondary storage units, which are not directly accessible to the processing unit but instead are connected to the processing unit through the main storage. Collectively, the total amount of all the data in storage is referred to as a *data bank*.

Each register, or location, in a memory unit holds one *word*. This may consist of up to 20 digits or letters. A word is the basic measurement of storage capacity. Typically, a computer will have 10,000–15,000 registers, but some large scale machines contain over 4 million registers. Since references are made to memory and storage units during the processing, the accessibility and capacity of these units and their operation in the computer are paramount. Specifically, we are concerned about the time required to refer to a specific register (location) and obtain the information from it. This is known as *access time*. In addition, the storage capacity of the memory and storage unit is important for we must have enough registers to handle all the information to be processed.

Memory and storage devices in use today are:

**1. Magnetic Core.** This is illustrated in Figure 10–21. It consists of a series of very tiny cores, or rings of magnetizable material, with wire passed through the opening in two directions. When an electric current is sent through the wires in one direction the core becomes magnetized with a positive charge; in contrast, when the current is sent through the wire in the opposite direction the core becomes magnetized with a negative

FIGURE 10–21. Magnetic Core Plane As Used in a Computer.

charge. Thus, the core stores either a positive or negative value, an on or off condition, which represents a portion of a binary configuration.

Magnetic core offers compact size and relatively low access time. The number of cores in a plane and the number of planes determine the storage capacity. Advances in computer design seem to indicate that, for the magnetic core, future reduction in the cost per storage location is a distinct possibility. Access time now is in excess of 5,000 registers per second.

**2. Magnetic Drum.**    A magnetically coated surface of a cylindrically shaped object is the data-bearing medium of a magnetic drum. The data are coded in the form of the location of magnetic spots or dots on this surface. Figure 10–22 illustrates the magnetic drum means. A magnetic drum is mounted on its axis and is rotated to bring the desired information to a magnetic head that reads the information. More than 1,000 characters can be stored within a square inch of surface and are available at a rate of about 25,000 characters per second. Because of design considerations, the magnetic drum is not used extensively in latest model computers.

FIGURE 10–22. Magnetic Drum Storage. In this illustration there are 200 characters per section, 10 sections per channel, and 40 channels per drum. This makes 80,000 characters per drum.

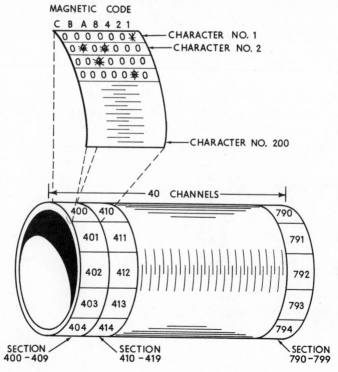

MAGNETIC  CODE

**3. Magnetic Disk.** This medium is similar to a phonograph record. The disks are coated on both sides with ferrous oxide recording material and mounted on a vertical shaft. Data are coded and stored as magnetized spots located in concentric tracks. Reading heads mounted on access arms read or write as directed by the computer controlling unit. Storage efficiency is very satisfactory, the access time is excellent especially when several access arms and read-write heads are used. In some designs, the total image is something like a comb of arms interleaved among a number of possible disks; in other designs, the disk is quite large being some four feet in diameter, thus providing large storage capacity. Figure 10–23 shows disk storage units (right) in a computer system.

FIGURE 10–23. A Computer System Installation Showing Various Units Including That for Disk Storage on the Right.

*Courtesy: International Business Machines Corp.,*
*White Plains, N.Y.*

**4. Magnetic Tape.** This medium can be described as a metallic or plastic ribbon of tape with a magnetic surface. Data for storage are coded and recorded on the tape as spots similar to that of the magnetic drum or disk. Magnetic tape is a common medium for secondary storage. It has too great an access time for wide usage as the medium for main storage.

## PROCESSING UNITS

There is always a central processing unit made up of a control and arithmetic-logical section. The former integrates automatically the operation of the entire computer system in keeping with the program of instructions. This includes controlling the data within the computer such as regulating the input devices, moving data into or out of memory and storage units and between memory and storage units and the arithmetic-logical section, and controlling data entering the output units.

As its name implies, the arithmetic-logical section performs arithmetic and logical operations. These include performing according to algebraic equations and calculus as well as basic processing operations such as reading, sorting, transmitting, comparing, and storing.

## CONSOLE CONTROLLING UNIT

By means of this unit the operator can gain a continual picture of the internal operations of the computer. One can view the console controlling unit as actually an integral part of the central processing unit. The operator can start and stop the computer, interrogate for data in memory units, and load data into the computer by means of the console controlling unit. With reference to programming, it is possible to use sense switches to stop processing or to select predetermined program paths. Hence, the flexibility of the program is increased.

There are also cases where not all the program is stored in and accessible to the computer. In such cases, by means of the console controlling unit, programs can be entered directly into the computer step by step as the processing work progresses. Also, the console controlling unit permits tracing a system or a procedure one step at a time and affords high human operator or external control. In some instances, limited data can be entered directly by control buttons on the console. In addition, limited output information may be obtained, thus enabling the console operator to supervise the computer operation.

A magnetic data inscriber console and a tape cartridge reader make it

FIGURE 10–24. Computer Unit to Enter Information into the System in Order to Update Information to Be Processed.

*Courtesy: International Business Machines Corp., White Plains, N.Y.*

possible to capture information on magnetic tape and then enter it automatically into a computer system. In Figure 10–24, the operator at the console types information on the keyboard to record it on tape housed in a small cartridge. After typing, the cartridge is placed in the reader (right) which feeds the data into the computer system at nearly 1,000 characters a second. This arrangement is specially helpful where punched cards are not required as a record—usually applications involving continual updating of records already stored in the computer in random order.

## QUESTIONS

1. Is there any significant relationship between systems and electronic data processing? Elaborate on your answer.
2. Set forth the main difference between a digital computer and an analog computer.
3. For a computer, name the basic components and function of each component.
4. Explain in some detail the meaning and the designing of programming for computer processing.
5. *a)* Give the binary number for each of the following: 19, 162, 10001.
   *b)* Give the regular number for each of the following binary numbers: 1101, 01100110, 100111.
   *c)* Answer (*a*) above by using four-place binaries for each regular number.
6. Discuss three different memory devices that are used in computers.
7. Identify clearly each of the following:
   *a)* Magnetic tape ledger record.
   *b)* Decision table.
   *c)* Console controlling unit.
   *d)* Nanosecond.
8. Enumerate and give the chief characteristics of three common media for communicating input data for computer processing.
9. Discuss the use of machines that read in the processing of data.
10. Explain the meaning of Figure 10–17 in your own words.
11. Explain the purpose and the methodology illustrated by Figures 10–3 and 10–4.
12. What are the important differences between programming for processing business data and programming for processing scientific data? Elaborate on your answer.

## CASE PROBLEMS

### Case 10–1. Yost Company

During a supervisors' meeting, Miss Dolores Denton was explaining the work of programming for computer processing. She stated that when a computer needs data, it goes to a specific address in its storage facilities, reads the data contained in that address, interprets the data read, and does what the instructions say to do. In computing the weekly pay for an employee, let us assume that the amount equals the total hours worked multiplied by the employee's wage rate less federal income tax withheld less other deductions. If over 40 hours are worked within the given seven-day period, one and one-half times the wage rate is paid for all time over the 40 hours.

Representing the data required to process the payroll is Exhibit 10–1A showing

**EXHIBIT 10–1A.**

| 1. Subtract 40 from the figure in 11. If answer is minus or zero, go to address 2. If plus, go to address 3.<br>Go to 3 | 2. Multiply figure in 11 by figure in 13.<br><br>Go to 7 | 3. Multiply figure in 13 by 40; put answer in 16.<br><br>Go to 4 | 4. Subtract 40 from figure in 11 and multiply by 1½.<br><br>Go to 5 |
|---|---|---|---|
| 5. Multiply answer in 4 by data in 13.<br>Go to 6 | 6. Add answer for 5 to figure in 16.<br>Go to 7 | 7. Subtract figure in 14.<br>Go to 8 | 8. Subtract figure in 15.<br>Go to 9 |
| 9. Record answer.<br><br>Go to 10 | 10. Store new data in 11, 13, 14, and 15.<br>Go to 1 | 11. Value of $A$, total hours worked. | 12. Blank. |
| 13. Value of $B$ employee wage rate. | 14. Value of $C$ federal income tax withheld. | 15. Value of $D$ total other deductions. | 16. Data from 3. |

16 storage addresses. Observe that in a storage box we have information telling (1) where to go to get the needed data, (2) what to do with the data, and (3) where to go to find the next instruction after completing the present one.

Assume for employee No. 333, the data are:

Address 11: 38 hours    (hours worked)
Address 13: $ 4.50    (employee wage rate)
Address 14: $16.20    (federal income tax withheld)
Address 15: $ 8.65    (total other deductions)

Following the instructions beginning with address 1, we get a negative answer (38 minus 40 equals a minus 2). The next operation at address 2, 38 multiplied by $4.50 gives $171 which is calculated by the computer. Address 2 instructs to go to address 7 which tells us to subtract figure in 14, that is, $171 minus $16.20, equals $154.80. Address 7 tells us to go to address 8 which tells us to subtract figure in 15, that is, $154.80 minus $8.65 equals $146.15, and on to address 9 with instructions to record answer.

## Questions

1. Describe the instructions for employee No. 777 who has a wage rate of $5, worked 45 hours, has federal income tax withheld of $21.60, and total other deductions of $9.60.
2. Chart the payroll processing using Figure 10–6 as a guide.

3. Determine the storage addresses for processing the answer to $4X^2 + 8X + 7$. Hint: Develop this expression by a series of elemental steps, starting with $X$.

## Case 10–2.   Gibbons Sales Service

A specific problem for a stored-program of a computer deals with the calculation of sales commissions. Currently, salesmen are paid 5 percent of their sales on the first $100 of sales each day and 10 percent on sales in excess of $100 for the same day. To encourage salesmen to sell the higher-priced units, the plan is being revised so that the higher commission will apply before the $100 daily sales level is attained. To this end, the amount by which the average price of units sold by the salesman exceeds $10 will be subtracted from the $100 sales level to determine the amount on which the 5 percent commission will apply. Commissions on sales in excess of this new level will be 10 percent.

To illustrate, salesman James Hendrick sells $150 worth of merchandise, the average price of which is $15. As the plan now is, salesman Hendrick will receive $10, calculated as follows:

$$
\begin{array}{lr}
\text{5 percent of \$100}\dots\dots\dots\dots\dots & \$\ 5 \\
\text{10 percent of \$ 50}\dots\dots\dots\dots\dots & 5 \\
\hline
\text{Total}\dots\dots\dots\dots\dots\dots\dots & \$10
\end{array}
$$

Under the contemplated revised plan, salesman Hendrick will receive $10.25, calculated as follows:

$$
\begin{array}{lr}
\text{5 percent of (\$100} - \text{[\$15} - \text{\$10])}\dots\dots\dots\dots\dots & \$\ 4.75 \\
\text{10 percent of [\$150} - \text{(\$100} - \text{[\$15} - \text{\$10])]}\dots\dots\dots\dots & 5.50 \\
\hline
\text{Total}\dots\dots\dots\dots\dots\dots\dots\dots\dots\dots\dots\dots\dots & \$10.25
\end{array}
$$

The various detailed operations in proper sequence must be determined so that the work can be processed by the computer.

## Questions:

1. Draw the diagram of computer operations for salesmen's commissions, using the present plan of compensation. Refer to Figure 10–6 and use it as a guide.
2. Draw the diagram for salesmen's commissions, using the contemplated plan of compensation.
3. Briefly discuss the observations you have made in preparing these diagrams, especially from the viewpoint of programming.

chapter **11**

# Computer processing— current developments

Every manager must today ask himself: what can you do that a computer can't do?
—*Frederick Pamp*

GREATER and greater speed, access, accuracy, convenience of use, and virtually unlimited memory are characteristics of the current computer. With the development of micro-miniaturization and integrated circuitry technology, the computer size in relation to ability has been steadily shrinking. The microscopic monolithic integrated circuits now used in computers are dwarfed by an ordinary paper clip. See Figure 11–1. Each tiny circuit is the equivalent of dozens of transitors and other components thus contributing greatly to the computer's smaller size.

Further, the power requirement is lower, and the capacity is higher. Since 1960, it is estimated that while the computer has decreased to one tenth its former size, it has increased its speed 100 times. At the same time, it has been steadily lower in cost to use, easier to use, and many times more versatile.

Already the computer has passed through three technological revolutions, sometimes called "generations." These include: (1) vacuum tubes, 1950–1961, in which speeds were measured in milliseconds (1/1,000 sec.), (2) transistors, 1961–1965, in which speeds were measured in micro-seconds (1/1,000,000 sec.), and (3) integrated circuitry, 1965–, in which speeds are measured in nanoseconds (1/1,000,000,000 sec.). And the "fourth generation" is just around the corner and will vault computer

248

FIGURE 11–1. Tiny Integrated Circuits Used in Today's Electronic Data-Processing Systems Are Shown in Comparison to the Size of an Ordinary Paper Clip. The illustration on the right shows a paper clip and the circuits in actual size.

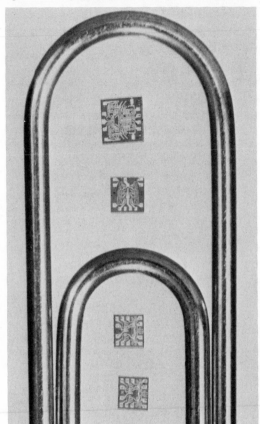

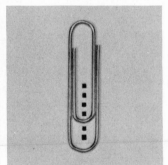

*Courtesy: Burroughs Corp., Detroit*

processing to unbelievable heights. We are certain to see the variety and sophistication of computer use multiply even more rapidly over the coming years. And this will be attained even though, as pointed out earlier, the computing power has been expending rapidly in the United States every year since 1955.

We have witnessed a great proliferation of electronic data-processing units. Figure 11–2 illustrates some of the units in varying combinations that are presently included to meet the user's needs. Illustrated are multiple tape listers, systems memory, magnetic tape clusters, memory input-output cabinets, central processor, on-line disk files, line printers, magnetic ink character reading document sorter and reader, magnetic tape units, paper tape reader, and paper tape punch.

FIGURE 11–2. Illustrating Some of the Many Units Now Available for Electronic Data Processing to Meet the User's Needs.

*Courtesy: Burroughs Corp., Detroit*

## CURRENT COMPUTER CHALLENGE

As the computer is becoming increasingly accessible to those needing its services, the links between it and the business society proliferate both in number, amount, and complexity. The relationship between man and the computer is becoming an integral part of our society. History shows that man and his machines are an unavoidable partnership, and it also reveals that sometimes these are happy unions, sometimes not. Usually man has feared each new machine.

There are, on the one hand, information managers widely enthusiastic about the computer and predicting its ability to help solve all manner of their managerial problems. On the other, there has been a reluctance to utilize computers for work where their capacities would count to greatest advantage. Some lethargy is to be expected, but the computer developments have now advanced to the degree that management members must embrace them. Computer processing is now an established fact of business life, if not the fact. In matching managerial needs with the growing resources of current computer technology lies the greatest portion of the answer to further progress.

A central current challenge of the computer is confrontation with change by managers. Much has been accomplished, but there is still much to be done. The need is to grasp the full scope of the management job in the computer era. The opportunities and demands of the future should be viewed in light of the tremendous computer assistance available and the placement of the computer to work in *strategic areas*. This means a closer bond between management and the computer.

## ON-LINE AND TIME SHARING

Among the most widely publicized recent developments are the advances in being on-line with a computer and the progress in time-sharing applications. Improvements in the early general purpose digital computer greatly expanded its logical power and flexibility. The use of magnetic tape, as a recording and storing means, made possible more complete banks of information, as well as quicker response to information requests. As a result, the use of the computer increased and more and more requests for information were made, and an increasing number of reports were prepared. However, "batch processing" was followed, meaning that "batches" of data were accumulated before making changes in the data stored. The data to be changed, arranged in the same sequence as the master file, were built up and then used to update the master file during a selected period only. This procedure necessitated that for each updating, the entire master file had to be processed, irrespective of the number of changes—obviously a time-consuming and costly task.

This condition sparked technological efforts to develop the "direct-access" technique in which each record in the master file stored in the computer was tagged, and changes required "accessing" only those records requiring change. Further, a sequential order for the input data was unnecessary, thus eliminating sorting work. They could, in fact, be in any order and were processed in the order they were received or "on-line." Hence, the terms *random-access* and *on-line* were born. The improved computer had the ability to search and find a particular record directly and in a minimum of time. Better storage media were developed. The whole development led to converting from a batch approach to an in-line or nonsequential approach, using direct-access equipment.

The feasibility of seeking out directly a particular record at terrific speed and accuracy logically led to greater computer accessibility serving multiple users. Called time-sharing, it means the operation of a computer system so that several users can make use of the computer simultaneously. It makes for highly effective use of the computer. Actually the users queue or wait in line to use the computer, but the computer's operations are so quick that each user has the impression that the computer is solely for him. The maximum convenience of this on-line arrangement is to have the users remotely located, i.e., not all in one geographic area. This means the provision of a communication link such as a telephone line between the computer and a device which permits the user to be connected to the computer. Such a device is commonly called a "terminal device" or just "terminal." The net result is that the user is connected to the computer by a communication link, he is on-line with the computer, and he has the means to carry out information tasks with the computer in a conversational mode. That is, the user and the computer can react to the inquiries and responses by each other. We will say more about communication links and terminal devices in the following pages.

Technical improvements in the hardware now permit the overlapping of input and output and of the processing activities. Results: a great lessening of computer idle time and fuller utilization of its components. Common now is "multiprogramming," a practice whereby programs are segmented and each portion executed before any complete program is finished. In other words, a program segment need not be finished before another is started. Along with multiprogramming has come "multiprocessing" which refers to the processor and is the use of two or more processors in a complete system having a common jointly addressable memory unit. Further, to make time-sharing practical, the modern computer system allocates small time increments on a rotating or sharing basis to users. To do this a computer timer, or hardware feature, is incorporated in the system. Most common practice is to follow a first-come, first-serve basis or some predetermined priority levels.

Paging, memory protection, and dynamic relocatability are impressive sounding software features fundamental to time-sharing. By paging is meant the segmenting of each user's program into pages, or small portions. These pages are stored in a high-speed secondary storage device. When scheduled for processing, the appropriate page is brought from the secondary to the main memory of the computer. This transferring of pages may require considerable time, and significant improvements in having the required data available to the processor are being gained. It is essential that pages transferred be deposited in the correct location of the main memory. To insure this, the memory protection features of the computer are utilized. Further, the meaning of dynamic relocatability is the capacity to put a page into any vacant location in the main memory, thus eliminating the need for always returning each page to its initial location in the main memory. Again flexibility and speed of the system are featured.

## COMMUNICATION LINKS FOR DATA

The concept of data communication is fundamental for an understanding of many modern uses of the computer system. Technically these needs will be met by electronic techniques employing either wire, cable, or microwave channels which are high frequency radio waves. These media have dimensions or physical properties that control the quantity of communication that can be handled per a unit of time. Important among these physical properties are bandwidth of the electronic channel, transportation loss—a kind of friction, and the amount of force or push conveying the data transmitted.

Communication facilities can be leased for exclusive use, leased for the time used only, or purchased. Leasing involves agreements with existing common carriers such as American Telephone and Telegraph Company and Western Union Telegraph Company. Leasing for exclusive use provides a private communication system. If full use is not made of it, the cost is prohibitive and the better arrangement is to lease on an as-used basis. For example, the user dials his call on the regular telephone network and is charged only for the time he utilizes. Under a lease arrangement, certain technical limitations to the transmission quantity he can transmit may be present, but usually they are not serious. Finally, he may purchase his own system. This entails a large first cost for installation and continuous maintenance costs, hence, it is practical for very large users only. Since 1965, private parties may apply and receive exclusive use of radio frequencies in the microwave range, a condition widening the alternatives available to a private communication user.

Outstanding improvements have been won in the communication of data. Increased capacity and bandwidths are now being used. Transmission speed in excess of 1.5 million bits per second are specified, and there are developments being used on the threshold of wide application that are unbelievable. Employing space satellites, for example, and lasers in connection with the quantum aspects of light energy are illustrative of progress in the communication field.

**DATA-PHONE**

Both the transmitting and the receiving of computer coded data are handled by means of regular or private telephone lines. What makes this possible is Data-Phone which accepts data signals from the computer or other data machines in either punched card, perforated tape, or magnetic tape medium; converts these data into proper tones for telephone transmission; and converts tones to data signals for use by the computer or other machine at the receiving station. There are no intermediate steps. An illustration of this equipment is shown by Figure 11–3.

To utilize the Data-Phone, a user picks up the telephone and dials the service number of the particular receiver wanted. An answer or a dial tone signals connection whether or not computer is ready to receive or read information. If ready, an identification card is inserted into the device attached to the telephone, or the required vocal identification is supplied, thus confirming the user's right to transmit. Then the data in the language of the computer—punched cards, perforated tape, or magnetic tape—are fed into the device; and these data are transmitted at speeds of up to

FIGURE 11–3. The Units to the Left Constitute Data-Phone. To the Right, Punched Cards Are Being Prepared.

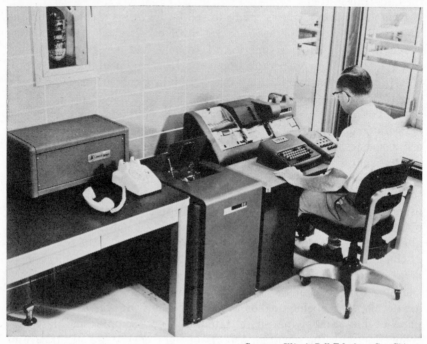

*Courtesy: Illinois Bell Telephone Co., Chicago*

2,700 words a minute directly into the computer. Machines talk to one another, cross-town or cross-country. Payment for each Data-Phone call is made just like an ordinary telephone call. Its potential is believed to be so great that in the not too distant future, conversations between machines over regular telephone lines may equal 70 percent of the total telephone communication.

### TELETYPE

Another widely used data transmission machine is Teletype. It transmits taped information to widely dispersed receiving stations. Units can reproduce anything a computer can express in ASCII code, charts, equations, chemical or mathematical equations.[1] Two-color printing is available allowing questions and answers to be easily distinguishable. Both upper and lower case letters can be used. The speed for both perforated tape and page copy is at a rate of 150 words per minute.

In Figure 11–4, upper left shows this modern versatile transmission

---

[1] ASCII stands for American Standard Code for Information Interchange.

FIGURE 11–4. The Modern Teletype Machine Gives Comprehensive Data Interchange.

*Courtesy: Teletype Corporation, Skokie, Ill.*

Upper left is the heavy-duty complete data terminal, Model 37 ASR (Automatic Send-Receive) unit; upper right is the efficient unit that receives and prints data only. Bottom illustration shows a dependable and well-designed Teletype machine in actual use.

machine; upper right is unit that receives data only. It features impact printing whereby characters are formed from electronically controlled ink nozzles. No buffer storage is required, and long and short printed lines can be intermingled without the use of fill characters. The lower portion of Figure 11–4 illustrates a Teletype machine that expedites and combines data of collecting, handling, and transmitting. Fixed data (customer's name, address, terms, and so forth) are obtained from perforated tape and variable data (date, quantity, and so forth) from the machine's keyboard, thus supplying a finished paper product with carbons for processing and filing. In addition, a perforated composite tape of the complete document is made and can be transmitted simultaneously by the machine to several destinations at the same time (cross-country or cross-office) or to a computer, or placed in storage. The unit illustrated features dual readers that automatically interoperate, a tape punch that simultaneously prints and perforates, and a four-row alphanumeric typewriter keyboard.

## INFORMATION UTILITY

The ability to have on-line, time-sharing, and communicating links has made possible the condition whereby the computer can be asked questions and can answer them through an information network of which the computer is the hub. Thus, an entirely new concept in information automation is developing and with it not only a host of different devices augmenting the input-output means, but also the processing itself. Computers can now be given questions through keyboard sets, drawings on a TV-like screen, or by voice. The answers come back through print, computer media, on a screen, or by voice. A multistation system allows hundreds of stations across the country or even the world to query a centrally located computer from their desk sets and receive instantaneous replies in a preferred form.

This makes for a powerful data communicative capability that can be diagramed something like that shown in Figure 11–5. The transmission control unit sorts the messages and permits the computer processing center to accept simultaneously transmissions up to about 30 lines without the need of a separate stored program device.

This gives rise to the use of an "information utility" which is a service for information similar to a public utility being a service for water, electrical power, or natural gas. To illustrate, there is a law research service having an index of law cases in computer memory. For a nominal fee, lawyers can interrogate the computer by means of a convenient terminal device and receive an immediate reply of relevant cases. Also, a nationwide credit information system is available covering buyers in some 80 large U.S. centers. Similarly, the information utility concept is being used by several companies joined together to share time of one large

FIGURE 11–5. The Computer Facility Existing with the Use of Multi-Terminals.

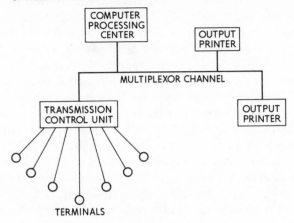

TERMINALS

computer the use of which none of the companies can afford separately. This means that each member company has a direct line to the computer, and can send, receive, and process its data when it wants to and from terminals located within its building. Many feel that this is the future arrangement of the service bureau which now performs information work for clients by bringing the work to its central computer, processing, and then delivering the processed work to the client.[2]

## TERMINAL DEVICES

As already stated, devices connected to the computer by means of communication lines are known as terminal devices. Until recently, most terminal devices were typewriter-like machines, but a wide range of new devices is now available. Which device to use depends upon the characteristics of the work to be done with it. For example, small quantities of data sent frequently may suggest a different device from that where large quantities are sent infrequently. The operator's skill and whether a printed copy is needed are further considerations.

In other words, because of developments in terminals, computer systems are now in the unique position to give users meaningful information at the very moment when the information is wanted. The computer maintains a complete master file that can be drawn from by many persons, for many purposes. Information can be pulled out again and again, as required, and it can also be reprocessed in keeping with the requirements for specific uses.

---

[2] Service bureaus are discussed in detail in chapter 22, p. 522.

Terminal devices serve as either input or output (or both) devices to the computer. Input devices extend from Touch-Tone telephones, tape devices, cathode ray tube (CRT) devices, magnetic ink readers, and optical character readers (OCR) all remotely located from the computer. Various types of documents can be handled; the input data may be financial information, time cards, production or sales data, and cash register tapes. Finger-driven or keyboard-oriented devices are still quite popular, yet their input speeds are directly related to the operator's speed which is far below the capacity of the computer.

In contrast, output terminal devices are highly dependent upon the computer characteristics, especially its speed. The availability of a wide variety of output terminals offers much freedom of choice. Popular are the Touch-Tone telephone, line printers, CRT devices of various types, typewriter-like units, TV-screen units, and audio-response or "answer-back" devices. There is an output terminal available to meet about any information need.

Figure 11–6 shows a visual terminal input-output unit. As the data are typed for input, a proof-copy appears on the screen. This is checked for accuracy and, if error free, the material is released to the computer by simply pressing a push button. Likewise, for output, the information is flashed on the screen where the operator can read it. If a hard or permanent copy is desired, the device will supply it within seconds.

The output printer, shown by Figure 11–7, extends the print-out capability of a computer system. Masters for this printer are prepared directly by the computer output as a by-product such as from a listing of a routine report. From these masters, the printer automatically transfers a clear

FIGURE 11–6. A Visual Terminal Unit.

*Courtesy: Burroughs Corp., Detroit*

FIGURE 11–7. This Transfer Printer Transfers a Direct Impression onto Unit Forms. It uses a master prepared at normal operating speeds of the computer. Hence, the computer print-out capability is increased.

*Courtesy: Addressograph Multigraph Corp., Cleveland*

and legible impression directly on the documents or forms which are positioned quickly. Certain attachments are available that convert the speed of this printer to speeds of up to 7,200 impressions an hour.

Voice recognition has reached the development stage where it is becoming in common use. The "answer-back" has been possible for some time, but this is being extended to vocal inquiries and responses to a computer system. Thus, true conversation with the computer is a reality and utilized where it is believed to be superior for a particular application. To illustrate, a large department store in Chicago now utilizes a computer-directed credit authorization system that gives a verbal reply to a salesperson's inquiry in less than 30 seconds. All sales-floor telephones in 12 different stores are hooked to the central computer which can handle 10,000 credit approvals daily. However, the computer's capacity is so large that credit applications use less than 5 percent of its time. Hence, the computer is used to prepare over 6 million customer statements a year, write reminder notices to customers, print sales promotion material, and identify probable bad debt accounts. In another example, an employee in a branch factory in Colorado can obtain informaton about inventory from the company's computer in Cincinnati by dialing a telephone number. Seconds later he hears a verbal reply to his inquiry.

Portable terminals, about the size of a large book, enabling an individual to question the computer from his desk or from his home by simply plugging it in the telephone line, stimulates the imagination as to future changes in our present mode of doing things. Such units are offered on the market. They can create, for example, entirely new approaches to managerial control and a different mode of operation for technical and research personnel. And its educational applications appear limitless.

FIGURE 11–8. A Remote Computer Terminal.

*Courtesy: Transcom Inc., Bloomfield, Conn.*

An interesting remote computer terminal provides instant verification of data sent or received and a permanent printed record in tape medium of every transmission. Input and output are accomplished by a push-button phone keyboard, and the machine is also effective for a voice answerback medium. Figure 11–8 shows this machine. The numbers on the tape indicate the following: 4–324, the account number 324; 71–5426.31, the receivable debt of $5,426.31; and 61–2869, the date of February 8, 1969.

## PERIPHERAL EQUIPMENT

Strictly speaking, any unit of equipment distinct from the central computer system makeup can be considered peripheral equipment or that which surrounds or is on the edge of the computer. Today, we do not think about just the computer. Our thoughts must be more comprehensive and include those important units that augment the computer and give flexibility to information technology. It has been estimated that by 1972, some three fourths of the expenditures for a computerized work will be for peripheral equipment.

The validity of this prediction will depend in great measure upon what is considered peripheral. Actually, this is a somewhat academic question. We know peripheral equipment is required and for some time have used machines of this type, that is, to convert information from one medium to another, interpret data, and so forth. Some classify all terminal units as peripheral, an assumption certain to increase the peripheral population. One may attempt to consider peripheral units (1) closely related to the computer processing and (2) in close proximity to the central computer so that a public-type of communication link is unnecessary. Following this line of thought, terminals are excluded from the peripheral classification for they normally do not meet either of these criteria. In this discussion we will include several units under the peripheral banner because they seem to belong in this category. But it is possible to justify their inclusion elsewhere.

## COMPUTER GRAPHICS

The area of computer graphics refers to a user communicating with a computer by means of graphic symbols such as lines and curves. In essence, sketching and drawing are added to the input-output of a computer. A cathode ray tube is used. Drawing directly on the scope face of this tube with an electronic stylus pencil permits communication with the computer in a form of graphic symbols. Further, the computer displays graphic information for interpretation by man. Computer graphics appear to offer substantial reduction for the design process. All design work is tentative—an assumed design is determined, stresses are calculated, and the strength and cost properties are ascertained. If not entirely satisfactory or to improve, if satisfactory, a modified design is assumed and the same calculations are made for it. Finally, the so-called best design is evolved. Man's design efforts are tentative and approximate, but a computer works with exact data toward a specific goal. As yet, we have not developed a practical means for having the computer design primarily because designing is creative and we don't know exactly for what we are looking. However, the computer can greatly assist the human designer in his trial-and-error approach.

Given restraints by the sketches on the scope face, the computer can be helpful in determining how this mechanical arrangement will probably perform. Most of the possible design parameters can be analytically determined, designs formulated and tested, and drawings provided. The designer gains increased analysis capability which is more complete in both scope and detail than previously attainable. Hence, favorable results include improved product quality, elimination of prototype developments, and enormous savings of design time. More precisely, it is believed that with success in near future developments of computer graphics, the design time for a new automobile might decrease from two years to five months. The use of hard-copy drawings will be minimized. Needed visual information will be obtained from a display terminal tied to the central computer. In turn, this will lessen the errors arising from outdated drawings—highly significant in a dynamic industry. Further, so-called interference problems will be substantially reduced. These problems arise when the specialty work of many designers is assembled into the one master design and the resultant misfits and noncoordinated components are eliminated.

## DIGITAL PLOTTING SYSTEMS

We know that a computer can produce thousands of pages of printed output in a single day. This processed information results from calculations and comparisons, updating of data, and the working out of thousands of courses of action. Because it can do all these things it has been accepted as a management tool. But it can do even more. The information needed from the usage of output data can be produced in readily compre-

FIGURE 11–9. Hookups and Machines to Obtain Computer Output Data in Graphic Form.

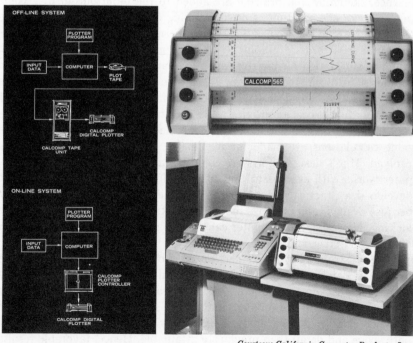

*Courtesy: California Computer Products, Inc.,*
*Anaheim, Calif.*

hended chart or graphic form—automatically. This is accomplished by means of a CALCOMP digital plotter. In some cases, particularly for the larger computer, the signal instructions are received by a medium for subsequent use by the plotter off-line. In other cases, direct coupling can be followed with a special adapter used to connect the computer output to a form suitable for driving the plotter. The hookups are shown in the left portion of Figure 11–9. In the right bottom portion of this figure is a time-sharing remote plotter working in conjunction with a teletypewriter for two-way communication with a distant computer. The view in the lower right position is a close-up of the plotter. Data for preparation of a learning curve are being plotted. This is a drum-type plotter. The completed chart is removed in a manner similar to that of taking a piece of paper from a roll of wrapping paper. There are also plotters in which fan-fold paper is stored flat in the unit with the plotter moving over this flat horizontal area.

Significant applications include emergency drawings, isometric-piping drawings, economic charting and analysis, critical path drawings, and ray tracing. The list of applications is constantly expanding. It is not necessary to spend long and tedious hours manually plotting data into graphic form. Figure 11–10 illustrates a geologic chart produced automatically by CALCOMP plotter from computer data.

FIGURE 11–10. Example of Chart Drawn Automatically from Data in a Computer.

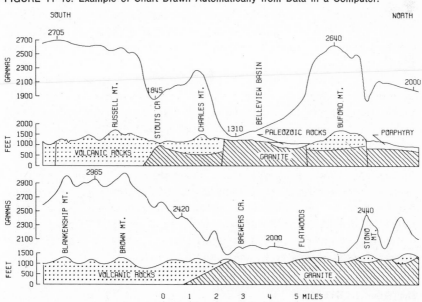

STRUCTURE AND LITHOLOGY FROM AEROMAGNETIC PROFILES OVER THE ST. FRANCOIS MOUNTAINS

*Courtesy: California Computer Products, Inc.,*
*Anaheim, Calif.*

The plotter can also be connected to a cathode ray display terminal, thus expanding the utility of the terminal in scientific application and also making it possible to produce a hard copy of any image on the display screen. A button is pressed on the keyboard of the display terminal and the chart or diagram is produced by the plotter.

The plotting is produced by movement of a pen relative to the surface of the paper. Each input impulse causes a very minute step on either the $X$-axis or the $Y$-axis. A deflection on the $X$-axis is produced by motion of the drum, on the $Y$-axis by motion of the pen carriage. Signals raise and lower the pen as required. Each step can be in any one of the 24 basic step combinations or directions made up of its $X$ and $Y$ values, i.e., the basic step direction for a plotted point can be any of 24 directions within the 360-degree quadrant made up of $X$ and $Y$ values of .01 or .005 inches.

## DIRECT-DIAL FROM TERMINAL TO COMPUTER

Efficient management reporting, faster customer service, and better utilization of a computer are possible by use of a machine which integrates an information network. The concept involves the capturing of data at the point of origin for processing by computer and transmitting these data to the computer center via telephone lines. In essence, the arrangement serves as a two-way data transmission between company field locations and its computer center. In addition, any terminal of the system can send to and receive from other terminals, store and retrieve data, double as an automatic typewriter for writing letters and reports, and serve as an extra desk and typewriter station whenever not in use as a terminal.

Figure 11–11 demonstrates an employee typing a sales order. She is receiving the phoned-in order from a local salesman or customer. As information is typed it is recorded on a magnetic tape cartridge shown in the open drawer of the desk. Each cartridge has a capacity of 200,000 characters. At the end of the day, the stored data for all the orders that day are transmitted over the telephone lines to the computer center hundreds or thousands of miles away. There the data are ready for instant input without additional conversion steps. The operator has at her command a memory unit for storing and retrieving information frequently used in an order to expedite her typing of the order. This memory unit is at the right end of the desk in the illustration. The system is also capable of receiving data prepared by the computer center.

## VIATRON SYSTEM

The Viatron System 21 features distributed data processing whereby the user can distribute the capabilities of the computer to those places in

FIGURE 11–11. The Communitype System Features a Removable Tape Cartridge That Has Extensive Storage Capacity (in Desk Drawer) and a Memory Unit (Right on Desk) for Retrieving Fixed Data Such As Programmed Formats Equivalent to Having 1,000 Punched Cards at Your Fingertips.

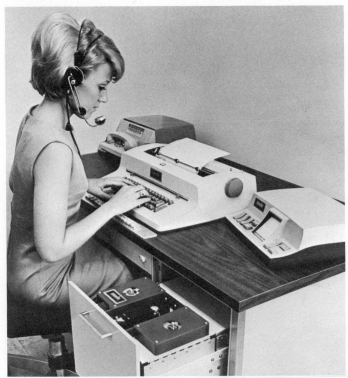

*Courtesy: Communitype Corp., New York*

an organization where they are needed most—executives, engineers, clerks, warehouse supervisors, and sales office personnel. The elements of the system are a display unit, a microprocessor, and a keyboard. The display unit shows either the results of keyboard entry, for visual verification, or the contents of a Viatape cartridge in which data are stored. Basic to the system is the microprocessor into which are built various microprograms designed to satisfy the specific application. Four input-output channels are tied to the microprocessor, two of which are for reading or writing from the recorders, and the other two for in- and out-putting data to other devices. A control panel on the microprocessor console permits the operator to control operations of the recorders, monitor the operation, and select information to be shown on the visual screen. Figure 11–12 shows the configuration of the components and the appearance of the unit in operation.

FIGURE 11–12. Employee Using the Basic Components of Viatron's Basic System 21. The system can be used in either a centralized data-processing facility or in a remote site.

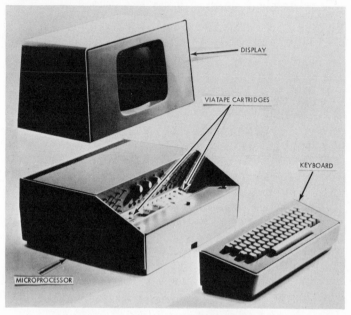

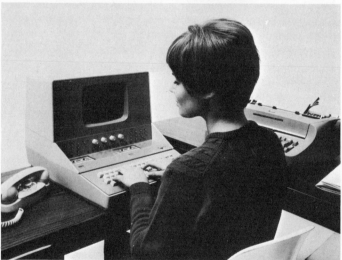

*Courtesy: Viatron Computer Systems Corp.,*
*Burlington, Mass.*

The Viatron system features a very low cost package for data entry, communication, display, storage, and retrieval. Its proponents envision the economic feasibility of its use on many desks—where the information is needed quickly. For example, data in a form for reports or insertion into a computer are expedited with a minimum of programming. On the screen may be displayed a blank invoice so the clerk just fills in the proper entries. The unit can be tied into larger data-processing systems by connection to direct wire links or to telephone lines.

## AUTOMATED CARD CONTROL TERMINALS

In this age of information automation, we are seeing more and more applications of input from cards conveying data on credit, security, time payment, reorder, production control data, and so forth. This input data must be compared with information stored in a computer for the requested action to take place, that is, grant the credit or ship the merchandise.

Consider the example of accounts receivable. The sales slip is entered on the cash register for store accounting, and customer's credit card and clerk's card are inserted in a Decitron Communication Systems Terminal. See Figure 11–13. The dollar amount and the type of transaction are keyed in the terminal unit machine and the transmit button is pushed. The computer checks credit. If OK, the transaction is recorded and stored in computer for billing. Later the computer prepares the customer's statement.

## AUTOMATING THE HANDLING OF CUSTOMER INQUIRIES

A large public utility receives annually nearly a million and a half customer inquiries. About one third of this number concerns a bimonthly bill, and most of the balance relates to application for or discontinuance of service. Although the average daily work load is 6,000 inquiries, during certain peak periods as many as 2,000 inquiries an hour may come in. Prior to automation, the manual system followed consisted of clerks looking up information in a central file, a time-consuming task. If the inquiry came to a branch office, the branch clerk telephoned the central group for needed information. Further, if the customer did not know his account number, a manual search in the customer directory was required. On service calls, the customer's name and address and the nature of the request were taken, the requests were filed, and promises made to return the call with confirmation or answer.

An on-line computer system handling both billing and customer service inquiries was installed. Large random access storage and speed of operation were considered essential. The data base includes customer name,

FIGURE 11–13. Diagram of Steps Taken to Verify and Record Instantaneously an Accounts Receivable Transaction and Machine Used for This Purpose.

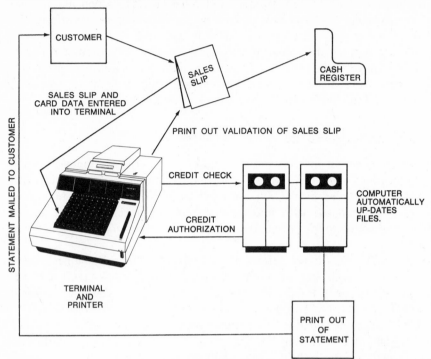

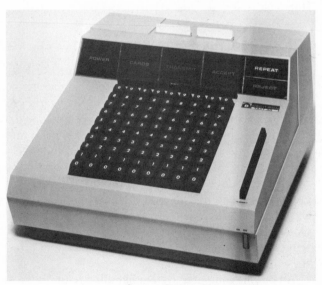

*Courtesy: Decitron Communication Systems, Inc., Brooklyn.*

address, one-year billing history, credit history, as well as meter, transaction, and service records. Over 100 terminal display units were included in the network with about 75 percent of them located in the central office, the balance in local offices. An incoming call is routed to an open line display terminal and the clerk determines the purpose of the call and the caller's identity. Within seconds all data pertaining to the call are flashed on the screen and the inquiry can be handled on the spot. Complicated cases are referred to higher clerks who give the solution in a return call to the customer. If incoming calls are not "on display" within one minute, they are referred to separate telephones handled by backup operators. Also, the screen shows any pending orders on the account, thus duplication of inquiries, a condition arising when several members of a family inquire about the same account, is eliminated. Output data are typed on the terminal's keyboard; the data are later printed out by means of a printer. Subsequently service calls are dispatched by radio-telephone to a service man in the field. In contrast, data on processed and billing inquiries are routed to the proper computer for required handling.

The loop from inquiry to service fulfillment is followed. Upon completion of required services, the field man fills out a form which is read optically and the data put into a computer where service required is matched with service given. Thus, the service history of an account is updated and is accessible when desired. Complete control over servicing is afforded, such as the efficiency of the repairmen doing the work noted, questions answered, whether additional training is needed, the proper replacement of parts used, and the frequency of repairs on an account.

## COMPUTER TRAFFIC CONTROL

Traffic flow, an enigma of modern society, is being regulated by a computer system. Traffic flow information is transmitted to a computer from pressure-sensitive devices imbedded in the pavement at strategic locations. This information is analyzed and the best different traffic-light timing sequences are determined in keeping with changing traffic demands. In other words, the traffic-light configuration is adjusted to maximize the flow of traffic. As traffic needs vary so does the system of traffic lights. The computer serves as a monitor. From the overall traffic viewpoint, engineers claim waiting time for lights to change is reduced 20 percent, the number of stops by about 10 percent, and a decline in accidents by nearly 10 percent.

A specialized application of total traffic control is that pertaining to better entering onto a freeway or busy expressway. Known as ramp metering, the arrangement calls for sensing devices along the right lane to detect gaps in traffic during peak hours. When a gap is detected, the computer changes a red ramp traffic light to green. The number of cars permitted to move at one signal change is determined by the size of the traffic gap. Experience shows higher traffic volume, and a lower rush-hour accident rate are achieved. The system is expandable to include the prediction of traffic stackups, precise locations of scenes of accidents, and the operations of traffic signals to warn and guide motorists of traffic impediments ahead.

## MEDICAL PRACTICE AND THE COMPUTER

Computers are assisting physicians to cope with the explosive growing body of medical paper work problems. Assistance in the diagnosing of disease is provided by the analysis of questions used for identifying medical problems. Further, this computer arrangement can be used for training by employing computer-simulated patients. For a given list of symptoms, the computer promptly furnishes a list of all diseases. The heart condition of patients in Michigan can be analyzed by computers in Boston via long-distance transmission of cardiograms. In a large medical center in New Jersey, a computer maintains patient records, handles drug orders, and selects dietary meals for patients. Assistance is provided so that comprehensive physical checkups can be given 300 people a day. Each checkup includes over 30 tests including blood tests, chest X ray and eye examinations, all completed in less than three hours. Laboratory results are fed into a computer as the patient goes from station to station. If abnormalities are found, additional tests are specified.

Blood tests, important in the early detection of disease, are now computerized and are ten times faster than when laboriously done by hand. A small sample of blood is divided into minute specimens upon which a dozen tests, from albumin to sugar levels, are performed. One computer can service many hospitals and at a cost substantially less than if each hospital had its own computer for such testing purposes. It is the belief of many hospital administrators that the popular future arrangement will be a cooperative program which allows 10 to 12 hospitals to share common computer facilities of improving patient service and hospital administration. And eventually perhaps a nationwide hospital information system will be in operation to benefit patients, members of the medical profession, and hospital administrators.

## ADVERTISING DECISIONS BY COMPUTER

The best selections of advertising campaigns and media schedules for various prospective products represent tough decisions faced by every advertising executive. A few calculations from data on a rate card are insufficient. Today, there are variable information on area rates, special editions, discounts, premiums, and the like. Further, the effectiveness of the advertising media varies with the type of product or service. In this situation, the computer is used to simulate activities in hundreds of hypothetical situations in order to select the superior decision. To illustrate, a computer can be used to analyze vast quantities of market and product data and recommend what advertising media should be used and how many dollars to spend in order to achieve predetermined marketing goals. Basically, the purpose is to minimize subjectivity in marketing decisions that involve a high residue of measurable factors.

The purchasing cycle for a particular product usually merits intensive study. The speed with which the product is purchased measured in terms of (1) steady buyers, (2) casual buyers, and (3) potential buyers reveals the purchasing cycle. The potential buyers' group is calculated by comparing the purchasing cycle with pertinent data of the major marketing or trading areas of the United States, which data typically concern people by number, age, income, sex, and family size for each area. Then, the potential buyer's group is compared against potential media. Repeated exposures within a given media, the extent of motivation to purchase what they see or read about, and local marketing costs and situations are taken into account. The result is an evaluation of the number of potential buyers against the number of buyers' needs, and against the type and schedule of media available. The printed report shows a complete breakdown of a potential product marketing program. This entails a tremendous amount of work, some six million calculations being necessary to provide such information. But this is accomplished in a relatively short time by the computer.

## COMPUTER PROCESS CONTROL (CPC)

In this the computer starts actions and acts upon the results of such actions, thus achieving complete automation of a series of activities such as exist along a production line. Under this arrangement, the computer makes a running analysis of the process and compensates for changes as they occur. The general arrangement followed is graphically represented by Figure 11–14.

The computer is connected to many and various instruments which provide pertinent readings on variables critical to the process. These readings are analyzed, related, and processed at fantastic speeds, thus recording if the process is progressing satisfactorily or what, if any, part of the production process needs remedial action. If the latter is the case, the computer dispatches back through the communicative network a series of actions that cause individual controls on various pieces of production equipment to make necessary adjustments.

Different processes put different demands upon CPC. Chemical industries typically require a large number of calculations; other industries

FIGURE 11–14. The General Arrangement for Computer Process Control (CPC).

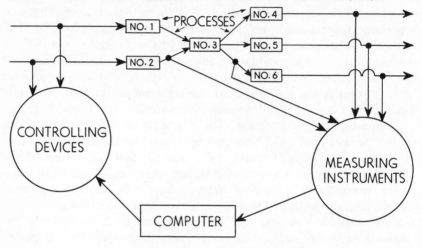

may necessitate relatively few checks, but they must be made with great rapidity. Complete CPC may cost upward of $1 million, depending upon the complexity of the process. But CPC can be achieved by stages, starting with the computer being used, not as an integral part of the process, but to assist human operators who have complete control of the manufacturing process. Gradually more and more control is given the computer.

Illustrative of CPC is the adaption of blast furnace operations in steel mills to computer control. This arrangement enables the blast furnace operators to know the ideal and exact conditions for the most efficient operations for producing the best-quality finished product. Indications of difficulties and mechanical failures are detected in advance. A typical blast furnace consumes daily 4,800 tons of raw materials, mainly iron ore, limestone, and coke, and turns out 1,700 tons of iron. The grade of ore, quality of limestone, amount of heat, iron composition and purity desired, and a host of other variables are representative of the type of information which must be properly coordinated to operate the furnace in keeping with predetermined goals.

### INVENTORY CONTROL DATA PROCESSING

Like many applications, the work of inventory control, as it is normally thought of, must be modified so that it is in a form that meets the physical operational requirements of computer handling. In this respect, a common arrangement for inventory control by computer is the cumulative or "cum" system, in which all activity is directed toward the new cum or total quantity. Information can be thought of as being gathered by degrees, and quantities increase in number until the entire records are started again from a new base. In essence, if cum is available, inventory is available at the proper time and in the proper quantity.

An understanding of the basic operations performed is essential for comprehending the working of the inventory control data processing. Hence, before discussing what the computer does, a brief description of the basic operations will be given. The initial step is the sales forecast, which is reviewed monthly and adjusted in light of market conditions. A "release for production" is made against the sales forecast, which release authorizes procurement of materials, production schedules, and final assembly. Comparison is made between the cumulative requirements and the amount available. If the latter exceeds the former, no order for parts is entered. On the other hand, if the amount available is less than the cumulative requirements, the deficit is filled by ordering the parts.

**The Data Utilized.** In Figure 11–15, the top illustration shows that for Model 124, the amount released is 5,000; shipped, 2,400; February scheduled shipment, 1,000; March scheduled shipment, 1,500. Thus, the cum for February is 3,400 and for March, 4,900. The data are converted to weekly amounts, as indicated by the middle illustration of Figure 11–15. So far, our data are by model, and each model may require a number of components. Quite probably, some of these components will be common to several models. Our need is to determine the total number of each component that will be required for the scheduled product mix represented by the various models. Assume the monthly data illustrated by the bottom illustration of Figure 11–15 represent these values. The amounts required will be determined primarily on the sales forecasts of each model, with important modifications for in-plant lead time. This is to say that some components are required for subassemblies, others for the final assembly; those for subassemblies must be available in the plant for consumption before the components intended for final assembly. In many instances, the same type of component will be used for the subassembly and again in the final assembly.

For each component, comparisons are now made between the cum and the availability. Based on this comparison, the decision to "order schedule" is determined. Referring to Figure 11–16, the cum requirements for component 1 are 13,400 for the "used to date." As indicated in Figure 11–15, the requirements for the first week of February are 1,500, making the cum 14,900; for the second week, 1,500, making the cum 16,400; and so forth. The availability of component 1 is 22,000, which, compared to the cum of February week A, shows ample supply; hence, no order schedule would be made, and the value of 0 is entered under week A. In like manner, it can be seen that no order schedule for component 1 would be issued during any of the weeks of February. Even the last week shows

FIGURE 11–15. Data Utilized in "Cum" Method of Inventory Control.

| Model | To Date Release | To Date Cum Shipped | February Release | February Cum Shipped | March Release | March Cum Shipped |
|---|---|---|---|---|---|---|
| 124 | 5,000 | 2,400 | 1,000 | 3,400 | 1,500 | 4,900 |

| | February Week A | | February Week B | | February Week C | | February Week D | | March Week A | | March Week B | | March Week C | | March Week D | |
|---|---|---|---|---|---|---|---|---|---|---|---|---|---|---|---|---|
| | R* | CS* | R | CS | R | CS | R | CS | R | CS | R | CS | R | CS | R | CS |
| | 250 | 2,650 | 250 | 2,900 | 250 | 3,150 | 250 | 3,400 | 375 | 3,775 | 375 | 4,150 | 375 | 4,525 | 375 | 4,900 |

Component 1 for All Models

| | February Week A | | February Week B | | February Week C | | February Week D | | March Week A | | March Week B | | March Week C | | March Week D | |
|---|---|---|---|---|---|---|---|---|---|---|---|---|---|---|---|---|
| | R | CS | R | CS | R | CS | R | CS | R | CS | R | CS | R | CS | R | CS |
| | | 1,500 | | 1,500 | | 1,500 | | 1,500 | | 1,625 | | 1,625 | | 1,625 | | 1,625 |

* R = Release; CS = Cum Shipped.

FIGURE 11–16. Component 1 for All Models

| Used to Date | February | | | |
| --- | --- | --- | --- | --- |
| | Week A | Week B | Week C | Week D |
| Cum requirements..........13,400 | 14,900 | 16,400 | 17,900 | 19,400 |
| Available................22,000 | 22,000 | 22,000 | 22,000 | 22,000 |
| Order schedule............. | 0 | 0 | 0 | 0 |

the cum will be 19,400, with 22,000 available. Production planning is quite unlikely to match exactly sales forecasts because of the varying need for finished goods inventory, variations in estimated lead times, rates of production, and capacity to produce exactly to requirements. But the system provides reasonable checks between weekly needs and availability, so that deviations are kept within practical limits; thus, satisfactory inventory control if achieved.

*Automating the Process.* A computer equipped with a random access is used. The various accounts may be posted in random order. For example, interrelated transactions might involve (1) securing raw materials, for which the transaction is posting receipts to raw material record; (2) making up subassemblies, for which the transactions are posting production of subassemblies to subassembly account and deducting components used in subassemblies from components accounts; or (3) shipping finished goods, which requires for the record a deduction from the finished goods account by the amount of finished goods shipped.

In this application, the equivalent of 62,500, 80-column punched cards, or 5,000,000 characters, is stored in the storage device of the computer. A total of 50,000 different records of 100 characters each constitutes the master information and previous balances. These 50,000 are prorated among the types of basic information and constitute addresses or identities by which specific records can be located by the computer. This is shown graphically by Figure 11–17.

*The Processing by Computer.* Each part contained in the bill of materials for each model has a parts record stored in a separate section in the computer. For example, the parts record for a purchased part contains the part number; the percentage allowance for loss, waste, or spoilage; the origin; the cum receipts; and the balance due on open purchase orders.

For the given period of 13 weeks, a master schedule or sales forecast by week by models is punched on a tape which is fed into the computer. This schedule is first processed by a bill-of-material section, or portion showing the materials needed. The computer calculates requirements by periods, namely, by multiplying usage by schedule by shrinkage factor. Next, the

FIGURE 11-17. Each of the 50,000 Records Has an Address or Specific Location on a Disk of the Storage Unit of the Computer.

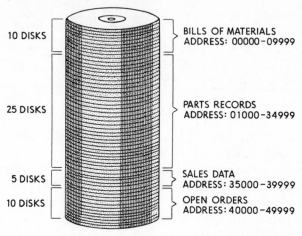

10 DISKS — BILLS OF MATERIALS ADDRESS: 00000-09999

25 DISKS — PARTS RECORDS ADDRESS: 01000-34999

5 DISKS — SALES DATA ADDRESS: 35000-39999

10 DISKS — OPEN ORDERS ADDRESS: 40000-49999

schedule period is adjusted for lead time on each piece part. These data are carried forward to the parts record, where they are stored awaiting information from other models. As this information from other models becomes available, it is combined with other like information so that the cum requirements by periods are accumulated on the parts record for each component. When and how much to purchase or make is determined by comparison of the accounts scheduled with the amounts available for each component, as discussed above.

What was previously long, tedious labor required for inventory control is now accomplished in several hours by means of the computer. In addition, it is now a simple matter radically to revise the production program. Information can be quickly obtained regarding the position materialwise if a new production plan is attempted. Shortages and excesses of materials are pointed out, and the status of all components is revealed.

## THINGS TO COME

Experiences of the present, although limited, suggest possible changes to be expected due to information technology. It appears that many of our present ways of performing information work fall by the wayside. More and more of our writing and calculating will be done automatically by machines which will operate from sound. Communicative devices will revolutionize further the distribution of information. Common will be permanent networks of central computers hooked to many terminals.

These computer facilities will form the bases of major processing means of the future. New concepts will prevail in the filing and storing of records. Papers common to our present office will be replaced by such media as miniaturized pictures and electronic impulses.

It is reasonable to predict that decision making will be improved. The quantification of data will not only improve the amount and the quality of facts but will reveal pertinent relationships among them. The availability of a wider range of alternatives evaluated factually could reduce decision making based either on intuition or on historical data projection. Also, decision making will be carried out on a broader base. Company goals, not departmental goals, will be stressed; and the interaction of decisions pertaining to departments will be emphasized.

Lastly, it is logical to state that the information manager's work will take on greater importance. With larger amounts of information handled, the various means available for its accuracy and timely processing, and the increasing demand for information, it is safe to state that information management will gain greater status and win more widespread acceptance than known heretofore.

## CONCLUSIONS ON COMPUTERS

To take advantage of current information technology, managers must analyze their operations in detail and completeness. When this is done, the common result is that many of the information segments can be done better by a computer. The tendency is to underestimate the significance of computer technology and likewise to understate the problems involved in harnessing this tremendous tool to bear on the needs of the enterprise. Today, we have information power that will not be denied. The organization that does not utilize and develop it simply will be passed by.

To reiterate, office automation stimulates thinking of information work as a whole, not just of a component of it. The larger concept is emphasized. Automation is geared to volume. There must be a sufficient quantity of work and, frequently, this means grouping the components and performing the work for all. Office automation offers numerous benefits, yet difficult decisions are required and deeply entrenched habits and beliefs must be dispelled. Office automation necessitates high caliber management.

Finally, remember that change is always taking place; the direction and degree of this change in the way information work is accomplished is, and will inevitably be, modified by the computer. Everywhere, the tempo of technological advance has quickened. The need for more and more information is being accelerated. Discoveries not yet imagined will be made. In such an era, the computer will occupy a role of increasing importance in the hopeful advances of human progress. Properly understood and applied, the computer will assist man in employing his talent, his time, and his ideas most effectively in the pursuit of values which make man so distinctive and his accomplishments so significant.

## QUESTIONS

1. What are terminal devices and what is their contribution in the handling of information?
2. Relate your understanding of "on-line" computer processing pointing out its relative importance in electronic data processing.
3. Explain Figure 11–9 in your own words relating what a digital plotting system is and the meaning of the diagram at the top of this figure.
4. Do you feel that the major areas of computer applications can be considered fairly well explored as of the present? Substantiate your answer.
5. Identify each of the following:
    *a)* Computer graphics.
    *b)* Multiprogramming.
    *c)* Computer process control (CPC).
    *d)* Data-Phone.
6. To what extent do you feel "information utilities" will develop. Justify your viewpoint.
7. Describe the work performed by the machine shown in Figure 11–13.
8. Discuss the use of Teletype in computer data transmission.
9. Could the cum method of inventory control be used for noncomputer data processing in this managerial area? Why?
10. Discuss the subject of "Medical Practice and the Computer."
11. Consult several business periodicals and read a report on a CPC installation. Relate the interesting aspects of this installation and what would seem to be the limiting factors of additional installations of this particular type.
12. Other than the applications described in this chapter, give examples of computer usage based on your reading or work experience. Discuss.

## CASE PROBLEMS

### Case 11–1.   Griffin Wholesale Company

PETER K. GRIFFIN (*president*): I have asked you to make this call in order that I might discuss with you personally the possible uses of a computer in our company.

RICHARD C. ALM (*representative of National Computers, Inc., NCI*): I am delighted to meet you Mr. Griffin and to give you any help that I can.

GRIFFIN: Good. You know we are in the wholesale hardware business. This is our 47th year in business. This company was founded by my paternal grandfather, Arnold C. Griffin.

ALM: I see.

GRIFFIN: Let me get down to business by asking you what wholesalers such as ourselves are doing with computers today. Is that a fair question?

ALM: It certainly is. And I'll try to answer it. The computer can be thought of as an all-purpose information machine. I have selected data from a copy of a recent study that is pertinent and will interest you. (*Takes Exhibit 11–1A from briefcase and hands it to Mr. Griffin.*)

First of all let me state that these replies are based on a representative group of wholesalers and for the most part will apply to a business such as yours. May I add that nearly one half of the wholesalers are using computers and the user group is mainly the larger wholesaler. This follows because the computer is geared to volume, and proper information is of special importance to management of these firms in order to reach the best decisions.

EXHIBIT 11–1A. Computer Usage by Hardware Wholesalers.

| Data-Processing Function | Use by Wholesalers |
|---|---|
| 1. Invoicing | 90% |
| 2. Accounts receivable | 67 |
| 3. Accounts payable | 52 |
| 4. Customer analysis | 85 |
| 5. Sales by type merchandise | 58 |
| 6. Vendor analysis | 72 |
| 7. Picking tickets | 68 |
| 8. Out reports | 81 |
| 9. Stock status | 70 |
| 10. Inventory control | 64 |

As you can see, invoicing is a common application. 90 percent of the wholesalers having computers use them for this application. Accounts receivable is 67 percent.

GRIFFIN: Yes. Interesting. Very interesting. What is number seven, Picking tickets?

ALM: Picking tickets? Yes. By means of a computer, wholesalers have analyzed sales by item and by line to compute the proper size to provide maximum efficiency of warehouse space. The size of the item, the average . . .

GRIFFIN (*interrupting*): Pardon me. Will you say that again, please? I didn't get it.

ALM: Certainly. Wholesalers have used a computer to analyze sales by line and by item and from these data have calculated mathematically what the proper bin size or space allotted to each item should be for maximum space utilization. Average inventory, frequency of orders, weight of items, and other selected factors are used. In other words, the warehouse is replanned based on the physical characteristics of the merchandise.

You can find out how many picking trips are made to what bins of what items to determine whether those items should be relocated in the warehouse to speed receiving and shipping. Also work loads can be scheduled so that the movement of goods between sections and floors maximizes warehouse performance.

The picking tickets deal with what we call, sequential order-filling documents. They guide the picker to items on the order in a sequence that saves time and effort and also to items having similar handling and receiving problems. For example, mowers are stored near children's wagons and tricycles, not grass seed. Order pickers seek the proper bin number, they need not be familiar with stock locations.

GRIFFIN: Yes. Vendor analysis is much higher than I would have guessed. It's 72 percent here.

ALM: Yes, sir. Vendor analysis takes many forms, some consider it a part of inventory control which is listed separately here. It is the last item on the list. We recommend Distribution by Line Value Reports which shows the dollar volume you produced annually from each vendor's line of merchandise. One benefit from this is to eliminate slow-moving items, reduce inventories of some, and increase others to provide better service.

GRIFFIN: Proper inventory has always been a problem.

ALM: I understand that two out of three respondents in this survey streamlined their stocks by eliminating some 2,800 items. Of course, the data must be interpreted. You, for example, may decide to handle a slow mover if it is a specialty and high profit item or one that you handle for a special customer.

GRIFFIN: Well, you are always going to do the great majority of your business with a relatively few number of accounts. It's the 80 percent of sales with 20 percent of accounts story.

ALM: That's true, and you can get quite detailed reports on that from the computer if you want. But as you know we were speaking of balancing your inventory in keeping with sales and there are savings to be had in that area.

GRIFFIN: What about inventory control that you show here—64 percent?

ALM: All right. In our opinion a computer will assist a wholesaler to control his inventory so that he will realize a turnover of six times annually. We have installations where 7.1 and 7.8 have been reached, but we feel this is a little high.

GRIFFIN: That's pretty good, I'd say.

ALM: You bet it is. We believe one of the big challenges concerns the inventory necessary to improve the order-filling percentage, for example, to minimize back-ordering. Our studies show that the inventory investment required to fill above 96 percent equals the gross margin produced from the added sales. The computer helps you determine helpful information like that, Mr. Griffin.

GRIFFIN: This is all very interesting. I would like for you to mail me some of your literature and I'll explore this matter further with my associates. I'd say we are interested, Mr. Alm.

ALM: I'll be glad to mail you our latest brochures and talk with your group at your convenience. I am confident we can be of help.

GRIFFIN: Thank you very much, Mr. Alm.

## Questions:

1. In general, what type of information would you expect to find under the heading of "Customer Analysis?" Discuss.
2. What is your understanding of "Out Reports?" Of what value are they? Discuss.
3. Give your reaction to Mr. Griffin's interviewing. What's your opinion of Mr. Alm? Justify your viewpoints.

## Case 11-2.   The Burton Company

One of the largest department stores in the entire United States, the Burton Company, operates six stores located within a large city and adjacent shopping areas. Studies conducted by the controller, Mr. Lief Huff, show that the company's paper work has been growing at a rate exceeding that of sales. Information efforts dealing with company purchases and inventory are considered satisfactory by Mr. Huff. However, excessive costs exist for handling papers created by store customer relations, the preparing of billings, and the processing of accounts receivable. Currently, for this work the company uses accounting machines purchased some seven years ago.

A customer extended open credit by the company produces her charge plate at the time of making a purchase. This plate is inserted into a small unit on the counter by the sales clerk. The plate imprints the customer's number, name, and address upon the purchase order made out by the clerk in longhand. At the same time, the customer's number is relayed to the central credit department, where a check is made to determine the credit standing. If satisfactory, approval is relayed to the originating small unit, and the sales clerk proceeds with consummation of the sale. In contract, if credit is unsatisfactory, the customer is politely informed by the clerk, who terminates the sale unless cash payment is made on the account or for the current merchandise being purchased. In some instances, it requires five to ten minutes to get the check on credit. Copies of the orders written by the sales clerks are sent to the accounting department where reports and records, including monthly statements to customers, are compiled.

Mr. Huff is thinking of using a computer. The company has approximately 300,000 customers sold on open account. Of the total number of sales transacted, some 22 percent are cash sales. Peak loads occur during the Easter period, late summer before school starts, and the Christmas period. Accounts are divided by stores, with the statements sent out for each store on approximately the same day of each month. During the past five years, the number of accounts has increased an average of 3 percent per year. It is believed that this growth will continue and may even rise to 5 percent per year.

## Questions:

1. What approach do you recommend that Mr. Huff follow? Why?
2. In your opinion, what are some major considerations that will help determine the feasibility of the use of a computer by the company? Discuss.
3. For computer application, give some important general specifications of the computer recommended and discuss the step-by-step procedure of the computer processing that might be followed.

chapter **12**

# Information
# distribution

Hear one man before you answer, several before you
decide.

—*Danish Saying*

A PART of the processing of data is the distribution of data to people and
machines performing the processing efforts. This concluding chapter in
this section on Planning for Data Processing is directed to information
distribution. In previous pages, we discussed certain developments for
transmitting information which have taken place in keeping with the
information automation revolution. But by no means is all data distribution mechanized. A large segment is performed by manual and nonautomated means which are discussed here.

## SELECTING THE DISTRIBUTION MEANS

Typically, a business enterprise has a variety of information distributive means available to it. These include mail, messenger service (either
personal or mechanical), telephone, intercommunication systems, television, and a host of others which will be included in this discussion. Before
the proper means can be selected, however, it is necessary to know what
the real distributive needs of the company are. Various considerations
enter into the picture. To provide a coordinated distribution system
tailored to serve best a company's requirements, these major considerations deserve high priority:

*1. The Quantity and Type of Information to Be Provided.* This information, segregated for supervisors, salesmen, customers, vendors, and the general public, will provide a helpful, factual basis for the system.

**2. The Cost of the Distribution Medium.** An approximate cost range from the minimum to the maximum, and related to the service provided, is helpful.

**3. The Importance of Speed.** Certain devices transmit messages in a matter of seconds, others require several days. Adequate planning commonly reduces much of the need for speed.

**4. Is Written or Oral Information Needed?** The former tends to be more specific, provides evidence, and helps to lessen misunderstandings. In contrast, the oral is quicker, costs less, and is superior when an exchange of ideas to reach a mutual agreement is desired.

**5. The Length or Amount of the Information.** Certain media are ideal for lengthy communications, while others are designed for short, terse messages.

**6. The Effect of Peak Load Periods.** Volumes vary and the capacity of the selected means must satisfy the peak load.

To gain a quick comparison of various distributive means, Figure 12–1 has been included. This indicates differences for basic considerations among the several means. Discussion of these characteristics is contained on the following pages.

FIGURE 12–1. Comparison of Communication Means on Basic Service Characteristics.

| | Characteristics | | | |
| --- | --- | --- | --- | --- |
| *Communication Means* | *Recipient's Presence Required* | *Contains Illustrations and Drawings* | *Oral Message* | *Written Message* |
| Mail | no | yes | no | yes |
| Personal messenger | no | yes | yes | yes |
| Mechanical messenger | no | yes | no | yes |
| Telephone | yes | no | yes | no |
| Teletypewriter | yes | no | no | yes |
| Intercommunication | yes | no | yes | no |
| Telegraph | no | yes (Wiretax) | no | yes |
| TELautograph | yes | yes | no | yes |
| Electrowriter | yes | yes | yes (Data-Phone) | yes |
| TV | yes | yes | yes | no |

## MAIL SERVICES

It is doubtful that a modern enterprise could exist without mail; it is imperative that some written means of offering the services of the enterprise and of issuing answers to inquiries, statements, and invoices be available. Promptness, accuracy, and reasonable cost are the major requisites of satisfactory mail service.

One of the greatest steps forward in mail addressing is the Zip Code which should always be included because it expedites delivery. Postal authorities offer assistance in providing Zip Codes. The five digits making up a Zip Code quickly identify the destination area and facilitate optical reading. The first digit designates one of ten national service areas. The second digit identifies the service subdivision, the third digit the post office in that subdivision, the last two digits the post office station from which the mail to that addressee is delivered. Figure 12–2 shows the Zip

FIGURE 12–2. The Zip Code National Areas and Authorized Two-Letter Abbreviations for the Various States.

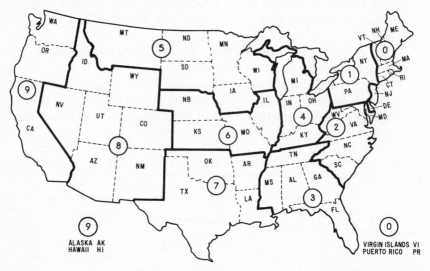

Code National Areas along with authorized two-letter state abbreviations. Using these abbreviations will enable city, state, and Zip Code to be written on one line by most addressing machines. Note that Colorado is CO, Connecticut is CT, Illinois is IL, and Texas is TX. National code area number 6 includes Illinois, Missouri, Kansas, and Nebraska. Figure 12–3 shows the Zip Code for Illinois. Chicago, for example, is 606; the second digit—0—identifies the northeast part of Illinois, the third digit—6—identifies the Chicago Post Office. To these three digits is added the local zone number in Chicago. Hence, a Zip Code for an address in Chicago, Illinois, is 60611.

There are nearly 600 major post offices and sectional centers and about 42,000 different Zip Codes. Mass users of second- and third-class mail are required to update and sort their mailing by the full five-digit Zip Code.

FIGURE 12–3. Zip Code for Subdivisions in State of Illinois.

*Courtesy: Post Office Dept., Washington, D.C.*

Use of proper envelopes also contributes to satisfactory mail service. Standard-sized envelopes are best suited for most purposes. The No. 9 or No. 10 envelope for correspondence is preferable, since only two horizontal folds in the enclosed material are necessary.

The postage-saver envelope permits third-class rates, yet gives the appearance of first-class mail. Also, the two-in-one combination envelope is recommended where a folder or booklet is sent with a letter. With this type of envelope, the letter or other first-class mail is in one compartment, while the folder or other third-class mail is in another compartment. Illustrations of the postage-saver and the two-in-one envelope are shown in Figure 12–4.

By using window envelopes the risk of getting a letter in the wrong envelope and the necessity of sending individually addressed envelopes to the mail room are eliminated. There is also a saving in cost. With regular envelopes, the labor costs for addressing are about $14 per thousand (assuming a rate of three a minute and wages at $2.50 per hour). Window envelopes cost about $4.00 per thousand more than regular envelopes, so the net saving realized by using window envelopes is $10 ($14 less $4) per thousand, or about 71 percent. However, some people believe that window envelopes are less attractive and dignified than regular envelopes. Certain

FIGURE 12–4. A Postage-Saver Envelope and a Two-in-One Combination Envelope.

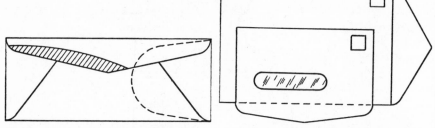

A postage-saver envelope requiring only third-class rate can be top-sealed like a first-class envelope. One end of flap remains unsealed to permit postal inspection.

With the two-in-one combination envelope, first-class mail in one compartment and third-class or fourth-class mail in the other can be mailed as a unit.

types of correspondence are probably best handled by regular envelopes. The final decision in this matter rests with the manager.

Further, to increase returns and lower costs from mail promotions, it is advantageous not to enclose regular stamped envelopes but business reply envelopes. To use them, a no fee permit is required. The postage for such envelopes is of a collect-on-delivery type for which the initial sender pays 8 cents for each reply, based on a 6 cents regular charge plus 2 cents for return privilege. If the return is less than 75 percent of the original mailing, a common result, the use of business reply envelopes results in savings. When regular stamped envelopes are enclosed, the postage for 100 replies is $6; likewise postage on 75 business reply envelopes is $6.

## MANAGEMENT OF MAIL ROOM

The work of the mail room is greatly simplified and performed more quickly by using the proper type of equipment and an orderly procedure. Mail handling is an important activity and warrants adequate planning of space facilities and competent personnel. The work of handling *incoming mail* consists of fairly well-defined and uniform steps including:

*1. Receiving and Opening the Mail.* Some companies have a representative call for its mail especially for first morning mail which can be distributed by the time the office formally opens. When this is the practice, employees handling incoming mail report for work about one-half hour before the regular opening office hour.

Mail is opened either by hand or by machine, depending upon the volume of mail. For manual means a good standard is 15 pieces per minute. Machines will open as many as 500 letters per minute. Mail marked "Personal" or addressed to specific individuals is not company mail and may or may not be opened, whichever is the policy of the company. The common practice is not to open it. In some instances, mail so addressed is forwarded immediately to the employee's home address.

**2. Sorting and Time Stamping.** The next step is to remove the contents of the envelopes and, at the same time, sort the mail according to who handles the particular type under question; this might be a department, a division, or an individual. Usually, the name of the person or of the department to whom the letter is addressed determines where it is to be delivered. When this is not given, a quick scanning of the paper is necessary to determine its proper destination. In exceptional cases, the entire contents must be read.

FIGURE 12–5. Handling the Incoming Mail in a Large Bank.

*Courtesy: First National Bank in Dallas*

Figure 12–5 shows a portion of a large mail room. The man in the foreground is opening letters by means of a machine. The man in the background is sorting to the proper compartments in the sorting racks. The general pattern of the various compartments in the rack is similar to that of the mail stations in the office, for in this way the sorted mail can be kept in a logical order for ultimate distribution.

In the case of mail containing money or checks, a listing showing the senders' name and address and the amount enclosed is made out by the mailing department. The cash and checks, along with the listing, are later sent to the cashier department. In other instances, the check is attached to the letter; or in the case of cash, the money is placed in a small envelope and attached to the letter, with appropriate notation. The checks and cash are then delivered to the cashier department.

A letter referring to previous correspondence can either be delivered to the department concerned, which, if necessary, requests the file from the filing department; or it can be sent to the filing department, where the needed file is attached and forwarded to the proper correspondent. The method used depends chiefly upon the number of such letters received and the system of filing used.

At the time the mail is read and sorted, it is customary to stamp the hour and date received on each piece of correspondence. This provides a timed receipt that can be used as evidence in controversial matters regarding the correspondence. It can also be used for checking the efficiency of mail distribution in the office.

**3. Distributing the Mail.** This is the final step in the handling of incoming mail and is usually done by messengers, although other means, such as conveyor belts and pneumatic tubes, may be utilized.

For *outgoing* mail, the major areas of mail handling are as follows. Normally, the same employees handle both incoming and outgoing mail.

**1. Collecting and Grouping by Destinations.** To help in collecting, outgoing mail is usually placed in special desk trays specified as mail stations. Upon receipt at the mail room, the mail is first grouped according to geographical area, then by city, and then by name of addressee. Sorting racks are commonly used for this purpose. All mail of a similar class, and addressed to the same wholesaler, branch, or company, is put together so that it can be mailed as a single piece. Frequently, large Manila envelopes with the address printed or stenciled thereon are used for these large firm mailings. In some instances, each of the outgoing sorting racks contains an addressed envelope which is handy for instant use. Replenishments are made either the first thing in the morning or at regular intervals throughout the day.

**2. Inserting, Sealing, and Stamping.** If necessary, the material is folded and inserted by the mail department. When ordinary envelopes are used, the name and address on the material must be checked with that on the envelope. Sealing and stamping can be done either by hand or by machine; the volume of mail should determine the method used. It is possible to seal and stamp around 350 letters an hour by hand. Machine rates are much higher. Figure 12–6 shows major equipment in a modern mail room. The machine in the foreground automatically folds, inserts, seals, stamps, and counts the mail.

Key mail personnel must know the postal costs and requirements, so that the proper amounts of postage—no more and no less—are affixed. Knowledge of the various classes of mail is basic. Recommended is use of the *United States Postal Guide* obtained from the Superintendent of Documents, Washington, D.C. 20402. In general, first-class mail includes

FIGURE 12–6. Machines Make Sending Mail As Pleasant As Getting It.

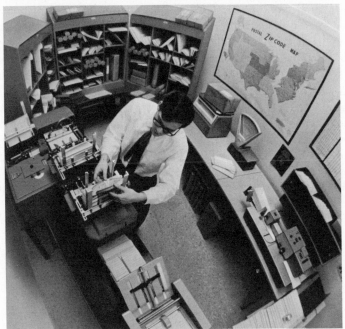

*Courtesy: Friden Division, The Singer Co.,*
*San Leandro, Calif.*

correspondence, securities, and documents; second-class mail, newspapers, magazines, and other periodicals; third-class mail, unsealed printed matter and form letters; fourth-class mail, packages and parcels. Special services, such as registered mail, certified mail, special delivery, and special handling, are available but should be used only under the right circumstances.

It is advisable to appoint one mail-room employee as sole custodian of postage. In the case of a manual method, he should affix the postage to the letters or packages personally or he should see the letters or packages it is going on before issuing postage to someone else.

The machine method employs a meter-mail machine that imprints the postage seal either directly on a letter or, in the case of a package, on an adhesive paper tape which is affixed to the package. At the same time the postage seal is imprinted, a "meter ad," postmark, and date are also imprinted. This is illustrated by Figure 12–7. The machines are offered in an array of capacities and designs; many seal as well as stamp the envelope.

An important part of this machine is the meter, which is a detachable, portable unit containing the printing die for the postage and a recording mechanism. In buying postage, the meter is taken to the post office and set for a lump sum which is paid in advance. The set meter is then returned to the place of business and inserted into the machine, from which metered stamps can be printed as and when needed. In essence, *a postage-meter machine is a government-licensed device for affixing postage.* Figure 12–8 illustrates postage-meter machines. Meter mail has many advantages, including the following: (1) Time and effort are saved; (2) stamp losses are stopped; (3) accurate accounting of postal expenditures is provided; (4) date of mailing is shown; (5) quicker handling is provided by the originating post office, since no canceling is required; (6) the prestige of the user is increased; and (7) postmark, slogan, and advertising are added.

**3. Mailing the Material.**  It is advisable to post mail at regular intervals

FIGURE 12–7. Illustrative of Metered-Mail Imprints, Showing "Meter Ad," Postmark, Date, and Amount of Postage.

(⅔ actual size)

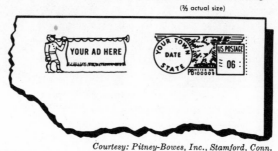

*Courtesy: Pitney-Bowes, Inc., Stamford, Conn.*

FIGURE 12–8. Postage Meter Machines.

*Courtesy: Pitney-Bowes, Inc., Stamford, Conn.*

On the left is shown the Touchmatic desk-model, 10-key keyboard model; on the right is a fully automatic mail unit for the one-man processing of heavy volume mail.

throughout the day. This practice smooths out the work load, minimizes the usual late afternoon peak, and helps the post office to deliver mail promptly. On distant mail, this practice might save a day. Also, knowledge of train and plane schedules is helpful in expediting mail. It is necessary to deliver certain classes of mail to the post office.

## MESSENGER SERVICE—PERSONAL MEANS

Usually, many papers including notices, letters, and memorandums must be delivered within an enterprise. For this purpose, either a personal or a mechanical messenger service can be used. The selection depends upon such factors as the number and frequency of the papers, the number of delivery points, the distances between these points, the maximum allowable time between these points, and the cost.

The personal means is common. The service should be regular and frequent; calls about every half hour are recommended. However, the schedule will vary depending upon the individual needs. In some cases, calls every 15 minutes might be required; in others, calls every hour might suffice. It is common to have calls made with greater frequency in the early morning and late afternoon business hours, in order to take care of the peak loads. Preferably, deliveries should be made on a desk-to-desk basis, since this insures that the person intended to receive the material actually gets it, that messengers do all the messenger work, and that the distribution and collection are accomplished with a minimum of effort and confusion.

A common practice is to include some of the mail personnel in the messenger group. In the opinion of some managers carrying messages provides excellent training for certain new, inexperienced employees. They can quickly learn the names of key employees, location of their work stations, layout of the office and plant, and the work of each organizational unit. Personal messenger service requires close supervision and adherence to these practices:

1. Each route with its designated stations must be defined and the allowable time for one trip must be known. Between trips, rest periods amounting to about 20 percent of the total travel time should be provided.

2. All stations must be visited on each trip.

3. Messengers should confine their efforts to the delivery and pickup of written materials along the prescribed routes. The running of errands should be forbidden.

4. Each messenger has an accordian file and sorts the papers as they are collected so that on each trip deliveries can be made to stations not yet called upon. Papers designated for stations already called upon are delivered on the next trip. The file can be portable or mounted on wheels and pushed from station to station.

5. A designated area or receptacle for "incoming" and another for "outgoing" messages should be used at each station.

6. Control over messenger activities is exercised by having messengers at selected stations either check in with the supervisor or pick up a card and replace it with another of a different color or number. By using different cards each trip, a quick check is provided. To inform of the last collection, leaving a card printed "Last collection has been made" or the messenger saying, "Good night," can be followed.

## MESSENGER SERVICE—MECHANICAL MEANS

When the work volume to be distributed is large, fairly constant, and the stations are fixed, the use of mechanical conveyors is recommended. Conveyors can include turns, end of channel stackers, and remotely controlled gates or brush-off stops to deposit at a specific station. It is also possible to transfer materials from one moving channel to another automatically. Figure 12–9 illustrates a conveyor belt being used to transport inquiries within a credit bureau office.

*Pneumatic tubes* are effective, easy to use, and do not require special skill to operate. Material is carried quickly and accurately to its destina-

FIGURE 12–9. Conveyors Being Effectively Used to Transmit Data in an Office.

*Courtesy: Data-Veyors Corp., Oakland, Calif.*

tion. The initial cost of the tubes is rather high, but the maintenance cost is low. The use of pneumatic tubes is most economical where the volume of work is large. Different-sized tubes and tube carriers are offered. For example, a "4-inch tube carrier" is a popular size and has maximum inside length of 14 inches. Rectangular-shaped carriers are also available for handling bulky items. In the case of a large aircraft manufacturer, the installation of pneumatic tubes linking seven buildings into one unit resulted in annual payroll savings of over $100,000. For a medium-sized metal processor, messenger service costs were cut $4,200 a year by use of pneumatic tubes.

## TELEPHONE

Verbal distribution of information is entirely satisfactory in many cases and for this purpose the telephone is very effective. Good telephone practices aid in building the good will of any enterprise, save time and energy, and help get work accomplished. Much of the wide usage of the telephone has come about because it provides an inexpensive, convenient, and rapid means of verbally communicating information. But the telephone is also important in transmitting information such as in Data-Phone, already discussed in chapter 11, and further in the use of the Teletypewriter, to be discussed later in this chapter.

Telephone systems can be classified into three types: (1) the outside telephone with extensions handled through a company switchboard (PBX), (2) the private internal telephone (PAX), and (3) Centrex telephone service. The first provides service for external calls coming into or going out of the office and for internal calls between telephones within the office. However, by using the Dial PBX, outbound calls are dialed directly from every desk, so the telephone attendant can handle incoming calls and perform other work. Figure 12–10 shows a Dial PBX. In the second type, private internal telephone (PAX), "inside" calls do not go through the switchboard. Since, in the typical company, more than one half of the telephoning is internal—between telephones within the company—use of the private internal exchange relieves the regular telephone lines. This clears the way for better service on "outside" calls—those from customers and other important callers. The third type, or Centrex telephone service, features Direct Inward Dialing (DID), that is, all incoming calls, local or long distance, can go directly to the extension, which carries its own number—the usual seven-digit number. Centrex needs no switchboard attendants to handle most calls, insures maximum privacy on every call, saves about one-half minute on each call by dialing directly, and provides itemized telephone billing by individual telephone station. Interoffice calls are handled simply by dialing the last four digits assigned to the extension that is called.

FIGURE 12–10. The New Dial PBX Provides an Easy, Part-Time Job for the Attendant.

*Courtesy: Illinois Bell Telephone Co., Chicago*

## PROPER USE OF TELEPHONE

Conversing over the telephone places the participants in a relationship whereby they can hear but cannot see each other. The impression must rely entirely on the voice—its tone, clearness, and pleasantness; the selection of words; and the manner of speaking. All of these factors, properly blended, constitute the art of telephoning, which can be acquired.

For the switchboard attendant, a clear, well-modulated voice and the employment of certain phrases and words are assets. To illustrate, it is effective to identify the company immediately by saying "Good morning, American Manufacturing Company." If the caller must be delayed, the attendant should so advise. If the caller agrees to wait, he should be advised every 30 seconds that the line is still busy. When able to complete the call, "I'll connect you now. Thanks for waiting," is appropriate. When the caller cannot wait, his name and number should be obtained and the call returned.

From the viewpoint of the individual telephone user, it is basic that the telephone be answered immediately and identification supplied, such as "Cost Department, Mr. Allen." If answering for someone else, give his name and then yours. Say "Mr. Brown's office. Miss Willis speaking." Some incoming calls will have to be transferred and when this occurs the calling party should be so advised so he knows what is taking place. Also, in case it is necessary to leave the line, tell the caller why and for how long—"Excuse me a moment. I must look at our file on this." And on an outgoing call, always introduce yourself promptly so the other person knows to whom he is speaking.

There are, of course, technical aspects to the effective use of the telephone. For example, the switchboard attendant must know the correct routing of calls and how best to handle unusual requests, dial numbers, and write messages. On the other hand, the individual user should remember to speak directly into the transmitter, place his hand over the mouthpiece to hear better in a noisy place, move the contact button slowly and evenly to attract the operator's attention, and, to keep the line alive, replace the receiver gently after finishing a conversation.

Periodic checkups on the use of the telephone by company personnel are in order. All calls should be handled in the company's prescribed manner. Data can be obtained on the time required to handle calls and on the manner of speech. Concentrate on the promptness in answering the telephone, helpfulness on all calls, and a pleasing telephone personality. Employees should be informed that periodic checkups are made. When necessary, remedial action should be taken without delay. Helpful suggestions are provided by communicating with the telephone company's special representative.

## AUXILIARY TELEPHONE SERVICE

It is possible for several executives in different parts of the country to hold a conference by means of a simultaneous telephone hookup known as *conference call service.* The savings in time and trouble from this type of service are obvious. In some instances, the connections are monitored or recorded for possible future reference. When this is done, approval by the parties is necessary. The signal that the call is being recorded is a "beep" tone every 15 seconds.

A perpetual telephone receptionist is afforded by the *automatic answering device.* This unit, about four times the size of a telephone, is linked to the telephone. Incoming calls are answered by a recorded message something like this:

This is the Avenue Realty Company. Your call is being answered by an automatic answering device. Will you leave your name, telephone number, and message after you hear the "beep" tone? You may leave a half-minute message for me, and I'll call you when I return. Thank you.

After returning to the office, all messages recorded by the unit are audited and the return calls made. The device is especially convenient not only for small, one-man offices and for medical doctors, but also for large offices during the nonworking hours, thus providing around-the-clock service.

*Radio-telephone service* provides communication between moving units and any Bell System telephone. It is particularly adaptable for use by trucking, taxicab, and public service companies, and by police and fire departments. For a two-way communication, a mobile unit is called by means of a regular desk telephone. A request is made for the mobile service operator who, by means of radio, signals the driver of the mobile unit. This is done over an approved radio channel. The driver answers the call on his dashboard telephone, and the conversation takes place. In a similar manner, the driver can call his office from his mobile unit. In contrast, the one-way service signals only to the mobile unit. By means of a code, the driver translates the message, such as "Go to Warehouse R immediately."

FIGURE 12–11. A Teletypewriter.

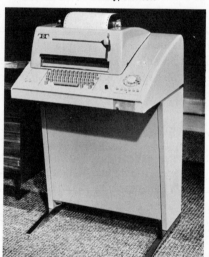

*Courtesy: Illinois Bell Telephone Co., Chicago*

The *teletypewriter,* or TWX service (pronounced "twix") of the telephone company, provides some 60,000 subscribers with a two-way teleprinter transmission. Speed averages about 75 words a minute. The machine used resembles a large typewriter that transmits messages between stations using telephone lines. Basically the keyboard of the machine is standard and when the keys are depressed, electric impulses reproduce the message in typed form on one machine or on many similar machines, the number being determined by the number of connections desired. To send a message, the TWX subscribers' directory is consulted, the call is placed by number, and the connection is made. Any two teletypewriters can be connected for communication in the same way as two telephones. The communication is two way; a written conversation can be carried out. The service is especially effective over long distances. Charges are made on the basis of time and distance, similar to the long-distance telephone. Rates are approximately two-thirds to one-half those of the telephone. Figure 12–11 shows a teletypewriter.

Additional services include:

*WATS, or wide-area telephone service.* This provides unlimited interstate telephoning within specific areas for a flat monthly rate. It is designed for the customer who makes frequent calls to widely scattered and distant points.

*Leased Private Lines.* These insure availability of the circuit for the customer who is provided exclusive use between two or more locations for a scheduled period each day. This service is preferred when a large volume is sent regularly to a small number of fixed points.

*Dataphone.* Machines are able to talk to each other by means of this service. It is very important in the transmission of data in the language of a computer. Dataphone is fully discussed in chapter 11, page 253.

## INTERCOMMUNICATION SYSTEMS

Quick verbal communication of information is provided by means of intercommunication systems. Within an enterprise the various individuals or stations are each equipped with a speaking-talking unit. By turning a switch or pushing a button, instant right-of-way is obtained with anyone in the circuit, and conversations can be conducted with great clarity of tone. When privacy is desired, the microphone in the unit can be turned off and a handset substituted.

Many different capacities and features in units are available. It is advisable to consult with the manufacturer or sales representative for specific data regarding individual requirements. The units can be connected in various circuit arrangements, depending upon the needs of the particular enterprise. Figure 12–12 shows models of intercommunication units.

FIGURE 12–12. Combining Functional Beauty with Great Versatility, These Intercommunication Units Enable the User to Converse with Any Other Master Station in the System.

*Courtesy: Executone, Inc., New York*          *Courtesy: Scan-Am Co., McHenry, Ill.*

## PAGING SYSTEMS

Important in most companies is the means of locating people through the use of flashing lights, tone bells, and buzzers. These paging devices are usually run by the telephone switchboard operator, or they may be a part of a private internal telephone system or of the intercommunication system. The light or noise outlets are located throughout the office and plant, so that key personnel are free to leave their desks without fear of missing any calls. By means of a code, such as two long and two short rings for the president, one long and one short ring for the controller, and so on, these men are notified of calls. By calling either the switchboard operator or a designated person, the message is obtained. The system is quite effective, for it is convenient and is a time-saver to all concerned. The latest paging units feature soft sounds in quiet areas and adequately loud sounds in noisy areas.

## TELEGRAPH

A well-known means of handling informational communications over relatively long distances is the telegraph. Telegrams secure attention, provide terse businesslike messages, and impel immediate action. They are used for practically all subjects or phrases of business activities.

Telegraphic communications can be sent by any of four main ways: (1) over the counter—giving it to the operator at any branch office; (2) by messenger; (3) by telephone—similar to an ordinary telephone call, charges being made to the telephone account or paid by coins dropped into a public pay telephone; and (4) by mechanical tie lines, such as direct telephone connections which is simply a direct wire between the sender's office and the local telegraph office. There is also a *Telex* service offered by the telegraph company. This includes a teleprinter network so that any Telex subscriber can communicate with any other Telex subscriber. The teleprinter is a machine similar to a typewriter which transmits the typed message electrically to the telegraph office. Transmission is at the rate of 66 words a minute. The message is recorded on paper tape both in the sending office and in the telegraph office. The former serves as the sender's reference copy; the latter is used to transmit the message to a circuit for its destination. Telex subscribers pay special low rates for this service. In addition, telegraphic means for transmitting data are a part of some automated data-processing arrangements discussed in chapter 11. Figure 12–13 shows a Telex machine.

The cost of regular telegraphic communications varies with length of message, distance, and speed of delivery. Domestic messages are classified into (1) telegram, and (2) overnight telegram. The former gives the speediest service, delivery usually being made within an hour or so. The minimum rate applies for 15 words or less; excess words are charged at a low extra word rate. The second type, or overnight telegram, can be sent anytime during the day up to midnight for delivery at destination the following morning. The minimum rate applies for 100 words or less; again, excess words are charged at a low extra word rate. For comparable distances, a 100-word overnight telegram costs less than a fast 15-word telegram. Different rates apply for intrastate and interstate messages.

Cablegrams or services to foreign countries have a different classification and include: (1) ordinary—the standard full-rate service, (2) urgent —priority over all other messages except government messages, (3) deferred—no priority over other types, and (4) night letter—messages permitting overnight delivery.

Code words are sometimes used for telegraphic communications in order to reduce costs or to insure secrecy. For example, the code word "ROEUZ" might mean: "What action shall I take?" Commercial codes are available, or a special code can be created.

FIGURE 12–13. A Dial-Direct Telex Machine.

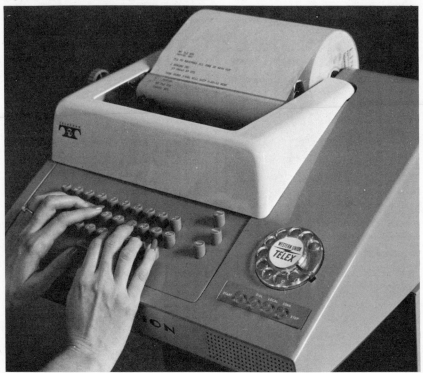

*Courtesy: Western Union Telegraph Co., New York*

Anything printed or drawn, such as layouts, drawings, or charts, can now be transmitted instantly and accurately by WIREFAX, a special service using telegraph equipment. Actually, WIREFAX is a public facsimile system that transmits in units up to 7½ by 9½ inches. Cost depends upon amount and distance. Charges for the initial unit between Chicago and New York are about $5, and each additional unit is about 50 cents.

There are also machines supplying the transmission of printed documents, drawings, and charts. A popular unit, called Desk-Fax, employs facsimile telegraphy which is a fast, accurate, and economical means. The user simply writes or types his message, places it on the drum of the machine, and pushes a button. The rest is automatic. Desk-Fax is illustrated by Figure 12–14.

Machines are also available that convert any written material, chart, or

FIGURE 12–14. Desk-Fax Machine for Transmitting High-Quality Facsimiles.

*Courtesy: Western Union Telegraph Co.,*
*New York*

photograph into electrical signals which are sent over telephone lines and reconstructed into an exact facsimile in black and white by a receiving machine. The reproduction is an exact copy of the original. The transmission is rapid, an 8½ by 11-inch page requiring about two minutes. Figure 12–15 shows a unit of this type.

FIGURE 12–15. Datafax Machine for Transmitting Graphic Facsimile Communication. Any document or photograph can be transmitted anywhere there is a telephone.

*Courtesy: Datafax Corp., Chicago*

## TELAUTOGRAPH

Another well-known means for transmitting messages is the telautograph. As the name suggests, it transmits a handwritten message. The writing is electrically reproduced mainly, but not exclusively, over comparatively short distances. It is popular for communication between main office and receiving room, department and department, and warehouse and main office. In order to send a message, a switch is turned on, and the message is written with a metal stylus on a metal platen. To see what is being written, the sender watches the pen of the instrument writing on a roll of paper. Figure 12–16 illustrates a telautograph. As the message is written, it is reproduced almost simultaneously at one or a number of connected points.

A telautograph provides economical and high-speed transmitting and receiving of messages. Handwritten records are furnished and can be attached to such things as inquiries, notices, and shipping instructions. It is possible to carry on a written conversation—messages can be sent and received.

FIGURE 12–16. TELautograph Receiver and Transmitter Instruments Which Handle Handwritten Messages, Including Special Symbols and Sketches.

*Courtesy: TELautograph Corp., Los Angeles*

## ELECTROWRITER

The Electrowriter sends and receives your handwriting as fast as a call on the telephone transmits your voice. No typing, coding, or copying of the information is necessary. Sketches and graphic information can be included in the message. It operates over any distance to any number of units and receives unattended. Economical to own and operate, the compact unit weighs 25 pounds and provides about 18 square inches of writing area. It uses telephone lines employing Data-Phone. This permits audio or the talking of information alternately as writing and receiving take place. Also, a third party can be included to verify the information. Figure 12–17 shows an Electrowriter.

FIGURE 12–17. A Machine to Transmit Handwritten Messages to Speed an Order, Request a Service, Schedule Parts, or Dispatch a Quantity of Material. A message written on the unit on the left is received by the unit on the right automatically.

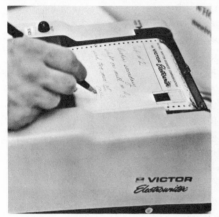 

*Courtesy: Victor Comptometer Corp., Chicago*

## CLOSED-CIRCUIT TELEVISION

Currently application in business is somewhat specialized, but television holds much promise for the future. By means of closed circuits, it is possible to transmit and have instantaneous receipt at many points. Television presents the message visually and in motion—a series of events. However, it does not provide a written record of the information to the recipient.

An interesting application concerns railroad freight car reporting wherein cars move by a TV camera stationed at a strategic point in the freight yard. Pertinent data are viewed on the side of the car and transmitted to a policing and recording center. Floodlights provide proper illumination for both day and night operation.

A television-telephone, enabling the caller to see as well as hear the party at the other end of the line, is available. When the caller lifts the television-telephone, his image appears simultaneously on one half of his screen and upon one half of that of the party being called. When the party answers, his image appears on the remaining halves of the two screens. The unit is about the size of a conventional television table model set. Maximum effective distance is several miles. Television-telephone applications include those in large industrial plants to compare drawings and materials, in banks to check signatures, and in penal institutions to serve as an electronic guard.

## TAPE AND WIRE RECORDERS

For purposes of distributing information covering such activities as inventory counts, personnel interviews, laboratory tests, and sales talks, the use of tape and wire recorders is especially effective. For inventory counts, the person taking the count is equipped with a microphone attached to the recorder in the office. As the inventory count is obtained, it is spoken and thus recorded. A typist then plays the recording and types the inventory lists. Intermediate paper work, tally sheets, and the like are eliminated. Likewise, interviews with prospective employees or, in the case of lawyers, talks with clients can be recorded and studied for complete information—a more effective practice than the use of handwritten notes, which often inhibit the speaker. However, when conversations are recorded, approval by both parties is necessary. Tape or wire is used in the operation of the machine. The tape is a narrow, thin, flexible, paperlike material coated on one side with magnetic oxide of iron; when wire is used, it is of a special type.

## QUESTIONS

1. Discuss a satisfactory approach to the determining of a company's communicative needs.
2. Discuss the use and management of intercommunication systems in an enterprise.
3. Mr. Burns comes to you for advice concerning the management of the personal messenger service of his company. What specific suggestions would you give him?
4. State concisely the difference between each of the following:
   a) A window envelope and a business reply envelope.
   b) An automatic answering device for a telephone and Telex service.
   c) Metered mail and first-class mail.
   d) Postage-saver envelope and regular standard envelope.
5. What practical suggestions would you give to a newly hired head of the mail room of an office in order to help him succeed on the job?
6. Clearly identify and discuss TWX service in office communication.
7. For what general types of applications would you as an office manager recommend the use of mechanical conveyors for the distribution of office papers? Why?
8. In your opinion is the handling of incoming or of outgoing mail the more difficult to manage? Justify your viewpoint.
9. Describe briefly each of the following, pointing out for what type of communication and under what circumstances it is best suited:

*a*) Centrex telephone service.
*b*) Telautograph.
*c*) WATS telephone service.
*d*) Closed-circuit television.

10. Under what general circumstances would you suggest that an enterprise use (*a*) the telegraph, (*b*) the long-distance telephone, (*c*) an airmail letter, (*d*) the teletypewriter, and (*e*) the telautograph? Give reasons for your answers.

11. What is an Electrowriter and under what general conditions would you recommend its use? A Datafax?

12. Enumerate key considerations in the effective use of the telephone in a modern office.

## CASE PROBLEMS

### Case 12–1.  Harold Swink

Several months ago Harold Swink, age 19, was hired as a messenger. He is one of three messengers in a large office located in the center business district of a large eastern city. Harold is proving to be an excellent employee; he is accommodating, reports early every morning to help sort the mail, and radiates a cheerful and pleasant personality. He seems to like his work and appears to be a worthy addition to the office employees.

Harold Swink began to let his hair grow and also acquired long sideburns. Some of the office employees kidded him about his hair, but neither of his fellow messengers approximately the same age as Harold said anything. They wear their hair in a military style and are clean shaven. Several weeks later, Harold Swink began wearing to work clinging pink pants, wide belt, and boots. He also added a necklace with a big medallion. He looked the image of the world of mod.

Many of the employees of the office made comments of a light vein to Harold about his dress. Most were made in a spirit of fun, but several criticized him for wearing such attire. The office manager believed Harold had carried the matter too far. He asked the purchasing agent, father of two teenagers, to have a serious talk with Harold and suggest that he stop wearing the mod clothes to work. Several days later the purchasing agent did so. Harold's response was that what he wore was his own business. His work not his dress should be the basis of judgment. He felt the purchasing agent was of another generation and not tolerant of new ideas.

The purchasing agent reported his experience to the office manager who the next day called Harold to his office and informed him that the accepted customs of the office forbid wearing clothes such as he was wearing. The office manager stated that an employee is expected to abide by the accepted standards of office dress and warned Harold that he must cease wearing such clothes to work or face serious consequences. Harold replied that he saw nothing wrong with what he was wearing. He was simply expressing himself; his clothing was not offensive. Why should he dress like everyone else?

During the following week, Harold Swink continued to wear his mod clothes. At the end of the fifth day, the office manager personally informed him that his employment was terminated effective immediately.

Questions:

1. Was the action taken by the office manager correct? Why?
2. As Harold Swink, what would you do now? Justify your viewpoint.
3. As the office manager, would you have taken any action different than what was taken? Discuss.

## Case 12–2.  Hoosier Pharmaceuticals, Inc.

This company sells a variety of pharmaceuticals to a large number of customers, including hospitals, drugstores, and physicians' supply stores. Distribution is nationwide, and the company is well known and established. About 75 percent of the company's shipments are in small packages—not over 8 x 8 x 6 inches.

Many of the packages are sent by (1) airmail, (2) special delivery, or (3) special handling, because the customer usually wants the pharmaceuticals as soon as possible. Mailing the packages in this manner incurs additional fees charged by the post office. Special delivery provides immediate delivery at the post office of the addressee; special handling applies to fourth-class mail only and insures prompt and expeditious handling by the post office. Starting at 3:00 P.M., several truckloads of packages are taken to the post office. The last load leaves the company building at 4:30 P.M.

A careful investigation by Mr. Charles Meyers, the office manager, showed that a great majority of the packages could be sent by regular mail, provided the packages were ready to go at stated times throughout the day, and would reach their destinations as quickly as by the use of special mailing services. Mr. Meyers estimated the savings from planned scheduled mailing and the use of regular mailing service at about $65 a day.

He feels that some loss is suffered due to stamp pilferage. Currently, stamps are kept in a desk drawer of the packing room and distributed by Mr. James Lange, the foreman. However, this distribution is loosely handled, in the opinion of Mr. Meyers. The foreman contends that he cannot sit at the desk all day long to issue the proper amount of stamps, nor can he check each package mailed for correct postage. Mr. Meyers has observed that frequently emergency letters or packages must be sent out at times other than regular working hours, that is, at night or on Saturdays and Sundays, during which time an employee not fully familiar with postage rates may be handling the mail. The suggestion has been made that orders to the same customer on the same day could be grouped and packed in the same box, thus reducing handling expense as well as being more convenient for the customer. However, Mr. James Lange disagrees, pointing out that the postage will be about the same and the time spent in grouping orders to the same customer will slow the work of his men.

Questions:

1. Do you agree with the viewpoints advanced by Mr. James Lange? Why?
2. What action do you recommend be taken? Justify your viewpoint.
3. How should Mr. Meyers proceed in this situation?

## Case 12–3.  Reba Products Company

Office manager Albert Stahl firmly believes in employee initiative, self-discipline, and self-imposed responsibility as the marks of a top-notch office employee. "Give them freedom to operate, permit them to see what's to be done, and help them do it the best way," is his manner of expressing it. For office employees to receive personal telephone calls at the office was all right in the views of Mr. Stahl. Generally, the employees did not abuse the privilege. However, Elmer Willis had frequent long personal telephone conversations. Neither Mr. Stahl nor any of his supervisors had talked to Mr. Willis about it. Mr. Stahl hoped that Elmer Willis' own common sense, or that other office employees, would tell Elmer that he was endangering the telephone privilege for all.

One morning the general manager, in showing the office to a good customer, walked past Elmer's desk and observed him talking quite loudly on the telephone. The gist of the conversation marked it as a personal call. Some time later the general manager, in returning to his office, found Elmer still talking on the telephone. Intrigued by the length of the conversation, he waited until it ended, then told Elmer he talked too long on the telephone and that during working hours the telephone was primarily for business calls. Elmer replied, "Yes, I know that. But that call was not more than five minutes and that's certainly reasonable."

The general manager felt Elmer was flippant about the affair and, checking with the switchboard operator, was informed the call was from a suburban area, was paid for by the caller, and lasted 43 minutes. The general manager called Elmer to his office and gave him the information he had received. Elmer insisted the call was not more than five minutes. He added that the switchboard operator must "have it in for me" to report any greater time. When asked, "What do you consider reasonable time for a telephone call?" Elmer replied, "That's too general a question to answer intelligently. Frankly, I figure the telephone is there to help me. As long as I can do my work satisfactorily and the calls are paid for by the caller, I can't see any useful purpose in your playing Sherlock Holmes." At this the general manager informed Elmer that his employment was terminated and told him to get his paycheck from the cashier.

### Questions:

1. What conditions led to this situation?
2. Discuss the practices and controls you advocate for use of the telephone for personal calls in an office.
3. What action do you recommend in this specific case?

# PART IV

# PLANNING FOR RECORDS MANAGEMENT

Managing the storing of information, retrieving it when wanted, and making copies of it as required point to the need for proper planning of these activities, the same as any other major activities. Some of our greatest needs as well as phenomenal developments have occurred in this records management area. They are discussed in three chapters "Storing and retrieving information," "Managing the information stored," and "Managing copying and office supplies."

chapter **13**

# Storing and retrieving information

The man who thinks he knows everything about a
subject renounces all hope of learning anything
more about it.
—*William J. Stevens*

AN IMPORTANT AREA of information management is commonly known as
"records management" which deals primarily with the storing and retrieving of information. Opinions differ regarding what precisely constitutes
records management, but most students of this field concur that responsibility for filing of records, establishing retention and destroying schedules,
transferring records, microfilming, and copying of records can be considered important activities with which records management deals. Some
claim the complete life cycle of a record is within the concept of records
management and hence would include the record's creation, distribution,
maintenance, retention, preservation, retrieval, and disposal.

We have already discussed record creation and distribution in previous
chapters dealing respectively with conceptualizing the information work
to be done and data processing. Hence, our attention now will be directed
toward the more important remaining concepts which for clarity we will
term: storing (filing or maintaining), retrieving, microfilming, retention,
and copying of records. Further, we will start with storing and retrieving
information by automated means, since this means is more recent and
becoming widely used. However it should be pointed out that the still
dominant means of storing and retrieving during the early 1970's remains
the manual and nonautomated means.

311

## COMPUTER INFORMATION RETRIEVAL

As pointed out in chapter 11, common to many modern computer applications is an information network capable of storing, retrieving, and printing large quantities of data at high speeds. Scientists and technicians are especially interested in the retrieval of certain information from a massive bank of data. Such facilities exist including an automated data center for engineering information. Many more are destined to be established and grow. Heretofore, much of the money and time spent for research and development have gone for searching, scanning, and noting data pertinent to a particular study. Efforts were duplicated, and frequently not all pertinent knowledge was reviewed because of physical limitations. These inadequate methods will be replaced by vastly improved information retrieval.

Computer information retrieval can be thought of as the automation of the intellectual effort of information input to provide quick accessing to voluminous information on any of a multitude of subjects. In the future we undoubtedly will have many specialized libraries in a form that utilizes automated information retrieval.

Different but closely associated with information retrieval is the belief by many that the computer will help bring about the common world language so long sought. The belief is that as man learns to communicate with machines, this communication will spread to man-to-man communication. Thus, computerese may end language barriers. On the other hand, it seems that to eradicate any language of long standing will certainly not be an overnight accomplishment. But communication between men of different languages is an accomplished fact of the computer. It can translate information from one language into another. Such units are feasible, but although important, this application to date has been relatively minor compared to the host of other uses to which computers have been applied.

However, the automation of information retrieval is not confined to the computer itself. Other arrangements using media in addition to that of the computer have emerged and offer exciting possibilities. Before presenting these additional automated storing and retrieving means, a discussion of microfilming is included, since it is basic to many of the automated arrangements.

## MICROFILMING

Microfilming is a photographic means of retaining information at a reduced size on film. It has been aptly termed, "information miniaturization on film." Microfilm was first employed extensively in banks where it was used in connection with checks. The list of applications grew steadily and its applications are now associated with many types of information. Microfilm is available to the small as well as the large enterprise. There are outside enterprises specializing in microfilming and they will micro-film records either in the client's office or their own. The cost is nominal being about $7 for each 1,000 records.

An important function in which microfilm can be effective is conserva-tion of space. A reel of microfilm will occupy about 2 to 3 percent of the space required by the original records, i.e., two or three drawers of microfilm hold the equivalent of about 100 drawers of original paper records. Also, with microfilm the records are protected from possible wear

FIGURE 13–1. Common Microfilm Media Forms.

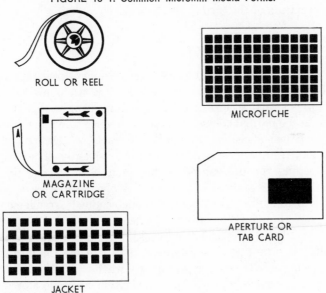

ROLL OR REEL

MICROFICHE

MAGAZINE
OR CARTRIDGE

APERTURE OR
TAB CARD

JACKET

and tear; a uniform size consistent with an effective filing arrangement and index are supplied; and the fire hazard is reduced because the film is of a noncombustible type. Further, microfilm can serve as the desired information medium in the system followed. Quite often, the filing can be done as a by-product of the processing work. In addition, the usefulness of records can be extended such as duplicate copies of original information can be made easily or copies of unique and helpful data can be acquired.

Figure 13–1 shows the five microfilm media forms currently in common use including roll or reel, magazine or cartridge, jacket, microfiche, and aperture or tab card. These are all microfilm; they differ only in format. The roll or reel resembles a 16-mm. movie film with the pictures in sequence along the roll. The same is true for the magazine or cartridge except in this case the film linage is smaller and the cartridge is more portable. A jacket is about 4 inches by 6 inches and accomodates 16-mm. film in several rows or channels across the jacket. For charts or engineering drawings, a larger or 35-mm. film may be used, which when included in a jacket may require two channels so that perhaps three drawings in one broad channel plus channels of standardized microfilm might make up one jacket. Microfiche is a transparent sheet of film containing multiple rows of microimages. A 4-inch by 6-inch microfiche may have 7 rows with 14 "views" or frames per row, or a total of 98 frames, the equivalent of 98 ordinary pages of data. The aperture or tab card is a single microfilm frame mounted into a punch card which carries identifying and classifying data of the microfilmed subject and permits rapid and accurate access to the information of the card.

## STORING-RETRIEVING ACTIVITY

An important segment of information management concerns the proper storing of information and the retrieving of it when needed. That is, information is stored according to some arrangement so that it is readily available. In the normal course of affairs, reference to written information concerning plans, decisions, thoughts, contracts, obligations, drawings, research, and transactions is utilized quite frequently. The storing consists of keeping the information either in a business machine, as for example the storage unit of a computer, or placing papers or records in acceptable containers. A well-defined predetermined arrangement is followed so that any stored information, when required, can be located and retrieved quickly and conveniently for use. The storing and the retrieving are equally important and are interdependent. Storing the information is essential; being able to retrieve it promptly when wanted is vital.

Each year, greater quantities of information must be stored and retrieved. Problems arise regarding how best to handle the information for quick reference, what arrangement to follow, what policies to adopt, and what equipment to utilize. The office is unique in that it stores many of its "products." This is a necessary part of information service. As we create more records, demand more information, and require more controls, storing and retrieving information has grown in importance. Every record and paper created and processed must have proper disposition. If it does not, or if we permit nonessential information to be stored, we are adding to the problem of achieving efficient records management.

## COMPUTER OUTPUT MICROFILM (COM)

The converting of computer output information on magnetic tape to microfilm, COM, in readable form and at magnetic tape speeds (300 pages a minute) illustrates an automation breakthrough into the storing-retrieving activities of records management. The process, sometimes referred to as "micromation," can be briefly described as follows. Data on magnetic tape from the computer are translated into readable text produced on a cathode-ray tube and printed on film. This film is then viewed, as required, at visible inquiry stations or terminals, or used to produce hard copies. Microfilm is an effective medium for this process and some estimate that by 1975, probably one half of all microfilm used will be for this process.

The micromation steps are illustrated by Figure 13–2. Beginning at

FIGURE 13–2. The Micromation Steps Providing a Distribution Method Handling Output Data at Computer Tape Speeds by Combining the Immediacy of the Cathode-Ray Tube Inquiry Station with the Permanency of Print.

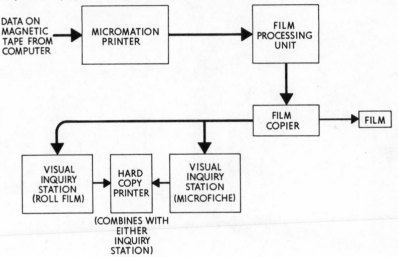

upper left, data on tape enter the Micromation Printer where the tape-to-film conversion takes place. Information requiring hours to print on paper is put on film in minutes. Next, the film is developed by a film processing unit which operates at same speed as printer and accepts various film widths. Copies of the film are made by the copier to eliminate multiple print-out-runs and reduce the cost of copies. Either roll film or microfiche can be used. A page per frame can be handled on roll film. On a 4-inch by 6-inch microfiche up to 224 pages of data can be placed. Access to the filmed data is by visual inquiry units or stations as indicated by Figure 13–2. Any small portion of the filmed data can be retrieved quickly—in a matter of seconds.

These visual inquiry units highly magnify the film for easy recognition by the human eye. The equivalent of thousands of pages of information can be viewed quickly and, if desired, a hard copy of any document can be made. This is done by a hard-copy printer which displays and copies the information in full size.

An illustration of the Micromation Printer is shown by Figure 13–3. It moves the output information at computer speeds, gives speedy retrieval time, and reduces storage space of records. Also, fixed images, such as a photograph, can be merged with the computer information during the print-out run. Many different types of business documents can be pro-

FIGURE 13–3. The Micromation Printer.

*Courtesy: Stromberg Datagraphics, Inc.*
*San Diego.*

duced without expense of preprinted paper forms. Extra copies can be produced without involving the computer.

Other machines offering various features are also available for COM operations. Microimage conversion systems are destined to increase in importance and flexibility. A complete cycle is possible using microfilm and the computer which includes recording data by microfilm (visual form), reading the information into a computer, modifying the data by means of computer techniques, and recording the new data by microfilm (visual form). The applications are many. For example, a large railroad microfilms nearly 600,000 pages of information each month consisting of weekly revenue accounts to daily listings on interchange cars and contents. The COM operation requires only two hours whereas a comparable printout takes 14 hours. Figure 13–4 depicts microfilm output and its possible uses. From the computer tape output, the conversion supplies two microfilm copies, one for active use, the other for archival storage. From the microfilmed information, active references can be made in any of several ways. See left portion of Figure 13–4.

FIGURE 13–4. Possible Steps from Computer Tape Output to Microfilm Output.

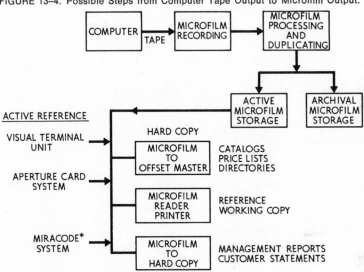

*\* MIRACODE in a trade name of Eastman Kodak Co.*

## TECHNIQUES OF MICROFILM INDEXING

A common method employed for indexing roll or cartridge film is Code-Line which is an address to document location on the roll. Black lines between frames are created at the time the film is created. These lines are changed in a straight progression after about each 20 frames. To locate a frame, reference to an outside index is made in order to obtain the Code-Line number relating to the wanted frame location. When advancing the film at high speed in a reading device, the code lines appear as a solid line and are interpreted by means of the scale adjacent to screen to locate the desired frame.

Another method widely used is Image Control. For this an opaque mark is placed on the film under the image. This mark is created during filming. Again, an external index is consulted for the index number to the wanted frame. This number is inserted in a keyboard; the reader logic counts the marks, locates, and displays the document desired.

Referring to Figure 13–4 again, the second type of microform is the aperture or tab card. Such media are sorted by the key punches in the card in order to locate the card desired.

Lastly, Miracode System composed of several machine units offers an automated system featuring the most advanced and sophisticated method of indexing roll film. At the creation of the film, the identity of each frame or group of frames is recorded in binary code adjacent to the frame on the film. To find a specific frame, the operator inserts the magazine in which the document is recorded in the printer-reader on the console. The identity of document is then punched into the system's keyboard. The machine searches, finds, and displays the desired frame on the screen of the display unit.

As shown in Figure 13–4, the information of the microfilm can be transferred to an offset master which is used to print catalogs and price lists, reference working copy, or hard copy for management reports or customers' statements.

## AUTOMATED MICROIMAGE RETRIEVAL SYSTEM

Also available is automated storage and retrieval systems for microfilm. By this means computer-produced film is readily accessible. In one popular system, the information in microfiche form is stored in large quantities in a centralized location. This microform repository in standard size has a capacity of nearly 50,000 microfiches, which at 98 frames each is equal to nearly 5 million pages. The repository accommodates intermixed formats, a unique random-access selectivity being used. Desktop viewing terminals are tied in with the repository. Up to ten terminals, each up to about a mile from the repository, can be used. By means of a control panel, the desired microform is selected, positioned, and enlarged on the screen. A six-digit address is entered on the keyboard and this triggers the automatic retrieval and closed TV circuit to the specific location of the storage module. The entire search requires but a few seconds. Hard-copy printers as well as real-time computer interfacing are optional. Available is an electrical lockout which prevents unauthorized viewing of confidential information. A view of the display unit and the central repository is shown at the top of Figure 13–5. Lower part of this figure diagrams the retrieving of wanted microform.

## MICROFICHE FOR STORING AND RETRIEVING

The use of microfiche is expanding rapidly for storing and retrieving applications because it is easily accessible for frequent and quick reference. COSTI (Committee on Scientific and Technical Information) speci-

FIGURE 13–5. An Automatic Microimage Retrieval System That Provides Any Number of Individual Remote Viewing Stations, Retrieves Intermixed Microimage Sizes, and Affords Instantaneous Retrieval from an Unattended Central Repository.

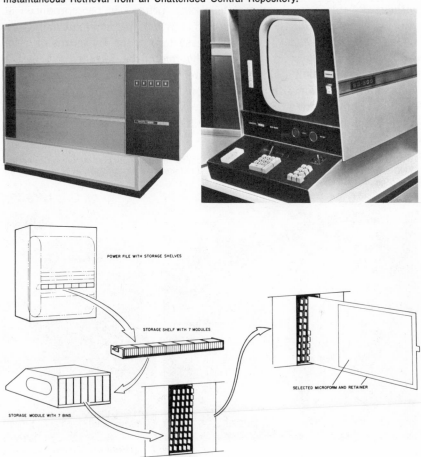

Courtesy: Sanders Associates, Inc. and Diebold, Inc., Canton, O.

fications state recommended sizes and formats of microfiches to be used, especially when interchange with government fiche is anticipated. Any widely adopted classifying and indexing system can be applied to microfiche. The heading should be well planned so that accurate identification is quickly made. Included are the classification number, document title, source, and other basic information. The pattern followed for storing varies depending upon the type of information, updating requirements, and related factors. Frequently the fiches are arranged in numerical sequence with new fiches added to the end.

Microfiches provide small, easy-to-handle units. Additions and deletions to the total information are expedited by discarding the old fiche and replacing it with a correct new one. Also, additions can be interfiled without difficulty. Duplicates or hard-copy prints can be reproduced at low cost with retention of sharpness and clarity of original material.

The microfiche reader or viewer is easy to operate. By means of a coordinate indexing system, keyed to the microfiche format, getting the correct image location is simple. It is a matter of moving an alphanumeric index pointer horizontally, vertically, or diagonally to the coordinates of the desired image. Magnification can be chosen from 18 times to 38 times. While used for most types of information, the microfiche principle is

FIGURE 13–6. Before and After Pictures of Records of Research Library Files Converted to NCR Microfiche. The information from nearly 300 legal-size file drawers is now contained in two small cabinets.

*Courtesy: The National Cash Register Co., Dayton*

especially popular for storing and retrieving. It is used to handle thousands of government monthly reports, as well as producing and distributing them to a multitude of governmental agencies and information centers. Figure 13–6 shows an interesting illustration of the savings in space and the gain in neatness by use of microfiche.

Storing and retrieving work utilizing the microfiche principle has been greatly enhanced by the process, PCMI Microform System, developed by the National Cash Register Company. This process permits tremendous reduction rates to be used in filming the material. The fiche produced by this process is called ultramicrofiche or mastermicrofiche. For example, over 1,200 printed pages of the Holy Bible are reproduced on about 2 square inches of film. This means that a million book pages can be contained in a stack of film cards about 6 inches high, or the contents of over 50,000 books could be stored in one drawer of a filing cabinet. The micro-images are initially made on a special material, photochromic dye. This is erasable by light, thus making it possible to inspect an image and if unsatisfactory erase and redo it. When all images are satisfactory, they are transferred to a photographic plate by contact print.

The PCMI process offers a new dimension to the microfilm industry; it has been called a way of "microfilming microfilm." By it, the storing and retrieving of an enormous quantity of information on microfiche is possible. To illustrate, the entire parts catalog system of a leading automobile

FIGURE 13–7. (Left) An Up-to-Date Output Microfilm Reader; (Right) a Service Man Using a Parts Catalog System, Each NCR Ultramicrofiche Holds the Equivalent of 3560 Catalog Pages of Information.

*Courtesy: The National Cash Register Co., Dayton*

manufacturer is available on eight 4-inch by 6-inch microfiches. When projected to the 9-inch by 11-inch screen of a viewer, a clear reproduction of each frame equivalent to the size of a catalog page is provided. Only the ultramicrofiches and the viewer are required. The desired ultramicrofiche is slipped into the compartment of the viewer and the directional finder moved to view any frame. Effective indexing permits quick finding of desired image. Revisions in material are handled by making a new ultramicrofiche and discarding the old transparency. Time is saved in retrieving precise information, the cost is very low, and the handling of heavy bulky catalogs is eliminated. Figure 13–7 shows a popular reader unit and its use in industry.

## TERMATREX-OPTICAL COINCIDENCE

Another interesting means for handling storing and retrieving work is the use of Termatrex cards and the principle of optical coincidence. In this methodology there is a card for each characteristic and each card has 10,000 positions or coordinates. A coordinate is a location expressed by so many spaces horizontally and vertically on the card. The serial number of an item is represented by the coordinates at which location a hole is drilled through the card. Using a simple example, suppose we want to retrieve information from a large personnel file to identify which personnel have the specific qualifications of administrative experience, radar designing, and electrical engineering background. Termatrex cards marked with these qualifications are superimposed, placed in a Termatrex Reader so that coincidental holes visible as light spots will reveal employees having these characteristics. In Figure 13–8 (upper right), the coordinate 25 spaces vertically and 11 spaces horizontally, designate number 2511, which is employee William Crawford. If the light spot shows through at this coordinate when the cards for each characteristic are superimposed, it means that William Crawford has the sought-for qualifications. The actual search procedure is shown in the upper left of Figure 13–8.

Available is an automatic scanner which totalizes coincident holes appearing in one or more cards. Also an available machine allows direct conversion from computer-punched cards to Termatrex cards so that a direct line connection can be utilized. This machine is shown in the left portion of the lower illustration of Figure 13–8. The operator is inputting information into the system. Completely modular, the arrangement comprises an inexpensive self-contained system as well as one compatible with the use of punched cards and computers.

## MOTORIZED FILES

Representative of less automated yet highly effective storing and retrieving means are motorized files. When the work requires access to a large quantity of original data, the motorized file is extremely useful. Operated electrically it brings to the seated operator any tray of material in the unit at convenient writing height. This means elimination of nonproductive times for walking to storage container, reaching to place materials at the top portion of the storage container, and stooping to utilize the lower portion of the container. Hence, every record is made available at the level where maximum labor efficiency is attainable. This has significance since research indicates that with the nonmotorized file, about 73 percent of the total storing and retrieving costs are for labor. It

FIGURE 13–8. An Information Search System Utilizing Optical Coincidence.

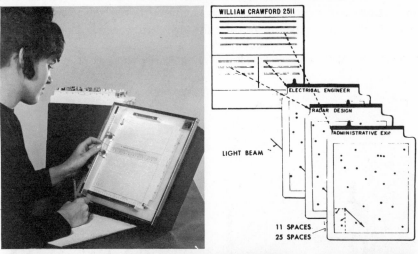

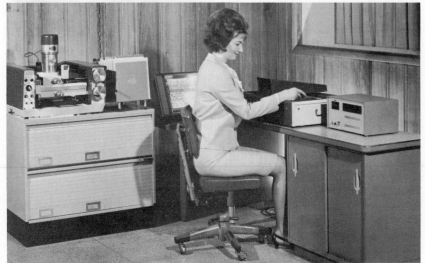

*Courtesy: Jonker Corp., Gaithersburg, Md.*

Upper left shows an employee taking a reading, upper right gives details of the operation. The lower view shows input data being prepared by direct conversion from computer-punched cards to Jonker or Termatrex cards.

is another reflection of work simplification—the operator does not go to the records, the records come to her. Further, power storage containers utilize the full space from floor to ceiling, thus in many cases doubling the cubic feet for storage per unit of floor space over that of nonmotorized arrangements. Figure 13–9 shows motorized files; the unit on the right handles cards, that on the left, letter-size documents. Also available is a motorized visible card file where the material is filed horizontally with margin exposed to expedite locating the filed card when needed.[1]

FIGURE 13–9. Motorized Files Providing Effective Work Station with Access to a Large Quantity of Data.

*Courtesy: Diebold, Inc., Canton, O.*

## NONMOTORIZED FILES

In this category are many familiar types. Selected for discussion here are pull-drawer, lateral, reciprocating, rotary, card automatic, and visible. The first, or pull-drawer, is available for various size cards, letters, and legal papers, and in types of one to six drawers. The one- and two-drawer models are used on a desk or table; the two-drawer is desk height and is usually used beside a desk, providing ready accessibility to papers frequently used. Three-drawer models are used for counter purposes. The five- and six-drawer files provide extra filing capacities for the floor space occupied. A standard four-drawer file holds about 5,000 sheets of paper, 300 file folders, and 26 file guides.

While the mechanical details differ among manufacturers, most pull-drawer files feature a ball bearing, full progressive sidearm suspension which provides smooth rolling action of the drawer and permits easy

---

[1] Visible card file is discussed fully on page 329.

opening and closing. Some feature storing the material in suspending folders which transfer the weight from the drawer bottom to two top rails on either side, running the length of the drawer. Suspended folders provide fingertip ease of filing and the folders cannot slump.

**Lateral Files.** Proponents of this category stress the ease of getting to the stored material; the fast handling of storing and retrieving work—25 percent more than that of other types; and savings in floor space—about 50 percent compared with a pull-drawer of four drawers using the basis of filing inches per square foot of floor area. See Figure 13–10. Lateral filing cabinets can be divided into four groups: (1) drawer, (2) box, (3) shelf type, and (4) suspension. For the first, the drawer opens from the side.

FIGURE 13–10. Lateral Filing Cabinets, Drawer Style, Are Popular for Use with a Desk Arrangement and for Areas Where the Depth Dimension Is Limited, i.e., along the Side of a Corridor.

*Courtesy: Oxford Filing Supply Co., Inc.,*
*Garden City, N.Y.*

These units can be equipped to handle either regular or suspension folders. All material can be reached easily. The second, or box, consists of top and side open-edged metal boxes or trays hooked onto the rails of a freestanding metal frame, which is assembled without nuts, bolts, or screws. The frame is tailored to fit individual needs and the boxes, into which the material is placed, hang at a slight angle, creating a stair-step effect to expedite the filing work. Top- or side-tab folders can be used. Figure 13–11 shows the detail of this type filing. The third, or shelf type,

FIGURE 13–11. Detail of the Cutaway Box Permitting Working Folder Corners. The box type is for records not requiring closed storage.

*Courtesy: Tab Products Co., San Francisco*

features compartments of filed material exposed for ready accessibility, as shown by left portion of Figure 13–12. Folders can be slid out instead of lifted out, separators within compartments can be supplied if desired, and open file doors serve as work surfaces. In the fourth, or suspension, filed material is contained in special folders suspended from a pair of rods. The folders, provided with labels at front edge, are available in many different sizes to accommodate different sizes and weights to be filed. Figure 13–12 (right) shows the detail of this file. Modification of the shelf and the suspension types, or so-called open-shelf type is widely used for odd-sized items such as magnetic reels, paper tapes, art-work, photographs, and line drawings.

**Reciprocating Files.** This type permits the operator to remain seated with necessary machines and tools located within easy reach, and the file can be moved forward and backward as required. Use of this type reduces

FIGURE 13–12. (Left) Shelf-Type Steel Filing Cabinets with Retractable Doors. (Below) Detail of Suspension File Construction.

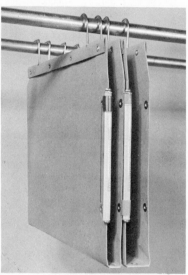

*Courtesy: Tab Products Co., San Francisco*

*Courtesy: Robert P. Gillette Co., Inc., Columbia, S.C.*

employee fatigue, travel, and waiting time. It also assists supervision in that all files are at desk-level height and under full view of the supervisor.

A useful modification of the reciprocating file is the arrangement whereby files can be moved along tracks, thus utilizing conventional aisle space for storage space. Figure 13–13 illustrates this idea. Only one "floating" aisle is used. The units can be moved from side to side to gain access to any one unit. For heavy shelving loads, electrical power can be employed. To operate, a pedal in front of the aisle is stepped on causing the units to open. A safety cord extending between the units is then removed, thus disconnecting the motor to prevent it operating as long as the employee is in the aisle. When ready, the employee walks out of the aisle, replaces the safety cord, and any bay of the arrangement is ready to be moved.

**Rotary Files.** This name applies to filing cabinets either (1) mounted on a platform which revolves or (2) held to the periphery of a wheel which revolves, thus affording a ready and quick locating means at writing height. The first type is designed to expedite work methods. It frequently makes one large set of records quickly available to several employees with work stations around the edge of the common file. It can be thought of as a reciprocating file with a circular pattern. See Figure

FIGURE 13–13. Movable Files Permit Greater Storage and Utilization of Space.

*Courtesy: Lundia, Myers Industries, Inc.,*
*Decatur, Ill.*

13–14. In the second type, posting is convenient without removal of the filed material. This wheel-type unit provides speedy handling—large motion savings up to 75 percent have been estimated—and compactness. The range of sizes is from small units about the size of a telephone to large units approximately 36 inches high. The capacity varies, of course, with the size of the wheel; for example, a unit having a 21-inch-diameter wheel, handling 5 x 8-inch cards, has a capacity of 6,000 cards. In most cases the filed cards have punched openings at bottom to provide a gripping effect to a retaining rod, but units are available which hold nonpunched cards, folders, photographs, and drawings. Both single- and multiwheel units are offered, as well as a special mechanism for stabilizing the rotation.

**Card Automatic Files.**   In this type equipment the cards are filed usually according to a particular code. By pressing the proper buttons on a small console, the wanted cards are slightly raised automatically, hence retrieval is very fast. It is possible to file cards by a code which permits information pertaining to a common subject, but on different cards, to be

FIGURE 13–14. Six Clerks Have Immediate Access to 60,000 Customer Account Records in This Rotary File.

*Courtesy: Acme Visible Records, Inc.,*
*Crozet, Va.*

retrieved quickly from all cards on which the desired information is located. Also, the code can be confidential so that filed information is not accessible to unauthorized personnel. Figure 13–15 on page 330 shows a card automatic file unit.

**Visible Files—Cards Horizontal.** These files assist retrieval efforts for they provide the user, at a glance, visible information in the file. The cards are filed horizontally in a shallow slide or tray in such a manner that the bottom margin of each card is exposed, providing for quick visibility. In this margin are pertinent data concerning the information on the major area of the card. Capacity per tray averages about 80 cards. Each card is fastened in such a way that it can be raised and flipped about the top edge. Thus, the complete information on any card can be viewed in full, or additional data can be written on the card with the tray used as an armrest. For an illustration of this type file, see Figure 13–16 shown on page 331.

In some equipment, the top edge of the card is fastened directly onto the tray; while in other equipment, "pockets" made of strong kraft paper are fastened directly onto the tray and the card is held in place by

FIGURE 13–15. In This Filing Unit, by Pressing Several Buttons the Wanted Material Is Raised Slightly So That It Is Retrieved very Quickly.

*Courtesy: Randomatic Data Systems, Inc.*
*Trenton, N.J.*

inserting the bottom edge into a flap made by a U-shaped plastic strip at the bottom of the pocket. The top of the card is held by inserting the corners into slots precut in the pocket.

Effective signaling to denote certain information on the card is one of the outstanding features of this visible arrangement. By sliding different-colored plastic markers along the visible margins, definite dates or quantities, which are signals for specific actions, are brought out in bold relief. By such signals, a whole tray of cards can be scanned and the items requiring immediate attention quickly spotted. Figure 13–17 illustrates a signaling system for accurate follow-up.

**Visible Files—Cards Vertically.** Another type of visible file is that designed for use where cards are filed vertically. With this type, common card sizes are from about 3 to 20 inches in width and 5 to 12 inches in height. They are similar in appearance to the printed forms for machine- and hand-posting work. It is common practice to cut away one or both of the upper corners of the card to provide diagonal indexing margins; in addition, the horizontal and one of the vertical margins of the card are used for indexing. An offset arrangement is followed in placing the cards in the file so that the top, diagonal, and side margins of the card are

FIGURE 13-16. Visible File Equipment Where Cards Are Filed Horizontally. The illustration is of a manually operated type. There are also motorized files of this type.

*Courtesy: Sperry Rand Corp., New York*

FIGURE 13-17. An Effective Follow-Up Signaling System. On the top card, the signal over the 4 indicates April, the month in which follow-up should be made. The signal at the right of the card at the 3 indicates the day of the month on which the follow-up is due.

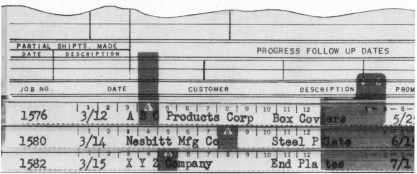

*Courtesy: Sperry Rand Corp., New York*

exposed or visible. The card is held in position by means of a notched arrangement at the bottom of the card which fits into a receiving device at the bottom of the file, and the design is such that cards can easily be inserted or removed. Both sides of the card can be used, and signaling devices similar to those already discussed can be employed. Figure 13–18

FIGURE 13–18. The Arrangement of Cards in a File. Groups of cards can be removed and replaced just as easily as one card. This is commonly called an open tub file.

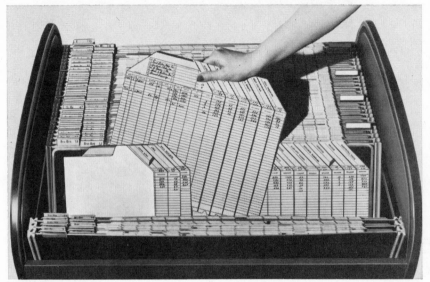

*Courtesy: Acme Visible Records, Inc., Crozet, Va.*

shows the arrangement of cards in the file. With this equipment, the retrieving time is minimized, thumbing through cards is eliminated, and exceedingly quick scanning over large numbers of cards is possible—for example, nearly 7,000 cards, 10 x 5 inches in size, can be accommodated in one file unit.

Visible card storing arrangements are also available in book form. Approximately 2,000 cards can be kept in one binder. The book form affords portability and a posting surface always at desk height. Binders are made to lie perfectly flat when open, to lock against any possible accidental shifting of record sequence, and to lift and guide sheets into proper position when the binder is closed.

**Filed Strips.**     Another type of nonmotorized file is the so-called filed strips used when quick reference to records containing a small quantity of data is needed. It is useful for maintaining lists which undergo changes, such as names and addresses of customers, prices, rates, bin locations, directories, reservations, hospital indexes, telephone and switchboard data, and routings.

Either of two methods can be followed. The first consists of writing the data on small die-cut cards which snap or button on a holding frame. This places the cards in an offset arrangement with the upper margin of the card plainly visible. The second method consists of typing or otherwise writing the data on scored and special sheet material, which is made of

FIGURE 13–19. Two Types of Visible Reference Record Equipment Used Where the Amount of Data Is Small and Where Fast, Frequent Reference Is Required.

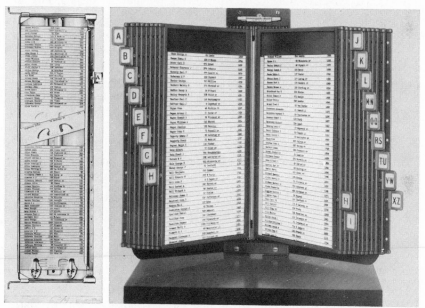

*Courtesy: Sperry Rand Corp., New York*

resilient veneer covered on both sides with paper; separating the sections by breaking along the scored line; and placing the strips in a frame by bending them slightly and snapping the ends under the side channels of the frame. With either method, the frames can be suspended on desk stands, wall brackets, and rotaries. Figure 13–19 shows illustrations of these files. To indicate special conditions applying to a particular name, a signaling device of a shape and color code is either slid over, or attached to, a record. Different-colored strips and cards are also available and can be used for signaling purposes, if desired.

## ARRANGEMENTS FOR STORED MATERIAL

We have already noted that the arrangement for stored material within a computer system can take one of several different patterns. It is not, for example, always in numerical sequence or in a time sequence. In some instances it is random, but the computer's access ability makes instantaneous retrieval possible. The arrangement for the stored information is taken care of by the computer programming followed.

In contrast, when manual means are followed, it is essential that a satisfactory storing arrangement be determined and followed. The most important of these arrangements merit discussion not only because they are basic to effective storing and retrieving by manual means, but also because they are helpful in understanding better the automated storing and retrieving means being followed.

For manual means, there are numerous ready-made arrangements available. Commonly called "filing arrangements," they reflect different features by different manufacturers, but all emphasize provision of ample divisions for the information, allowance for possible expansion, and ample inclusive constraints to cover all information to be handled. A total of four basic arrangements are available: (1) alphabetical, (2) numerical, (3) geographical, and (4) chronological. Modifications and combinations of these are commonly used. For example the alphabetical-numerical plan is often employed, and in many alphabetical files, the material in each subdivision is arranged chronologically, i.e., the latest paper always on top. Likewise, under the geographical plan it is customary to arrange the subdivisions alphabetically.

### ALPHABETICAL ARRANGEMENT

Possibly the most widely used, this arrangement stresses the name or topic as the important item. If the first letter is not sufficient for determining the proper place of the material, the second and, if necessary, the third and fourth succeeding letters are used. For any given total of names, the probable number which will occur in each subdivision of the alphabet is known. For example, names beginning with the letters $S$, $B$, $M$, and $H$, respectively, are most common; those beginning with $X$, $Q$, and $U$ occur least frequently. For a given quantity of names, there are usually about three times as many names under $B$ as under $A$, twenty times as many under $H$ as under $I$, and ten times as many under $T$ as under $U$. Information of this sort is utilized scientifically in determining filing guide subdivisions, which can be purchased as standard equipment. Sets ranging from 24 to some 2,600 subdivisions are available.

To provide for expansion, sets are available that permit the inserting of additional subdivisions to the original set. For example, a set of 300 subdivisions is converted into one of 400 subdivisions simply by adding an expansion package of 100 subdivisions. None of the original subdivisions are discarded; there is no waste.

The advantages of alphabetical filing are that direct reference is provided, a quick check is offered on misfiled material, and common names are grouped. It is sometimes considered "the natural way to file." Figure 13–20 illustrates an alphabetical storing arrangement for correspondence. From this illustration, the following can be observed:

1. The primary guides, or partitions segregating the material, give the chief breakdowns of the alphabet and are identified by green tabs occupying the first three positions which are shown along the top left portion of the guide.[2] These tabs are marked with letters and numbers, i.e., $A = 1$, $Abr = 2$, $Ad = 3$, $Ag = 4$, and so forth. The number expedites the filing work. When considering the letter $d$, it is a little difficult to recall that $d$ is between $c$ and $e$. In contrast, less thought is required to remember that the number 3 is between 2 and 4.

2. Individual folders containing regular correspondence are filed behind their proper primary guide and tabbed in the fifth or extreme right position: "1. Aaron, Carl"; "1. Abbott, A. M."; and so forth.

3. Miscellaneous folders, used for occasional and miscellaneous correspondence, are marked with red tabs in the first three positions. These folders correspond in identification and number with the primary guides and are placed in the back of each primary-guide spacing.

4. Auxiliary guides, tabbed in the fourth or right-center position, are used to simplify and to speed the filing by dividing primary-guide spacings according to individual needs. Auxiliary guides may include (*a*) common titles and names, such as "American," "Brown," "Smith," and "United States"; (*b*) alphabetical listings which segregate the material under the common title or name—"American Art Works" or "American Bridge Co.," for example; and (*c*) monthly listings which separate the material under the common title or name by months—"Baker Bros.— Jan.," "Baker Bros.—Feb.," and "Baker Bros.—March."

5. Out guides are tabbed with blue in the fourth position and are inserted in the file when any folder is taken out. Each out guide is equipped with a holder device for a charge-out card. Entries on this card show when a folder is removed, by whom, and when returned. Out guides are also available in folder form, in which case spaces are ruled on the side in order to record data on removals.[3]

---

[2] Tabs are located by position along the width of the guide. At the left is the first position, and moving to the right are the second, third, fourth, and fifth positions; the fifth position is at the extreme right.

[3] The subject of charging material out is discussed in chapter 14, p. 352–54.

FIGURE 13–20. Filing Arrangement under a Modern Alphabetical Correspondence-Filing Plan.

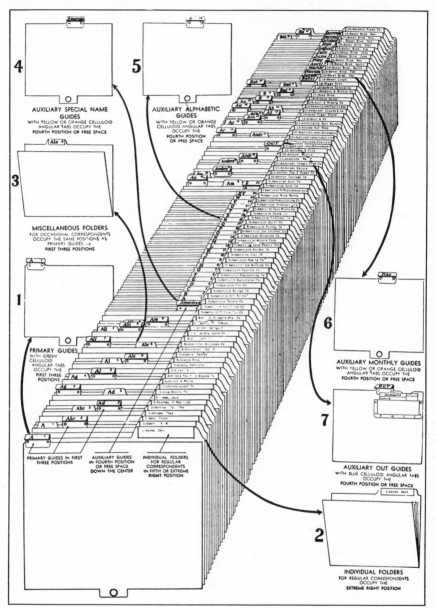

*Courtesy: Globe-Wernicke Co., Cincinnati, O.*

## MODIFICATIONS OF ALPHABETICAL ARRANGEMENT

Two major modifications of the alphabetical arrangement are (1) subject, and (2) phonetic. In the former the material is arranged according to subject or descriptive feature instead of name. For example, all material pertaining to insurance is put in one main division and all material on taxes in another division. If necessary, subdivisions of each subject are made. For Insurance, the subdivisions might be Accident, Fire, and Group; and the material is usually filed alphabetically under each classification. The choice of subject heading should be inclusive and descriptive of the contents. Any logical grouping based on usage is permissible. Idiomatic terminology should be used. Subject filing places all material of a common descriptive feature together, so that it can be used conveniently.

The second, or phonetic, is based on the pronunciation or sound of the stored identity, usually a name. For example, the name "Bohlin" is pronounced the same but can be spelled "Bowlin," "Bowlyn," and so forth. Under which spelling is such a name to be placed in a file? Poor handwriting and errors in transcribing might add further to the problem. In such cases, the phonetic arrangement is helpful under which all names are coded by use of the "Soundex Code," which is:

| *Code Numbers* | *Key Letter Equivalents* |
|---|---|
| 1 | $b, f, p, v$ |
| 2 | $c, g, j, k, q, s, x, z$ |
| 3 | $d, t$ |
| 4 | $l$ |
| 5 | $m, n$ |
| 6 | $r$ |

The letters *a, e, i, o, u* and *w, h, y* are not coded. In addition, the following practices apply:

1. The initial letter is not coded but is used as a prefix to code a number which always has three digits.
2. The zero is used where there is no key letter equivalent.
3. Doubled key letters are coded as one, that is, *rr* as *r*.
4. A key letter and its equivalent are likewise coded as one, that is, *ck* as *c*.

To illustrate, the name "Bohlin" would be coded B—450; "Bowlin," B—450; and "Bowlyn," B—450. Thus, all names which sound alike, although spelled differently, have an identical filing location and thus can be quickly located. Note that the phonetic modification is of an alphabetic-numeric type. The phonetic arrangement provides these advantages:

Ninety percent of all family names are grouped automatically, duplications are detected, unlimited expansion and flexibility are provided, the effect of transcribing errors is minimized, and a uniform and precise indexing method is provided.

## NUMERICAL ARRANGEMENT

In this arrangement, each item filed has a number, and location of the material is by numerical sequence. This arrangement is popular for such material as bank checks, invoices, engine numbers, and papers pertaining to freight cars. However, it is not confined to prenumbered material. Items such as letters, memorandums, and notices are also filed according to this plan; and in such cases, an auxiliary alphabetical card file is employed to learn the proper filing number. The system of numbers can be basically one of two types: (1) serial—to provide unlimited expansion, or (2) coded—to indicate specific types of items. An illustration of the latter type is given below:

*Divisions*

| 100. *General Sales* | 200. *Production* | 300. *Research* |
|---|---|---|
| 110. Recap of orders booked | 210. Purchasing | 310. Consumer studies |
| 120. Recap of sales shipped | 220. Payroll | 320. Radio ratings |
| 130. Expenditures | 230. Budget | 330. Television surveys |
| 140. Budget | 240. Recap of items completed | 340. Readership records |
| | | 350. Product testing |

The numerical plan offers simple provisions for expansion, some degree of secrecy, ease and speed of operation, and an effective means of identification. Numbers are easy to work with; in fact, most alphabetical arrangements use numbers in addition to letters.

In terminal-digit filing, a variation of the regular numerical arrangement, numbers are used, but they are read from right to left instead of the conventional left to right. Hence, records are filed according to the last digit or, more commonly, the last two digits, then the next two or subdivision thereof. To illustrate:

| *Numerical* | *Terminal Digit by Last-Two Numbers* | *Terminal Digit by Two Last-Two Numbers* |
|---|---|---|
| 160 79 | 3 25 41 | 5 17 41 |
| 174 63 | 5 17 41 | 3 25 41 |
| 325 41 | 1 74 63 | 1 74 63 |
| 517 41 | 1 60 79 | 1 60 79 |

Why file this way? To eliminate misfiles from misreading six or more digits, as happens in regular numerical filing, and to disperse filing activity—the newest records are not placed at one end of the file, causing congested activity in that part of the file.

## GEOGRAPHICAL ARRANGEMENT

The main divisions for stored material in the geographical arrangement include states, counties, cities, branch-office territories, and salesmen's areas. Usually, the subdivisions are arranged alphabetically; for example, a sales area by cities in alphabetic order, and each city by customers' names in alphabetic order. An effective arrangement of the geographical plan of filing is shown in Figure 13–21.

The geographical arrangement, sometimes called location arrangement, is easy to understand, simple and direct, and can cover the overall work division, particularly that of sales. The files are generally less unwieldy than is frequently the case with the other basic arrangements. Also, several people can work at the files simultaneously—for instance, one in the Philadelphia file for "Cupper Manufacturing Company" and the other

FIGURE 13–21. Geographical Filing.

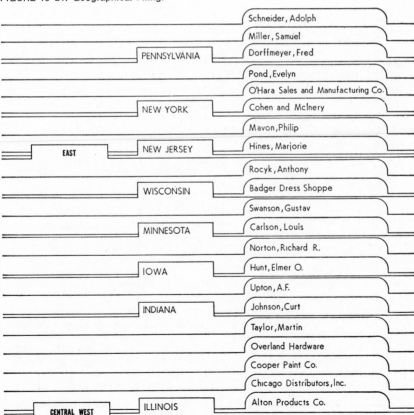

in the Los Angeles file for "Cizzla Sales Corporation." In addition, the geographical arrangement makes it comparatively simple to compile mailing lists by states or cities; and the segregation of material for tax, political, or mailing reasons is readily provided.

## CHRONOLOGICAL ARRANGEMENT

Segregating material according to its time sequence is the essence of this arrangement. The main divisions are either months or weeks, with the subdivisions being days. Some correspondence, bills, and pending accounts payable can be handled on a chronological plan. The advantages of this plan are simplicity, ease of filing, and a convenient signal or reminder of unfinished work, which is shown by the material in the file with reference to a specific date. The widely used "tickler file" is an adaptation of the chronological arrangement. Future matters requiring attention are filed under due dates or the time when action should be taken. A glance at the file shows for any given period what is to be followed up, what is behind schedule, and what must be handled in the near future.

FIGURE 13–22. Filing Guides.

1. Use enough guides and folders to help place and find the material quickly. Usually this means a guide for each inch of filing, a folder for about every six to eight papers.

2. File materials *behind* the guides.

3. Use colored tabs and labels to increase identification.

4. Put the latest material at front of a folder.

5. File each name according to (*a*) surname, (*b*) given name or initial, (*c*) middle name or initial, and (*d*) title, if important to retain.
 Alexander, Charles D. (Dr.)

6. File "nothing before something."
 Carter
 Carter, George
 Carter, George L.

7. File alphabetical material in exact sequence of letters, *A* through *Z*, to the last letter of the last word.
 M & A Stores, Inc.
 Maag, Robert C.
 MacArthur, Thomas P.
 Mack, Henry
 MacTavish, Sam W.

8. Treat compound words as one word.
 Cohen, Julius I.
 Co-operative Sales
 Co-workers Order of Bart

9. Spell out abbreviated names.
 Safety Tool Company
 Saint Louis Poultry Company
 Saint Paul Club
 Salk, Meyer L.

10. Spell out numerals and abbreviations.
 Three Thirty-Three Lake Building
 Young Women's Christian Association

11. When names are identical, file by city; then state; then street address.
 Carson, John M.
  Bangor, Maine
 Carson, John M.
  Springfield, Mass.

12. To save time with alphabetic material, sort by first segregating into four groups, such as A–F, G–L, M–R, and S–Z; then, sort each group according to the first letter. For numeric material, first sort 0–2, 3–5, and 6–9; then sort each group by the first digit.

## MAINTAINING AN EFFECTIVE ARRANGEMENT

Figure 13–22 lists some guides which should be followed to have an effective arrangement when manual means for storing information are followed. In most cases adherence to them will bring the most satisfactory results. However, they are suggestive only; individual circumstances may suggest deviations which work out better.

## INDEXING

The following material could be indexed in any one of the several different ways indicated:

| *Material* | *File According to:* |
|---|---|
| Catalogs | Date, name of company, or name of product |
| Correspondence | Date, subject, name of company, name of customer, name of seller, point of destination, or point of origin |
| Invoices | Date, name of customer, or number |
| Personnel application forms | Name of applicant, or type of work (subject) |
| Purchase orders | Date, name of vendor, name of product, or number |
| Tax reports | Date, subject, or name of taxing body |

That is, an index is a finding tool. It furnishes the key to how the materials are arranged. For any given set of material, a choice is made from several possible indexes. In some cases, the subject is the best index; in others, the name of the customer or the point of destination might be most useful.

Flexibility is of prime importance in an index so that needed changes can be made simply and quickly. In most manual applications and to a lesser degree in those that are automated, the collection of information keeps growing or changing so that the index must grow and change. Answers to questions such as the following aid in planning the superior index. What is being indexed? Are individual items easily identified and located? Are other indexes already in use and accepted by custom? What form should the index take—a list, on cards, in a manual? It is advisable to avoid the use of synonyms. Information on various types of rentals, such as house, townhouse, apartment, and store should be indexed under the heading, Rentals. If a distinction appears needed, use two headings: Rentals-domestic, Rentals-commerical. The advantage of adopting well-chosen headings is that a logical location is provided to assemble all of the items on a particular subject, and there will be only one place to look. Cross indexing is used when more than one subject is covered by the material or when several indicators are helpful in finding it. A report dealing with the subjects of market expansion and finances could be filed under the subject of markets, sales, future sales, finances, or costs. Cross indexes provide information as to where to place and to find the report; however, numerous cross references should be avoided in order to simplify the work as much as possible. Cross indexes can be well maintained in a separate card file. A typical card might read:

| | |
|---|---|
| Wages | *See also* Compensation |
| | Fringe Benefits |
| | Job Evaluation |
| | Salary |

That is, information about Wages may be found under all five terms. Some feel that when an alphabetical arrangement is used, the cross-reference index should be by number or code. In contrast, when the numerical arrangement is followed, the cross index should be alphabetical.

Essential in most offices is a *basic classification index* which is a categorical grouping of subjects with appropriate detailed subheadings. In addition, *a relative index* is helpful since it shows, in a dictionary type listing, all possible words and combinations by which the material may be requested. All indexes to stored material should be kept current by making new entries for additional classifications as they occur. Main new sources will be key words, new terminology, or any other means by which material may be requested.

## QUESTIONS

1. Discuss your understanding of the storing and retrieving activities in information management.
2. Relate your understanding of storing and retrieving information by the PCMI Microform System and include explanation of Figures 13–6 and 13–7 in your answer.
3. Explain in your own words the work done by the retrieval system shown by Figure 13–5.
4. As an office manager under what general conditions would you approve the use of motorized files?
5. What is meant by Computer Output Microfilm (COM) or micromation? Discuss its importance and potential in information management.
6. Point out the significant differences as well as the similarities between the Microimage retrieval and the Termatrex-Optical Coincidence means of storing and retrieving information.
7. Discuss the subject of indexing as an important part of filing.

8. Identify and discuss application of the suspension type, open-shelf type of lateral filing.
9. Identify each of the following, and explain how it is used:
   *a*) Image control for indexing microform.
   *b*) Terminal-digit file.
   *c*) Computer information retrieval.
   *d*) Card automatic file.
10. Explain the filing arrangement illustrated by Figure 13–20.
11. For each of the following filing troubles, suggest a feasible solution:
    *a*) Correspondence papers piled up in miscellaneous folders.
    *b*) Necessity of fingering many folders before finding the right one.
    *c*) Need to search through many papers in a folder to find the one wanted of a certain date.
    *d*) St. Louis correspondence may be found under "St. Louis," "Saint Louis," or "Missouri."
    *e*) File drawers jammed tight with material.
    *f*) Too many files in which a needed paper might be found.
12. Explain Figure 13–17 in your own words, using an application of this type filing to illustrate your answer.

## CASE PROBLEMS

### Case 13–1.   Evans-Nagle Company

This progressive mail order company processes much of its information by a modern computer installation. Current operations are running smoothly, but Mr. Victor Lucas, the information manager, believes there is always room for improvement. He cites the present work in connection with the customers' directory as an example. The company maintains a customer file showing name, address, and number. The latter or customer's number is an important means of identification and must appear on all input data handled by the computer.

It is not uncommon for a customer to send in an order without including his number. Much has been done to get the customer to include his number, but the general feeling is that there will always be some orders received without it. This lack of number requires a clerk to check a master customer directory, find the number, and mark it on the order before processing the order. If the order is from a new customer, a number must be assigned to him.

Currently the customer directory is a printed output of the computer. The information has been found to be quite accurate, but consists of many pages. It is cumbersome to use. Printed every three months, it is growing bigger and bigger with each issue. Mr. Lucas anticipates more problems with the present system in the future. The number of order-processing stations is increasing and will jump at least an additional 260 when the pending arrangement is soon settled for Evans-Nagle Company to establish catalog sales outlets in the stores of a large retail chain in which it has a substantial financial interest. Further, limited study by Mr. Lucas shows that the search time to find the number is increasing and lookup errors are rising. Mr. Lucas feels a better means of providing the customer's information must be found and adopted.

## Questions:

1. What is your recommendation to Mr. Lucas?
2. Explain how your suggested arrangement would operate.
3. Justify your recommendation.

### Case 13–2.    Metcalfe Power Corporation

According to Polly Dubonne, classification and accounts payable manager, her department handles 650 file actions daily including the storing of nearly 200 purchase orders. Miss Dubonne estimates that as many as 9,000 current purchase orders are on hand at one time and perhaps 15,000 pieces of related paper. All materials pertaining to purchases and accounts payable are considered active for two years from date of purchase and are retained in the department's files. This period was arrived at quite arbitrarily, but since its adoption some five years ago, has worked out quite well. At the present time, 80 four-drawer filing cabinets are in the department. The policy of the company, strongly entrenched, is to maintain all these cabinets in the general area of the department. Not only does this make for convenience but there is ample space available.

Estimates are that file expansion will take place at an annual rate of 18 percent. Considerable turnover is being experienced among file clerks. Currently the material is filed alphabetically. Beginning in the very near future a new computerized system will be inaugurated which will deliver material to Miss Dubonne's department at a rate faster than ever before.

The records manager, Mrs. Ethel Reynolds, believes that modification in the present storing and retrieving practices is desirable. Faster access to the material is needed in her opinion. Miss Dubonne agrees and points out that at least a part of the problem is a shortage of help for which she recommends an upward adjustment in wages for filing help. She adds, "The filing load is increasing steadily, but we have less people now than last year." Mrs. Reynolds observed informally on several occasions last week a clerk standing at the end of the file waiting her turn at the file. Also, she recalls several backshifts of the entire filed contents and transfer of material into additional filing cabinets.

## Questions:

1. In your opinion, what are the major ways to gain faster access to the filed material?
2. Based on the information given, what is your recommendation to the management of this company? Why?
3. What additional information about this case do you feel it desirable to have?

### Case 13–3.    Hennings Construction Company

Custom-built houses in the $27,500–$30,000 price range are constructed by the Hennings Construction Company, which maintains a main office, two construction offices, and an on-the-site sales office. The two construction offices are about 35 miles apart, and the main office is approximately 20 miles from the sales office or either of the construction offices.

The sales office and the construction offices require immediate information on costs, delivery of materials, and dates subcontractors performed work on the houses, and telephone the main office for this type of information. Unfortunately, the desired data are not always available, primarily because the three bookkeepers in the main office are two to four months behind in their work, and each bookkeeper keeps all the pertinent information in her desk drawer until she has posted the cash receipts and the payments to the subtrades, or put the sales through the books.

When a call is received from the sales department or from the construction department, the bookkeepers usually cannot get the information requested until the following day—or in some cases, not for several days. This is because, to find the data requested, it is frequently necessary to search through many papers in the desk drawer and six wooden filing cabinets along the wall of the office. Completed records are placed in these filing cabinets. All information pertaining to purchases, for example, is filed alphabetically, no attention being given to date purchases were made.

Under the present state of affairs, canceled checks and monthly bank statements are not reconciled for periods of two to three months. This work is handled by the chief bookkeeper, Betty Dougherty, who guards the canceled check work and permits no one else to perform this work. Some difficulty is experienced in getting the checks written for accounts payable. None of the bookkeepers want to do this check writing because it takes time from their bookkeeping work.

The situation became so bad that Carl Hennings, president of the company, called in Professor Franklin Swope from a nearby university to review the situation and make recommendations regarding what corrective action to take. Professor Swope studied the entire operations and at the end of two days discovered that:

1. The company managers do not believe in overtime work.
2. Office morale is low.
3. Any change to improve the office operation will be welcomed by Carl Hennings.
4. One key area for improvement is to get the processed papers into the files in accordance with an arrangement that will expedite usage of the filed material.
5. Carl Hennings is thinking of firing the entire office force.
6. Carl Hennings has no objections to the company's having two checking accounts—one for general payables, the other for payroll.

## Questions:

1. What pertinent recommendations do you feel Professor Swope should make to Mr. Hennings? Be specific.
2. What contributions do you believe improved filing management practices and procedures can contribute to this company? Why?
3. What difficulties do you anticipate in implementing the recommendations you feel Professor Swope should make? How would you overcome these difficulties?

chapter **14**

# Managing the
# information stored

THE IMPORTANCE of storing and retrieving information in any enterprise demands that adequate management over this work be provided. Too often neglected, or viewed as an adjunct to a major office activity, it simply exists and fends for itself as best it can. Some have termed it the "universal blind spot of office management"—an overstatement, indicating the challenge of this vital area.

## PRESENT STATUS

With the advent of more and expensive machines, storing and retrieving activities undoubtedly will capture the eyes of more managers. The number of machines and the selection of them will help bring this about as well as the current thrust toward greater realization of effective storing and retrieving contributions toward improved services of information management. Currently manual labor represents by far the lion's share of the total storing and retrieving expenditures. Yet we can not rely on mechanization alone to bring about progress. The records manager must do his part.

This means that better managerial practices must be applied not only for mechanized, but probably more important for nonmechanized installations. Although excellent machines are available and will gain acceptance more and more, we will still perform much storing and retrieving work by nonmechanized means. Consideration for basic factors such as volume of records, cost, and deeply entrenched customs in this area will make this so. For example, the small enterprise will no doubt continue with nonmechanized methods unless centralized storing and retrieving centers flourish far beyond our present expectations. And there is the somewhat unexplainable affinity for retaining the original document. Some are dissatisfied with a copy or a small reproduction of the original. To illustrate, many courts prefer original documents, but will accept microfilmed material when failure to produce the original is adequately explained. In time, these barriers will go by the wayside. Microfilm, for example, is proving an excellent medium and is destined to gain wide acceptance and permanency in many of the mechanized operations.

## MANAGEMENT OF MECHANIZED MEANS

With direct connections to a computer and the use of other sophisticated machines for information storing and retrieving purposes, it seems paramount to have a responsible person head up these activities. Only in this way will specific goals be pursued and needless overlapping of efforts and of records maintained minimized. In addition, legitimate growth or contraction of storing and retrieving activities will be won in keeping with the individual mechanized means being utilized. Further, having an active head over these activities gives recognition to their importance, potential contribution, and proper management.

The mechanized arrangement makes for centralization of this work which, in turn, raises some interesting managerial questions. One is the control over the number of copies. With automated printouts and hard copies readily available, there may be a tendency to provide an excess of such copies. Thus, the retrieval gates might be opened too widely and the office flooded with papers not required. Another problem is the proper maintenance of confidential information. Many machines are equipped with lockout arrangements preventing machine operation to unauthorized personnel. But there remains the question of what information stored in a machine is not confidential and, further, who determines what personnel are authorized. To this can be added, what information should be stored in the first place? The answers, of course, are supplied by competent managers. Again pointing out that the machine is basically an extremely capable tool of management, but not management itself.

In contrast, it should be observed that the centralization effect of mechanization is minimized by the use of many terminal units in the case of computers or of many widely dispersed units in the case of other mechanized arrangements. Further, the rapid transmission of information from one part of an organization to another tends to negate the presence of centralization. Fundamentally, however, the core of the work efforts are performed in a centralized area and it is over these efforts that management is concentrated.

Cost is relative and in the case of mechanization should be considered in light of what volume of work and service—speed, accuracy, and convenience—is being supplied. High volume is usually required for sound economic mechanization. In the case of computerized storing and retrieving, the total computer expense is small. If the computer is already available, the managerial information cost is minimal, nevertheless it should be made to reflect reasonably accurate cost data. In an application of microfiche, the cost is about $700 annual rental per viewing unit. Charges for the microfiches vary with the quantity, but are reasonable. Against these costs must be weighed the extra time required to find the information from several manuals, the expense of printing the manual sheets, purchase of binders, and the supplying of fresh copies.

Because of difficulty in establishing, the use of work standards may be ignored in managing storing and retrieving under a mechanized means. This is a mistake. Reasonably accurate standards should be sought and applied. Records of accomplishments should be maintained and expected work outputs mutually agreed upon between the manager and the employees. The need for management is not lessened because the operation is mechanized.

Finally, there is specialized training to provide. Efficiency in operating the machines is aided by adequate instruction in the use of the machines by the personnel. The machine manufacturers commonly supply all the operational information required, but the selection, placement, and instruction of the personnel in performing the work remains the task of the company management.

## MANAGEMENT OF NONMECHANIZED MEANS

Here again and for the same reasons mentioned above, there should be a management head of storing and retrieving activities. The person should have adequate authority to direct and maintain the activities. He may have committees to assist in certain phases of the work and he may consult with department heads. But the ultimate responsibility for managing the storing and retrieving is his alone. One person in charge helps promote needed study and improvements. He must, of course, exercise strong leadership, otherwise the efforts are not properly coordinated and directed. Locating stored information convenient to those frequently using it is recommended. But to implement this recommendation requires decisions as to where the information will be stored, the number of copies to be retained, and some screening of information to ensure retention of information which has value or a reasonable expectancy of future certainty.

Cost is used by many enterprises to keep nonmechanized storing and retrieving work within reasonable limits. Some overall cost constraints usually are helpful and should be established. The average expenditure for a typical four-drawer cabinet is about $250 annually. Fifty files, therefore, mean $12,500 annual cost. Cost data on other equipment should be sought. The expenditures for labor and space will vary depending upon the particular location, but cost for equipment is relatively uniform. For this latter, an average cost figure is 35 cents per cubic foot of information stored. However, this may be inappropriate for some types of equipment; the cost of lineal inches of storage space may be better. The number of records is of little value because of the wide variation in type, content, and size of records. Surplus equipment should be transferred to an area where it is required and any purchase of equipment should be reviewed carefully to determine its essentiality.

Ratios, helpful for managerial purposes, can be derived. To illustrate, the maximum cubic feet of information per employee can be determined. The amount permitted will depend upon the type of enterprise. In public utilities, for example, an amount of 5 cubic feet of records per employee on payroll is considered satisfactory. For an assembly plant a comparable figure may be only 1 cubic foot of records; whereas in a purchasing department, the amount may be as great as 12 cubic feet, yet qualify as an acceptable amount.

Helpful ratios can also be derived. To illustrate, a "usage" ratio reveals the extent to which the materials stored are being used. The formula is:

$$\text{Usage ratio (in \%)} = \frac{\text{Retrievals} \times 100}{\text{References filed}}$$

For example, if last month, 200 retrievals were made from 20,000 items stored, the usage ratio in percentage would be 200 x 100 divided by 20,000 or 1 percent. This ratio for stored materials will seldom exceed 5 percent. For active materials, it should run about 15 to 20 percent. Further analysis of usage ratios can be made, taking into account the rate of reference by type of record versus the age of the record. Such studies assist in better controlling of storing and retrieving efforts.

Another ratio is the "accuracy" ratio, which is calculated by this formula:

$$\text{Accuracy ratio (in \%)} = \frac{\text{Number of items not found} \times 100}{\text{Number of items found}}$$

For 10 items not found and 10,000 found, the ratio is 0.1 percent. For a rating of excellent, the accuracy ratio should not be greater than 0.5 percent. A value of 3 percent or more signifies that remedial action is required.

Work expectancies should be developed and followed. With these as a guide, along with periodic follow-ups, the manager can determine whether prescribed methods are being followed and whether the level of work is satisfactory. Spot checks for accuracy are advisable. For this purpose a committee can be used in order to generate more interest in the work and enhance an awareness of needed improvements. Expectancies will vary among different enterprises due to a number of variables, chief of which are the type of records and the general work environment. However, to demonstrate what can be done, the following expectancies are shown, based on data from a number of companies:

| Task | Units per Hour |
|---|---|
| Sorting letters and filing alphabetically | 180 |
| Filing 5 x 8-inch cards in an alphabetical vertical file | 315 |
| Locating and pulling letters from an alphabetical file | 110 |
| Filing vouchers numerically | 700 |
| Marking one-page letters for filing | 220 |

From the viewpoint of organizing, nonmechanized storing and retrieving commonly are on a decentralized basis, which provides accessibility for those needing the information, flexibility in arrangement, and reasonably satisfactory service. But desirable coordination may be lacking. This prompts some to suggest that perhaps an arrangement centralized from the viewpoint of managerial operation and decentralized as to the physical location of files is superior. With centralized management authority, the best of storing and retrieving knowledge and practices from the overall company viewpoint can be put into use. However, the exact organizational plan depends upon individual requirements and understanding them. The needs are not always the same. The type of material, the work habits of the employees using the files, the normal filing usage, the flow of work, and the frequency of records are several of the more influential considerations.

One of the major realistic difficulties is better placement of personnel for storing and retrieving work. In too many instances, the attitude prevails that the untrained office employee who cannot be fitted in elsewhere because of lack of skill should be given filing work. Entirely overlooked is the fundamental truth that storing and retrieving personnel should possess certain attributes, including a sense of orderliness, accuracy, manual dexterity, quick reading comprehension, and a liking for detail.

To gain the best efforts of personnel the following program is offered. First of all, the manager of storing and retrieving must instill a feeling of confidence in the work. Each employee must believe in what he is doing, its importance, and its contribution. It is also necessary to make sure that all requests are clear and complete. Frequently, the file clerk is expected to have an ability to find a piece of paper even though she has never seen it and does not know what it was about, who it was from, or when it was written. In addition, a manual supplying information on the procedures and practices to storing and retrieving personnel is also helpful. Data on the type of material stored, the indexing system, and specific duties should be written clearly and made available to anyone whose work is affected by storing and retrieving. Such a manual is extremely beneficial for obtaining better understanding and for training purposes. Further, with the assistance of the employees, the manager should select suitable equipment and create a favorable physical work environment. In addition, an upward adjustment in pay should be seriously considered. Nonmechanized storing and retrieving can never be more efficient than the people doing the work. Improved pay scales assist in acquiring better skills, lowering turnover, and stimulating improved effort.

## PROCEDURE FOR MANUAL STORING AND RETRIEVING

The chief steps in such a procedure include:

*1. Checking Release for Storing.* Before any material is stored, it must first be checked to be sure it is released for storing. Material which is still being processed or referred to, or which, because of policy, is not retained by the company, should, of course, not be stored.

*2. Reading and Marking.* Reading is done to determine the proper storing classification. A marking to indicate this classification can be shown by underscoring or circling a word or two on the paper or by stamping or writing the proper file data in the upper right corner. A colored pencil usually works very satisfactorily, as the contrast aids future reference. If there is a possibility of storing under several headings, it is helpful to consult the cross-reference index to insure use of the best classification for the material.

*3. Sorting.* Next, the material is sorted by mark showing the storing classification. Sorting can be performed entirely manually or with the use of a sorting device. In the former, the material is divided into neat piles on a table or desk, each pile being of a different classification. When this method is followed, it is best to sort all material according to major divisions, then each major division by subdivisions, and finally each subdivision as required. For example, for alphabetic material, sort by first segregating into four groups, such as A-F, G-L, M-R, and S-Z; then, sort each group according to the first letter. For numeric material, first sort 0–2, 3–5, and 6–9; then, sort each group by the first digit. Figure 14–1 shows sorting devices being used in a large office. The device consists of dividers properly indexed and hinged, at intervals of about ¼ inch up to 1 inch, to a common base section. Thus, a series of pockets is formed, and each item of the material to be sorted is dropped into the proper pocket.

FIGURE 14–1. Sorting Waybills in a Large Office. Approximately three million waybills per year are sorted in this office.

*Courtesy: Erie Railroad, Cleveland*

Different sizes are available, ranging from around 30 up to as many as 2,000 divisions or pockets.

**4. Storing.** Each piece is stored under the proper classification, with the newest addition always on top or at the front of the contents in its respective folder. This actually amounts to placing the material into its proper place and quickly checking the work as it progresses.

**5. Retrieving Information.** A definite manner for handling the removal of papers from the container is necessary in order to maintain the file and to know where items are, in the event that several people want the papers at the same time, and also to minimize indiscriminate removals from the files. Records of charged-out materials can be handled in any one of four ways as illustrated by Figure 14–2: (*a*) by substitution card, (*b*) by out folder, (*c*) by out guide, or (*d*) by multiple charge-out form.

When the removed material is a single card or piece of paper, its place in the file can be occupied by a substitution card showing the name of the person to whom the material is issued, along with the date and the initials of the employee issuing the material. Upon return of the material, the entries on the substitution card are lined out, and the card is reused. Out folders are ordinary file folders with one side printed for the recording of

FIGURE 14–2. Media Used in Controlling Charge-Outs from Filed Material: (*a*) Substitution Card, (*b*) Out Folder, (*c*) Out Guide, and (*d*) Multiple Charge-Out Form.

data concerning removals from that folder. The out guide is a pressboard guide with tab printed "Out" and a pocket or device to hold a single charge-out slip. It replaces a folder taken from the file and serves both as a record and as a marker for the borrowed material. When the withdrawn material is to be transferred from one user to another, a multiple charge-out form is used. As shown in Figure 14–2 the date, identification, and is attached to the substitution card, out folder, or out guide. A second route of material are written on the multiple forms. One copy of this form copy is filed in a tickler file for follow-up. Other copies are attached to the material so that, as each individual or department using the material finishes with it, a line is drawn through the name or department on the route list; the top copy is returned to the issuing storing and retrieving department; and the remaining copies and material are forwarded to the next name on the route list. As copies are retrieved, they are attached to the tickler file copy; thus, there is a record of who has the material, without clearance of the material each time through the department.

## RECORDS RETENTION

The storing of records cannot continue indefinitely. Containers become filled to capacity and many records stored have outlived their usefulness. Periodic culling of the stored material is required. You cannot file and forget.

The life cycle of all records consists of three stages (1) active use— quick access is important, (2) storage—for possible use, and (3) elimination—no longer of use. Succinctly stated, worthless records should never be stored, records stored should be reviewed periodically to eliminate those that have become useless, and those stored having either permanent or possible future use should be transferred to inexpensive storage areas. These concepts are the essential makeup of records retention, an important part of records management. Formally stated, *records retention deals with the disposition of records and concerns storing those that must be retained and destroying those that are or become worthless.*

## ADVANTAGES OF RECORDS RETENTION

A records-retention program can be quite extensive, nearly everyone in an enterprise is affected by it. A great deal of foresight, judgment, and especially a steadfastness of purpose are required. The rewards are high. Better storing and retrieving efficiency is gained since inactive material is removed, thus reducing finding time. Space savings are also achieved— throwing out records that have become useless means less space is needed. Also, storing useful but inactive records in an inexpensive storage area means dollar savings. And avoidance from accidental or premature destruction of records is assured. Furthermore, the retained records are better protected and safeguarded. Equipment designed especially for storage can be utilized, and the records are not subject to possible mutilation as a result of frequent handling.

Typically, records retention brings about these results: 26 percent of all stored material is retained as active, 16 percent is placed in inexpensive storage for possible future use, and the balance, 58 percent is eliminated. Think of it. Only one paper in four remains in the office file. The savings in finding time and space are tremendous. The National Records

Management Council, Inc., a nonprofit organization, estimates only 5 percent of all records filed are ever referred to after a year and 5 percent of the references made deal with records over five years old. A large public utility reported to be spending nearly $24 million to maintain some 200,000 filing cabinets, adopted a records retention program and trimmed this cost to $17 million and with better service and efficiency. The gains by several other companies are shown by Figure 14–3.

FIGURE 14–3. Typical Disposition of Records by Companies Without and Those with Records-Retention Programs.

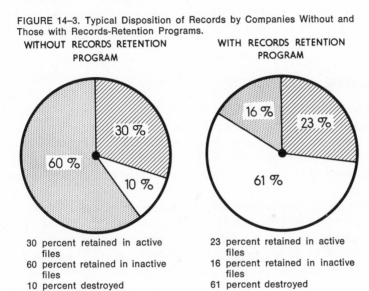

WITHOUT RECORDS RETENTION PROGRAM

WITH RECORDS RETENTION PROGRAM

30 percent retained in active files
60 percent retained in inactive files
10 percent destroyed

23 percent retained in active files
16 percent retained in inactive files
61 percent destroyed

## TAKE INVENTORY OF RECORDS

The objective of a records-retention program is to retain only needed records only as long as they are needed. To this end the first step is to find out what records you have and evaluate them. We shall term this step, take inventory of records.

The study might begin with a cursory review of the entire enterprise to obtain background and understanding of the current work and to spot what records are used and what ones are filed for satisfactory operation. Following this, a survey is in order to determine (1) what is filed; (2) how much is filed—its size and quantity; (3) where it is filed—including the copies, if any; (4) how often it was used during specific preceding periods; (5) when, if ever, it is permanently removed from file; and (6) what is done with permanently removed material. In some instances, this inventory work is expedited by classifying the material by type or by department. Information applicable to several departments can be studied as a group, thus relating the types of information common to the several units. Usually a simple form is used upon which to record the data.

From the survey data, the value of each record is weighed. Questions decided are: Should this record be filed at all? How long should this record remain in the file? Is it advisable to retain this record in storage? Only material considered to have future worth should be stored. Keeping worthless materials out of storage is easier than getting them removed once they are stored. It is helpful to pay particular attention to records presently having long-term retention because frequently their retention times can be cut measurably below the periods formerly believed necessary.

## DETERMINE RECORDS-RETENTION PERIODS

Determining records-retention periods is the next step which deals with the problem of how long to retain active and inactive file material. This, in turn, depends primarily upon the usefulness of the material to managers, and the legal requirements. The period of retention differs among companies, but there is a tendency toward the development of standard practices.

What papers to retain and for how long a period can probably best be decided by members most affected by these issues. Usually, the controller, the legal counsel, the tax counsel, and the manager of records retention should be included in this group; they usually are well qualified for such decision making. For the most part, this group sets forth policy instructions on which operating decisions can be based by the manager of records retention.

Papers that are essential to the company's security should be kept. Proof of assets and liabilities is important. Papers giving proof of ownership, property, inventories, machinery, and buildings are included in this category. Insurance is recovered on proof, not guesswork. Records dealing with transactions should be saved. These include receipt of money, proof of payment, proof of expenses or puchases, and payroll. Also, documents providing proof of usage should be retained, for they are vital in matters dealing with research, engineering, and patents. If the company becomes involved in infringement or other patent-suit claims, certain drawings, properly coded, numbered, and preserved, form the basis for prosecution or defense. Historical data of various types often prove valuable in that they provide trends and statistical analysis helpful in the company's planning efforts. Such data should be retained if there is a reasonable possibility that they will be used in the future or will be referred to for improving decision making by relating the reasons given *why* certain decisions were made in the past with the outcome of such decisions.

FIGURE 14–4. Suggested Schedule for Retention of Various Records in Years.

| | | | |
|---|---|---|---|
| Accounts receivable | 10 | Insurance—property | 8 |
| Agreements with employees | P* | Labor clock records | 5 |
| Annual and monthly reports | P | Labor earnings records | P |
| Articles of incorporation | P | Medical histories | P |
| Attendance records of employees | 7 | Minute book of directors meeting | P |
| Bids | 3 | Paid bills | 8 |
| Cash books | P | Patent records | P |
| Charge slips | 10 | Registered mail | 5 |
| Checks canceled | 10 | Requisitions | 3 |
| Correspondence— | | Sales expenses | 6 |
| credit and collection | 7 | Shipping tickets | 6 |
| —purchase | 5 | Tax bills and statements | P |
| Delivery receipts | 3 | Time and motion studies | P |
| Dividend checks | 10 | Union labor contracts | P |
| Financial statements | P | Wage rates | 8 |
| General ledger | P | | |

\* P = Permanent

Figure 14–4 shows selected retention periods for various records. These values represent the consensus of authorities on record storage and reflect current thinking in this area. However, the statute of limitations, which varies for different documents among states, regulatory activities by government agencies, and personal preferences should be considered in the choice. The statute of limitations specifies the length of time a record is alive according to law.

Based on the information obtained from the inventory of records, suggested retention periods, and judgment, records of varying importance can be classified as to their retention. For convenience, they can be divided into four groups:

*1. Nonessential.* Records so classified should never be stored. Since they have value for a short period only—perhaps a few seconds—retaining them is wasteful. Included are pencil notations, routine inquiries, and announcements.

*2. Helpful.* Records in this group can assist, but only for a very limited time, perhaps four to five weeks. After this period, their usefulness is completed. If filed, they should be placed in a separate drawer or cabinet and destroyed as their helpfulness ceases. An example is general correspondence, most of which has a useful life of not over four weeks.

*3. Important.* These include records containing information of value for relatively long periods—up to five or six years. They should first be stored in the office for handy reference; but ultimately, as they lose their current usefulness, they should be transferred to an inexpensive storage area. How long they remain in the office depends upon the type of record and the retention period established. Many firms keep records such as invoices, accounts receivable, sales records, quotations, and financial statements in active files for one to two years, then transfer to a storage area.

**4. Vital.** As the name implies, these records are paramount. They are retained permanently. They may be transferred to the storage area after a given period of time, but they are never destroyed. Vital records include legal papers of incorporation, titles to ownership, deeds, and reports to stockholders.

## PROVIDE A GOOD STORAGE AREA

The third step is to provide a clean, dry area to serve as an inexpensive and safe storage area. Proper conditions of temperature, circulation of air, and humidity should be provided. The storage areas should be regarded as attractive work areas. The floor area must withstand a relatively high weight, as much as 250 pounds per square foot. Location can be either on-site (same as office) or off-site (away from office).

Various types of equipment can be used for storing records. Of special interest is a specially designed fiberboard drawer file which combines the drawer, shelving, and base, all in one unit. A steel framework carries the entire weight load. The drawer files are interlocking, each drawer locking to the one below and the one above it. The unit "builds its own steel framework as you stack it." As many as 20 drawers can be stacked in one tier. There is no buckling, sagging, or warping. Different sizes are available for punched cards, letter, and legal-size papers. The total space is devoted to drawer units, which results in a compact, efficient use of storage space giving the high storage ratio of 8 to 1, i.e., the cubic feet of records to square feet of floor space. For bulk storage where reference is infrequent, larger containers with the same interlocking feature can be used. Each container is about 15 inches by 24 inches and holds two boxes, one of which can be used for letter, the other for legal size. Details and illustrations of this storage equipment are shown in Figure 14–5.

For records in storage, a system of indexing should be adopted, so that all such material can be located quickly. The information can be kept on small index cards or on sheets in a loose-leaf notebook. It should include subject classification, shelf number, box number or name, and scheduled date for ultimate destruction. It is important that each container be labeled plainly.

At least once a year, a list should be prepared showing what stored original records should be destroyed. It can be compiled readily from data on the index cards. This list is then submitted to the records manager or designated executive for approval and authority to proceed. When this has been granted, the material is destroyed and the list filed permanently for future reference.

FIGURE 14–5. Storage Boxes Slide into the Stacking Shell. These shells are stacked one upon the other forming a unit of interlocking fiberboard drawer files which is compact and sturdy.

*Courtesy: Bankers Box Record Storage Systems, Franklin Park, Ill.*

## TRANSFER RECORDS

The last step of a records-retention program is transfer records. Several moves are necessary, including transfer from active to inactive files and from inactive files to a low-cost storage area. In each case the transfer may also lead to a decision for their destruction should the records at that stage be considered worthless. Reference to Figure 14–6 is helpful in discussing the various tranfers.

FIGURE 14-6. A Program of Records Retention.

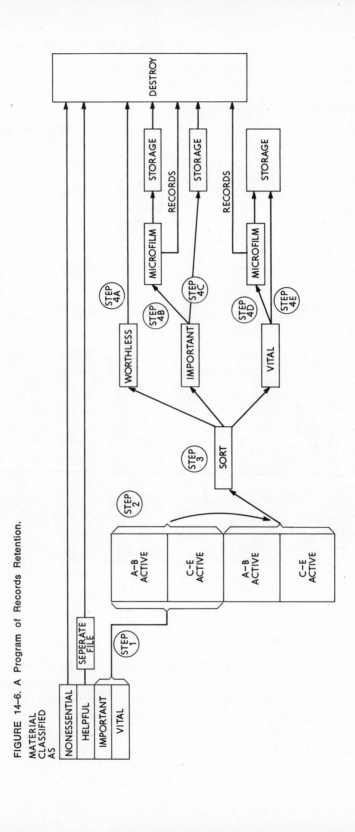

To reiterate, material classified as nonessential should never be filed, but should be destroyed immediately. "Helpful" material is filed in a separate file for the limited period, then destroyed. Material considered important or vital is stored (step 1) and subsequently transferred to the inactive file as a normal practice (step 2). With a four-drawer filing cabinet, the top drawers can be used for current material and the bottom two for inactive material. This arrangement affords convenient reference to inactive material which is necessary from time to time. When the five-drawer file is used, a common arrangement to follow is illustrated by Figure 14–7.

FIGURE 14–7. Arrangement for Active and Inactive Material in Five-Drawer Files.

| 1 INACTIVE | 3 INACTIVE | 6 INACTIVE | 8 INACTIVE |
|---|---|---|---|
| 1 | 4 | 6 | 9 |
| 2 | 5 | 7 | 10 |
| 3 | 4 INACTIVE | 8 | 9 INACTIVE |
| 2 INACTIVE | 5 INACTIVE | 7 INACTIVE | 10 INACTIVE |

The transferring of material can be done in one of two main ways: (1) the entire unit, or periodically; and (2) the individual, or perpetually. The former requires that all material be transferred at a scheduled time. Usually, an annual basis is used—at the beginning of the calendar year, fiscal year, or busy season. The material remains in the original folders and is moved bodily. New folders are used for the new material in the current file. The individual, or perpetual, means places time limits on individual papers by appropriate marks on the folders. Then, periodically, at intervals of about two or three months—or perpetually, at irregular intervals—the files are screened, and papers found to have been in the file past the allowable limit are transferred to the inactive file. In cases where the transaction is terminated, i.e., a settlement granted or a sale closed, the material is transferred immediately, regardless of date.

From the inactive files all materials are removed periodically and sorted (step 3 of Figure 14–6). The material in these files is now classified as either worthless, important, or vital. Worthless material is destroyed as indicated by step 4A; important material follows either step 4B or 4C; and for the vital information either step 4D or 4E is adopted. This program may be somewhat modified for certain individual applications. For example, microfilm may not be used at all, or it may be found more practical to eliminate step 3 (sorting), microfilm all records, and use the microfilms for reference in all cases.

At the time records are placed in storage, many records managers suggest determining the future life period of that material. Thus stamped on the box is a notice such as "Destroy July, 1976," or "Retain permanently." In any event, as stated above, all transferred material should be classified, properly labeled, and indexed so that it can be found if needed.

## QUESTIONS

1. Discuss the managerial consideration for cost, standards, and number of copies in storing and retrieving work when mechanical means are used.
2. In your opinion will the management of information storing and retrieving become more or less important in the future? Justify your viewpoint.
3. Do you recommend having a responsible person head up storing and retrieving activities regardless of whether mechanized or nonmechanized means for handling the work are followed? Why?
4. For how long a period do you suggest each item in the following list of filed material be retained:
   a) Sales prospect lists.
   b) Invoices from suppliers of raw materials.
   c) Real estate deeds.
   d) Payrolls and pay rates.
   e) Application forms from prospective employees.
   f) Quotations to customers.
5. Suggest ways to improve the efficiency of storing and retrieving personnel.
6. Last month, storing and retrieving sorted 4,640 items in preparation for filing, performed 850 successful retrievals, failed to find 38 requested retrievals, and received additional equipment valued at $690. It is estimated that there are a total of 65,000 items in the files. What is the accuracy ratio? The usage ratio? Is any remedial action suggested by your values for either of these ratios? Explain.
7. What is the meaning of records retention, and of what importance is it?
8. Describe the meaning of Figure 14–6 in your own words.
9. Discuss major considerations in providing a good storage area for records retention.
10. Write a two-sentence identifying description of each of the following:
    a) Life cycle of all records.
    b) Fiberboard drawer file.

*c*) Multiple charge-out form.
*d*) Statute of limitations.

11. An office which has never had a records-retention program is now interested in establishing one. Suggest an approach which can be followed to meet this purpose.

12. Do you favor the entire-unit or the individual method in the transferring of filed material? Why?

## CASE PROBLEMS

### Case 14–1. Quebec-Fortier Services Corporation

Mr. Conrad Boggan, assistant information manager, estimates that 50 file drawers or 75 cubic feet of material are annually placed in records storage. He is not sure, with all the alternatives now available to the corporation, that the best program is being followed. In bringing up the subject with Mr. Michelle Angone, the information manager, an interesting discussion developed during which it was agreed that Mr. Boggan should study further major alternatives to that of the company's present practice.

The first alternative is to microfilm all inactive material removed from the files. A few documents would be stored in their original form, but for purposes here we can consider all material placed in the storage area will be in microfilm. Mr. Boggan talked with a representative from a microfilm service company and was quoted $6.50 per 100-ft. reel which quotation includes total costs, i.e., machine, material, and labor. Approximately 3,500 documents are photographed on a 100-ft. reel and there are 3,000 documents per cubic foot. According to Mr. Boggan, about 140 documents are retrieved yearly from the storage area. The representative indicated that such retrievals with the material on microfilm would cost about $1.25 each. This includes cost of a viewing machine depreciated over a ten-year period.

Mr. Boggan believed the answer might be a sorting of the documents removed from the files into (1) present form storage (2) microfilm and store, and (3) destroy useless material. For this alternative, Mr. Angone secured some cost estimates including ten man-hours of labor at $2.50 an hour, one third of the material microfilmed, and two thirds destroyed. As above, some stored material will not be microfilmed, but it will be a relatively small amount and can be considered microfilmed for purposes of this analysis.

The third alternative is to obtain microfilm records of computer output at time of initial processing using the COM, or computer output microfilm arrangement. These microfilm records would serve as the storage copies for all computer-processed data. There would also be noncomputer processed papers such as customers' orders and correspondence which Mr. Boggan estimates will be 25 file drawers annually, or one half of the present amount now annually removed from the active files. These could be handled as under the first alternative, i.e., microfilmed and to the storage area. Mr. Angone advises that COM cost per year for the computer-processed papers can be estimated at $360. He also noted that the current total cost for retrieving an original record from the storage area is $8.00.

## Questions:

1. Are there other alternatives to the problem of records retention that should be considered? Explain.
2. Make a table by listing the present practice and the three alternatives vertically with cost and other important considerations horizontally. For each alternative fill in the total cost and note the other important considerations.
3. What decision do you recommend be made? Why?

### Case 14–2.  Martin-Durkee Manufacturing Company

RALPH HESS: Come in, please. You're Mr. Fred Ford, the management consultant?

FRED FORD: Yes. Thank you very much.

HESS: I'll be glad to assist you in every way. I suppose you'd like me to start by discussing what we do here?

FORD: Yes, if you will.

HESS: The engineering design division is divided into three sections: design, administration, and design drafting. I am in charge of the latter. We are responsible for all mechanical drafting work in the designing of new products, improvements in the design of existing products, production drawings relative to the building of prototype products, and products to be built under contract to customers.

FORD: You handle improvements in existing design?

HESS: Yes, sir.

FORD: What does the design section handle?

HESS: They handle the design of new products only. Now, to be able to use the latest commercially offered items as components of design—and this is true for new product design as well, that is, for the design section—it is necessary to have readily available a file of catalogs and design manuals offered by various manufacturers. All these cabinets you see in the room out there are filled with such material. In addition, we have correspondence, blueprints, original drawings, and even samples of various items. Some of these, both papers and samples, are odd sizes and shapes, and are difficult to store; and my guess is that part of what we have out there could be discarded.

FORD: Do the files out there represent all the stored reference material?

HESS: No. There are stacks of stuff in a basement room. The material is stacked up in neat little piles on the floor; each stack is tagged, but it's a mess to find anything down there.

FORD: Do you have need to go to this basement room from time to time?

HESS: Yes, every once in a while. The men resent being sent there to look for something—all except Harvey Pair, who doesn't seem to mind. In fact, I guess you could say he even enjoys it. Gets lost down there for half a day at a time.

FORD: About how frequently do you refer to the files out here in this next room?

HESS: That's hard to say. Sometimes, quite often; at other times, maybe just once or twice a day.

FORD: How is the material arranged in these files?

HESS: It's supposed to be alphabetical by manufacturer's name, that is, for the design manuals. General literature from vendors is kept in a separate tier of cabinets, by vendor's name. Several times a week, a young lady from the main office brings current material and files it. But my designers and draftsmen are constantly coming to me and complaining they can't find the material they want, and they insist it was in the files. Sometimes, we find it misfiled; sometimes, the young lady tells us we never did have the material; sometimes, it is lost but turns up later.

FORD: What do you think should be done?

HESS: Well, now. . . . I understand you're the expert, so what I say may not make any sense. But for whatever it is worth, I think there is too much junk in the files—stuff we'll never use. And some way to find what we want would be a big help, too. Why, we've requested new copies of booklets and catalogs from a supplier only to discover before we receive them that we have the same booklets or catalogs in our file. Just could not find them when we wanted them.

## Questions:

1. What further information do you feel Mr. Ford should obtain from Mr. Hess?
2. As Mr. Ford, would you hold any other interviews or make any observations within the company? Why?
3. What recommendations would you make to the company's managers? Discuss.

chapter **15**

# Managing copying and office supplies

COMMONLY considered a part of records management in offices are a
number of activities closely related to records storing and retrieving. In
the large office they represent a sizable quantity of work, frequently that
of a department, and require adequate supervision and a watchful eye
over the costs and services supplied. In the small office, this work may be
performed by typists or clerks along with their normal work duties. In
this instance it would be common for outside agencies to be used to meet
any large requirement such as making 500 copies of a 20-page sales report.

## EXPANSION OF COPYING

Copying is one of the current fast-growing areas of information efforts.
Today there are over 50 manufacturers offering nearly 400 different
models of copying machines. The cost per copy has dropped, but the total
expenditure for copying has increased. The reasons for this growth are
numerous but of prime importance are the need to have the information
quickly, the relative inefficiency of manual means, and the availability of
high quality machines providing copies at low unit cost. The convenience
of quality copies has modified many former practices followed in information management. This ability to produce a number of copies of the
original material gives the manager another new tool with which to devise

better ways to get information to people that need it and want it. The simple requirement of just having the information at your fingertips when it is needed—no processing of the data involved—can now keep pace with the hastening tempo of the other activities of data handling. No longer must an employee laboriously copy material word for word on a typewriter or by manual means. This work can be mechanized. Further, the wide variations in machine speeds and sheet sizes, which can be accomodated, provide a range to meet the individual requirement of the particular application.

In this discussion we are employing the single word, *copying*, to include all written reproducing and duplicating of information. For the sake of simplicity, this seems satisfactory, but there are differences and it is advisable to state now what they are. Reproducing is making an exact image of the original. Usually the same size is obtained; art and graphic material are included exactly as in the original. In contrast, duplicating is substitute printing and involves preparing a master from which copies are produced. It is found when many copies are required. Art and graphic material can be included, but they must be a part of the master used. There are copying machines or copiers and duplicating machines or duplicators.

## MANAGEMENT OF COPYING

With the expansion of copying and the innovating of information activities has come the demand and challenge for adequate management of copying. From the overall view, this implies performing copying that assists in the essential work being done and that is in keeping with the major goals sought. Fundamental questions arise. For example, "Are copies really needed?" If so, "What minimum number will suffice?" "Is it better to print computer output on regular forms, or on transparent paper or direct-image master plates for reproduction?" "Should we make or buy most of our office printing needs?"

These are not easy questions to answer; they require sound managerial decisions and actions which are subject to both periodic review and interpretation. A basic consideration is the quantity, quality, speed, and flexibility of the copying service. Determining what these attributes should be is provided by securing facts on both future work that will be done and present work being done that involves or should involve copying. This resolves into sound planning for future copying. For existent copying efforts a yearly usage report is recommended. This includes such information as the type of documents being copied, the equipment used, copies made, and the cost of operation. In addition, a monthly log of each machine showing similar types of information is helpful.

Analysis of such data will spot areas to be corrected and suggest changes for general improvement of the copying service. Specifically, what appears to be excessive cost can be investigated from the viewpoint of what documents are being copied, what use is made of these copies, whether the machine is a purchase or a rental, whether a special operator is required, and how many copies are made of each document? This latter information is usually quite helpful because it indicates the number of different job setups, whether the runs are short or long, and what type of machine is best suited for this type flow of work.

Improvement in copying management takes many different forms; for example, selection and location of the proper type copying machine for the specific requirements, elimination of existent copying abuses, control of copying costs, reduction of the size of the document, placement of copy on both sides of the paper, and the use of a different color paper to provide needed distinguishing purposes. We will look at several of these approaches more closely.

Proper machine selection includes consideration for speed, capacity, quality of copying, and freedom from maintenance—all as they influence the service required. Machine location brings up the question of whether placing a copier near the department having the most need for it is better than establishing several copying stations throughout the office and plant, or having all copiers within a single department location. Usually when the volume is relatively small, but the cost of travel time of an operator is high, it is recommended to locate a small copying machine in each of the several key departments and in each department let the supervisor have jurisdiction over the copier. Other arrangements entail consideration for loss of labor due to travel, work interruptions, and unnecessary corrections which collectively more than offset the cost of the copier. In contrast, advocates of the centralized arrangement correctly point out that distinct advantages exist under this choice and cannot be ignored. They include better and more complete service, since time loss of highly paid employees is avoided; better utilization and maintenance of machines is feasible; several types of machines can be included yet without costly duplication; and unauthorized use of the machines is minimized. Generally speaking there is a tendency to utilize copiers on a decentralized basis and duplicators on a centralized basis.

Abuses exist and in some cases are extremely difficult to eradicate. Included are the running off of more copies than are needed, copying materials when it is less expensive to purchase it from the outside, and making copies for personal use. There are also the unexplainable habits of rerunning copies to see if the "next ones are of better quality" and of utilizing a more costly machine when a smaller, more economical one will do the work satisfactorily.

To control copying cost it is first necessary to know not only what the cost should be, but also what present cost is being incurred. The common situation is a complete lack of any cost data for this area. Hence, the initial order of business is to set up a system to obtain such information and enlist the active support by employees to the system. Beyond this, the controls utilized should include scheduling of copying to gain better usage of machines from the viewpoint of both time available and type of copying performed. Also, the controls should include security of classified information, some flexibility to meet changing needs, and allocation of cost to the units for whom the copying service is being provided.

Urgency of delivery of duplicated material is usually requested. However, a practice of a first-come, first-serve basis is usually satisfactory. Wherever possible a grouping of the work and establishing its sequence for each duplicating machine give desired orderliness. Some controls over the issuance of papers are usually in order and for this purpose the use of a requisition form showing the process preferred, the number of copies, size of paper, date needed, destination, and general comments is effective.

Likewise an accounting of how much time is spent on each job is normally needed to exercise really effective control. A form like that illustrated in Figure 15–1 can be used. Reasonable levels of performance

FIGURE 15–1. Comparative Data Are Helpful in Controlling the Work of Copying.

| REPORT OF COPYING | | | | | | | |
|---|---|---|---|---|---|---|---|
| HOURS AND ACTIVITY REPORT | | | | WEEK ENDING | | | |
| Regular jobs: Special jobs: Machine down time: | | | | Total paid hours: Time available: | | | |
| | | | | *Standard Hours* | | | |
| *Standard Hours* Operation | *Unit* | *Activity* | *Std.* | *All.* | *Taken* | *Diff.* | |
| Stencils Run copies Gather and staple Plastic binding | Stencil Copy Copy Fin. unit | | .040 .00008 .00004 .025 | | | | |
| Material 20# stock | Ream | | | | | | |

should be established and made known to the employee. The lack of proper work loads per employee results in poor management of this service.

Basic training in the operation of each copying machine is paramount. Excellent machine instructions given in a step-by-step, easy-to-follow manner and amply illustrated are provided by most machine manufacturers free of charge through their sales representatives. In addition, the employees need definite copying work goals. The nature of this work seems to require that a sense of accomplishment be emphasized by management. Also, the employee's desire to have the manager know what is being achieved must be satisfied. Furthermore, full utilization of employee's time should be stressed. Too little or too much work can result in a dissatisfied employee. Or expecting the work to be accomplished within practically no time at all can dull the employee's enthusiasm. Team effort is especially important because those in duplicating may perform several different tasks throughout the day. It is therefore desirable to maintain a congenial and cooperative group.

## SYSTEMS AND COPYING

Copying is an essential component in many systems. In some applications, basic information is put on a master and subsequently duplicated as needed onto paper forms designed to direct and control a particular business activity. For example, in purchasing, master sheets for duplicating can be prepared. When an item is to be purchased, its master is withdrawn from the file, and the needed information duplicated on all the purchasing forms. These forms are then processed, and the master is returned to the file for future use. The result is accurate, fast work and much saving in writing time.

An interesting variation of this procedure is used when several of the requisitions to purchase can be assembled for the preparation of one purchase order for one supplier. The requisitions are sent to the purchasing department, where the buyer groups them respectively under the names of the vendors whom he selects. The card for each selected vendor is removed from the vendor file and assembled with the requisitions which will make up the purchase order to that vendor. These are placed in a shingled or overlapping position and held in place by a large clip. In addition, a variable information form is added, so that the composition of the purchase order can be completed. Figure 15–2 shows the purchasing requisitions, giving complete specifications, assembled on the left, with the variable information such as purchase order number, date, and quantities being written in on the right. When entries are completed, the entire assembly is placed over a purchasing order master giving heading and shipping instructions—common to all purchase orders—and duplicated. Thus, a complete purchase order is prepared with a minimum of manual writing.

The practice is growing in record retrieving of never releasing any document from a file. A wanted document is located, removed from the file, copied, and immediately returned to the file. The copy is sent to the person requesting the document. The chance of losing the original document is practically nil. As pointed out in chapter 6, more and more routine

FIGURE 15–2. Preparation of Purchase Orders from Component Parts Is Expedited by the Use of a Duplicating Machine.

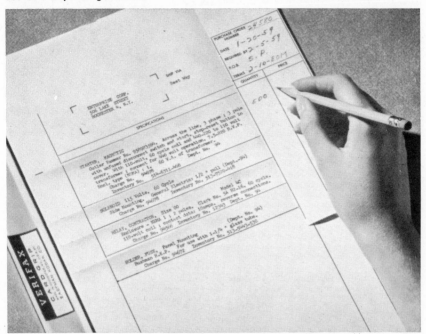

*Courtesy: Eastman Kodak Co., Rochester, N.Y.*

correspondence is being answered by the "reply at bottom" type of letter. To reiterate, in this type, the answer or comment is written at the bottom of an incoming letter. A copy is then made and sent to the initiator, the original being retained for the files. Thus saved are considerable typing and filing space and the chances for errors are minimized. Another practical example pertains to the preparing of account receivable records wherein the use of copying makes for an efficient and effective system. Customer account receivable ledger cards are used as a source document in preparing statements. Data on the ledger card are typed on a translucent paper and retained as a permanent copy by the company. At the end of each month, a copy is made of the entire statement and is sent to the customer. The need for the writing of headings is eliminated, the customer receives an itemized accounting of his account, and laborious transferring of information by typewriter or by hand is eliminated. Fast, convenient follow-up reminders can also be used for delinquent accounts.

## COPYING PROCESSES

Basic knowledge of various copying processes is helpful in selecting the process to utilize. Figure 15–3 shows pertinent information on a comparative basis for a number of different duplicating processes. The contact process, for example, is a reproduction process, has a relatively high cost per sheet, enjoys average usage, is usually economical for up to ten copies, is suited for typed or printed material, script, drawings, and pictures, and is produced at the rate of eight copies a minute. Individual requirements should govern the selection and take into account not only the type of data in Figure 15–3, but also such factors as the cost of the equipment

FIGURE 15–3. Comparison of Various Copying Processes.

| Process | Relative Cost of Copied Sheet | Usage | Usually Economical for Number of Copies up to: | Main Type of Material for which Suited* | Speed in Sheets per Minute | Reproductive (R) or Duplicative (D) |
|---|---|---|---|---|---|---|
| Contact | High | Average | 10 | T-S-D-P | 8 | R |
| Xerography | High | Average | 15 | T-S-D-P | 6 | R |
| Stencil | Low | Wide | 5,000 | T | 200 | D |
| Direct | Medium | Average | 300 | T | 150 | D |
| Offset | Low | Average | 10,000 | T-S-D-P | 150 | D |
| Indirect | Medium | Limited | 300 | T | 200 | D |
| Multigraph | Low | Average | 10,000 | T | 150 | D |
| Whiteprint | Medium | Limited | 500 | T-S-D | 8 | R |
| Photocopy | High | Limited | 5 | T-S-D-P | 5 | R |
| Carbon | High | Wide | 18 | T | 5 | R |
| Noncarbon | High | Limited | 4 | T | 5 | R |

* CODE   T = Typed or Printed   S = Script   D = Drawing   P = Picture

and the supplies to run it, the quality of copy desired, time and place considerations, and employees' preferences.

The various descriptions of these duplicating processes are:

*1. Contact.*  This means is rapidly growing in popularity and consists basically of placing a sensitized paper in contact with the material to be reproduced and inserting it into the machine, which exposes, develops, and fixes the copy sheet. The process is technically known as thermography and means literally a "burning" process. Dark areas, such as typewritten words, absorb more heat than the blank areas. Exposure to infrared light causes the words of the original to burn an image onto the heat-sensitive copy paper. Representative of the contact process is Thermo-Fax and Readyprint. Figure 15–4 shows a Thermo-Fax copying machine, which makes direct copies in a matter of seconds. Exposure timing is set on the dial on the right of the unit. The original and sensitized papers are placed together and inserted into the machine, which starts automatically and makes the copy. It gives ready-to-use, dry copies and emits no detectable odor. The process is effective wherever carbon is present in the writing, as with pencil or typewriter. Readyprint gives exact copies of letters, includ-

FIGURE 15–4. Thermo-Fax Copying Machine Featuring Speed, Economy, and Convenience.

FIGURE 15–5. Readyprint Copier for Fast, Single-Copy Needs up to 8½ × 14 Inches.

*Courtesy: Minnesota Mining and Manufacturing Co., St. Paul*

*Courtesy: Eastman Kodak Co., Rochester, N.Y.*

ing original letterhead and signature, and other papers, is always ready to go, produces top quality copies, and is easy to operate. Figure 15–5 shows a Readyprint Copier.

**2. Xerography** (pronounced zē-rog′-ra-fē). This word stems from the two Greek words meaning "dry printing" and is identified as a dry, fast, electrophotographic copying process. Xerography uses light and static electricity to make copies of anything printed, typed, written, or drawn. Copies are made on ordinary paper in a matter of seconds. Figure 15–6 diagrams how this process works. Copy paper input is at (1) in the figure, and the original document is placed at (2). An oscillating mirror (4) scans the document and reflects document to another mirror (5) and from there to a selenium-coated drum (6). The drum is given a positive charge of electricity by the charge corotron (7); negatively charged toner (8) is poured between the drum and the electrode (9) which concentrates the charge in the image area. The transfer of image (10) takes place drawing the image and toner from the drum. Heat from the fusing lamp and reflector (11) causes the image area to become molten and fuse into the paper. If no image, the toner does not fuse into the paper. The operation is completely automatic. Figure 15–7 shows the popular Xerox 3600 III office copier. Some feel that the xerography principle will be applied to the printing of most books in the future. While tremendous expansion has been achieved, it is not as yet being offered widely for this application.

Another popular model of an electrostatic copier with interesting features has an automatic flip-up exposure lid making the hands free to slide the original out with the right hand and slide a new original in with the

FIGURE 15–6. Schematic Plan of Xerox 3600-III Operation.

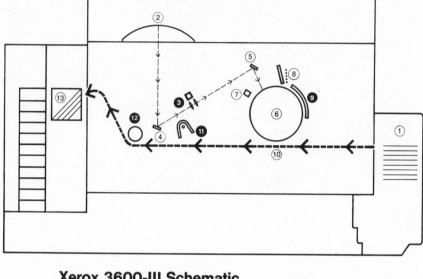

## Xerox 3600-III Schematic

| | | |
|---|---|---|
| | ④ Oscillating Mirror | ❾ Electrode |
| | ⑤ Fixed Mirror | ⑩ Image Transfer |
| ① Copy Paper Input | ⑥ Drum | ⓫ Fusing Lamp and Reflector |
| ② Original Document | ⑦ Charge Corotron | ⓬ Copy Brush |
| ❸ Photo Cell - Lens Iris | ⑧ Toner | ⑬ Output Tray |

*Courtesy: Xerox Corp., Rochester, N.Y.*

left hand. It is streamlined for convenience and speed to make every move count. The machine shown by Figure 15–8 on page 376 is recommended for up to 1,800 copies per hour.

**3. Stencil.** This is a common means and consists of "typing a stencil," either by typewriter with ribbon removed or nonoperative, by special hand tools (styli), or by a die-impressed operation performed by the manufacturer. The openings thus made in the stencil, i.e., openings caused by the stencil coating being pushed aside and exposing the base fiber, permit ink to pass through so that paper held against the surface receives the image. Even, sharp, and clear strokes on the stencil give the best results. Corrections can be made on the stencil by using a special fluid to reseal the surface and then retyping. It is also possible to block out and remove an area and replace it by attaching a new portion of stencil. The image or printing is usually in a jet-black color, although several other colors are also available. It is possible to store the stencil for use at a later time; about 5,000 copies can be made from one stencil.

**4. Direct or Liquid Process.** In this process, the material to be re-

FIGURE 15–7. The Widely Used Xerox 3600-III Turns Out Copies at the Rate of 60 per Minute from Original Documents or Half-Tone Photographs.

*Courtesy: Xerox Corp., Rochester, N.Y.*

produced is put on a master sheet which has behind it a special carbon layer. The carbon places the image in reverse on the back of the master sheet. Different carbons are used for different colors. The master is placed in a machine, and copies are made directly from it in this manner: The copy sheet is slightly moistened with a special fluid before contacting the back side of the master; and as the copy sheet presses against the master, a very small layer of the carbon is removed and impressed on the copy sheet. Four colors can be reproduced in a single machine operation, and about 300 copies can be made from one master. Master sheets can be stored for reruns.

**5. Offset.** The offset process is subject to many variations. Basically, the principle involved is that the material to be reproduced is (1) prepared on a plate, which is (2) transferred to an intermediate agent, which is (3) printed on the paper. Frequently, the intermediate agent is made of rubber.

One important offset process is photo-offset. The material to be reproduced is photographed, and the negative is transferred to a sensitized

FIGURE 15–8. High-Quality Copies, Uninterrupted Productivity, and Dependability Are Featured by This Copier.

*Courtesy: Dennison Manufacturing Co., Framingham, Mass.*

plate. This plate is then used in a photo-offset printing unit. Slight variations in this method are commonly termed "planographing" and "offset lithography." Frequently, a xerography process is used for making offset master paper plates.

A well-known process known as "multilith" is based on this offset principle. Either a metal or a paperlike master can be used. The latter is more widely used, since it can be handled like a piece of paper. That is, a regular typewriter plus pencil, pen, ink, brush, or crayon furnished by the supplier are used in preparing the master. Erasures and corrections are handled as with ordinary paper, and the paperlike masters can be filed in the office like paper sheets. The process is recommended for quantities—over 500 and up to 10,000 copies.

**6. Miscellaneous Processes.**   There are many more reproducing processes—too many to include all of them here. In addition to the above, however, mention of several others is warranted. The *indirect* process, also known as the gelatin process, consists of putting the material on a master sheet made of special paper; the master sheet is pressed against the gelatin, thus depositing the image on it. Copies are then made by pressing the sheets against the image in the gelatin. *Multigraph* employs either an imprinting or a ribbon process of reproducing. In the former, type, rubber strips, or electrotypes are used. The medium is inked and paper coming in contact with the wet type forms the copy. In the latter, or ribbon process, the duplicating is done through a ribbon similar to that used in standard typing, and the finished work closely resembles original typing. The type used is held in a segment or blanket and consists of up to 70 lines of type. Signature attachments are available, changes or corrections can easily be made in the type, and the process is speedy, as over 10,000 copies can be run in one hour. *Whiteprint* provides a black on white directly from translucent originals. Additions to the master is a feature. This is the process commonly used in the handling of accounts receivable discussed above. The process is flexible and can handle large sizes of paper. Either the copy is given a light coating of a special solution to develop the copy permanently or it is exposed to controlled aqua ammonia vapors. *Photocopy* is one of the oldest copying processes. By photographing a negative, it is possible to make a positive paper print, that is, black lines with white background. Prints can be made in the same size as, or larger or smaller than, the original. *Carbon* includes a typewriter and carbon paper. This means is widely used, especially when the information is original and the need does not exceed about 18 copies. For ordinary work where three or four copies suffice, the manual typewriter with soft platen is satisfactory, but for more copies, the electric typewriter with hard platen should be used. *Noncarbon* utilizes carbonless "NCR paper" of the National Cash Register Company. The bottom side of the first sheet is coated with a colorless chemical and the top side of the second sheet with another chemical. Writing on the first sheet reproduces instantly on the second sheet, and similar reaction takes place between the remaining sheets of the pack. Clear copies are obtained, smears and smudges are eliminated, and hands and clothing are not soiled.

## COMPOSITING, COLLATING, AND BINDING

Type compositing, collating, and binding are tasks frequently connected with duplicating work. Type compositing is preparing the type for the master copy. Different styles, sizes, headings, and the like are commonly utilized to make the duplicated material more readable and to highlight important facts. For this work office composing machines are widely used. They bring the versatility of a well-equipped printing shop into the office and are used to prepare type of all sorts for reports, bulletins, booklets, catalogs, price lists, and house organs, where variety in composition is desired.

Figure 15–9 shows an office composing machine. It resembles a typewriter in both appearance and operation. Each type face is on a removable disk which can be quickly inserted into or removed from the machine. Each disk is complete with capital and lower-case letters, numerals, and symbols. Over 600 different sizes and styles of type, ranging from 5½-point newspaper style to 14-point Heavy Gothic type, and including boldface headings and italics, are available. Even margins on both the left and the right, similar to those of regular typeset composition, are obtained by typing each line twice. To illustrate: line 1 of the copy is typed in the regular manner on the left half of the piece of paper. Then, it is retyped on the right. The machine spaces the second typing so that both margins are even. The procedure is repeated for each line. When completed, the typed material on the right half of the paper constitutes the finished or master copy.

Collating is the assembling of several different sheets of paper to form

FIGURE 15–9. Changes from One Type to Another Are Accomplished Quickly by Means of Small Type Fonts Weighing Less Than One-Fifth of an Ounce. Two such fonts fit into the machine at one time, and changes are made in less time than it takes to refill a mechanical lead pencil.

*Courtesy: Addressograph-Multigraph Corp., Cleveland, O.*

a report or booklet. This work can be done manually or by a hand or electrically operated machine. The general concensus is that if 15 man-hours a week are spent on collating by hand, the same work can be done with a collator in only three hours, and serious thought should be directed toward obtaining a collator. Designs vary; either pigeon holes or stationary and expanding racks are employed. In a mechanically operated unit, the operator depresses a foot pedal causing one sheet to slide off each stack of papers arranged in a double row of pigeon holes. Units with different capacities or number of stacks are offered. There are also automatic collators available for high volume collating.

FIGURE 15–10. An Automatic, 200-Station Sorting Machine Which Handles Sheet Sizes from 5 × 8 to 12 × 18. The control panel in front-center provides for automatic starting, indexing, bin shifting, and bank selecting.

*Courtesy: Pitney-Bowes, Inc., Stamford, Conn.*

Ingeniously designed sorting or distributing machines are available to permit simultaneous sorting of material direct from printing or duplicating. Thus, in effect these sorters arrange printed material in desired stations or groups. Models from 20 to 200 stations are available. Figure 15–10 shows a 200-station machine.

In many cases, the material is held together by a binding, of which there are many different types. First, there is side wire stitching, i.e., on the side. Also, there is saddle wire stitching, i.e., through the fold at the back of the booklet. Usually, the latter is preferred, since it enables the sheets to remain flat and open once they are placed in that position. Mechanical fasteners are used extensively, including ring or loose-leaf binders, prong fasteners, or screw-post fasteners. Also the use of wire and of plastic bindings has won widespread favor. Wire binding is spun or coiled onto the packet of punched paper; plastic binding is fastened onto the paper via punched holes by means of a clasping action. Plastic binding equipment is available for use in the individual office. Such a binding has won considerable favor holding together a variety of different stock including cards, papers, and charts, such as found with program documentation or different-size papers, photographs, and samples as required for advertising manuals. Also, it is inexpensive, durable, and permits revisions in the bound material to be made quickly right in the office. Binding is increasing in importance as more and more paper printouts of computers are employed. Such unbound information is difficult to refer to and to transport. Binding reduces these difficulties.

## ADDITIONAL MECHANIZATION OF COPYING

There are a number of additional machines available for work that can be classified under the general category of copying. The list is far too long for inclusion here, but we feel two machines merit mentioning. The first is a converter of computer hard-copy output to the conventional 8½ x 11-

FIGURE 15–11. Precise Copier to Reduce Computer Printouts to 8½ X 11-Inch Copies.

*Courtesy: Graphic Communications Corp., Moonachie, N.J.*

FIGURE 15–12. A Web Printed Offset Duplicator Designed to Provide Operating Economy, Efficiency, and Professional Print Quality.

*Courtesy: Diddle-Glaser Co., Emporia, Kansas*

inch size; the second is a Document Reproducer of professional print quality operating at fantastic speeds.

Printouts of most computers are about 11 x 15 inches, a size considered by many to be awkward to handle, file, or bind in a folder. The machine shown by Figure 15–11 is a versatile and accurate electrostatic copier reducing any sized original up to 12 x 16 inches to 8½ x 11 inches. It does this at the flick of a switch and will turn out as many sharp, fresh copies of each original as you wish—automatically. Same-size copies can also be obtained as well as copies of just about anything including three-dimensional physical objects.

The Document Reproducer is a web fed and printing offset duplicator providing precision one- or two-color printed 8½ x 11-inch sheets at 25,000 copies an hour. Printing can be on both sides; an optional accessory punches holes in the margin operating simultaneously with the printing. Fed by a roll of paper, the printing is continuous and the paper is cut to size after printed automatically by the machine. The capacity of this machine provides expanded capacity for the printed information requirements. Figure 15–12 shows the Document Reproducer.

## OFFICE SUPPLIES MANAGEMENT

Information employees need proper supplies if maximum productivity is to be accomplished. The lack of writing paper, a typewriter ribbon, an order pad, envelopes, or letterheads might cause serious delay in getting important office work finished when required. Also supplies represent an investment of capital. On the average for every information employee it is quite likely that some $100 worth of office supplies are on hand. Lack of adequate management over office supplies may result in extravagance, needed items being out of stock, excessive prices paid for certain items, and obsolete material remaining in the stockroom.

Among the initial actions in managing office supplies is to decide on the location of the stockroom or stockrooms as the case might be. The location should be in a convenient space that is not desirable for clerical work. Be sure it is clean and dry. Enclose the area, and keep it under lock and key. Provide adjustable shelving and arrange for easy accessibility to supplies. The effective use of storage space can be calculated by dividing the cubic volume of the items stored by the cubic volume of available storage space. A value of 45 to 55 percent should be sought. This sounds low. But, when considering aisle space and nonuse of space adjacent to the ceiling, it is realized that a higher percentage figure is normally not attained.

The stock arrangement should follow some orderly plan. If possible, store related items near each other. Place heavy items on the lower shelves and light items on the upper shelves. Those items with a relatively fast turnover can be located close at hand—near the entrance. It is best to eliminate old or seldom used items. They are costly to store and clutter up the stockroom. Index all items stored by number or code and have a handy reference available to locate any item quickly.

Establish realistic maximum and minimum quantities for each item, as well as the ordering point. These can be based on judgment guided by past experience. The analysis of the requirements for each item will help attain a balanced inventory of supplies. As a normal practice, it is usually best to buy small quantities at frequent intervals. For each item, the amount purchased should be in line with the rate of consumption, the time required to receive a replenishment from the supplier, the quantity considered minimal for the functioning of effective management, and the savings in cost, if any, which are achieved through larger quantity purchases of the item.

It is an effective policy to limit the quantity of supplies issued at any one time to about a two-weeks supply. Large quantities encourage waste; too-small quantities involve excessive requisitions and trips to the stockroom. In many cases, it has been found that packaging supplies in small units helps to economize their use. Further, all issuances might be confined to one day out of the week or to certain dates during the month. In the event that supplies are needed in the interim, a special requisition and approval can be required, a practice which tends to discourage requests for supplies at irregular times.

Supplies should be issued only upon authorized written requisitions, which should be made out, in most cases, by the department head or by the supervisor of the unit receiving the supplies. By filing these requisitions, it is convenient to maintain a journal or record by departments of what is issued, when, and to whom. A periodic inspection of such record is helpful to ascertain if consumption of supplies appears to be normal in the light of past requirements and volume of work handled.

## PERSONNEL AND OFFICE SUPPLIES

One person should be put in charge of the stockroom. He should have complete authority over its operations and be responsible for the decisions and their implementation affecting the storage and issuance of supplies. He must, of course, enlist some assistance in carrying out his managerial work, but the ultimate job of managing the stockroom is his alone.

Among his relationships with co-peers, the person in charge should inform supervisors, by means of monthly statements, of the costs of office supplies issued to their respective units. This will help to keep the supervisor conscious of the importance of office supplies; and the supervisor, in turn, will reflect this attitude to the individual employees. In addition, it is recommended that from time to time a campaign be held to encourage reduction of waste of supplies by employees. The creating of an intense desire by employees to stay within prescribed limits of usage and to conserve supplies ranks among the most effective measures to develop.

Also, it is beneficial to determine if less costly items can be substituted for certain present supplies. Actually, this is a joint adventure by all employees, for its success depends upon how well motivated the employees are about trying to reduce the cost of supplies. An arrangement for pretesting different products, or at least a willingness to try them out, is in order. Also, success in reducing the number of items used normally expedites stockroom management and lowers cost. Closely allied to the effort of finding a satisfactory substitute is that of ascertaining if what is now being used is needed and, if so, if it meets requirements. To this end, select at random a requisition for supplies and investigate it thoroughly. Find out how the item is used, who uses it, what the user thinks about it, whether it is the best for the specific use, and whether the price paid for it is reasonable and in line competitively. Answers to these questions either will confirm that a satisfactory job of acquiring supplies is being done or will uncover areas which require remedial action.

## QUESTIONS

1. How do you account for the rapid increase in copying machines in offices? Is this growth good or bad? Why?

2. What considerations do you feel should be taken into account in determining the location of a copying machine in an office?

3. Discuss the major controlling activities you recommend over copying machines.

4. Point out the major differences between the concepts in each pair of the following:

   a) Multigraph and multilith duplicating processes.

   b) Document Reproducer and Photocopying.

   c) Office composing machine and collating.

   d) Side wire stitching and saddle wire stitching.

5. Enumerate and discuss several improvements as illustrative of possible improvements in copying management.

6. Relate several examples of copying being used as an essential component of an office system or procedure.

7. As you see it, in the management of copying, which is most important: planning, controlling, organizing, or actuating?

8. As an office manager, what actions would you take to provide adequate management over office supplies?

9. Do you favor having copying work on a centralized or on a decentralized organizational arrangement? Why?

10. Explain for what purpose and how the machine shown in Figure 15–9 is used.

11. Discuss the subject of "Personnel and Office Supplies" from the viewpoint of office management.

12. What duplicating equipment would you recommend for each of the following?

    a) Eight copies of a chart 8½ x 11 inches.

    b) Copy of a letter.

    c) A company president's speech of 15 pages, copy to be made for each of 8,000 employees.

    d) Copy of photograph.

    e) One hundred copies of a one-page announcement.

    f) A copy of a map 8½ x 15 inches.

## CASE PROBLEMS

### Case 15–1.   Investment Institute, Inc.

Commonly referred to as the "Three Eyes," Investment Institute, Inc., is a successful group of 2,200 members who are interested in receiving financial news and investment counseling. Now in its 18th year, it is enjoying sound operations after a difficult initial period of establishing its services. The institute confines its activities to (1) bonds—both municipal and corporate, (2) stocks—listed and unlisted, and (3) mutual funds—closed and open end. It provides an advisory service only and does not handle any investment transactions.

Each member pays an annual dues for which he receives a monthly publication, *Innovative Investing,* and one evaluation annually of his portfolio without charge. Any member can also obtain a special investment study upon written request and payment of a special fee. The amount charged depends upon the type of study requested, but normally it is based on a low percentage figure of the amount of capital being invested. In addition, throughout each year a member is entitled to write six questions dealing with investments and have them answered by the institute's experts. A reply within three days of receipt of letter by first-class mail is a long-standing practice of the institute. The average response per member is 4.81 letters of inquiry per year.

Until about 18 months ago, these investment inquiries were answered by individually typed letters. However, with growing membership and the popularity of the service, the task of getting out all these individual letters became too burdensome. Several alternatives for handling the answering were considered. The use of form paragraphs and letters were believed the best answer, and a manual providing such help was prepared and given to each correspondent. After several months, however, this solution did not appear to be working out too well. The typists complained, costs were still high, and some members wrote in stating the institute's letters were stilted and "all the same."

After several months a new arrangement was followed. It consisted of writing an effective letter for each of 150 questions which it was judged would probably be asked most frequently. A quantity of 1,000 copies of each of these letters was printed so that an attractive and complete reply to each question could be given. Members have complimented the institute on the "new and attractive information leaflet." However, after using this approach for the past year, the institute finds that questions asked have not followed the predicted pattern. Consequently, many individual letters have had to be written and substantial quantities of the printed replies are on hand. Costs remain high, and competent correspondence help is extremely difficult to obtain.

## Questions:

1. Enumerate the alternatives available to the institute.
2. What do you recommend be done? Why?

## Case 15–2. O'Reilley Products Company

Stencil-duplicated material has been processed and used in the office of the O'Reilley Products Company for a number of years. Last year, for example, there were duplicated 1,780 memorandums of one page each, 307 reports of six pages each, and 225 reports of eight pages each. For each memorandum, an average of nine copies was made; for the six-page reports, eight copies; and for the eight-page reports, six copies.

Current costs of the company are 20 cents each for a stencil; ink, about $20 a year; labor for typing or operating the duplicator, $2.20 per hour; paper, $1.90 for 500 sheets when purchased in quantity. It requires approximately one minute per line to prepare stencils. The memorandums average 15 lines and the reports are 20 lines to a page. It takes about 8 minutes to put the stencil on the machine, adjust it, and later remove and file it. Speed of the machine is 80 sheets a minute. For hand collating and stapling of reports, a flat rate of 12 cents per report can be used.

Since the present duplicating machine is worn and must be replaced in the near future, the office manager believes that in addition to the stencil method, both the contact and the xerography methods should also be investigated for possible adoption. With this thought in mind, he has compiled cost data as follows. For the contact method, sensitized paper, one of which is needed for each page duplicated, costs 6 cents each, depreciation on the contact machine will be $65 per year, compared to $85 per year for a new stencil machine. Material costs, in addition to sensitized paper sheets, will approximate $30 per year for the contact machine, which it is estimated will produce 150 copies an hour. This includes the work of loading the machine. For xerography, output can be estimated at 350 copies an hour, machine lease cost at $375 a month, and machine supplies at about $0.001 per duplicated sheet. For either the contact or the xerography method, work of adjusting the stencil and removing it from machine is not required.

## Questions:

1. Based on cost, which duplicating process should the office manager select? Substantiate your answer.
2. In addition to cost, what other important factors should be considered by the office manager in arriving at a decision?
3. What should be the decision of the office manager? Why?

### Case 15–3.  Clenndenning Company

Ted Woodruff filled out a form for one pad of paper, a box of paper clips, and six large manila envelopes. He deposited this form in the office supplies control basket on the table near the door to the office supplies room. Ted was following the "help yourself" supplies arrangement which had been followed by the company for some time. The filled out forms were collected and reviewed weekly by Craig McKelvey, the assistant office manager, who used the information for reordering supplies reaching a low inventory. Actually, the current system did not work too well. Shortages of items were frequent and Craig McKelvey believed that some employees failed to fill out the required form correctly or, in some cases, not at all. He therefore spent some of his time watching the action around the storeroom to see if he could discover the cause or causes of discrepancies in the supplies. He observed Ted entering the storeroom and emerging ten minutes later with a large wrapped bundle under his arm. Going to his desk, Ted placed the bundle in a desk drawer and resumed his work.

Later, at quitting time Craig observed that Ted removed the bundle from his desk drawer and started down the aisle with other employees leaving for home. Just before passing the doorway leading to the reception room and then to the outside, Ted was stopped by Craig who inquired if the package he had was his own. Ted said that it was. Craig's questions and disclosures resolved that the bundle contained expensive company supplies. After further questioning Ted admitted he was taking the supplies home for use by himself and his family. He added that he frequently did company work at night in his home. Relieved of the bundle, Ted was permitted to go home, but was requested to report to Edward Lasser, the office manager, first thing in the morning.

Next morning Mr. Lasser told Ted his action was strictly against company policy and he was discharged. Ted asked for another chance, pointing out that he had been with the company four years, and other employees took supplies all the time from the storeroom without filling out any form whatever and many of these supplies were taken by the employees to their homes.

## Questions:

1. What major conditions have contributed to this situation taking place?
2. Evaluate Ted's behavior. Craig's behavior.
3. Did Mr. Lasser handle the situation correctly? Why?

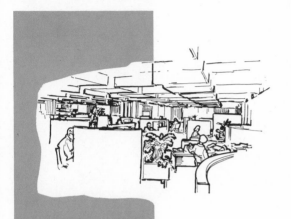

# PART V

# ADDITIONAL PLANNING REQUIREMENTS

To complete our total planning efforts, we now discuss these efforts in selecting the office location and office furniture. Further, the physical facilities must be arranged to expedite the work flow and to maximize accomplishment of expected work assignments.

Three chapters are offered including "Office location and furniture planning," "Office space planning," and "Office environment."

chapter **16**

# Office location and furniture planning

In the field of observation, chance favors only the prepared minds.

—*Louis Pasteur*

THE PROBLEM of selecting a new office location is encountered by an office manager from time to time. A move is almost inevitable for a growing business and perhaps also for a contracting one. While not a common occurrence, the problem does arise, and when faced it is best to view it as an opportunity to improve office efficiency.

## MAJOR ALTERNATIVES

Most offices are located in one of the following places: (1) in the factory building, (2) in a separate building adjacent to or near the factory building, or (3) in an office building far removed from any factory building. In the first two cases, the office location depends upon the factory location which is usually determined with reference to factory needs only. However, in the third case, the office location can be determined in line with the particular needs of the individual office. Since many location problems arise due to the need for more space, the major alternatives are either expand at the present location—build an additional building at present site, rent another floor, or find a brand new location. However, experts tell us that generally speaking, *it costs less to occupy a new building than to modernize an old one.* Hence, in many cases a new building is preferred and usually this entails the problem of selecting a location.

FIGURE 16-1. The 100-Story John Hancock Center in Chicago.

*Courtesy: Cushman and Wakefield, Inc., Chicago*

This is not to say that modernization should never be followed. Many considerations enter the picture such as the prestige of the current address, convenience, suitability of remodeled quarters, and the cost of modernization and who pays for it. Individual conditions govern each case.

## LOCATION AND SPACE REQUIREMENTS

With the growth in the economy and especially in the information field, the amount of office space has expanded. Evidence of this is all around us particularly in the number of new office buildings built each year. Many of these are in the large metropolitan areas where certain commercial advantages are maximized. Most of these new office buildings have architectural beauty, are a real asset to the community, and encompass conveniences and efficiencies unknown a generation ago. Figure 16–1 illustrates the 100-story John Hancock Center incorporating outstanding excellence in man's design and construction ability. Located in Chicago, this building reaches 1,100 feet above the ground with television antennas accentuating the structure as an imposing landmark. Among its many features are elevators traveling at 1,800 feet per minute, parking for 1,200 cars, glare-reducing glass, acoustical ceilings, resilient tile flooring, exclusive

FIGURE 16–2. Tabulated Information to Expedite Determining Present and Future Space Requirements for Office.

| | Space Requirements for Office | | | | | | | | |
|---|---|---|---|---|---|---|---|---|---|
| | Today | | | 5 Years Hence | | | 10 Years Hence | | |
| Usage | Space per Unit (Sq. ft.) | No. | Total Requirement (Sq. ft.) | Space per Unit (Sq. ft.) | No. | Total Requirement (Sq. ft.) | Space per Unit (Sq. ft.) | No. | Total Requirement (Sq. ft.) |
| Private offices | 400 | 1 | 400 | | | | | | |
| Private offices | 200 | 8 | 1600 | | | | | | |
| Private offices | 90 | 14 | 1260 | | | | | | |
| Purchasing | 175 | 1 | 175 | | | | | | |
| Accounting | 600 | 1 | 600 | | | | | | |
| Computer | 200 | 1 | 200 | | | | | | |
| Sales | 1000 | 1 | 1000 | | | | | | |
| Filing | 1400 | 1 | 1400 | | | | | | |
| Telephone Switch-board | 200 | 1 | 200 | | | | | | |
| Reception | 500 | 1 | 500 | | | | | | |
| Interviewing | 100 | 2 | 200 | | | | | | |
| Conference | 250 | 1 | 250 | | | | | | |
| Stockroom | 500 | 1 | 500 | | | | | | |
| Storage | 600 | 1 | 600 | | | | | | |
| Miscellaneous | 1500 | 1 | 1500 | | | | | | |
| Total | | | 10,385 | | | | | | |

stores and shops, restaurants, and an observatory. Column-free office space is provided from 26,400 to 34,500 square feet. The 46th floor upward through the 93rd floor is devoted to apartments.

Although large metropolitan areas offer many advantages, many enterprises have located their offices in suburban areas. Locations 15 to 20 miles from the downtown area have become commonplace. Manufacturing, publishing, insurance, and research offices are prominent in this movement to suburbia. Major reasons are lower cost, a happier work force, and open space. In addition, new offices located away from the larger cities permit ample room for expansion, provide satisfactory mailing and shipping facilities, and have excellent labor availability.

Fundamental to renting office space or constructing a building for office use is the amount of space required now and for a reasonable period of the future. It is advisable to give this rather detailed planning; otherwise unexpected serious difficulties may arise. Effective is the tabular arrangement of the estimates, similar to that shown in Figure 16–2.

## LOCATION FACTORS

A number of factors can be considered in determining an office location. To illustrate, for banks, population, income per household, penetration by competing banks, traffic flow, prominence of site, and rate of growth for the area are given top priority. Bank location stresses consumer retail service and is not typical for many office locations, but it points out the usual need of evaluating many factors in any location problem. And this in turn raises the issue of the proper weight to be given each factor. To meet the problem, a chart like that shown in Figure 16–3 can be used. By this means either an existing space can be evaluated or the requirements of a space yet to be constructed are identified.

Eight selection factors are listed on the left, and beneath each factor are statements designed to help identify the intended meaning of the factor. Opposite each factor is a series of numbers indicating the range of points or values which have been assigned to that factor. Also, the points assigned reveal the relative importance of each factor. Those shown are suggestive only. In an actual case, the factors selected and the weights given each one are determined by the evaluator. However, to make comparisons among different possible locations valid, the same chart is used for evaluating the several sites under consideration.

## ADAPTABILITY OF THE SPACE

Top priority is accorded adaptability of the space, for that which is selected should permit suitable arrangement of the various office organization units; it should be of adequate size and shape. For the most part,

FIGURE 16–3. Chart Used to Determine Office Location Selection.

| | Excellent | Good | Fair | Poor |
|---|---|---|---|---|
| 1. Adaptability of space:<br>Is the space adaptable to the needs of the office?<br>Is there room for expansion? | 60 | 45 | 30 | 15 |
| 2. Building facilities:<br>Are entranceways, wiring arrangements, outlets, ducts, fire protection, and other *fixed* facilities adequate? | 60 | 45 | 30 | 15 |
| 3. The proximity of office building to business factors:<br>Is the building near to customers; to transportation facilities; to shopping centers, restaurants, and hotels; and to mail facilities? | 44 | 33 | 22 | 11 |
| 4. The cost involved:<br>Is the rate reasonable and in keeping with competitive prices? | 40 | 30 | 20 | 10 |
| 5. Natural lighting and ventilating provided:<br>Is the exposure on the north, east, south, or west? Does it have large glass areas? Do windows face the street or open lots? Are ceilings high? | 28 | 21 | 14 | 7 |
| 6. Characteristics of the building:<br>Does the building have a favorable appearance, good name and address that are easy to pronounce and remember, and adequate floor load and ceiling height? | 24 | 18 | 12 | 6 |
| 7. Freedom from dirt and noise:<br>Is the general area free from dirt and noise? Is the area itself clean and quiet? | 24 | 18 | 12 | 6 |
| 8. Stability of tenants:<br>Do tenants of the building tend to stay put (are moving and transferring the exception)? | 20 | 15 | 10 | 5 |
| Maximum total......................... | 300 | 225 | 150 | 75 |

rectangular shapes are best; and where requirements permit, occupancy of an entire floor is usually preferred. Individual circumstances alter cases; but normally, it is more economical to travel 10 feet vertically, i.e., between floors, than 150 feet horizontally, i.e., on the same floor.

Preferably the space selected should permit future alteration and office expansion. Future requirements mean more than just securing space greater than that needed for current requirements. Consideration must be given to where and how future changes will alter present space provisions. Usually, future considerations are taken care of either by leasing entire floors and subleasing what is not now required or by securing options on adjoining areas. Some office executives feel it is desirable to provide space arrangements to accommodate at least five years of future expectations.

The difference between a site's "rental space" and "usable space" should be noted. Usually, one pays for rental space, which is the area measured between the inside surfaces of the outer boundaries. It includes areas for columns, projections, pilasters, and window arrangements necessary to the building. The usable space is the effective area which can be used for the office. Frequently, 10 percent of the rental space cannot be used, and commonly the figure is higher.

## THE BUILDING FACILITIES

A building facility includes any device or feature incorporated in or attached to the building which assists in using the space with convenience and efficiency. It must be fastened to the building, or installation is required to finish the building. Building facilities include a long list of items, among which are entranceways, elevators, stairways, wiring arrangements, air conditioning, hallways, columnar spacing, janitor closets, water accessibility, noise control features, means of fire protection, and other fixed facilities.

Adequate wiring facilities are one of the big considerations in building facilities today. Separate runways are used for (1) low voltage, including telephone and communication systems, and (2) high voltage for normal electrical current as well as that of higher voltages. For electrical current, many older office buildings are wired for about 2 watts per square foot of floor area, whereas the current recommendation, due to the number of electrical machines, is about 6 watts per square foot. Wiring capacity is limited by the cross-sectional area of the conduit, and to increase wiring capacity requires either larger conduits or new-type conductors. The former is expensive, since most conduits are buried in concrete. One alternative is to attach a new, larger conduit on the surface. A better solution is use of a new type of wire with very thin but effective insulation. Its use permits greater copper capacity in the conduit; hence, in some instances, the old wiring can be replaced with this new type and the present conduits employed.

The modern need for quantities of electrical wires has given rise to the use of cellular steel floors. At the top left portion of Figure 16–4 is shown a series of galvanized steel cells spaced close together, providing continuous in-floor passageways throughout the entire floor area. Various cross-sectional areas and spacings of the cells are available. These steel cells serve as a subfloor over which the concrete is poured. However, before pouring concrete, steel header ducts are fastened directly on top of the steel cellular flooring and at right angles to the cells. In turn, the header ducts are connected to the desired distribution lines in the cells, from whence the proper distribution line is connected to an outlet. In the illustration, two outlet fittings are shown. Easily installed anywhere along the cell length, they are available in many designs to meet various functional requirements. For example, in the top right illustration of Figure 16–4 are shown the components of a compact aluminum outlet fitting for telephone service; it features three connecting blocks with a capacity of 15 pairs of telephone wires or 30 separate wires. Additional flexibility is made available by cellular steel floors in that, via conduits beneath the cells, additional wire connections between designated points can be utilized. The cellular steel floors also provide unobstructed underfloor ducts for heating and air conditioning, as well as for other uses. The bottom illustration of Figure 16–4 suggests a combination of air, electrical, and telephone cells.

It should be noted that construction and remodeling work is subject to building code requirements, which specify the design and the type of construction that is permitted. Use of certain materials may be forbidden, or stated design principles must be followed for certain structural parts. To reduce the fire hazard, it may be required that all buildings have at least two entranceways. In most building codes some flexibility is pro-

FIGURE 16–4. *Top Left:* Close-up of Cellular Floor Construction. *Top Right:* Components of Telephone Outlet Fitting. *Bottom:* Suggested Arrangement for Use of Cellular Floor for Telephone, Power, and Air Needs.

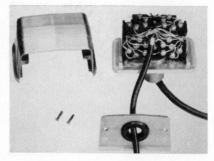
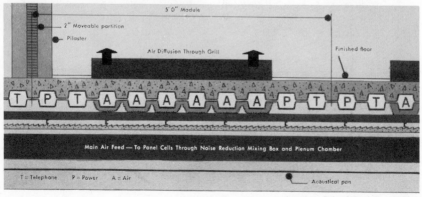

*Courtesy: Inland Steel Co., Chicago*

vided, certain alternatives and choices being designated. Portions of some building codes have remained the same for a number of years, while others have been modified from time to time. Code requirements are enacted and enforced usually by local government.

## PROXIMITY OF OFFICE BUILDING TO BUSINESS FACTORS

When the location covers an office building, the following factors should be given careful consideration:

*1. Customers and Others in Same Business.* The proximity of the building to those who are in almost daily contact with the office is a very important consideration. In the first place, closeness to customers is generally considered advantageous. This is true when personal interviews and associations are frequent, but relatively minor when activities with customers are by telephone or by correspondence. Secondly, closeness to others in the same line is viewed with favor. This closeness encourages discussions of common problems among occupants, helps simplify the problems of the building manager, and adds to the convenience of customers and clients dealing with occupants of the building. There is, for example, a tendency for offices of financial houses, law firms, real estate firms, insurance agencies, and public utilities to locate in buildings in the financial district. Also, in many cities, specialized buildings to accommodate particular types of business offices are available; for instance, motion-picture offices may be located in the film exchange building and stockbrokers' offices in the stocks and bonds building.

*2. Transportation Facilities.* Convenient and low-cost means of getting to and from the building must be available not only to employees but also to outside representatives, visitors, and delivery and messenger men. Out-of-the-way places, necessitating transferring and long waits for buses, trains, or taxicabs, are a distinct disadvantage.

*3. Retail Stores, Restaurants, and Hotels.* Convenience to retail stores might well contribute to the growth of the business. For example, domestic financing enterprises have found it helpful to locate in or near retail stores. The availability of restaurants is another consideration. Employees like to have a selection of handy eating places for noon lunch, or for evening meals when overtime work is necessary. A lack of eating places might necessitate providing a company cafeteria or dining room. Also, nearness to hotels is, in many cases, a distinct advantage in the location of an office.

*4. Mail Facilities.* Good mail facilities should always be secured and given consideration in the selection of an office location. Frequent pickups and deliveries, with convenient accessibility to a post office, can contribute very materially to operating efficiency.

## THE COST INVOLVED

The cost of office space is of cardinal importance; however, it should always be considered along with the other location factors discussed. The cost of office space is expressed in dollars per square foot per year. To illustrate, assume an office measures 30 × 40 feet and the rental is $5 per square foot. The cost per year is 30 × 40 × $5, which equals $6,000, or, on a monthly basis, $6,000 divided by 12 equals $500.

The cost per square foot varies with many factors, such as the size of the city and general business conditions; but in order to gain some idea of the range in rates, a high of around $9 to a low of around 25 cents per square foot can be used. The top figure represents space in the better locations and buildings of the larger cities, while the latter may be converted factory space in a relatively poor location. Included in the square foot cost are services such as air conditioning, running water, wall maintenance, and elevator service. In many respects, the price is subject to negotiation with regard to what is included.[1]

## NATURAL LIGHTING AND VENTILATING PROVIDED

Since lighting is very important in an office, the availability of daylight and the building facilities for providing artificial light should receive prime consideration. Any area that provides much daylight is normally favorable. Exposures facing the north are generally preferred, as northern light is of a steady and soft type. Eastern exposures are next in preference, followed in order by southern and western exposures. Normally, the outside wall areas should utilize a maximum of glass area and be not less than one fifth of the floor area. Windows extending almost to the ceiling permit a maximum amount of natural light to reach the inner areas of the floor space. Artificial light, however, will also be required and for this purpose adequate fixtures, electrical outlets, and lighting provisions must either be available or be provided. Agreement on the amount of artificial light to be utilized and the cost of installing and maintaining the necessary fixtures is a further important consideration.

It is imperative that an office be well ventilated. Careful observation should be made of the prospective space area to determine if adequate ventilation is possible. Spaces with few windows, a small number of openings to air ducts, low ceilings, and window openings on inside courts normally do not provide sufficient ventilation. However, with air conditioning, many of these shortcomings can be overcome.

---

[1] See also page 402 for discussion of "Provisions of Lease."

## CHARACTERISTICS OF THE BUILDING

The general appearance of the building, its size, reputation, age, available services, and technical factors should be taken into account. In considering these things, decisions are made based on such factors as whether the building is modern or old, whether the building name is in good repute, whether the name and address are easy to pronounce and remember, and whether the building is well advertised. Also considered are the building services, including the elevator service, janitor service, and night protection.

An important technical factor is the allowable floor live load. At least 75 pounds per square foot are needed and a value of 100 pounds is desirable for complete versatility of layout. The floor-to-ceiling heights should be a minimum of 8 feet; however, for large areas, 10–12 feet is more appropriate. Low ceilings create a feeling of congestion and make the office difficult to ventilate; high ceilings make lighting, noise-reducing, and heating efforts difficult. Furthermore, columnar spacing must be considered, for it affects office layout, especially the location of main partitions that are joined to columns. A spacing of 20 × 20 feet or more is acceptable; spans less than 18 feet are normally unsatisfactory for efficient office utilization. Along the outside walls, a constant dimension of approximately 5 feet, center to center of window sections, or alternating windows and piers, expedites locating partitions and accommodating new units of equipment and machines.

## FREEDOM FROM DIRT AND NOISE

Certain elements are extremely disturbing to office workers and should be avoided whenever possible. Dirt, smoke, and soot are objectionable, and their presence in an office location and area should be avoided. Street noises are bothersome and interfere with efforts of mental concentration. In addition, the surrounding tenants' types of businesses, with special reference to the amount of traffic and the operations performed, might also be important from the viewpoint of noise.

## STABILITY OF THE TENANTS

Generally it is considered advantageous to locate an office in a building where the tenants are stable. Frequent moves by tenants in and out, and alterations, are undesirable from the viewpoint of solid, substantial enterprises. Various studies seem to indicate that real estate companies, law firms, and financial houses are among the most stable. Their office needs remain fairly constant, and they seem disposed to remain in one location for relatively long periods. In some cases, their tenure in the same location extends for 25 years and longer. In contrast, manufacturers' agents and advertising agencies tend to move more frequently. However, many of these remain in the same location for 10 or 15 years; and while this is relatively less, it still reflects a strong element of stability.

## OWN OR LEASE

In most discussions regarding the office location, the question arises: "Is it better to own or to lease?" This question involves policy and can be answered only by the top managers. Like many decisions there are advantages to each course followed. For example, ownership permits the building to be tailor-made for, or remodeled within technical limits to meet, the particular needs of the enterprise. However, needs change; sometimes the building becomes obsolete or at least not as convenient as first planned. Also, there is prestige for an enterprise in owning its own office building. The name of the enterprise can be used for the building, and the publicity value can be quite high. Further, a relatively safe investment is provided. An office building usually represents a fairly secure equity, and income from renting out a portion of the building is a possibility. When this portion is rental, some flexibility for future expansion is supplied. In addition, permanency of location is obtained. This adds stability to the enterprise and permits continuity of a desired name and street address.

In contrast, the main advantages of leasing include freedom of top managers from care and worry in connection with ownership. The problems of building maintenance and repairs are avoided. The leasee retains financial flexibility; he does not have large amounts of capital tied up in one relatively long-time investment. He is free to invest any surplus in the most productive channels. Further, changes in office location can usually be made more freely. The enterprise is not wedded to one location. And for the small enterprise whose requirements are not elaborate, a satisfactory arrangement is supplied.

The "sale and lease back" arrangement, being heard of more and more, describes a transaction in which an investor buys a building from a seller and in the same transaction gives the seller a long-term lease on the building. The seller continues to occupy the building, pays rent, and is free of the responsibility of building upkeep and operation. For the seller, the deciding issue to enter into a "sale and lease back" arrangement is his financial position, especially that of taxes and his desire for liquidity of his capital. For the buyer, or investor, the arrangement provides a known income from a known source at an agreeable rate of return. In a variation of this plan, a builder will construct a new office building to the tenant's specifications and lease it to him for a long period. Thus, the tenant gets a building especially designed for his needs without a large initial capital outlay. The builder may retain ownership of the building or sell it to an investor.

## PROVISIONS OF LEASE

The legal right of a tenant to occupy a given office space is consummated by means of a lease. Actually, *a lease is a form of contract by which one party conveys real estate to another party for a period of time at a specified compensation.*

A lease is in effect for a stated period of time. Office leases usually run for one, three, five, ten, or twenty years, and in some instances longer. Payments are usually made monthly, with the first payment due at the time the lease is executed; this first payment customarily applies as rent for the first month or stated period. Sometimes, an advance of three months' rent is made at the beginning of the lease period, and this is held by the lessor as evidence of good faith and intentions on the part of the lessee.

The different agreements or clauses contained in a lease depend upon the type and value of the real estate involved and the number of subjects upon which the lessor and the lessee believe a definite written agreement is advisable. A lease can be specially written, or it can be a standard form. Normally, the lessor provides janitor service, heat, running water, elevator service, window shades, and fire-protection apparatus. He usually has the right to change the name and street address of the building; designate all sources for sign painting, ice, towel service, and the like; have pass-keys to the premises; and enter the premises at all reasonable hours for inspection, repairs, and alterations. On the other hand, the lessee usually provides floor coverings, partitions, Venetian blinds, awnings, ventilators and fans, and intercommunication units. Normally he has the right to remove them at his expense at the expiration of the lease.

It is good practice to spell out in the lease what building services, such as elevator, window washing, daily cleaning services, are included. Most leases provide for subletting rights which means the lessee retains the right to sublet or assign the lease. Further, an escalation clause may be included whereby the tenant pays for increased taxes and labor costs or for some agreed percentage thereof up to a certain stated limit. This relieves the lessor of certain increased costs and also lets the lessee know his maximum liability. From the lessee's viewpoint, it is desirable to have a cancellation privilege even though if exercised a penalty is incurred. Also, the lessee should try to obtain the right to renew the lease.

## FURNITURE PLANNING

In chapter 7, under Part III, "Planning for Data Processing," we discussed the planning for machines since they are *directly* related to information processing. In addition to machines the office includes various types of furniture for which planning is vital. Up to this point we have not discussed furniture planning. Office furniture is *indirectly* related to information work, and it represents an essential and intimate part of office planning efforts. Many of the planning concepts, including the most significant selection factors for machines as stated in chapter 7, are equally applicable to office furniture. There are, however, in the case of furniture, additional specific considerations and these will be included in the following pages.

Office furniture tends to be used for long periods and it represents substantial expenditure. Hence, care in its selection and use is paramount. Actually, it represents investment for assisting personnel in performing work efficiently. It has been termed an important working tool of the office employee—a very apt description. Furniture adaptable to the needs of its user plays an important role in keeping good people on the job and in controlling costs. Suitable office furniture influences morale favorably and facilitates the work to be done by economizing on the physical exertion required and facilitating speed of the necessary operations.

## OFFICE CHAIRS

The office chair is probably the most important physical facility in an office. It is personal to the employee and vitally affects the ease and comfort with which the work is done. Most office work is of a sedentary nature, a fact that further stresses the importance of the office chair. Certain features merit careful consideration. With respect to upholstering, vinyl is suitable for chairs in high traffic areas where a strong material with easy cleaning qualities is desired. Fabric upholstery offers cooler seating, a softer appearance and an extremely wide range of colors and patterns from which to choose. Leather provides elegance, comfort, and easy care. Seat cushions should be wide enough so that a person can sit in the chair comfortably. The cushion should not "bottom out" when occupied, but should provide a firmness that will support adequately. Caster wheels made from relatively hard material are usually best for use on carpeting, while casters of softer material should be used on composition tile and wood flooring. Glides are another consideration. Will they protect floors and carpeting? Will they last a lifetime without corrosion or breaking and, if replacement is necessary, can they be replaced? Among the many types of office chairs are the familiar straight-back chair, the

FIGURE 16–5. Contemporary Styled Office Chairs Featuring Rugged Construction, Lasting Beauty, and Comfort.

*Courtesy: Steelcase, Inc., Grand Rapids, Mich.*

swivel chair, chairs that tilt, the posture chair, plain or upholstered chairs, wood or metal chairs, and chairs with or without armrests. Figure 16–5 shows various types of office chairs of modern and practical designs.

Most office chairs are intended to fill a definite need or use. Of special importance is the posture chair which has three adjustments thereby making it possible to "tailor-fit" the chair to the occupant. These adjustments include:

1. *The seat height*—so that the feet are comfortably placed on the floor and no undue pressure is present on the underside of the leg just above the knee.
2. *The backrest height*—so that support is provided the small or lumbar region of the back. The swivel joint of the backrest should be approximately one inch higher than the top of the hip bone.
3. *The backrest horizontal position*—so that the muscles covering the two pelvic bones, i.e., the glutei muscles, overhang slightly the rear edge of the seat, thus placing the body weight forward on the underside of the leg muscles.

Even though available, these adjustments are frequently not used, thus incorrect seating exists as illustrated by Figure 16–6.

FIGURE 16–6. Examples of Common Incorrect Seating.

Chair Too High
Seat pressures nerves and stops circulation just above the knee.

Chair Too Low
Steady pressure on spine causes great fatigue.

Chair Back Too High
No needed support to spine, causing slumping and a strain on back and shoulder muscles.

Chair Tilts Back Too Far
Occupant easily gets off balance, with excessive back strain.

The major consideration about a posture chair is that it be used properly. Simply supplying a posture chair seldom assures that the benefits of the chair investment, namely good posture seating, are being enjoyed. The occupant must know how to sit in the chair and must sit that way. The proper use of posture chairs improves the appearance of office employees, reduces fatigue, improves morale, and aids in the functioning of important body actions, including breathing, circulation, and elimination.

## OFFICE DESKS

An office desk provides a work surface, a temporary storage for materials being processed, and a convenient area for selected tools and machines required in accomplishing the work. The trend in desk appearance is toward smooth, streamlined surfaces. Supports touching the floor are recessed in order to conceal them from view, to permit ample toe room when standing near the desk, and to facilitate cleaning the floor. Steel desks are equipped with linoleum or plastic; lighter colors and finishes seem to be preferred. Many wood desks are finished with light stain and bleached colors. Hardware and exposed metal parts are of dull finish to avoid annoying highlights.

FIGURE 16–7. A 60 × 30 Double Pedestal Desk Available with Various Drawer Combinations and In-Drawer Conveniences. The center drawer is optional.

*Courtesy: The Shaw Walker Co., Muskegon, Mich.*

FIGURE 16–8. Suggested Desk-Drawer Layout to Meet Individual Requirements for Order Department Manager.

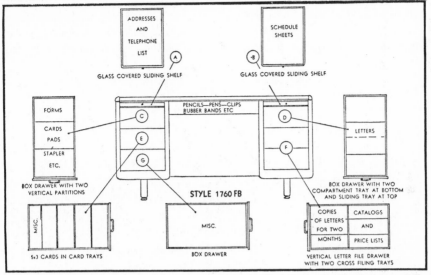

*Courtesy: Art Metal Construction Co., Jamestown, N.Y.*

To reiterate, a desk is actually a basic working tool, and this should be kept in mind when planning. Viewing a desk as a working tool emphasizes the meaning of desk efficiency, which is influenced by (1) the design features of the desk and (2) the person using the desk. The former stresses the old adage: "A place for everything, and everything in its place." The desk and its interior are planned to give maximum service to the user. Tailor-made desk-drawer arrangements are available to aid work production. As new requirements arise, the drawers can be interchanged and rearranged as desired. Figure 16–7 illustrates a modern desk offering a choice of more than 100 standard drawer variations. It is actually "programmed" to simplify the kind of work to be done with it. The popular clerical desk, for example, can have as few as 2 and as many as 17 drawers work-organized and free from clutter. Figure 16–8 suggests efficient arrangements of materials in desk drawers to meet specific requirements.

The second factor—the person using the desk—emphasizes the influence of the desk user's work habits and attitudes upon desk efficiency. The personnel element is vital and necessitates adequate instructions, training, and supervising. To assist in achieving desk efficiency, the following guides are listed:

1. Work on one task at a time and finish it before starting another. Abstain from trying to do several tasks at the same time.

2. Keep the desk free from excess papers and supplies. Have only those items on the desk that are needed. The desk top is a work surface and should facilitate immediate action.

3. Shelve material that is not urgent. For example, insert slips in magazines to articles to be read and then put them to one side for reading in off moments.

4. Strive to keep the work moving over the desk. Take action on each paper coming to the desk as quickly as possible.

5. Act on important paper work first. Have a daily schedule, and make use of a desk calendar to guide the sequence of work.

6. Dispose of all mail before going home. Do not permit a stack of mixed-up papers to remain overnight and cause a poor start the next day.

Regarding desk design, a multitude of types are available to serve particular needs. Among the most popular are those for executives, junior executives, stenographers, typists, adding and calculating machine operators, and billing clerks. Desks are available in single- and double-pedestal styles. The pedestal is the support or foundation of the desk, and it contains the drawers or a foldaway platform which houses a typewriter or some special machine. The single-pedestal desk is used in cases where a single tier of desk drawers and a smaller-size top are sufficient. Figure 16–9 illustrates several different types of desks designed to serve particular requirements.

FIGURE 16–9. Various Desk Designs: (Upper Left) Overhanging Top, (Upper Right) General-Purpose, (Lower Left) L-Shaped with Machine Platform, and (Lower Right) Fixed-Bed Typewriter Desk.

*Courtesy: Art Metal Construction Co., Jamestown, N.Y.*

FIGURE 16–10. (Top) a Functional Modern Design Desk, (Middle) an Executive "L" Desk, (Bottom) a Work Organizer Desk.

The "conference desk" has an oversized top that overhangs the pedestals at one or both ends and at the back. At meetings, it is possible for five or six people to sit comfortably around a conference desk, since ample work space and leg room are provided. The conference desk has become quite popular; it adds prestige to an executive's office. Other desks featuring contemporary design and emphasizing certain work conveniences are also available. Attractive functional desks of this type are shown in Figure 16–10 (page 409).

**Desk Dimensions.** Dimensions of desks vary with the type of desk, the material used, and the manufacturer. Executive desks are usually the largest, sizes ranging from 76 x 36 inches to 60 x 30 inches being the most common. For general office work, sizes from 60 x 34 inches to 42 x 30 inches are popular. The trend is toward smaller desks. For example, most new general office desks are 50 to 55 inches wide instead of the former 60 inches, and 30 inches deep instead of 34 inches. In some companies, however, certain sizes are specified for certain uses. For example, in one company, the following applies:

| *Employee* | *Desk-Top Size* |
|---|---|
| Department head | 78 x 38 inches, triple overhang |
| Supervisor | 60 x 36 inches, front overhang |
| Staff | 60 x 30 inches or special-purpose desk |
| Clerical | 60 x 30 inches |

Desks are made of various heights. Currently the preferred height is 28½ or 29 inches. It is claimed that for the average employee this height is better since it helps to maximize the employee's comfort.

## MODULAR OFFICE FURNITURE

This type of furniture consists of easily and quickly assembled modular components which, when assembled, comprise an effective functional and modern arrangement. Basic units include such "building blocks" as desk tops, desk pedestals, auxiliary tops, end supports, and filing and shelving units. In a number of installations, modular components have been put together to form a U-shaped desk and platform arrangement as illustrated by Figure 16–11. Partition panels for privacy can be added to meet individual requirements. Components are standard and interchangeable, thus supplying flexibility and many various combinations.

An interesting modular-type furniture is the Centiform which is designed to promote an environment of friendliness and of communication. Initially developed for use in a bank, the intent was to make the customer feel that he was with bank personnel who were genuinely friendly and were not inhibited in their communicating by office furniture of standard design. An open, yet closed, effect was sought because customers want to see their banker, but they also want privacy. Figure 16–12 shows the

FIGURE 16–11. Modular Office Components Assembled to Provide an Efficient U-Shaped Unit.

*Courtesy: Invincible Metal Furniture Co. Manitowoc, Wis.*

FIGURE 16–12. The Centiform Arrangement Providing Privacy Yet Promoting an Environment of Friendliness.

*Courtesy: Lehigh-Leopold Furniture Co., New York*

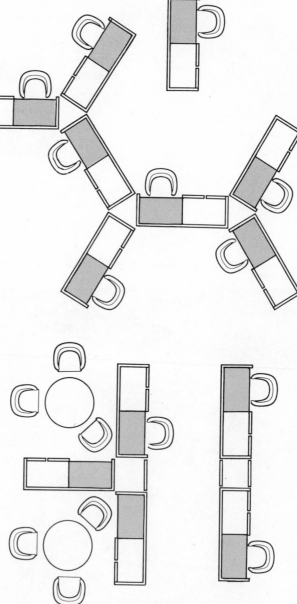

FIGURE 16–13. The Centiform Offers a Variety of Arrangements.

Centiform which offers the facilities of four private offices, yet occupies less floor space than four desks, cabinets, and chairs. Each work station includes a cork board and light fixture, a clothes closet for customer convenience, file drawers, and shelving for storage. Note the traditional desk is replaced with the nonformal conference table and an ample writing area is provided to the back and side of the unit. Communication barriers are minimized. The Centiform creates an effective interviewing-conference area, saves space and time.

A variety of arrangements is possible. Instead of the four-unit arrangement shown, three- or two-unit components are used as well as a chain of three- or four-unit arrangements as illustrated by Figure 16–13.

## CABINETS AND STANDS

A variety of cabinets is available to house records being worked on more or less continuously. Figure 16–14 shows a widely used arrangement

FIGURE 16–14. Convenience and Speed to Record Reference Are Enhanced by Use of These Storage Cabinets and Writing Surface. Insert shows a close-up of the storage cabinet.

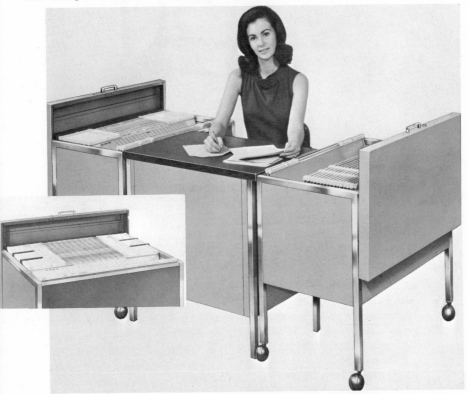

*Courtesy: Diebold, Inc., Canton, O.*

with cabinet on either side of a writing area. These cabinets are made to accommodate virtually every type of record including papers, cards, and punched tape. Speed and convenience to record reference are achieved by use of these units. Instant record location, full-range scanning speed, and indexing plans to spotlight attention to only those items requiring action are among the outstanding features.

Stands for typewriters, copiers, or other office machines are also popular. They supply easy portability and a vibration-proof support assuring operator comfort and machine safety. Certain models include one or two king-size drop leaves thus providing a convenient work area. Figure 16–15 illustrates a popular style.

FIGURE 16–15. A Popular Office Machine Stand.

*Courtesy: Tiffany Stand Co., St. Louis*

## QUESTIONS

1. What are some important features to take into account when acquiring chairs for an office?
2. As an office manager, would you favor the "sale and lease back" arrangement in connection with acquiring suitable office space? Why?
3. Enumerate the major advantages in a company owning its office building. The major disadvantages.
4. Define each of the following:
   *a*) Rental space.
   *b*) Allowable floor live load.
   *c*) Work organizer desk.
   *d*) Lease.

5. Select two office buildings in the community in which you now live, and make a survey to determine their suitability with respect to (*a*) the characteristics of the building, (*b*) the cost involved, (*c*) the adaptability of the space, and (*d*) freedom from dirt and noise for each of the following prospective tenants:

   *a*) A sales representative requiring desk space and a room for small samples.

   *b*) An insurance office requiring a total of about 1,800 square feet, including a reception room, a room about 15 x 25 feet for salesmen, and general office space.

   *c*) A medical doctor who needs a reception room, an examining room, and, if possible, a small room to one side for his records and library.

   Write your results in a suitable form, using a sentence outline type of presentation.

6. Of the various major factors given consideration in locating an office, which two factors do you believe are most important? Justify your viewpoint.

7. Discuss the subject of building facilities as applied to office location and building.

8. For an office employee to achieve desk efficiency, what are four guides she may follow?

9. In your own words explain how the chart shown in Figure 16–3 is used.

10. Select two companies that have moved their offices within the last two years. Find out the reasons for each locating where they did. What conclusions do you draw from your study?

11. Does the supplying of a posture chair insure that the office employee who occupies it will have good posture while seated? Why?

12. What is Centiform, why is it used, and do you favor its use?

## CASE PROBLEMS

### Case 16–1.   Johnson-Snyder Corporation

Located in a town of less than 15,000 population in Iowa, Johnson-Snyder Corporation makes automotive specialty items. The "J-S" line is well known and widely used both for original and replacement use. Business has been very good and the corporation must expand.

The production manager, Mr. Orville Sagar, has suggested that the office move to Detroit and the present office space adjacent to the manufacturing plants be converted and used for production purposes. He believes it may be advantageous for the office to be in Detroit where important buyers of the corporation's products are located. Further, the modern and rapid communication means of information would join effectively the new office and the factory. He feels that the move he proposes might be the first step in the total project of relocating the entire business, office and manufacturing, in the Detroit area where he feels it belongs.

Vice president of sales, Mr. Charles L. Stanwood, has no compelling beliefs about moving the office. He claims the sales force will operate successfully from any location. Customers are really widely disbursed and considerable sales travel and expense will be incurred no matter where the office is located. He admits that the corporation's chief competitors are in the Detroit area. Perhaps better service and closeness to auto manufacturers' headquarters might give sales efforts an added edge; he says he really doesn't know.

Tom Kennedy, the office manager, violently opposes any office move. He points out that it would be disturbing a successful operation. The biggest problem, he points out, would be replacing office employees who do not want to leave Iowa. In his informal conversations with many of them, he has confirmed his hunch that many would not move with the company. The reasons are that they don't want to leave their families and friends, and they prefer to live in a small town. He is of the opinion that if more manufacturing space is needed, it should be acquired near the present plants. Plenty of ground is available.

## Questions:

1. In general, what are the probable major alternatives available to the corporation?
2. How do you suggest the issue be settled? Substantiate your viewpoint.

### Case 16–2.  Nikko-Sanwon Chemical Company

This company, an integrated manufacturer of vinyl plastics, produces and sells three major categories of such plastics, including (1) vinyl chloride polymer resins, (2) "PUC" compounds, and (3) calendared vinyl sheeting and polyethylene film. These products are used in a variety of applications such as insulation for wire, flooring, toy components, luggage, and bookbinding.

The sales office of the company is located in the Merchandise Mart, near the Loop in Chicago. In this office, 12 salesmen and 26 clerical personnel are employed. The office is convenient for buyers and is a prestige location where a representative can bring customers and impress them favorably. In addition, "the Mart" is very accessible for employees, who can live in any part of the greater Chicago area and reach the office without trouble.

One of four manufacturing plants of the company is located in the southwest area of the city, some nine miles from the Loop area. Adjacent to this plant is a large warehouse which was constructed two years ago. There is ample space available in the warehouse to house the sales offices, now in the Merchandise Mart. In the opinion of Mr. Tashio Umeda, president of the company, the sales office should be removed to the warehouse. This would reduce overhead and consolidate Chicago operations in one location. However, through Mr. Leonard Griffin, the vice president of sales, Mr. Umeda discovers that many of the salesmen and office personnel do not favor such a move. Some of them have stated that they will quit if the move takes place.

Mr. Umeda strongly feels that the move would be best for the company from the long-range viewpoint. However, he wishes to retain all his present employees if this is possible and suggests that the company (1) reduce the working hours to $7\frac{1}{2}$ hours daily from the present 8 hours, but keep the pay the same; (2) establish a free service to assist employees to find satisfactory housing quarters in the southwest area of the greater Chicago area; and (3) organize car pools, with the company compensating the employees whose cars are used.

## Questions:

1. What additional information do you feel appropriate for Mr. Umeda to consider before reaching a decision on whether to move the sales office?
2. Outline the program of action that you recommend Mr. Umeda take. Substantiate your recommendations.

### Case 16–3. Security Insurance of Saint Louis

For the past several months, discussions dealing with modernization of office facilities have been held by executives of Security Insurance of Saint Louis. At the last meeting, approval to proceed was passed, and a committee was authorized to formulate a complete plan and submit it to the president of the company within 60 days. Approval of the committee's recommendations would be a routine matter. The prime purpose of the committee was to determine what office equipment to purchase and to keep expenditures within the authorized limits. The committee consisted of the office manager, the controller, and the personnel manager.

Since the prescribed expenditures were somewhat limited, the committee decided to purchase what was probably most important—desks and chairs. It was believed this would be a good start in the company's office modernization program. Suppliers of this type of equipment were called in and requested to submit bids. It soon became apparent that the company's tentative appropriation for this purpose was insufficient to purchase as many desks and chairs as the committee had in mind.

The controller suggested that a survey of the present equipment be made and purchases be limited to what was most in need of replacement. Several suppliers agreed to make this survey free of charge and to take the used equipment as partial payment on the new equipment. The personnel manager, however, objected to this plan, explaining that for an office employee with a new desk and chair to work alongside an employee with an old desk and chair might cause difficulty and some misunderstanding among employees.

The idea was also advanced that either new desks only or new chairs only be purchased. But disagreement over which should be purchased existed among the committee members. One committee member strongly advocated new desks, since these provide the working areas, are in full view, and contribute a great deal toward improving the general appearance of an office. In contrast, it was pointed out that a new comfortable chair probably would mean more to an employee and would result in more favorable comments by the employees.

The office manager rejected the idea that the project be held in abeyance pending the availability of more money to purchase both desks and chairs and perhaps other modernization work. He believes a beginning must be made now and eventually the entire office probably will be improved. In his opinion, to delay will bury the office modernization program indefinitely.

## Questions:

1. Evaluate the viewpoints of the controller; of the office manager.
2. What alternatives are available to the company?
3. What action should be taken? Why?

chapter 17

# Office space planning

The superior man makes the difficulty to be overcome his first interest; success comes only later.
—*Confucius*

ONE OF the most challenging areas of office management is office space planning. With the system and flow of work decided, the office location and space acquired, and the various machines and furniture identified, we are now bringing these together forming a physical arrangement or a floor plan whereby the information work can be performed. Office space planning is more than simply locating machines and furniture conveniently. It is this plus facilitating a good flow of work, assisting supervision, adding to the employee's comfort, and providing for future expansion or contraction. Formally stated, office space planning can be defined as *the arrangement of all physical components within the available floor space to provide maximum effectiveness and the coordination of these components into an efficient and attractive unity.*

At the outset it is wise to recognize that space planning is not all factual or technical. We use dimensions, lengths of work flows, percentages of effective space, and the like, but in addition to these data we must take into account the managerial climate, principal likes, and attitudes. For example, answers to basic questions such as these are needed: What image or impression should the space convey? Which is most important —cost, prestige, or appearance? Are functions performed or organization status or some other consideration to dictate the location and design of private offices? Recognizing these nontechnical factors makes the plan-

418

ning program realistic and lends assurance that the layout as developed will be adopted. Endless modifications are avoided.

## BASIC CONSIDERATIONS

Everyone seems to have ideas about office layout. Some of these ideas are excellent, while others are so impractical or incomplete that they are useless. In most instances, the help of an office layout specialist is recommended, for this assures that efficient office layout work will be done. This approach, however, does not prohibit the office manager or any executive from talking with the layout specialist and contributing to the task of evolving the best office space plans. Some companies have found that a planning committee works out very well to encourage participation in office layout work.

In order of their increasing difficulty, office layouts are for either new, remodeled, or currently used areas. New areas normally permit the most effective space utilization; completely coordinated space planning is possible. The next group—remodeled areas—sometimes poses difficult-to-solve problems, in that the building facilities are inadequate or the space modernization is incomplete. Finally, the planning of existing areas for space improvement can be both fascinating and frustrating, in that considerable improvement in space utilization can usually be brought about, but certain rigidities prevent a desired level of space efficiency being attained.

Space planning is usually a continuous type of activity. It arises when (1) a new or modified system or procedure is adopted, (2) an increase or decrease in either work or personnel is made, (3) a change in organization is made—either adding or taking away from a unit, and (4) complaints from employees are heard about their work areas suggesting elimination of the poor areas that infest the office layout.

Ineffective use of office space is a continuous liability. It contributes to office inefficiency daily, and continues to do so until an improved layout is planned and put into effect. The individual daily loss may be small; but when consideration is given the cumulative amount—for a month or a year, for example—the importance of proper layout is brought into bolder relief. Office space represents a definite cost. While it does not represent the largest portion of office expenditures, it usually does represent a sizable outlay, and it should be kept within reasonable limits.

From the viewpoint of space planning, most large offices are made up of four separate types of areas, including (1) private offices, (2) general office area, (3) service areas, and (4) storage areas. It helps to keep these in mind when preparing office layouts so that the overall viewpoint is maintained and the essentials for each type of area are included.

## SPACE PLANNING AND INFORMATION SYSTEMS

From the rational and technical viewpoint, space planning is governed and coordinated by the systems followed in performing the information work. What papers, people, and machines are used and what is done at each stage of work dictates what space planning should provide. Systems planning should always precede space planning and the latter is never divorced from the former.

Every resource in the office area is a tool to help do the work. As such each has a purpose as a coordinated unit and the space arrangement should help in integrating these various contributions. Some refer to this as "integrated space planning." It means that the acquiring of harmonious efforts toward common office goals is promoted by the office layout, that is, office systems not only guide but in turn are helped by the office space plans.

Emphasis should also be given to certain practices and conditions which influence the layout. These include the office and personnel practices followed, the way the manager wants to run the office, and the physical facilities of the building. Included in the latter are the number of elevators, location of the electrical distribution system—high voltage and low voltage, water, stairways, receiving and shipping areas, and special plumbing.[1] Also important is the difference between the usable and the gross square feet area of the building. In some buildings this amounts to 30 percent of the building area, which is taken up by service cores, offset walls, columns, and primary corridors. Although frequently not recognized, it is the low efficiency created in the construction of many buildings that accounts for many inefficiencies in office layout.

### SPACE PLANNING AND FUNCTIONAL ANALYSIS

Many agree that space planning should be functional. It should serve to get the specific work accomplished. But to what should space planning be functional? The answer: to (1) organization, (2) function, activity, and duty, (3) office equipment and machines, and (4) communication. This leads to four types of functional analysis in office space planning.[2]

*1. The Organization Analysis.* A study of the organization is made to determine all personnel to be housed in the facility, the level of each, and formal lines of communication. Projections by organization unit for five years and for ten years are recommended.

---

[1] See also chapter 16, p. 396.

[2] These four types are from a statement by a prominent authority in office space planning, Mr. William I. Sohl, President, Concept Products, Inc., New York.

**2. The Function, Activity, and Duty Analysis.** Information in this area can be obtained from study of the office systems, procedures, and methods prescribed. Usually this is supplemented by observations at the procedures and methods levels. It is also practical to observe and record the personnel activity and from this information determine what the present workflow is. The work and the conditions required to execute it adequately are determined and evaluated. Also, probable needs for five and ten years are forecast. A review of operations at each level with corresponding management member is now made and if any special studies seem appropriate, they are referred to the space planning head or committee.

**3. .The Office Equipment and Machine Analysis.** Along with the information obtained under part 2, data are also secured on the equipment and machine requirements to perform each function, activity, and duty. Working closely with the systems and methods personnel is very helpful. Also recommended is observation of office practices followed, work station arrangements, reports prepared and used, common office policies followed, and control of traffic. We need an inventory of currently used equipment and machines, where they are located, and whether they appear suitable for continued use under either the present or a proposed layout. The need for special equipment warrants careful investigation. All these types of information are gathered during this third part.

**4. The Communication Analysis.** This includes a survey of present facilities and an evaluation of their adequacy both for the present and for the contemplated facility. Not only are the number, type, and location of units important; but also the communication aids of the physical facility itself, including size and location of ducting, floor conduits, and power lines which are required to employ the communication units advantageously.

The data from all these analyses are recorded on specially designed sheets to facilitate study. Some include questions to ask, others diagrams to fill in, and still others call for listing specific information under designated columns. This latter means, for example, is followed for recording the inventory of machines and furniture. Figure 17–1 shows a portion of work sheets developed from the communication analysis. If such data are not compiled and used, it may subsequently be found that telephones have to be changed, outlets are incorrectly located, and unsightly conduits must be attached to the floors and ceilings.

It is extremely helpful to determine by organization units the approximate space needed. This is derived from data of the above analyses. Space requirements result not only from the people on the payroll but also, and more important, from the machine and furniture requirements of each member. We need therefore to keep the following data for each employee: name, functional title, units of furniture and size of each, machines and

FIGURE 17-1. Telephone Work Sheets Used in Space Planning.

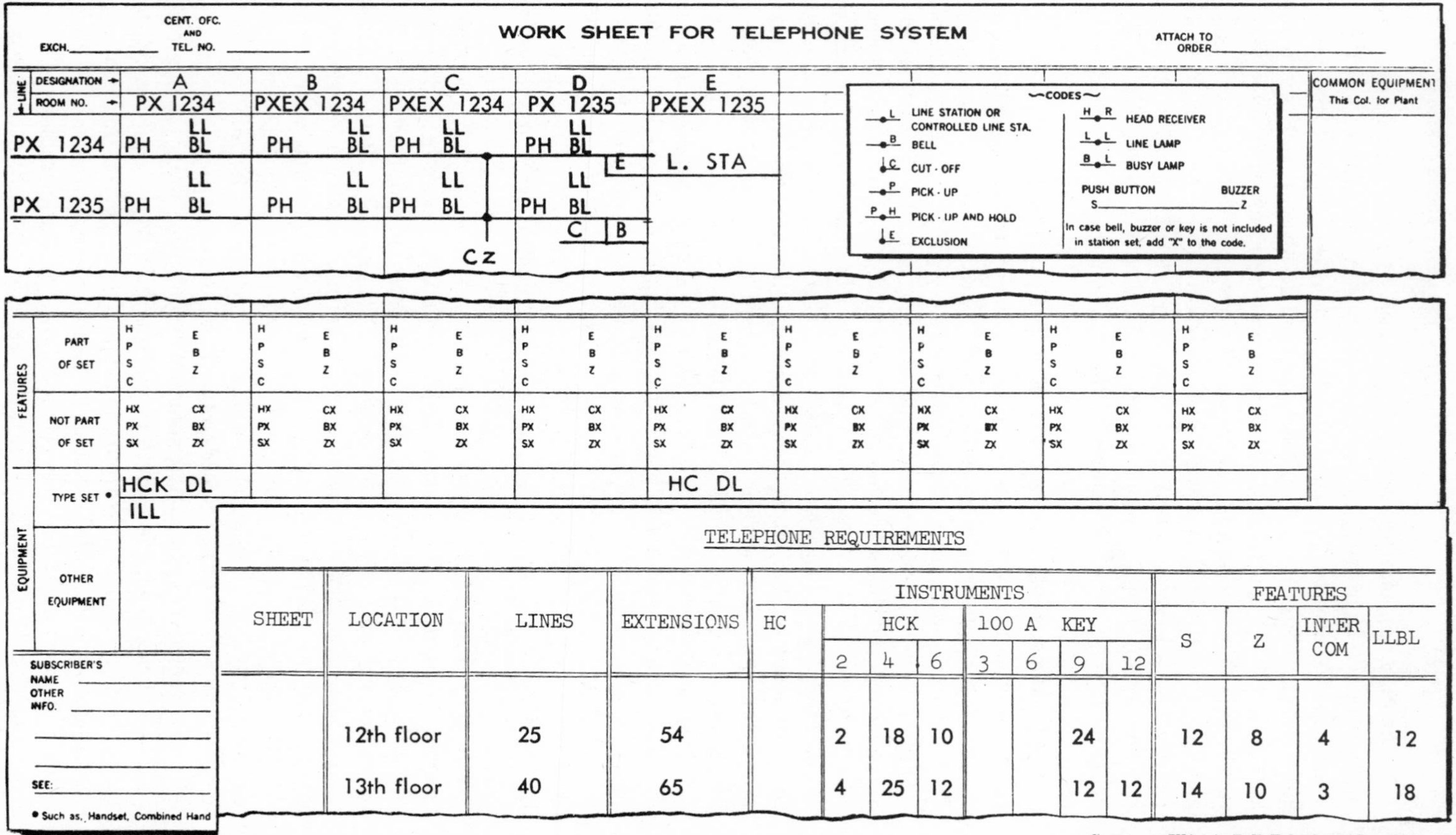

# WORK SHEET FOR TELEPHONE SYSTEM

EXCH. _____    CENT. OFC. AND TEL. NO. _____    ATTACH TO ORDER _____

| LINE / ROOM NO. → DESIGNATION → | A | B | C | D | E | COMMON EQUIPMENT This Col. for Plant |
|---|---|---|---|---|---|---|
| PX 1234 | PX 1234   LL BL | PXEX 1234   LL BL | PXEX 1234   LL BL | PX 1235   LL BL | PXEX 1235 | |
| | PH | PH | PH | PH | E → L. STA | |
| PX 1235 | PH   LL BL | PH   LL BL | PH   LL BL | PH   LL BL | C   B | |
| | | | C z | | | |

CODES

L — LINE STATION OR CONTROLLED LINE STA.
B — BELL
C — CUT-OFF
P — PICK-UP
P H — PICK-UP AND HOLD
E — EXCLUSION

H R — HEAD RECEIVER
L — LINE LAMP
B L — BUSY LAMP
P S — PUSH BUTTON
BUZZER — Z

In case bell, buzzer or key is not included in station set, add "X" to the code.

## FEATURES / EQUIPMENT

| | | | | | | | | |
|---|---|---|---|---|---|---|---|---|
| PART OF SET | H P S C | H P S C | H P S C | H P S C | H P S C | H P S C | H P S C | H P S C |
| | E B Z | E B Z | E B Z | E B Z | E B Z | E B Z | E B Z | E B Z |
| NOT PART OF SET | HX PX SX | HX PX SX | HX PX SX | HX PX SX | HX PX SX | HX PX SX | HX PX SX | HX PX SX |
| | CX BX ZX | CX BX ZX | CX BX ZX | CX BX ZX | CX BX ZX | CX BX ZX | CX BX ZX | CX BX ZX |
| TYPE SET • | HCK DL | | | | HC DL | | | |
| | ILL | | | | | | | |
| OTHER EQUIPMENT | | | | | | | | |
| SUBSCRIBER'S NAME | | | | | | | | |
| OTHER INFO. | | | | | | | | |
| SEE: | | | | | | | | |

• Such as: Handset, Combined Hand

## TELEPHONE REQUIREMENTS

| | | | | | INSTRUMENTS | | | FEATURES | | | |
|---|---|---|---|---|---|---|---|---|---|---|---|
| SHEET | LOCATION | LINES | EXTENSIONS | HC | HCK | 100 A | KEY | S | Z | INTER COM | LLBL |
| | | | | | 2 4 6 | 3 6 9 12 | 12 | | | | |
| | 12th floor | 25 | 54 | | 2  18 10 | | 24 | 12 | 8 | 4 | 12 |
| | 13th floor | 40 | 65 | | 4  25 12 | | 12 12 | 14 | 10 | 3 | 18 |

Courtesy: Illinois Bell Telephone Co., Chicago

size of each, and other or miscellaneous area requirements. These can be the heads of columns for our spread sheet. Projections for future periods can be included in the extreme right columns, if desired. Incidentally, such data will show the specific makeup of personnel accounting for the anticipated greater space requirements. From these sheets detailed space needs are easily obtained.

A quick and helpful comparison should now be made. One should calculate the square feet of usable space and compare it with the square feet of space needed. This will reveal whether there is too little, too much, or enough space. If there is too little, some rigorous adjustments must be made at once. If there is too much, the surplus should be either utilized for additional purposes, screened off in readiness for future expansion, or rented. Leaving it open and idle may well result in adjacent units spilling into these areas, and after this happens, space control is lessened and an orderly expansion program is ignored.

## WHO GOES WHERE?

The next task is to determine the general location of the various units within the total usable space. For this purpose, functional flow studies are used. They result in showing the relationship of components and can be illustrated graphically by a block diagram as given in Figure 17–2. Each block identifies the department or unit to be included in the layout. The width of the line joining two blocks indicates the quantity of work flow

FIGURE 17–2. Block Diagram Showing Relationship of Components.

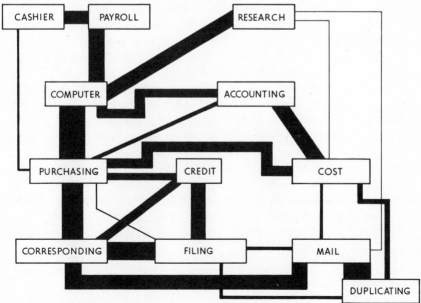

and the physical requirements for communication between these two units.

These efforts show who works with whom and what goes where. Flow is either (1) by papers or (2) by people. We try to minimize the latter, but both must be used. Usually there are key papers about which work of certain units revolve. Tracing the movement of such papers supplies clues as to what units should be related and in what sequence. Data from the communication analysis are also beneficial in this respect. Probably the most reliable data come from an analysis of the systems. Even though time-consuming and somewhat complex to carry out, it is normally well worth the work.

Keeping in mind these relationships of components, the overall work flow, and the nontechnical factors fostered by top managers, the space planner strives to fit the requirements into the usable space so that the work can be accomplished efficiently and under pleasing physical conditions. In this evolving of the layout, knotty problems arise. Trial and error, patience, and experience assist, but also helpful are utilizing certain layout guides and space standards, and following certain layout steps. However, before presenting these latter aids, a brief comment about the use of CRAFT should be made.

## CRAFT

One of the newer and more interesting means for determining the best relationship of components is CRAFT (Computerized Relative Allocation of Facilities Technique).[3] This technique gives an answer which is difficult to improve upon. A diagram is drawn showing how the units are related to each other. Adjustments are then made to find the arrangement of units having the best relationship contributing to the effectiveness of the totality, as measured by cost or time (some measurable unit) for the various work flows and communication efforts. Input data to the computer start with the total cost of work flow and communication for a given pattern. Then, the change in the total cost brought about by two units exchanging positions is calculated. Subsequently calculations by the computer proceed through all combinations of exchanges among the units. For 20 units or departments, and using paired exchanges, some 190 calculations are required. If any unit is to be considered not a candidate for exchanging positions, it can be so programmed. Hence, by means of a computer, the relationship among components to provide the total minimum cost of work flow and communication can be precisely determined.

The printed computer output shows the physical locations. Each

---

[3] E. S. Buffa, G. C. Armour, and T. E. Vollmann, "Allocating Facilities With Craft," *Harvard Business Review,* March–April, 1964.

printed column and each line represent a given measurement like 10 feet, so that 5 columns by 20 lines, or 50 feet by 200 feet, represents 10,000 square feet. Within this area the letter F, for example, in 2 adjacent columns and of 3 adjacent lines deep represents an area 20 feet by 30 feet, or 600 square feet for filing. Its position is the best for filing, considering the total layout, and is shown relative to that of all other units or departments. Armed with such information, we know what units to locate adjacent to what other units and have the structural framework for the most effective layout.

## BASIC APPROACHES

Up to this point we have emphasized the acquiring and organizing of facts considered essential to office space planning. But as stated in the beginning of this chapter, space planning is not all factual or technical. This does not mean that we ignore basic facts in the space planning, but rather that we consider them along with ample consideration to nonfactual factors. As a result, there are today two basic approaches that can be followed (1) the symmetrical-technical, and (2) the flexible-personnel.

The symmetrical-technical is the older and more familiar approach. It is highly engineered and favors gridlike forms where symmetry and uniformity are king. Communication requirements are recognized, a neat orderly appearance is obtained, and employees are put in comfortable boxes reflecting their relative position in the organization hierarchy. The emphasis is upon tradition, efficiency, work, and cost expenditures.

The flexible-personnel approach is the newer and less known approach. It strongly emphasizes that in laying out new offices or refurbishing old ones, we must avoid monotony. A monotonous office usually makes work seem tedious and creates subtle tensions. Some variation in the office layout should be provided. Private offices can vary in size and shape. Walls can be of different colors and the furnishing need not be uniform. Striped partitions can be attractive. Further, the layout should encourage employee communication. The interaction of people is given high priority as well as personnel involvement and team effort. Human behavior and its environment are emphasized. Open spaces are featured with great force placed on lines of work flow.

## OFFICE LANDSCAPING

Representative of the flexible-personnel approach is office landscaping which stresses office layout following communicative and work flow needs and a minimizing of privacy and privilege. Its pronounced visual innovation is a large open landscape rather than enclosed or separated areas. Office landscaping emphasizes the viewpoint of the user, not the outsider.

Work flow, traffic patterns, and communication networks are recognized and studied, then a landscape is built to meet these needs. The flow pattern of work, people, and tools, essential for effective performance, are encased to form a production unit, rather than encasing the units within a series of symmetrical containers. Study may indicate, for example, that the executive staff should be in the center of the landscape because of frequent consultations and closeness in getting the work performed. Simi-

FIGURE 17–3. An Office Space Arranged in Keeping with the Concept of Office Landscaping.

*Courtesy: E. I. DuPont de Nemours and Co., Wilmington, Del.*

larly, it would also indicate who should be adjacent to the computer room, purchasing, and so forth.

Privacy without isolation, visual control of personnel, and instantaneous communication are stressed by the landscaped office. Screens and dividers of varying height replace walls, the use of thick carpeting absorbs sound, and furniture and machines are spaced in functional clusters. An executive office area is distinguished by more space, a larger desk, or the character of accessories. The functional arrangement can be maintained, even as sections expand or contract, thus providing flexibility to the arrangement. Both the functionalization and the freer, open idea of office landscaping make for irregularly arranged work stations which are developed from the work flow and traffic pattern of the organization. The free-form series of groupings and the orientation of the individual pieces vary from group to group and frequently within groups. One may face south while its neighbor faces 15 degrees west of south, and another faces west. The purpose is to give personal identity to each group and thus to the individual within the group. This irregular orientation of work stations permits control by sight lines. This aids supervision. Yet it is customary to restrict any view to about 30 feet in order to retain intimacy and not expose an employee to the total area. Further, landscaping by its physical nature permits the free flow of information, suggestions, criticisms, and collaborations so essential in leading to a free intercourse of ideas and to prompt decision making and implementation. Figure 17-3 shows an office landscaping installation.

Ideally the space for this type office layout is a minimum of 10,000 square feet and neither dimension less than 75 feet. It will not work well in an area too small or too narrow. Column spacing should be 25 feet or more with ceiling height a maximum of 9 feet. A rigid basic requirement is good acoustics to ensure quietness. Several surveys to determine how office landscaping is being accepted by employees indicate some minor problems but the vast majority like it.

## ADMINISTRATIVE SUBSTATION

Rapidly gaining acceptance in office space planning is the administrative substation which is a compact work station handling numerous information activities closely related but traditionally thought of as separate functions. It may include a secretarial services unit, messenger services, storing and retrieving of certain records, mail room, and copying services. Ideally, substations are joined together with other substations forming a framework linked to the computer information center.

Each substation has a supervisor who oversees work input and output of that unit. Frequently this is a private secretary who because of her knowledge of company operations can perform this work competently. They serve as deputies of the information manager or his assistant in that they translate requests for information service into working programs. All personnel of the work station are upgraded because they acquire additional skills to perform their varied tasks. Their work is more interesting and challenging.

The concept of an administrative substation evolved from the development of the landscaped office. It can exist, however, in an office layout either as a feature in the flexible-personnel approach or as an important modification of the symmetrical-technical approach. In perspective, it is a workable office layout idea that captures the availability of human skill and ability as well as improved utility of many modern furniture pieces and machines of this present day.

## PREPARING AN OFFICE LAYOUT

The initial step is to obtain a drawing or blueprint of the available area. If no print is available, the space should be measured and the dimensions indicated on a neatly drawn hand sketch. A convenient scale is $\frac{1}{4}'' = 1'$, which means that $\frac{1}{4}$ inch on the drawing is equal to 1 foot of actual floor dimension. The exact location and size should be indicated for windows, building offsets, and door swings, and the location of columns, pipes, electric light outlets and wiring, ducts for telephone wiring, running water facilities, entrances and exits. Frequently, the ability to adapt a suggested layout depends upon the completeness and accuracy of these data. A building offset incorrectly spotted, or the omission of a column, can necessitate alterations in a proposed layout or even rejection.

Next, from the total area, locations for main traffic movement should be determined. These locations will depend upon such things as the size and shape of the space available and the general type of office. Building facilities such as entrances and exits, stairways, elevators, rest rooms, and the like will suggest areas of greatest travel. From this information, the location of the main corridors, storage rooms, reception rooms, and wardrobe rooms in the layout will be suggested. These represent space required for other than personnel occupancy.

Third, tentative answers can now be formulated regarding the use of reception room, conference rooms, and private offices. Discussion on the use of these areas is made later in this chapter. For the present, our decision will be based in part on the approach to office layout that we are taking—whether symmetrical-technical or flexible-personnel. In either event, we should approximate the amount of space for these accommodations and include in our listing of the physical facilities to be provided.

Fourth, the data from the organization, activity, machine, and communication analyses are now studied and digested. Efforts to coordinate the information into an overall picture is not easy, yet it is not especially difficult. We can identify the number of employees and the equipment and machines required for each organization unit. We also have the total size of the area needed for each major unit, and we know, as stated above, the relationship among the units in terms of flow and communication—as shown in the block diagram. Matching the major segments of the space requirements against usable space available sounds like a herculean task and the work does resemble working a jigsaw puzzle. But bit by bit, an adjustment here and there, key areas begin to shape up and the entire layout begins to unfold satisfactorily. Consultation with the leaders of those to occupy the tentative spaces can be used. Valuable suggestions are received and conflicts, such as several groups wanting the identical space, can be resolved.

We are now ready to work out specific details which begin by making templates to scale of all physical units (or use models) and identifying each. A template is a scaled pattern, made of cardboard or paper, which is used to represent the floor area occupied by a physical unit. The scale of the templates must be the same as that of the drawing showing the available area; as already pointed out, a scale of ¼″ = 1′ is convenient. Frequently, the shape of the templates is confined to that of a square or a rectangle; and in most cases, this is satisfactory; but there are instances where the details of cutoff corners, rounded corners, and the like should be included in the templates, as the final arrangement may hinge upon these considerations. A separate template is made for each physical unit considered in the layout.

For purposes of identification, the name of the unit and of the basic group by which the unit is to be used should be stamped or printed on each template. It is also possible to use different colors representing different physical units to help visualize the work. Where a conference room and private offices are considered, templates covering the overall floor dimensions should be included.

Instead of templates, small-scale, three-dimensional models of the physical units can be used. These office models are dimensionally accurate and show at a glance the arrangement of the office. Many people can visualize the layout more clearly from scale models than from a technical drawing with which they may be unfamiliar. Complete kits, consisting of several hundred pieces including desks, chairs, files, machines, coat racks, and building columns, are available.

Also available are magnetic templates and magnetic models that can be used along with a steel-covered piece of plywood serving as a base. The magnetic templates or models hold fast to the steel-plywood base, yet they can be moved to show different layouts. The base can be attached to a wall, thus providing convenient viewing adequate for a group of people.

The templates or models are arranged for each basic group within its respective tentative area. The layout is determined by moving and shifting the templates or models to various positions so as to arrive at an effective arrangement. This phase of layout is a tentative trial-and-error process. It requires considerable time and cannot be rushed. If magnetic templates or models are used, they can be moved about as desired; yet, when released, they hold a fixed position. When the contemplated layout is completed, a picture of it can be taken and white paper copies made so that convenient reference sheets are provided.

Next, the entire tentative layout is reviewed and minor adjustments are made as required. In other words what we believe may be the best arrangement is checked as a totality to see that it is a well-knit arrangement which will meet the particular needs. Attention is directed to the contribution of every major unit. A check is made of the work flow through the entire area and the probable general appearance of the entire layout.

Appropriate markings are added to indicate the major flows of work, the telephone and electric wiring, and the name of the employee to be located at each unit. This information is necessary to gain a complete understanding of the layout. Proper planning for telephones can prevent much inconvenience and the location of electric wiring outlets is especially important where groups of electrically driven machines are used. The name of the employee at each work unit is helpful to the office executive in visualizing the arrangement.

Finally, a recheck is conducted with each interested group. The first group to consult, of course, is the top managers. Point out to them where they will be located, what facilities are provided, and the chief considerations determining the recommended layout. Generally, minor changes will be suggested, and they can usually be incorporated. The same approach is followed with each group head. If consultation was practiced as suggested previously, the suggested plans are usually viewed favorably. However, if there are doubts and questions, an explanation of the recommended layout should be made, with the reasons carefully pointed out. After all groups have OK'd their respective layouts, the entire plan is submitted to the top managers with the statement that this layout has the approval of each group head. Acceptance by the top managers is then usually little more than a formality.

## BASIC LAYOUT GUIDES

There have been developed a number of layout guides which when followed help to provide an effective office arrangement. Not all of these can be followed in any one layout. The basic approach followed has significant influence. The list includes:

1. Utilize one large area in preference to an equivalent area of small parcels. The single large area permits better lighting, ventilating, supervising, and communicating.

2. Give major preference to the dominant flows of work and communication needs. Provide for good work flows and avoid backtracking, crisscrossing, and unnecessary movement of papers.

3. Place related departments adjacent, and keep jobs of a similar nature in close relationship.

4. Locate departments which normally have many visitors from the outside near the entrance; or if this is not feasible, make provisions so that this traffic will not disturb other departments.

5. Locate vending machines, fountains, and bulletin boards where they will cause least distraction and congestion.

6. Provide for maximum work loads.

7. Anticipate and provide for future changes. Keep the layout flexible.

8. Locate supervisors in such a manner that they can easily observe what goes on in the work area.

9. Have the work come to the employee, not the employee go to the work. Keep employee flow to a minimum.

10. Arrange desks so that ample natural light comes from a little back and over the left shoulder.

11. Avoid private office locations which cut off natural light to the adjacent general office area.

12. Do not have the employee facing a window, too near heat sources, or in line of drafts.

13. For necessary walls, use movable partitions as they are easy to install; part-way partitions with plain or opaque glass permit good light and ventilation.

14. Provide sufficient floor electrical outlets for office machines.

15. Place units making much noise in a soundproof area to avoid disturbance to others.

16. Put files and frequently used machines near the employees who use them. Abstain from putting all files at dead wall space.

17. Arrange filing cabinets back to back.

18. If a corner is required, consider the possibility of providing it with filing cabinets.

19. If possible, provide lounging areas where employees can relax during rest periods, talk informally, and eat lunch.

20. Provide convenient and adequate rest-room facilities.

## OVERALL SPACE ESTIMATES

Studies show that a value of 60 square feet of usable space for each *ordinary clerical employee* is a desirable standard; and when an office layout calls for this amount, the space utilization is considered by some to be highly satisfactory. The value of 60 square feet per ordinary clerical employee is arrived at in this manner:

54-inch desk and chair, 54″ x 72″ = 27.00 sq. ft.
Aisle per desk, 18″ x 72″ = 9.00 sq. ft.
Miscellaneous (files, aisles, etc.) = 24.00 sq. ft.
Total = 60.00 sq. ft.

But space requirements vary with the machines and furniture needed, and hence, so-called allowances of square feet per employee are unrealistic and fluctuating. They are at best foggy guides. Some surveys show 75 to 80 square feet per clerical employee as typical in a fairly large clerical area. A value of 90 to 100 square feet per employee is more realistic. Estimates for other personnel include:

Top executive ..................... 400–450 sq. ft.
Intermediate executive .............. 275–300 sq. ft.
Supervisory executive ............... 110–125 sq. ft.

These data are more valid primarily because there is more uniformity in what machines and furniture and executive or a supervisor is provided. They are helpful as broad estimates.

FIGURE 17–4. Minimum Standards for Back-to-Back Arrangement of Desks under Different Floor Plan Layouts.

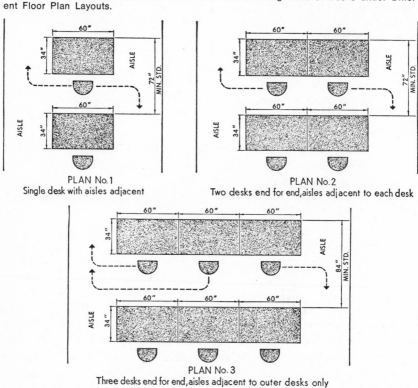

PLAN No. 1
Single desk with aisles adjacent

PLAN No. 2
Two desks end for end, aisles adjacent to each desk

PLAN No. 3
Three desks end for end, aisles adjacent to outer desks only

However, to repeat, there is no fast rule for the standard number of square feet per office employee. The amount of space to allow is influenced by many factors including the nature of the work, the available total area, the extent of service areas, the need for privacy, the number and type of equipment and machines, and the shape, exposure, and obstructions within the total space itself. One office with a value of 77 square feet per clerical employee may have an excellent layout, while employees of another office with 77 square feet per clerical employee struggle under cramped office conditions.

Over a period, certain prescribed space usages have gained acceptance as representing effective space utilization. Some consider them space standards which in a sense they are, but they should not be viewed as rigid measurements, but rather as the result of reliable practices which assist in providing a satisfactory layout. For the most part they apply only to the symmetrical-technical approach.

For desks, suggestions are shown in Figure 17–4. For example, referring to the top illustration, when 60 x 34-inch desks are arranged as single units with aisles adjacent, or when they are arranged in pairs, end for end, with aisles adjacent to each desk, the minimum space standard from back to back of desks is about 72 inches. These arrangements provide about a 3-foot strip for the chair and for getting to and from the desk. The bottom illustration of the figure shows space standards for three desks placed end for end. Of the three plans shown in this figure, plan No. 2 requires the smallest area per clerk; in contrast, plan No. 1 requires the most.

FIGURE 17–5. Recommended Aisle Spaces for Active Files according to Their Arrangement.

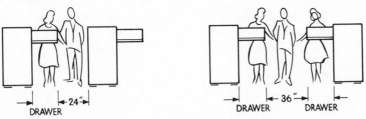

Main corridors should be from 5 to 8 feet wide, depending upon the amount of traffic to be handled. A 5-foot aisle can normally accommodate around 850 people in five minutes. Main aisles in an office area should be from 4 to 5 feet wide, and the range of secondary aisles should be from 3 to 4 feet wide. Cross aisles should be provided about every 50 feet.

The spacing of filing cabinets depends upon frequency of use and functions of the material filed. Pertinent data include:

| Material | Type of Cabinet | Position of Filing Cabinets | Aisle Space |
|---|---|---|---|
| Active | Ordinary pull drawer | Facing same direction | Drawer depth plus 24 inches |
| ″ | ″ ″ | Facing each other | Two drawer depths plus 36 inches |
| Inactive | ″ ″ | Facing same direction | Drawer depth |
| ″ | ″ ″ | Facing each other | ″ ″ |
| Active | Side or lateral | Facing same direction | 24 inches |
| ″ | ″ | Facing each other | 30 inches |

The first two arrangements are illustrated by Figure 17–5. When a quantity of ordinary pull-drawer filing cabinets are used, always arrange them facing each other, i.e., back to back, to save space. Likewise, for lateral cabinets, the most economical arrangement is having them face each other.

## THE COMPUTER ROOM

Computer space requirements are demanding and include quality and reliability of electrical power, supply of water and raw air for air conditioning, satisfaction of insurance (especially fire) requirements, accessibility, and ample space for storage of input and output materials and for expansion and future development. Line-to-line voltage tolerance usually must be maintained plus or minus 8 percent of the normal rated voltage measured at the receptacle when the computer system is operating. Also the illumination of the computer room should be somewhat equalized over the machine area as frequently personnel must work behind the various machines. Most computers generate a considerable amount of heat and to maintain good operating conditions, year-round air conditioning is required. This, in turn, necessitates large quantities of water and raw air, provisions of which are mandatory. Many managers recommend a cooling system separate from that of the building. Computer systems are connected by cables of limited length and this requires accessibility and working positions which define the work area. In addition, large quantities of cards, tapes, disks, paper printouts, and microform records require a convenient and large area for storage and quick retrieval. The computer room houses a center of vital information. Many records flow into it, many flow out of it. And the computer personnel usually must work closely with other personnel. All of these considerations help to determine the location of the computer room.

## THE PRIVATE OFFICE

Decisions regarding the use of a private office should be made only after ample consideration has been given to the individual circumstances. A private office should be employed when its use is dictated by facts and unbiased judgment. It should never be provided simply because it has always been provided for a particular job or because requests and sometimes pressure have been brought to bear.

Those in favor of a private office commonly seek to justify their views by emphasizing the need for prestige. It is for this reason that most top management members are supplied with private offices. This helps add weight, influence, and respect to this group in the eyes of other employees and of visitors to the office. In addition to top managers, there are others who, for reasons of prestige, probably merit private offices. They include department heads and professional people.

Also, in support of the private office is the provision of a suitable space for work requiring high concentration. It is contended that creative work, such as writing advertising copy and preparing difficult reports, usually justifies a private office. Likewise, employees doing intricate analysis, original planning, close mental work, and work requiring exclusive attention with a minimum of distraction merit a private office.

Finally, the providing of proper accommodations for confidential work, significant in research, planning, control and consolidating recapitulations of important statistics is offered. Also, conversations during personnel-selection interviews are of a confidential sort and should be conducted in a private office. But note that a conference room can be used for this purpose. It is not difficult to overemphasize the importance of confidential work. Hence, extreme care should be exercised in determining whether this consideration actually warrants a private office. Figure 17–6 shows several suggested layouts for private offices. Note the additional furniture that can be accommodated in the larger office.

On the other hand, the use of private offices may interfere with supervisor effectiveness. The closeness of the supervisor to the employees, his familiarity with problems as they arise, and his being at the heart of all happenings in his unit are the types of things that are usually lost when the supervisor is segregated by a private office. In order to see that an order is carried out properly, it is frequently best to be close at hand to give instructions, check performance, and provide encouragement. For example, in the main office of a large aircraft manufacturer, there are no interior walls or room dividers. The only sign of top executive status is placement in corner areas furnished no differently from the nonexecutive areas. This is in part compatible with the flexible-personnel approach to office layout.

Furthermore, private offices complicate the heating, ventilating, and lighting of these areas as well as of adjoining areas. Individual segments of space, set off from the large area, require special arrangements to supply these services, all of which mean additional materials and labor.

Also, the relatively high cost of the private office is a paramount objection. By their use, space utilization is reduced to 35 to 50 percent that of the open-area arrangement. And the buying, erecting, maintaining, and, in case of alteration, moving of partitions entail expenditures which cumulatively amount to quite sizable figures.

## MOVABLE PARTITIONS

For segregating the private offices needed and dividing the office space as the approved layout requires, movable partitions are widely used. Made of metal or wood they are easily erected, dismantled, and relocated.

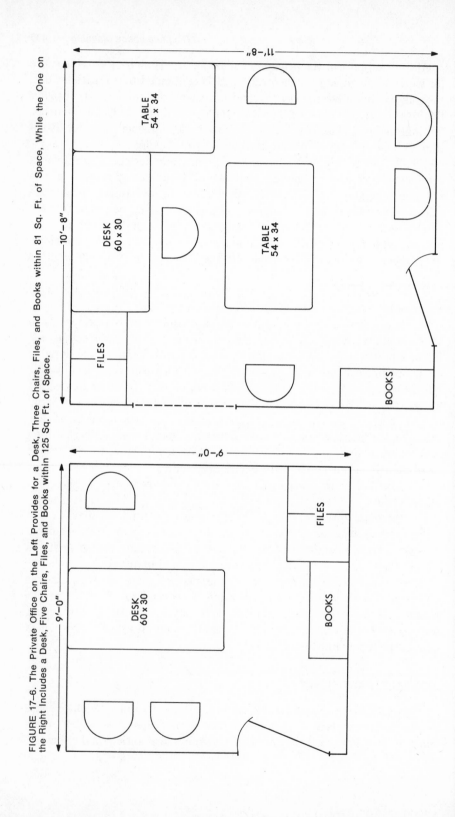

FIGURE 17–6. The Private Office on the Left Provides for a Desk, Three Chairs, Files, and Books within 81 Sq. Ft. of Space, While the One on the Right Includes a Desk, Five Chairs, Files, and Books within 125 Sq. Ft. of Space.

Wiring and outlets are laid in the baseboards and joints. The partitions are factory finished and offered in a variety of styles and colors. All are soundproof having insulating material in the core or center. Panels with recesses for bookcases, alcoves for drinking fountains, provisions for door openings, door units, and with or without glass (crystal or obscure) in the top areas are among the many available kinds offered to fit requirements for every type of working space. See Figure 17–7.

Movable partitions afford not only great flexibility in office layout, but also space control and high material salvage. The panels can be used over and over again. Changes in layout can be made overnight or during a weekend. In many instances, the cost of erecting movable partitions is only 15 percent of that of immovable tile and plaster walls. Furthermore, eliminated are objectionable inconveniences such as noise, commotion,

FIGURE 17–7. Effective Use of Movable Office Partitions.

*Courtesy: General Fireproofing Co., Youngstown, O.*

debris, waiting for plaster and paint to dry, and, after partition installation, the cleaning of rugs, draperies, and furniture.

Various heights, ranging from the railing to the ceiling, are available. The heights of 36 inches to 84 inches are popular. They provide privacy, yet do not interfere with the ventilating and lighting. Railings have been used in banks, for example, with outstanding success. Executives are located in open areas of the bank area, with offices, if divided, separated by low railings. This arrangement is of relatively low cost, minimizes the need for special lighting and heating facilities, makes a pleasing appearance, and is convenient for both the officers and the customers.

## MODULAR ARRANGEMENTS

Modular furniture and its availability with partition panels was pointed out in chapter 16. Such units are preferred when a compact and individual unit is wanted. A number of arrangements are offered. These are assembled from interlocking, interchangeable, component units.

Modular-type arrangements save floor space and increase efficiency. Figure 17–8 illustrates a comparison between conventional desk units and modular units, with a saving of 22.4 percent of floor area resulting from

FIGURE 17–8. A Comparison of Conventional Desk Units with Modular Units Shows That, for the Same Number of Employees and Approximately the Same Desk Areas, the Modular Units Save Nearly 23 Percent of Floor Space (8,160 Square Inches Compared with 6,664 Square Inches).

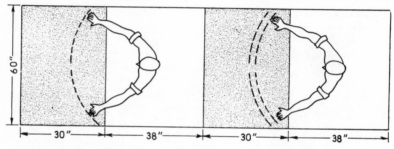

DESK AREAS = 3,600 SQ. IN.    TOTAL AREA OCCUPIED = 8,160 SQ. IN.

CONVENTIONAL DESK UNITS

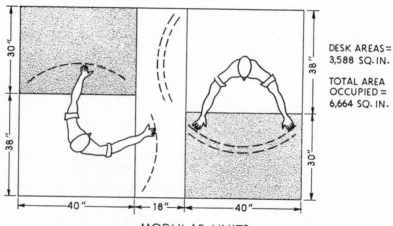

DESK AREAS = 3,588 SQ. IN.

TOTAL AREA OCCUPIED = 6,664 SQ. IN.

MODULAR UNITS

*Courtesy: Globe-Wernicke Co., Cincinnati*

the use of the modular units. At the same time, the smaller space is more convenient and provides an adequate work area.

## RECEPTION ROOM

The reception room and the receptionist create the initial impression of the enterprise upon the visitor, and initial impressions are often lasting ones. The reception room should be inviting. Displays of the company's products or services are very effective and assist in building good will. Keeping the room clean is basic. Chairs should be kept in a straight line, with newspapers and magazines arranged neatly on a table, and ash trays should be kept clean. It is also well to include cloakroom facilities adjacent to this area. If possible, the reception room should not handle ordinary and necessary traffic between different areas in the office because this creates a disturbing influence and distracts from the dignity of the entire office. To prevent this condition, provide a passage for regular office traffic which bypasses the reception room.

The receptionist should be friendly and extend visitors courteous and prompt treatment. Her job is to find out with which person, if any, the visitor should talk and arrange for the visitor to see the proper person quickly. She needs to be fully familiar with what matters are handled by each employee who has callers. Normally a guide or booklet is available for reference. As a matter of record, it is a good practice to have the receptionist keep a report of callers, including the date, the name of each caller, the name of his company, and the person called on. When individual conditions permit, the receptionist might also perform office work of sorting, stuffing envelopes, typing, or operating the telephone switchboard. However, if there is too much extra work, the regular duties of the receptionist might be neglected and the supervisor should watch this carefully.

## CONFERENCE ROOM

For meetings in privacy, a conference room is highly recommended. Most private offices are not suited for the handling of meetings. With a conference room, the participants can be arranged more satisfactorily, a greater number can usually be accommodated, and each one can have a convenient place to write or to take notes. Furthermore, the meeting is placed on a businesslike basis, with a minimum of interference and distractions. The conference room should be located conveniently where traffic in and out of the room will be least disturbing to the other office employees. Figure 17–9 shows dimensions of a well-planned conference room layout.

440   *Office management and control*

FIGURE 17–9. Layout of Conference Room for Ten People. The table is 4 x 10 feet. For each two additional people to be accommodated, add 2 feet 6 inches to table length and to room length.

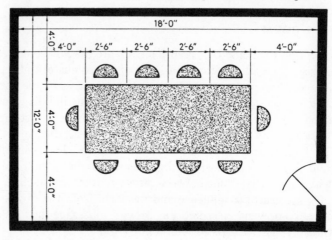

## WARDROBE FACILITIES

Wardrobe facilities can be provided either by having separate rooms—locker or cloakrooms—or by placing wardrobe racks in the office areas. If the former plan is used, provision should include separate rooms for men and women. When racks are used, they can be located throughout the office areas. Units are available which provide storage for coats, hats, overshoes, umbrellas, and the like for as many as three persons per square foot of floor area.

## PLANNING THE OFFICE MOVE

Office layout changes necessitate moves—sometimes small, sometimes large. It is best that these be well planned. A detailed office layout should be developed. The approach should be along the lines outlined in this chapter. This means that employees will know of the move, and they should. When the layout is determined, inform them of decisions they will want to know about, such as the general decor to be used, where they will be located in the new layout, the approximate time of the move, and outstanding features of the new arrangements. When the layout is finalized, number each item in it. Then tag and number all equipment and machines to designate their exact location in the new layout. For large moves a code of different colors and letter prefixes is effective, i.e., red (second floor), C (cost department), yellow (third floor), L (library), and so forth.

It is recommended that a moving committee be appointed. Usually a top executive becomes chairman with all department heads as members. Each of the latter selects two assistants from his own department and the three serve as a departmental subcommittee. They get things in their department ready for the move. On the day of moving they serve as deputies helping to coordinate the move, direct traffic, check to see that items are placed in correct locations in their areas, and answer questions.

FIGURE 17–10. Check List in Preparation for M-Day (Moving Day).

Arrangements for:
1. Building directory—show new locations.
2. Cleaning all furniture, carpets, rugs, and draperies, if not replaced.
3. Moving company.
4. Stationery—purchase new letterheads, envelopes, and other printed matter.
5. Telephone—request service well in advance.
6. Teletype—request service well in advance.
7. Utilities—request service well in advance.

Follow up on delivery of new furniture and machines:
1. Accessories.
2. Chairs.
3. Desks.
4. Machines.

Notify:
1. Customers and suppliers.
2. Government—Internal Revenue Service, Social Security, State Unemployed.
3. Insurance companies.
4. Local post office.
5. Publishers of periodicals.
6. Western Union.

Sell obsolete furniture.

Drawing up a check sheet of "things to be done" in connection with the move helps direct efforts to the many tasks that are to be taken care of. Representative of such a list is that shown by Figure 17–10.

It is best to schedule the move over a weekend or vacation period, allowing a maximum of 60 continuous hours (Friday 6:00 P.M.—Monday 6:00 A.M.) and arranging for an adequate number of trucks and crews. It is also preferable to move one section of the office at a time. Attempts to move two or three sections at the same time can result in a serious tie-up Items to be placed in remote and farthest areas should be moved first, after which should come those located adjacent to the entranceway. The movers, electricians and carpenters, and other personnel should be informed of the schedule.

## QUESTIONS

1. Do you agree with the following statement: "Office space planning is a continuous type of activity." Why?
2. Enumerate what is included in "the function, activity, and duty analysis" as applied to office space planning.
3. What information does Figure 17–2 convey and how is this information used in office space planning?
4. What are some office space standards that you would use in making an office layout?
5. Identify each of the following:
   *a)* Physical facilities of a building.
   *b)* The symmetrical technical approach.
   *c)* Office space planning.
   *d)* Templates.
6. Identify and compare the basic approaches that can be followed in office space planning.
7. Discuss the meaning and use of administrative substations in an office layout.
8. What are the major features of office landscaping?
9. Approximately how much office space would you allot to each of the following:
   *a)* Two desks end for end (60 x 34-inch desk), aisle adjacent, chair for each desk.
   *b)* Private office for a supervisory executive.
   *c)* General office space for six clerks.
   *d)* A main aisle running the long distance of an office area 20 feet by 28 feet.
10. Give some realistic suggestions for an office manager to utilize when planning the office move.
11. The computer room requires special attention by the office space planner. Why is this? Justify your answer.
12. Describe the layout of an office with which you are familiar, and point out several ways in which you feel it might be improved. Give reasons for your suggested changes.

## CASE PROBLEMS

### Case 17–1.   North American University

Professor Henry D. Matisoff is joining the faculty and is looking forward to his new assignment at North American University. His work will include not only teaching classes, but also much counseling of students. He will have a secretary three mornings a week to assist him in any clerical work he may have. She will have a work station in Professor Matisoff's office.

Office space is at a premium around the university but the Dean has succeeded in locating a vacant office in a temporary campus building. The office is 12 feet by 10½ feet exclusive of two large closets. There are two windows on the north side of the area, entrance is on the south. Details are shown in Exhibit 17–1A. Professor

**EXHIBIT 17–1A.**

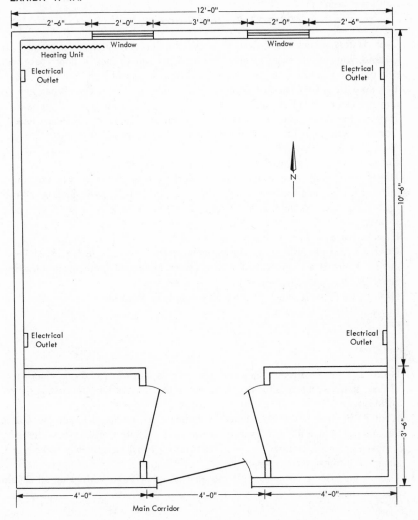

Matisoff is advised that he can select what furniture he wants from the following: two 58 x 30 desks, two bookshelves 42 x 10, two four-drawer filing cabinets 15 x 28, four desk chairs, three straight back chairs, one 36 x 24 typist desk, one 18 x 18 stand, three table lamps, and one three-drawer filing cabinet 15 x 28.

## Questions:

1. Develop two office layouts that you recommend for Professor Matisoff's consideration.
2. Point out the advantages and disadvantages of each layout.
3. What is your recommendation to Professor Matisoff? Why?

## Case 17–2.   Iola Products, Inc.

Tom Hance (*sales representative*): Absolutely. Side filing is efficient. Mr. Conrad, you can file twice as much material per square foot of floor space with side filing as you can with the conventional four-drawer file.

Bernard Conrad (*office manager*): That's difficult to believe. What are the dimensions of a side filing unit?

Hance: The dimensions are 13 inches by 36 inches. The unit is 36 inches long.

Conrad: And the regular four drawer file is about 15 inches by 28 inches?

Hance: Yes, that's right.

Conrad: What's the capacity in filing inches of a side file?

Hance (*referring to manual*): In filing inches, let's see. Here you are. Filing inches for a 13-inch by 36-inch side filing unit are 204. For a 15-inch by 28-inch four-drawer filing cabinet, it is . . . ah . . . 102 filing inches.

Conrad: 202?

Hance: No. It is 102.

Conrad: All right, 102. Now, our available space is 9 feet 6 inches by 21 feet 2 inches. There is a 30-inch door in the center of one 21-foot-2-inch side. How many side file units can I get in there?

Hance: I'll figure it out. Will you wait a couple of minutes?

Conrad: Surely. Go ahead.

## Questions:

1. Is this statement correct? "You can file twice as much material per square foot of floor space with side filing as you can with the conventional four-drawer file." Substantiate your answer, showing calculations.
2. What is the answer for Mr. Hance in reply to Mr. Conrad's inquiry regarding the number of side filing units in the given area? (Hint: Consider first the units arranged mainly lengthwise—along the 21-foot-2-inch dimension, and second, along the 9-foot-6-inch dimension.)
3. Aside from space requirements, briefly discuss other factors Mr. Conrad should take into account.

## Case 17–3.   Pelkey Company

Now in the process of constructing a new district sales office, Mr. Robert Sheller has the task of bringing together the various company's personnel space wishes and the constraints of the proposed building. After holding numerous conferences, Mr. Sheller has concluded that the following space needs should be provided:

 1 General manager's office, 14 feet x 10 feet
 1 Assistant general manager's office, 14 feet x 7 feet
 1 Accounting department area, 11 feet x 35 feet
 1 Transcribing room, 7 feet x 11 feet
20 Private offices, 7 feet x 11 feet
 1 Reception room, 14 feet x 11 feet

1 Conference room, 14 feet x 11 feet
1 Library, 10 feet x 11 feet
1 Supply room, 11 feet x 11 feet
1 Mail and shipping room, 11 feet x 16 feet
1 Records storage room, 11 feet x 11 feet
1 Machine room, 10 feet x 11 feet
1 Lounge, 11 feet x 14 feet
1 Cafeteria, 10 feet x 30 feet
1 Stairway to basement, 3 feet x 11 feet
1 Women's toilet, 11 feet x 11 feet
1 Men's toilet, 8 feet x 11 feet

The column-free overall space will be 70 feet by 70 feet with an inner court area 16 feet by 16 feet. This inner court, or atrium, will be located in the exact center of the overall space. A roofed open gallery will entirely surround the overall area. It is 10 feet wide. The general manager has stated that he would approve possibly two or three offices or facilities located in the atrium if needed and if it also contributed to the overall layout, but he felt the pleasing effect of the open gallery depended on it being an open space.

Most business callers see either the general manager, one of six representatives (housed in private office), or someone in the accounting department. It is believed the transcribing room should be near accounting. Likewise, services of the cafeteria are used mainly by the accounting personnel. Further, the library is used most by the assistant general manager, but he prefers that it be located convenient but not adjacent to his office. He also feels it is better to have his office located away from that of the general manager's.

## Questions:

1. Prepare an office layout that meets the company's specifications. A scale of ¼ inch equals 1 foot is satisfactory.
2. Point out the desirable features of your proposed layout.
3. Design a suggested detailed sketch of the furniture arrangement for the general manager's office.

chapter **18**

# Office environment

Pain makes man think. Thought makes man wise.
Wisdom makes life endurable.
*—John Patrick*

T<small>HE</small> <small>GENERAL</small> physical working conditions under which office work is done makes up an additional area where proper planning can be of genuine help. Employees respond to their surroundings physically and emotionally so that study to create the best possible work environment is very much worthwhile. For our purpose, we will discuss five environmental factors including (1) light, (2) color, (3) music, (4) air, and (5) sound. Usually the services of specialists in these factors are utilized in the planning efforts. The information manager should be familiar with the basic knowledge and practices in each area to ensure that his specific objectives are attained and the various efforts are properly synchronized.

Planning for these factors should not be handled separately. They are all interrelated, not only among themselves, but also with location, layout, machines and furniture, and all the other major planning areas already discussed. To illustrate, lighting is dependent somewhat on the color scheme employed, and color conditioning is tied in with office layout. All planning must be carefully coordinated.

## IMPORTANCE OF OFFICE ENVIRONMENT

It is now an established fact that many factors influence an office employee's performance. Among them are experience, inherent abilities, attitude, and age. These all are individual characteristics, but for a given

446

set of conditions, we know that any individual's performance is significantly conditioned by the environment in which the employee works. The cumulative effect of his total work environment is a strong determinative in how well he marshalls his abilities and skills, his attitude toward his work and his co-peers, and his enthusiasm for his work.

We are interested in environment not only because of its direct effects upon productivity, but also because of its indirect effects which can likewise be quite beneficial. Consider light, for example. For proper environment, we want enough light so that we can see rapidly, accurately, and with the least effort. There are physical requirements. However, in addition, we want enough light, not too much not too little, to create and influence an emotional response. Hence, there is an aesthetic and spatial environment to which light contributes. In other words there is a psychological gain as well as an economical one. However, in some cases, gains other than productivity to be derived from supplying the proper environment, are likewise economic. For example, heat generated from a lighting system can now be used to optimize the heating and cooling of a building. Called "electrical space conditioning," it exemplifies an advantageous economic by-product derived indirectly from the supplying of a desired environment.

## OFFICE LIGHTING

Adequate light is one of the most important considerations in an office. Many office tasks are of an exacting and close nature. Small print, carbon copies of typed material, and poorly handwritten notes are among the regular hard-to-see materials that must be handled. The advantages of good lighting are illustrated in Figure 18–1.

FIGURE 18–1. A Well-Balanced Program of Lighting in the Office Provides Many Advantages.

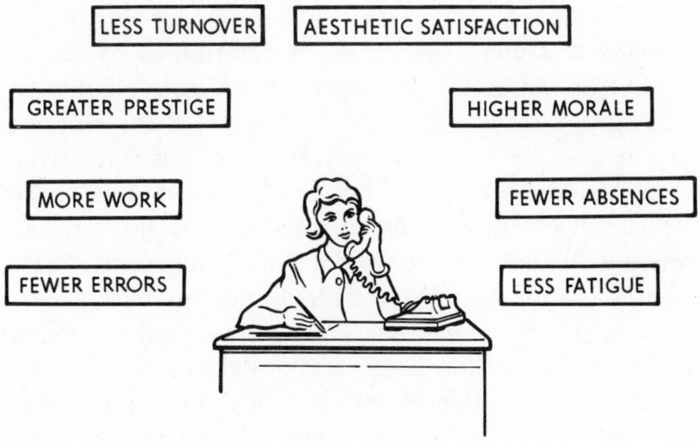

Without light, there can be no sight; and for light itself to be seen, it must be *associated with surfaces*. Light and surfaces are closely linked. It is the light reflected from the surface that enables a human being to see. Also, for an object to be seen, it must stand out from all other things around it. That is, contrast is necessary. Let us examine these concepts further by considering three characteristics of light: (1) quantity, (2) brightness, and (3) diffusion. These are crucial in any study of lighting.

**1. Quantity of Light.** A common measurement of light is a footcandle which is *the amount of direct light one foot distant from a standard candle.* A rule of thumb for rough estimating is that, for small rooms, one watt per square foot of area provides 15 footcandles. Thus, a 100-watt bulb in a room 10 feet x 10 feet will provide approximately 15 footcandles of light. The amount of light also depends upon the distribution of the light sources; for example, that provided by a single 100-watt bulb will differ from that supplied by four 25-watt bulbs, because of the difference in the light diffusion. Recommended values of illumination are shown in Figure 18–2.

FIGURE 18–2. Recommended Values of Illumination for Office Work

| *Type of office or work* | *Footcandles recommended on working area* |
|---|---|
| Detailed drafting and designing | 200 |
| Difficult seeing tasks | 150 |
| such as auditing and accounting, business machine operation, transcribing and tabulating, and bookkeeping | |
| Ordinary seeing tasks | 100 |
| such as private office work, general correspondence, and work in conference rooms, active file rooms, and mail rooms | |
| Casual seeing tasks | 30 |
| such as in inactive file rooms, reception rooms, stairways, washrooms and other service areas | |

Source: Illuminating Engineering Society, New York.

**2. Brightness of Light.** Brightness is determined by the amount of light reflected from an object. To repeat, the effective light for seeing is the reflected light, not the light from the source. If the object to be seen reflects very little of the light cast upon it, the object is relatively difficult to see and in this case possesses a low reflectance value. The ratio of the light a surface reflects, divided by the amount of light it receives, is the reflectance value of that surface. The finish of the surface, its color, and type of material are major influences regulating the reflectance value. For example, a smooth finish in white has a reflectance value of about 0.90, or 90 percent; in medium yellow, 0.65; and in dark green, 0.07. Figure 18–3 shows recommended reflectances for room and furniture surfaces in the office. These values are higher than normally found which means that

FIGURE 18–3. For Good Office Lighting These Light Reflectance Values for Room, Furniture, and Machine Surfaces Should Be Attained.

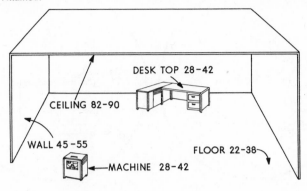

DESK TOP 28–42

CEILING 82–90

WALL 45–55

FLOOR 22–38

MACHINE 28–42

many office areas are improperly lighted, not because of the fixtures or amount of light supplied, but because the office surfaces do not reflect the light sufficiently for good seeing conditions.

Brightness is also important because it controls contrast, which affects seeing. The human eye sees best when the areas within its field of vision, such as a desk and its immediate surroundings, are approximately of the same brightness. An undesirable situation is that in which the light is concentrated on the desk area, and the surroundings are dark. Under these conditions, the pupils of the eyes are continually expanding or contracting in their adjustment to the bright and dark areas. This makes for eye fatigue and difficulty in concentrating on the work. For the visual area, which is generally described as about 30 degrees in all directions from the eye, the ratio of the brightness of the light source to its background should not exceed 3 to 1. Lighting fixtures and their arrangements influence this ratio. From the practical viewpoint, too great a brightness contrast can cause glare, which comes either from the source of light or from smooth, highly polished surfaces. (See Figure 18–4.)

Greatest visibility is usually reached when there is a maximum color contrast between writing and its background. It is difficult to read when there is little contrast between the paper and the printing, for example, white on white, white on cream, or black on black. On the other hand, white chalk marks on a blackboard or black print on white paper affords a high contrast and helps the seeing process.

**3. Diffusion of Light.** In order for an object in any spatial position to be seen clearly and easily, diffusion of light is required. Light should not be absolutely uniform. To illustrate, daylight is most uninteresting when it is most uniform. A heavy overcast day is representative. Sight and interest are greatest when black clouds are dissipated by bright sunlight for this includes a whole complex of values and relationships. The same

FIGURE 18–4. Glare Prevents Office Employees from Working Effectively.

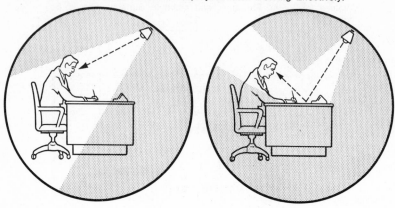

holds true for lighting an interior area. The entirety is done with a feeling for the total environment and in relation to the details of the specific visual tasks within the environment. Actually this is one of the big challenges of lighting: how to add variety but preserve the proper lighting for each task and a feeling of lighting unity for an entire large area.

Light must be supplied discreetly. The light need not be monotonous in order to supply the amount required. A tentative arrangement of fixtures may give nonuniform light at work surfaces located by the layout. Closer spacing of fixtures is suggested, but this brings up the question of proper brightness and of the choice of shielding material. Further certain parts of the area may need an emphasis of light. This can be a vertical surface, a planter, a wall, a picture, or even drapes over a window opening to give a warm sunlight effect.

Delicate contrasts and shadows provide variety and this effect is normal to the eye. In contrast, harsh, strong, contrasting shadows are annoying and should be avoided. Well-diffused light is sometimes referred to as a "soft" light. Proper diffusion of light is obtained by having light in different amounts come from an adequate number of sources and directions.

## OFFICE LIGHTING AS AN INVESTMENT

Expenditures for proper office lighting represent a sound investment. A well-coordinated lighting system represents about 2 percent of total operating costs of a large office, compared with 0.5 percent normally spent for obsolete, inadequate lighting. This increase of 1½ percent is minute when related to all the comfort, greater accuracy, and psychological advantages of proper office lighting. And it is even more so when compared with office productivity where many studies show 10 to 15 percent gain obtained from providing proper lighting.

Maintenance has a significant bearing on any lighting investment. The practice of replacing bulbs on a regularly scheduled basis is gaining favor. This simplifies maintenance and maintains proper lighting levels. Also needed are periodic cleaning of the luminaires, proper wattage of bulbs, and correct voltage. In one study involving eight locations, the footcandle output was raised from an average of 11.8 to 46.2 footcandles, or an increase of over 350 percent, by cleaning the dirty fixtures, using color of high reflecting value for the walls and keeping them clean, replacing aging bulbs, and supplying the correct voltage.

## SOURCES OF LIGHT

Sources of office lighting include natural, fluorescent, and filament bulbs. Natural light varies throughout the day and from day to day, and usually other sources of light must be used to maintain the required amount of light. Natural light has beneficial psychological effects. An employee usually feels better and has a sense of less confinement when he can look out occasionally and see daylight, observe the weather, and the like. It would seem advisable to have natural light visible even in cases where it is a very minor light source, but a number of modern offices have solid outside walls and rely on artificial light exclusively.

Fluorescent light enjoys wide acceptance in offices. Practically all new offices and most of those remodeled are using this type of light source. Fluorescent light is closer than any other artificial light to the color of natural light, and it provides large amounts of illumination at relatively low operating costs. To illustrate, the light output of a 40-watt fluorescent tube is nearly twice that of a 40-watt filament bulb. Also, the surface area of a 48-inch-long fluorescent tube is roughly ten times that of the filament type; this characteristic helps to distribute the light more uniformly.

Filament-bulb light is still an important source of artificial lighting. Improvements in filament-bulb shape, type of glass, and length of life have been achieved. However, the filament bulb has certain objectionable characteristics, including the yellowish color of its light that looks different from the color of natural light, the large number of bulbs that are necessary to supply a sufficient amount of light under today's office-lighting requirements, and the heat generated from these masses of bulbs.

Sources of light can also be classified as either (1) general lighting or (2) supplementary lighting. In the former, the entire area is lighted to a prescribed level of illumination. The source is usually a number of fixtures in or suspended from the ceiling. The second, or supplementary lighting, consists of illuminating a relatively small area, like a desk top or a portion of an office machine. Supplementary lighting is used advantageously not only in providing the desired decor in private offices, reception rooms, and hallways but also for increasing the illumination of a fixed office work position or where the area involved is relatively small.

## BASIC DESIGNS OF LIGHTING SYSTEMS

The five basic designs of lighting systems are: (1) direct, (2) semidirect, (3) indirect, (4) semi-indirect and (5) general diffuse. Under direct lighting, light from the luminaire is permitted to travel directly to the working surface. This gives a "hard" type of light, and diffusion is not too good. Glare may be high, shadows are sharp, and the ceiling is usually dark. Generally, it is the least preferred type.

The design of semidirect lighting allows some of the light from the luminaire to travel upward to the ceiling, whence it is reflected downward to the working area. Most of the light, however, travels downward directly to the working area. A semidirect system illuminates the ceiling and lessens the effect of deep shadows.

In the case of indirect lighting, the light travels upward to the ceiling, where it is reflected downward to the working area. This provides a light which is "soft" and relatively free of sharp shadows. Actually, the ceiling is the source of light to the work area; therefore, it should have a high reflection value. But since the employee cannot completely ignore the ceiling, the possibilities of glare and too intense ceiling brightness must be taken into account.

With semi-indirect lighting, most of the light travels upward to the ceiling and then down to the work area, but some of the light is allowed to travel directly downward. As with indirect lighting, the ceiling is, in effect, the main source of light. The direct light helps increase the amount of light on the work area, but consideration must be given to its possible contribution of objectionable shadows and glare.

Under general diffuse lighting, about one half of the light on the working surface comes directly from the lighting unit; the remainder is contributed by reflection from the ceiling and upper wall areas. A common identification of this type is the use of a large enclosing globe which assists in diffusing the light. Normally, this type should not be used to provide high levels of illumination since the globe may become too bright both for the direct and the reflected light. Genuine diffuse lighting gives a relatively high illumination for a given wattage, but shadows are more noticeable and there may be a slight reflected glare.

Figure 18–5 shows an office with excellent lighting. The level is 175 footcandles. The equipment is recessed 2-feet by 4-feet fixtures using glass control panels, each unit containing four 48-inch, 40-watt fluorescent lamps.

FIGURE 18–5. Recessed Fixtures with Glass Control Panels Provide Excellent Lighting in This Office.

*Courtesy: General Electric Co., Cleveland*

## ARRANGEMENT OF FIXTURES

Generally speaking, with fluorescent lighting, it is more comfortable to view the fixtures *crosswise*, not lengthwise. Especially is this true in a large office. In a small office, this consideration is relatively unimportant. However, there is one important exception—the use of luminous-sided fixtures with glass or plastic sides. These units should be viewed lengthwise for greatest comfort, regardless of the area size.

Some uniformity or symmetry of the lighting fixtures is usually desirable for better general appearance. The arrangement should bring out the architectural and decorative features that assist in producing a cheerful working environment. Long rows of fixtures may be interrupted or designed with an occasional break, but the foremost considerations are proper lighting without serious glare and a coordinated lighting system. Fixtures can be suspended from the ceiling or recessed into it. The design of having the ceiling completely luminous is also popular. For this purpose, "floating-panel luminaires" can be used. They are economical, easy to install, and create a pleasant atmosphere. Figure 18–6 shows an installation of this design.

## COLOR CONDITIONING IN THE OFFICE

Color not only beautifies an office but also improves conditions under which office work is performed. The gains from color properly used can be

FIGURE 18-6. An Office with Ceiling Completely Luminous Supplies Effective Light.

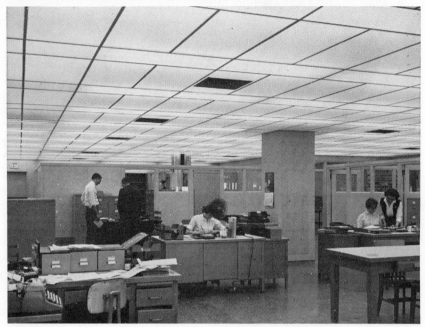

*Courtesy: Illuminating Engineering Society, New York*

economic although they are usually thought of as being only aesthetic and psychological. Color cannot be used indiscriminately in the office. Its use requires an understanding and an appreciation of color harmony and compensation.

It is now well established that color affects the human emotions, senses, and thought processes. For example, color usually has an important influence upon one's blood pressure and disposition to relax. A certain color will impress the minds of some individuals with a particularly favorable feeling or thought; another color will have the opposite effect. Some colors give a lift; others impart a depressed feeling. Some tend to hasten mental action, others to retard it.

Colors in the range of yellow, orange, and red are regarded as "warm" colors; they usually have the psychological effect of encouraging warmth and cheer. In contrast, cool colors, including blue, violet, and dark green, generally produce a subduing effect of restraint and calmness. Tints such as buff, beige, and ivory are moderately stimulating, while pale violets and blues are depressing.

For example, during August, the walls of a New England office were painted blue. The following winter, the employees complained of the office being cold, even though the normal temperature of 70 degrees was maintained. Then, the temperature was raised to 75 degrees, but complaints still continued. The blue walls were then redecorated to warm yellow and green. The temperature continued at 75 degrees. Now, the employees protested that the office was too warm. A return to the temperature of 70 degrees resulted in the ceasing of the complaints.

## SELECTION OF COLORS

The general color scheme of an office can follow one of many arrangements, depending upon individual preferences. A proper color balance, however, is needed and this means the use of a few colors correctly, not a variety haphazardly. The monochromatic approach is popular. This describes the use of various shades of one color for floors, walls, and draperies, together with one bright accent color. As a beginning point, the desk is selected in a particular color. With this basic color determined, the floor covering is selected to harmonize correctly with the desk. Then, lighter shades of the floor covering can be used for walls and draperies. The accent color can be in the chair or accessories such as pictures, desk pieces, and lamps. Figure 18–7 shows a suggested color guide to obtain a coordinated color pattern in an office.

FIGURE 18–7. Suggested Color Guide for a Coordinated Color Pattern.

| *When Desk Is—* | *Use Carpet of—* | *Use Walls of—* | *Use Draperies of—* | *Use Chair, also Pictures, Desk Accessories, and Lamps of—* |
|---|---|---|---|---|
| Gray | Gray | White | Gray | Red |
| Gray | Rust brown | Light gray | Rust | Yellow |
| Walnut or ma-hogany | Green | Beige | Chartreuse | Dark yellow |
| Walnut or ma-hogany | Beige | Light blue | Light blue | Dark yellow |
| Bleached or blond finish | Light brown | Beige | Beige | Orange |
| Bleached or blond finish | Charcoal | Gray | Yellow | Coral |

Additional specific color suggestions include:

1. *For the general office.* Ceiling in white, walls faced by employees in soft, cool colors; one or more of the walls may be in a warm color such as light yellow. Wall colors should harmonize.
2. *For the conference room.* Light and neutral colors are preferable, but some carefully utilized strong colors are usually necessary to stimulate occupants.
3. *Reception room.* Neutral colors are usually best. Avoid sharp contrasts. Limited and careful use of vivid colors is in order.

**4. Corridors.** Light colors are usually needed because of lack of daylight.

Other color schemes can be used. For example, two walls in the same room can be painted different colors. The effect can be surprisingly favorable. However, dark colors can be used opposite windows, but they should not be used on the window side because the contrast between the dark colors and the window exceeds that for visual comfort. Color is an excellent medium to express individual preferences. Certainly not all offices should follow identical constraints and feature cream-colored ceilings, beige walls, gray steel desks with dark green chairs.

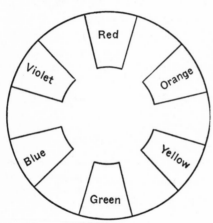

FIGURE 18–8. Sketch of Color Wheel, Showing Relationship of Primary Colors—Red, yellow, and Blue. Secondary colors are made by mixing adjacent colors named on the wheel. A combination of all the colors shown produces a neutral gray.

The use of a color wheel also aids in proper color selection. A sketch of this wheel is shown by Figure 18–8. The primary colors are red, yellow, and blue; they are located on the wheel at equally spaced distances. Secondary colors are obtained by mixing adjacent colors on the wheel. For example, red and yellow give orange. Colors directly opposite each other on the wheel are complementary colors. Green, for example, is the complement of red; blue, of orange. Toward the center of the wheel are the grayer shades which color experts use to minimize the possibility of color violence. The main ways to secure pleasant and harmonious color effects are:

|  | *Such As* |
|---|---|
| *Use* | *(Refer to Color Wheel, Fig. 18–8.)* |
| 1. Complementary colors | Red and green, the colors directly opposite each other. |
| 2. Split complementary colors—actually a triad, two colors adjacent to the direct complement of the third color | Green-blue and green-yellow, the two colors adjacent to green, the direct complement of red. |
| 3. Triads—three colors equidistant from each other | Red, yellow, and blue. |

## COLOR AND LIGHTING

As implied in the early part of this chapter, color has a significant influence upon the lighting of an office. Light colors increase the utilization of light; dark colors decrease the lighting intensity. This is because light colors reflect the light rays, whereas dark colors absorb the light rays. For these reasons, any normally dark area will lighten up when lighter colors are used for the ceiling, walls, and floors.

Natural lighting varies slightly in color. Light predominantly from one particular direction usually has a characteristic tinge; to compensate for this condition, the use of complementary colors is usually recommended. This is illustrated as follows:

| *When Predominant Natural Light Source Is—* | *Light Is Slightly Colored by—* | *Recommend Use of—* |
|---|---|---|
| Northern light | Bluish tinge | Warm color |
| Eastern light | Neutral | Neutral color |
| Southern light | Yellowish tinge | Cool color |
| Western light | Reddish tinge | Cool color |

Furthermore, the use of color influences the apparent proportions of an area. This is due to the reflecting and the contracting light effect brought about by the different colors. Dark colors seem to advance an area, light colors to retreat it. Hence, the dimensional effect of a long narrow room can tend to be equalized by the use of a dark color on the end walls and a lighter shade of the same color, or of a harmonizing hue, on the other walls. Similarly, the proportions of a square area can be made to appear elongated.

## MUSIC CONDITIONING

Music serves as an environmental aid because the physiological and psychological power of music may be used to produce and improve the behavior pattern. Music can make you alert or relaxed, happy or blue. "Music while you work" programs are designed to improve working conditions, relieve mental and visual fatigue, reduce nervous tension, and make the employees feel better in general. Such programs are popular and they are effective.

In a survey of over 35,000 employees, 90 percent stated they liked music while they worked; an equal number credited music with making their work more enjoyable; and nearly 85 percent said it helped to break the monotony of their work.[1] The types of office work showing the

[1] *An Answer to Worker Tension* (a booklet published by the Muzak Corporation, New York, 1960).

maximum benefits include filing, mail room, typing, reception, keypunching, and verifying. In a large public utility, the productivity of cards punched increased 18 percent when music was added. Common gains in other offices include a decrease in absenteeism of from 5 to 10 percent, a reduction in clerical errors of 37 percent, and a noticeable lessening of nonessential employee conversations.

The music is functionally controlled, which means that it is specifically arranged, orchestrated, and recorded to accomplish a specific goal. Distracting and attention-getting music, such as heavy brass effects and solos, is excluded. The music is stimulating and designed to fit the specific office work as well as the temperament of the employees. The music is enjoyed subconsciously. The employee doesn't actively listen to it. His attention is not distracted because action-impelling factors of the music are avoided. Music during the first part of the morning consists of a bright opener followed by moderately bright music, such as several waltzes. Music of maximum stimulus is played during late morning and afternoon. Light classics and slower swing tunes are usually predominant in programs for office employees. The music is played for specific intervals only because best results are usually obtained from this type of pattern. It is either "piped" from a central sending studio, or a self-contained unit providing the music is installed in the office. The expense is nominal and is paid either on a per diem basis or at a monthly rate per employee. The inexpensive addition of a microphone to the subscriber's equipment automatically converts the installation to a public-address system.

## AIR CONDITIONING

Air conditioning regulates atmospheric conditions by controlling the four basic elements—temperature, circulation, moisture content, and cleanliness. It is possible to control only three, or two, or, in fact, just one of these elements; but such control is more correctly termed partial rather than complete air conditioning. Either a central or individual units can be used. Varying sizes and capacities are available. Individual units for a small group of offices or for part of a floor area have grown in popularity. Some are designed for a single room and are portable. The cost of air conditioning is reasonable. Not only does it aid health and comfort, but it also offers economic advantages. More consistent and higher productivity along with decreases in cleaning and decorating costs are prominent.

## TEMPERATURE, HUMIDITY, AND VENTILATION

The temperature in many offices is too high. This leads to discomfort and drowsiness. Regulators should be installed on the heating apparatus so that excessive temperatures are not reached. It is well to become "thermometer-conscious" and to keep the office temperature within reasonable limits, that is, 70 to 74 degrees Fahrenheit. If air conditioning is used, the recommended temperature range is from 68 to 82 degrees Fahrenheit, depending upon the outside temperature. Too great a differential between outside and air conditioned areas is undesirable.

Humidity, or the amount of moisture in the air, definitely affects the comfort and efficiency of a human being. At the same temperature, moist air feels hot and dry air feels cool. Excessive dampness may cause physical discomfort of a respiratory nature and induce a heavy, languid feeling. Likewise, excessive dryness or very low humidity frequently induces a feeling of parchedness and nervous irritability. "Relative humidity" is the term used to describe the intensity of moisture saturation in the air. A recommended relative humidity for an office is from 40 to 60 percent. When the relative humidity is 20 percent, the office air is too dry; when the humidity is 70 percent, the air is too moist.

Lack of proper ventilation can make a person feel sleepy and unduly tired. At 70 degrees Fahrenheit, an adult human body at rest gives off a small amount of heat, which must be carried off by the surrounding air; otherwise, the body becomes unduly heated. The normal ventilation requirement is about 2,000 cubic feet of air per person per hour. Drafts should be avoided. Usually, the best practice is to have the air circulating from a number of outlets so that it is distributed evenly over the entire area. For nonair-conditioned areas, fans help considerably in providing adequate ventilation. Also, window ventilators permit incoming fresh air without causing direct drafts to blow on any one person. The practice of opening windows and airing the office for short, stated periods during midmorning, noon, and midafternoon does much toward expelling stale air and freshening up the office.

## SOUND CONDITIONING

A noisy office is seldom an efficient office. Noise is unpleasant, distracting, and costly. It makes for difficulty in concentrating, in using the telephone, and in turning out accurate office work. According to physicians, noise causes transient changes in blood and brain pressure, a quickening pulse rate, and indigestion. So-called "getting used to noise" is misleading. One may temporarily be unaware of its effects; but over a period of time, one becomes excessively fatigued and irritable as a result of noise.

Noise has no definite pitch and quality, whereas in a musical tone, these properties are fairly well defined. Sound can be defined technically as "vibrational energy." The oscillation of these waves of energy, or sound waves, traveling through the air stimulates the auditory nerves; and this, in turn, results in a perception of the sensation and a consciousness of sound. Among the chief characteristics of sound are (1) pitch—frequency of the vibrations, (2) intensity—the energy of the vibrations, (3) quality —the mode or type of vibration, (4) reverberation—the sustaining qualities after the sound has stopped at its source, and (5) the expectancy and acceptance of the individual. Of greatest concern is loudness, which is primarily determined by both intensity and pitch, with emphasis on intensity. Actually, the phenomenon of increasing loudness follows a rather complex physical law. To have a relative measurement of the range of sound intensities, a unit of measurement called a "decibel" is used. One decibel is about the smallest change in sound that the human ear can detect. The decibel scale shows the relative values from the lowest to the highest human audible sound intensity. For convenience, the scale is measured logarithmically. The lowest value is zero, the beginning of human audibility, to approximately 110, which represents the sound of thunder. Figure 18–9 shows a table of sound identification and the corresponding decibel ratings.

FIGURE 18–9. Value of Noise Levels Expressed in Decibels

| | |
|---|---:|
| Threshold of hearing | 0 |
| Noise in average home | 32 |
| Quiet office | 37 |
| Quiet radio in home | 40 |
| Noise in city (residential district) | 45 |
| Restaurant clatter | 50 |
| Noisy office | 57 |
| Stenographic room (large office) | 70 |
| Noisy factory | 85 |
| Boiler factory | 97 |

Source: *Encyclopedia Americana*, Vol. I (New York: Americana Corporation, 1955), p. 107.

Probably the best way to control noise in the office is to locate the office in a quiet space. The top floors of a building are usually less noisy, since they are further removed from street traffic. Relocation within the building to avoid direct exposure to noise sources or to highly congested areas can also be made. In addition, when practical the sources of office noise can be segregated from the rest of the office. Noisy machines can be located in a separate room or in an area off to one side. If this is not feasible, concentrate the chief noise sources in one area; this is better than having them scattered all over the office. Also efforts to reduce and, if possible, eliminate the source of the noise can be taken. For example, placing felt pads or rubber cushions under typewriters, calculators, and other types of machines gives satisfactory results. Soundproofing cabinets such as illustrated in Figure 18–10 are effective. Proper lubrication of file drawers, doors, desks, and chairs contribute further to noise reduction.

FIGURE 18–10. The Cabinet over the Machine Is an Effective Noise Reducer.

*Courtesy: Gates Acoustinet, Inc., Santa Rosa, Calif.*

Appeals to employees can be made, stressing consideration for others and the importance of eliminating unnecessary conversations. Lastly, sound-absorbing materials should be used for office floors, ceilings, and walls. Sound travels in waves and is reflected from glazed or nonporous surfaces in the same way that light is reflected. Under these conditions, sound continues to travel in all directions and bounces back and forth until its energy is absorbed; then the sound dies out of its own accord. This condition usually makes for a noisy office.

When acoustic treatment or sound-absorbing material is used, the sound dies out faster. The same sounds exist as before, but they are not permitted to reflect repeatedly until dissipated. Carpet eliminates virtually all floor noise. Also, drapes and curtains made of soft fabrics help to absorb sound. Acoustic material for covering ceilings and walls is available in several forms. One common type is a fibrous mineral tile, about 12 x 12 inches in size and perforated. It is available in thicknesses ranging from ½ inch to 1¼ inch, and can be attached either by a special cement or by means of nails or screws. Another common variety is a mastic type material which is spread on the surface and dries, leaving a porous surface. In some instances, a loose, fibrous material is used, along with a separate hard facing material that has numerous perforations.

## QUESTIONS

1. Are you of the opinion that the general physical working conditions of an office should be of major concern to the office manager? Why?
2. Discuss the subject of color selection for office use.

3. Define each of the following:
    a) Decibel.
    b) Footcandle.
    c) Monochromatic approach in color selection.
    d) "Soft" light.
4. Of the five major factors of physical working conditions in an office, which one do you believe is most important? Justify your answer.
5. Discuss the key considerations in the arrangement of lighting fixtures in an office.
6. Do you personally favor having music while you work? Why?
7. Discuss the relationship between color and the lighting of an office. Between sound and music in an office.
8. Relate basic general information about sound conditioning with which you feel an office manager should be acquainted.
9. Discuss the importance of light quantity, brightness, and diffusion upon the attainment of adequate lighting in an office.
10. Mr. Ron Costello has received estimates from different contractors to modernize his general office space. The lighting fixture installer believes productivity will increase some 20 percent due to improved lighting. The air-conditioning people state it is common for their commercial customers to experience 15 percent or greater productive increase due to the comforts offered by air conditioning. The painting contractor states that the newly decorated walls and ceiling will have a favorable effect upon the work done by the employees. He estimates a gain of at least 12 percent. Does this mean that Mr. Costello can expect a productivity increase of 47 percent as a result of his improved lighting, air conditioning, and newly painted general office? Justify your answer.
11. At an office management meeting, Mr. Alexander Messinger, an office manager, tells you that his general office is quite noisy. What suggestions can you give Mr. Messinger to combat the office noise?
12. An office manager heard many favorable comments concerning the adoption of "music while you work" in various offices. Believing this might be desirable in his office, he arranged, through the office supervisors, to ask his entire office force if they would like to work to music. The response was overwhelmingly in favor of having music. Accordingly, the office manager purchased a wide selection of long-playing records and two record-playing machines—one machine for each of the two main office areas. What benefits or difficulties do you feel might result from the office manager's action. Explain your answer.

## CASE PROBLEMS

### Case 18–1.  Webb Company

Office manager Ivan Burger believes that ventilating, heating, and air conditioning are probably the most important elements which affect office behavioral attitudes. Complaints by employees about the lack of ventilation have been frequent and lately have grown in intensity.

During the last several months as sort of an interesting hobby, Mr. Burger has from time to time noted the office temperature as well as the relative humidity. For nearly 75 percent of his readings, the temperature has been 80 degrees Fahrenheit or more and in about 45 percent of the cases, the relative humidity has exceeded 60 percent. Conversations with heating and ventilating suppliers confirm that the office can be made comfortable the year round. Quotations for necessary equipment installed range from $18,485 to $27,120. Annual estimates for operating the equipment are from $800 to $1,050.

Mr. Burger feels that the installing of adequate heating, ventilating, and air conditioning would prove to be a good investment. He judges, for example, that office employee productivity would increase at least 10 percent. He bases this increase on a spot review of records of summer absenteeism in his office reportedly caused by weather conditions; his observation of time being wasted during a hot, humid spell; and the slow pace that prevails during uncomfortable days. There is a total of 15 nonmanagerial employees whose average weekly wage is $93.77.

Mr. Burger's superior, Mr. Bert Bleyer, claims that if installation of the equipment is to be justified on the basis of increasing employee productivity, the best decision is to forget the whole proposition. "Ivan, let me tell you something," stated Mr. Bleyer. "You won't get any more work after installing that equipment than you are getting now. They know what is expected of them and on certain days they may have to work a little harder. People adapt to their office environment. On certain days they expend more energy for the same amount of work than on other days. Personally, I would not give too much weight to complaints. If they aren't griping about no air conditioning, they will be complaining about the office machine not working properly, too many telephone call interruptions, or something."

Mr. Burger replied that there certainly were intangibles involved—risks are inherent. In his mind an overruling consideration was whether the company had available money for an expenditure like this. A comfortable place to work could hardly be called a luxury.

To these comments, Mr. Bleyer responded quickly with, "We've got the money. If you decide to go ahead, we can finance it OK."

## Questions:

1. Evaluate the concepts advanced by Mr. Bleyer.
2. Do you feel Mr. Burger is justified in deciding whether to install the heating, ventilating, and air conditioning in the office? Justify your viewpoint.
3. What decision should Mr. Burger make? Why?

### Case 18–2. Dixson and Kerr, Inc.

At long last the office of Dixson and Kerr, Inc. is to be renovated. Sidney Epperson, assistant to the president, has worked long and hard to secure the money and approval for the project. The executive committee has long taken the stand that available funds should be invested, the office is not too bad in appearance, and the frugal thing to do is make the present physical environment last as long as possible.

Mr. Epperson engaged the services of an interior decorator, Edna Bukovitz. After several weeks, she submitted a very attractive plan and sketches of the "new office." Difficulty was the estimated cost, which was three times what Mr. Epperson had to spend. Miss Bukovitz stressed redoing the whole office including the purchasing of new items not only where functionally needed, but also where required to obtain the proper impression of the entire office. She felt strongly that the present walnut wood desks should be discarded, and recommended that carpeting be installed to reduce noise and add to the appearance of the office. It was her contention that unless a properly coordinated and complete remodeling job was done, the renovating efforts would look like an unfinished job. "You really can't do anything with those old desks," she explained. "They don't go with anything in the office and to retain them will spoil the entire effort. If you are going to fix up, if you want a modern, attractive office, if you want to give a modern, progressive impression, you should start improvements from the floor and work up."

Mr. Epperson conceded that her points were well taken, but he insisted that the dollars for a complete change simply were not in the budget. He was inclined to go ahead with what they could afford, otherwise they may end up with nothing. Accordingly, Miss Bukovitz reluctantly revised her designs and offered them to Mr. Epperson with the statement that she did not want to engage actively in the change, since it would not represent what she thought really should be done. Somewhat surprised, Mr. Epperson offered his regrets, said he would get in touch with her if he could swing the entire remodeling deal, and suggested he would gladly pay for her time and asked her to submit her bill.

Mr. Epperson along with his secretary then took over the renovation as sort of a personal project. The revised plan of Miss Bukovitz suggested the beige tile floor to remain as is; walls were to be painted a pastel blue; drapes were to be new of a coarsely woven material and very dark blue in color; ceiling painted white; the present wood desks would be retained; seat and back covers for the office chairs were to be a dark yellow or mustard color.

The correspondence employees, all less than 24 years of age, found out about the contemplated remodeling through Mr. Epperson's secretary. Shortly thereafter, they visited Mr. Epperson in his office and asked if they could have their area fixed up the way they wanted it. Mr. Epperson stated that he thought they could, but cautioned that due to a limited budget, the beige tile floor, walnut desks, and present chairs would have to remain. Several days later, they submitted their plans.

All the correspondence personnel face north in their area which is located off to one side from the general area and is connected by a 6-foot corridor to the general area. On the 25-foot-long west wall, about one third of the wall area is occupied by four separate large windows; the entrance is at the northeast corner on the 35-foot-long north wall. The plan offered by the correspondence personnel called for the north and east walls painted yellow, the west and south walls painted black; drapes were to be new of a synthetic material, white with black stripes; covers for chair seats and backs were to be maroon. The cost for these changes are within Mr. Epperson's budget.

## Questions:

1. What is your reaction to the decision made by Miss Bukovitz?
2. In your opinion should Mr. Epperson have deferred the remodeling until a complete renovation could have been handled? Why?
3. What decision should Mr. Epperson make with respect to the plan offered by the correspondence personnel? Why?

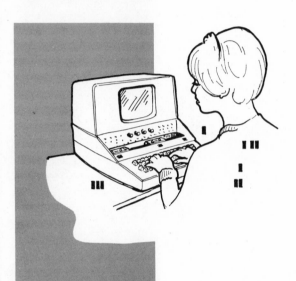

# CONTROLLING

Controlling, a fundamental function of office management, consists of determining what is being accomplished, evaluating it, and, if necessary, applying corrective measures. Basically, controlling is performed to see that what is planned is being accomplished.

Controlling is extensive; it is applied to the use of time, the accuracy of office work, the amount of work, and the dollars expended. Five chapters comprise Part VI of this book; they cover completely the essentials of managerial controlling as applied to office work. Included are "Office controlling and standards," "Office time-use," "Quality and quantity control," "Cost and budgetary control," and "Office manuals and audits.

# chapter 19

# Office controlling
# and standards

Nothing in life is to be feared. It is only to be understood.
—*Marie Curie*

LACK OF adequate control in the office is reflected by the growth of clerical
payroll, the number of pieces of paper on everybody's desk from the
president down, the amount of money spent for office forms, and the
number and frequency of management reports. As pointed out in chapter
1, controlling is a fundamental function of management and is performed
to insure results in keeping with the planning. Logically, we can say that
lack of controlling stems from lack of planning. Without a plan, we have
nothing to which to direct our control efforts. Controlling and planning
are intimately related. With but a modicum of planning, we need controlling. And in most cases there is some planning, even though insufficient, so
that controlling is needed to orientate and to evaluate what is being
accomplished.

## MEANING OF CONTROLLING

Some view controlling as the familiar follow-up either to confirm
operations as satisfactory or to reveal deviations that necessitate corrective actions. The experienced information manager knows that what he
plans for and hopes to achieve does not always take place. He must know
what the actual results are if he is to manage effectively. To this end
verbal and written reports are made to supply information as to what is
being accomplished. These reveal whether the prescribed process is being

467

followed, the proper number of people employed for each type of work, the quality of work attained, the amount of expenditures, and if the work is being completed when wanted.

A formal definition of controlling is that it consists of (1) *determining what is being accomplished,* (2) *evaluating it, and* (3) *if necessary, applying corrective measures.* These three steps are basic and universal in controlling. They exist in every type of control.

Some view controlling as of two types (1) management controlling and (2) operational controlling. The former deals mainly with the assurance that resources are obtained and used effectively, the latter with the assurance that specific tasks are performed effectively. This segregation is actually by management level and points out the broad spectrum of controlling. Actually there is no clear-cut line of demarcation between the two. Nevertheless the concept is useful and helps determine the type of information needed to exercise the control. For the most part, management control necessitates considerable human judgment whereas operational control is largely routine and can be programmed on a computer for processing.

It should also be noted that the application of controlling is aided and abetted by information—the contribution of the information manager. We must have current and accurate information in order to control adequately. Information is fundamental to the controlling process—the three controlling steps enumerated above.

## APPROACHES TO CONTROLLING

In most instances managers do not know precisely where the plans are not being followed, where real waste in the information work is taking place, or where ineffective work is being permitted to exist. This state of affairs exists not only because of a lack of appreciation for the controlling techniques available, but also because of viewing or pursuing only one part of the total problem.

A particular office may have troubles stemming from many sources. To employ but a single technique may result in an inadequate solution. A broad-gauge approach is the answer. An awareness of the various types of office problems is mandatory and the capacity to select the particular and appropriate techniques that would seem to offer help is essential.

This leads to two approaches. First is the generalized approach where a broad view is taken to decide if what is received seems satisfactory or is worth the effort and cost of the controlling efforts. For example, a careful and somewhat detailed observing of the storage containers may be made to see if material called for can be quickly retrieved, to note whether drawers are too crowded, and to spot any dissension among the storing and retrieving employees. In a sense this is in the nature of an audit covering a reasonably large segment of the total office. In essence, this generalized approach seeks to determine cost-value relationships.

Second is the functional approach where all phases of selected functions are reviewed and those deemed most important are chosen for further study intended to correct the existing difficulty. In this respect, typical functions are systems, procedures, policies, physical facilities, forms, service, and standards. Usually the preferred selection from these functions is that which influences or affects all or a large part of the entire operation. Office forms, for example, are of this nature and usually represent an effective approach to controlling. For discussional purposes, we will take the areas of forms, reports, and telephone calls to illustrate the use of controlling. Each area will be discussed in turn.

## CONTROLLING OF OFFICE FORMS

In nearly every enterprise, forms have a tendency to continue indefinitely regardless of need. The root of much office inefficiency stems from this situation. In addition, new forms are started whether the information desired is now contained in existent forms or can be secured by a slight modification in these forms. These facts are recognized by many executives who believe operations in their respective enterprises would be greatly improved if proper control over office forms were exercised. In addition, many studies show that the *functional* considerations of forms —time spent in using the forms and their aid in getting information recorded, transmitted, and processed—represent by far the greater cost of forms as well as the greater opportunities for improvement. *Physical* considerations—size and weight of paper, and printing cost—are important and must be taken into account, but they are relatively minor. For each dollar spent to purchase forms, somewhere between $15 and $25 are spent to process the forms. Taking the average of $20, this means that a multiple-copy form costing $60 per thousand involves a processing cost of $1,200. By eliminating unneeded forms, much time, effort, and money can be saved.

Well, what can be done about it? The answer: Exercise effective forms controlling. Start with the first step, common to all controlling, stated above. It is: Determine what is being accomplished.

## DETERMINE WHAT IS BEING ACCOMPLISHED

For this purpose, current information on the various forms now being used, what respective purposes they serve, and specific data on their contents and identification are required. To these ends, the following steps are recommended.

1. Announce to all employees the existence of the forms control unit,

and explain its function and its authority. Be specific as to who is the head of it. In many cases, the head may be the office manager. Other members of the unit should include key personnel who are qualified and can give support to the office forms control efforts from different departments of the enterprise.

2. Freeze all forms activity at its *status quo*. Announce that any additions or changes must be taken up and cleared through the forms control unit.

3. Obtain at least two copies of every office form used in the enterprise. Use one copy for a centralized forms control file, the other for purposes of analysis, as described below.

4. Make out a tabulating card for each form indicating its (1) function, (2) numerical designation, and (3) construction features. File these by numerical designation and use as cross-reference with the centralized file. Office forms are employed to assist in any of the following functions: report, request, record, instruct, follow up, authorize, cancel, order, apply, acknowledge, estimate, route, schedule, and claim. Segregating the forms by their major function assists analysis.

5. File each form in the centralized file according to function. This will bring together every form that is similar in nature regardless of its design, its name, or where it is used.

6. Secure a listing of all the office systems and procedures used in the enterprise.

7. Mark all forms in the centralized file according to the system or procedure in which they are used.

With the big growth in SDA (source data automation) and computer usage, the trend in forms procurement has been to consider all forms of one system or procedure at the same time. This approach recognizes the interrelatedness of the forms. Suggestions are made and bids are received for the complete form requirements per system or procedure. This way, better prices and services are obtained.

## EVALUATION OF PRESENT FORMS

The second step is to evaluate what is being accomplished. That is, in our controlling sequence we now seek to determine how well the present office forms are serving the enterprise. For this purpose, several different but related activities can be undertaken. Questionnaires sent to those using the forms frequently prove effective. It is helpful for the person in charge of forms control to meet separately with each department head and discuss improvements. These meetings can be followed by group meetings for all department heads in order to decide what improvements can be made in forms that affect more than one department.

In evaluating the present office forms, it is not uncommon to analyze the existent forms to determine if any can be (1) eliminated, (2) combined with others, or (3) improved. The emphasis is upon functional considerations. The form's adequacy to meet the work requirements consistent with efficient office management is of foremost importance. Results achieved are sometimes amazing. In the case of one prominent Chicago company, the total number of office forms was reduced from 1,182 to 368.

Figures 19–1 and 19–2 show how forms can be combined to improve office efficiency. Originally, four separate forms—shipping label, invoice, shipping memorandum, and packing slip—were typed separately. Subsequently, the four forms were combined and now require only one typing. In Figure 19–2, a copy has been raised to show the shipping label in the upper left corner, the receiving memorandum in the upper right, and the packing slip below. These are separated by tearing apart at the perforations.

In addition, physical considerations are taken into account—the size of the forms, correctness for filing, cut without waste, and easy folding for enclosure in an envelope. Also, the weight of paper for the original and each carbon, the use of different colors of paper, and their essentiality in the particular form are carefully reviewed. Specifications are checked—the type of ink, punches, and perforations are investigated. The ordering quantities and rates of consumption are compared.

These indicated efforts actually point up two major activities: (1) the disclosure of possible improvements in the current work accomplishment and (2) the establishment of standards. The former can be justified as a planning activity, but the activity is triggered by controlling and the closeness of these two fundamental activities is demonstrated by this illustration. Often the controlling simply poses questions as to what might be done, but the actual doing of it and working out the details is delegated to the planner. Also, it must be added that the evaluating does not always include attempts to improve. In many cases it is simply a counting or a measuring task. For example, consider control of quality. Usually the evaluation is to grade the quality being achieved. Is it satisfactory or not? There may be no suggestions or direct attempts to improve the quality being attained. The assignment is either to accept or to reject what is made. Of course, this is a limited and narrow viewpoint; it fails to maximize its possible participative contribution from its advantageous position.

The second major activity mentioned above is the establishment of standards. Standards are discussed later in this chapter, but for now they are identified as *base lines of reference*. That is, to evaluate what is being accomplished, we compare it to its standard. In the case of office forms, for example, we would develop standards we believe suited for the company's needs. Such standards for forms would give stability, uniformity, and continuity to our controlling efforts. This does not mean that the work of forms control becomes static. Quite the contrary; it is dynamic. As the

FIGURE 19–1. Forms Used by a Clothing Manufacturer; Top to Bottom: Shipping Label, Invoice, Shipping Memorandum, and Packing Slip.

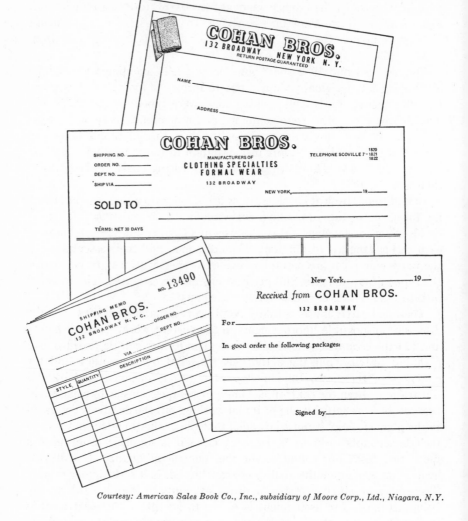

*Courtesy: American Sales Book Co., Inc., subsidiary of Moore Corp., Ltd., Niagara, N.Y.*

needs of the company change, the standards and the forms used will also change.

## APPLYING CORRECTIVE MEASURES

The third step in controlling is to *apply corrective measures, if necessary.* This includes redirecting the efforts in a manner to insure that the recommended modified work means are followed. In the case of office

FIGURE 19–2. A Combination of the Four Forms Shown in Figure 19–1. Now, the same amount of work is accomplished in one typing operation instead of in four.

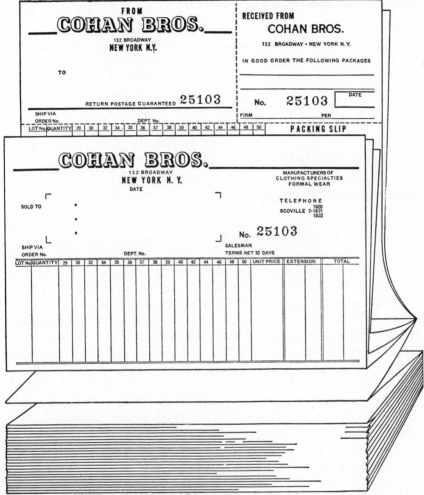

*Courtesy: American Sales Book Co., Inc., subsidiary of Moore Corp., Ltd., Niagara, N.Y.*

forms, controlling includes bringing about the establishment and use of office forms deemed proper and effective. Also, the forms controller or organization unit would have the authority to purchase forms and to review and pass on any and all forms if it were concluded that this was the best way to acquire the forms the company should have. The personnel involved in this phase of controlling should have sufficient status so that others will take them seriously. They must work well with others in the company. Suggestions by others should be encouraged and their cooperation won.

## GAINS FROM CONTROLLING FORMS

What is gained by having effective controlling of office forms? In a numerical arrangement, the answer is (1) retention of only necessary forms, copies, and items on forms, (2) prevention of issuing unnecessary forms, (3) improvement of forms to allow for ease of data entry, filing, and reference, (4) distribution of forms for those having justifiable reasons for receiving them, (5) production of required forms by the most appropriate process, (6) reduction of limited-use forms and expansion of general-purpose forms, and (7) review periodically of all forms in use in order to keep them in line with current needs of the enterprise.

## CONTROLLING OF REPORTS

The cost of preparing reports can be surprisingly high when the supervisory, clerical, machine, distribution, and storage expenses are taken into account. Further, the information in these reports may be presented in several formats so that a simple comparison is difficult to obtain and the efforts to evaluate each report on its own merits poses a real challenge. The duplication of effort, while acceptable to some degree, results in higher costs than are necessary. To obtain significant evaluation requires an accurate inventory of current reports, evaluation of them by recipients, objective analysis of these evaluations, and determination of the need for each report in relationship to the service it supplies and its cost of preparing, handling, and use.

For these purposes, certain steps are taken. The first is to send out a cover letter to the originators of reports explaining the "Reports Controlling Program" and requesting a copy of each report they prepare be attached to an executed report questionnaire. Figure 19–3 suggests the contents of this questionnaire. Next, each recipient of reports listed on the returned questionnaires is requested to evaluate each report he receives with reference to necessity, use, and value of information contained. Again, a covering form letter and a questionnaire are used. The report evaluation questionnaire is illustrated by Figure 19–4. These returned questionnaires are now tabulated. Shown for each report on a spread sheet are the type of information contained, the source of information, and the estimated cost of preparation. Meetings are held with management members and other report recipients to determine the need and possible improvement for each report. Recommendations are evaluated regarding what reports can be eliminated, combined with other reports, improved, or simplified. Subsequently, all approved reports are assigned a report control number which is used along with its title for purposes of identification in the future. Further, a list of reports eliminated is prepared showing the reasons for such action and the estimated savings from their termination.

Like the action taken in a forms control program, some managers recommend that centralization of authority over report writing be established. When this is done it frequently is either the director of correspondence or the head of the systems and procedures department. The purpose is to prevent the spawning of new reports and to require formal approval

FIGURE 19–3.

REPORT QUESTIONNAIRE

Title of Report _____ Originating Dept.
Name, and No. _____

Name and Title of Person
Responsible for Preparation
of Above Report _____

1. Description of information      1A. Sources of information (forms,
   the report contains                  reports, or original)

2. To whom is this report distributed?

        Name of recipient      Title        Location
   a.
   b.
   c.
   d.
   e.
   f.
   g.
   h.

3. Report is usually:

   Size_____ No. of pages _____ No. of copies____ Frequency_____

   Prepared by_____ method (handwritten, typed, duplicated, etc.)

4. Estimated cost:

   Initial writing            Typing
   cost (hrs. X rate)_____ (hrs. X rate)_____ Material_____

   Reproduction
   cost _____ Total cost_____

5. Signature of person
   filling out this form _____ Your title_____

   Date today_____ Your superior_____

from a centralized agency before issuing any additions to the reports membership. Thus, controlling of reports is exercised.

## TELEPHONE CALL CONTROLLING

Several areas usually attracting the center of attention in telephone call controlling are long-distance calls, personal phone privileges, and

FIGURE 19–4.

REPORT EVALUATION QUESTIONNAIRE

To:                    Location: (Dept.)                Date:

It is our understanding that you receive a copy of the report indicated below.  Please answer the following question regarding this report and return to _____ dept. by _____. Thank you.

1.  Do you use this report?  Yes_____ No_____

    If No, your questionnaire is complete.  Please return to us at once.

    If Yes, is report required for:

    a.  Making decisions  Yes _____ No _____
    b.  Checking accuracy  Yes_____ No _____
    c.  Keeping informed  Yes _____ No _____
    d.  Other (please write in)_____

2.  Would elimination of this report affect your operations?  Yes__No _____
    Comments _____

3.  Would elimination of certain items or portions of this report meet your approval?  Yes _____ No _____
    Comments_____

4.  If the report in total or in part is necessary, could lessening of its frequency be made?  Yes_____ No _____

    If Yes, what minimum frequency would be acceptable _____

5.  Do you retain your copy of this report?  Yes_____ No_____

6.  About how often do you refer to it after its original use?_____

7.  Is the report destroyed after its useful life?  Yes_____ No_____
    Comments _____

8.  Please give any additional comments or suggestions you have regarding this report. _____

Your signature _____ Date _____

Title of Report_____

excess message units. Under the QZ billing for long-distance calls, each employee who frequently uses long distance is assigned a telephone number, such as 4Z1-1234. When he places a long-distance call, the outside operator is dialed directly. He gives her the number he is calling and his special billing number. Employees infrequently making long-distance calls use a special number assigned to each department. At the end of the month, the long-distance expense is itemized by the telephone company so that a quick and accurate check can be made of who called whom and when. Allocation of telephone expense to departments is made and the supervisor of each unit can review his employees' usage of long distance. This places responsibility for the telephone expense where it belongs. In addition, the company's switchboard operator can concentrate on incoming calls and give better service.

Reducing the number of personal calls by employees on company telephone and time is a fertile field for telephone controlling. It is possible to obtain data on the numbers being called by means of the "Optional Detailed Message Unit Billing" offered by the telephone company. This service must be taken for at least two complete billing periods and supplies a monthly listing of calls for which a charge of two or more message units is made. Study of such data reveals what numbers are dialed frequently and whether they are personal or business numbers. Appropriate action can then be taken. However, creating the proper psychological climate to use the telephone only when necessary and to minimize personal calls appears to bring about the best mutual results. Getting responsibility placed on the person making the call is essential. Explain that in general the company telephone does not have unlimited "free" calls as provided in many private home installations. Knowing this fact will help to reduce the abuse of excess personal calls. And letting it be known by means of bulletin board notices and supervisors' actions that the personal call privilege must not be abused helps to bring about desired results and satisfactory control in this area.

In large metropolitan areas, calls to outlying areas are charged extra message units, depending on the distance and the length of each call. To minimize this excess cost, an enterprise can have installed "foreign ex- change" trunks which enable calls to be made to distant areas at less cost per call. To do so the proper level (a certain number like 8 or 9) must be dialed to get an outside line, depending upon the geographical area or the exchange prefix being called. To assist in making the proper selection, memos can be distributed or stickers located adjacent to the telephone can be used. In some instances a map of the area may be shown with different-colored areas indicating the "dial 8" and "dial 9" locations. Trunk selection errors are thus reduced and savings can be substantial. In one medium-sized company, the excess message units, averaging $450 a month, were reduced subsequently to $235 a month.

## HUMAN RELATIONS AND CONTROLLING

It follows from what has been stated that controlling is influenced greatly by the human relations existing in a given situation where controlling is applied. The reactions of personnel to controls are vital in the design and administration of those controls. Controlling is not simply a mechanistic measurement of accomplishment or a comparison of numbers. We are dealing with people and what we accomplish or do not accomplish is going to be in large measure because of the people doing the work.

Controls can create extreme tension and put pressure on employees. When the employee sees no personal benefit in having the controls, he may be critical of them. He may feel that the work expectancy is unfair and view the controlling as a threat to his personal security. Unfortunately in some instances his fears appear to be justified, but in the great majority of cases the real difficulty is the failure of managers to explain the reasons for certain controls and to use them as a positive assistance rather than a negative hindrance. Better explanation of controlling and why it is required both for the enterprise and the employee are needed. Effective communication is likewise important so that a means is available to relate ideas, suggestions, and grievances. Truly effective controlling is beneficial both to the manager and the nonmanager.

## CONTROLLING AND STANDARDS

Returning to our three basic steps of the control process—(1) determining what is being accomplished (2) evaluating it, and (3) if necessary, applying corrective measures,—it is evident that evaluation of accomplishment (2) is essential. To assist in this evaluation, a manager uses standards. They are so important that the balance of this chapter will be devoted to them. Standards are also important for other managerial uses as we will indicate in the following pages, but for the discussion at hand, think of standards in their relationship to controlling and the important role that they play in this fundamental function of management.

First, a clear understanding is needed of what is meant by "standard." *A standard is something established by either custom or authority in order to gauge such things as quality, performance, and service of any factor used in management.* It may be thought of as a basis of reckoning, i.e., a basis of comparison. Most standards represent the best current knowledge of an item or practice formulated and accepted to meet the needs of present conditions.

Specifically, standards do not imply or reflect perfection. A material standard for paper designated by the manager of an office means that paper of these particular specifications is the type desired by the manager and is satisfactory for the specific purpose in mind, taking into account such things as the type of printing press, the price range, and the desired finished product. The standard provides him with a reference line to evaluate the paper.

Standards not only facilitate controlling, but they are also important to the other fundamental functions of management, including planning, organizing, and actuating. For example, in planning, standards are the essential media for determining what components are required for establishing the sequence of successive operations. In other words, standards provide the common language for carrying out managerial work in areas such as expressing what is to be done, discussing, allocating, and instructing.

## EXTENT OF STANDARDS

Standards apply to all factors of an enterprise. For example, there exist, in management, standards for each of the six M's—i.e., Men, Materials, Machines, Methods, Money, and Markets. This means that modern managers have established recognized bases of reference for each of the six factors. For example, concepts such as "standard material" and "standard machine" are common in the office, but less commonly identified standards are "standard man" and "standard money." The concept of a standard man is frequently used in personnel work when considering what qualifications a man must possess to fill a particular job, while standards in money or the financial part of an enterprise are very well illustrated by expressions of standard costs.

In many offices, the basic types of standards, along with the type of area covered by each, are shown by the following:

| *Basic Standard* | *Area* |
|---|---|
| Work: | Measurements of the quantity and the quality of accomplishment |
| Tools: | Desk, file, machine |
| Conditions: | Amount of space, equipment layout, lighting, floor covering |
| Process: | Filing methods, mail distribution, handling of accounts receivable, duplicating process |

Under tools, for example, a standard for a machine might designate the specific type, capacity, speed, and possibly the name of the manufacturer. Furthermore, this designated machine would probably be expected to be used for certain work. In this case, the machine standard serves for purposes of controlling.

## MEANS OF EXPRESSING STANDARDS

Various means of expressing standards can be used, including the following:

*1. Written Specifications.* Simply a detailed statement of the requirements that must be followed or that must be met by the factor under consideration.

**2. Model.** A typical sample, a miniature representation, or an exact representation of a specimen of the factor considered standard.

**3. Accepted Rule or Regulation.** An established course or guide prescribed by a person in authority.

**4. Unwritten Customary Procedure.** The habitual usage or generally recognized practice as shown by past experience.

**5. Verbal Communication.** The conveyance of thoughts and opinions concerning the standard by means of spoken words.

Convenience has tended to associate or group certain of these means with certain factors employed by managers. For example, a standard method is usually expressed by one of three means—a written specification, an unwritten customary procedure, or a verbal communication. In contrast, a standard material might be expressed by any of these means plus a model. Figure 19–5 shows the means most commonly used to

FIGURE 19–5. The Means Most Commonly Used to Express Standards According to the Factors of Management.

| Factor | Written Specification | Model | Accepted Rule or Regulation | Unwritten Customary Procedure | Verbal Communication |
|---|---|---|---|---|---|
| Men | X | ... | X | X | X |
| Materials | X | X | ... | X | X |
| Machines | X | X | ... | ... | ... |
| Methods | X | ... | ... | X | X |
| Money | X | ... | X | X | ... |

express standards according to factors. To illustrate, for machines, the standard is usually expressed by a written specification or by a model. Figure 19–6 shows a methods standard expressed by means of a written specification. In this case, the method is precisely stated; it tells exactly what to do and minimizes the possibility of misunderstanding.

## CHANGE AND STANDARDS

Standards are changed primarily for two reasons: (1) to gain improvement and (2) to recognize the interdependence of standards within an enterprise. Experience shows that after a standard has been set, it is common to try to improve it. This is as it should be, for progress in management is dependent in large measure upon improvements in standards. In addition, the setting of a standard seems to place a level below which future standards will not be set.

The interdependence of standards can be comprehended best by consid-

FIGURE 19–6. A Methods Standard in the Form of a Written Specification.

Every error which is made in posting a passbook or ledger card must be corrected by an adjusting entry on the savings machine, as described in the following paragraphs. No erasures are permitted.

If the wrong old balance is posted in the machine, the correction should be made as follows:

1. If the old balance is picked up incorrectly and detected immediately, the Clear and Sub-Total lever is merely brought to the "Clear Balance" position and the balance cleared.

2. If the error is found after posting the old balance and the deposit or withdrawal, but before extending the new balance, the incorrect old balance is to be set up and the Overdraft key depressed (with the book and card out of the machine), and the correct old balance is to be set up on the Old Balance key. The book and card are then to be inserted and the correct new balance extended.

3. If the error is not detected before the new balance is posted, the correct old balance is to be picked on the Old Balance key (with the book and card out of the machine). If the entry was a deposit, the amount is to be recorded under the Overdraft key. The card and book are then to be inserted and set to the line immediately below that on which the incorrect balance appears and the correct new balance extended. The word "Balance" is to be written beside it and an ink line drawn through the incorrect balance.

4. If the error is not detected until the cards are proved at the end of the day, the procedure in (3) above is to be followed, except that the card only can be corrected. A Caution signal should be placed on the card so that the book will be corrected when next presented. The customer should be advised of the error and asked to present his passbook for verification as soon as possible.

Source:  *Manual for Savings Tellers*, First National Bank of Boston (Boston, 1943), pp. M1 and M2.

ering an illustration. For a given task in an office, assume standards have been set up for the material, machine, and method. These three standards are interdependent and may be called "associated standards." The employee, in order to accomplish the task, must use the standard material in the standard machine and follow the standard method. Figure 19–7 in the second column, illustrates the present standards for the material, machine, and method. The employee is to use 12-pound, $8\frac{1}{2}$ x 11-inch paper in an $11\frac{1}{4}$-inch-roll typewriter, and he is to make five copies, using $\frac{1}{2}$-inch spacing between vertical columns.

Now, suppose that a change is made in the standard of the material from 12-pound, $8\frac{1}{2}$ x 11-inch paper to 16-pound, 17 x 22-inch paper. In order to handle this new weight and size of paper, it is necessary to change the machine standard from an $11\frac{1}{4}$-inch to a $19\frac{1}{4}$-inch-roll typewriter and to change the methods standard from making five copies to four copies and from allowing $\frac{1}{2}$-inch spacing to a 2-inch spacing between vertical columns. These changes in standards and the reasons for making them are shown in concise form in Figure 19–7.

*In general, a manager should review all standards when any one*

FIGURE 19–7. Illustrating the Interdependence of Associated Standards.

| Factor | Present Standards | Standards after Changes | Reasons for Changes in Standards |
|---|---|---|---|
| Material | 12# white bond paper, size 8½″ x 11″ | 16# white bond paper, size 17″ x 22″ | New sheet size requested by top management members. Larger sheets necessitate heavier paper. |
| Machine | 11¼″-roll typewriter | 19¼″-roll typewriter | Larger roll needed to accommodate new paper size. |
| Method | Insert paper in machine, make five copies, leave ½″ spacing between vertical columns. | Insert paper in machine, make four copies, leave 2″ spacing between vertical columns. | Number of copies reduced from five to four because of heavier paper used. Increased spacing improves appearance of sheet. |

Note: The standard for material was changed upon request of top management members. This change in the standard for material necessitated a change in the standard for machine and also in the standard for method.

*standard is revised.* This is especially important for associated standards, but it also applies for standards of a similar group. All methods standards, for example, should be reviewed whenever a change is made in any one methods standard, because in this way possible sources of improvement and the bettering of all methods standards can be discovered and adopted. To repeat, *standards are not independent, they are interdependent.*

## ADVANTAGES OF STANDARDS

The use of standards in management provides tremendous advantages, including:

*1. Aid Managing.* The performance of the management process is expedited by the use of standards. Identification and measurement of quality, performance, and capacity of the factors used by a manager constitute the supports upon which the managerial functions can be predicated.

*2. Provide a Common Basis for Understanding.* Standards provide a common terminology, or a common language, between the employee and supervisor or between the buyer and seller. Through the use of standards, it is possible to determine exactly what is being discussed or investigated.

*3. Aid in Securing Coordination.* Standards serve as focal points around which revolve most problems of management. The synchronization of the various factors used by a manager depend, in the final analysis, upon the synchronization or interplay of the various standards which are brought together.

**4. Reduce Waste.** Standards help to determine definite requirements. Losses resulting from obsolete equipment, inefficient methods, and excess materials are kept at a minimum when good standards are employed and strictly enforced.

**5. Promote Better Utilization of Employees.** Standards help to achieve the goal of utilizing personnel within carefully defined and known limits. Executives are encouraged to do executive work—not routine work. Likewise, supervisors are expected to carry out the job of supervising—not that of an operative employee with only the title of supervisor.

**6. Encourage Simplicity.** Standards tend to eliminate unusual and complicated practices. The very nature of standards and their interrelatedness tend to encourage the use of simple descriptions and easily understood terms. Also, wide usage encourages understanding of the standard.

**7. Act As Stimuli to Research.** Standards help to localize areas in which improvements might be made. They serve to help state the problem and to assist the researcher in concentrating on a problem of relatively limited scope.

**8. Provide Effective Connecting Links between the Findings of Research and the Application of Research Results.** Standards serve as the contact points for the application of research findings. New discoveries and improvements are introduced via the standards; and in this manner, the beneficial contributions of research are utilized with a minimum of time and effort.

**9. Provide Interchangeability of Part and Machine.** Each component may be so specified and accurately determined by the use of standards that it is entirely feasible to use any one of a group of similar components. By means of standards, it is possible to insure that all units of part $X$ will be identical within the limits set up by the standards.

**10. Make Mass Production Possible.** Standards permit the handling of each component separately; thus, specialization may be practiced and the gains thereof realized. Difficult and complex jobs requiring long and strenuous training periods are reduced by the use of standards to relatively simple tasks, yet at no sacrifice in the total amount of work accomplished.

## AMERICAN STANDARDS ASSOCIATION, INC.

For some years the American Standards Association, Inc., and the Administrative Management Society (prior to 1963 known as the National Office Management Association) have worked together in efforts to establish office standards which it is hoped will prove useful to many managers. The American Standards Association does not set standards; it provides the machinery whereby every group concerned in any project has a right to participate in the setting of the standards. The program includes the establishment of office standards for each of the following major groups: office equipment and furniture, paper for office use, office supplies, business machines, personnel, physical and physiological factors, and office forms, records, and procedures. Figure 19–8 shows an office standard for basic sheet sizes and standard stock sizes for bond papers and index bristols. By its use, a reference level for managerial controlling is provided.

FIGURE 19–8. A Written Office Standard.

**Division 2**
**Paper**

**N2.1 - 1955**

# OFFICE STANDARD

Reg. U. S. Pat. Off.
**X2.2.1 - 1955**
*UDC 676.3.001.3:389.172

Basic Sheet Sizes and Standard Stock Sizes
for Bond Papers and Index Bristols
(An American Standard)

**1. Scope**

1.1 The scope and purpose of this standard is to list the basic sheet sizes and standard stock sizes of bond papers and index bristols in order to encourage the use of normally available sizes.

**2. Definitions**

2.1 For purposes of this standard, the terms listed below are defined as follows:

2.1.1 **Basic Sheet Size,** as defined in the Dictionary of Paper* is a certain sheet size recognized by buyers and sellers as the one upon which its basic weight is figured. Usually, it is also the one which prints, folds, and trims most effectively.

2.1.2 **Standard Stock Sheet Sizes** are the sizes of paper normally stocked by most paper merchants and most paper mills and from which the sizes commonly used in the office are cut with a minimum of waste.

2.1.3 **Bond Paper** is a grade of writing or printing paper originally used where strength, durability, and permanence are essential requirements, as in government bonds and legal documents. Its use has extended into other fields, such as business letterheads and forms, where strength and permanence, though important properties, are not so essential; this accounts for the wide range of quality in this type of paper. These qualities are obtained through the use of rag pulp, bleached chemical wood pulps, and mixtures of these fibers in the manufacturing process. Although bond paper is a typical writing paper, almost all of it is subjected to some form of printing before use. Therefore, it must have good printing qualities which, however, are not as important as writing and erasing qualities, clean-

liness, formation, finish, color and freedom from fuzz. It is usually made in basis weights from 13 to 24 pounds (17 in. x 22 in. per 500 sheets).

2.1.4 **Index Bristols** are bristols used principally for index records, business and commercial cards. They are a group of cardboards made on the Fourdrinier or cylinder machine of homogeneous stock (such as rag, sulphite, or bleached sulphate pulp) or by pasting together two or more plies of the same kind of paper, and finished and sized for pen and ink work. The usual basis weights are 180, 220, 280, 340, and 440 pounds (25.5 in. x 30.5 in. per 1000 sheets).

*The Dictionary of Paper, published under the auspices and direction of the American Paper and Pulp Association, 122 East 42nd Street, New York, N. Y. (Copyright Second Edition 1951.)

**3. Standard Stock Sheet Sizes†**

(All Dimensions in Inches)

| Bond Papers (Rag Content or Chemical Wood Pulp) | Index Bristols (Rag Content or Chemical Wood Pulp) |
|---|---|
| 17 x 22‡ | 20½ x 24¾ |
| 17 x 28 | 22½ x 28½ |
| 19 x 24 | 22½ x 35 |
| 22 x 34 | 25½ x 30½‡ |
| 24 x 38 | |
| 28 x 34 | |
| 34 x 44 | |

† The Standard Stock Sheet Sizes listed in this standard, except for the 22½ x 35 size Index Bristol, are identical with those listed in Simplified Practice Recommendation R22-40 for Paper of the U. S. Department of Commerce.

‡ Basic Size.

NOTE: When the direction of the grain is important, it should be specified.

## OFFICE STANDARDIZATION—MEANING AND IMPLICATION

The wide adoption of a limited number of standards in a particular area can lead to standardization. For example, when a company adopts certain stated standards regarding the type and size of desks it will use, the practice is known as standardization. A degree of uniformity is implied in all standardization. In many instances, standardization deals with an industry, not with just one enterprise. Both the needs and the benefits of standardization are in proportion to the complexity of managing the particular enterprise or industry.

Typically, a number of considerations must be included in standardizing an office item. For desks, the considerations might include size, appearance, utility, comfort, interchangeability, construction, maintenance, depreciation, and initial cost. How much weight to give to each of these factors is primarily a question of judgment, although weights in proportion to the relative costs of the factors might be developed. Standardization can be applied to any number of office areas, such as chairs, files, machines, lighting, forms, procedures, employment qualifications, and training programs.

From an *economic* viewpoint, there is little doubt that office standardization is beneficial. Such economic factors as simplified control, greater quantities of work achieved, advancement of office production techniques, and assistance in managerial decision making are among the virtues generally pointed out.

However, from the *social* viewpoint, there has been much discussion, and differences of opinion exist. Proponents claim that due to standardization the level of both the skilled and the semiskilled employee has been raised; a measurement of performance is provided; the uniformity among similar jobs has widened the market for employee's services; and the employee can develop proficiency in a definite, prescribed area of endeavor. In contrast, those opposed to office standardization claim the employee is deprived of his dignity as an employee—valuable skill and enthusiasm for his job are lost; the range within which the employee may exercise his skill is narrowed; the employee is without the overall picture, of which his efforts are a small part; and the dull and drab work life, with work interest and outlook impeded, can make the employee an undesirable citizen in his community.

## QUESTIONS

1. Give an example, respectively, of the generalized approach and the functional approach to controlling.
2. Explain the purpose and use of information derived from Figures 19–3 and 19–4.

486    *Office management and control*

3. Discuss controlling of telephone calls in an office.
4. Give a brief explanation for each of the following:
   *a*) Optional detailed message unit billing.
   *b*) Interdependence of standards.
   *c*) Base line of reference.
   *d*) Associated standards.
5. Discuss the extent and importance of standards in the field of office management.
6. Can controlling take place without the use of a standard? Elaborate on your answer.
7. Elaborate on the statement: "Effective controlling of office operations should be viewed as a positive assistance rather than a negative hindrance."
8. Discuss the evaluation of present office forms as a definite step in the controlling of office forms.
9. Can controlling exist without planning? Planning without controlling? Management without controlling? Explain your answers.
10. In your opinion, what are the three most important advantages of standards in office management? Point out and discuss your major reasons for selecting these three advantages.
11. State three benefits derived from the controlling of office forms. Discuss one of these benefits in some detail.
12. Do you favor office standardization? Cite reasons to support your viewpoint.

## CASE PROBLEMS

### Case 19–1.  Lullen Company

Mr. Anthony Cristo (*controller*): Gentlemen, I have called this meeting to discuss our report writing. As I indicated in the memorandum given each of you last week, all company records show our costs for preparing reports are way out of line—nearly double what they were three years ago. During this same period with the same product mix, our sales have increased about 45 percent. Mr. Friedman [the president] is quite disturbed about present status of our report writing. Our getting together today to discuss it and hopefully to formulate a workable plan to improve it has his full support.

Scott Condon (*sales and market research*): I certainly hope we can come up with the cure. Personally, I've devoted much time trying to develop my staff to write just a satisfactory—not a good report. They simply can't write. That's the whole trouble. I suggest that we call a teacher or expert in report writing and have some good training sessions. It would be a good investment.

Cristo: Here in our office?

Condon: Yes. You can have them anyplace you like. What I am saying is that it's a personnel problem. We have to develop writers, that's all.

William Sanders (*accounting*): I don't believe it's that easy. At present we have no prescribed level of expectancy. Anything goes. All sorts of formats are used, some of our reports are reasonably well written, many are mediocre. But at least a part of our present difficulty is due to our lack of insisting that certain standards of report writing be met and following up to see that they are met.

JOHN HOWELL (*production*): There are standards for report writing?

SANDERS: Certainly.

HOWELL: I never knew that. Anyway, I go along with improved quality of reports, but I don't think that's the big problem. As I see it, and I'm talking now mainly from my own experience which may not be adequate in this field, the big problem is far too many reports. I receive one almost every day and on Mondays I get four big reports and over the first four days of every month, I must receive eight or ten. They're not all needed. I do not have time to study them. I suggest, Mr. Chairman, that we cull our present reports, do away with the excess, and concentrate on what is vital. And the way to do this is to slash arbitrarily 20 or 25 percent, or whatever we need, from the present allocations for reports. What we have to do is write fewer reports.

CONDON: Well, isn't what you suggest going to result from establishing training sessions which is what I suggested. And isn't the training sessions a better means of obtaining our goal?

HOWELL: I don't think it is, if you're asking me.

CRISTO: Frankly, I don't know. That's what this meeting is all about. Do we really know what reports we do need? I feel that's where we should start.

SANDERS: I don't believe we do know, to answer your question. We have never spelled out what we expect either in quantity or quality.

CRISTO: I have sometimes thought that we should hire several specialists in report writing and have them prepare all the reports. Effective report writing actually requires the services of a specialist. Perhaps it is unrealistic to expect high caliber reports from experts in areas other than writing.

## Questions:

1. What do you believe are the major contributing factors to the company's present dilemma? Why?
2. What's your reaction to the ideas advanced by Mr. Cristo? Mr. Sanders?
3. What is your recommendation to the managers of this company? Justify your stand.

### Case 19–2.   Benton-Donohue Company

For the past several months, Mr. Richard E. Schubert, the office manager, has been giving serious consideration to the establishing of standards for posture chairs which his company purchases. Mr. Schubert believes that standards are necessary for three chair classifications—executive, supervisory, and clerical. For each of these groups, a particular model, design, upholstery, and color would be determined and used throughout the entire office.

To substantiate his viewpoint, Mr. Schubert points out that the use of such standards would greatly improve the appearance of the office and save much time in purchasing. Also, chair purchases could be made at better prices for the company. But probably of even greater importance would be the elimination of comparison of chairs by employees of the same general organizational level. For example, one supervisor would not compare his chair to that of another supervisor and feel that he had a better or an inferior chair by comparison. Chair equality would be attained.

The controller suggests that the employees of each office division should be permitted to select the chairs they want. In other words, chair standards should extend within an office division only. Any other standards arrangement would conflict with personnel interests and possibly with the type of work performed. Furthermore, he believes that the company should give its chair business to several suppliers. Competition should be encouraged; otherwise, the company might find itself at the mercy of one supplier.

The president of the company does not see anything wrong with employees of the same organizational level using different chairs, and he asks two questions of the office manager: (1) "How are you going to determine the standards for chairs in our office?" and (2) "What are the tangible savings from adopting the use of chair standards?" As the president sees it, the answer to question one is so involved that the company should not undertake the project. In addition, many employees would question the results and their use regardless of what would be determined. In answer to the second question, it appears that additional expenditures, not savings, would be incurred. Not one, but groups of chairs would probably have to be purchased if chair standards were adopted. Also, the possibility of taking advantage of lower prices on the chair market would be minimized, and further improvements in chair design and manufacture would be discouraged.

## Questions:

1. Do you agree with the viewpoint of the controller? Discuss. Of the president? Discuss.
2. What action do you recommend that the office manager take? Why?

 **Office time-use**

It is difficult to live in the present, ridiculous to live
in the future, and impossible to live in the past.
—Jim Bishop

TIME-USE is a major area of office controlling. It deals with the accomplishing of work *within specific time limits*. The office work is to be completed, but how long should it take to do it in keeping with fair, reasonable, and adequate time controls? To determine what is being accomplished, we encounter the problem of office work measurement to which time values can be prescribed. A time control of 3.0 minutes implies a given quantity of work is to be completed within this period.

## OFFICE WORK MEASUREMENT

To measure means to determine quantity. For control of time-use, we measure work, we measure time, and relate the two together. To illustrate, it is common to speak of so many orders processed within a given time. The number of orders becomes meaningful when tied with the quantity of time.

Measurement of work concerns accomplishment or productivity. It has to do with results; it does not deal with the amount of energy expended, although in many cases this may be in direct proportion to the work output. Work measurement not only helps a manager to distribute work loads fairly, but it also enables him to define work success in tangible units, evaluate employee performance, and highlight where remedial help is needed.

Much of the work in an office can be measured fairly accurately and inexpensively. The extent in any given case will depend upon the particular type of office tasks performed; but usually from two thirds to three fourths of all work in an office can be measured. It is true that difficulty in measurement is encountered, for example, when the office work is nonrepetitive and irregular, or when it is primarily mental rather than manual. These are impediments, but they are also used as excuses for nonmeasurement far more frequently than is justified.

## MYTHS AND MEASUREMENT

Excluding office work from measurement stems from several myths. First is the *judgment myth* under which the viewpoint is held that office work entails mental processes of such a high order that it is not possible to measure them. Although held in good faith, this viewpoint is erroneous in the vast majority of cases. Much office work requires simple decisions of the Yes-No variety and work measurement makes allowance for this fact. The decision making is routine and after a reasonable length of time on the job, the decisions become somewhat automatic and involve very little or no real judgment. True, an employee may be called upon to decide whom to call if a query comes up or where to store a certain document, but these cannot be classified as situations requiring judgment.

There is also the *creativity myth*. Frequently this is a holdover from the past. At one time the work may have required creative thinking such as the determination of systems and procedures, but no longer is this true. Or confusion between what the job occupant offers and the job's requirements may be the source of difficulty. Experience or special knowledge of the employee performing certain work may lead erroneously to believing creativity is essential to the performance of that job. The question is, of course, are these special qualities indispensable attributes for performing the job competently? In many cases, they are not.

Also, the *human relations myth* is encountered. Some argue that office work measurement inevitably results in pushing employees for greater amounts of work and ill feelings between operative and nonoperative employees. Properly handled work measurement will not have this effect; in fact, it should improve human relations. To employees who work fairly and consistently the work measurement will formally identify such employees and point them out as outstanding. For those who perform most of their work say during the morning and then space what work remains over the afternoon hours, work measurement will show they perform a full day's work but can produce more if they have a mind to do so. A practical solution is to offer bonus pay for all work accomplished in excess of the norm. Lastly, the employee group turning in low performance will be revealed by work measurement. This is part of the current conditions that need correction and which controlling assists in disclosing. A remedy here is to provide training and better supervising. Also, transferring to other work which is better suited to their limited capabilities, in which they have greater interest, or in which they will be in a better suited work group for them may be followed.

## MEASURING UNIT

To measure requires a recognizable unit. There are many different units that can be used, the selection depending mainly upon the type of office work. For example, typewritten work can be measured by typing area or sheets, and purchase orders by the number written. Sometimes, the quantity can be determined very easily by means of counting devices on machines; and frequently, the relationship of the weight of paper to the amount of work can be employed. Other examples of work-measuring units in the office are the number of invoices written, the amount of postage (dollar value) used on outgoing mail, the weight of incoming mail handled, the reams of paper used in duplicating work, the number of paychecks prepared, the inches of card stacks filed, and the number of credit investigations made.

The unit used should be easy to identify, count, and understand. For each related application, it should possess uniformity of scope and definition. Generally speaking, the unit preferred is that which comes into existence as the result of an essential, clear-cut office operation. This characteristic aids identifying and counting.

In some instances, the selection of a satisfactory unit is extremely difficult; while in other cases, there are several available and acceptable units. In the latter case, for example, typewritten work can be measured in units of (1) pages, (2) standard-length lines, (3) key strokes, (4) square inches of typed material, or (5) cylinders or disks from which material is transcribed. The choice is guided by the individual characteristics of the work under consideration. No one unit is best under all conditions. For example, the number of pages is satisfactory provided the pages are approximately uniform in the amount of typed material and in difficulty.

Accurate measurement is desirable and should be sought; but in the case of office work, this can be carried to uneconomical extremes. Too precise or too detailed measurements can result in bulky and sometimes cumbersome data which are ineffective in practical application.

## MODIFIED WORK MEASUREMENT UNITS

A modified unit to measure office work is frequently used. To illustrate, the unit of a purchase order of a company may not be satisfactory because all purchase orders are not identical. Some require five lines of typing, others eight lines, and for exceptional orders, the filling out of special forms is necessary.

To combat these hurdles, modified work measurement units can be employed. One common example of this is to use a "block of orders" instead of a single order as the basic measurement unit. A quantity of 200 orders may make up a block of orders. The content of the individual order may vary considerably, but the content of 200 orders will normally be quite like that of another 200 orders. Thus, a work measurement unit possessing reasonable comparability is provided.

Also, the work measurement can be considered over a period of time, i.e., for 10 or 15 days. During such a period, the average makeup of the modified unit will be fairly constant, that is, comparing one 15-day period with another 15-day period.

Another approach is to employ what can be termed "the core operation." Under this modified work measurement unit, the office work of an entire system or procedure, or any part of it, is expressed by a single unit, considered the core or the most important operation and the one around which most of the other work of the system or procedure, or the totality being measured, depends. To illustrate, the incoming order might be considered the core. All processing in connection with this order, such as credit investigation, correspondence, billing, and the like, is tied up with the handling of the incoming order. These activities increase as the incoming orders increase, and vice versa. By measuring the core, it is feasible to get a reasonably accurate measurement of all the work. Common core operations include number of policies handled, applications processed, orders received, items on order, units shipped, sheets duplicated, bills sent out, requisitions made, or checks written.

## TIME AND WORK MEASUREMENT

For purposes of control, time is associated with work measurement. Time is the element which is basic and common to all work. The important question is: Within what time limits can this amount of work be done? How long should it take? How much time should elapse from the start to the finish?

Time identified with work measurement is known as "time study." Formally defined, *time study is the determination of a satisfactory work output and of the time required to complete a given number of work units regularly.* The unit may be an entire task or any part thereof. Time is usually expressed in minutes per piece or 100 pieces, or at a rate of so many pieces per hour.

The values from time study are called "time standards" and are used by managers as bases of reference for controlling. More specifically, time standards help the manager of office work, in that:

**1. A Basis for Work Distribution Is Provided.** Time standards give the office manager the means for determining the volume of work and the number of employees required to get the work out. They afford the establishment of a "fair day's work," and they make it possible to plan the office operations.

**2. The Office Work Can Be Scheduled.** Knowledge of the time to be allocated to different tasks expedites the arrangement of the order of work according to a predetermined timetable. By this means, full utilization of all production factors can be more nearly attained. And better control over scheduling and individual work assignment are possible. Information on the starting and completing dates for the various tasks can be determined and the office can supply excellent service.

**3. Effectiveness of Department, Division, or Individual Can Be Determined.** An indication of what the working force should accomplish is provided. The question is not "Is the employee always busy?" but "What does the employee accomplish?" The actual productivity compared with standard productivity is known. It is therefore possible to distinguish the efficient from the inefficient employee or group. Remedial action to improve the work of the inefficient personnel can be taken.

**4. Control over Labor Costs Can Be Exercised.** Time standards make it possible to compare standard against actual labor costs. Control can thus be applied and corrective action taken if costs are out of line. Also, the tendency is to reduce labor cost where good time standards are used.

**5. Morale and Labor Relations Are Improved.** With time studies, the employee knows what is expected of him, and this makes office work more interesting. Having an objective—an end in view—lends encouragement so that office work does not seem like an endless mass of detail. Generally, the employee will be happier and do better work when he knows what and how much he is supposed to do, and upon what basis his efforts will be judged. Time standards remove favoritism; they provide factual information and treat all employees alike. In addition, by means of standards, basic data are obtained which provide help in measuring supervisory effectiveness and formulating employee promotions.

## PRELIMINARY ESSENTIALS

Before attempting to set any office time standard, it is well to observe several key considerations. The first essential is to gain top management support on the need for this type of program. Depending upon the time, place, and situation, this may or may not be a difficult endeavor. Generally this is not a one-meeting session with top managers. Several formal and informal gatherings are common. It must be remembered that problems will arise, some will try to point out the flaws of the proposed program and will bring up the judgment, creativity, and morale issues discussed previously. Also, care must be exercised to avoid the impression that the program reflects on the management members' ability to manage their departments effectively.

After top management support is assured, talent to man the program should be selected. Mental quickness and ability to grasp details and functions performed are requisites. Experience and education in systems and procedures work and in work measurement are desirable. Normally it is helpful to have some of the analysts taken from the company's personnel and some from outside or from a consulting firm.

Also important is to gather background data including statements on company policies and authority distribution, information on the organization, job descriptions, budget estimates, systems and procedures, and the office layout. Armed with information of this sort, the analysts are in a much better position to gain their acceptance by department heads, their assistants, and the operating employees.

Interviewing with management members supplements the analyst's knowledge of what is being done and the problems involved. The analyst should explain the purpose of the program, major reasons why it is being undertaken, and the general plan of action. He then should obtain answers to questions pertaining to the department's organization structure; the general flow of work; the work volume, trend, and backlog; overtime requirements; and other pertinent remarks. A friendly, cooperative atmosphere should be created.

At the conclusion of this interview, an informal meeting with all employees of the unit should be held. During this meeting the purpose of the program and what will be expected of each of them are explained. Questions are encouraged and answered.

Subsequently, the work of each employee is carefully identified, and the time standards determined and discussed with all interested parties. If any question arises the analyst should indicate his willingness to discuss it at the manager's or nonmanager's convenience. Implementation of the standards follow, and some adjustments probably will be needed in order to get the program operating smoothly. During any of these phases, there must be complete cooperation among analysts, management and nonmanagement personnel because the ultimate success of the program depends upon this cooperation.

The selection of the most appropriate means for determining the time standards is a prime decision. Different means exist and they vary in respect to various criteria as shown in Figure 20–1. For example, the cost of determining the time standard varies from low to high, among the various means included. These data are relative and serve as a guide only.

FIGURE 20–1. Comparison of Office Time Measurement Techniques.

| Criteria | Subjective Judgment | Past Performance Records | Work Sampling | Standard Time Data | Stopwatch Study | Standard Data from Stopwatch Study | Report Activity System |
|---|---|---|---|---|---|---|---|
| 1. Cost of determining | Low | Medium | Medium | High | High | High | Medium |
| 2. Time to measure and establish standards | Fast | Fast | Average | Slow | Average | Slow | Average |
| 3. Training and skill required | Low | Low | Low | High | Average | High | Low |
| 4. Relative preciseness | Low | Medium | Medium | High | High | High | Medium |
| 5. Group or individual work application | G or I | G or I | G or I | I | I | I | G or I |
| 6. Assistance in methods improvement | Low | Low | Low | High | Average | High | Average |
| 7. Satisfactory for work variation by volume | Yes | Yes | Yes | No | No | No | Yes |
| 8. Satisfactory for work variation by type of work | Yes | Yes | Yes | No | No | No | Yes |
| 9. Acceptance by employee | High | High | Medium | Medium | Low | Medium | Medium |
| 10. Interruptions to work operations | Low | Low | Medium | Low | Medium | Low | Medium |

Individual considerations determine which means to utilize in a specific case. Discussion of these means will now be made.

## SUBJECTIVE JUDGMENT

Time standards set through subjective judgment are sometimes referred to as rule-of-thumb standards. They are based only on the experience and guess of the management member. It is strongly recommended that the manager refrain from the use of such time standards. Even when an accurate guess in establishing the standard has been made, it is extremely difficult to explain and justify the estimate. Frequently, disagreement over the guess arises and may cause problems.

## PAST PERFORMANCE RECORDS

This means consists of recording what is happening. To illustrate, assume billings written as the work unit. The recordings will show accomplishments day by day or week by week as follows: the number of units on hand at the beginning of the period, the number received during the period, the number completed, and the number at the end of the period. These are basic data. The actual performance time standard is derived by dividing the number of total man-hours worked by the number of billings processed. Trends, variations, maximum work loads, and the like can be evolved and subsequently utilized in controlling the work.

Figure 20–2 illustrates the development of a time standard from past records which have been maintained for purposes other than time control. Also, as will be pointed out, estimates concerning these past records have been used. It has been decided to use a previous month as a base period. Attendance records show how much time was actually worked. The volume of work turned out was obtained from production records maintained by the supervisors. An estimate was made on how each employee divided his time on each type of work. For example, the total time of 735 hours for the five clerks was divided 147, 441, 147 to corresponding, copying, and storing and retrieving respectively. The total time for each work category is divided by the completed work volume to give a standard time per work unit as indicated on the bottom line of the figure.

Time standards derived in this manner are helpful. They identify areas for further investigation and they serve as a reference for future accomplishment. Effective for interoffice comparisons and inexpensive, they give some idea of how much time is being taken and raise the question of whether this appears reasonable. They are also usable in federal offices where watch time study may be prohibited by clauses in appropriation bills. The approach can be refined to apply to smaller identifiable types of work, and accurate counts of both the time spent on each work type and the number of each work units can be achieved. For these purposes it is helpful to follow these steps: (1) determine the basic operation being performed, (2) summarize these operations to know what is performed by the total organization or the portion of it being considered, (3) ascertain the time spent in performing each of the basic operations, (4) keep a count of the work units produced under each operation, (5) relate the time spent and the work count of steps 3 and 4, and (6) utilize the time standard so derived to determine future effectiveness of each of the included organizational units.

A simple and common technique followed for finding out the amount of time spent on different operations is the *time ladder approach.* This is a log of employee time usually conducted by the employee himself. Each

FIGURE 20–2. Data Used to Develop Time Standards from Past Performance Records.

| Job Classification | Rank Number | For Month of April, 197– | | Hours Spent on | | |
|---|---|---|---|---|---|---|
| | | Days Worked | Hours Worked | Corres- ponding | Copying | Storing and Retrieving |
| Supervisor................. | 3 | 22 | 462 | 154 | 154 | 154 |
| Assistant Supervisor......... | 2 | 22 | 308 | 154 | | 154 |
| Correspondents............. | 4 | 20 | 560 | 560 | | |
| Transcribers................ | 6 | 20 | 840 | 840 | | |
| Clerks..................... | 5 | 21 | 735 | 147 | 441 | 147 |
| Storing and retrieving sorter. | 1 | 21 | 147 | | | 147 |
| Storing and retrieving clerks. | 4 | 20 | 560 | | | 560 |
| Total time................ | | | | 1,855 | 595 | 1,162 |
| Completed work volume..... | | | | 2,610 | 9,915 | 4,150 |
| Standard time per work unit. | | | | 0.71 | 0.06 | 0.28 |

employee keeps a record by minutes of how he spends his work days and gives this information to the superior or analyst who calculates the standards. Normally at least a period of at least two weeks is used to include the effect of cyclical work characteristics. The name, *time ladder,* comes from the fact that the data are recorded on survey sheets listing time by minutes in columnar form such as 9:00, 9:01, 9:02, 9:03, and so forth. The employee writes opposite these time values indicating how he spends his time. For example, between 9:00 and 9:20, he may write "reading mail," and between 9:20 and 9:25 "sorting mail."

As already indicated, time standards from past performance have management value. It should be observed, however, that in the final analysis, such standards are really *records of "what is," rather than "what should be."*

## WORK SAMPLING

Work sampling is a means employing random observations whereby the ratio of delays and of elements of work to the total process time is determined. It is based on the law of probability. If a comparatively large number of observations are taken at random intervals, the ratio between the observed frequency of a particular activity to the total number of observations taken will approximate the correct percentage of that activity. The technique consists of random but frequent spot checking of the activity of one or more office employees and the recording of the activity at the moment it is observed. From the work sample obtained, the time spent on each type of operation in relation to the total time available is determined.

FIGURE 20–3. Determining Time Standards from Work Sampling Observations.

| Type of Work (1) | No. of Observations (2) | Percent (3) | Minutes (4) | Work Volume (5) | Unit Time Standard [(4) ÷ (5)] (6) |
|---|---|---|---|---|---|
| 1. Type | 540 | 29.8 | 6,700 | 5,135 | 1.31 min. |
| 2. Calculate | 217 | 12.0 | 2,698 | 5,135 | 0.53 |
| 3. Check | 154 | 8.5 | 1,911 | 5,135 | 0.37 |
| 4. File | 142 | 7.9 | 1,777 | 7,460 | 0.24 |
| 5. Sort | 80 | 4.4 | 989 | 7,460 | 0.13 |
| 6. Telephone | 133 | 7.4 | 1,664 | 514 | 3.24 |
| 7. Misc. | 120 | 6.6 | 1,484 | — | — |
| 8. Idle | 105 | 5.8 | 1,304 | — | — |
| 9. Personal (includes lunch) | 319 | 17.6 | 3,958 | — | — |
| Total | 1,810 | 100.0 | 22,485 | | |

Figure 20–3 clarifies the manner of establishing office time standards from work sampling. Column 1 shows the different types of work observed and column 2 the observations of each type, making up a total of 1,810 observations. Column 4 reveals that the total work time period over which these observations were made was 22,485 minutes. From official records and counts, we obtain the data of column 5 on work volume for the total work time period. With these basic data, we calculate the remaining data as shown in Figure 20–3. To illustrate, referring to line 1 the calculations for the value under column 3, 540 divided by 1,810, or 29.8 percent; for column 4, 29.8 percent of the total units, 22,485, or 6,700 minutes; for column 6, 6,700 minutes divided by 5,135 units, or 1.31 minutes per unit. The time standards by type of office work are shown in column 6. We have assumed that the total of 22,485 minutes was spent in the same proportion as the observations made.

By work sampling, it is possible to determine effective utilization of time, causes and extent of interference with effective accomplishment, flow of work through an office, and the amount of time devoted to various activities by an employee. The office manager of a large insurance company found, by means of work sampling, that a low utilization of personnel and machines existed in the company's data-processing center. Using these facts as a springboard, the manager, within eight months, by means of control programs, increased machine utilization 17 percent, released 12 rental machines, and won enthusiastic support of supervisors and employees for work sampling as a technique for making jobs less complicated and more productive. Many believe work sampling is one of the most practical and economical means for appraising the time required to perform office work.

Work sampling data can be secured by means of observations by the supervisor. The degree of reliability obtained is increased by increasing the number of observations. The method is economical and measures cyclic effect, a very important concept in most office work. However, it is not practical to take a sampling of too many breakdowns of a job. Work sampling is better suited to broad operations. It is recommended for standards for purposes of cost control, group effectiveness, planning personnel needs, and for taking corrective action. Care must be taken to avoid purposeful behavior by the employee being observed. For example, when the observation starts, the employee may not continue to work at his normal pattern but strive to appear busier and begin moving papers, straightening up his desk, and engaging in similar activities. Such actions decrease the accuracy of the data. To combat this, use the supervisor or a stationary observer throughout the study so that the employee does not know when to exercise purposeful behavior. However, the stationary observer eliminates cost advantages of work sampling and reverts to the all-day study with its relatively high costs. Probably the best ways to eliminate purposeful behavior are (1) to use and train the supervisor as the observer and (2) to explain thoroughly the need and manner of performing the study in order to win the employee's complete cooperation.

## STANDARD TIME DATA

The data for this means of determining time standards are based upon fundamental motions or muscular movements for which basic time standards have been developed. The time values vary with the nature of the motion and the conditions under which it is made. For example, movement of an arm 4 inches is given a certain time value, turning the wrist has another value, and so forth. Most standard time data are expressed as tables of values. To utilize this material, the standard time data man analyzes each manual operation into the basic motions which are necessary in performing the task. The time for each required basic motion is taken from the table of values and added to determine the time standard for the entire task.

Figure 20–4 shows the standard time values for the elemental motions required to obtain and put an original sheet of paper into a typewriter. On line 4, for example, right hand, the elemental time of 0.0016 of a minute is the time allotted for a motion, *F1*, meaning fingers open 1 inch; and the elemental description is *Gr*, meaning grasp. Similarly, on line 5, the

FIGURE 20–4. Data from a Standard Time Study.

OPERATION NAME: Obtain and put an original sheet of paper into typewriter  DEPT. Sales Analysis  SHEET 1 OF 2

| NO. | ELEMENTAL DESCRIPTION (LEFT HAND) | MOTION ANALYSIS | ELEM. TIME | CUMULATIVE TIME | ELEM. TIME | MOTION ANALYSIS | ELEMENTAL DESCRIPTION (RIGHT HAND) | NO. |
|---|---|---|---|---|---|---|---|---|
| 1 | | | | | | | | |
| 2 | | | | .0080 | .0080 | A20 D | R to sheet | 1 |
| 3 | | | | .0080 | - | Ct Gr | 1st Gr | 2 |
| 4 | | | | .0103 | .0023 | F1P | Separate | 3 |
| 5 | R to sheet | Wait / A20D | .0119 / .0080 | 0119 / 0199 | .0119 / .0016 | F1 | Gr | 4 |
| 6 | Gr sheet | 1/2 Fl | .0008 | 0207 | .0199 / .0080 | A20D | M sheet to typewriter | 5 |
| 7 | Approach typewriter roller | A1SD | .0034 | 0241 | .0207 / .0008 | Hold | | 6 |
| 8 | A1 (OTS-TD .074") | 1-1/2A1SD | .0051 | 0292 | .0241 / .0034 | A1SD | Approach typewriter roller | 7 |
| 9 | GD 5" | 1-1/2A1SD 30%.0005 | | 0307 | .0249 / .0008 | 1/2 Fl | R1 sheet | 8 |
| 10 | IND | A1SD | .0034 | 0341 | .0303 / .0054 | A8D | R to roller knob | 9 |
| 11 | INS | A1D | .0026 | 0367 | .0311 / .0008 | 1/2 Fl | Gr roller knob | 10 |
| 12 | R1 paper | 1/2 Fl | .0008 | 0375 | .0367 / .0056 | Wait | | 11 |
| 13 | R to carriage release | A80 | .0054 | 0429 | .0398 / .0031 | FS180° | Turn roller knob | 12 |
| 14 | Gr carriage release | 1/2 Fl | .0008 | 0437 | .0406 / .0008 | 1/2 Fl | R1 roller knob | 13 |
| 15 | | | | | .0437 / .0031 | FS180° | R to roller knob | 14 |
| 16 | | | | | .0445 / .0008 | 1/2 Fl | Gr roller knob | 15 |
| 17 | | Wait | .0192 | 0629 | .0601 / .0156 | .0078x2 | Repeat elements Nos.12-15 | 16 |
| 18 | Depress carriage release | F1 | .0016 | 0645 | .0629 / .0028 | FS45°SD | Turn to final line | 17 |
| 19 | Push carriage to 1st position | VA4SD | .0048 | 0693 | .0645 / .0016 | Hold | | 18 |
| 20 | A1 (OTS-TD .100") | 1-1/4A1SD | .0043 | 0736 | .0693 / .0048 | VA4SD | Pull carriage to 1st position | 19 |
| | | | | | .0736 / .0043 | 1-1/4A1SD | A1 (OTS-TD .100") | 20 |

TOTAL SELECT TIME: _____ X _____ CONVERSION = _____ HPC   STANDARD PRODUCTION PER HOUR (100 ÷ HPC) _____ EHO

REMARKS:

*Courtesy: Wofac Corp., Moorestown, N.J.*

standard time value of 0.0080 of a minute is given *A20D*, arm extended 20 inches to *M*, or move, sheet to typewriter.

Standard time data are predetermined time values for definite basic motions. By their use, time standards can be set before the work is actually performed—especially useful in planning a new or a changed system or procedure. Standard time data are best suited for high-volume, repetitive tasks where manual motions predominate. Even though applicable for reading and mental computations, it is often difficult to convince employees of the data's validity for such work. The better known standard time data systems are Work Factor, Methods-Time Measurement, and Office Manning Controls.

## STOPWATCH STUDY

The time standard developed from this source applies to specific work done under specific conditions, including the workplace, method, and material. It is not a universal time standard. The work selected for study should be repetitive and of sufficient volume to warrant careful analysis. The proper workplace should be resolved and the work motions economized. There is no point in establishing carefully set time values for work that is performed ineffectively and is soon to be improved. The variable job elements which are affected by changing conditions should be under control. The stopwatch should be one which reads directly in one hundredths (0.01) of a minute. Keeping all values in these units simplifies calculations.

The employee selected for observation should be an above-average type, not because he accomplishes more work, but because he will probably have the best motions and rhythm in his work. This does not mean that the time standards to be determined will require an above-average worker. Discussion of this point will be given in later paragraphs. Complete cooperation of the employee must be secured. This means, among other things, explaining what is being done, and why, plus answering any questions the employee may have. When ready, take a position a little to one side of and behind the employee. To become familiar with the task, watch the completion of it several times.

The job is divided into components or small motions that can be observed and timed. An illustration of such components for the work of posting material requisition notices on card files is shown by Figure 20–5. The eight components heading up a like number of columns are hand-printed across the top of the form.

Next, the time observations are recorded. Under each column appear the letter $T$ for *elapsed* time, and the letter $R$, for the *reading* of the watch. In the "continuous reading" method the watch is permitted to keep running, the watch reading being noted at the completion of the element and recorded on the form under the $R$ heading of the proper column. Subtracting the preceeding from the immediately following cumulative reading gives the value of $T$, or elapsed time. To illustrate, under column 2, first horizontal line, the value of 9 is obtained by subtracting 12, the previous $R$, from 21, the immediately following $R$ value.

In the illustration, nine cycles (horizontal lines) or readings were made. Usually this number, a total of about 15 to 20 minutes, is required to derive satisfactory results. It is possible to determine mathematically how many cycles represent a reliable sample. Sometimes interruptions occur as shown on the third line under element 5. It is coded by letter $A$

and is explained under "foreign elements" space on the extreme right of form.

For each element, or vertical column, the average time is calculated. Since we want the time standard for the average employee we adjust this average observed time to the time of the average employee. We do this by "leveling." On the far left, evaluation of the observed employee's skill,

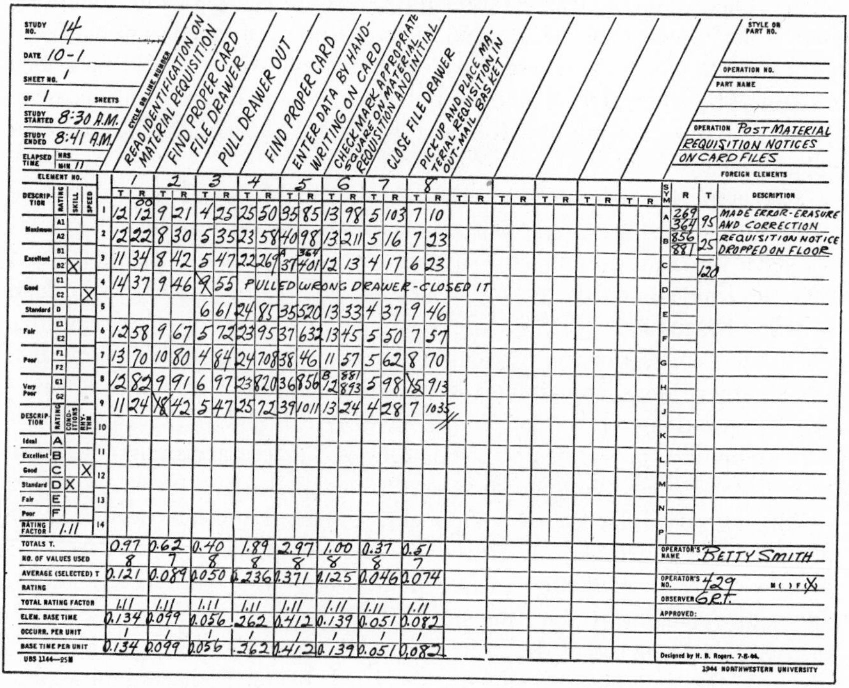
STUDY NO. 14 — DATE 10-1 — SHEET NO. 1 OF 1 SHEETS — STUDY STARTED 8:30 A.M. — STUDY ENDED 8:41 A.M. — ELAPSED TIME HRS / MIN 11

Elements (CYCLE OR LINE NUMBER): 1 READ IDENTIFICATION ON MATERIAL REQUISITION; 2 FIND PROPER CARD FILE DRAWER; 3 PULL DRAWER OUT; 4 FIND PROPER CARD; 5 ENTER DATA BY HAND-WRITING ON CARD; 6 CHECK MARK APPROPRIATE SQUARE ON MATERIAL REQUISITION AND INITIAL; 7 CLOSE FILE DRAWER; 8 PICKUP AND PLACE MATERIAL REQUISITION IN OUT-MAIL BASKET

| ELEMENT NO. | 1 T | 1 R | 2 T | 2 R | 3 T | 3 R | 4 T | 4 R | 5 T | 5 R | 6 T | 6 R | 7 T | 7 R | 8 T | 8 R |
|---|---|---|---|---|---|---|---|---|---|---|---|---|---|---|---|---|
| 1 | 12 | 00 12 | 9 | 21 | 4 | 25 | 25 | 50 | 35 | 85 | 13 | 98 | 5 | 103 | 7 | 10 |
| 2 | 12 | 22 | 8 | 30 | 5 | 35 | 23 | 58 | 40 | 98 | 13 | 211 | 5 | 16 | 7 | 23 |
| 3 | 11 | 34 | 8 | 42 | 5 | 47 | 22 | 269 | A 37 | 364 401 | 12 | 13 | 4 | 17 | 6 | 23 |
| 4 | 14 | 37 | 9 | 46 | 9 | 55 | PULLED WRONG DRAWER-CLOSED IT | | | | | | | | | |
| 5 | | | | | 6 | 61 | 24 | 85 | 35 | 520 | 13 | 33 | 4 | 37 | 9 | 46 |
| 6 | 12 | 58 | 9 | 67 | 5 | 72 | 23 | 95 | 37 | 632 | 13 | 45 | 5 | 50 | 7 | 57 |
| 7 | 13 | 70 | 10 | 80 | 4 | 84 | 24 | 708 | 38 | 46 | 11 | 57 | 5 | 62 | 8 | 70 |
| 8 | 12 | 82 | 9 | 91 | 6 | 97 | 23 | 820 | 36 | 856 | B 12 | 881 893 | 5 | 98 | 15 | 913 |
| 9 | 11 | 24 | 18 | 42 | 5 | 47 | 25 | 72 | 39 | 1011 | 13 | 24 | 4 | 28 | 7 | 1035 |

Skill: Excellent B2 (X); Speed: Good C2 (X). Conditions: Standard D (X); Rhythm: Good C (X). RATING FACTOR 1.11

| | 1 | 2 | 3 | 4 | 5 | 6 | 7 | 8 |
|---|---|---|---|---|---|---|---|---|
| TOTALS T. | 0.97 | 0.62 | 0.40 | 1.89 | 2.97 | 1.00 | 0.37 | 0.51 |
| NO. OF VALUES USED | 8 | 7 | 8 | 8 | 8 | 8 | 8 | 7 |
| AVERAGE (SELECTED) T | 0.121 | 0.089 | 0.050 | .236 | .371 | .125 | 0.046 | 0.074 |
| RATING | | | | | | | | |
| TOTAL RATING FACTOR | 1.11 | 1.11 | 1.11 | 1.11 | 1.11 | 1.11 | 1.11 | 1.11 |
| ELEM. BASE TIME | 0.134 | 0.099 | 0.056 | .262 | 0.412 | 0.139 | 0.051 | 0.082 |
| OCCURR. PER UNIT | 1 | 1 | 1 | 1 | 1 | 1 | 1 | 1 |
| BASE TIME PER UNIT | 0.134 | 0.099 | 0.056 | .262 | 0.412 | 0.139 | 0.051 | 0.082 |

OPERATION POST MATERIAL REQUISITION NOTICES ON CARD FILES

FOREIGN ELEMENTS

| SYM | R | T | DESCRIPTION |
|---|---|---|---|
| A | 269 364 | 95 | MADE ERROR-ERASURE AND CORRECTION |
| B | 856 881 | 25 | REQUISITION NOTICE DROPPED ON FLOOR |
| C | | 120 | |

OPERATOR'S NAME BETTY SMITH — OPERATOR'S NO. 429 M ( ) F (X) — OBSERVER GRT. — APPROVED:

UBS 1144—25M — Designed by H. B. Rogers. 7-8-44. 1944 NORTHWESTERN UNIVERSITY

FIGURE 20–5. Time-Study Data Sheet for an Office Task.

effort, working conditions, and consistency are given. These leveling factors give a total level rating factor of 1.11 (determined by consulting a table) which means our observed employee is above the average employee. To convert to the average employee, we multiply our observed time by 1.11, in effect allowing greater time to the average employee upon whom the standard is based. The leveled values (bottom line of the figure) are added giving a sum of 1.235. To this is added an allowance for personnel needs, fatigue, and unavoidable delays. Frequently this is 15 to 20 percent. Using 20 percent, the time standard is 1.482 (1.235 plus 20 percent of 1.235). This is in minutes. Expressed as units per hour, the value is 40.5 $\left(\frac{60}{1.482}\right)$.

## STANDARD DATA FROM STOPWATCH STUDY

This means utilizes predetermined or standard data values derived from the data of many actual stopwatch studies from which it is possible to determine the basic allowable times for elements which are common to many tasks. To do this, relationships between time and some meaningful variable, such as distance, size, or weight, are determined. For example, consider the element "pulling file drawer out." From many actual stopwatch studies, the time values for this element are obtained. Some of these values will be for pulling file drawers out a distance of 6 inches, others 10 inches, still others 14 inches, and so on. By mathematical analysis of these data, the relationship between time and distance traveled for the element "pulling file drawer out" can be determined. From this relationship, the amount of time for this element can be predetermined, based on the distance the drawer travels. In similar manner, relationships can be determined for the size of the drawer and the weight of the material in it. The relationships so developed can be expressed as tables of values, as equations, or as graphs.

## REPORTING ACTIVITY SYSTEM

Because of varied work load, short job cycles, and changes in work procedures, the more common means of applying time standards are sometimes questioned and believed inappropriate for office work. To meet the peculiar conditions of the office, the reporting activity system for office time controlling has been developed and is enjoying increasing favor. In this approach the various job functions in each office department are noted, and improved work methods instituted immediately, if possible. For each function, a reasonable time standard is established using any one of the methods discussed in this chapter. Measurement of the work by major types is then made so that manning tables showing the approximate number of employees required for each type of work can be determined. The supervisor is given these data for the work of his unit. The supervisor's key responsibilities are reiterated in specifics, for example, to regulate the work group in keeping with the work volume being handled, to eliminate idle time, to distribute the work fairly, and to improve human relations by stating reasonable goal expectancies.

A reporting system is applied to provide direct measurement of the work output and to maintain contact between the performance of individual employees and middle management members. A daily report is prepared by each employee showing the volume of work done and the time used. These data are segregated by equally divided intervals during the day, such as two periods in the morning and two periods in the afternoon.

FIGURE 20–6. Example of Data Used in the Reporting Activity System.

*Daily Individual Activity Record*

*Date:* Feb. 17, 197–     *Dept.:* S and R     *Name:* Kim Clements

| Activity | Measurement Unit | Target Minutes | Volume Completed | | | | Total Volume | Completed Minutes |
|---|---|---|---|---|---|---|---|---|
| | | | 7:45–9:45 | 10:00–12:00 | 12:45–2:45 | 3:00–5:00 | | |
| Prepare for sorting | items | 1.25 | 11 | | | | 11 | 14.0 |
| Sorting | card | 0.07 | 743 | 786 | | | 1529 | 107.0 |
| Sorting | paper | 0.11 | 140 | 70 | | | 210 | 23.0 |
| Placing in file | card | 1.15 | | | 40 | 49 | 89 | 102.0 |
| Placing in file | paper | 1.70 | | | 12 | 10 | 22 | 37.0 |
| Handling charge-outs | items | 2.90 | | 4 | | | 4 | 12.0 |
| Retrieving | card | 2.65 | | | | | | |
| Retrieving | paper | 3.85 | | | 5 | | 5 | 19.0 |
| Misc. clerical allowance | allow. | 60.00 | | | | | | 60.0 |
| Total minutes completed | | | | | | | | 374.0 |
| Total minutes worked | | | | | | | | 480.0 |
| Performance percentage | | | | | | | | 78.0 |

This arrangement provides the employee with helpful periodic checkups throughout the day and assists in making the program effective. Figure 20–6 shows the daily individual activity record. Note the activities are identified and, for each, target minutes are supplied. The volume of work completed is recorded four times daily. The overall performance in this case illustrated is 78 percent as shown in lower right of figure. These daily reports are consolidated into weekly reports from which it is easy to spot any improper utilization or coverage, a need for closer supervisory control, reassignment or education of personnel.

## EXAMPLES OF OFFICE TIME STANDARDS

The following office time standards have value in connection with various types of office work. They are included here to be helpful in a comparative way only. They were determined for specific conditions prevailing in a particular office and should be used as guides, not goals.

|  | *Units per Hour* |
|---|---|
| 1. Typing: | |
| Type name and account number on card | 180 |
| Type labels from typewritten copy | 135 |
| Type ledger cards | 105 |
| Type report, double space on 8½ x 11-inch paper, one original and one carbon copy | 10 |
| Type address on envelope | 85 |
| 2. Calculating and checking: | |
| Compute products of 3-digit number by 3-digit number, using machine | 500 |
| Add 20 numbers in a column (each number is 3 digits) by machine | 2 |
| Compare columns of figures on tape or report, with columns of figures in like order (number of digits per figure compared equals 5) | 4,800 |
| Count items on a tape, or lines on a sheet | 9,400 |
| 3. Accounting: | |
| Pull from source, post account to ledger sheet by machine, and replace sheet | 130 |
| Make entries in ledger (manual) | 40 |
| 4. Filing and sorting: | |
| Sort correspondence papers for filing | 480 |
| File correspondence papers in alphabetical file | 180 |
| Sort 5 x 3-inch cards alphabetically | 300 |
| Locate and pull addressing plates from alphabetical file | 420 |
| 5. Miscellaneous: | |
| Hand-fold 8½ x 11-inch sheet with one fold | 1,200 |
| Seal ordinary envelope (manual) | 450 |
| Assemble three sheets of paper, 8½ x 11 inches, and insert in large 9 x 12-inch envelope | 575 |

## PERT

Before closing this chapter a few words about PERT (Program Evaluation Review Technique) are in order. PERT deals with time controlling from the large, overall viewpoint of several related systems and procedures making up what can be termed a project or a network activity. Multistage industrial operations as the development of certain government defense projects or the construction of several buildings simultaneously by the same contractor may constitute the project. It is also used successfully for scheduling computer installation programs.

A chart is usually prepared to visualize better the composite necessary operations for the total project. From the beginning to the end of this network activity, there are typically several paths of work sequence that can be followed. Using the chart as a guide, the time required for the longest sequence of operations is computed; this is known as the "critical path," because it time controls the completion of the entire network. A delay in any task along this path would necessarily delay completion of the entire network. In contrast, delay in any other jobs of the project not included in the critical path could, within limits, be delayed without retarding the whole project. Usually some 85 percent of the individual jobs are found in this category; thus, 15 percent of the jobs are critical in content and sequence to the completion of the entire project within a stated period. In other words, PERT highlights the key or critical jobs or work.

Figure 20–7 shows a portion of a PERT chart which ties separate parts of a large project together. The circles with numbers inside are events and represent completion of certain work. The connecting lines are activities and indicate work being done. The time for each activity is shown by the three numbers accompanying each line. For example, the numbers 8–11–15 mean that the first number, 8, is the estimated optimistic time, the second number, 11, the most likely time, and the third number, 15, is the pessimistic time. From these values a weighted average is calculated; this is termed, $t_e$, or expected time. Various paths or chain of events are now searched for in order to determine possible paths and also the earliest possible and the latest permissible times for each event to be completed. For a complex chart, this work is done by a computer. In our illustration of Figure 20–7 which is a portion of an entire network, considering from event 25 to event 37, we can see that the possible paths are (a) 25–26–28–34–37, (b) 25–26–29–37, (c) 25–27–31–37, or (d) 25–27–31–32–36–37. Of these let's assume (a) is the longest or requires the most time. This is the critical path between events 25 and 37. Comparing routes (b), (c), or (d) to (a) means that (b), (c), or (d) will have extra or slack time in them because they must wait for (a) to be completed. Effort is now directed to trading off time now required in $(a)$ to either $(b)$, $(c)$, or $(d)$ so that the total completion time can be reduced. If impractical, the work is time controlled very carefully to $(a)$ so that the best available schedule is maintained.

Observe that what actions are taken depend upon the situation at each event. To illustrate, we have stated possible actions in terms of routes $(a)$, $(b)$, $(c)$, or $(d)$. But route $(a')$, 26–28–34–37, is longer than route $(b')$, 26–29–37, so that there is slack time available for use in $(b')$ when compared to $(a')$. The full solution takes all contingencies into account,

FIGURE 20–7. Portion of a PERT Chart.

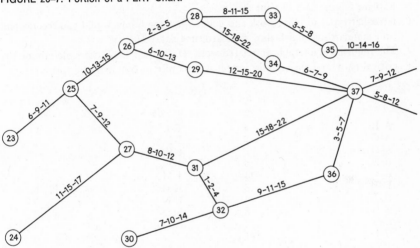

for as stated above, the situation at each event is determinant. Also, observe that there is neither a meaningful scale on a PERT chart nor do the lengths of activity lines have meaning. Values are determined from numerical values only.

## QUESTIONS

1. Discuss the meaning and use of modified work measurement units in office controlling of time-use.
2. Why is it necessary to measure office work? Why not just time the work and determine the time standard from these data? Discuss.
3. Explain Figure 20–2 in your own words.
4. Indicate what measuring unit you would recommend, and your reasons why, for each of the following:
   *a*) Duplicating a monthly report.
   *b*) Verifying the accuracy of bank checks written.

*c)* Answering correspondence dealing with sales.

*d)* Receiving office visitors.

5. Why should a stopwatch study be made only after the proper workplace has been provided and the motions economized? Are there any exceptions? Explain.

6. Discuss the human relations myth with respect to office work measurement.

7. Explain the following: "Past performance records are actually 'what is,' rather than 'what should be.' "

8. Distinguish carefully between the concepts in each of the following pairs:

*a)* Elemental time and time study.

*b)* PERT and judgment myth of office measurement.

*c)* Work sampling and "snap-back" watch readings.

*d)* Time ladder approach and leveling factor.

9. Explain Figure 20–3 in your own words.

10. For what types of office work and under what conditions would you recommend time standards established by standard time data? Discuss.

11. The following data apply to related work. Draw the PERT chart, determine the critical path, and answer how long it will require to complete the entire project.

| Activity | Expected Time (Days) | Activity | Expected Time (Days) |
|---|---|---|---|
| A-B | 4 | F-I | 2 |
| A-C | 2 | I-L | 2 |
| A-D | 3 | I-K | 1 |
| B-E | 4 | J-L | 2 |
| C-J | 11 | J-M | 2 |
| D-H | 3 | K-O | 6 |
| H-J | 4 | L-N | 5 |
| E-F | 8 | M-N | 8 |
| E-G | 3 | N-O | 5 |
| G-J | 1 | | |

12. Describe the reporting activity system for office time-use controlling and explain when its use is advantageous.

## CASE PROBLEMS

### Case 20–1. Ostlund, MacNamara, Shepard, and Marshall

Each partner of the law firm of Ostlund, MacNamara, Shepard, and Marshall is assigned a private secretary and each staff attorney shares the services of a secretary with another staff attorney. This arrangement developed quite informally as the firm grew. It worked out fairly well, but from time to time there were complaints about it both from the attorneys and the secretaries. Finally, Rodney Shepard, one of the partners, decided to do something about it.

First, he observed very carefully the work being done by each attorney and each secretary. He discovered that a considerable amount of work done by the secretaries was fill-in work and of a non-secretarial nature. Rush jobs were not always handled promptly. Some of the secretaries voiced displeasure at the lack of work at times and the mediocre tasks at other times that they were asked to perform.

Next, Mr. Shepard decided to secure factual evidence about the current arrangement. He asked each attorney and each secretary to keep a detailed record of how they spent their time each day, broken down into 12-minute segments. The notations were written in according to a code number to expedite tabulation. For example, a conversation by an attorney with another attorney about a pending case was number 7, dictating a brief was number 3. For the secretary, transcribing a brief was number 10, and a personal telephone call was number 44.

The attorneys balked at having to fill out the daily forms. They made derogatory statements about the request and among other things termed it "time-consuming" and "juvenile." Mr. Shepard, portrayed as a skinflint, tried to ease the objections by explaining the arrangement was used in many law firms. "It is not intended as a check on you," explained Mr. Shepard, "but is requested to provide information on the makeup of your activities with the hope that an equitable division of the work is made and a schedule followed to facilitate your efforts and increase interest in your legal work." The attorneys, however, continued their resistance. Forms were not turned in on time and many were incomplete. Mr. Shepard termed it "a peaceful resistance."

In contrast, the secretaries cooperated fully. After receiving these data for a period of four weeks, Mr. Shepard tabulated and analyzed the results. One conclusion to be made was that under the present assignment arrangement it is difficult to get maximum use of the secretary's skill because they must be available for the attorneys for whom they are working. The result is that at times some are required to work under great pressure while others are engaged in work that could be deferred.

Tentatively, Mr. Shepard concluded that a stenographic pool should be adopted. It appeared that the ten secretaries now employed could be reduced to seven. To this number would be added a typist to handle copy work requiring no secretarial skill. With this arrangement it was believed each attorney would have adequate secretarial help and the work would be divided fairly among the secretaries.

However, the attorneys objected to the pool suggestion. They argued that the secretary may be unfamiliar with the particular case—its background, spelling of names, deadline dates, and the like. Further, they had grown accustomed to working with one secretary and they believed that the advantages and rapport of this arrangement should not be destroyed.

## Questions:

1. How do you account for the resistance of the attorneys to Mr. Shepard's actions and suggestions? Explain.
2. In addition to those stated above, what advantages do you envision by adopting the secretarial pool?
3. What action should Mr. Shepard take? Justify your recommendation.

### Case 20–2. Lorne Company

A contact-type duplicating machine is located in the corresponding section of an office where it is convenient to make a duplicate of a letter with handwritten answer on the bottom of the sheet. Use of the machine, however, is for company business by anyone in the office. Both the manager of the credit section of the office and the assistant sales manager of the sales department office, immediately adjacent to the main office, have requested the general manager of Lorne Company to buy each of them a contact duplicating machine. The credit manager states that he uses the duplicating machine very little now because the one in corresponding is being used when he wants to use it. Many times a number of copies were being made and this means too long a wait for him to use the machine. The assistant sales manager points out that the present machine is being cleaned or temporarily out of order too much. He believes it would save his employees much time to have their own duplicating machine.

The general manager asks Michael Miller, the office manager, to look into the situation and give him recommendations as to what to do. Accordingly, Mr. Miller decides to conduct a work sampling study. After some observations and talking with the supervisor of corresponding, he reasons that there are logically eight categories for observation, including (1) machine nonavailable—being used by other than corresponding, (2) machine in use by corresponding for either 1, 2, 3, 4, or 5 or more copies, (3) machine not in use but ready for immediate use, and (4) machine being cleaned or temporarily out of order for any reason. He believes 450–500 observations over a three-week period will provide adequate data. Proceeding with the study, the following data are obtained:

|  | *Observations* | | |
|---|---|---|---|
|  | *Week No. 1* | *Week No. 2* | *Week No. 3* |
| Unavailable.................... | 22 | 19 | 18 |
| Being used for |  |  |  |
| 1 copy...................... | 24 | 30 | 41 |
| 2 copies..................... | 22 | 26 | 17 |
| 3 copies..................... | 3 | 1 | 6 |
| 4 copies..................... | 6 | 11 | 6 |
| 5 copies or more.............. | 5 | 7 | 4 |
| Not in use.................... | 46 | 55 | 57 |
| Being cleaned or temporarily |  |  |  |
| out of order................ | 13 | 13 | 10 |

## Questions:

1. Complete the table of data by calculating the number of observations (*a*) in each category, (*b*) in each week, and (*c*) in total for the study.
2. Determine the percentage of observations accounted for by each category and the corresponding minutes per workday (480 minutes) for each category.
3. Are the work sampling data complete and conclusive enough to provide the general manager with satisfactory answers? Explain.
4. What recommendation should Mr. Miller make? Why?

# chapter 21

# Quality and quantity control

It is a good rule to face difficulties at the time they arrive and not allow them to increase unacknowledged.

—*Edward W. Ziegler*

AN IMPORTANT AREA of office controlling is that applied to quality of work. Poor quality impedes the essential services of an office. A poorly typed letter, an incorrectly executed office form, an error in extending the cost data, or a misspelled name on a customers' list diminishes the effectiveness of information handling. Some of the work must be done over, some can be "fixed up" by additional expenditure of time and energy, and some is used "as is"—with errors or misstatements undetected, and promising the possibility of subsequent waste.

In reality no office processing is ever completely free of errors. The occurrence will vary depending not only on the particular operation but also on the definition established as to what constitutes an error. What, for example, is an error in letter writing? Is it a misspelled word, incorrect word usage, or an error in grammar? Or does it also include wordiness, inaccuracy of content, vague meaning, and repetition?

## QUALITY CONTROL PROBLEM

The problem of office quality control resolves into a balancing of the time and cost of checking against the benefits realized. Finding and eliminating errors must be compared with the value obtained to ascertain if the review is justified. Frequently, it is found that the checks and

511

imperfections followed are traditional, neither their adequacy nor their necessity has ever been questioned even though the procedures and methods have changed. The quality controls may be over- or underadequate, time-consuming, or ineffective.

Generally speaking, improper control over quality can result in several types of losses. Paper work errors can cause a wrong decision to be made. Failure to process an inquiry properly might result in the loss of the prospective sale from a very important customer. Or poor quality can jeopardize good will. A customer's payment improperly posted is illustrative. Further, detecting and correcting office errors results in loss of time and money. Frequently, this loss is unnoticed; nevertheless, it is present.

## IMPLEMENTING THE QUALITY CONTROL PROGRAM

Quality controlling does not put quality into any office work or service. It does provide information on whether the work or service is of the quality expected and, if not, points out the deviation which can be accepted, minimized, or eliminated. In the office, quality of work is conditioned more by the employee than by any other consideration. Discussion of errors with the employee committing them, encouragement for greater accuracy, and suggestions on ways to accomplish improvement are prime courses to follow. Ideally every error found should be reviewed with the employee committing it. As a routine practice, every office employee should be informed on the quality of his work and where greater care might be exercised. Of course, errors result from nonpersonal causes. Included are improper operation of machine, incorrect paper thickness, poor alignment of form, short circuit with machine, and so forth. Some errors can be eliminated entirely by the use of such techniques as process improvement and simplified office forms.

## SECURING INFORMATION ON PRESENT QUALITY

Because of the complexity of many office operations it is difficult to know exactly what the quality of work being processed is, or what quality each individual office employee is attaining. Therefore, among the first steps in determining what types and how much quality controlling should be taken is the amount of checking presently being followed and the results being obtained. Such data will reveal the adequacy of present quality controls used. To obtain such data means reviewing present systems and procedures and observing what types of checks are performed, how frequent such checks are made, which checks involve a large segment of the total work done, and which work is highly repetitive. These requirements may require many hours of time by the supervisor and senior clerks, but in many instances the personnel performing the

FIGURE 21–1. Tally Sheet for Recording Errors.

| Department: | Employee: | | | | | | |
|---|---|---|---|---|---|---|---|
| Week Ending: | Supervisor: | | | | | | |
| *Type of error* | *Mon.* | *Tues.* | *Wed.* | *Thurs.* | *Fri.* | *Sat.* | *Total* |
| Product name<br>incorrect | — | — | 3 | — | — | — | 3 |
| Product price<br>incorrect | — | 2 | — | 1 | — | — | 3 |
| Wrong extension | — | — | — | 1 | 1 | — | 2 |
| Incorrect heading | 1 | — | — | — | — | — | 1 |
| Transaction omitted | — | — | — | — | — | — | — |
| Other | 1 | — | — | — | — | — | 1 |
| Total errors | 2 | 2 | 3 | 2 | 1 | — | 10 |
| Total units | 48 | 51 | 46 | 50 | 50 | — | 245 |
| Percent of errors | 4.2 | 3.9 | 6.5 | 4.0 | 2.0 | — | 4.1 |

work can keep a tally of the work items reviewed and the errors found over a specified period, perhaps two to four weeks. Figure 21–1 shows a typical example. This concerns order writing and for the week indicates a 4.1 percent of errors.

## OFFICE QUALITY CONTROL APPROACHES

Maintaining an acceptable level of accuracy in the office work at a reasonable cost is accomplished by following one of several approaches. First, a practice of checking every segment of all work can be followed. This constitutes 100 percent inspection—i.e., each letter or each column of figures is gone over to verify the correctness of the work. Second, a policy of either spot or sample checking can be followed. In the case of spot checking, every third or perhaps fifth document or segment of work is checked. For sample checking, a group which is representative of the total is determined statistically and is subsequently checked to determine the quality level of the total work being performed. Third, the office work can be inspected by means of statistical quality control (SQC), an approach based on statistical methods and the laws of probability. It is more than a "look-see" after the work is completed. SQC provides signals and information that work is satisfactory or not as it is being processed. Thus, if errors are occurring beyond the acceptable limits, the processing can be stopped, corrected, and then resumed.

In all cases, the decision must be reached whether the present quality level is satisfactory. If not, efforts to improve this level are made such as training programs to instill quality-mindedness in employees, repair or replace present machine, and initiate a new procedure or method. When the quality level is satisfactory, the quality approach to be followed is made by the manager based on study of the data and his judgment and experience.

## CHECKING ALL WORK

Reading handwritten or typed copy and columns of numbers for accuracy is representative of 100 percent inspection. Shortcuts are possible, for example, proofing masters only of duplicated material, certain shortcuts for checking calculations, and proofing devices on office machines. For the most part, required is an exact comparison with the original or a general checking for correctness of intended meaning and satisfactory appearance.

When exact comparison is required, it is common for one employee to read from the original while another employee checks the material. A word-for-word comparison is made. The employee reading indicates headings, quotations, and punctuation marks, and spells difficult words. Care must be exercised by the employee checking to catch omissions, misspelled words, and incorrect syllabifications. Along with this, an examination is made to see that the general format, margins, and appearance are correct.

In checking numbers read the columns vertically. Place the original list side by side with the written list, so that the numbers are matched on the same line. This helps to eliminate possible error. The doubling of figures and using the comma division should also be practiced whenever possible. For numbers that repeat, use the expression "two times," "three times," and so forth. To illustrate:

| When the number is: | Say: | | | |
|---|---|---|---|---|
| 157 | One | fifty-seven | | |
| 2157 | Twenty-one | fifty-seven | | |
| 2,157 | Two | one | fifty-seven | |
| 3,845,157 | Three | eight | forty-five | one fifty-seven |
| 341<br>341<br>341 | Three | forty-one | | —three times |

Material requiring general checking is carefully read, but a word-for-word comparison is not made. Frequently, general checking work is done by one employee—commonly the one who wrote the material. The meaning of the material must be clear and the general appearance satisfactory. Special attention should be given dates and amounts. In this respect, comparison with the original is recommended.

## SPOT CHECKING

Spot checking can also be employed to obtain data for the quality audit. Usually this is conducted by the supervisor who each workday selects at random one of his subordinates and draws a random sample of the work done during the day by this employee. The supervisor checks this work for errors and records the results on a suitable form. As a month or two progresses, several samples of each employee's work are taken. Hence, a basis is obtained for calculating the accuracy of each employee's work. Statistical' measurements can be used to determine if the sample size is adequate for valid interpretation. Some managers prefer to sample the work being done for a specific period each day, say 50 minutes, rather than check a specific sample size for a quality review. Figure 21–2 shows an interesting format for a quality report. A separate sheet is maintained for each employee. However, these can be combined for a departmental report should this be preferred. In the illustration the date and number of documents reviewed are recorded. The error categories are identified so that the type of errors is known and any trend in a specific category can be quickly observed. Note that the errors are given weights in keeping with their respective seriousness. Although observations for only four days have been recorded to date, it appears that the employee needs corrective action for misspelled words, and the overall quality is too low—a total of 32 points from 120 items received.

## STATISTICAL QUALITY CONTROL

The third approach for quality controlling is statistical quality control. For this approach a large number of observations are made, generally over a fairly long period, the exact requirement depending upon the variety and complexity of the work being done. A description of each error, its probable cause, and an estimate of the time required to correct it provide additional information. Study and statistical calculation derived from the data determine the approximate quality level being achieved and also the consistency with which this level seems to be maintained. Basically all the data are used to form a nucleus of establishing statistical quality control which will now be fully discussed.

## BASIS OF STATISTICAL QUALITY CONTROL

Natural phenomena and their relationships are statistical in character. Repeated productive operations of the same thing will provide a distribution of values. This can be evidenced either by measurement on each of a

FIGURE 21-2. Employee Quality Check.

*Employee Name:* Agnes Nance      *Period:* From 3/21 to 4/3

*Dept.* Typing

| Date | Number of Items Received | Misspelled Word 3 | Strikeover 4 | Erasures and Smudges 4 | Soiled Appearance 5 | Improper Divisions 3 | Capitalization 2 | Poor Arrangement 3 | Carbon Copies Illegible 4 | Total Points |
|------|------|------|------|------|------|------|------|------|------|------|
| 3/21 | 20 | 1 | 2 | — | — | — | — | — | — | 11 |
| 3/22 | 35 | 2 | — | — | — | 1 | — | — | — | 9 |
| 3/23 | 30 | 1 | — | — | — | — | 1 | — | — | 5 |
| 3/24 | 35 | 1 | — | 1 | — | — | — | — | — | 7 |

quantity of similar items or by repeated measurements of the same thing on the same item. This follows because of the inherent characteristics of the measuring method.

The distribution of values can be shown graphically by means of a curve, with the values represented on the horizontal scale and the frequency of the values on the vertical scale. For our purposes here, it can be stated that when the phenomena are natural, sufficiently large, and of random selection, most of the values will cluster in the center around a representative average value, while other values in the group will tend to

FIGURE 21–3.

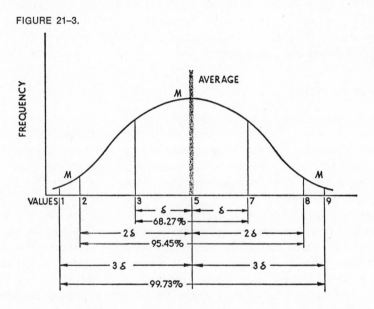

taper off to the left and to the right of this average. The result is what the statistician calls a normal, or bell-shaped, curve, as shown by the curve *MMM* in Figure 21–3. To illustrate, if the errors of inventory recorders are counted, it will be found that most commit, let us say, five errors, while a few commit three, and still fewer commit one error. Likewise, to the right (or greater than five errors), there will be some with seven errors, and a few with nine errors.

Based on statistical mathematics and the laws of probability, the statistician can determine the normal dispersion or spread of these data. Commonly, a value known as a standard deviation is calculated. Within a standard deviation to the left and to the right of the average are contained 68.27 percent of the values of the series. Within two standard deviations to the left and to the right are 95.45 percent, and within three standard deviations, 99.73 percent of the values. These concepts are shown in Figure 21–3.

## CHANCE AND ASSIGNABLE CAUSES

These statistical relationships are utilized in developing effective means to control the quality of work. For a series of data, it is known statistically what variations from the average can be expected on account of the inherent characteristics of the phenomena. Variation within a definable area is inevitable and is *the result of chance.* However, variation outside the definable area can be discovered and subsequently corrected. In other words, statistical quality control reveals when a variation is due to *other than chance,* i.e., when *an assignable cause* is present. But it does not tell what the cause is. Investigation and analysis are required to find and remove the assignable cause.

## CONTROL CHART

A graphic device known as a control chart is constructed and used for plotting data and showing variations from the acceptable goal or standard. The values of the limits placed on the chart are determined statistically. In this work, the statistical concepts of the normal curve, the average or normal quality value, and the limits of variations that are due to chance are determined.

Figure 21–4 illustrates a control chart. This can be thought of as developed from a normal, or bell-shaped, curve placed on its side, so that the area in which variations due to chance occur is represented by a horizontal band. In the illustration, this band is from 1.0 to 9.0 errors which are the limits set by three standard deviations above and three standard deviations below the average. The average or normal expectancy due to the inherent nature of the work is 5.0 errors; however, the quality of the work will vary from 1.0 to 9.0 errors because of chance. It is inevitable and is not assignable to a cause. When the quality measurement goes outside this pattern of variations—for example, as indicated by points 1 and 2—the cause is not chance but an assignable influence which should be discovered and eliminated. It might, for example, be a defective tabulating key mechanism on the typewriter, paper slipping in the machine, or a space bar that is not working properly.

In a control chart, the frequency of plotting the data depends upon the quality and value of the product controlled. Usually, the values are obtained from a sample of the work—that is, a representative number of the total are selected and checked. This may be once every 15 minutes, or perhaps once a day. The value of these selected units is representative statistically of the total being processed.

A different control chart is usually established for each control station.

This is done because the work being quality controlled at one station may differ considerably from that at another station.

To reiterate, SQC stresses preventive rather than remedial action. When more than 9.0 errors are found in a batch of work, indicated by point 1 in Figure 21–4, the work is stopped, and the reason for this assignable amount of errors is discovered and corrected before the work is permitted to continue. Thus, processing a large quantity of work and subsequently finding much of it defective is avoided. Usually, the trend of the readings is indicative. For example, the increasing readings climaxing to point 2 in Figure 21–4 point to the occurrence of such a reading as 2

FIGURE 21–4. A Control Chart.

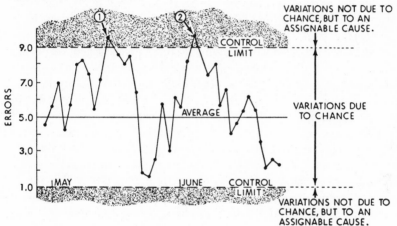

outside the control limits. Many feel that trends leading to readings near the control limits can be used as signals to look for an assignable cause without waiting for the actual reading to exceed the control limits.

## QUANTITY CONTROL

Prominent and important in office management is quantity controlling. In most offices the volume of work is likely to be quite large during some periods and, conversely, quite small during other periods. This fluctuation appears to be in the general nature of office work. A study of the demands upon an office over a comparatively long period of time will usually reveal a rhythmic pattern in office activities. For example, it may be found that peak loads are generally experienced on the first day of each week, every Friday, or the last few days of each month.

These conditions require controlling effort to minimize the fluctuation and make the work more manageable. When the peak periods are known fairly well in advance, quite adequate means for handling them can be determined. However, some unbalance is always present. The demands upon an office are continually changing, a condition which makes controlling difficult.

## OBJECTIVES OF QUANTITY CONTROL

The challenge is to provide adequate office service at reasonable efficiency. Many believe that getting the work finished when it is needed is paramount. Adequate quantity control can assist tremendously in this respect. But at what cost can this be achieved? Work fluctuation creates a "feast or famine" situation in the factors utilized in processing the work. A manager should have only the number of people and the facilities needed for the expected work volume. For any given period, this brings up questions such as how many people to hire, what machines to employ, and which methods to adopt. On the other hand, the reduction of idle machine and personnel time are paramount; still, lack of sufficient capacity in machine or manpower is of foremost consideration. Reliance cannot be placed on the designation of work as "special" or "urgent." Commonly such a designation is given to all office work and means very little in determining work priority. Furthermore, from his quantity controlling, the information manager likes to designate a completion date for a designated batch of work. Although complicated by work fluctuation, reasonably accurate information on the progress being made, the number of units completed, and the probable finishing time can be supplied by effective quantity control.

## QUANTITY CONTROLLING EFFORTS

Several fundamentals should be kept in mind when performing quantity controlling. First, it is mandatory that adequate knowledge and information about the things being controlled and which affect quantity of work are available and supplied. Data on personnel, systems and procedures, machines, cost, and due dates must be known. Of special interest is the policy defining the service to be supplied under various conditions. Second, the control efforts should be coordinated, viewing the totality of the work. Quantity control cannot be left to the individual employee. Unbalanced and sporadic work loads are eliminated in part by taking into account the complete and inclusive work requirements for definite periods. Also, the best practice is to have the controlling under the direction of one individual or an organization division designated to handle this function. Third, quantity controlling should be constructive in its ultimate effect. It is an energizing, positive action, not a depressant. The controlling should make it possible for the manager to give more attention to getting the work out, planning efforts, making decisions, improving methods, and reducing costs.

Expressing the work in measurable units is especially helpful for successful quantity controlling. We are dealing with amounts of work, and specific measurements of it are basic for the control efforts to have meaning and purpose. In this respect, the use of standards, as discussed in chapter 19 appear mandatory. "A lot of office work" is subject to an infinite number of interpretations. We also need accurate and fast means of communication between the one doing the controlling and the employee doing the actual physical office work. In the smaller office, or where the supervisor initiates his own means of control, no particular difficulty is encountered with this requirement. However, when centralized controlling is used, fast intercommunication service is necessary between the line operators and the controlling unit.

Evaluating what is being accomplished, an essential step in all controlling, takes on special meaning in controlling quantity. The planned sequence of operations for each type of work should be utilized, otherwise the controlling is usually diminished. In many instances, the office system or procedure will supply this information, but details covering a specific job are sometimes also necessary. This is especially true in the case of bottleneck areas. Emphasis should be directed toward getting the specific work accomplished. In controlling office quantity it is easy to digress and find the efforts really perpetuating a control mechanism or program as such. Care must be taken to direct and keep the evaluating of quantity "on the beam."

## MEANS OF CONTROLLING OFFICE WORK FLUCTUATION

The question now arises: "What specifically can the office manager do in order to meet the problems inherent in the fluctuation of the office work volume?" The answer lies in employing either initially, or subsequently as suggested by events as they unfold, one or several major means. Eight possibilities are offered here:

*1. Employment of Part-Time Help.* This possible solution is self-evident and will not be discussed in detail. In certain cases, the use of part-time help is entirely satisfactory; but experience seems to indicate, in general, that part-time help may not be as reliable, efficient, and cooperative as regular employees. Also, the cost of recruiting, hiring, and training part-time employees might be excessive. Flexibility of the work force, however, is gained by the use of part-time people.

It should also be noted that some service bureaus specialize in supplying skilled office help in the client's office for a specified short-term period.[1] Help obtained in this manner is usually competent and can be recruited upon short notice, but the cost is higher than that of regular employees doing the same work.

**2. Overtime Work.**    Although commonly resorted to, this solution to the problem of work fluctuation is not entirely satisfactory. For occasional overloads, it may represent the simplest solution. However, when the amount of work during regular hours is *light* and frequent peak loads are common, the working of overtime is open to serious question as the best way of handling the problem. For one thing, overtime increases unit labor cost considerably. Consider a common case in which an employee works eight hours overtime. These eight hours are paid for at the rate of time and one half. In effect, these overtime hours increase the unit labor cost by 8.33 percent, calculated by dividing 52, the hours paid for, by 48, the hours worked, or 1.0833, an increase of 8.33 percent.

There is also the question of employee fatigue. Over an extended period, there is reasonable question whether the rate of output during the overtime hours will be the same as that during the regular work hours. The rate of production during overtime tends to fall below the normal production rate. Most office managers will concur in the statement that an office employee working an extra two or three hours after a normal eight-hour working day will not produce an extra two-eights or three-eighths of a normal day's work. The amount will be less—in some instances, considerably less.

Furthermore, legal restrictions must be taken into account. Federal and state laws regulate the type of work and the hours which an employee can work in certain occupations. Where female employees are involved, the regulatory statutes may be of special importance.

**3. Forming Mobile Units.**    In some offices, it is possible to form "flying squadron" units which are moved from area to area to help handle excessive work loads. Normally, the office must be fairly large to utilize this method. However, the same idea is used informally in most small offices by shifting the employees around when and as the work requires. Utilizing mobile units necessitates employees with comprehensive training in a number of different types of office work. Hiring and maintaining such employees present some difficulties, but can be managed satisfactorily.

**4. Calling Service Bureaus to Do the Work.**    Office overloads or work which is of a special nature can be handled by outside enterprises which specialize in this type of work. Most of these so-called service bureaus are independently owned business firms, but some are units of office machine manufacturers. Service bureaus are located in all major cities throughout

---

[1] Service bureaus are discussed in several following paragraphs.

the United States; several are nationwide in scope. Some are specialists operating, for example, computer or punched-card installations only; but many offer complete services in typing, calculating, tabulating, filing, transcribing, duplicating, and direct mailing. In the case of a computer, a user can lease processing time on a central processor and peripheral equipment but commonly supplies the computer program required for the processing work. It is estimated that as of 1970, there were over 1,000 service bureaus in the United States. In addition, many banks sell time of their computers to outside enterprises.

Service bureaus offer vast experience and competent, specialized personnel to handle complex jobs. The service is fast. For example, one service bureau completed, for a client, inventory calculations involving 3,500 hours of work within three working days. In view of the service provided, the cost of service bureaus is usually reasonable.

It should be observed that these outside service bureaus are useful to the office manager for more than meeting peak loads or emergency problems. They are also helpful when purchase of particular office machines cannot be justified by the office because of its size or the amount or character of the work. Also, a service bureau can be engaged to serve as a laboratory to test the value of a new means of handling office work before the necessary equipment is purchased.

**5. Stress Centralization in Organization.** One of the strongest justifications for centralization in office organizing is the more effective handling of peak loads.[2] When the excess work is (1) mainly basic activities such as typing, computing, copying, sorting, and filing and (2) concentrated in different departments at different times, the centralized organizational approach has real merit.

**6. Use of Cycling.** Cycling is an arrangement whereby papers are processed throughout a period according to an orderly plan rather than as a group—for example, at the beginning or end of each period. In other words, by means of cycling, the work is spread out evenly throughout the period. The practice of cycling has been used in connection with the mailing of statements and is commonly referred to as cycle billing. The same practice, however, can be applied to other types of office work.

Cycling has been used for a long time by public utility companies in sending out their bills for service. Meters are read, for example, in a certain section of the city, bills mailed, and payments specified by a certain date. Several days later, other meters in another section of the city are read, bills mailed, and payments requested by a date which is a few days after that of the previous group.

Many department stores operate on a cycle-billing basis under which each account is posted once a month, but statements are mailed for a

---

[2] See chapter 24.

different section of accounts on different days throughout the month. The accounts can be divided into 20 or fewer groups, depending upon such things as the volume of postings, the number of accounts, and the number of trays required to house the accounts.

FIGURE 21–5. Chart Used to Establish Cycles in a Cycle-Billing System.

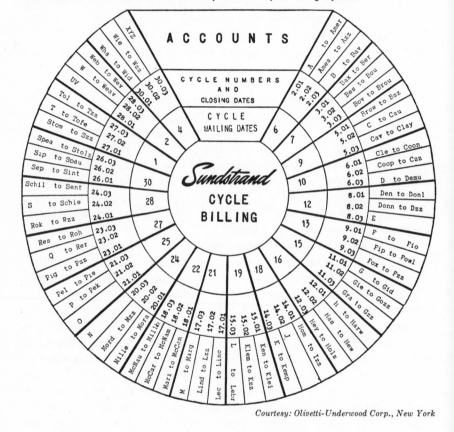

*Courtesy: Olivetti-Underwood Corp., New York*

Figure 21–5 shows a chart which gives the divisions for 20 cycles. Going from the outer to the inner circle of this chart, the data represented are, respectively, the accounts, the cycle numbers and closing dates, and the cycle mailing dates. For example, to the right of and slightly above the center of the chart, accounts "Cle to Coon" have cycle number 6.01. The 6 of this number indicates that the closing date is the sixth of the month. The cycle mailing date is 10, i.e., the tenth of the month, which allows four days after closing accounts to prepare the statements for mailing to customers.

**7. Maintain Work Backlog.**  This means utilizes a reservoir of work, so to speak, in order to level out the peaks and valleys of the office work flow. When certain work can be postponed or moved up, this approach works out quite satisfactorily. The attempt is to make each day an average day.

An alternate approach is to mix urgent with nonurgent office work. Certain tasks of the office, such as bringing records up to date, replenishing supplies, and putting headings on certain papers, can usually be performed during slack periods. When work having high priority is received, it is processed immediately, the nonurgent work being laid aside for the time being.

FIGURE 21–6. Flow of Work before and after Quantity Controlling.

|  | *Week 1* | *Week 2* | *Week 3* | *Week 4* |
|---|---|---|---|---|
| Items arrived forward | 2,740 | 1,860 | 1,280 | 890 |
| Items received | 5,228 | 3,740 | 4,195 | 5,075 |
| Total for processing | 7,968 | 5,600 | 5,475 | 5,965 |
| Items processed | 6,108 | 4,320 | 4,585 | 4,607 |
| Number of employees | 10 | 8 | 7 | 7 |
|  |  |  |  |  |
| Items arrived forward | 2,740 | 2,968 | 1,708 | 903 |
| Items received | 5,228 | 3,740 | 4,195 | 5,075 |
| Total for processing | 7,968 | 6,708 | 5,903 | 5,978 |
| Items processed | 5,000 | 5,000 | 5,000 | 5,000 |
| Number of employees | 8 | 8 | 8 | 8 |

An interesting example of maintaining a work backlog is illustrated by Figure 21–6. The top portion of the figure shows the work flow without quantity controlling, the bottom portion with controlling. Study showed that the work fluctuated in a fairly regular pattern each month, the highest weeks being the first and the fourth. Before quantity controlling was applied the number of employees varied to meet the work needs. Then a control of backlog was established. Study of past records showed the monthly work volume remained fairly constant throughout the year. The size of the work force was set at eight, using standards. Also note that approximately 4,600 units are processed by seven employees in weeks 3 and 4. Hence eight employees should easily process 5,000 units weekly. To maintain control, 1,000 units are released daily to the group of eight employees, thus providing a steady release and a feeling among the employees that the available work load is within the realm of reasonable accomplishment.

**8. Orderly Work Flow through Routing, Scheduling, and Dispatching.** This approach consists of establishing specific channels by which the office work is to be accomplished, placing time values on each successive step so arranged, receiving information on progress of work, and issuing authorization for work to proceed from step to step. It emphasizes the controlling of the work quantity and the use of time in work performance. Each of the major components of this approach—routing, scheduling, and dispatching—will be discussed.

## ROUTING

*Routing is the determining of the route or channel through which the work travels and the sequence of operations required for the completion of the work.* For most offices, routing is determined by the system and procedure used. In some instances, the choice of a particular machine or of a certain area may be fixed by the routing process, but this is the exception rather than the rule with most office work. Commonly, a route sheet, showing the sequence of operations, is prepared. In addition, for each operation, the allocated time and the department in which the work is to be performed are indicated.

A practice sometimes followed is to place the office work in a heavy manila envelope with the route sheet attached on the outside. A copy of the sheet is retained by the person or department doing the central control work. In some instances, the form of the route sheet is printed on the envelope to prevent possible loss of the route sheet in the office.

## SCHEDULING

*Scheduling is the assigning of time values to the work sequence—the determination of when each operation starts and when it should be completed.* The extent to which office work can be scheduled depends upon the individual circumstances; but usually, a great deal can be scheduled, including billing, key punching, tape perforating, tabulating, transcribing, check writing, order writing, and inventory taking.

The common practice in scheduling is to work backward from the time specified for completion. An allowance is made for each operation required by the work; and in this manner a starting time is determined. For example, if the time set for completion of a job is 4:00 P.M., Thursday, June 12, and the work requires 18 hours' time, this means that the work should start 18 hours before that time and date, or 2:00 P.M., Tuesday, June 10.[3]

The three common means of scheduling include use of:

*1. Folders.* In certain instances, this simple and quite effective informal means of scheduling office work can be used advantageously. Under it, a given number of units of work are placed in each of a number

---

[3] This is based on working hours from 8:00 to 12:00 noon and from 1:00 to 5:00 P.M., five days a week.

of folders. These are distributed by the supervisor, who notes to whom each folder is given, the starting time, the machine or workplace used, and the completion time the batch of work in the folder should take. The employee is told the amount of time the work should require. Upon return of the completed work, the time taken is noted, and the process is repeated. The supervisor is the key controlling person under this arrangement. He has knowledge of the work on hand, the amount completed, the amount in process, and when it should be finished.

Best results are obtained when the amount of work in each folder is a reasonable amount—probably that requiring an hour or less for completion. Some prefer to call this *short-interval scheduling* and are enthusiastic about the excellent results it brings. It features assigned amounts of work that an employee easily comprehends, frequent and certain follow-up, good time utilization, and adoption of the basic tenet that telling an employee when you expect him to complete a specific job before he starts it usually helps in meeting the schedule.

**2. Visible Index Cards.** Data required for formal and complete scheduling can be handled on cards. For this purpose visible index cards providing signals for control purposes work out very well.[4] A separate card is made out for each machine, desk, or workplace. The signals featured by this type of equipment are moved to specific positions along the margin of the card to designate specific scheduled times. Scanning the cards quickly reveals what equipment is available for work and what jobs are currently being worked on.

**3. Charts.** Another effective means of recording scheduling data is by the use of charts. One of the original types, called the Gantt chart, was devised by Henry L. Gantt. The basic principle used is that work planned and work accomplished are shown on the same chart in relation to each other and also in their relation to time. The items are listed in a column, with corresponding capacities or data on maximum scheduling loads shown in an adjacent column. Other columns are used for time units, such as hours, days, weeks, or months.

Figure 21–7 shows a Gantt chart representing the scheduling of work for department 13, in which six posting machines are used. In this figure, a main time column represents one week, as shown by the date filled in at the right and top of each time column. To illustrate, the column headed "Dec. 3" means the week ending December 3. In this case, there are five divisions under each main time column; the divisions represent the five working days in the week. The data for each machine are shown in the identified horizontal sections of the chart, i.e., machine No. 1–N by the top horizontal section, machine No. 2–B by the second horizontal section, and so forth. For each machine, the work, scheduled by weeks, is indi-

---

[4] See chapter 13 for discussion on visible equipment for filing.

FIGURE 21–7. Gantt Load Chart, Showing Graphically the Degree of Utilization of Machines, Idle Time, and Time Available for Scheduling.

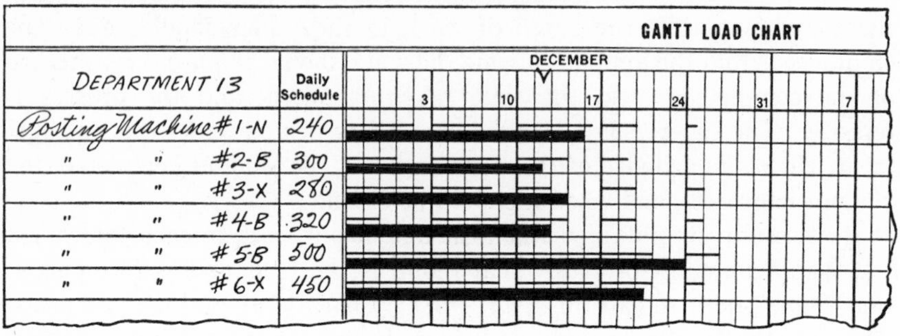

cated by the light line and the total cumulative work scheduled by the heavy line. Thus, for posting machine No. 4–B, work time scheduled for the week ended December 17 is three days, which represents 960 postings (3 × 320); and the total amount of time scheduled for this machine for the six weeks' work is twelve days. The **V** mark on the top of the chart shows that the chart represents the status as of that date, which, in the illustration, is December 14. This type of Gantt chart is termed a load chart, since it graphically represents the load assigned to each machine and likewise reveals the idle or available time. Successive additions can be made on the chart by extending the proper lines; a redrawing is not necessary.

Another type of scheduling chart combines the principles of the visible card and the Gantt chart. It has the general appearance of a large, visible card file with the overlapping card pockets hanging vertically. (See Figure 21–8). Scheduled items, such as operations, machines, or work stations, are shown in the extreme left column of the chart; time is indicated along the horizontal axis. A separate pocket is used for each scheduled item. At the extreme left of each pocket is placed a card which gives frequently used information about the scheduled item, with the identifying data appearing in the visible margin. The remaining portion to the right in each pocket is used to show graphically the scheduled operations and times allotted for the particular item. To do this, two types of cards are used: (1) operation cards and (2) time insert cards. The former are printed card forms used to indicate data about the operation and the scheduled time. Operational information is written on the card with the scheduled time information shown in the bottom margin of the card. The latter are printed strips of paper placed in the visible margin to show the time scale along the horizontal axis. The strips are folded lengthwise, with the turned-up stub showing the printed scale.

When the operation card is tucked in the visible margin and behind the insert card, only the colored strip of the operation card is visible; and the

FIGURE 21–8. Top: Close-up of Scheduling Chart. Bottom: Installation in Office of a Large Manufacturer.

Courtesy: Remington Office Systems Div., Sperry-Rand Corp., New York

length of this strip indicates the amount of time required to do the work. The exact placement of the card is determined by the scale of the insert card in the visible margin. Since a colored strip indicates scheduled time, it follows that white space indicates free or unscheduled time.

## DISPATCHING

Dispatching is putting into action and adequately following up the routing and scheduling plans; it represents true controlling and is made up of a signaling to go ahead and a checking to see that action is taking place when and where it is wanted. For office work, dispatching is usually quite simple. It is frequently done informally by the supervisor. An excellent example is the implementation of the short-interval scheduling mentioned earlier. Giving the folder of work to the employee, in effect, gives authorization to proceed with that amount of work and to complete it within a given period. Further, it assumes that by these actions this work is coordinated with the other work of the department. A common practice is to inform the employee that for work completed in less than the allotted time, the time savings (allotted minus actual time) is free time for him. To illustrate, assume the quota is 30 work items to be completed in 45 minutes and the employee finishes the work in 38 minutes. He is given 7 minutes (45 less 38) as free time. Some managers use this plan with great success. They claim such an arrangement is psychologically stimulating in that it creates a rhythmic motivation and sets a series of attainable short-term goals.

When the volume and different kinds of office work warrant, the dispatching can be quite sophisticated. Employees doing only dispatching work may be used advantageously. Quite often, it is desirable to use a central control board which graphically visualizes the dispatching of the many different jobs which are started, moved through the office, and completed.

Different types of control boards exist, including the three-hook, spring-clip, peg-string, and grooved-strip types. The last two are most adaptable to office work. Figure 21–9 shows a peg-string board, which has the controlled items on the left side and such things as time, operations, and departments in separate sections across the top. The board has a series of small holes into which pegs are inserted. For each item in the left column, there are two horizontal rows of holes. The top row is used to indicate the scheduled operations, the bottom for the actual progress. Thus, comparison between the two is easily made.

To show the scheduled operations, a peg with a string attached is

FIGURE 21–9. A Close-up View of the Peg-String Board.

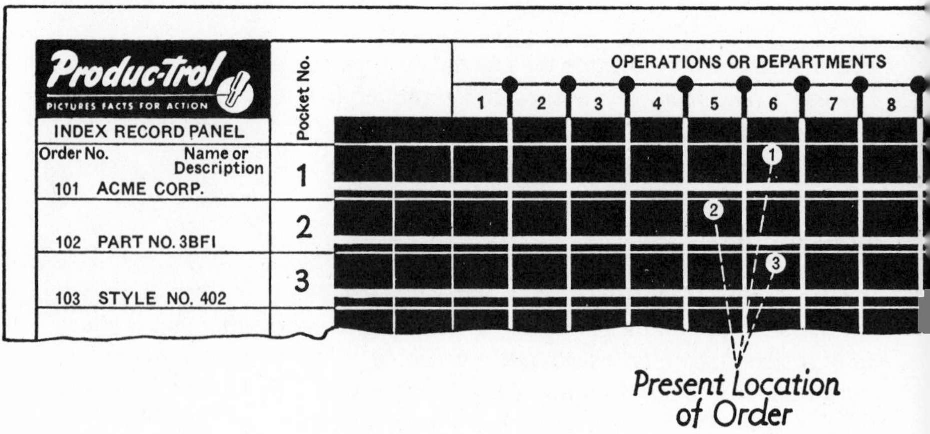

Present Location
of Order

inserted in the proper hole corresponding to the operation and time value. The string, which extends from the left of the board to the peg, is always taut, thus giving the impression of a horizontal line. Pegs inserted in the bottom row of holes show the actual progress. For quick reference, an assortment of different pegs, having contrasting colors, shapes, and markings on the top, is employed. A quick glance at the board shows the times for dispatching, what work is behind schedule, and what work is ahead of schedule. A vertical cord representing a specific time and date, frequently a "today line," is used to assist in visualizing these conditions. Each day, for example, the cord is moved to the right a distance equal to one day on the time scale. All data are kept up to date on the board by moving the pegs to the proper positions representing the current condition.

The first line, pocket No. 1, of Figure 21–9 covers order No. 101. The large round peg shows that this order is in department 6. To the right and under July, the small round peg indicates that the order was received July 11. The peg with the string attached to it is shown under July 25, which is the scheduled completion date of the current operation. The "today line" is at July 21. Hence, this order is to be completed in four days. In contrast, order No. 103, in the third pocket, was scheduled for completion on July 16 and is five days behind schedule. This order is in department 6, which should be consulted to determine what can be done to get the order moving. The square pegs to the extreme right of the board indicate the scheduled dates for finishing the orders. Order No. 101, for example, is to be completed August 12.

In contrast, the grooved-strip board has horizontal cardholder strips for insertion of tickets representing work lots. The extreme left column is used for work-lot numbers, and the remaining columns are headed by

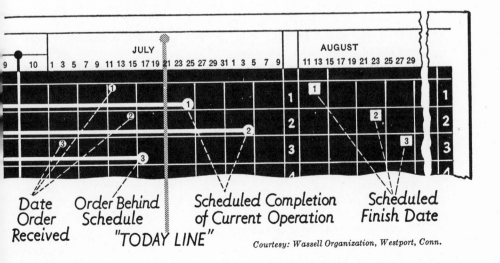

Date Order Received    Order Behind Schedule    "TODAY LINE"    Scheduled Completion of Current Operation    Scheduled Finish Date

*Courtesy: Wassell Organization, Westport, Conn.*

department names. Cards are made out for each work lot. As the work progresses, the cards are moved on the board to correspond with the correct department location of the work. In some instances, the time is shown horizontally. When this is done, separate tickets can be made for each operation on each work lot, as well as for the scheduled starting and finishing times indicated on each card. In this manner, the helpfulness of the board is increased by showing the scheduling function.

## QUESTIONS

1. What is the specific purpose of quality controlling, and discuss how the results of this effort is used by the effective office manager.
2. Discuss the use of spot checking in the work of office quality controlling.
3. Many feel that office work must be 100 percent accurate and free from mistakes. In light of statistical quality control, is this belief reasonable? Should an office manager expect this degree of quality? Discuss.
4. Identify each of the following:
   a) Unassignable cause in statistical quality control.
   b) Work backlog.
   c) Time insert cards.
   d) Gantt chart.
5. What different approaches can an office manager follow with regard to quality control? Discuss.
6. Explain the meaning of short interval scheduling, indicate where its application is probably most desirable and its relationship with dispatching.
7. Talk with an office manager and inquire if maintaining quality of work is a problem in his office. If so, evaluate practices followed to minimize it. If not, how do you account for its absence? Make a brief report of what you discover.
8. Explain the meaning of the data in Figure 21–6 in your own words.
9. As an office manager, would you favor forming mobile units to meet fluctuating work requirements? Justify your stand.
10. Indicate what means probably would be used to handle the peak office work load caused by each of the following:
    a) Granting discounts on all bills paid by the tenth of the month following the month in which purchase was made.
    b) Finishing a payroll by Friday morning of each week.
    c) Completing an inventory over a weekend for a large manufacturing company.
    d) Issuing licenses to car owners of a state during the first two months of the year.
11. Discuss the use of service bureaus as a means for controlling fluctuation in office work.
12. Point out the relationship, if any, in each of the following pairs:
    a) An error and 100 percent inspection.
    b) Quality control and dispatching.
    c) Scheduling and routing.
    d) Peg-string board and standard deviation.

# CASE PROBLEMS

## Case 21–1. Dommerich Company

The services of Roland Hopkins were engaged to establish statistical quality control (SQC) programs over several operations of the company. The question of SQC had come up for discussion several times during the past several weeks and, while not serious, it was believed the company had operations where effective practices for attaining quality should be followed. Mr. Hopkins was asked to start with the work of machine posting to documents by five operators. Errors in this work resulted in either an over- or an undercharge to customers or payments to vendors.

As his first activity, Mr. Hopkins talked with the supervisor and the five operators explaining his mission of establishing an SQC program. He pointed out that this consists of a statistically reliable sample of the work being checked before it is released. The supervisor will be designated to select and check a sample size of work and this is done in a routine manner. The results of these checks alert to an error situation that requires attention and corrective action. He suggested that if they had any questions about what he was doing to ask him about it, and he would try to give them the answer. They agreed to give him their full cooperation.

Next, Mr Hopkins decided what work categories to check. He reasoned that working with a percentage of errors may not be satisfactory if the errors range from $1 to $100. Hence, he stratified the work which the supervisor assured him could easily be handled by a simple presort and division of the work. The high-value postings represented a small amount of the total. Accordingly, Mr. Hopkins divided the work into three groups: (*a*) those postings over $50 to be given a 100 percent check, (*b*) those from $25 to $49.99 to be given a spot check, and (*c*) those under $25 to be given SQC.

A test period to determine the error rate in group *c* was then conducted. A total of about 30 random samples daily was taken over a period of six weeks. From a total of 1,080 samples, errors were discovered in 33, making an error rate of 3.05 percent. This rate was considered too high by the company managers. Several ideas to improve the accuracy were tried out over the next month. They included rearrangement of the work station, different paper forms, and improved lighting. Mr. Hopkins helped in these efforts, but while these improvements were taking place, Mr. Hopkins spent most of his time on an assignment in the factory. Eventually from daily samples of 30 extending over 40 days, an error rate of 1.65 percent was attained. This was considered acceptable.

Mr. Hopkins then calculated the value at which corrections will be made so that this 1.65 percent error rate is not exceeded. This is the upper control limit (UCL), calculated as follows:

$$ \text{UCL} = p + 3\sqrt{\frac{p(1-p)}{n}} $$

where $p$ = error tolerance; $n$ = size of sample

$$ \text{UCL} = .0165 + 3\sqrt{\frac{.0165(1 - .0165)}{30}} $$

$$ = .0181 $$

Since the daily volume of postings under $25 is 265, Mr. Hopkins recommended a daily sampling of 36 postings, adding that the error rate in this sample should remain consistently at or below .0181. When this exists, the statistical probability is that all the work is at or below the 1.65 percent which was decided is satisfactory. Mr. Hopkins recommended setting up a control chart as a visual means to determine whether the work is out of control, i.e., exceeds the UCL.

## Questions:

1. What alternatives for controlling quality were available to the company?
2. What is your reaction to the work of Mr. Hopkins?
3. What does the supervisor do if the error rate reaches 2.80 percent?

### Case 21–2.    Oakson Company

Shortly before quitting time at 4:45 P.M., supervisor Joseph Ayer noticed four employees of his department, the factory office, getting ready to go home. He called them over to his desk.

MR. AYER:    You are working overtime tonight—till 8 o'clock at least. (*The employees stared for a moment, then one of them,* WALTER BROWN, *spoke.*)

MR. BROWN:    Is there something wrong? How come we must work? I don't get it.

MR. AYER:    There is nothing wrong. We simply have to get caught up in our work. I told you day before yesterday we were working overtime tonight.

MR. BROWN:    Well, I can't work tonight. And I don't recall getting any notice about working overtime.

MR. AYER:    I told you while you were standing right where you are right now. And that's all you need.

MR. ROBIN (*another employee*):    Mr. Ayer, I did not get any memo about overtime tonight.

MR AYER:    You don't need a detailed written message delivered to you personally. I told you and that's sufficient.

The men worked past quitting time. About 5:30 P.M. Mr. Ayer told them that he was going down the street for a sandwich and cup of coffee and asked if they wanted to join him. All replied in the negative. When Mr. Ayer returned to the factory office at 6:05 P.M., he found that his four employees had gone for the day.

## Questions:

1. Assume you are Mr. Robin and first thing the following morning Mr. Ayer talks with you privately. What explanation or defense for your action would you give? Why?
2. What action do you recommend Mr. Ayer take? Why?

### Case 21–3.    Ferguson Company

Numerous complaints were being received dealing with the slowness of processing customer orders. The central office handles all order processing and sends documents to the company's 11 warehouses for shipment of merchandise. It is the general manager's desire to process all orders and send them to the mail room within 24 hours of receipt of order. He suspected this time requirement was not being met. To investigate the situation he conferred with the manager of systems and procedures, Mr. Herman Ottoman, and it was agreed that Mr. David Cosand, a systems analyst with the company, would talk with the general manager, study, and suggest measures to effect improvements. Subsequently, while interviewing the general manager, Mr. Cosand suggested that a study be undertaken to determine how long it was taking to process an order. However, the general manager believed a simple control record based on a sampling of orders should be tried. As the general manager saw it, from a portion of the completed work, the amount of elapsed time from receipt to completeness could be determined, but more important, the elapsed time up to each department or major work station could be found for any given department or station. Hence, a pattern of orders, such as orders station 1 from the first day after initial receipt, orders station 1 from the second day of receipt, and so forth, could be revealed.

Mr. Cosand agreed that this was entirely possible and practical. He expressed the belief that this would give some factual measurement of the problem, but would not solve the difficulty, namely, completing customer orders more quickly. He also pointed out that to him the proper control to attain was (1) knowing exactly what kind of service is being supplied and (2) comparing this against the service goals established by management. The former would be gained by following the general manager's suggestion. To this the general manager heartily agreed, but added that remedial measures would be needed to upgrade the service to the level desired and this, in turn, would require knowledge of how the orders are now processed.

Accordingly, Mr. Cosand studied the practices now being followed in processing the orders. He found that (1) orders are sent to the sales department, where they are reviewed; (2) when review is completed, usually around noon, orders are sent to credit department for checking; (3) thence they go to the order department, where orders are extended in dollar amounts and merchandise availability is checked; most of this work is not completed by 5:00 P.M. and it frequently extends until noon the following day; (4) orders passing credit and merchandise availability requirements are sent to invoicing; all orders being invoiced have been in possession of the company at least a day; (5) completed and checked invoices are sent to the mail room at 4:00 P.M. daily for mailing to warehouses.

## Questions:

1. Give your understanding of the general manager's concept of a control record to indicate the service being rendered, i.e., data showing the elapsed time for completion and likewise the elapsed time up to each department, and explain how these data could be used advantageously. Illustrate your answer with a chart, if you desire.
2. What additional types of information do you feel it advisable for Mr. Cosand to obtain? Why?
3. What recommendation do you believe Mr. Cosand should make? Why?

chapter **22**

# Cost and budgetary control

MANAGERIAL SUCCESS in many cases lies in getting the work completed satisfactorily within a certain cost. Today's information manager requires answers to what things cost, how these costs are figured, and the meaning of the final results in terms of cost. Such data are basic. Hence, the area of cost controlling in information management is of utmost significance.

As used here, cost means the *dollar amount expended for the owner-ship, use, or service of every component making up and employed in the execution of the work*. Cost is a matter of money outlay for manual or mental work planned, accomplished, or in process of being achieved.

## COST AND THE INFORMATION MANAGER

In the opinion of many, cost is the common controlling medium since other types, such as those for quantity, quality, and time-use, can be expressed in terms of cost. But other media of controlling should be used when they are believed to be superior under the particular circumstances. Cost is not an objective in itself, but simply a means, and an important one, used by a manager. It helps the manager, especially in the act of controlling, to direct the various activities so that within stated limits the goals will be realized.

Decision making is usually greatly influenced by the consideration of cost information. Whether to install a new procedure, to purchase a new office machine, to perform a new service, or to revise a form design are decided with the aid of cost information. Sometimes, the question is answered almost entirely on the basis of cost. In addition, cost also helps justify a managerial action. Recommendations for a change usually include the cost before and the cost (estimated) after the change is effected. Likewise, if an alteration has been made, the wisdom of this move is frequently confirmed by a "before and after" cost picture. Figure 22–1 illustrates one type of form that can be used.

An information manager keeps informed of many office practices by means of cost information. Many of the items in reports dealing with

FIGURE 22–1. A Cost Savings Estimate.

## COST SAVINGS ESTIMATE

DEPARTMENT NO. ___78_____

DATE _9/7/_____

DESCRIPTION _Adopt work layout and method described by M-240_____

NOTE: ALL COSTS FOR ONE YEAR

| COSTS | PRESENT | PROPOSED | SAVINGS |
|---|---|---|---|
| LABOR | $2875 | $2130 | +$745 |
| MATERIAL | 925 | 800 | + 125 |
| MACHINE TIME | 750 | 1035 | - 285 |
| OTHER (WRITE IN) | | | |
| TOTAL | $4550 | $3965 | $585 |

ACTION ___Recommended and approved on Oct. 3, 196_–by executive___
committee, R. C. McGinnis, Chairman._____

APPROVED AND PUT INTO EFFECT BY ___*CRW.*_____

accomplishments, and also in ordinary financial statements, are expressed in cost. The number of employees; supplies used; inventory on hand, in process, or finished; charge for floor space occupied; charge for office machine usage; and the like are expressed in dollar values, estimated from cost data.

Cost also serves as an effective medium for coordinating managerial activities. For example, it is helpful in determining the program of action that will achieve the required results, yet maintain the proper balance. The selection and extent of managerial efforts, their timing, and direction can be executed in an orderly manner. Actions predicated on guesses or on hit-and-miss bases are minimized.

Cost information provides the office manager with clues to places where waste can be reduced or eliminated. While curbing waste is a desired result of all controlling, it is especially so in the case of cost. The very nature of cost information focuses attention on what was paid out and what was received. This leads to waste reduction.

## COST-VALUE RELATIONSHIPS

Examining the purpose and value of each operation and determining how this same purpose might be accomplished at lower cost represent the essential meaning of cost-value relationships as used in information management. It is to a great extent a mental and questioning viewpoint. The

FIGURE 22-2. Cost-Value Relationship Used for a Report.

Subject: Trend report
Issued: Four a year: Jan., April, July, and Oct.
Approximate preparation time: 72 man-days per issue; 288 man-days annually.
Approximate cost: $450 per issue; $1,800 annually.

The purpose of this report appears essential. However, the format is questionable, the wording trends to be repetitive, and the real contributions of the report are buried in difficult-to-interpret charts. The report can certainly be simplified and made more readable. Detail required from operating decisions should be simplified and put in a format to expedite preparation of this report. In this respect, it would appear that mechanization at considerable savings in man-hours should be adopted. Furthermore, the timing of the work for preparing these trend reports coincides with other essential work of the personnel responsible for these reports. Reassignment of the writing duties is recommended and the possibility of either advancing or retarding the issue dates of the report should be considered.

purpose of each office activity is identified and what would seem to be an acceptable cost for achieving this purpose is set down. Judgment is used to arrive at this cost as well as knowledge of costs and their relationships applicable to other activities within the enterprise. Figure *22-2* shows analysis on a report using this cost-value relationship.

Asking certain questions helps in arriving at acceptable data. Significant questions include: Can the activity be eliminated? Does it provide more than is necessary for the basic purpose? Does it seem to cost more than it is worth? What substitute, lower cost methods might give equally satisfactory results? Is excessive quality being maintained?

This balancing of cost against value can be applied to a number of office situations. In each case, the approach is one of comparing mentally what is being done at present cost, quality, and performance to what might be done at another cost, quality, and performance. Comparison is basic to this approach.

## SUNK COST

Another cost concept which the information manager encounters from time to time is sunk cost. Commonly associated with an investment in a machine or facility, sunk cost is an expenditure which is submerged and of a more or less long-term holding which cannot be liquidated into cash at its approximate present net worth to the owner. Usually it is a cost representing a portion of the initial investment that is sacrificed when a substitute or something better is obtained to replace that for which the initial investment was made. Normally a sunk cost is thought of in connection with an investment in dollars, but it can also be in terms of time or effort or any combination of these.

An illustration will prove helpful. Suppose purchase of a second machine is contemplated to replace a present or first machine and the trade-in allowance on this first machine is very low. The difference between the present value of the first machine and its trade-in allowance represents sunk cost. It must be paid even though the first machine will not be used, along with the cost of the second machine. Or consider the example of a man feeling quite hungry and ordering a $5 meal at his favorite restaurant. Halfway through the meal he realizes he has had a sufficiency. He must pay the full $5 for the meal whether he stops eating in the interest of his comfort and health or finishes the meal to get his money's worth.

Typically, a manager encounters many situations where sunk cost is a factor. It is helpful to recognize them and to realize the responsibility that management has in these situations. In this connection two helpful guides will be offered. First, sunk cost tends to give emphasis to the past cost commitments. These should be considered but not excessively. It is the present and the future that are vital. For any present situation, even though adverse, the course of action to be selected is the one promising the best future results. Second, the presence of a sunk cost in a situation is usually a psychological impediment toward selecting the most objective course of action. The usual desire is to avoid writing off the cost, to backtrack, or to avoid drawing attention to a potentially embarrassing situation.

## APPROACHES TO COST REDUCTION

The effective use of cost information leads logically to the maintaining of satisfactory cost levels and, beyond this, to the lowering of these cost levels. Progressive reductions in cost appear to be a normal state of affairs in a progressive economy. The eternal challenge is to achieve better office work at less cost.

To gain significant office cost reduction, three approaches appear essential: (1) Concentrate on the items offering greatest cost reduction opportunities, (2) develop a cost-consciousness among all employees, and (3) establish an effective cost control program. This three-pronged attack, when efficiently applied, is practically certain to reduce costs.

## ITEMS OFFERING GREATEST COST REDUCTION OPPORTUNITIES

Certain items normally offer greater cost reduction possibilities than others. Those representing the big items, the ones on which the most money is now being spent, and those of a cumulative and repetitive nature usually offer the best opportunities for lowering costs. Some research and probing may be required to find this type of information for a particular office.

In most offices, however, the major expense is wages and salaries—employees are the key cost. Office cost segregation under typical conditions usually shows a pattern similar to the following:

| Item | Percentage of Total Costs |
|---|---|
| Office wages and salaries.......................... | 70% |
| Supplies, postage, telephone....................... | 15 |
| Purchase and maintenance of office equipment and machines, rent, light, and heat............. | 15 |
| Total costs............................... | 100% |

In other words, nearly three out of every four office dollar costs are for people. Interestingly this pattern has remained about the same during the past several decades, even though office automation is now used extensively. To increase efficiency, this suggests the use of less employees, or the more efficient use of those presently employed. Stressing people as the core of office cost reduction, Fred E. Shelton, Jr., suggests careful examination of four areas: (1) office supervision, (2) habit patterns, (3) servile attitudes, and (4) methods of administration.[1]

For better cost controlling, further segregation of the listed types of office cost should be made. For example, office wages and salaries should be broken down by various types of office work such as office supervisors, stenographers, billing machine operators, punched card operators, general clerks, and so forth. This procedure affords a complete detailed record of office personnel costs in terms of office functions.

## COST-CONSCIOUSNESS AMONG EMPLOYEES

Cutting cost is not a job restricted to managers. It is a job in which every employee can and should participate. Interest in costs is fundamental because it is a means contributing to employee security. To reduce

---

[1] Fred E. Shelton, Jr., "Wanted: Cost Reduction," *Office Executive* (June, 1956), pp. 9–11. This is an excellent article. Mr. Shelton is an executive of the Standard Register Company, Dayton, O.

costs is a way of keeping an enterprise fit so it can continue to operate successfully and meet its responsibilities.

Cost information can be used to develop a cost-consciousness among employees. A feeling of the importance of cost and its use throughout the entire enterprise must be achieved for cost to have greatest value. Every

FIGURE 22–3. Possibilities for the Reduction of Office Costs.

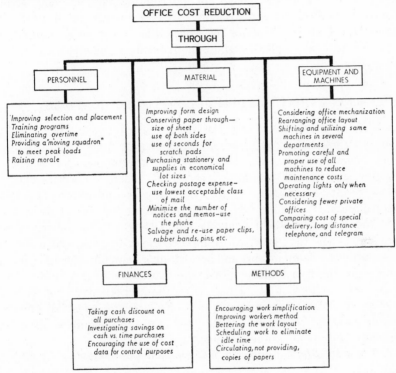

member on the payroll, from the top executive to the lowest employee, should be made aware of and encouraged to think in terms of cost. When the employees are cost-minded, a basic and broad beginning toward improving operations has been accomplished. Thinking in terms of cost is necessary for greatest efficiency.

To accomplish this aim, suggestions pointing out possibilities for lowering office expenses are helpful. Figure 22–3 shows this in graphic form and brings out the fact that cost permeates all office activities. Every employee has the opportunity to be cost-minded and to reduce costs. In addition, accurate cost information should be disseminated to all supervisors and employees who are charged with those costs and for which they are responsible. By this means, cost is given important and meaningful status. Employees are quick to recognize this and will seek to use cost as a guide in their everyday tasks.

## ESTABLISH EFFECTIVE COST CONTROL PROGRAM

As pointed out throughout these chapters on controlling, three steps make up controlling and consist of determining what is being accomplished, evaluating it, and applying corrective measures if necessary. These same steps hold true for cost controlling. A complete discussion of each step will be supplied, highlighting considerations pertinent to cost controlling.

## DETERMINING WHAT IS BEING ACCOMPLISHED COSTWISE

Obtaining the facts on cost, classifying them by type, and arranging them to expedite quick reference are fundamental in determining what is being accomplished costwise. Sources of cost information include ledgers, cost journals, payroll records, purchases, and records of service charges. Better results are usually secured by concentrating efforts in several selected areas. It is well to take into account these considerations:

*1. The Data Should Be Accurate and Timely.* In the modern office, frequent changes may be made to improve the operations. These changes are sometimes of a major sort and necessitate a new collection of cost data in order to reflect an accurate measurement of current expenditures. Even in the case of minor adjustments, the resultant effect may be sufficiently large to invalidate a considerable portion of previous cost information. Cost data should be closely affiliated and apply to the current situation; otherwise, their value is questionable.

*2. The Data Should Apply to Well-Defined Components.* Usually, in studying cost data, the most important figures are not the totals but the individual cost figures, covering each component of those which collectively make up the total cost. Sufficient details must be included in all cost information to maximize its managerial value. No single factor tells the whole cost story.

In addition, the "cost per unit" should be used. The unit cost is the important concept. Comparison of a $300 actual cost with a $200 expected cost is not valid. If the work accomplished is 150 units and the expected output was 100 units, the true values become:

$$\text{Actual} = \frac{\$300}{150 \text{ units}} = \$2 \text{ per unit,}$$

$$\text{Expected} = \frac{\$200}{100 \text{ units}} = \$2 \text{ per unit,}$$

which demonstrates that the actual unit cost did not exceed but is equal to the expected cost.

**3. The Data Should Be Completely Identified As to (a) General Type and (b) Individual Specifications.** A means of classifying cost is essential to effective cost controlling. In fact, the term *cost* in and of itself is practically meaningless. The varieties of cost are almost endless, the different types depending upon the degree and kind of work covered. To facilitate understanding, information concerning "cost of what to whom" is needed.

Several general type identification arrangements will be given. The first, based on the elements of material, labor, and overhead, includes the following:

| *Element* | *Segregation and Meaning* |
|---|---|
| Material cost: | Direct material cost—expenditures for materials which are or become a part of the product (office forms and letterheads, envelopes, and postage). |
| | Indirect material cost—expenditures for materials which are not a part of the product but are necessary in the carrying out of the work (typewriter ribbons, erasers). |
| Labor cost: | Direct labor cost—expenditures for labor attributable to and having a bearing upon the product or service (billing-machine operator, typist). |
| | Indirect labor cost—expenditures for labor not attributable to or in an unbroken connection with the product or service (methods man, janitor). |
| Overhead cost: | Expenditures which do not belong exclusively to any part of the material or labor (rent, light, heat, managerial expense, telephone). |

The second arrangement utilizing a functional basis consists of total costs made up of:

I. Production costs, under which are:
   A. Production overhead costs
   B. Production direct costs
   C. Office cost consisting of:
      1. Office overhead cost
      2. Prime office costs
         *a*) Direct office material cost
         *b*) Direct office labor cost
II. Sales cost, under which are:
   A. Sales overhead cost
   B. Promotion, travel, and advertising cost
   C. Salesmen's compensation cost
      1. Wage payment cost
      2. Commission and bonus cost

These arrangements are illustrative only and are not complete.

Many managers find that apportioning office costs for a specific period to the main office systems and procedures brings very satisfactory results. Specific estimated and actual costs for informational outputs or units of office production can be determined wherever appropriate. Many types of cost analyses are thus possible, such as determination of cost trends and expected office cost incident to various managerial decisions.

Identification as to individual specification is also necessary. This includes information of the particular office operation covered, such as date, location of operation, and operation number. A tabular arrangement of these data is usually satisfactory. In some instances, the data are written in a coded form to preserve their confidential nature. Either cards, letter-size papers, or large spread sheets can be used.

## EVALUATING THE COST EXPENDITURE

To evaluate the cost we need to (1) know what cost is satisfactory and (2) compare this actual cost with the cost deemed satisfactory. For the former, the amount can be determined in several different ways. One is to arrive at the amount from past experience, giving ample consideration to general economic changes and conditions. Another is a judgment or estimate of what is received for a given expenditure. This is in the nature of an educated guess. In addition, standard costs can be employed. These are predetermined costs calculated to represent the amount of expenditure for material, labor, and overhead considered normal for the performance of the work. Theoretically, when the work is done by a standard employee with standard material and under standard conditions, the total dollar expenditure should be the standard cost. Generally speaking, the evaluating of cost expenditures by standard costs is superior because they reflect an analytical, studied, and reasonably accurate cost expectancy. Where standard costs have been established some time ago, they must be adjusted to reflect current conditions. These adjustments are called variances and may be either positive, i.e., added to the standard, or negative, i.e., subtracted from the standard.

The use of standard costs gives rise to several outstanding advantages. Basic references are provided to orientate managerial efforts, strict accountability for deviations from the established standard cost can be placed on those responsible for the deviations, and cost analysis is simplified. In contrast, standard cost usage has its shortcomings. For example, the units of expression are dollars and hence are subject to fluctuating value; personnel must be especially trained for standard cost work so that proper interpretation and use of the standard data are made; and in cases of special work, standard cost data cannot be used unless serious adjustments are made. While all these objections are valid, they are not particularly serious. Dollar values tend to remain *relatively* the same even though they do fluctuate in absolute value. It is probably true that some guide to acceptability, although it be found wanting in many respects, is better than none at all. Also, most efforts to guide the performance of work must, of practical necessity, be tempered with judgment.

After we have a fairly firm idea of what cost is satisfactory, we can compare the actual cost to this expectancy and thus determine whether the actual expenditure is greater, the same as, or less than the acceptable level. From this comparison, the performance efficiency is revealed. If the expenditure is less than the amount considered satisfactory, an investigation is made to determine if the work performed was of acceptable quality and quantity and if the satisfactory cost level is proper. On the other hand, where the actual cost exceeds the established satisfactory level, an investigation might be made to check the satisfactory level or, more likely, to analyze the actual cost to see in what way it can be brought into line.

The comparison work is expedited by cost reports giving detailed information on expenditures and compiled at the end of each day, week, or month. For maximum assistance, the report should show the plus or minus deviations from the expectancy for each item and, what is very important, should include sufficient data to establish trends. In many instances, the comparison of actual with expected cost is included under budgetary control, which is discussed later in this chapter.

## APPLYING CORRECTIVE MEASURES IF NECESSARY

For the most part, this step includes efforts to reduce expenditures in those cases where actual costs are exceeding the satisfactory cost level. In many cases, the data apply to what has already happened, so that the corrective action is for some future date. However, it is vital to evaluate costs and to seek the reasons for present values. To illustrate, investigation of an increasing trend in office personnel costs may reveal poor selection techniques and high turnover. The remedial action might include a testing program, retraining of interviewers, and specific employee training efforts.

Although costs are detailed in terms of specific office functions, it is necessary to retain the overall viewpoint in deciding the corrective action. A reduction in one expense might increase another, making a total net gain in expenses. For example, centralized office costs may be reduced, but the work has been shifted to branch offices where the costs increase. Other illustrations are reducing the amount of light, resulting in an increase of time required to do the work; and eliminating interoffice telephone service, with the resultant increase in time spent by employees in delivering messages personally.

Another consideration is how to utilize all time and space gain or savings derived from the corrective action. The controlling is ineffective if it permits the former overage to dissipate among other work. For example, consider a six-hour task requiring eight hours to be completed. Through effective cost controlling the eight hours is reduced to the proper six-hour level. But actually the correction is effective only if these two hours saved as a result of the controlling are used to perform other work. Likewise, an additional office machine may save the time of one person out of three; but unless the third person is transferred and put to other work, the net result costwise is not a saving but only a machine added.

What we are saying is that for cost controlling to be effective, it is necessary (1) to check and see that the corrective steps are followed and (2) to know, as a consequence of these revisions, what the new results will be. The first point is achieved through personal means—observation and working with supervisors. For the latter point, some simple type of reporting can be instituted. For these reports to have greatest value, they should be made on a weekly and, in some instances, on a daily basis. It is important to know immediately if costs are getting back into line both for individual and for total costs. Receiving reports at relatively long intervals of time might mean needless continuation of costly practices or receipt of information when it is too late to do anything about it.

Cost controlling is a job that never ends. It varies in intensity with the particular needs of the office and the enterprise, the skill of the personnel assigned to and interested in it, and the beliefs of the top management members. It takes time and is laborious work, but it is well worth the effort. Best results are usually obtained from continuous, not sporadic, efforts.

## OFFICE BUDGETS

An important device for implementing controlling, usually associated with cost, is a budget. When a manager speaks of using a budget, he actually has two concepts in mind: the budget and budgetary control. Each of these can be defined formally in the following manner: *A budget is a device consisting of an orderly arrangement of data determined by computed guesses and covering all phases of the enterprise for a definite future period of time.* On the other hand, *budgetary control is the process of using the budget by comparing actual results with the computed guesses in order to correct either the estimates or the causes of the differences.*

The budget and budgetary control are interrelated and must always be considered jointly. A budget without budgetary control is useless from the managerial viewpoint; and budgetary control without a budget is meaningless.

## WHY USE A BUDGET?

Preparation of a budget requires planning, and practicing budgetary control necessitates orderly controlling. Thus, the use of a budget assists a manager in performing these two fundamental functions of management and in closely relating them for practical purposes. Specifically a budget helps the office manager by encouraging a desired balance among the various office activities. The overall viewpoint is promoted. The use of a budget also helps to reveal weaknesses in the office organizational structure. Those units in which expenditures are excessively high can be marked for managerial attention. Furthermore, the decision making of a management member is facilitated by the factual information of goals and respective accomplishments shown by the budget.

It should be noted, however, that a budget is a managerial tool—a means of assistance to a manager, not management itself. Budgets are not automatic in their operation. Care in their compilation and wise, meaningful interpretation of the data are required. In addition, the use of budgets requires time. Current ills are not cured overnight by budgets. The discovery, correction, or elimination of undesirable conditions cannot be hurried. Also, budgets are limited by the accuracy of the forecasts. Reviews about every month or three months should be scheduled so that new developments or changes of conditions are reflected in the budget. We will say more about budget reviews later in this chapter.

## KINDS OF BUDGETS

It is possible to draw up a budget for almost any department or division of an enterprise. Frequently, separate budgets are made for sales, production, purchasing, finance, labor, and general expense. These are then combined into one budget, which is sometimes termed the "master budget" or simply the "budget."

As stated previously, most budgets are cost-controlling devices and therefore are prepared in dollars, but physical units, or any other term which is useful and convenient, can be used. Quite often, where physical units are employed, the dollar values are also shown. When this practice is followed, it should be noted that not only units but also unit cost, i.e., price, must be forecast, and this can prove quite difficult.

It is sometimes desirable to show in a budget not only the allowances at a certain level of activity but also the allowances at various other levels. Such a budget is referred to as a *step budget,* and its value lies in predetermining and thinking through the action to be taken should variations from the estimated goal arise. Actually, the work of preparing a step budget is not as difficult as it may at first appear. Deviations are estimated from the allowances for the established goal. Some items will vary directly with the volume; others will tend to rise or fall with the operating level, but not in direct proportion to it; others will remain the same regardless of the operating level.

## ALL BUDGETS CONCERN THE OFFICE MANAGER

The office manager should use all the budgets employed in an enterprise to find out the plan or projected trends in operations which will affect the amount of office work. Included in the various budgets of an enterprise are those for sales expense, production, purchasing, and general expense, as will be mentioned in the following pages. From these various budgets, knowledge of changes such as an increase in advertising literature to be mailed, a change in the number of bills payable, the development of new sales markets, a new policy regarding billing practices, and a reduction in the number of purchasing orders can be ascertained and this information utilized to have the office provide its necessary functions.

Ordinarily, the office manager is active in the preparation of (1) the

FIGURE 22–4. An Office Expense Budget.

OFFICE EXPENSE BUDGET FOR THE YEAR 19—

| Item | January Estimate | January Actual | February Estimate | February Actual | March Estimate | March Actual |
|---|---|---|---|---|---|---|
| 1. Stationery and envelopes | $ 75 | . . . . . | . . . . . | $ 83 | $ 50 | |
| 2. Supplies | 50 | $ 68 | $ 35 | 21 | 35 | |
| 3. Postage | 35 | 35 | 35 | 35 | 35 | |
| 4. Telephone and telegraph | 185 | 173 | 185 | 186 | 185 | |
| 5. Reception and messenger service | 450 | 440 | 450 | 440 | 500 | |
| 6. Magazine and book subscription | 18 | 18 | . . . . . | . . . . . | . . . . . | |
| 7. Maintenance of machines and equipment* | 40 | 53 | 40 | 62 | 40 | |
| 8. Purchase of machines and equipment* | 440 | 291 | . . . . . | 165 | 200 | |
| 9. Rent | 80 | 80 | 80 | 80 | 80 | |
| 10. Light | 22 | 21 | 20 | 21 | 20 | |
| 11. Traveling expenses* | 80 | 135 | 80 | 40 | 80 | |
| 12. Employees' welfare | 50 | 60 | 50 | 47 | 50 | |
| 13. Clerical payroll* | 3,750 | 3,870 | 3,750 | 3,920 | 4,000 | |
| 14. Supervision payroll* | 1,140 | 1,140 | 1,140 | 1,170 | 1,300 | |
| 15. Miscellaneous (list) | 25 | . . . . . | 25 | . . . . . | 25 | |
| Install new electric outlet | . . . . . | 3 | . . . . . | . . . . . | . . . . . | |
| Fix door at north exit | . . . . . | . . . . . | . . . . . | 18 | . . . . . | |
| Total | $6,440 | $6,387 | $5,890 | $6,288 | $6,600 | |

\* These items must be justified by details on supplementary sheets.

Note: Supplementary sheets are used to show the details of certain items which are selected on the basis of judgment and experience.

cash budget and (2) the office expense budget. In the case of the cash budget, the extent of office activities affects the cash requirements of the enterprise. The purchase and trade-in of office machines and equipment, the expansion or contraction of any office function in order to keep it in balance with changes elsewhere in the enterprise, or simply action to cut down office expenditures are illustrations of the office's influence on the cash budget.

The office expense budget is the individual budget covering office activities and is one in which the office manager is vitally interested. Typical items include supervision, clerical payroll, stationery, supplies, postage, telephone and telegraph service, reception and messenger service, purchase and maintenance of office machines and equipment, rent, and light. As already indicated, comparisons are made with the estimated amounts.

Figure 22–4 shows a portion of an office expense budget. In this case, entries of actual expenditures have been made for the months of January and February. Expenses for February are nearly $400 in excess of the estimate. A study of the itemized data for this month shows that clerical payroll, machine and equipment purchases, and supervision payroll are the items chiefly responsible for the increase. Further investigation of these expenses should be made.

## PREPARATION OF THE BUDGET

An interesting graphic representation of the sequence of budget preparation is shown in Figure 22–5. The total estimated income is determined from expected sales and other sources of income. From this total estimated income are subtracted the expenses of sales, production, purchasing, and general expense. This gives the estimated net income or loss, which can be reflected in the financial budget, an estimated balance sheet, and an estimated earnings statement. The chart shows some of the details included under each individual budget.

Usually, the sales budget is developed first, since in many cases all other activities are predicated on what the sales expectancy picture is. Using the predicted sales as a basis, the plan for production, purchasing, and the like can be drawn up.

However, in some cases, this approach is reversed. The beginning is made by estimating the approximate income needed to provide a fair return on capital invested in the enterprise; then, one works back to determine the sales required, the production, and so on. There are variations of these two approaches, as well as other methods.

Most procedures for budget making consist of a series of steps somewhat like the following:

1. A conference of top management members is held to discuss trends

FIGURE 22–5. A Normal Sequence of Budget Preparation. The chart shows the coordination of the various individual budgets and the type of information found in each one.

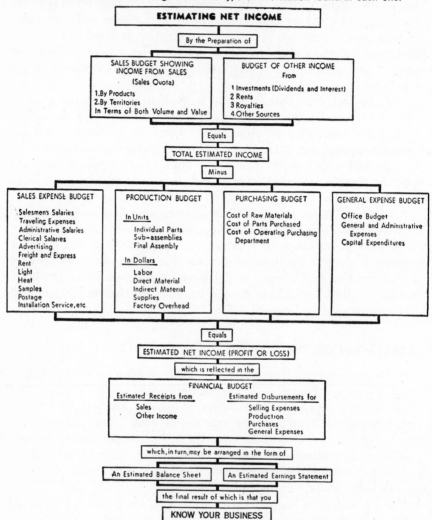

**ESTIMATING NET INCOME**

By the Preparation of

| SALES BUDGET SHOWING INCOME FROM SALES (Sales Quota) | BUDGET OF OTHER INCOME From |
|---|---|
| 1.By Products 2.By Territories In Terms of Both Volume and Value | 1 Investments (Dividends and Interest) 2 Rents 3 Royalties 4.Other Sources |

Equals

TOTAL ESTIMATED INCOME

Minus

| SALES EXPENSE BUDGET | PRODUCTION BUDGET | PURCHASING BUDGET | GENERAL EXPENSE BUDGET |
|---|---|---|---|
| Salesmen's Salaries Traveling Expenses Administrative Salaries Clerical Salaries Advertising Freight and Express Rent Light Heat Samples Postage Installation Service,etc | In Units Individual Parts Sub–assemblies Final Assembly In Dollars Labor Direct Material Indirect Material Supplies Factory Overhead | Cost of Raw Materials Cost of Parts Purchased Cost of Operating Purchasing Department | Office Budget General and Administrative Expenses Capital Expenditures |

Equals

ESTIMATED NET INCOME (PROFIT OR LOSS)

which is reflected in the

FINANCIAL BUDGET

| Estimated Receipts from | Estimated Disbursements for |
|---|---|
| Sales Other Income | Selling Expenses Production Purchases General Expenses |

which, in turn, may be arranged in the form of

| An Estimated Balance Sheet | An Estimated Earnings Statement |
|---|---|

the final result of which is that you

KNOW YOUR BUSINESS

*Courtesy: Art Metal Construction Co., Jamestown, N.Y.*

and general outlook and to formulate broad policies regarding activities throughout the coming year.

2. The basis for the entire program, including sales and net income, or some other entity, is first drawn up by the executive in charge of the particular activity. It is then submitted for discussion and approval to the remaining top management members.

3. Each department head then prepares a budget for his own separate activity, guided by the data in the basic budget.

4. These budgets covering separate departments are submitted to the officer in charge of the budget. Generally, this is the controller or the budget officer.

5. A conference between the designated officer and each department head is then held for the purpose of thoroughly discussing and, when necessary, revising the respective individual department budget. Sometimes, a budget committee is used, in which case the budget officer transmits the estimates to the committee along with his recommendations.

6. After a tentative agreement on each individual budget has been reached, the master budget meeting is called. At this time, each individual budget is submitted and discussed. If necessary, adjustments are made, and final approval is obtained. This approval is generally contingent upon a final OK by the general manager or the president.

7. When finally determined, the budget is written up in its approved form, and copies are sent to all persons charged with carrying out a major portion of the plan. In like manner, copies covering specific parts of the master budget are distributed to lesser executives who are responsible for the execution of a particular portion of the plan.

## BUDGET AND MUTUALITY OF UNDERSTANDING

Essential to the preparation and use of a budget is mutual understanding about it by all affected by it. This is implied in the discussion on budget preparation, but some elaboration of this point is in order. To assist the budget preparer, pertinent information for his planning should be provided along with the request for the budget. Copies of budgets used along with the results obtained for the past five years should be supplied. This budget history on his own department's activities is a valuable aid. In addition, the supplying of any ratios among operating expenses developed after years of experience in a specialized business will prove helpful. Also, the general attitude toward the tentative departmental budget makers should be, "This is your budget and you will be held responsible for the performance you expect of yourself." Periodic reminders of this responsibility are recommended. It is likewise effective to stress budget preparation as basically a careful planning opportunity to achieve desired goals. This places budget preparation in a favorable light and evinces the best efforts by all concerned.

## THE BUDGET PERIOD

The data of a budget apply to a definite period of time. The length of this period varies, however, because of several important considerations, one of which is the ability to make reasonable forecasts covering conditions affecting the work. All comparisons are made with the forecast data. It therefore follows that for valid comparison, the budget should cover only a reasonable future period, usually one year or less.

Other considerations include the normal cycle for completion of the work, the fiscal period utilized, and the intended use of the budget. That is to say, the budget period selected should be long enough to include any seasonal or characteristic variations of "up and down" changes brought about by sales and production cycles. When fiscal income and expenditure are key considerations, the budget period should coincide with or fit into the time pattern already existing for other financial controls. And if the budget is to serve as a quarterly check, the time period should include a three-month period. If the purpose is a semiannual check, a six-month period will be used.

The most common period covered is one year, with breakdowns for quarterly and monthly periods. The year usually coincides with the calendar year, although if operations are on a fiscal basis, the fiscal year is used. Customarily, the forecasts are subjected to revision and addition, either monthly or quarterly, as new conditions become known.

## REVISION OF BUDGET

Generally, the forecast will be made during November and December for the following year. Then, the revising and adjusting can follow any of a number of plans.

Periodic budgeting is quite popular. Under it, major revisions are made three times a year—in March, June, and September—for the remaining months of the year. For example, in March, a reforecast for the period April through December is made. If needed, revisions can be made at other times of the year as well.

Another plan is *progressive budgeting*. This arrangement furnishes definite times for major revisions through the year, such revisions covering definite periods following the revision date. For example, assume that revision times are bimonthly or at the end of February, April, June, August, October, and December, and that the period covered is six months. At the end of February, revisions would be made for the following six-month period, March through August; at the end of April, revisions are made for the period May through October; and so on. Revisions made at times other than the definite dates usually apply to the current budget only.

Also, *moving budgeting* can be followed under which a forecast for 12 months is maintained by adding a month as each month is completed. To illustrate, at the completion of October, 1968, a forecast for October, 1969, is added; therefore, the 12-month forecast would cover November, 1968, through October, 1969. Revisions in the forecasts covering the intervening months are made when necessary.

## MAKING BUDGETING MORE EFFECTIVE

Several salient points merit mention before closing this chapter. The effectiveness of budgeting is enhanced by:

**1. Formulating Broad Boundaries.** In the initial budget broad boundaries are formulated from the top down, subsequently filling in needed data from the bottom up. The best budget is everybody's budget. If the budget resembles the form of an edict from top managers, it becomes a punitive club instead of an effective tool of management. The general goals and necessary broad constraints are set forth by top managers, who are in a position to visualize these needs. To supply the practical means for reaching these goals, middle and supervisory management members should be given the opportunity to participate in the formulation of the budgets that affect them. Suggestions from nonmanagement members should also be encouraged. In this way, interest, enthusiasm, and acceptance of the budget by all personnel are developed.

**2. Setting Specific Targets.** Budgeting exists to help accomplish specific goals within specific expenditures. Budgets are not simply official means to approve or disapprove specific expenditures only. It is erroneous for a manager simply to accept $x$ dollars to run his department, for such a viewpoint fails to include a specification of the assignment to be accomplished for these $x$ dollars. How much informational accomplishment is to be expected, i.e., how many checks processed, letters written, or inquires handled?

**3. Providing for Emergencies.** To help in meeting day-to-day problems easily, budgeting should include plans for what to do, if. . . . Actions commonly change from those anticipated. The work force is increased or decreased, training is altered, layouts rearranged, promotions reduced. Flexibility is vital in budgeting. The successful meeting of objectives usually requires application of reason and intuition at all levels. Unless adequate provision for emergencies is made, budgeting can be feared as an inviolable instrument that instills unsurmountable rigidities into the operations.

**4. Including Realistic Goals.** The best budgets reflect neither undue optimism nor pessimism. They do not call for better results than sound judgment indicates will be achieved. Likewise, they don't view the future as unduly difficult, with things getting worse and resulting in the inevitable need to cut costs regardless.

**5. Looking at Favorable As Well As Unfavorable Variances.** The natural tendency is to be most interested in unfavorable variances and to take proper action to correct them. However, it is frequently beneficial to review the favorable variances too. Some may cover activities that can be improved by application of technical advances, while others may be combined with other activities or even eliminated in view of current requirements.

## QUESTIONS

1. What significance do you attach to the fact that approximately 70 percent of total office costs constitutes wages and salaries?
2. In your opinion, can an office be managed effectively without a budget? Defend your answer.
3. Name the major approaches to office cost reduction, and discuss briefly the one you feel is most important.
4. Discuss the use of cost-value relationships in office controlling efforts.
5. State concisely the meaning and give an example of each of the following:
   a) Sunk cost.
   b) Cost control.
   c) Cost-consciousness by employees.
   d) Overhead cost.
6. Do you agree with the following statement: "All cost reduction efforts should be considered from the overall office viewpoint, otherwise a cost reduction in one department may result in a cost increase in another department." Why?
7. Discuss the subject, "Mutuality of Understanding in Budgets and Their Use."
8. Do you agree with the statement: "All budgets concern the office manager"? Explain your answer.
9. Miss A believes that if an item is in the budget, it is sufficient justification for spending that amount in order to utilize funds advantageously and keep them in balance. In contrast, Miss B claims that, whenever possible, savings on every budget item should be made in order to keep costs at a minimum. With whom do you agree? Give your reasons.
10. As an office manager, what basic arrangement for revising the budget would you follow? Why?
11. Which of the following can serve as objectives of an office manager?
    a) Costs.
    b) Reduction of costs.
    c) Budgets.
    d) Standard cost.
12. Discuss the consideration of providing for emergencies in efforts to make budgeting more effective.

## CASE PROBLEMS

### Case 22–1.  Nelsen-Higham Company

Mr. James X. Mueller, information manager, recently called his employees together to discuss the cost of the work performed by them. In all there were an assistant, 12 managers including 8 supervisors, and 93 nonmanagement members. He criticized no one and stated he believed the overall record for his division was good. He added that Mr. Kiefer (executive vice president) was worried about current cost expenditures by the company and wanted to bring them down. While Mr. Kiefer did not single out any portion of the total operation for cost reduction, he did mention that overhead cost seemed high. From the company viewpoint, expenditures by the information division are included under overhead cost. In Mr. Mueller's opinion, there must be excess cost in the current information activities. He asked the members of his division if they thought they could and if they would like to try to do better than their current efforts.

The group responded strongly in the affirmative. Their interest and comments greatly encouraged Mr. Mueller. Once again he believed he headed one of the best group of employees anywhere. Some pertinent suggestions were made by the group members and the meeting adjourned on a note of optimism. Several days later requests from several supervisors were received by Mr. Mueller for current cost data. They pointed out that it was difficult to tell if improvement was being made when they did not know what costs the company expected or what current expenditures were. Mr. Mueller carried the requests to the cost department where he encountered opposition to releasing cost information such as he requested. It was a strict company policy not to release cost information to unauthorized personnel.

Mr. Mueller saw little possibility in securing the cost data requested. He called a meeting for his supervisors, informed them about the cost information requests, and related his turndown. He said he had some thoughts on what to do now, but would withhold them until the supervisors had a chance to offer their ideas. From this meeting it was decided that the supervisors would estimate the cost wherever feasible. Although an approximation, it would serve the purpose for cost reduction efforts. Records dealing with past performance would be useful. Laborsaving approaches should be sought. Every office employee should be made to feel he is competing with himself to gain cost reduction.

Accordingly each supervisor began to keep records of cost and to accumulate information which he believed helpful in his cost controlling efforts. After several months, Mr. Mueller was greatly encouraged by the progress being made. From the reports of his supervisors at the weekly meetings, the following cost reductions expressed on an annual basis were achieved:

| Week | Cost Reduction |
|------|------|
| 1 | 4.5% |
| 2 | 3.5 |
| 3 | 3.0 |
| 4 | 3.0 |
| 5 | 2.5 |
| 6 | 1.5 |
| 7 | 3.0 |
| 8 | 1.0 |
| 9 | 1.0 |

Yesterday, at a management meeting called by Mr. Kiefer, the divisional heads were told that the company's profits had sharply declined during the past two months. To stem this trend, strong cost reduction measures would have to be instituted. The chief offender is overhead cost.

## Questions:

1. Appraise the approach used by Mr. Mueller to reduce costs of the information operations.
2. Interpret the results of the cost reduction reported by the supervisors.
3. What action now do you recommend by Mr. Kiefer? By Mr. Mueller?

### Case 22–2.    Computermation, Inc.

Having successfully offered one-, three-, and five-day seminars for office work, the managers of Computermation, Inc. now contemplate a two-week or ten-day session program. They would like a minimum of 50 paid registrants and are mailing 3,000 announcements at a cost of 15¢ each for the mailing and $400 for preparing and printing these announcements. Each registrant will receive seminar materials estimated to cost the institute $36.50 per enrollee. Meetings will be held at the conveniently located Thunderbolt Hotel, which charges $35 a day for a conference room having a capacity of 92. The group will be served lunch each conference day in a special catering room of the hotel, for which a charge of $3 per person, including tips, is made. Also, hot beverages will be supplied at midmorning and again at midafternoon in the rear of the conference room. For this service, a charge of $1 per day per enrollee will be made. A total of 14 instructors will be used to cover the various subjects; but only two different instructors for any one day will be scheduled, each handling the group for half a day. Compensation for an instructor for half a day is $100 plus his lunch regardless of whether he instructs in the morning or in the afternoon.

As a policy, the institute invites ten prominent management members in office automation to attend the seminar free of charge. They are extended all the benefits of a regular fee-paying attendee. It intends to follow this same policy with the proposed larger session. Based on past experience, about one half of the invited guests attend. The institute requires a minimum margin of approximately 25 percent of the total income from a seminar. That is, if the total income was $1,000, the institute strives to keep expenses at no more than $750. Registrations from mailings for other seminars have ranged from 1.9 percent to 5.1 percent of the total number of mailings sent out. However, the managers of the institute are at a loss to know whether these response ranges are valid for a seminar such as they are now planning.

## Questions:

1. Discuss the major problem facing the institute.
2. Calculate the approximate registration fee that the institute should charge for the office automation seminar.
3. What plan of action do you feel the institute should follow? Why?

# chapter 23

# Office manuals and audits

Habit is either the best of servants or the worst of masters.

—*Nathaniel Emmons*

To ASSIST controlling efforts it is desirable that general information, instructions, and regulations be put into writing. Part of successful controlling lies in informing employees what is expected of them, when, and how. This requirement is assisted greatly by the use of complete and up-to-date office manuals. An employee fully informed can aid significantly in the controlling efforts. But management must spell out the requirements and make them known to all concerned.

By means of manuals, authorized information dealing with the policies and practices of the enterprise; recommended systems, procedures, methods, and standards to be followed; and the regulations regarding employment can be given in a simple, direct, and uniform manner. We can define office manual as follows: *An office manual is a written record of information and instructions which concern and can be used to guide the employee's efforts in an enterprise.* Actually, it is a guidebook—a source for data believed essential for the highest performance of the job.

## EVALUATION OF MANUALS

Essentially, an office manual is a device to assist in the orientation of employees. It can help to make instructions definite, to provide quick settlements of misunderstandings, to show each employee how his job fits into the total organization, and to point out how he can contribute to the achievements of office objectives as well as to maintain good relationships with other employees. Employee performance is boosted by having this information at the employees' fingertips. On the other hand, manuals aid management members significantly. Manuals relieve management members of having to repeat similar information, explanations, or instructions. They not only force decisions on policies and procedures—thoughts about them must be put into writing—but they also provide constancy to them. Employees come and go, but the manual stays. The training of newcomers is enhanced because the manual gives them the information they need in a readily available form. But manuals also serve as effective refreshers for employees who have been on the payroll for some time. Both the delega-

FIGURE 23–1. Basic Requirements for Success of Office Manuals.

1. Center authority and responsibility for the manual program.
2. Write to the level of the employee who will use the manual.
3. Maintain a distribution list—distribute only those manuals that are needed in each case.
4. Use color to emphasize identity of binder or printing matter.
5. Keep manual simple in arrangement of material and in language used.
6. Adopt adequate indexing and cross-referencing.
7. Use numerous visual aids—charts, illustrations, and cartoons.
8. Keep manuals up to date.
9. Highlight changes and revisions.
10. Audit the material periodically.

tion of authority and management by exception are promoted by the use of manuals.[1] Furthermore, manuals assist in reducing gaps, obsolete activities, and needless office work duplication.

In contrast, there are some managers who do not advocate the use of manuals for any of a number of reasons. Among the more common criticisms are that manuals "cost too much," "are too much work," "stifle initiative," or "won't work in our case." In some cases, these objections are no doubt justifiable; but for many enterprises, the use of manuals appears to be beneficial. The great majority of nonusers of manuals are small companies where informal communication and mode of operations are considered sufficient.

Figure 23–1 lists the basic requirements for success of office manuals. More will be included about these requirements throughout the pages of this chapter.

---

[1] Delegation of authority is discussed in chapter 26; management by exception in chapter 3.

## TYPES OF OFFICE MANUALS

Different offices have need for different manuals. The type is determined by answering the question: "What is the purpose to be served?" In some instances, a single purpose only is served; while in others, several purposes are to be fulfilled. The number and the kind of purposes are determined by the individual circumstances.

Manuals can be written to cover a variety of subjects, including policies, organizational structure of the enterprise, employment, indoctrination, supervision, job instruction, standard work practices, computer data processing, history of the enterprise, and specialized or departmental practices such as in the accounting, corresponding, filing, engineering, purchasing, or sales department. However, for convenience, the major types of manuals, along with their respective purposes, can be set forth as follows:

| *Type of Manual* | *Purpose* |
| --- | --- |
| Manual of policies | To state the policies of the enterprise or office. |
| Manual of operations, or standard practices manual, or job instruction manual | To inform employees of established methods, procedures, and standards. |
| Manual of office rules and regulations, or handbook on employment | To give concise information on benefits, operating rules, and employment regulations. |
| Historical manual | To provide historical information about the enterprise. |
| Multiple-purpose manual | To supply selected items from any area or subject deemed desirable and helpful in the work performance. |

## MANUAL OF POLICIES

A policy is a basic guide to action. It prescribes the overall boundaries within which activities are to take place and hence reveals broad managerial intentions or forecasts broad courses of managerial action likely to take place under certain conditions. To illustrate, promoting employees solely on the basis of merit is a policy. It states the guide for promoting, but it does not tell who will be promoted. Likewise, the payment of salaries above the prevailing amounts in the community for similar work, consistent with the economic well-being of the enterprise, is another example of a policy. Knowing the policies of an enterprise provides the main framework around which all actions are based. Policies furnish the background for an understanding of why things are done as they are.

A manual of policies puts into writing the policies of an enterprise. It has been said that a policy does not really exist unless it is in writing. To decide each case on its individual merits and to convey this decision verbally is not in keeping with modern management thinking. Proponents of a manual of policies cite these advantages: (1) Written policies require managers to think through their courses of action and to predetermine what actions will be taken under various circumstances; (2) a general program of action for many matters is provided, and only the unusual or exceptional matter requires the attention of the top managers; (3) a framework is provided within which the manager can operate freely; and (4) written policies help to insure equitable treatment to all employees.

On the other hand, there are those who object to having a manual of policies. Among the important points they mention are the following: (1) Policies are extremely difficult to write accurately and completely—the interpretation of words and phrases sometimes leads to serious misunderstandings; (2) written policies make it difficult to keep policies flexible, as is frequently required by changing conditions; and (3) knowledge of policies should be confined to those persons charged with their execution —the top executive, department heads, or supervisors, as the case might be.

## MANUAL OF OPERATIONS

A manual of operations can serve as a convenient source for information on how the work is to be done. The authorized steps can be listed; and supplementary information, in the form of diagrams, sketches, and charts, can be included in order to clarify the data. The standards and guides to be followed are usually included.

The contents of this type of manual can be directed in one of several directions. First, it can emphasize the performance of *individual tasks and jobs*. Illustrative is the manual which explains how to operate and use an adding machine. The importance of keeping accurate records can be emphasized and information included describing the parts and operations of an adding machine, practice lessons, and an explanation of the practices of the company. A glossary of terms is sometimes included to clarify the work. Figure 23-2 shows a portion of a page from a correspondence manual which includes assistance in how to write effective letters.

Second, the manual can be directed toward *departmental practices*. Manuals of this type contain a statement of the duties of the department. Its divisions are defined, the supervisors listed, and their responsibilities indicated, along with outlines and procedures for operating. The work of departments, such as sales, purchasing, storing and retrieving, accounting, and research is often set up and described in departmental manuals. An example of this type is shown in Figure 23-3.

The third area to which a manual of operations may be directed is *general practices in a special field*. This type of manual is becoming more popular, for it furnishes valuable general information which is usable in

FIGURE 23–2. Portion of a Correspondence Manual.

---

SEC. XI: WORDS, SENTENCES, AND PARAGRAPHING
The choice of the right word is a challenge to the effective writer. Put yourself in the place of the reader and visualize how best he will understand what you are trying to tell him. Develop an adequate vocabulary because choice of words is a matter of having a choice from available word material. Also, be willing to seek the right word and take the effort to do so.
All other things being equal, short words are preferred because they form a letter which is more easily comprehended and can be read quickly. Long words slow the reading and give rise to misunderstanding.
Strive for short sentences mixed with long sentences. Do not use a series of short sentences as they give an appearance of brusqueness. Let the subject and the verb be well identified. Avoid involved or complex sentences.

---

special lines of work. Its adoption is mainly in large offices, although in certain instances the small office can benefit from manuals of this type. Systems and procedures manuals and those for computer data processing are illustrative. Each of these very considerably in makeup. However, a somewhat typical page from a systems and procedures manual will give the number, title, and subtitle of the system or procedure, the organization units affected, a general statement of the system or procedure in one

FIGURE 23–3. Portion of a Storing and Retrieving Manual.

---

GENERAL INSTRUCTIONS
1. Accuracy is the prime essential in storing and retrieving work; make it your foremost consideration. Speed is important, but it comes after accuracy.
2. Guard against these common mistakes:
    *a*) Drawers and folders too full.
    *b*) Papers improperly indexed.
    *c*) Material in miscellaneous folder not filed alphabetically.
    *d*) Charge-out system not used.
3. When filing, always pull the folders part way out of the drawer in order to avoid placing papers between folders.
4. All materials are to be stored within the day following its receipt.
5. Most stored material is confidential. Therefore do not discuss the contents of any file with fellow employees or outsiders and never give a stored file to a person whose duties have no relation to the material requested. In case of doubt, see your supervisor.
6. The number of papers taken from the sorter to be worked on at one time should be equal to the quantity you can handle within about 15 minutes of your filing effort.
7. Acquaint yourself with office details other than those in the storing and retrieving department when such knowledge will assist understanding of how materials should be stored.
8. Suggestions for improvement are always welcome. Talk with your supervisor who will authorize the change if your suggested method is simpler and more efficient.

---

paragraph, an outline of the material classified by major headings, with important actions numbered and listed under each heading. Concluding are original issue date, revision date, and signature of authorizing manager.

## MANUAL OF OFFICE RULES AND REGULATIONS

Manuals are an excellent medium in which to explain employee benefit plans, including such things as group insurance, hospitalization, and

FIGURE 23–4. Page of a Manual Used by a Large National Distributor of General Merchandise.

---

GENERAL OFFICE ROUTINES

*Desks*—Keep your desk clean. It's a workbench, not a catchall. Never allow a lot of old-fashioned relics to accumulate on it. File everything away in its natural place, and dispose of obsolete matter. (The job of filing is an important one and is not to be neglected or allowed to pile up.)

Avoid having decorations on the desk that might tip and spill, such as flower containers, ink bottles, sponge cups, etc. Keep such things in safer places.

Clear all desks and tables before leaving the building. Any papers or letters of a confidential nature must be put away, never left on the desk top. All lights are to be turned off, fans and ventilators disconnected, and blinds raised. Typewriters should be covered when not being used.

*Dusting*—Each office is to be thoroughly dusted each morning—during the day too if necessary. No one need resent dusting—it's part of the job.

Pens should be filled, pencils sharpened, and water bottles filled first thing in the morning. See to it that ash trays are kept clean throughout the day. If blotters are used, make sure soiled ones are replaced.

Typewriters should be dusted morning and night, type cleaner applied weekly.

*Supplies*—If you are responsible for handling supplies for the office, check them regularly and make sure that you are not running low. Keep a list at your desk of supplies that will soon need to be requisitioned (use form 527 for ordering). All requisitions must be authorized by the department head.

*Hours*—Arrange hours if possible so the office will not be unattended at any time. If it is impossible for someone to be present during lunch hour, do not leave without making arrangements with someone else to take any important calls.

*Callers*—It is much better to have an understanding with your superior regarding his wishes in the matter of announcing callers, the persons he wishes to see and those he does not, rather than to guess at the proper procedure in each instance.

Keep an accurate, up-to-date list or notebook of telephone numbers and addresses, business as well as personal. Such a list should be readily accessible. Add to it regularly so it will be of value both to you and your superior.

---

*Courtesy: Butler Brothers, Chicago*
*Reproduced here by special permission.*

savings facilities. Questions regarding the use of the company library, cafeteria, and recreation club can also be answered. In addition, the prescribed guides for conduct are included and cover such items as sick allowances, the use of rest periods, conduct regarding smoking, solicitation for money in the office, the sale of tickets, hours of employment, holidays, vacations, office etiquette, rest periods, telephone usage, and recreational provisions. As already stated, a manual of this type is identified either as a manual of office rules and regulations or as a handbook on employment. However, for psychological reasons, the manual may be given a title like "You and the XYZ Company" or "Getting Along at XYZ." Such a manual helps to orientate and to inform the employee by giving him specific answers to all the elements of his work surroundings, thus promoting understanding and harmonious relationships. Figure 23–4 shows a sample of the type of information included in this kind of manual.

## HISTORICAL MANUAL

Many employers feel that it is important to give employees information regarding the history of the company—its beginning, growth, accomplishments, present management, and current status. This gives the employee an insight into the tradition and thinking behind the enterprise with which he is associated. It probably makes for better understanding, increases morale, and helps the employee to feel that he "belongs"—that he is a part of the company. Giving an employee a picture of the whole helps him to fit himself into the total picture. Manuals, of course, are excellent means for conveying this type of information to employees. The story of the enterprise usually can be told on several pages; and quite frequently, it can be a part of a message written by a major officer. Historical information is commonly included as the introductory portion to a manual of office rules and regulations.

## MULTIPLE-PURPOSE MANUAL

This type of manual represents a combination of any two or all of the types that have been discussed. The company's needs, the size of the enterprise, and the philosophy of the top managers usually determine the makeup. The outline of a multiple-purpose manual might include the following:

1. Title.
2. Foreword.
3. Table of Contents.
4. Company History.

5. General Policies of Company.
6. Organization.
7. Company Departments—Functions, Authorities, and Responsibilities.
8. Office Regulations.
9. Office Supplies and Maintenance.
10. Personnel Points—Hiring, Promoting, Terminating, Sick Leave, Employee Benefits, and Social Activities.
11. Miscellaneous.
12. Index.

## SOURCES FOR MANUAL MATERIAL

Probably one of the best sources of material for a manual is manuals used by other enterprises. Looking over what has been included in manuals of another company suggests what topics might be covered. However, the manual should be personalized to meet the particular needs of an enterprise.

Additional data can be secured from a number of other sources. Such data might include (1) minutes of board of directors' meetings, (2) reports of executive conferences, (3) speeches and published articles of executives, (4) bulletins and company circulars, (5) agreements with employees and contracts with unions, (6) grievance records, (7) company magazines or similar publications, and (8) interviews with executives, especially the personnel manager, training director, and supervisors.

Experience shows that, with time, it will be desirable to eliminate certain material and to add other material. The additional material might be secured from the sources mentioned or, because of the unique nature of the information, may be secured from a special source. For example, instructions in the correct use of a new office machine would probably be secured from the manufacturer or seller.

## PREPARATION OF MANUALS

Some orderly process must be followed in the preparation of manuals if they are to be inclusive and to be completed within a reasonable period of time. The process followed depends a great deal upon the individual in charge of this work. In general, however, it will be helpful to follow a procedure along these lines:

1. Announce to all members of the enterprise that a manual is to be prepared. Solicit their suggestions and ideas as to what should be included. Appointing a committee of employees often encourages their participation in the preparation of the manual. As a result, better understanding and greater acceptance and use are usually gained. Special

attention should be directed to supervisors, for they are usually rich sources of excellent material.

2. Draw up a list of all the subjects to be covered by the manual. The purpose of the manual, the cost, and managerial judgment will determine, for the most part, what items are included. Proper subheadings should be made under each main topic, and the list should be arranged according to the contemplated main divisions or sections of the manual. A big time-saver in this respect is to use a separate card for each topic and file behind guides. By this means, material can be classified quickly and the list or outline changed with a minimum of effort.

A logical arrangement of the material is most commonly used, but this sequence is not necessarily the most effective in all cases. Consideration should be given to placing the vital information or that which is most interesting in the beginning, using the last portion of the list for data of less importance.

3. Write the information under each subject. It is advisable to use headings—major and minor—so that the material is well organized and the reader can follow it easily. Check the source data to help insure accuracy in all writing. Source material can be numbered and indexed, and this means of identification tied in with the writing by means of marginal notes. Keep the prospective reader in mind—write so he will want to read the manual and understand what it is intended to mean. A simple, friendly, and sincere style is best. Short words and sentences should be employed. Narrative style is common, but the playscript format is very effective.[2] Include charts, cartoons, diagrams, and examples of proper forms, letters, and reports in order to gain greater clarity. These illustrations should be in an inexpensive, rough form until it is decided whether they will be included in the final manual. All material should be presented in the "normal flow of work" sequence. The amount of detail depends upon the importance of the subject.

4. Prepare a limited number of copies for key executives, supervisors, employee or union representatives, and several key employees. Have them read the manual and submit criticisms and suggestions. Quite often, better ways of expression are found in this way. Sometimes, subjects can be combined, major items previously overlooked can be added, minor points strengthened, and the entire manual improved.

5. Revise the manual and give it to top management members for approval. Corrections and suggestions from the previous step are incorporated. It is well to include a separate statement to the effect that the entire contents are in agreement with the philosophy of top management members and are acceptable to the employees.

6. Send the approved manuscript to the printer or the party doing the

---

[2] Playscript is discussed in chapter 6, p. 126.

actual mechanical production work. The manual can be published by any of several different processes, including xerography, mimeograph, offset printing, or letterpress.[3] The quantity, appearance, and cost will probably determine the process used. Details regarding size, paper, and type of binding must also be decided. Generally, it is well to seek competent advice in these matters.

The size $6\frac{1}{4}$ x $4\frac{1}{2}$ inches is excellent for a booklet intended for carrying in the pocket. If the manual is to be used as a reference book on a desk, an 11 x $8\frac{1}{2}$-inch size is very satisfactory. Other popular sizes

FIGURE 23–5. Helpful Suggestions for Preparation of Manuals.

---

PAGE SIZE—

If printed, the 6 × 9-inch page size is effective. This is the typical book size.
If typed, the $8\frac{1}{2}$ × 11-inch page size will be preferred by most employees.

ARRANGEMENT OF MATERIAL—

Place sections most frequently used at front of manual.
Related sections should be placed close together and interrelated by cross-references.
Set sections apart by stiff divider page of different-colored paper.
Either tab sections for ready reference, or use a divider of page size to facilitate a margin index.

REMEMBER TO—

Make the cover attractive by using a clear, brief title and well-selected artwork.
Include a table of contents and an index so that the reader can quickly find what he is looking for.

---

include $9\frac{1}{8}$ x 6 inches, $8\frac{1}{2}$ x $5\frac{1}{2}$ inches, and $5\frac{1}{8}$ x $3\frac{3}{4}$ inches. Pages of these sizes can be cut, with minimum waste, from sheet sizes usually carried by the printer.[4]

The number and size of the pages in the booklet generally determine the weight of paper used. When the number of pages does not exceed about 24, a thick paper can be used; but where a greater number of pages is involved, a thinner stock is used, to eliminate unnecessary bulk. For page sizes under about $8\frac{1}{2}$ x $5\frac{1}{2}$ inches, a paper of about 60 pounds is used. When the size is greater, paper of about 70 pounds is employed.

---

[3] See chapter 15 for discussion of copying processes.

[4] In the case of loose-leaf and many bound manuals, it is customary to give the dimension of the binding side first. Thus, an 11 x 8-inch size means the binding is on an 11-inch side. The dimensions used in this discussion follow this practice. In contrast, and at times somewhat confusingly, in specifying dimensions of index cards, the horizontal dimension is named first, followed by the vertical dimension. For example, an 8 x 5 card means 8 inches horizontally and 5 inches vertically.

Headings stand out on the page by the use of white space around them, or color may be employed. Color increases the cost; but in many cases, the effect brought about by such things as a colored border, headline, or illustration justifies the additional expense. For additional suggestions see Figure 23–5.

The type of binding may be either side or saddle wire stitching, screw post, prong fasteners, ring binder, and wire or plastic edge binding. The choice will depend primarily upon usage, amount of material, appearance, and cost.[5]

## DISTRIBUTION OF MANUALS

It is paramount in the distribution of the manuals to provide a copy to everyone concerned with and in need of the information the manual contains. The extent of distribution depends upon the size of the enterprise; in most cases, one copy of the manual should be available for ready reference in at least each department or division. In cases where manuals pertain to specific jobs, copies should be readily available to every employee on such jobs.

To increase the readership of the manual, it is sometimes given to the employee only during an interview. His attention is directed to specific pages, and he is encouraged to read the entire booklet. In some cases, depending upon the type of manual, it is mailed to the employee's home with an accompanying letter. Forewarning that the manual is to be used as the subject for a forthcoming meeting or group discussion is a very effective means of encouraging readership. In addition, sometimes the employee is requested to sign and to return an enclosed card in the manual as evidence of reading the complete booklet; and in other instances, questions are asked on the card to measure the employee's understanding of the manual contents.

## MANUAL MAINTENANCE

The problem of keeping the manual up to date is ever present. In most enterprises, changes are taking place constantly, owing to new work being added or improvements in current work being made. Revisions of and additions to manuals are constantly in process. New pages must replace the old and be distributed to all holders of the manuals. These changes may be covered either by single sheets or by entire supplements. Frequently, amendments are written on colored paper to attract attention to the change. Also, notations made in red ink in the manual will point out those parts which have been changed, omitted, or amended. When

[5] See chapter 15, p. 379, for detailed discussion of this subject.

many changes cause the manual to be difficult to read and use, it should be rewritten.

All changes in manuals should be cleared through a central control unit so that proper authorization and conformity in results are obtained. If this is not done, needless confusion and misunderstanding will result. The revised sheets should follow the established form of the manual. New material will probably be added every three to six months, together with certain modifications in the old material. Limited research shows that nearly 90 percent of all managers prefer a three-ring binder, which facilitates the insertion of revised sheets.

An old saying is that the three R's of manuals are easy reading, reference, and revision. Much emphasis is placed upon the last R—revision. To aid manual maintenance an excellent practice is to find out what users of the manual think of it. For example, do they believe it is:

1. Readable—effective writing style, good format, and easy-to-read print?

2. Illustrated—where needed, and in sufficient detail?

3. Practical—titled properly, directions clearly given, adequate coverage of material and effectively indexed?

4. Modern—attractive appearance, and up to date in content?

## AUDIT OF OFFICE OPERATIONS

Increasing in importance is the use of the audit to improve office operations. For our purpose, the audit will be viewed as a fairly exhaustive review and evaluation of information management using selected attributes as guides. It includes a sort of stock taking of all phases of the office's operations including an examination of systems, procedures, forms, correspondence, physical facilities, quality, service, and the like. While it is neither controlling in the concept adopted here nor does it follow the control process, the office audit is closely related to controlling and can be discussed here.

The idea of an audit is not new. It has been the practice of most enterprises to review and evaluate their financial accounts at least annually to be certain of their accuracy and to reveal any weaknesses in controls that may require correcting. "Auditing the books" and a periodic inventory of physical assets are accepted business practices. This sort of stock taking is followed for office operations.

The office audit normally should follow two stages. First is the broad, general survey which seeks to ferret out the major difficulties of current information management. While not exhaustive, it supplies a reasonable review of the information work as it is currently performed. The second stage is a detailed problem-solving study of each area requiring attention as shown by results of the first stage. For example, it may include an analysis and study of the office layout, of the forms being used, or ways to improve the systems now followed.

Audits necessitate the collecting of facts from a variety of sources. To illustrate, production records, work schedules, office organization charts, letters, and office personnel records may be assembled and studied in an audit project. In addition, key personnel at all levels, both supervisors and clerks, may be interviewed to verify information derived from written records. Also, their opinions and suggestions are obtained for possible improvements and changes. Hence, the value of an office audit is not only in ascertaining whether the work and service are being accomplished as desired, but also to access the adequacy and effectiveness of the work performed and to obtain recommended remedial suggestions where applicable.

Those performing the audit must decide what data they want along with why such information is wanted. For example, the decision to review work measurement reports may be made so that both the work flow and the approximate work loads involved in various duties may be evaluated. Also, personal observations of the work being performed may be followed in order to obtain first-hand impressions of the adequacy of the machine, desk, files, as well as the work travel, and work station arrangements. Information may also be obtained on the responsibility and authority of selected employees in particular work groups to ascertain if possible reassignment of duties or reorganization of work groups is advisable, to confirm that no duties overlap or are ignored, and to determine the real need and purpose for many duties.

## BASIC AREAS FOR OFFICE AUDIT

Usually, it helps to have a guide of problems to investigate so that audit efforts are concentrated in most productive endeavors and no important area is ignored. For each area, a number of questions are formulated, thus probing into a number of possibilities leading to either approval of present activities or recommendations for subsequent improvement. Among the common areas for an office audit are: forms, systems, procedures, machines, office space, scheduling and work flow, quality control, office organization, supervision, and office employee development. Not all of these are applicable for every office audit. The selection will depend upon the importance of each area in the individual case as judged by the auditor.

We will select three areas—forms, procedures, and scheduling and work flow—to show the type of audit questions that can be asked under each. Figure 23–6 shows this information.

Good auditing requires time. The work cannot be rushed as normally much reflective thinking is required to perform the work satisfactorily.

But within a reasonable period, a report on the findings from the audit should be made. It may well be that the report will include recommendation for further study and intensive investigative work in selected areas. Decisions on any follow-up are made by top managers. The office audit report, however, should be submitted without unnecessary delay so that benefits from it can be enjoyed and its status maintained in the normal conduct of the company's affairs.

FIGURE 23–6

---

ILLUSTRATIONS OF THE TYPE OF QUESTIONS TO ASK UNDER MAJOR AREAS OF INVESTIGATION IN AN OFFICE AUDIT.

Under forms, pertinent questions include:
1. Are similar forms completed elsewhere?
2. Is a definite need served by each present form?
3. Is the information requested on the forms purposeful?
4. Is the information arranged in best sequential order?

For procedures, these questions can be asked:
1. Is the procedure being used by the operating personnel?
2. Is it in written form? Should it be?
3. Is the procedure up to date?
4. Can any part, or all, of the procedure be eliminated?
5. Would elimination cause other work to be added, change policies, or involve organizational change?
6. What effect does present procedures have on employee relations? Customer relations?

For scheduling and work flow, ask these questions:
1. If peak load periods, what causes them? Can work be shifted to level them off?
2. Is work processed immediately upon receipt? Is this desirable?
3. Are there numerous rush jobs? If yes, why?
4. Are certain types of work deferred in processing?
5. Are machines and manpower capacities sufficient for work loads?

---

## QUESTIONS

1. List and briefly comment on six basic requirements for success of office manuals.
2. Is an office manual of greater importance in a large or in a small office? Justify your answer.
3. What are some common purposes for which an office manual can be used?
4. Distinguish carefully between the elements in each of the following pairs:
   *a*) Controlling and auditing.
   *b*) Historical manual and manual of policies.
   *c*) An 11 x 8½-inch manual and an 8½ x 11-inch manual.
   *d*) Managerial controlling and manuals.
5. Discuss some important considerations pertaining to the distribution of office manuals.

6. Name and evaluate the important sources of material for manuals.
7. For each of the following, indicate in what type of office manual you would expect to find the information:

   *a*) Practices to be followed in computer data processing.

   *b*) Conditions under which books from the company library can be borrowed and taken home.

   *c*) The philosophy and working principles followed by Jonathan Rosewell Heinmann, founder of Heinmann and Hertz, Inc.

   *d*) General office routines to be followed by all office employees.

8. It has been suggested that a manual be written that would be adaptable for use by all offices. Spaces for individualized "fill-ins" would be provided. Do you believe such a manual is feasible? Explain.

9. Enumerate and discuss briefly the major steps in the preparation of a manual.

10. Discuss the use of basic areas for conducting an office audit.

11. Discuss the subject of manual maintenance.

12. What are the two stages of office auditing and for what purposes are each conducted?

## CASE PROBLEMS

### Case 23–1. Yardis Manufacturing Company

Complaints were increasing about the company's handling of telephone calls. Most were from employees, but a number were from vendors and customers stating they could not reach their party after several attempts. Edward Wasson, the office manager, talked with the company's chief switchboard operator about the complaints.

WASSON: Here are some of the more serious complaints:

*a*) I always have trouble in reaching our production control department in auxiliary plant No. 2.

*b*) Why is purchasing's telephone always busy? I now walk to the department with the message. It takes less time.

*c*) There are entirely too many personal calls by employees in my unit. I have tried to curtail them, but since I'm not at my desk all the time it poses a problem. The switchboard people should check and not accept these personal calls.

CHIEF OPERATOR: That's really his job, don't you think? For us to police all outgoing calls is asking too much, don't you agree?

WASSON: Well, maybe so. Here's another.

CHIEF OPERATOR: No one has complained to me. Why have they gone to you with these troubles?

WASSON: I suppose they feel I am the one to handle them. Listen to this

*d*) Your sales department surely makes a fellow wait. I held on for fully ten minutes last week and then was told, 'The record on that appears to be misplaced. I'll call you when I locate it.' At the end of two or three minutes he should have told me that he would call me when he located it.

*e*) Many use long distance to reach me but find that I must call back later. When the return call is made to your office, I seldom reach your man. Later, he tells me he was in his office all the time waiting for the return call. What goes?

CHIEF OPERATOR: Well, that's because he places the call then doesn't notify us of his whereabouts. The call is returned and he isn't in his office and can't be located. Nobody knows where he is. Also, let me add that some of our people place a long-distance call and then hang up before the operator on the board can find out who is placing the call and if he is an authorized person. This takes time and it also means extra time spent in calling back and getting the needed information. I also know that some dial the wrong prefix number for outside calls and they commit the same error for inside calls. If I have explained it once, I've explained it a thousand times. But they don't seem to remember. Then too, we have a number of new people in the office.

WASSON: Yes, that's right.

CHIEF OPERATOR: Complete information, and I mean complete, is in the company manual. Either they don't read it or they don't pay any attention to what they read in it. If you'd enforce what is already in there, the telephone complaints would vanish.

WASSON: Do you tell that to an employee when he is having trouble using the telephone?

CHIEF OPERATOR: No, I do not believe it is my job to do so.

## Questions:

1. Is proper usage of the telephone an appropriate subject to be included in a company manual? Justify your views.
2. What major factors do you believe led to the telephone situation now faced by the company?
3. What action do you recommend be taken by Mr. Wasson? Why?

### Case 23–2.  Van Debur Corporation

After three days on her new job with Van Debur Corporation, Marilyn Veit, a private secretary for the treasurer of the corporation, had an interview with her superior. She expressed the opinion that the morale of the office employees seemed low, especially of those in the correspondence section. She believed it would help to prepare a manual for them which, among other things, would give information about the corporation's history and the importance of its products as well as definite aids in typing letters and sundry tasks of employees in the section. The treasurer listened attentively to the suggestions, congratulated Marilyn, and authorized her to get together her ideas and some samples of what the proposed manual would be like. He informed the office manager of his decision. The office manager reports to the treasurer.

Marilyn talked with the supervisor of the correspondence section, who offered to assist in every way possible. However, she told Marilyn that a manual would not improve morale. What the employees want is more money, but the corporation will not give it to them. She explained the work to Marilyn and gave her samples of work requested. When Marilyn suggested talking to one or two selected employees of the department, the supervisor countered that this was not advisable, so Marilyn dropped the request. Later, in talking with the treasurer, Marilyn learned that none of the office departments had a manual, that any conversation with office employees should be cleared with their supervisors, and that the corporation very infrequently changed systems in use, the tendency being to stay with established conditions and practices of conducting the work.

## Questions:

1. Enumerate the types of information you suggest be included in the proposed manual.
2. Do you believe the proposed manual is appropriate and will be helpful? Discuss.
3. What action do you suggest Marilyn Veit take? Why?

# PART VII

# ORGANIZING

Organizing is the subject of our next part. From the formal viewpoint, this includes apportioning the office work to be done, assigning the various parcels of work to specific members of the work group, and establishing the proper work relationships among them. Informally, employees find ways to cooperate or not and become active in groups arising from their working together.

Effective organizing is essential in managing an office. Five chapters are devoted to office organizing. They are "Organizing the information efforts," "Determining the formal office organization," "Authority and organizational relationships," "Informal organization and the office," and "Dynamics of office organizing."

# chapter 24

# Organizing the information efforts

> Let men decide firmly what they will not do, and
> they will be free to do vigorously what they ought
> to do.
>
> —*Mencius*

ORGANIZING is a fundamental function of management and it becomes a
necessity when two or more people work together. Decisions must be
made regarding who does what information work, who reports to whom,
what members are in a certain work group, and who decides what types of
issues. Organizing deals with these basic questions.

Answers to these questions provide an organizational framework
within which talented individuals can contribute to the common goal of
both their enterprise and themselves. The framework or structure utilized should assist and promote the collective efforts, but in the final
analysis it is people, and only people, who determine the success or failure
of organizing efforts.

Organizing makes possible the effective operation of a group. Organization is the basis for necessary teamwork among the various members of a
common enterprise and helps blend together their efforts. In essence, the
value of each individual's contribution is enhanced and, at the same time,
the accomplishments of the group are increased. Every member, management and nonmanagement, knows how he and his work fit into the total
picture, what he is to do, when and where he is to do it, and who, if
anyone, helps him. Also, organization reveals logical personnel advancements and the normal sequence of promotions.

## MAKEUP OF ORGANIZING

From the rational viewpoint, organizing is concerned with (1) *work—* how to distribute it among employees, (2) *employees—*who is going to do what work, (3) *relationships—*what is the relative authority and responsibility among the "organizational units" formed by work and employees, and (4) *work environment—*what tools and workplaces will best contribute toward maximum work accomplishments and employees' satisfactions. As already implied, organizing results in an organization structure about which these components are interrelated and centered in order to achieve orderly and desired actions. Stated formally: *Organizing is the allocating of the total work to be done among employees, establishing the relative authority and responsibility of each individual who is placed in charge of each work component, and supplying the proper work environment.*

## OBJECTIVES AND ORGANIZING

Organizing, like the other fundamental functions of management, is influenced and guided by the objective being sought. Organizing is, or should be, performed to achieve a definite objective, and this goal determines the type of work performed, the people selected to do it, and the formal relationships established among them.

To evaluate competently the results of organizing efforts requires relating these to the particular objective for which the organization structure is designed. The question "For what objective is the group organized?" is a cardinal consideration in organizational efforts. The paper work required in one enterprise may differ from that in another enterprise. The centers for paper work processing are not identical in all organizations. Top managers' ideas of what information work should be performed by what departments differ among enterprises. Some companies are local, others national, and still others international in scope. Also, some have only one line of related products, while others have multiple lines of products. These considerations help shape the objective and, in turn, are utilized to mold the organization.

## BENEFITS OF EFFECTIVE ORGANIZING

It will be helpful to point out the major benefits of effective organizing at the beginning of our discussion. Organizing enables a manager to enlarge his scope or influence; with organizing he can accomplish much more than is humanly possible working alone. Activities are placed into manageable units the work for which can be planned effectively, expanded or contracted as required, and adequately controlled. Further, misunderstandings among management members concerning coverage of their respective authority are clarified. Organizing spells out the relative authority for each manager. Areas in which decisions and their enforcement are authorized are clearly established; they are not left to chance.

Organizing provides a satisfactory climate for achieving a satisfied work force. It avoids needless duplication of effort. Formal communication is expedited. Organization gets individuals to work effectively as members of a team, not separately as single individuals. This unity of effort is carried to a degree that permits some leeway and freedom of action to the employee in the decision making regarding his particular efforts and his work. Confusion and misunderstanding as to who is to do what work is avoided as is also "buck-passing," an excessive number of managers and nonmanagers, and misinformed members of the group. Further, effective organizing provides a basis for evaluating performance and capabilities of employees inasmuch as specific work is assigned and the accountability for its performance is known.

## RELATION OF OFFICE TO ORGANIZATION OF ENTERPRISE

It is helpful first to consider office organization in relation to the organization of the entire enterprise of which the office is an important part. It is common to think that in the typical organization, the major activities to be performed are production, sales, and finance. Each must be done satisfactorily if the enterprise is to survive. The creating of a utility for others is basic for most enterprises. This, in turn, necessitates selling efforts, so that the product or service is made available to buyers. The producing and selling efforts necessitate financing activities, in that ample capital must be obtained and maintained.

In addition to these three major activities, there are frequently personnel and the office, which are included to assist the main functions. Many feel that both personnel and the office are major activities, and that each should be accorded organization position and status on a par with production, sales, and finance. Sound arguments can be advanced to justify this viewpoint. In the case of the office, for example, the trend toward more and more automation, the use of computers, and the general recognition of the vital contribution of information give increasing weight to this viewpoint.

Any attempt to justify one major activity as the most important in an enterprise is purely academic. Actually, all the major activities are needed. For example, production requires sales, financing gives rise to paper work, personnel assists production, and paper work expedites sales efforts. Our interest here is organization in the management of the office; and the vital concept for our purpose is to remember that office work is done to help fulfill other major functions—it is not performed apart from them. Production activities such as cutting, sewing, machining, assembling, painting, drying, and packing are assisted by the work of the office. Likewise, typical sales activities such as merchandising, analysis of markets, and selling efforts are helped by the office. And the same is true of finance and personnel, for many records and papers are needed in each.

## ORGANIZATIONAL CONTENT AND PLACEMENT OF THE OFFICE

The questions can now be asked: "What activities should be included in the office?" and "Where should the office organizational unit be placed in the organization of the entire enterprise?" The answers must be known so that organizational relationships can be identified both within the office itself and between the office and major organizational units of the enterprise. These relationships can be termed (1) intradepartmental—among the activities making up the office, and (2) interdepartmental—among the office and other major organizational units of the enterprise. The interdepartmental viewpoint is especially helpful because it emphasizes the facilitating and service aspects of office work.

Actually, to designate an organizational unit as "the office" can be confusing, for it is likely neither to be in one location nor to include all information activities. To reiterate, office work is not an activity in and of itself; it is a part of and employed in almost every function. Information is needed to perform the major functions of production, sales, finance, personnel, and other functions, such as engineering, research, and purchasing, which are necessary in a particular organization.

Logically, from the organizing point of view, the required office work should be located where it can be performed at lowest cost, assist best in achieving the stated objectives, and supply the highest service to those using it. This is determined by giving consideration to a number of factors, of which the following are important:

**1. Type and Nature of the Enterprise.** The content and the placement of the office function are affected greatly by the dominance of the production, sales, finance, or personnel activities. If the enterprise is primarily one for production—a large manufacturer, for example, selling its entire output to several large buyers—the office unit probably will be of relatively small importance. However, in a predominantly financial enterprise, the work will be of relatively great importance. To illustrate, in a bank or insurance company, office work is usually of much greater importance than it is in a manufacturing company. Likewise, in a governmental enterprise, the office unit normally occupies a position relatively high in the organizational structure.

**2. Importance Attached to Office Work.** If top managers of an enterprise recognize the work of the office as of relatively high significance, the tendency will probably be to bring it together into one organizational unit and place this unit high in the organizational structure. But if office work is considered minor, although necessary, it probably will be performed by the department needing it and coordinated as completely as possible with the primary activities of the respective department.

**3. Degree of Office Mechanization Used.** Up to a certain level, the adoption of office machines has small effect upon the organization structure. But when machines capable of processing huge quantities of work or of performing work historically handled by several departments are adopted, the result organizationwise is to consolidate the work, shrink the department, combine departments, and change the organizational framework. This can readily be seen in the case of computers and their impact upon office organizing. Significant changes take place likewise when source data automation (SDA) is adopted, and also to some degree when high-speed accounting machines, punched-card machines, automatic typewriters, and duplicating machines are installed.

**4. Extent of Centralization of Office Functions.** Since office work occurs throughout the entire enterprise, from the president's office to the lowest-paid clerk, it is possible to have it performed in dispersed locations, under the jurisdiction of the unit in which it arises. When this practice is followed, the office function is dispersed and either combined with, or made subordinate to, other organizational units. In its fullest application, this dispersion extends to the smallest and lowest organizational unit of the enterprise. In contrast, a directly opposite arrangement might be used. In this case, the office work is fully concentrated and is placed in the hands of a single executive who is completely responsible for all office activities in the organization.

These two conditions, however, are extreme. From a practical viewpoint, seldom is either used. An intermediate or modified arrangement between these two extremes is commonly followed:

1. Office work is located and performed by major departments, and each department head is fully responsible for the office activities in his own department.

2. Office work is distributed among all departments, but one person is placed in charge of this office work in order to achieve reasonable coordination.

3. Certain office work is centralized in one unit and placed under one manager. The remaining office work is performed in the unit in which it arises and is supervised by the regular department head of that unit. This arrangement is quite popular. It is interpreted in different arrangements, and the more common of these are discussed in the following paragraphs.

## THE OFFICE SERVICES ARRANGEMENT

By office services are meant corresponding, report writing, mail and office communicating services, copying, and manually operated storing and retrieving. In some enterprises these services are included in one organizational unit and placed under the "office services manager." However, all these services are not always centralized, the notable exceptions being corresponding, report writing, and manually operated storing and retrieving. Furthermore, even when all these services are referred to as being centralized, they are only partially so—some of certain services being located in various units throughout the entire organization structure.

The adoption of an "office services" unit arrangement means that the manager in charge of information work has a dual managerial task. First, he should manage the services unit; and second, since information work is being performed in various other units in which it arises, he should counsel with the executives of these various units and help them accomplish their information work in the best manner. This second task is of paramount importance and in many respects establishes the true status of the information manager in any organization structure. Actually, it is identifying what information work is and demonstrating to other managers in the organization how best to accomplish this type of work, in essence providing the information viewpoint to all managers of the enterprise. All use information; hence, help in how to use it effectively constitutes a real service. Figure 24–1, top left illustration, shows graphically the office services arrangement.

## THE SYSTEMS AND PROCEDURES ARRANGEMENT

As recognition that the "systems approach" can increase office efficiency, many companies have established an organization unit to facilitate this particular viewpoint and effort.[1] The exact format, content, location, and authority of this organizational unit vary considerably from company to company. For our purposes here, it is identified as the "systems and procedures department"; but other common titles are systems department, procedures department, methods department, or business services deparment. Probably none of these titles identifies completely and clearly the work performed. For discussion purposes, we have assumed that this unit is subordinate to the major unit of finance. It is also common to subordinate it to the controller's office. Any or all of the following activities may be included in the systems and procedures unit: (1) office systems, procedures, and methods design and implementation—to determine and use the proper office operations, their best sequence, and the manner of performance to get the office work accomplished efficiently; (2) computer analysis and programming to operate the computer; (3) analysis of other office machines and equipment in order to advise what

---

[1] The systems approach is discussed in chapter 2, p. 25.

FIGURE 24–1. Various Organizing Arrangements of Office Work with Reference to the Entire Enterprise. The shaded areas approximate the relative amount of office work.

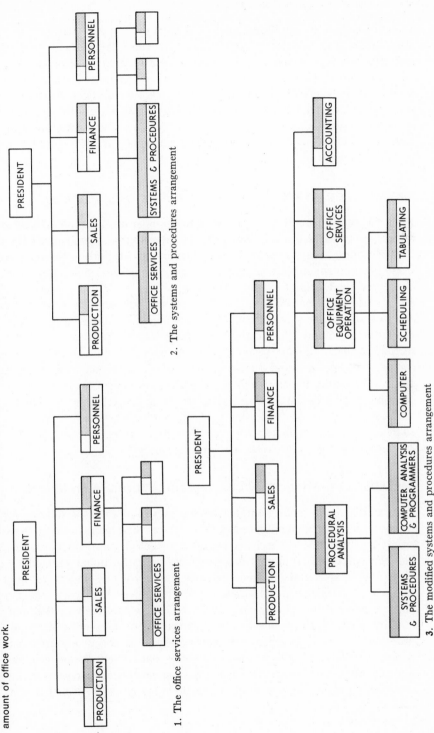

1. The office services arrangement

2. The systems and procedures arrangement

3. The modified systems and procedures arrangement

type of machine or equipment should be used for a specific type of office work under the prescribed conditions; (4) office layout and working conditions—to recommend the most effective arrangement of office facilities and the physical surroundings to supply; (5) office standards—to relate useful levels of performance or frames of reference in order to evaluate achievement; and (6) office work simplification—to point out ways to eliminate waste of all kinds and get the office work out more effectively. The systems and procedures arrangement is illustrated by the top right illustration of Figure 24–1.

## THE MODIFIED SYSTEMS AND PROCEDURES ARRANGEMENT

As computer usage has increased, some companies have adopted what might be termed a modified systems and procedures arrangement. Here the procedural analysis for systems and computer facilitation is separated from the implementation of the machines. Experience has shown that above certain levels or volumes of activity, the work of computer and other office machine scheduling and usage are best segregated from the design and analysis functions for these machines. The bottom illustration of Figure 24–1 shows this arrangement. Note that the procedural analysis section includes (1) *all* systems and procedures work throughout the company in one unit and (2) the work dealing with computer analysis and programming in another unit. The head of the procedural analysis section coordinates the activities of systems and procedures men and that of the computer analytical personnel. Also, observe that the computer analysts and programmers make up *one* unit in order to maintain close organizational ties between these related activities.[2]

## THE ADMINISTRATIVE SERVICES ORGANIZATIONAL ARRANGEMENT

Primarily because office automation has increased and especially as the strong trend toward computers has taken place, the organization of those supplying information has been modified to better meet current needs. The concept of an "administrative services" organizational unit on par with other major units of an enterprise has developed and is winning favor. This arrangement places most of the information work under a single administrator. The top illustration of Figure 24–2 shows the administrative services arrangement. For illustrative purposes only, the units under administrative services are shown as systems and procedures, machine operation, and office services. Observe that the efforts of designing how the work will be accomplished (systems and procedures) is segregated from that of implementation (machine operation). Also, that ana-

---

[2] See chapter 2, p. 39.

FIGURE 24–2. Two Administrative Services Organizational Arrangements Each of Which Provide Top Recognition and Status to Office Work Efforts. The shaded areas approximate the relative amount of office work.

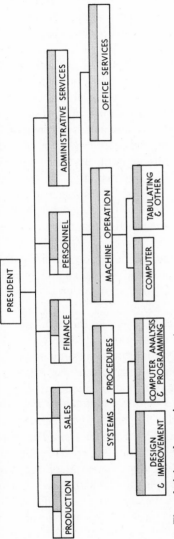

4. The administrative services arrangement

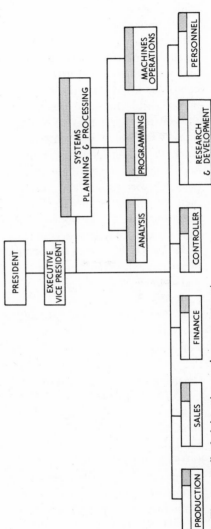

5. The top staff administrative services arrangement

lyzing and programming essential for computer usage is concentrated in a separate unit from that of the efforts designing the means to be used for the paper work in general. Modern electronic machines make it feasible to handle a large part of the paper work of an enterprise in one organizational unit. However, even under the administrative services arrangement, some office work is performed in other major units, simply because it is easier, more convenient, and of greater service to perform some of the office work in these other units.

Having an administrative services unit is a departure from the initial and still widely used arrangement of having the office unit include the computer group and the entire unit under the finance or the controller major unit. The main reason for favoring the finance vice president or the controller was that he could move with freedom across organizational lines, was already associated with office machines and systems, and the work to be done by the computer—notably payroll, accounts payable, and accounts receivable—was already his responsibility. But as experience was gained and applications broadened, the automatic assignment of computer stewardship to the finance executive or controller was questioned. It was reasoned, and quite correctly, that the office organization should take into account:

1. **The Objectives of the Computer Usage.** Is reduction of office cost or improvement of managerial information primary? Can a computer assist and take an increasing role in the overall management process of the enterprise?

2. **The Scope of the Applications.** The broader the range of applications, the stronger the reasons for a separate administrative services unit. For example, if the usage is broadened in scope from processing of routine data to sophisticated management decision making, the chances are that a separate unit will be the more effective organizational vehicle.

3. **The Organizational Strength of the Finance Executive or the Controller.** It is readily apparent that the man in charge of an activity determines its contribution and importance. The manager should comprehend the tremendous contribution of better information, creating effective systems and procedures, and harnessing the huge potential of the computer. In addition, competence in working effectively with, and securing action from, major executives and having the support and confidence of top management are essential. In many instances, the finance executive or the controller meets these requirements fully while in other instances there appears to be an inadequacy.

## THE TOP STAFF ADMINISTRATIVE SERVICES ARRANGEMENT

The bottom illustration of Figure 24–2 (p. 585) is a simplified form of a large enterprise with an extensive informational services unit and largescale electronic data processing. Responsibility for all this work is fixed in a department executive reporting directly to the executive vice president. This department serves as a service group to all other departments including the vice president of finance or the controller. Also, the department head has charge of small paper work staffs maintained by some of the major departments such as sales and research and development. These small staffs are not shown in the figure.

This arrangement permits companywide coordination of all paperwork systems. It identifies informational activities with the top management and enhances the enlistment and support of department heads. The informational needs can be determined objectively without predisposition to a particular means or solution. Either manual, semimechanical, or complete computer application can be evolved and installed after all alternatives have been carefully evaluated. An avowed goal of this arrangement is to improve the quality of information made available to management members.

## ILLUSTRATIVE EXAMPLES

In a large public utility the responsibility for the computer system has always been a part of the accounting function. Figure 24–3 shows the or-

FIGURE 24–3. A Public Utility Organization Chart.

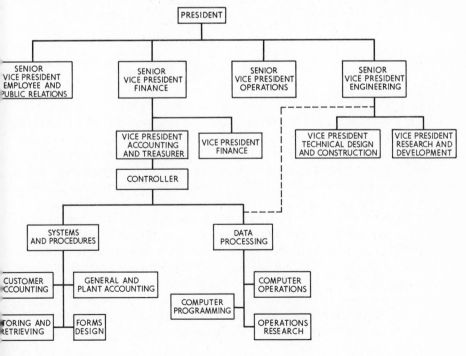

ganization chart. Historically the first application of the computer by the utility was customer accounting because this was the area where greatest immediate savings could be realized. Today the major portion of all accounting is done by computer. Caution marks any efforts to move into new areas of computer use which is viewed solely as a management tool. Engineering and research and development make some use, but a very small portion, of the computer complex.

It is top management's view that computer location should be determined by the computer's use. In view of the general nature of the public

FIGURE 24–4. Corporate Level Organization of Retailing Conglomerate.

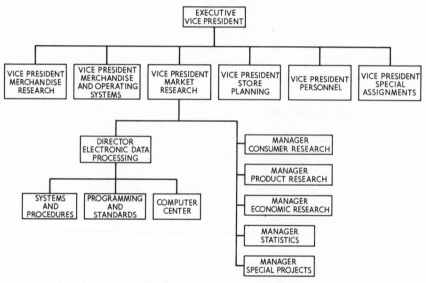

utility's activities, and the requirements for many reports which must be filed with regulatory agencies, it appears that electronic data processing will remain in the accounting function. Systems development, programming, planning, and computer operations are the responsibility of the corporate vice president of accounting who is also the treasurer. This arrangement appears firmly entrenched.

Another example is a retailing corporation made up of a large number of highly autonomous subsidiary companies the managers of which operate their own respective stores. The only formal relationships that exist between the companies and the corporate level are the presidents of the companies and the corporate president. The corporation exercises financial controls and provides services as requested by the company managements. Over a period of several years the corporate management developed attractive information services including inventory-control methods, accounts payable systems, product-profit analysis, and return on investment programs. All of these are computer processed. In most of the companies computer capabilities now exist, but for the most part they are utilized for processing routine information such as payrolls, customer billings, cash-flows, and budgetary data.

Figure 24–4 shows the director of electronic data processing who reports to the vice president of market research who, in turn, reports to the executive vice president. The latter deals with the operations of the corporation's many stores. The functions included under the vice president of market research and of the electronic data-processing director are indicated on the chart. The functions are so aligned in order that maximum information service, designed to improve store operations, can be supplied to the companies' managements.

## CURRENT CHANGES

Research shows that the organizational location of the computer or central system processing center is moving toward the top levels in the organization structure. And increasingly the trend is toward computer activities centralization, but this does not necessarily lead to centralized decision making.[3] Actually in many cases the top management intention is to guard against such a practice and to take measures to insure that decentralized decision making is followed. The significant factor in what arrangement is followed is the characteristic management style and philosophy. For example, a company may use a centralized computer operation to help decentralize its operations.[4]

Organizational conflicts arise from the intended placement of the computer and the existent relationships. The fear of a centralized computer system eliminating departmental or divisional autonomy is frequently present. And managers of major functional units initially assigned responsibility for computer operation are usually reluctant to release their hold. But when considering the vast potential of the computer and its effect upon the individual manager and his operation, it is no surprise that its organization location has given cause to debate. However, with the passage of time and the expanding computer applications, satisfactory means for overcoming internal rivalries appear plausible.

## CENTRALIZATION AND OFFICE ORGANIZING

"Centralization of information activities" means the physical concentration of such activities into a single group, with the management over

---

[3] Centralization is discussed in detail on the following pages.

[4] See Robert R. Reichenbach and Charles A. Tasso, *Organizing for Data Processing* (New York: American Management Association, 1968).

FIGURE 24-5. The Four Possibilities of Centralization.

POSSIBILITY 1

PHYSICAL LOCATION : CENTRALIZED
MANAGEMENT :              CENTRALIZED

COMMENT: COMMON CONCEPT
OF CENTRALIZATION

POSSIBILITY 2

PHYSICAL LOCATION : NOT CENTRALIZED
MANAGEMENT :                   CENTRALIZED

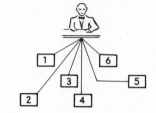

COMMENT : COMMON BUT SOMETIMES
NOT FULLY COMPREHENDED
AS A TYPE OF CENTRALIZATION

POSSIBILITY 3

PHYSICAL LOCATION : NOT CENTRALIZED
MANAGEMENT :               NOT CENTRALIZED

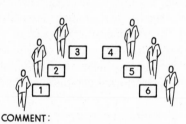

COMMENT :

SERIES OF INDIVIDUAL UNITS.
ACTUALLY NO CENTRALIZATION
CONCEPT EXISTS

POSSIBILITY 4

PHYSICAL LOCATION : CENTRALIZED
MANAGEMENT : NOT CENTRALIZED

COMMENT :

RELATIVELY RARE CONCEPT OF
CENTRALIZATION - LITTLE USED

them vested in one person. For example, in centralized corresponding, all corresponding work for an entire office is done by a corresponding section and managed by a corresponding chief. Centralization is concentration.

Actually, the concept of centralization can be considered from the viewpoint of (1) physical location or (2) management. This, in turn, permits four possibilities, namely, (1) physical location centralized and management centralized, (2) physical location not centralized and management centralized, (3) physical location not centralized and management not centralized, and (4) physical location centralized and management not centralized. Illustrations of these four possibilities, along with comments for each, are shown in Figure 24-5.

A key consideration in office organizing is the degree of office work centralization from the management viewpoint which is adopted. As already indicated, the degree of centralization of "office services" varies among different enterprises; by no means do all enterprises have either a department akin to the systems and procedures department, or some form of an administrative services department. Equipment analysis, for example, may be handled by the executive handling the particular function for which the equipment will be used; likewise, the executive of the operating department may have charge of standards applying to paper work in his unit. A computer may be located solely within one department such as accounting or research and development.

## EVALUATION OF OFFICE CENTRALIZATION

The current trend appears to be toward centralization. Office automation, use of computers, consolidating fragmented clerical functions, and taking organizational measures to stop the spiraling of overhead costs are among the major reasons for this trend. A suggested approach to determine the feasibility of centralization of office work is discussed in Chapter 28. Specifically, the advantages of office centralization include:

*Flexibility is given the organization.* Work peak loads can be readily handled, office machinery utilized fully, and the effects of labor shortages reduced to a minimum.

*Equitable wage schedules are fostered.* The measurement of office output is encouraged, and comparisons of wages for similar work are possible.

*Training of office employees is expedited.* New employees can be added to centralized groups without seriously affecting the operations of the group. The retraining of old employees for new jobs is also well adapted to a centralized type of organization.

*Methods of office operation can be applied uniformly and quickly.* Standards common to several organizational units can be established.

*Cost of performing office work is decreased.* Supervisory costs are lowered, the costs of investment and maintenance of machines are lowered, and the amount of floor space is frequently reduced.

*Labor specialization is practiced.* Employees become highly efficient and are continuously employed on work necessitating their highest individual skill and ability.

On the other hand, there are many who feel that better results are obtained from a noncentralized, or decentralized, organizational arrangement of the office work. To substantiate their view they point out that:

1. Much office work is confidential and should be handled by the unit in which this confidential trust is placed.

2. The work is performed by those who may not be familiar with the detailed requirements. Minor changes and corrections cannot be made on the spot.

3. Effective planning and controlling are difficult to exercise since the executives most familiar with the use and purpose of the paper work are not near at hand.

4. Work is done without regard for urgency or importance to the individual office unit. Delays may take place. The efficiency of each unit may be hampered.

5. Costs may increase due to nonproductive transporting and handling time required.

6. Employees of a "generalist" nature are not developed. Some versatile persons with overall viewpoints are essential in all enterprises.

It should also be added that for a noncentralized office arrangement to provide satisfactory results, certain organizational requirements should be met. Foremost is an understanding and an agreement among all information management members with respect to the information goals and policies to be followed. This is basic. Also, there should be written statements concerning decision making for information work made by noninformation managers. Further, such decision making by these managers should be reported to the chief information manager so that such decisions can be noted and communicated to other management personnel. It is also helpful to have a follow-up and postdecision audit to evaluate the decisions made and institute modifications believed necessary.

## QUESTIONS

1. Enumerate the major benefits derived from effective organizing.
2. Discuss the possible conflicts that arise due to the placement of a computer in an organization.
3. Discuss the office services arrangement of office organizing efforts.
4. Identify each of the following:
   a) Work division as an essential of organizing.
   b) Organizing.
   c) Decentralization.
   d) The administrative services arrangement of office organization.
5. What relationship, if any, exists between managerial objectives and organizing? Discuss the significance of your answers in the study of office management.
6. Explain why organizing enables a manager to enlarge his scope of operations.
7. Briefly discuss what in your opinion are the four most important advantages of centralization. Of decentralization.
8. Point out the essential organizational differences as shown between Figures 24–3 and 24–4.
9. Justify your answer to each of the following:
   a) Does centralization give flexibility to an organization structure?
   b) Is work environment an essential component of organizing?

*c*) In the typical manufacturing enterprise should a computer be located under finance?

*d*) Is coordination the main purpose of organizing?

10. If specialization helps in getting work accomplished, should not all office work in an enterprise be performed in a centralized location and under the management of one head? Justify your answer.

11. Discuss the relation of the office to the organization of a large company. Is this relationship important in office organizing? Why?

12. Relate where you believe the computer should be located organizationwise in a medium-sized manufacturing company. Justify your answer.

## CASE PROBLEMS

### Case 24–1.    Zeis-Jaffe, Inc.

MR. HERSCHEL JAFFE (*president*): Acquiring a computer involves a great many people, and it should because as you know a computer affects all the operations of an enterprise. We are a large manufacturer of technical products requiring a great deal of engineering design and testing. We had several small computers before the new one was selected.

MR. MORTON CONE (*a business friend*): This big job was not your first computer?

JAFFE: Oh no. Actually we were among the first ten users of computers in this state.

CONE: Is that right.

JAFFE: The desirability of a big modern machine that can do just about everything was the idea not of any one individual, but of all our management team members. They wanted the best. We had computerized much of our technical design computations, inventory control, engineering specifications, cost estimating, sales forecasting, payroll, and accounting records, but the need to perform these faster and in different formats suggested consolidating them on a single modern computer.

I suppose you could say that the start was made by our factory accounting manager who got the ball rolling initially by his discussion with our data-processing manager, our systems and procedures director, and our special projects technical director. In turn, they discussed the possibilities with the factory manager who in turn discussed the matter with his general shop superintendent. He talked with the data-processing manager, the systems and procedures director, and the factory accountant.

CONE: I am confused. Do you have an organization chart of your company? I'd like to visualize the setup so I can follow you better.

JAFFE: Oh sure. Let's step in the next room. A chart on the wall there will show what you want.

CONE (*looking at chart shown in Exhibit 24–1A.*): Yes, this will do it.

JAFFE: Now you see, I was talking about the factory accountant, data-processing manager and they are shown right here [points his finger to chart]. All right. The factory accountant also discussed the big computer idea with the controller, manager of computer operations, and the chief engineer. All in all a number of discussions were held. They were informal and took place over a period of three to four months. Then we held formal meetings at which three or four managers would attend. The policy we followed here was that only the need for a new computer was discussed. You could say what you wanted, but it had to apply to the subject at hand. This prevented the meetings from drifting. Some lasted quite a long time. I remember one which I understand went for six hours without a break.

CONE: Six hours—golly.

JAFFE: There was opposition to the suggestion of getting one large computer. Some believed it would lead to job losses, others expressed a preference for the work done manually, and still others preferred to maintain the status quo. After

EXHIBIT 24–1A. Zeis-Jaffe, Inc.

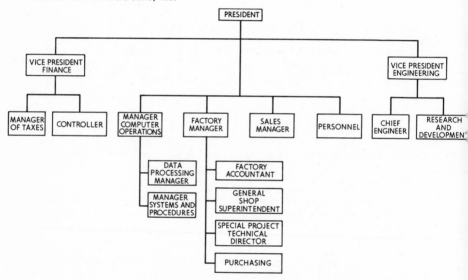

nearly eight months had passed, the manager of computer operations and the factory manager agreed to approve the obtaining of a new computer. This was brought about in part by feasibility studies conducted by various major units of our organization. Reports were submitted periodically to interested parties. This continued, I would judge, perhaps eight months or so. All these reports were studied, weighed, advantages developed, disadvantages noted, and a final composite report was prepared.

CONE: Who prepared this report?

JAFFE: Our automation committee made up of the factory accountant, factory manager, manager of computer operations, sales manager, and the vice president of engineering, if I remember correctly. Let me see now. Yes, this committee handled this and the makeup was as I just gave you. Anyway, copies of this final report were submitted to the vice president of finance. His approval was required before we could go ahead.

CONE: Didn't you have to approve, Hersch?

JAFFE: No, I stayed out of it. I figured the men handling it knew far more about it than I. To continue, in due time the vice president of finance approved. Then the automation committee selected five computer manufacturers to provide specifications, potentials, and prices of a computer to fill our requirements. We invited representatives of each to visit us and showed them examples and drawings of what we wanted to get from the new installation. In addition, the factory manager, the chief engineer, and the manager of computer operations visited other enterprises using similar computer equipment to what we had in mind. They observed what was being done and asked questions. Also, the factory manager and the manager of computer operations interviewed the computer manufacturers' local sales representatives asking them many questions and, in turn, answering many questions they posed. Following this, our factory manager and manager of computer operations went over these matters with the controller, the factory accountant, and the vice president of engineering. Upon recommendation by the factory manager and the manager of computer operations to the controller for acquisition of a particular computer, the controller studied the recommendation, approved it, and submitted it to the vice president of finance where final approval was given.

## Questions:

1. Superimpose on the organization chart, lines showing the various communication held among the various members of this company and with outside people.
2. From study of this drawing you have made, what general conclusions do you reach regarding organization and communication? Organization and the computer? Discuss.
3. Elaborate on the statement that organization is a means for people to work together toward a common goal.

### Case 24–2. Harper and Reeves, Inc.

The corporation maintains three offices, one for each of its three separate manufacturing plants in Chicago, Boston, and Oklahoma City. All consolidated reports of the corporation's activities are prepared in the Chicago office, which is considered the main office. Six months ago, new machines were installed in the Chicago office and just ten days ago it was announced that most accounting as well as all statistical tabulating work used primarily for forecasting and sales purposes now performed in Boston and Oklahoma City were to be moved to the Chicago office. The move would start in 30 days and require approximately 40 days to be consummated.

This change gives rise to organizational problems. In the Chicago statistical tabulating unit, for example, there were initially six employees, and the supervisor Paul Isham directed the group informally and kept a close personal touch with all the employees and their work. With rapid increase in sales and a demand for more precise data, Mr. Isham's unit has grown to ten employees during the last 120 days. Now with the centralization of statistical tabulating services in Chicago, Mr. Isham's unit is expected to acquire an additional 12 employees, one of whom is the former supervisor of the Oklahoma City statistical tabulating unit. The office manager is concerned about providing adequate supervision so that the new tab summaries and reports are correctly and promptly prepared and that the old established work is continued satisfactorily in the future as it has been in the past.

## Questions:

1. What are some major alternatives open to the corporation?
2. What organizational arrangement do you recommend for the Chicago statistical tabulating unit?
3. Evaluate this recommended organization unit, discussing important advantages as well as disadvantages.

# chapter 25

# Determining the formal office organization

Every person who pursues a career, as distinct from
a jobholder, should expect to continue his education
for the rest of his professional life.
—*Harry Levinson*

FOR ORGANIZING to take place, work is divided forming clusters of tasks,
and people are assigned to these tasks. The resulting "work division-peo-
ple assigned" segments provide the nuclei of organization units. These
units are then related by means of authority as will be discussed in the
following chapter. For the present, we are concerned with developing
these organization units which brings up the question of how to divide the
work and what people to assign to what work.

## WORK AS THE INITIAL BASIS

We start with work and its division because, in the great majority of
cases, this is the superior approach. A manager must coordinate what is
being done, not who is doing it. Also the work is relatively permanent, it
changes less frequently than the interests and abilities of personnel.
Furthermore, to formulate organization units primarily on the basis of
personnel often results in unusual combinations of duties that are difficult
to manage and for which the securing of replacements is arduous. However, the "people–work" division approach is used and in some instances
with outstanding success.

The objectives and the nature of the enterprise determine for the most
part the work to be done. Using this work as the initial basis for the

organization promotes the objective viewpoint and minimizes subjective influences. Further, concentration of attention on the work helps to develop clear concepts of what activities must be performed and helps prevent uneconomical overlapping and duplicating as well as excess work.

## WORK DIVISION

Dividing the work can be accomplished by various means including (1) by function, (2) by process, (3) by customer, (4) by product, (5) by territory, and (6) by project. An organizer can use any means he desires, and commonly several means are employed in the same organization structure. What best helps to achieve the objective should be used. In a bank, for example, for the top levels, functions may be used; whereas the loan department may be divided by customer—loans to manufacturers of plastics, chemicals, and paper; loans to manufacturers of food processors and package machines; or by product—commercial loans or personal loans. Office work division by territory is common for offices designed to serve sales organizations. The territory divisions constitute the main segments of the sales organizational structure, and the offices serving such organizations are likewise segregated and located throughout the country. Work division by project in office organization has been used very little as of now. It utilizes the idea of work division being a project or a major and complete program. Assigned to a project is a complete team which is permitted to work on the project assigned until either successful completion or an authorized termination is ordered, at which time the team is disbanded and new projects are activated with newly formed teams believed appropriate for the new work involved. Large research development agencies of government are using project organization with great success. In the future it may become an important segment of office organizing.

The most common means of departmentation is by function, which can be defined as *the normal or characteristic operation of an activity*. Copying, for example, is a function in that it is an activity which always has characteristic identities, and these identities are usually considered the proper action of copying. In management, it is common to speak of "functions." Observe that the same function may be performed by two or more people, and likewise, the same person may perform two or more functions. Illustrative of the former is a group of clerks all doing the same work, for example, checking billings in a department. The latter is illustrated by the receptionist who greets and directs visitors, opens and sorts the mail, and types letters.

Any function covering a broad scope of action such as processing can be broken up into component functions of relatively limited scope. The extent of this functional work division is guided by considerations for the organization unit to be formed. The desired size of this unit, the quantity and scope of work, the way it is done, the need for verifying the work of one unit by another, the extent of continuous flow, and the permanency of the work are usually of prime importance. The advantages of specialization are sought, but not at the expense of employee job interest.

The grouping together of similar functions provides strong major groups for the organization; the tendency to split activities is minimized. This grouping also affords great strength and flexibility to the organization; functions may be modified, new functions added, and old functions eliminated easily and simply without disturbing the essential structure of the organization.

Further, it must be remembered that the organizational units being created will be influenced by its manager and the employees performing the operative work and their relationships to all other employees in the total organization. Hence, we should keep in mind the type of management member who will take charge of this unit, that is, his special attributes, his shortcomings, ambitions, accomplishments, and education. If no manager is currently available, we need to answer what qualifications will be sought, and is there a reasonable possibility that such a manager can be hired. Also, adequate thought must be given to evaluating the proposed nonmanagement members of the unit, the capacity and skills required, personnel relationships to be integrated, and the wishes of the contemplated prevailing management member.

In addition, work division to form an organization unit is affected by the organizational relationships that will be established as a unit of organizing. If a unit includes a relatively large work scope, it usually will tend to have a prominent position in the organization relationships and its manager will have much authority. In contrast, units of small groups usually have relatively minor authority.

## EXISTENT DIVISION OF WORK

For an existent organization, data on the current work divisions as well as who performs the different tasks can be surveyed and recorded on a work distribution chart. Basically this is a spread sheet which shows, for a given time period—usually a week—the type of work and the time spent on each job by each employee in the office organization unit under review. The basic information can be obtained from the supervisor or the employees. Probably more objective data are obtained by observing each employee and recording information on his activities. However, this approach is relatively expensive.

Figure 25–1 shows a work distribution chart. A vertical column is used for each employee, along with one to indicate the time spent on each activity. The functions performed are listed in the first column on the left. This chart gives a graphic, overall picture of the work done and the work divisions in effect. In addition, it reveals the relative amounts of time put

FIGURE 25-1. Work Distribution Chart.

| OFFICE FUNCTIONS | TOTAL MAN HOURS | LOIS MILLER Unit Supervisor | MAN HOURS | BETTY HEIDT Stenographer | MAN HOURS | RUTH TOPFF Order Clerk | MAN HOURS | EDITH WRIGHT File Clerk | MAN HOURS | SYLVIA GAZEL Telephone Switchboard Operator | MAN HOURS |
|---|---|---|---|---|---|---|---|---|---|---|---|
| Correspondence | 54 | Read and route Dictation | 9 10 | Takes dictation Transcribes | 10 20 | Types labels and materials for files | 5 | | | | |
| Computing | 32 | Figures prices | 3 | Figures prices | 2 | Figures prices | 15 | Figures prices | 12 | | |
| Filing | 21 | | | | | Files correspondence Finds letters in file | 2 5 | Files correspondence Finds letters in file Classifies correspondence | 4 6 4 | | |
| Handling mail | 26 | Opens mail Time stamps mail | 2 5 | Stamps mail | 2 | Opens mail | 5 | Stamps mail | 4 | Opens mail Stamps mail | 3 5 |
| Miscellaneous | 67 | Answers questions Answers telephone inquiries Supervises | 8 2 1 | Cleans typewriter Gets supplies Arranges advertising stuffing material | 1 2 3 | Answers telephone inquiries | 2 | Errands for postage stamps and supplies Maintains tickler file for follow-ups | 2 8 | Operates switchboard | 32 |
| | 200 | | 40 | | 40 | | 40 | | 40 | | 40 |

on each office function and the extent of work division. From the "people assigned" viewpoint, the chart shows what skills are required, whether special skills are being wasted, whether too many employees are performing the same function, and whether an employee is doing too many unrelated tasks.

## INDIVIDUAL JOB CONTENT

From the organizing viewpoint, individual job content is the contribution to the objective made by the individual performing the particular job. The activities assigned or the individual job content can be viewed as what the employee is required to perform because of the organizational position and relationship occupied in the organization structure.

Effective organizing requires that each employee have definite tasks that he understands, can perform, and that encourage his personal development. When these requirements are met and the necessary physical facilities and adequate supervision are provided, the individual is in a work situation where real accomplishments are possible.

The division of work to be done must be carried out to the individual job level. That is, the department functions must be divided ultimately into jobs for each individual. Unless this is done, the formal organizing is incomplete, and the group of people connected with the enterprise may experience difficulty in ascertaining a unity of action.

## JOB SPECIALIZATION

All organizing requires some specialization. Most managers agree that no one person can do everything equally well. The need for allocating total work and capitalizing upon what a person can perform best have resulted in job specialization. Complex work is divided into relatively simple components, each accomplished effectively by employees specializing in that single operation or in a group of similar operations. The question is not whether to have job specialization but to what extent job specialization should be carried. In organizing, the office manager must decide this question as exemplified by determining the work makeup of each organizational unit and what is done by each member of that unit. Job specialization avoids too many and too varied tasks for one employee.

However, in some companies an attempt to broaden the job scope has been advanced. This is commonly referred to as *job enlargement*. These efforts have given excellent results, such as reduced office costs, improved quality of work, better teamwork, and lower absenteeism. While these results must be interpreted carefully, they seem to indicate that there are both economic and social limits to job specialization. The degree and form of job specialization to follow presumably depend upon the type of office work and the individual doing it. More specific information is needed to derive definite recommendations. The current prevailing belief is that jobs of limited scope should not be used as from them arise monotony and lack of employee interest in his work. In some instances, job rotation among employees within a unit is followed to improve morale.

## WORK DIVISION ARRANGEMENTS

Generally speaking, work divisions for the top level of an organizational structure are made on the basis of functions. Divisions for the intermediate levels usually are either by type of product, by customer, or by territory. Common at the lower office organizational levels are work divisions by any of these three arrangements: (1) serial, (2) parallel, and (3) unit assembly. Work division by product, customer, or territory is self-explanatory; but further discussion of the serial, parallel, and unit assembly is warranted and illustrated by Figure 25–2. In this illustration the work consists of handling customers' orders and is made up of three separate operations: (1) credit approval, (2) inventory check, and (3) pricing. Assumed is a work force of three employees, Nancy Brown, Sharon Hewitt, and Virginia Walker.

In the serial arrangement, shown at the top of the figure, the work division is extended to a series of small tasks, each task being performed by a specialist in that particular type of work. Moving progressively from task to task, the work advances until completed. The serial arrangement is the same basic plan as the familiar factory assembly line, commonly found in production plants. In some quarters, the term "production line basis" is used to describe the serial arrangement in the office. "Consecutive handling" adequately describes this arrangement.

FIGURE 25–2. Illustrating the Serial, Parallel, and Unit Assembly Arrangements of Work Division.

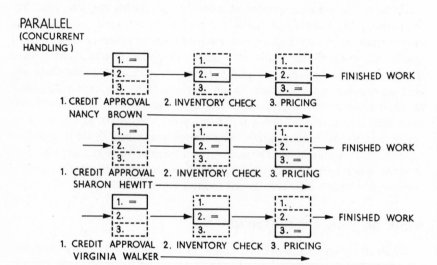

SERIAL
(CONSECUTIVE HANDLING )

1. CREDIT APPROVAL   2. INVENTORY CHECK   3. PRICING
   NANCY BROWN          SHARON HEWITT         VIRGINIA WALKER

FINISHED WORK

PARALLEL
(CONCURRENT HANDLING )

1. CREDIT APPROVAL   2. INVENTORY CHECK   3. PRICING
NANCY BROWN

FINISHED WORK

1. CREDIT APPROVAL   2. INVENTORY CHECK   3. PRICING
SHARON HEWITT

FINISHED WORK

1. CREDIT APPROVAL   2. INVENTORY CHECK   3. PRICING
VIRGINIA WALKER

FINISHED WORK

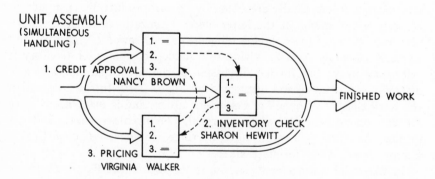

UNIT ASSEMBLY
(SIMULTANEOUS HANDLING )

1. CREDIT APPROVAL
   NANCY BROWN

2. INVENTORY CHECK
   SHARON HEWITT

3. PRICING
   VIRGINIA WALKER

FINISHED WORK

The parallel arrangement, or concurrent handling, shown in the center of Figure 25–2, permits a series of needed and separate tasks to be performed by one individual or a work team. The employee or employees, as the case might be, do not specialize in performing one task but gain proficiency in accomplishing several tasks. Frequently, the tasks are related, but this is not necessary. In our illustration, the total customer order-handling work has been divided into three parts that parallel each other. Each part consists of all three separate tasks of the work, that is, credit approval, inventory check, and pricing. As illustrated, employee Nancy Brown performs all three tasks or operations, and so do each of the other two employees, Sharon Hewitt and Virginia Walker.

The unit assembly arrangement illustrated at the bottom of Figure 25–2 provides for different employees to perform different work steps upon the same work items at the same time. It can be termed "simultaneous handling." Specialization is practiced by each employee, but the work sequence is not identical for each item. Nancy Brown performs credit approval; while at the same time, Sharon Hewitt performs inventory check, and Virginia Walker does pricing. Coordination of the various tasks is a prime requirement under this arrangement, for the separate tasks usually do not require identical times to perform. The unit assembly arrangement can be thought of as a cross-blending between the serial and the parallel arrangement.

## WHAT ARRANGEMENT TO USE

Like many other practices, the question of whether to use the serial, parallel, or unit assembly arrangement cannot be fully answered by a "Yes" or "No." Normally, for any given office, the tendency is toward the prevalence of one, but seldom will it be used exclusively. Individual circumstances govern, with consideration given to cost, employees' interest in their jobs, quality of work, preferences of managers and employees, and the overall objectives.

More specifically, the serial arrangement of work division requires a sufficient work quantity of a particular type to keep an employee fully occupied in its performance. Quantity and specialization are close "buddies." Also, mechanization tends toward a serial arrangement. Most office machines handle a large volume of work, and their cost usually requires a high percentage of utilization throughout the workday. In some instances, the job content is so complex and the tasks so heterogeneous that some breakdown in the work is necessary to acquire and maintain employees for the work. When this is the case, the serial arrangement is usually followed. In addition, some office work, if performed by one employee, would incur a sizable loss of time in shifting from one operator to another. For example, a job consisting of typing, then calculating, followed by checking and resumption of typing, may show low efficiency. Selecting the serial plan frequently follows when the skill needed is of a special type, due to scarcity or the amount of training that can economically be provided. It is usually not feasible to dilute the efforts of the employee possessing a needed skill in a specialty. An expert in operating punched-card equipment should not type and operate the copying machine as a part of her regular job duties. Another condition normally suggesting the adoption of the serial arrangement is when great uniformity in handling certain portions of the office work is required. The signing of checks and bank drafts can be cited as an illustration.

In contrast, the parallel arrangement is usually followed when better work performance appears to be associated with a complete understanding and handling of the particular subject matter. An overcharge in a billing to a complaining customer might best be handled in its entirety by one employee. Furthermore, when the "start to finish" period for the work performance must be reduced, the parallel arrangement may be superior. Under this pattern, delay in work processing, or loss in time by papers traveling from operation to operation, is avoided. Less handling and idle time generally result when the papers are processed by employees working under a parallel arrangement. In some cases, by keeping the division of work too small, an employee is deprived of helpful overall checks in the work. When this situation exists, the parallel arrangement automatically provides the solution. It should also be observed that with parallel groups performing similar cycles of work, it is possible to hold contests, compare work accomplishments of each group, and inject other competitive devices in managing the work. Such measures help stimulate high productivity. In addition, the parallel arrangement helps to eliminate duplication of efforts such as reading and checking if such is present when high specialization is followed. Under the parallel pattern, one employee familiarizes herself with the contents of the paper by a single reading and a single checking. Finally, the parallel arrangement is suggested where the circumstances indicate that greater interest and enthusiasm by employees probably will be gained from having a greater variety of work in the job makeup.

The unit assembly arrangement permits work to start at an operation other than the first in the sequence of tasks. This makes it possible to start processing the work simultaneously at different operational stages. In other words, the performance of work operation number 3 need not wait until number 1 and number 2 are completed. In certain situations, this is a definite advantage. Furthermore, flexibility in machine utilization and in work scheduling is provided. Usually, completed work is obtained more rapidly under the unit assembly arrangement; for this reason, it is employed for special rush and emergency work. Specialization is practiced to a great degree under this arrangement; but as stated above, sometimes the coordination of the individual work processing poses a difficult problem.

## JOB ANALYSIS

Job analysis is a formal means of determining the job content. It can be defined as follows: *Job analysis is the process of critically examining the components of a job, both separately and in relation to the whole, in order to determine all the operations and duties.* In short, job analysis deals with facts about jobs and what is required for competent performance. Typical of data included are the forms and materials handled, the equipment and machines used, the methods utilized, the frequency of the operations, the amounts and kinds of skill required, and the degree of concentration needed. Such information is extremely useful in management because it can be used to define the scope of the job. Furthermore, by use of job analysis data identity of a certain job name to certain work becomes fixed, and a definite association between the job title and the content is established.

Job analysis is customarily and quite correctly thought of as an activity logically a part of personnel activities because it is basic in the performance of many personnel department functions. For example, job analysis is the basis for determining the relative worth, compensationwise, of jobs; it facilitates hiring and placing, can be used for formulating developmental needs, and serves to identify promotions and transfers. These are truly personnel functions in character and are discussed in Part 8 of this book. However, inasmuch as job analysis does identify the job and its content, it is included in this discussion dealing with organizing. As already pointed out, really effective and complete organizing work requires specific work divisions at the individual level. Job analysis helps supply this requirement.

## OBTAINING JOB ANALYSIS DATA

In the case of new work or a new organizational unit, the manager doing the organizing must decide the characteristics of the newly created job or jobs. In a going office, however, three methods of securing job analysis data are possible: (1) interview and observation, (2) conferences, and (3) questionnaires. For the first method, the analyst goes to the employee, asks questions about the job, and observes what the content of the job is. While this method is satisfactory for office jobs, it is probably most popular for factory jobs. In the second method, the employee is called into conference and verbally describes his job to the analyst, who records the information. This method usually requires more time than the others, takes the employee from his job, and may interfere with the work routine. In the third method, a questionnaire is sent to the employee, who fills in the information. This method is used in cases where the employees can intelligently handle clerical details and are more or less accustomed to paper work. It is commonly used for most office work. The federal government has employed this procedure successfully for over 50 years. Frequently the questionnaires are supplemented with short observations and interviews, especially for the more important jobs.

Whatever method is adopted, it is advisable to secure within practical limits as much information as possible about each job. It is usually better to have too much than too little data. Commonly the data are recorded on a prepared form which serves as a reminder to answer definite questions and thereby secure all the needed facts, so that no part of the job is overlooked. It also expedites recording the data in a standardized manner, thus making it easier to handle and interpret the information. Figure 25–3 shows a portion of a job analysis form.

FIGURE 25–3. Portion of Questionnaire Used for Job Analysis.

JOB ANALYSIS

Present title of job _____ Department _____

1. What is the general purpose of this job?
2. What duties are performed in the *usual* course of the work? (Tell from where work is received, what is done with it, and where it is sent.)
3. What duties are performed only at stated intervals? (Give answers by daily, weekly, monthly, etc.)
4. In what organizational unit is this job presently located?
5. Does the job entail supervising other employees? (Explain.)
6. If there are any special training courses essential in order to perform the duties of this job satisfactorily, name them.
7. What past experience is *necessary* for a new employee to have in order to perform the duties of this job?
8. What are the *most* difficult parts of this job?
9. What are the *least* difficult parts of this job?
10. About what proportions of this job require sitting, _____%; standing, _____%; moving about, _____%?
11. What machines or other equipment are operated?
    Regularly:
    Occasionally:

## JOB DESCRIPTION

The information on the job analysis form actually describes the job. However, when this information is written in a more descriptive style, the term "job description" is frequently used. While the format used for writing these descriptions varies, they usually contain a summary of the job, the work performed, and the qualifications generally considered essential. (See Figure 25–4.)

Job descriptions are useful in the work of organizing. The duties and the lines of authority, if any, are clearly set forth. Job descriptions also help bring about better understanding within an enterprise because they point out the qualifications required of an employee on the particular job, help in selecting persons best fitted for the requirements of the job, and assist in acquainting the new employee with his job.

Either the job descriptions or the definitions of each job in a special

FIGURE 25–4. A Job Description Written in an Effective Form.

# JOB DESCRIPTION

DATE_____

JOB TITLE__ JUNIOR ACCOUNTANT _____GRADE_VI____CODE _____

SUMMARY:  Under general direction of Comptroller and immediate supervision of Accountant, performs general accounting duties and prepares special reports as assigned.

WORK PERFORMED:  Maintains records of cash receipts and/or disbursements, posts related subsidiary records. Posts various journal entries and adjustments, maintains record of Supply Department receipts and prepares minor financial statements.

Handles correspondence, verifies tabulations and reconciles bank statement. Assists in distributing work to temporary help, prepares monthly reports and special statements. Performs related work, such as figuring per capita and expense ratios. Operates office machines as required.

May supervise work of accounting clerks, typists for temporary periods, etc. and performs similar duties as assigned.

QUALIFICATIONS:  Normally requires three to five years' training and experience, including two years' general accounting training plus three years' company accounting experience as an Accounting Clerk.

*Courtesy: J. D. Moore Organization,*
*Ann Arbor, Mich.*

format can be collected and utilized in designing and maintaining a formal organization structure. For maximum utility, the definition should include the duties, authority relationships, and the responsibilities of its occupant. Frequently, this information is included in an organization manual. Getting this information down in black and white helps the organizer to visualize more clearly the division of work and the organizational relationships formally established. Such work also helps to utilize constructive and creative thought in the organizing. Also, the organization manual is helpful for training purposes and provides official answers to organizing questions for the given enterprise.

Current practice tends to use the terms "job description," "job state-

FIGURE 25-5. Job Statement of Programming Manager.

*Programming Manager:* Reports to director of procedural analysis. Supervises administrative assistant programmer. Is responsible for planning and organizing all programming activities for the computer; maintaining essential records of the programming department; directing, motivating, and evaluating personnel; and participating in the planning of computer usage.

ment," and "job title" to identify progressively contracting descriptions of the job. A job statement is used to furnish a quick picture of the job. To illustrate, in Figure 25-5, the job content of "programming manager" is condensed to a single paragraph. A job title is simply a common name for a job. However, job titles are commonly inadequate to identify a job satisfactorily. For example, the title "secretary" is used to identify jobs of different makeup, as illustrated by the two job statements in Figure 25-6.

FIGURE 25-6. Job Titles May Be Identical, but the Respective Job Statements May Differ.

*Secretary:* Takes dictation, using shorthand, and transcribes the dictated material into a neat typed format; makes appointments for executive and reminds him of them; answers and makes telephone calls; handles personal and important mail; writes routine correspondence on own initiative; maintains executive's files.
*Secretary:* Takes dictation, using either shorthand or a machine; transcribes dictation from either shorthand notes or a machine; interviews people coming into the office, directing to other employees those who do not warrant seeing the executive; answers and makes telephone calls.

*The title plus the job content are necessary for accurate identification.* This is important in office organizing where work division and organizational unit creation must be decided.

## IMPORTANCE OF PEOPLE IN ORGANIZING

As stated in the beginning of this chapter, organizing can logically start with work division, and the divisions created serve as focal areas for organizational units. In turn, the work within each organizational unit must be accomplished, directly or indirectly, by people. Up to this point, attention has been directed to the work aspect of organizing; but equally important, and in the opinion of many of greater importance, is the "people aspect" of organizing. In fact, it would be difficult to overemphasize the importance of people in organizing.

Successful organizing helps provide the means for getting effective results through people's efforts. It provides for the adequate development and placement of people. While work division and assignment are important, they are not the end objective in organizing. The main goal is to make it possible for a group of people, called employees, to work cooperatively and efficiently. The total work is segregated by functions so that each individual of the work group can perform a portion of the total work in the best possible manner. The expression "Organization is people" is trite; nevertheless, it stresses the importance of people in the work of organizing. It brings out the basic idea that people constitute the center about which revolve the organizational concepts of the work to be done, the authority, and the work environment.

In the final analysis, the organization structure is a tool—it provides the grouping of specific activities and of people for the purpose of applying management. Work is accomplished by people or machines operated by people. Organizing does not accomplish any work objective; it must be implemented with people. Hence, one of the biggest jobs of a manager is to form or maintain an organization which permits the proper placement and the development of employees. Some claim that almost any organization structure will prove satisfactory as long as the right people are operating it. Others lay great stress on the proper division of work and relationships. No doubt, both are important. However, the point here is that people are vital in organizing; they can make or break any organization structure.

It follows, therefore, that good organizing is necessary for effective employee performance. This is true because organizing deals with and sets forth such basic issues as what is to be done and by whom, and who decides what. This view of organizing has been compared to that of writing the story for a motion-picture film. It sets the stage and predetermines what is to take place. How well it takes place, i.e., the quality of the motion picture, depends in great measure upon the actors—the personnel element.

Each employee should be assigned to work that is best suited for him. This necessitates considerable knowledge and skill in placement for maximum benefits to all concerned. Let us direct our attention, more specifically, to this task of assigning the right person to the right job. For this purpose, we must first obtain applicants for the work, in the case where none are available, and second, in selecting from these or from the present employees the person to be assigned to the work of a specific organizational unit. This brings up the important subject areas of recruiting, sources of help, and the techniques of personnel selection.

## RECRUITING

The recruitment of employees is a permanent activity. Increased emphasis is placed upon this work during peak business periods, but the problem of securing the right employees confronts most offices most of the time. There are always separations because of marriage, illness, voluntary leaves, terminations, and death.

Recruiting has several major aspects. First is knowing the quantity and quality of candidates to seek and when to seek them. This establishes the needed goals. Also, an evaluating of the recruiting process for different types of office jobs is needed. People with the required attitude and interest should be the target for recruiting efforts. Contacts are also required to obtain the referrals of candidates. In addition, many office managers have found that appropriate recruiting literature is definitely helpful in aiding their recruiting efforts.

Limited data reveal that the number of applicants hired to the number rejected is in the ratio of 1 to 7, and that over $200 is spent for each office employee hired. These data suggest that recruiting can be improved. What can be done? Probably foremost is the use of more accurate and complete job specifications. When the job requirements are vague, the likelihood of finding a satisfactory candidate is considerably lessened. No available source can supply its maximum recruiting assistance when the information supplied is insufficient and not clearly stated. Another improvement possibility is speeding up the selection process. In too many cases, a qualified candidate is lost because of a lack of promptness in dealing with the applicant from the time of application to the time the decision to hire or not to hire is rendered. A third area is developing the reputation of the particular office as being a good place to work. The office possessing this valuable public good will commonly has a satisfactory group from which outstanding candidates can be selected.

## SOURCES OF OFFICE HELP

Generally speaking, a variety of labor sources is desirable and needed to meet recruitment goals. The "best" source usually must be qualified regarding the type of office job, the geographical location, the prominence of the company, and the skill with which the recruiter uses a particular source. The proper personnel viewpoint is to work with a number of different sources of office help. Better people usually can be selected if there is a group from which to choose.

Among the more common sources are:

*1. Persons Recommended by Present Employees.* This is usually a very good source, but caution must be exercised to avoid favoritism. Some companies post notices on bulletin boards encouraging employees to recommend friends who might be seeking employment.

*2. Former Employees.* This group constitutes an excellent source. However, careful screening and selection techniques are required to avoid a "come and go" atmosphere. Frequently, satisfactory part-time employees can be obtained from this source.

**3. New Employees.** The person just hired usually knows somebody else who is looking for a job. Satisfactory results are usually obtained if candidates are put through the regular selection channels.

**4. Employment Agencies.** It is well to utilize this source. Some agencies are public, others are private. The former charge no fee; the latter do, and the charge commonly is made to the employer. Agencies have broad contacts and experience; they try to supply likely candidates for vacancies.

**5. Schools—Including Vocational Advisory Boards.** This is one of the better and larger sources of office employees. Some companies keep in close touch with high schools, business colleges, and universities, and send representatives to talk with students about to graduate. Many schools have placement offices and will cooperate fully with prospective employers. It is well to develop schools as a source of office help. The candidates usually have formal training but limited business experience.

**6. Institutions for the Rehabilitation of Handicapped Persons.** Frequently, very capable people can be secured from this source.

**7. Voluntary Applicants.** It is a good practice always to see people who come in looking for a job. Frequently, this source offers excellent personnel, but it cannot be relied upon as the sole source of help.

**8. Advertising.** Newspaper, radio, and television advertising are effective media for securing a number of candidates. Good coverage is usually obtained; but all respondents will not be fully qualified, and the normal weeding-out process must be used.

## SELECTION OF OFFICE HELP

Choice of a candidate (new applicant or present employee) is normally based on a comparison between (1) what the job requires for successful execution and (2) what the candidate has to offer. For the most part, the better the balance between these two factors, the better the selection work, and the more likely is the attainment of a satisfactory working force. Under job requirements are such attributes as the amount of formal education, knowledge, experience, and physical considerations. Under what the applicant offers are his fund of knowledge, experience, intelligence, physical attributes, and personality. This matching effort, however, must not be thought of as an exacting operation. On the contrary, it is quite flexible. Job requirements should be used as a guide. Frequently, a satisfactory person does not have the *exact* qualifications desired; but with time and experience, he may well prove satisfactory on the job.

The use of vocational requirements facilitates the selection. For example, the suggested minimum vocational requirements for the job of beginning stenographer might be established at ability to type at a rate of 55 words per minute on straight copy material for a ten-minute period, with five errors or less; to perform shorthand writing at 100 words per minute;

to transcribe notes of unfamiliar material at the rate of 35 words per minute for a ten-minute period, and to produce work of mailable quality; to transcribe from a machine, at the rate of 10 to 12 letters per hour each letter consisting of two to three paragraphs. During the past decade much progress has been made by various associations in getting office managers to request employees who meet definite vocational standards and in getting schools to train students toward these standards.

## TOOLS OF PERSONNEL SELECTION

There are a number of selection tools that assist in deciding which candidate should be placed in what job of an office organization. Discussion here includes the tools of (1) application form, (2) interview, (3) references, (4) physical examination, and (5) tests.

**1. Application Form.** *The application form is a written record providing a means of securing and maintaining the more obvious personnel information, such as identification, education, work history, and activities of the applicant.* Sufficient information should be obtained, but superfluous information should be avoided. All questions asked should serve a definite purpose in evaluating the candidate's possible value to the office.

For the higher level jobs, it is often quite helpful to ask several questions designed to gain some insight into the candidate's general attitude toward life and his ability to write and to organize material. To illustrate, questions such as the following might be asked: "In narrative form, give us a résumé of your major accomplishments, hopes, and ambition." "Will you tell us about your special qualifications not covered elsewhere in this application?" "What unusual business situations have you encountered, and what did you do about them?"

**2. Interviews.** The opportunity to meet the applicant and observe his verbal ability, appearance, general personality, and attitude are extremely helpful in selection work. The face-to-face meeting with the applicant offers possibilities of information afforded by no other means. The objectives should be to exchange information and to make a favorable impression upon the applicant. Unless these conditions are accomplished, the interview is not wholly satisfactory. The exchange of information is essential to intelligent selection. Creating a good impression establishes a favorable attitude by the applicant toward the office, whether he is hired or not.

Figure 25–7 shows interviewing practices that are effective. In addition, it is a sound practice for the interviewer to have a list of items he wishes to cover. The accuracy and quality standards on previous jobs held by the candidate, the supervisory practices liked, and the grades received in school are illustrative of areas to cover that will make for effective interviewing. Rating charts can also be used so that the relative intensities of the important factors are recorded. Use of oral trade questions is recommended. An idea of the candidate's competency is obtained by such questions which deal with names of office machines, office operations, general knowledge of office jobs, and the like. Fourth, an interviewer's guide, designed to help secure essential information, can be used.

**3. References.** Managers usually like to obtain information on the applicant from previous employers and responsible persons currently acquainted with him. Reference checking is helpful in appraising the candidate's cooperation, dependability, skill, interests, and abilities. On the other hand, some believe that references are frequently unreliable claiming that inaccurate evaluations are provided and either excessive praise or excessive criticism is supplied.

FIGURE 25-7. Follow These Practices for Effective Interviewing.

---

1. Put the applicant and yourself at ease.
2. Explain the duties, responsibilities, chances for promotion, and working conditions of the job. If possible, read or let the candidate read the job description.
3. Encourage the applicant to talk by asking questions that begin with *why, when,* and *how.* Avoid questions that can be answered by a "Yes" or "No."
4. Interrupt the applicant only when what is being said is irrelevant. Start speaking after the applicant has paused for at least ten seconds.
5. Use language appropriate to the educational and experience background of the applicant.
6. Let the applicant ask questions.
7. Grant sufficient time for the interview, but do not prolong it to the extent of useless repetition.
8. Keep interview fresh. Periodically change the questions and the sequence in which they are asked.

---

Qualifications for reference givers include being fully familiar with the demands of the job, knowing the candidate extremely well, supplying information with absolute honesty, and exercising sound evaluating judgment. These qualifications appear to be filled best by professional people and former employees. Telephone reference inquiries commonly produce better results than mail, possibly because people giving references are usually more willing to speak frankly than to put the same comments in writing. If possible, reference information should be obtained *before* a full interview. Data can be checked, and selected areas for discussion or further probing can be chosen for the interview.

**4. Physical Examination.** The main purpose of the physical examination is to determine whether the candidate is physically suited to perform the office work under consideration for him. Testing of the eyes is especially important for office work. Physical examinations help to raise the standard of physical fitness, to increase work output, to lower accident rates, to decrease turnover, and to lessen the amount of absenteeism caused by sickness.

**5. Tests.** This is the last personnel selection tool to be discussed. *Tests are measurements of personnel aspects secured by scientific methods of observing and recording in certain standard situations.* The measurements are normally qualitative and are believed to be related to success in performing the work. But tests determine what a candidate can do, not what he will do. A test score is an indication of the probability of the candidate's success or failure as determined by his possession of the attributes measured and the importance of these attributes in the work accomplishment.

By *validity* of a test is meant the relationship between the test score and accepted facts about the attribute measured by the test. To illustrate, the most desirable employees among the present employees should make a high score; the average employees, a lower score, and the least desirable employees, the lowest score. *Reliability* of a test deals with the consistency of the test in yielding similar results when given on different occasions. When a test has been found, through a process of experimentation, to have both validity and reliability, it is commonly referred to as a *standardized* test. A series of numbers indicating performance scores of large numbers of persons who have taken the test are called *norms* of the test. They serve as guides for comparison of scores.

Today, there are a great number of tests designed to measure many different attributes. The National Business Entrance Tests, sponsored jointly by the Administrative Management Society and the United Business Education Association, offer a battery of tests covering machine calculation, stenography, typing, bookkeeping, filing, and business fundamentals. Those who pass these tests are given a card or certificate of proficiency. A 12-hour examination program is utilized for Certified Professional Secretary candidates. The examination, prepared annually, consists of personal adjustments and human relations, economics and business organization, business law, secretarial accounting, decision making, and business procedures. Successful candidates are given a CPS identifying card and are permitted to wear a CPS pin.[1]

Among the many types of single-trait tests, the following are probably of greatest importance in office management: (1) the intelligence test, (2) the clerical test, (3) the personality test, and (4) the interest test. Figure 25–8 shows a comparison of these four types of tests, revealing for each one the contribution, general content, basic implication, names, and main purpose.

---

[1] For further information on the National Business Entrance Tests, write the Administrative Management Society, Willow Grove, Pa.; for information on the Certified Professional Secretary tests, write National Secretaries Association, 1103 Grand Ave., Kansas City, Mo. 64106.

Testing is a specialized field, and best results are usually obtained when the work is performed by qualified testing experts. Trained personnel, either on a part- or full-time basis, can be engaged.

## MANAGER'S ATTITUDE AND ORGANIZING

From what has been stated in this chapter, it is evident that organizing reflects a manager's attitude and reveals his understanding of the essentiality of the human element and how this resource is to be regarded. Allocating the work and assigning employees efficiently are vital in organizing. Likewise, the creating of certain working relations among the organizational units must be handled with great care. There is genuine skill in having logical work divisions tie in respectively with an adequate consideration for who is to do each respective component of work.

An information manager implements his regard for the human element in his organizing efforts by recognizing and appreciating the value, as well as the limitations, of his employees. This is not a one-shot proposition but a continuing, ever searching effort to keep up to date the placing of each employee on the type of work best suited for that employee and of directing all efforts toward the common goals sought. The supervisor in charge of the mail room, for example, reflects from the human-element viewpoint the office manager's thinking, organizationwise, of the supervisor's value, including his strong and weak points for his particular supervisory job. The job content, a result of work division, is presumably what the information manager thinks it ought to be; likewise, the authority granted is what the office manager thinks it ought to be—all or at least a big portion of it is with reference to the office manager's human-element evaluation of the supervisor. In this sense, it is sometimes said that an organization structure reflects the shadow of its manager. However, it appears more appropriate to state that an organization structure *reflects the light or understanding* of its manager.

Concentration on men's strengths pays organizational dividends. A manager holding firm convictions about an employee's abilities to perform the work competently tends to instill confidence in the employee and develops his will to do successful work. At the same time, the manager must realize that not all men can do all things. To assume otherwise can lead to disaster in his organizing. Yet, by proper managerial motivation, leadership, and lifting a man's vision to higher planes, the common man can be stimulated to achieve uncommon things.

However, the office manager who experiences the greatest success in organizing is a realist and accepts people available to him for what they really are. He recognizes that most organizations, and particularly the area of which he is a part, are the result of many decisions which took into account various considerations, some of which were controversial and

FIGURE 25-8. Comparison of Various Tests on Significant Factors.

| Name | Contribution | General Content of Test | Basic Implications | Examples of Standard Tests | Main Purpose of Test |
|---|---|---|---|---|---|
| Intelligence and mental alertness tests | Indicates one's adequacy in a number of types of work. | Problems on information and of judgment and reasoning. Questions dealing with contrast or comparison. Memory tasks. | What a person has absorbed is a fair indication of what he will or can absorb. Differences in background are not taken into consideration. Little indication of how the indicated ability may be applied. | Army Alpha (Original and Several Revisions) Benge Test of General Knowledge The Henmow-Nelson Test of Mental Ability The O'Rourke General Classification Test Otis Self-Administering Test of Mental Ability The Pressey Senior Classification and Verification Psychological Corporation Scott Company Mental Alertness Test | To make preliminary selection To gain an insight to the applicant's ability to understand and to manage ideas. |
| Trade and clerical tests | Helps to show the degree of achievement possessed by a candidate for this specific type of work. | Questions appraising vocabulary level. Ability to notice details. Problems in simple calculations and arithmetic reasoning. Competency in performing clerical work. | Candidate having achievement of certain level and above will probably execute the job requirements most effectively. | Benge's Clerical Test Blackstone Stenographic Proficiency Tests Minnesota Vocational Test for Clerical Workers National Business Entrance Tests O'Rourke's Clerical Aptitude Test Psychological Corporation Shellow's Intelligence Test for Stenographers Thurstone Examination in Clerical Work, Form A | To determine applicant's knowledge of a specific trade or profession. To select candidates having at least a certain minimum of relative ability to perform work in a particular field. |

FIGURE 25–8 (continued)

| Name | Contribution | General Content of Test | Basic Implications | Examples of Standard Test | Main Purpose of Test |
|------|-------------|------------------------|-------------------|--------------------------|---------------------|
| Personality tests | Indicates the presence or absence of traits, or group of traits. | Single item questions which are answered with "Yes" or "No." Single words suggested—applicant names words which he associates with this single word. | Applicant will answer questions honestly. The make-up of the personality is related to the situational demands of a job. | Beckman Revision of Allport A-S Test California Test of Personality Heidbreder's Personal Traits Rating Scale, Form 2 Humm-Wadsworth Temperament Scale Laird's Personal Inventory C-2 | To appraise those qualities which are pivotal in a situation and probably will determine the degree of future success of candidate on the job. |
| Interest tests | Aims to determine the extent of the candidate's genuine interest in a particular type of work. | Questions to indicate the correct use or identity of machines and devices. | One's latent or developed interest in a certain type of work is closely related to the energy, persistence, and contribution which he gives to that work. | Brainard-Steward Specific Interest Inventory Strong's Vocational Interest Blank, Form A Thurstone Vocational Interest Schedule | To determine the degree of interest which a candidate has for different types of work. |

contained imponderables. He also realizes that organizing is a "give and take" proposition between what is to be done and who is assigned to do it. Essentially, it has a compromise characteristic. The chief criterion, however, is to get the work accomplished adequately and maintain a continuity of satisfactory work achievement.

## THE RATIONALITY OF FORMAL ORGANIZING

There is a strong "rational" feature about formal organizing. The necessary work is divided, employees are assigned to specific and carefully defined jobs, and the "work-employee" components are purposely related. The justification for such activities is that to do otherwise would be wasteful and haphazard. On the other hand, there is some question whether this rational approach provides the best organization possible. And does an organization derived rationally meet current day requirements?

Strong differences of opinion exist regarding the answers to these questions. It appears, however, in light of current knowledge that the degree to which organizing can be rationalized and considered an economic entity has limitations. Further, to ignore these limitations may result in planting the seeds of organizational difficulties that can bloom into major problems. More will be discussed on this subject in chapter 27.

## QUESTIONS

1. In performing the work division of formal organizing, should consideration be given to the type of management members who will take charge of the units so formed? Why?
2. Elaborate on the statement: "Organizing, a fundamental function of management, does not accomplish any work objective."
3. What is the unit assembly arrangement used in organizing and what are its advantages, if any?
4. Many writers and composers have achieved greatness working alone—without an organization at all. Does this demonstrate, in part, that perhaps in management there is a tendency to overemphasize the importance and contribution of organization? Why?
5. Do you agree with this statement, "People constitute the essential makeup of an organization. Hence, it is logical as well as advantageous to begin organizing efforts by finding out what people are available and what each of them can do best." Justify your answer.
6. What are the significant differences between the concepts in each of the following pairs?
    *a*) Job description and project organization.
    *b*) Office function and work divisions.
    *c*) Serial work division arrangement and validity of test.
    *d*) Job enlargement and job specialization.

7. Discuss the meaning, obtaining, and utilizing of job analysis data.
8. In what ways do you believe the recruiting of office employees can be improved? Are you of the opinion that these improvement means are practical and can be accomplished? Explain.
9. Explain Figure 25–1 highlighting the main concepts that this illustration shows.
10. Regarding tests for selection purposes, answer each of the following:

    *a*) What is the main contribution of personality tests?

    *b*) What is the main purpose of trade and clerical tests?

    *c*) What are the basic implications of intelligence and mental alertness tests?
11. Discuss the effect of a manager's attitude upon his organizing efforts.
12. A friend of a present employee has been interviewed, tested, and her references checked. She is recommended to the supervisor of department K-5, who hires her. At the end of a four-week period, it appears she cannot perform the work satisfactorily. Is the personnel selection, supervision, company, or employee at fault? Explain your answer.

## CASE PROBLEMS

### Case 25–1.   Roxworthy Company

CECIL HOWELL (*office manager*):  Of course, there are gaps and overlaps in our job descriptions. We try to avoid this but it is very difficult to describe precisely and completely every job especially when you have as many jobs as we do.

EDGAR WOOD (*an employee*):  That's exactly my point. If certain work isn't covered in the job description, it isn't a part of the job. How can a different conclusion be made?

Edgar Wood, a clerk in computer processing, has developed into a valuable employee. He has contributed a number of suggestions that were adopted for electronic processing of various types of data. Last year he attended night school studying programming and has acquired proficiency in this area. Last week when work was slack in the computer room, Mr. Richard McGill, the supervisor, asked Edgar Wood to help in rearranging the stockroom, marking and indexing the stored items and getting it in better shape. Reluctantly, he abided by Mr. McGill's request. He dislikes stockroom type of work and after four days of it, he had a confidential talk with Mr. McGill voicing the opinion that he was supposed to be given computer processing work only, that's what was stated in his job description. Mr. McGill replied that straightening out the stockroom would indirectly benefit processing. It was work that had to be done. Employees are expected to operate as a team with group efforts coordinated toward given goals. Not satisfied with this explanation, Edgar Wood requested and received permission to discuss the question with Mr. Gail Howell, the office manager, who requested that Mr. McGill attend the meeting.

HOWELL:  Well you see Mr. Wood, cleaning up the stockroom is needed and Mr. McGill is trying to get it finished with the manpower he has available.

WOOD: I'm for getting the stockroom in shape. That's fine. But why should I be put on this work? My job description clearly lists the duties of my job and it doesn't include cleaning up a mess some jerks left.

HOWELL: I would say the company has a right to direct its work force and make assignments.

WOOD: Right. They have. But the company also has job descriptions that it used to build its present organizational structure. If you throw your job descriptions to the wind, your organization is going to suffer. Any employee can be changed to any kind of work. You have no organization.

McGILL: It's like I told you Edgar. We have to work as a team. There's work to be done, let's get together and do it. You simply cannot list every duty in a job description. Because a specific task is omitted, doesn't mean a man should not be required to do it. Isn't that right, Mr. Howell?

HOWELL: Well, yes. Within limits, of course. I'd say a job description should be specific, but not detailed. It outlines in definite terms what the tasks are, but not how to do them.

WOOD: That's what I say. There is no definite statement in my job description about cleaning stockrooms.

HOWELL: Job descriptions serve as guides to fit the company's goals. Included are the activities that must be carried out. Now goals change, at least the subgoals, or the day-to-day variety. That's occurred in this case. The question here, I believe, deals more with utilization of job description than with its contents. A job description must be used by both the manager and the employee with a great deal of flexibility. Certain elements will expand, others contract. Some will be deleted, others added. But this doesn't necessarily result in a complete rewrite of the job description. Usually the emphasis or interpretation needs to be placed differently.

I want you to know Mr. Wood that we think very highly of you. This stockroom deal is temporary and will be over in a matter of days—a week perhaps at the most. Then we want to get you back on the computer.

WOOD: Yeah, that's where I want to be. Your ideas on job descriptions are quite different from mine. From what you say Mr. Howell, job descriptions can mean just about what the user wants them to mean.

## Questions:

1. What is the problem in this case?
2. What's your general opinion of Mr. Howell? Why?
3. As Mr. Edgar Wood, what action would you now take? Discuss.

## Case 25–2. Doran, Inc.

An opening exists for a draftsman in the engineering and designing department of Doran, Inc., a heavy machinery manufacturer. The corporation has always taken considerable.effort to place the person on the job that best suits the applicant. Much attention is given to maintaining good relationships among employees especially those working together within a department. Doran, Inc. has a reputation as a good place to work. Currently there are 17 men in the engineering and designing department.

The personnel department recruits, holds preliminary interviews, and screens applicants for work. Those believed satisfactory are referred to the supervisor of the department where the applicant will work. The final decision on whether to hire is made by the supervisor. For the draftsman opening, the personnel department has referred two candidates to supervisor Bart Osgood.

One candidate is Leonard Baker, age 42, high school graduate, married, two children, just retired from the U.S. Army after 21 years of service, honorable discharge, rank of sergeant. Most of his time in the U.S. Army was spent in engine maintenance work. He studied drafting, engine design, and carpentry from a correspondence school.

The other candidate is Mildred Morse, age 20, single, since graduation from high school has worked as a sales clerk in a local department store. Likes machines, has a brother who is a mechanic and together they have torn down and rebuilt several racers. She says the drafting job is just what she has dreamed of.

During interviews with Mr. Osgood, neither candidate impressed him as highly favorable. However, realizing the labor market is thin, he chose Leonard Baker and advised personnel of his choice.

When Mildred Morse heard of her rejection, she was bitterly disappointed. In her opinion the company is violating the civil rights law which forbids hiring discrimination because of sex, marital status, creed, color, or national origin. Relating her experience to governmental officials, Miss Morse said she knew she could do the work because a friend of her brother works as a draftsman for Doran and she can do the work that he does. Further, while waiting in Mr. Osgood's office for the interview with him, she overheard the conversation between two draftsmen adjacent to the office. The one stated that Bart was talking to a young woman for the drafting job that was open, but he'll never hire her because that would really upset the department. The other one agreed, stating words to the effect that "I hope Bart handles this right. The last thing we want here is a woman. I don't see why he is even talking with her. And I'll never understand why a woman would want to do this kind of work. I'm against it. If a female is hired, heaven forbid, I'll tell you what will happen. She'll get all the easy work and make a silly old fool of Bart."

## Questions:

1. Comment on the action taken by Mildred Morse.
2. What effect do you believe the civil rights law may have upon the "people of an organization" in the future? Discuss.
3. What is your recommended action for the company? Why?

### Case 25–3.  Foster-Myers Company

Experience with personal interviews and background checking for personnel selection and placing was proving unsatisfactory for Jack Echols, office manager of Foster-Myers Company, a regional chain of variety stores. To correct the situation, Mr. Echols decided to enlist the help of tests designed to measure learning, memory, alertness, adaptability, creativity and flexibility in thinking. The results obtained proved extremely satisfactory, so much so that in talking with the president of the company about this program, Mr. Echols was urged to use these tests throughout the office organization. Currently, the company needed a typist in the purchasing department and a typist in the sales analysis department. Of seven applicants, Mr. Echols, by interviewing, selected five to be tested and from the results of testing selected the two best girls. They were placed in the jobs and were well received. The supervisor of purchasing congratulated Mr. Echols on his providing such an excellent new employee. However, at the end of the eighth week the girl placed in the sales analysis department quit and three weeks later, the girl in purchasing was absent and telephoned her supervisor that she had decided to leave the company. Upon hearing this news, Jack Echols stated, "I'm through with tests. It's like I've been saying, the best approach is to hire any likely candidates and just try them out. Maybe they stay a few days, a few weeks, a few months, perhaps a few years. But you never know. Scientific personnel selection and placement? That's a schoolroom term."

## Questions:

1. Evaluate the actions and beliefs of Mr. Echols.
2. What action regarding selecting and placing of employees should the company follow? Why?

chapter **26**

# Authority and organizational relationships

No one is so rich that he does not need another's
help; no one so poor as not to be useful in some
way to his fellow man.

*—Pope Leo XIII*

THE VARIOUS organizational units made up of work divisions and people
assigned to them must be related, or formally tied together, so that they
provide a unified group which can operate effectively toward obtaining
common objectives. Relating these units leads to the subject of authority.

*Authority is the right to act or to exact action by others, within a
prescribed area.* With the concept of authority is associated the power to
make decisions and to see that they are carried out. The compliance
aspect of authority is not confined to coercion or force; more commonly,
it is gained by means of persuasion and requests.

## CHARACTERISTICS OF AUTHORITY

Authority has definite limitations. First of all, it must, from the
management point of view, be used in conformity with the efforts to
achieve the accepted goals of the organizational unit. It is not used by an
office manager as his whims or wishes might suggest. Also, the use of
authority is influenced by the people with whom it is being employed. The
exacting of certain actions by others must be within their capacity to
perform. To illustrate, trying to enforce a decision impelling an inexperienced file clerk to operate a modern bookkeeping machine would be a
ridiculous misuse of authority.

The relative position in the organization structure normally indicates the degree of authority from the formal viewpoint. But the amount of decision-making power and ultimate enforcement may be modified by the popularity or acceptance of the one in authority by the person being influenced by that authority. Managerial competence to gain enthusiastic cooperation, to acquire respect, and to inspire may be lacking despite the formal authority established by position in the organization structure. This also means that a person with little or no formal authority established by reason of his position in the structure might actually possess extensive authority due to his integrity, knowledge, and skill. In punched-card accounting, for example, others may seek suggestions from a certain individual and do what he recommends. Although the person may not be formally in charge, he actually possesses significant authority. Situations of this type may be of a temporal nature or may exist for long, continuous periods.

In many office organizational units, situations of an unusual or emergency nature arise from time to time. They may not be provided for in the regular organizational arrangement. In such circumstances, the person assuming the authority has derived it from what is called the "authority of the situation." This usually is temporary and exists until the person normally in charge assumes authority over the unusual event.

The relationship established by authority is either of two major types, (1) vertical and (2) horizontal. Vertical authority relationships are those between different organization levels and concern the superior-subordinate association. Horizontal authority relationships deal with organizational units within an organizational level and concern the manager-to-manager association within the same organization level.

Lastly, authority is dynamic. Within prescribed limits, its makeup is changed according to the specific conditions and requirements of the group or the individual. It is not always applied to the same degree or intensity. This characteristic emphasizes the manager's skill or application of his authority.

## RESPONSIBILITY

When a management member is given or assumes authority to perform specific work, an obligation to perform the work is created. The acceptance of this obligation is known as responsibility which can be defined as follows. *Responsibility is the obligation for the carrying out of a duty and what one is accountable for in the execution of an assigned task.* That is, responsibility can be viewed as having two parts: (1) the obligation to secure results and (2) the accountability to the one from whom the authority is received. Commonly responsibility takes the form of a list of duties. These are general statements—they do not spell out every detail of what is to be performed.

Being obligated to secure results and being accountable automatically puts a person under pressure and develops his sensitivity to gain satisfactory results. Typically, in a business enterprise the board of directors appoints a president who is expected to manage the business. His obligation to secure results and his accountability are well known. In turn, by means of organizing, he shares his authority and responsibility with individuals. In fact, this is one of the main purposes of organizing.

Efforts to develop responsibility in management members take many different forms, but an effective practice is to provide the holder of authority and responsibility with a list of questions to improve the exercise of his authority and to stimulate his enthusiastic acceptance of

FIGURE 26-1. Questions to Develop Management Responsibility.

1. Do you make a continuing review of excess office processing capacity?
2. What five office work areas require most of your time? Should they?
3. Have you investigated to find out if your instructions are understood?
4. Are you keeping up with the latest developments in office machines that might be used in your organizational unit?
5. Are written procedures brought up to date?
6. Do you receive any useless reports or documents?
7. Do you take an individual interest in each of your subordinates?

his responsibility. Figure 26-1 illustrates the type of questions that can be asked.

## AUTHORITY AND RESPONSIBILITY—DEFINITE AND COEQUAL

Both authority and responsibility should be definite and known to all concerned. Defining the authority assists in gaining the needed coordination among the various component efforts, and especially it enables vertical coordination between superior and subordinates throughout the entire organization to be effective. However, this defining of the authority does not mean spelling out every detail of what a manager can and cannot do. It prescribes in what broad areas the manager shall make decisions; and by means of objective identifications, policies, and communication, the manager directs his efforts to specific work. By this formal rationale it is believed the manager's initiative, creativity, and enthusiasm are stimulated, not thwarted.

Responsibility implies an individual trust, a dependence upon an individual to perform an assigned task promptly and efficiently. When this is defined and made known to an individual, he knows that it is up to him and to him alone to see that the job is carried out satisfactorily. Defining responsibility tends to develop the individual and to increase his reliability. Knowing exactly the task and the activity for which he is being held fully responsible, he tends to overcome common obstacles and to perform his tasks promptly and thoroughly. Human beings like to measure up to the requirements made of them. In addition, the use of definite responsibility aids in work accomplishment. With knowledge of whom is responsible for each particular activity, the proper person for a specific function can be seen quickly and directly, without waste of time.

Responsibility should be fixed at a level as low in the organization structure as is consistent with the capability of the personnel at that level to assume responsibility. The lower the level, the greater the benefit to the total organization personnel. Furthermore, benefits of developing future managers of the enterprise, increasing the individual's feeling of worth, and minimizing disciplinary problems can be cited.

The authority of any manager should be coequal with his responsibility and, vice versa, his responsibility coequal with his authority. The association between authority and responsibility is intimate and where one exists so does the other. This relationship is akin to an object and its image in a mirror. If one exists, the other exists also in a coequal status. Authority commensurate with responsibility is needed before responsibility becomes meaningful; and likewise, responsibility without commensurate authority has dubious managerial value.

## SPAN OF AUTHORITY

In writing of relationships among organizational units, the question arises: How many immediate subordinates can a manager manage effectively? The number is commonly referred to as "span of control" or "span of management." For our purposes here, it is believed the term "span of authority" is appropriate and helpful.

In a given case, there is probably an optimum number of persons who should be immediately subordinate to a manager in order that most satisfactory managerial results are obtained. The number should be large enough to utilize the manager's full time and ability, yet not so large that his efforts are diluted over too wide a span. The proper span of authority depends upon many considerations.

The organizational level at which the managerial work is performed appears to be important. At the higher levels, few might report to their immediate superior; while at the lower or operative levels, many might report to one superior. Also, the type of work is important. To illustrate, a supervisor of draftsmen might adequately direct the work of 15 draftsmen, depending upon the particular type of drafting work performed.

Generally speaking, a relatively broad span of authority can be used. In addition, adequate consideration must be given to whether all the immediate subunits are of equal size and importance, whether they must be given equal attention by the supervisor, and whether the caliber of personnel requires a large or a small amount of supervision. Where the makeup of the work is fairly stable and little communication between units is required, a broad span of authority usually proves satisfactory. Furthermore, the geographical distance between activities affects the span utilized.

Some managers prefer a span numbering from four to eight. Originally, this quantity came from the military, where rapid change in plans and operations may be necessary because of enemy action. However, in business organization, the span should be determined by keeping in mind the considerations mentioned above. The number used may well be four to eight, but it need not necessarily be this amount. The span of authority appears to be increasing in many business enterprises. In some instances, successful operations are reported with spans of 10 to 12 persons at the top levels and with 20 to 25 persons at the lower levels. In the final analysis, the number of subordinates reporting to a manager should be limited to what he can effectively manage.

It is appropriate to point out that span of authority deals with the number of persons reporting to a manager, not the number of persons having access to a manager. The two can be greatly different. Also, span of authority is confined to *formal* authority relationships. Actually, in most enterprises, there are usually many informal authority relationships. These result from the existence of social interests and relationships among employees and are frequently different from the economic formal relationships established.[1]

Wide spans of authority make for relatively few organizational levels; short spans make for many organizational levels. With wide spans the organizational structure is referred to as a "flat organization," with short spans as a "tall organization." Coordination vertically is relatively easily obtained in the flat organization; and in contrast, it is more difficult in the tall organization because of the depth created by the organizational levels. On the other hand, and because of the same reasons, coordination horizontally is relatively easy within the tall organization, but relatively difficult within the flat organization.

With respect to organizational relationships, their number increases rapidly as the number of persons supervised increases. First, consider a manager, M, with two supervisors, A and B. In this case, there are six relationships: M with A, M with B, and A with B, plus the reverse of each, assuming the initiative is taken by the second-named party; i.e., the

---

[1] See chapter 27.

additional three are A with M, B with M, and B with A. Now, assume that M increases his number of supervisors from two to three, or an increase of 50 percent. What happens to the number of relationships with which M may now be concerned? They increase from 6 to 18, or an increase of 200 percent. The third supervisor, C, makes for these additional 12 relationships: M with C, B with C, A with C, M with AB, M with BC, and M with AC, plus the reverse of these six relationships. This is summarized in Figure 26–2. It should be noted that not all the relation-

FIGURE 26–2. Data Showing the Rapid Increase in Organizational Relationships as the Number of Persons Increases.

| MANAGERS | SUPERVISORS | ORGANIZATION RELATIONSHIPS |
|---|---|---|
| 1 | 2 | 6 |
| 1 | 3 | 18 |

ships are of equal importance, but they should be taken into account when determining the span of authority.

## DELEGATION OF AUTHORITY

Another important concept of authority in organizing is the delegation of authority. This is the granting or conferring of authority by one manager to another. Usually it is thought of as being from a higher to a lower level, as is commonly the case within business enterprises. However, in some organizations of government and some religious groups, delegation of authority is from a lower to a higher level and from one level to another on the same plane. Hence delegation can be downward, upward, or outward.

By means of delegation, an executive spreads his area of managerial influence and makes an organization meaningful. Without delegation, an executive restricts his managerial actions to those that he himself can perform. In fact, organizing does not become fully effective until delegation of authority is practiced.

Figure 26–3 illustrates the importance of delegation of authority in an organization. At the top of the illustration, office executive A has three assistants, 1, 2, and 3. In turn, assistant 1 has chiefs 11 and 12 reporting to him; likewise, chief 11 has subordinates 21 and 22; and chief 12, subordinates 23 and 24. The employees reporting to executives 2 and 3 are shown by the illustration. President A delegates proper authority to his executives 1, 2, and 3. The former two, 1 and 2, delegate authority to their subordinates; and in turn, these subordinates delegate authority to their subordinates. In contrast, executive 3 is trying to do all the managerial work of his organizational unit himself. He does not delegate authority to either 15 or 16, who likewise do not delegate to 29, 30, 31, or 32. This failure to delegate authority actually paralyzes this portion of the organization under executive 3. To a great extent, the employees reporting to executive 3 may just as well not be management members of the organization. There is in reality no formal authority structure below executive 3.

In delegation, the delegator always retains his overall authority for the delegated duties. He does not surrender or permanently release his authority. He does grant the right for others to act officially within the specific areas. Only the authority needed to carry out successfully the assigned functions is or should be delegated. This makes for the tapering concept of authority and simply means that in most organizations the

FIGURE 26–3. Failure to Delegate Authority by Office Executive 3 Tends to Paralyze the Organization Established Under Him.

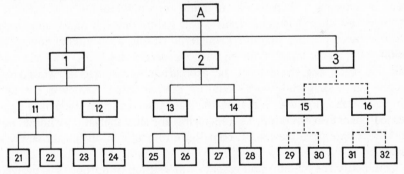

authority becomes successively smaller or tapered as successively lower horizontal levels of the structure are considered.

Since an authority delegator retains in the ultimate all his authority, he likewise retains in the ultimate all his responsibility. He cannot evade a failure of a subordinate by saying it was the fault of the subordinate. The superior retains the ultimate responsibility and is accountable for what is or is not achieved by his organizational unit.

From the practical viewpoint, delegation of authority is either specially granted or inherently implied in the job. In the former case, it is given to an individual in order that he may act to perform the management which is essential in achieving the objective. In the latter case, the authority is inherently tied up with the job, so that whoever holds the job automatically possesses the authority which goes with that position. In any enterprise, therefore, authority is contingent upon such things as the delegation of those already in authority, the traditional structure of the organization, and the character and mental characteristics of the individual.

## PROBLEM OF DELEGATION

Many managers are reluctant to delegate; and frequently, delegation is practiced to a limited degree only. To request a manager to delegate seldom brings about the desired practice. A fear exists that if authority is delegated, the right decision may not be made, and the work will not be handled correctly. The nondelegator believes that he must keep in close touch with activities and decide most issues. In some instances, failure to realize the amount of authority needed by a subordinate to get the work done properly may exist. In other instances, the manager states that he has delegated authority but at the same time criticizes his subordinates when they make and enforce decisions without his advice.

Delegation of authority is not easily acquired. The natural tendency is to do work yourself if you are the one charged with doing it. And if the work is important, there is all the more reason for doing it yourself to make certain that it is done right. These habits develop quite commonly because most persons acquire managerial status after doing nonmanagerial work. The latter type emphasizes doing the work yourself and doing it well; the reward can be promotion to managerial work. But success in managerial work requires getting work achieved by and through others. Failure to realize this fact plus difficulty in making the needed change in thinking, i.e., acquiring the managerial viewpoint, not the direct operative viewpoint, contribute to the lack of delegation by a manager.

Commonly the amount and extent of delegation of authority is arrived at informally by trial and error. The subordinate makes a decision or tries out a certain practice; and if no reprimand results, he assumes the management work performed is within his province. In many cases, the status of delegation of authority is the result of an infiltration process over a long period of time. Slowly but surely, authority for certain matters has been turned over to the delegatee. Commonly, verbal statements establish the amount of delegation of authority; and in a relatively few instances, the superior gives specific delegation of authority in writing.

## DEVELOPING DELEGATION OF AUTHORITY

The first requirement for developing delegation of authority is to realize the need for it. A manager must recognize that as long as he is limited to doing what he can accomplish himself, he will always be short of time and limited in his achievements. The alternative is to acquire aides, train them, and permit them to do the job, even if their manner of doing it differs from how the manager might have done it. Competent aides are mandatory for group efforts to reach greatest heights. A manager's need is to multiply himself. It is nonsense to try to lead the band and play all the instruments, too.

Also needed is the establishing of a work climate that encourages delegation. Managers must be made to feel that turning over carefully selected assignments to their subordinates is the proper thing to do and that their superiors approve of such action, even when the subordinate does not perform the assignment in the same manner that the manager would and the results are short of the expected accomplishment. The deficiency is charged to the development of managerial skill. The underlying theme is that a manager grows most when he builds subordinates the most.

Furthermore, for delegation to work effectively, certain criteria can assist materially. Important is the establishment of definite goals and clear policies, for these give guidance to the subordinate and keep him from going too far astray in the fulfillment of the tasks. Work which is routine and which is covered by definite policies should offer little delegation difficulty. Clear and timely communication, complete instructions and orders, and definite job identifications are also helpful. And the use of broad controls expedites delegation, for they can supply the desired checks to determine whether the work is being accomplished satisfactorily.

Lastly, belief in delegation is necessary. An office manager must want to make delegation successful; he must strive to help it succeed. Among other things, he will not interpret delegation as distributing the work to others, sitting back, and observing if they make good or not. Rather, he will select the delegatee carefully and offer counsel readily to him, being careful not to give him answers, but to help him find the answers himself. Effective delegating does not just happen. From the very beginning, it takes much effort, time, and persistence to develop the art of authority delegation and to keep it alive.

## LINE AUTHORITY AND STAFF AUTHORITY

Full comprehension of organizing also requires knowledge of the types of authority, their respective characteristics, and when to use what type for which purpose. The two main classifications of authority are (1) line and (2) staff. A manager can have either or both. When a manager has line authority, he is called a "line manager" and normally exercises direct command over the work of all members in his unit, but there are certain exceptions, to be discussed. Characteristically, the authority relationship is of a superior-subordinate type, forming "a line" from the top to the bottom of the structure. It is the authority used to accomplish directly the major goals of an enterprise and exists at all levels of the organization structure.

Staff authority, the second major classification, is made up of several different types including (1) advisory staff, (2) functional staff, (3) service staff, and (4) control staff. All of these are commonly termed "staff authority," yet they are dissimilar in important respects, and the common identification of staff is unfortunate. A manager with staff authority is a staff manager. A clear understanding of these various types of staff authority helps clarify vital relationships in organizing. All are in use and are believed necessary. Their specific application depends upon the individual organization.

## ADVISORY STAFF AUTHORITY

The word "staff," according to Webster, means "a pole carried in the hand for support." Therefore, staff authority pertains to assistance or

FIGURE 26–4.

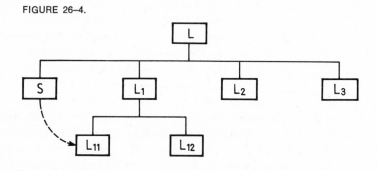

support, and this concept was the initial identification and use given staff authority. Much of this assistance and support takes the form of being advisory and is appropriately called advisory staff authority. Specifically, a manager with advisory staff authority normally counsels or advises, in his specialty, the manager having line authority. Advisory staff is a manager-to-manager relationship and can exist within any organizational level.

In Figure 26–4, line manager L has four subordinates, S, $L_1$, $L_2$, and $L_3$. The latter three are line executives, while S is an advisory staff executive. His job essentially is to counsel and advise L in his (S's) specialty so that L can do a better job. The counsel and advice of S can be accepted in whole or part and utilized by L in managing the organizational group; or L can reject the advice of S, since L is in direct command of the unit. In some companies, the practice of "compulsory staff service" is followed. This requires a line executive to listen to his staff executives, but the final decision and enforcement rests with the line executive. When the managers are competent, this practice aids them in their respective tasks. Also, in some enterprises, the "completed staff work" doctrine is followed. This emphasizes the presentation of complete solutions by the advisory staff to the line executives. Piecemeal recommendations are avoided; and stress is placed on supplying assistance, not placing the line man in a predicament with questions regarding what he wants investigated or what data should be included in a report. Of course, the line man and the staff man should talk things over, but in a constructive way, with each making contributions.

## FUNCTIONAL STAFF AUTHORITY

In information management, the use of functional staff authority is especially common. It concerns specific functions only and is delegated from one manager to another manager who is not related to the former by formally established authority channels. It can be conferred by a line to a staff manager, or vice versa. To illustrate, in Figure 26–4, line manager L may delegate to his subordinate staff executive, S, the authority for S to issue orders concerning a specific work activity directly to $L_{11}$, who is a line manager. In this case, the authority possessed by S is functional staff. Actually, L is delegating a qualified amount of line authority for a specific activity to S. The delegated authority is limited to a particular activity and applies only to the authority relationship in this activity between S and $L_{11}$. Good management practices would include L's informing $L_1$, $L_{11}$, and $L_{12}$ that this functional staff authority exists. Functional staff authority expedites efficiency and is convenient. Its use, however, must necessarily be limited; otherwise, established authority relationships are neutralized. Some specialized activities of the office from time to time require a competent office executive to explain and enforce office procedures to nonoffice personnel in order to insure proper handling and good administration. Such situations are solved by the use of functional authority.

## SERVICE STAFF AUTHORITY

When speaking of office organizing, the term "service unit" commonly arises. Its justification is primarily economy and improved work performed or service offered by the unit. Purchasing, mail, telephone, and reception service, and legal counsel are examples of service organizational units. Generally, the head of such a unit possesses service staff authority which actually includes some line authority, as persons are expected to request the service organization unit to perform for them a service included in the service unit's makeup and, furthermore, to be bound by the decisions made by the service unit in its specialty. To illustrate, the manager of billing may not purchase supplies and equipment. This is done for him by the purchasing unit, and the billing manager abides by the decisions and actions of the purchasing unit.

Service staff authority applies both within and outside of the service unit as it pertains to this specialized service work. In addition, some service organizational units utilize functional authority when delegated, that is, they have jurisdiction over specific work performed by others not normally or formally under the authority of the service unit. In some instances, the service unit's authority is limited to the strictly advisory. The unit recommends and counsels in work regarding its specialty, but the decision as to what to do and its enforcement are not within the province of the service unit.

## CONTROL STAFF AUTHORITY

In many organizations, there are units that perform essential work for achieving the major goals of the enterprise; yet, their work is of a specialty nature and is not supplied on a strictly advisory basis. The contribution is indirect insofar as the chief objectives are concerned; but when necessary enforcement of decisions is present, considerable line authority over the particular function in the enterprise may be present. For example, these conditions frequently exist for an auditing unit, or a procedural analysis organization unit, or one dealing with office standards. Requests by such a unit to line managers to supply certain financial information, to use financial standards supplied, and to abide by prescribed auditing practices are not on a "take it or leave it" basis by the line managers. The requests are essential for required managerial control and when they can be enforced by the auditing unit, such a unit has control staff authority. In a very real sense, it includes aspects of ultimate line authority. Enforcement is usually voluntary because the line managers realize that the specialty offered is important and that, if necessary, compliance with requests can and will be forthcoming.

## ORGANIZATION CHARTS

*An organization chart is a graphic representation of an organization structure.* It can be thought of as a picture of the organization structure; it shows the organizational units, the relationships, and the existing lines of authority.

To draw an organization chart, use the outline approach. First, list the main functions; next, place those functions which are subordinate to the main functions under the proper main function in the outline list; then, place under each subordinate function the minor functions which properly belong under the respective subordinate function. In this way, a list is developed which shows the main functions, the subordinates under each main function, and the minor functions under each subordinate. This outline form is then transformed into the graphic form which makes up the organization chart.

The chart may also be prepared by starting with the person of highest authority in the organization structure and working down by determining who reports to this top person and what activities each person handles. This procedure provides the information for the first level of management below the chief executive and may be followed for each consecutive layer. From the information so gathered, the organization chart can be constructed.

An organization chart simply helps in visualizing the organization structure; it insures neither good organization nor good management. However, it does compel the organizer to put down in black and white what the structural relationships are. This crystallizes his thinking and clarifies fuzzy, but important, details which might otherwise be overlooked. Specifically, the main advantages of an organization chart can be listed as follows: (1) a clear, overall concept of the organization is obtained; (2) the main lines of authority and responsibility are brought out in full relief; (3) promotional possibilities are provided; and (4) the assignment of titles is simplified.

## THE LINE ORGANIZATION

The line, or scalar, type of organization, which was used extensively in our early industrial development, is one of the oldest organization forms. It uses line authority exclusively. This type of organization is still quite popular and is frequently employed by proprietors of small businesses and for other enterprises where the number of employees is small.

The line organization is characterized by direct lines of authority from the top executive to the various assistants, and direct from them to the employees at the operative level. Each member is fully responsible for the carrying out or the actual performance of the job to be done. Throughout the entire structure, each member is in complete charge of all activities within his particular organization segment. Authority and responsibility are greatest at the top, and reduce as successively lower levels of management are considered.

The advantages of the line organization include the following: Authority and responsibility are definitely fixed, and the person who has that authority and responsibility is known to all; the structure is very simple and hence readily understood by all personnel; discipline is easily maintained, since each superior and each subordinate knows what is expected of him and in which areas he is to operate; decisions can be quickly reached; the fact that a single superior who is in complete charge makes for a minimum of delay in decision reaching; and lastly, the line organization offers splendid training opportunities for the development of managerial talent. The line manager is charged with getting things executed; he must be a doer; he must get the work accomplished.

In contrast, the line organization also has its disadvantages. Perhaps most outstanding is that, relatively, specialization of work is not practiced. Particularly is this true at the intermediate and supervisory management levels. Another disadvantage is the difficulty of securing coordination. Each lord is master of his own house or his unit of the organization, and the coordination between any two line units of the same organizational level is obtained solely by the strong leadership of the man at the top in charge of the several line units. The tendency is for the head of each unit to develop a rather independent unit and to think only of his own unit's activities, without much regard for other necessary functions of the enterprise. In fact, some believe that the line organization probably places too much emphasis on the managers. Another disadvantage is the difficulty of forming organizational units; this is particularly true in cases where the unit is not suggested by the process. Frequently, insufficient opportunity is afforded to modify and to change existing units from the viewpoint of the total organization structure.

## THE LINE AND STAFF ORGANIZATION

When staff authority relationships are added to a line organization, the resultant organization is called a line and staff organization which is extensively used. In this type, line managers have line authority to carry out the activities, but their efforts are qualified by staff managers who have authority to carry out their particular work. Both line and staff managers are considered essential, and all are believed needed to accomplish the work effectively. More precisely this means that the line and the staff managers comprise a winning team of managers with varying degrees and types of authority. In the team effort, all are required. None should be thought of as inferior; for if in fact they are, then either they should be replaced or their area of operation should be eliminated.

The chart of a line and staff organization is shown in Figure 26–5. Under the vice president of information are the managers of data processing, storing and retrieving, communication services, and research. The organizational units under each of these managers are indicated on the chart. The managers of units without dotted circles around them have line authority, those encircled have staff authority. Likewise, under the vice president of finance are shown the units of line and of staff authority.

FIGURE 26–5. A Line and Staff Organization.

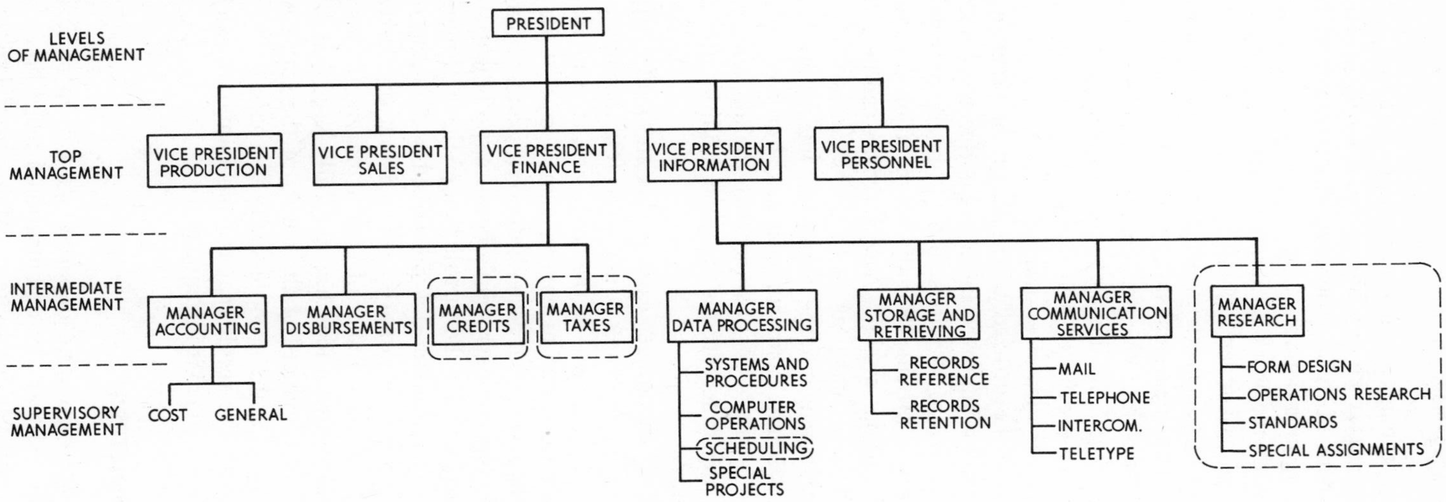

LEVELS
OF MANAGEMENT

TOP
MANAGEMENT

INTERMEDIATE
MANAGEMENT

SUPERVISORY
MANAGEMENT

PRESIDENT

VICE PRESIDENT PRODUCTION
VICE PRESIDENT SALES
VICE PRESIDENT FINANCE
VICE PRESIDENT INFORMATION
VICE PRESIDENT PERSONNEL

MANAGER ACCOUNTING
MANAGER DISBURSEMENTS
MANAGER CREDITS
MANAGER TAXES
MANAGER DATA PROCESSING
MANAGER STORAGE AND RETRIEVING
MANAGER COMMUNICATION SERVICES
MANAGER RESEARCH

COST
GENERAL

SYSTEMS AND PROCEDURES
COMPUTER OPERATIONS
SCHEDULING
SPECIAL PROJECTS

RECORDS REFERENCE
RECORDS RETENTION

MAIL
TELEPHONE
INTERCOM.
TELETYPE

FORM DESIGN
OPERATIONS RESEARCH
STANDARDS
SPECIAL ASSIGNMENTS

Note that even though a function is staff, the organization for carrying out that function may be of a line organization type. To illustrate, under the vice president of information, the management of the research unit is staff to the organization as a whole, but the research unit itself is a line organization with the work of forms design, operations research, standards, and special assignments under it. Also observe that a staff unit can exist at various management levels. The chart is intended for illustrative purposes only. Organizational units under the vice president production, vice president sales, and vice president personnel have not been included.

The advantages of the line and staff organization are many. First, the lines of authority are fairly well fixed, good discipline can be attained, decisions can be reached after desirable deliberation, and the principle of specialization can be utilized to the extent of practical limits. Second, coordination can be improved because the line officers are supplied with factual data concerning activities both within and outside their own units. Third, flexibility is provided for the organization structure to expand or contract, as conditions warrant. New activities can be added and old ones discarded without seriously affecting the organization structure. Fourth, proper balance among all the activities, line as well as staff, can be maintained. Fifth, more opportunities are afforded to match the desires, capacities, and interests of personnel with the job, since a greater variety of jobs involving different duties, responsibilities, training, and background is required.

In contrast, disadvantages exist in line and staff organizations. These disadvantages tend to center around the relationships existing between the line and staff managers. In the first place, the line manager may tend to ignore the advisory staff manager's counsel, so that the expert information provided is never used. Second, the staff manager may tend to ignore the ideas of the line manager simply because specialization and expertness are supposed to be under the jurisdiction of the staff manager. Third, the staff manager may overstep his prescribed staff authority and even attempt to take over line authority which is out of his realm of activity. Fourth, a considerable number of staff managers are not good salesmen, and many staff contributions are not fully used partly because other managers are not convinced of the merits of the staff's work. Fifth, line orders, staff advice, and staff orders may be confused by members of the organization, with the result that misunderstanding exists and cooperation among the managers is incomplete.

## USE OF COMMITTEES

Committees constitute an important part of most organization structures. They can exist at any organizational level, be of short or of long life, and deal with various subjects. Many are delegated line authority, that is, they not only discuss and decide issues but also secure compliance of others with the decision. Such a committee is sometimes called a "plural executive." However, probably most committees have advisory staff authority. Their purpose is to discuss and recommend. In some cases, they simply receive information, classify it, and make it available for others to use.

The committee may be viewed as an important modification or addition to the main type of organization. Just as staff modifies the line to form a line and staff organization, so the committee may also be added to form a line, staff, and committee organization. In this case, the committee element adds an excellent medium to the organizational structure for discussion and educational group meetings. Also, the committee acting in an advisory capacity serves as an excellent addition.

A committee offers several outstanding advantages. First, it permits organization members to take an active part; thus, better cooperation is obtained. Second, it helps to secure coordination. Men and women from different departments have the chance to see the organization's needs as a whole; they have a chance to discuss these problems with their fellow supervisors and employees. Third, the committee is an excellent source of collective advice, ideas, and opinions of top managers. Fourth, the committee offers an excellent medium for educational and training purposes.

In contrast, a disadvantage of the use of a committee is that it divides responsibility. There is no single individual fully responsible. Second, the committee is weak in carrying out activities. It commonly lacks decisive action and follow-up. Third, most of a committee's decisions are the result of compromise—a "straddle the fence" variety. Usually, the majority rules; and this might tend to bring prejudice, secret agreements, and bargaining, rather than facts only, into the committee's decisions. Fourth, committee meetings usually require a great deal of the members' time. There appears to be little doubt that a sizable amount of this time is wasted and might better be spent by members on their individual tasks.

## QUESTIONS

1. In your opinion which poses the more serious problem; a manager deficient in authority or a manager deficient in responsibility? Discuss.
2. Outline the identity, implication, and importance of span of authority in organizing.
3. Do you agree with this statement: "Authority should filter down in an organization and reach the person at the lowest management level, in contrast, responsibility should be fixed at a high management level so that effective management is feasible." Why?
4. Point out the difference between the terms in each of the following pairs:
   *a*) Span of authority and horizontal authority relationships.
   *b*) Service staff authority and a flat organization.

*c*) Organization chart and authority.

*d*) Compulsory staff advice and plural executive.

5. Describe a situation illustrating difficulties encountered due to a lack of utilizing the completed staff work doctrine.

6. Briefly discuss the advantages in a manager using a line and staff organization.

7. Enumerate the major reasons why managers do not delegate authority. What inferences do you draw from this state of affairs?

8. Describe an organizational arrangement illustrating the use of service staff authority. Of control staff authority.

9. What is management responsibility and how can it be developed in a management member?

10. Do you agree with this statement: "Delegation of authority is seldom set forth by means of a formal or special grant by the delegator." Why?

11. Discuss several ways in which the delegation of authority by an office manager can be developed.

12. Relate the advantages and disadvantages in the use of committees in office organization structures.


## CASE PROBLEMS


### Case 26–1.   Jordon-Huss Company

Returning from the monthly management meeting, Supervisor Hugh Zeigler of the tabulating and processing department, walked by two of his employees, operators of card-punching machines, and said "No more overtime. The chief is really on the warpath. Be sure to leave when quitting time arrives." They did and so did Mr. Ziegler.

The following morning Mr. Ziegler's wife telephoned the office that her husband had the flu and would not be in for a few days. That same day about midafternoon, the assistant marketing research manager, Mr. Russell Pruyn, came to the tabulating and processing department with work which he described as an emergency and asked the card punchers to start it immediately and stay with it till finished. The female operators replied that Mr. Ziegler told them not to work overtime. "Forget it. I don't care what you were told," shouted Mr. Pruyn. "Finish this job, work as late tonight as necessary."

The operators talked it over and decided to ask the personnel manager what they should do. "I can't tell you," was the reply. "I know top management has just issued an edict, No more overtime. You'll have to decide what to do." The operators decided not to work overtime.

First thing next morning, Mr. Pruyn called for his tabulated data, but the cards were not finished. Upon finding that the operators did not work last night, Mr. Pruyn became furious and stalked directly to the office manager's office. Within a few moments, a telephone call requested the two operators to come to that office. The office manager asked the operators to explain why Mr. Pruyn's work was not finished. They related that Mr. Ziegler told them not to work overtime. They also asked for advice from the personnel manager who told them to decide for themselves. They did.

## Questions:

1. What conditions led to this problem?
2. What is your recommendation to avoid such situations as this in the future?
3. What action should the office manager take? Why?

### Case 26–2.  Mathews Company

It is true that Mr. Paynter is a very busy man. The work load is heavy, but based on much organizational study and carefully established work standards, there are ample work divisions and employees in each division. Mr. Paynter reports directly to the vice president of finance, and reporting to Mr. Paynter are six supervisors, including, respectively, the heads of (1) corresponding, (2) order billing and invoicing, (3) office procedures and methods, (4) mailing, (5) filing and records retention, and (6) office services. Mr. Paynter is known to run a "tight ship." He permits his supervisors to make routine decisions only and frequently there are differences of opinion as to what is a routine decision. He sees to it that he is in on every decision affecting (1) any hiring, promoting, or terminating of an office employee, (2) any office employee's pay adjustment, (3) any change in currently followed procedures or methods, (4) any purchase of office equipment, machines, or supplies, and (5) any contemplated change in office policies. In addition, Mr. Paynter personally directs the office suggestion system, edits and approves changes and modifications in the office manual, and supervises the receptionist, two telephone switchboard operators, and the four members of the office janitorial staff working day and night hours.

The president of the company has expressed his dissatisfaction with the office to his immediate subordinates, the vice presidents of sales, production, and finance, respectively. He states that he waits an unduly long time for office information, there are many delays in preparing reports, processing customers' orders seems to take longer than it should, and "it takes a month and three summers to get a new idea adopted in the office." He has observed idle office machines during his walks through the office. He personally likes Frederick Paynter who is a hard worker, always willing to help, is extremely agreeable, dresses well, and is conscientious about his work. If anything, he appears overly cooperative. With all the office employees, now 83 in number, the president feels the office should be far more effective than it is.

## Questions:

1. As you see it, what is the major problem?
2. What action do you recommend the president of Mathews Company take? Why?

### Case 26–3.  Paul Lawrence Chadwick

Paul Lawrence Chadwick is the head of a staff unit, the office work simplification unit; he reports to the office manager. In turn, the office manager reports to the president of the company. Chadwick works hard, has a multitude of ideas, and at times becomes discouraged because of the delay and inactivity on many suggestions for improvement made by his organization unit.

What he believed to be an excellent suggestion, from the viewpoint of both less effort required to do the work and lower cost, was submitted to the office manager in a report some six weeks ago. Since that time, Chadwick has asked the office manager several times what he thinks about the suggestion and receives the answer: "We are looking into it." Chadwick feels, however, that the office manager is just "stalling."

A few days after the last time Chadwick spoke to the office manager, the latter suffered an injury in an automobile accident. It was announced that he would be unable to come to work for at least four weeks; while he was absent, his duties would be taken over by the assistant office manager. Chadwick has little respect for the assistant office manager's abilities. Likewise, the assistant office manager feels that Chadwick is too precise and spends company money on a lot of impractical ideas. The two do not get along too well.

Chadwick believed the suggestion embodied in the last report to the office manager to be so important that, in the company's best interests, delay in its adoption should not be tolerated. Based on past experience, he was convinced the assistant office manager, now in charge, would take no action on it. Accordingly, he explained the new procedure to the supervisor whose department, direct mail, is affected and to a small number of line employees in that department. At Chadwick's insistence the new means was tried out. For the next several weeks, careful records of time expenditures were made by Chadwick, and these were compared with expenditures under the previous arrangement. Savings of $23 a day, or approximately $6,000 a year, were indicated through the use of the new means. Chadwick wrote the report concerning the installation and the results obtained and submitted it to the president of the company, with a copy of the report being sent to the "office of the office manager."

Two days later, the office manager returned to his job; and during the course of "welcome back" conversations, the president referred to the report and asked a few questions about it, which the office manager could not answer, explaining he was not familiar with it. Returning to his office, the office manager called in his assistant and inquired about the new process being used in the direct-mail department. The assistant knew nothing about it. The office manager's secretary, overhearing the conversation, located the copy of Chadwick's report to the president and gave it to the office manager.

## Questions:

1. What action do you feel is proper for the office manager to take? Why?
2. Do you approve of Mr. Chadwick's action? Justify your answer.
3. What general impression do you gain concerning the organization of this company?

### Case 26–4.  King-Mullin Corporation

Manufacturers of devices to control, confine, and utilize the flow of liquids under pressure, King-Mullin Corporation has grown tremendously during the past five years. Its fluid system components are being used in the aircraft field, missiles, lift trucks, hydraulic accumulators, air control valves, and similar applications. Headquarters are in Los Angeles where the general manager runs the business for several owners. There are 156 employees in production which is headed by the production manager. Reporting to him are members of the research and development unit. The office personnel and the work done by each follow. The number in parentheses following each title indicates the number of employees with that job.

*1. Assistant to the Purchasing Agent.* (1) Types the letters of this department and handles the files of this unit. Reports to the purchasing agent and personnel director.

*2. Assistant Sales Manager.* (1) Handles advertising; works with the advertising agency; plans catalogs and brochures, displays, and sales portfolios; corresponds with distributors and customer. Reports to sales manager.

*3. Billing Clerk.* (1) Types the invoices, maintains her own files of the customers billed. Reports to the controller.

*4. Bookkeeper.* (1) Keeps the books, types bills, and also does some filing work. Reports to the controller.

*5. Controller.* (1) Directs the work of the accounting department; makes up various financial reports, cost analysis, and office employees' payroll; and hires new employees for the office. Immediate superior is the general manager.

*6. Correspondent.* (2) Dictates letters on machine and sometimes to a file clerk or typist, makes up shipping schedules and cost estimates. Reports directly to the sales manager.

*7. Cost Accountant.* (1) Makes up factory payroll, assists the controller with cost analysis work and other reports, and does some typing and filing. Reports to the controller.

*8. File Clerk and Typist.* (2) Alternates between filing and typing, takes shorthand, and is responsible for office supplies. Is under the direct supervision of the sales manager.

*9. General Manager.* (1) Actually the president of the corporation, he coordinates the entire operations of the corporation, makes major decisions, and interprets broad policies.

*10. Order Clerk.* (1) Enters incoming orders and is secretary to and reports directly to the sales manager.

*11. Purchasing Agent and Personnel Director.* (1) Handles all purchasing and is personnel director for factory workers only. Immediate superior is the general manager.

*12. Sales Manager.* (1) Handles contacts with customers, either personal or by mail; travels about 50 percent of the time; and manages the work of the sales department. Reports to the general manager.

*13. Salesman.* (6) Calls on prospects and customers, secures orders, takes care of customer inquiries by telephone. The sales manager is the immediate superior of all salesmen.

*14. Secretary to the General Manager.* (1) Performs secretarial work for the general manager, which work requires about 35 percent of her time; during the remainder of her time, she helps the other departments. Reports directly to the general manager.

*15. Switchboard Operator.* (1) Operates the telephone switchboard and does some typing. Reports to the general manager.

Within the next four months, a small computer will be delivered and installed at the company. This addition is mainly the result of the efforts of the general manager, who is confident that it will prove very valuable for problems in the company's research and development work, analyzing sales, and improving office work. For this latter application, he has received little or no encouragement from the controller, who, to date, has shown little interest in the forthcoming computer or its application to the regular paper work of the corporation and prefers not to disturb the present means of processing papers.

## Questions:

1. Draw an organization chart of the company.
2. Evaluate the present office organization, pointing out what may be its strong and weak points.
3. Where do you suggest the forthcoming computer unit be placed from the standpoint of organization? Why?

chapter **27**

# Informal organization
# and the office

In order that people may be happy in their work,
these three things are needed: They must be fit for
it, they must not do too much of it, and they must
have a sense of success in it.
—*John Ruskin*

THE TRUE MAKEUP of organization consists in many respects of the
patterned activities of a number of individuals or employees. These
activities are interdependent, repetitive, and relatively enduring. They
exist and take place in relation to the attainment of goals although the
activities may not always be purposive and representative of the most
efficient endeavors. It is a common state of affairs for an organization to
include more than is indicated by the design of its founder. Some activities become distorted in operational practice, others take on unforeseen
embellishments, while others, assumed to be present, are lacking.

It is with these important properties of organization, over and above
those developed logically and rationally, that we shall deal in this chapter.
Various attempts to deal with the latent, in contrast to the manifest,
functions of organization have been made. And approaches along the line
of studying anticipated and unanticipated consequences of organization
functioning have been pursued. But these studies are incomplete in that
we lack knowledge of the real purpose of the major organizer and,
furthermore, are unable to discover the mental designs of the organization
that he possesses.

645

## ORGANIZATION OBJECTIVES

We commonly speak of organization objectives and seek to define and use them in our efforts to understand and improve an organization. But the stated purposes of an organization can be misleading. They can idealize, distort, or even omit some important purposes of the organization's operations. And commonly there is no universal agreement among the managers and the nonmanagers on the real mission of the organization. The same stated goal is given different interpretations or shades of meanings. The intent and priority of actions in the planning designed to attain the objectives are further evidence of misunderstanding or disagreement on what the objectives are. We are dealing with human beings and their beliefs and behaviors. Many actions are generated that have little to do with the rationale of the organization, yet they constitute strong influences that must be reckoned with in organization study.

For example, the president of a company may describe the purpose of his enterprise as one of supplying high-quality and wanted food products to discriminating buyers; his sales manager sees it as realizing an above average amount of profits; the research director as creating new knowledge about food technology; the information manager as demonstrating the essentiality of processing paper work efficiently and obsoleting certain office practices long followed by the enterprise. These objectives are not necessarily diverse. With mutual explanation and some minor adjustments, they might well be quite compatible. Yet an elaboration by each of his objectives would certainly lead to additional differences. Again, we must realize that we are dealing with different people in an organization and they have different values, ambition, viewpoints, and behaviors.

## ORGANIZATION AS A SYSTEM

Viewing organization as a system is winning favor. If for no other reason, this approach offers the advantage of beginning organizational thinking with concepts that do not require identification of the designer's purpose and subsequently correcting for them when not fulfilled. In the systems approach, we start with three components: (1) input, (2) functioning of organization as a system, and (3) output. That is, the input into the system, the processing and transforming within the system, and the output or results are the major concepts with which to be concerned. It is these concepts to which the stability or recurrence of activities is examined. In the office, for example, these include the information and the human labor as the input, the patterned activities of data processing transforming the information, and the output, which is the report, letter, or information in an acceptable form representing the finished product or service.

The members who perform the activities are themselves interrelated by the organization system. What they do and don't do, think and don't think, believe and don't believe are interdependent with the established formal organization, the tasks to be accomplished, the customers, the unwritten rules about expected behavior for a member, and the personalities of others who are members of the organization. Hence, the behavior of any one manager is determined, not only by his motives and personality with those needs, but also by the interaction of his motives and personality with those of his colleagues. Also exerting some influence are the nature of the work being performed, the rewards, the controls, the formal relationships, and the expectancy of how a manager should behave. All these determinants are interrelated by the organization system.

Advocates of the systems approach to organization point out that it supplies the overall inclusive viewpoint necessary to understand the true meaning and influence of organizing. Many organizations are so large and complex that much past research about them has been limited to a segment or constrained aspect of organization. The true functioning of an organization as a whole has not been fully explored. Some studies have centered on offices performing a limited variety of tasks and technical conditions. It would seem that findings from such a study cannot be generalized to apply to all office organizations and certainly not to offices that are a part of different total organizations. To illustrate, the office of a mail-order company may be significantly different from that of a governmental unit or of a small job-shop manufacturer. Further, the environmental conditions are neither identical nor constant and we know now that such conditions must be taken into account in order to reach sound organizational decisions.

## GROUP'S EFFECT UPON THE INDIVIDUAL

Organization places the individual in a group relationship, and this differs from that of an individual being alone or in an individual-to-individual relationship. Individuals usually act differently when they are alone in comparison to when they are with other individuals. The presence of a group stimulates a person in that normally he produces a larger quantity of physical work when a part of a group. On the other hand, an individual is less inhibited and more free-ranging in his answers when tested before audiences or under a group situation, than he is when quizzed alone.

There appears to be some commitment, implied or otherwise, by the individual to the behavior and attitude of a group of which he is a member. A person joining the employment of an enterprise emphasizing modern information management is likely to become interested in and make contributions to this type of management. The group influence upon the individual is strong and, hence, organizational influence is strong.

Several generalizations regarding group-individual relationships will be stated. First, change in a group's belief and behavior is easier to accomplish than is change in belief and behavior of individuals separately within the group. For example, a group decision on a debatable subject commonly eases the effectiveness of outside social pressures that might be directed toward an individual should he take the same stand as an individual. In brief, the individual is protected by the group within which he hides his identity.

Another generalization is that group attitude changes are more likely to be permanent than are individual attitude changes. In part, this arises from the individual's desires to meet the norms of the group. The stronger the group's bonds, the more deeply imbedded are the individual's attitude with the group's standards. From the practical point of view, this means that bringing together affected persons to a joint meeting and trying to establish a group norm among them is superior to meeting each individual singularly and establishing an individual norm for each. The group is quite likely to ignore the individual norms. But observe that group influence creates momentum. Future change within the group is quite probable; permanency of group behavior is not assured. With new external pressures forthcoming shifts are quite likely.

In addition, the individual members of a group should participate in the group's decisions if the group is to be truly effective. We first stated this generalization back in chapter 4, but it merits mentioning again. A human being will most readily accept ideas and decisions that he has assisted in shaping. In essence, he is supporting his own thought and concepts. To illustrate, an information manager acts in a certain manner in part because of his particular personality and in part by the effect of his peers and superiors upon him. He will behave as he does to some degree because of expectations he shares with his comanagement members. Further, the formal relationships established will have some influence on his behavior as will also the particular set of operating conditions including the controls exercised, the exact nature of the technology applied, and the importance given to cost.

## FORMAL ORGANIZATION PRESSURES

Once a formal organization is created, it generates pressures for its growth, change, and survival. By the very nature of organization, the interaction of environmental requirements and personal needs and desires of members make dynamics a normal state of affairs. This means that the full comprehension of organization cannot be wholly understood in terms of past or present. Organization is a living entity and emphasizes future influence.

The dynamic characteristic derives mainly from the condition of organ-

ization members sharing a common fate, interest, and norms for carrying
out their respective activities. In addition, the existent common values
among the members provide a basis for a rationale to implement changes.
There are a number of identifiable dynamics. We will discuss only the
most important which include: (1) technical proficiency, (2) stability
maintenance, (3) adaptive adjustment, and (4) compromise and control
technique.

**1. Technical Proficiency.** Task accomplishment is the prime force and
ideology in the technical proficiency dynamic. Getting the task done is
given a position above all others. The major responsibility of each organization member is directly related to some aspect of the major task. To
this end work specialization is followed and the work itself is fractional-
ized to components in order to expedite the work processes. This fraction-
alization is derived by rational analysis. Standards are recommended for
work segment and accomplishment is checked against these standards. As
pointed out in Chapter 25, allocation of jobs is usually on the basis of
work similarity in terms of process, but other bases are used, for example,
the location or place the work is done, the people who do the work, and
the buyer or clientele served. Selection depends upon individual circumstances and the judgment of the organizer.

However, the fact that the divisionalization of work is logical and that
the measurements of work output are precise and accurate do not, as such,
automatically guarantee that the work will be accomplished with high
technical efficiency. The attitude or propensity to produce by the employees may be negative for any number of reasons. Turnover may be high, a
lack of enthusiasm toward work observed, and an absence of genuine
cooperation noted on matters of importance to the enterprise. Technical
efficiency may be approached, but organization efficiency is considerably
distant from its maximization.

**2. Stability Maintenance.** In some organizations the major dynamic
can be characterized as one of preserving a steady equilibrium. It is
evidenced by different forms such as preserving the pattern of existent
authority relationships by seemingly constant adjustments, spelling out
organizational concepts to bring about rigidity, and maintaining the
status quo in absolute terms. Pressures from within toward formalization
and "to keep things as they are" develop and become quite potent. The
key is stability and predictability.

To illustrate, specific practices and mechanisms are adopted to preserve
this constant organizational state. Applicants are screened to select only
those believed most likely to adopt to this stable status. In fact, indoctrination is commonly undertaken to assist new members to fit into the
organization mold. Seniority is a sacred part of the organization, decisions
are deeply seeped in precedent, uniformity is viewed as ideal. The attempt
is to formalize all organization behavior by prescribing operating proce-

dures which are the accepted relevant human behavior. When achieved, it means that stability is accomplished and predictability is certain.

Most organizations have some element of stability maintenance about them. At least, this is true for the short run. This conservatism stems in part from the organization's attempt to maintain itself. And this has been the case with many offices. As an organization unit, the office has attempted to maintain itself even while other major units with which it is associated have changed quite drastically. Without doubt, this condition is due to the beliefs and behavior of the people of the office organization, but it is worth noting that to some degree it is found in all service organization arrangements which include the office to total enterprise organization.

External demands normally exert pressures for change. In the business organization these demands are usually first recognized by leaders in either sales or manufacturing. They have contact with outside environmental influences and are concerned with the primary tasks to be done. The office, research and development, and engineering are more insulated from external forces. Yet indirectly they are affected by that to which the externally exposed components are subjected. Some activities of the office, for example, may become obsolete or the office may be asked to meet demands for which they lack adequate resources. The office is in reality concerned with not only its own survival, but that of the entire organization as well.

**3. Adaptive Adjustment.** Closely related to stability maintenance but representing a separate and important organization dynamic is the adaptive adjustment. In brief, this identifies the characteristics of an organization unit to exploit a changing environment rather than be exploited by it. Research is a good example in that in discovery of new basic knowledge, improving services or products, and investigating the needs of a changing economic and social order served by the enterprise the adaptive characteristic is emphasized. This makes for survival in a changing world by ability to be adaptive to the changing situations. Likewise, the information efforts of an office have undergone numerous changes during the last several decades, but they have survived and occupy the position they do today because of successful survival of new developments.

The adaptive activities within any enterprise are conditioned mainly by the enterprise's type of output and the external environment to which it is subjected. The office output of a research foundation, for example, is quite different from that of a mail-order house and, further, because of its sparse contact with outside reality, the research foundation office will be subjected to different nonenterprise influences than will be that of the mail-order house. Some offices enjoy relatively few transactions with the total enterprise's external environment and have no means of collecting data on changing demands and how best to meet these demands. From this arises a poor adaptive response to the eventual massive demands and the unit quite likely will be forced to make drastic modifications, if it survives.

One can say that the adaptive functions from the inside out, while maintenance functions from the outside in the enterprise. Yet both tend to preserve constancy in the conditions of the organizational life. Adaptive seeks environmental constancy by bringing the outside forces and changes under control. In contrast, the adaptive seeks to achieve environmental constancy. However, the adaptive can move in either direction to (1) attain control over external forces, or (2) strive for internal modification of its own organization structure to meet the requirements of a dynamic environment. Which approach is better will depend upon the leaders and their judgment in which course offers the greatest possibility of success.

Human beings tend to prefer a status quo with internal arrangements and blame outside causes for any malfunctioning present. It is easier to attack the external images and concepts. If the services of an office are not being fully accepted, new services or new ways of supplying the old services are more likely to be conducted than rigorous efforts made to find out exactly what information recipients really want and need. If new employees are performing the office work poorly, we prefer to raise the hiring standards rather than modify the training and work standards. An internal structural change is viewed as a threat to the organization. In contrast, resolving a difficulty by changing the environment is not viewed as a threat, but actually a confirmation of the rightness of the existent organization.

**4. Compromise and Control Technique.** The three dynamics already discussed are often in conflict and are kept in bounds by means of the compromise and control technique or dynamic. By means of decisions the difference is either resolved or the decision is one of compromise. Within an office organization, for example, the information manager finds it easier and reasonably expedient to settle conflicts between the computer section and bookkeeping or between system and machine selecting on a current day-to-day basis, making concessions first to one and then to the other. Reorganization by logical analysis involves decisions involving imponderables—what to do with the long-standing organization unit, or the faithful but obsolete employee. Further, the lack of knowing which decision will bring the best results, and the absence of the ideally qualified new employee leads to the "alternate concession" approach. It is not difficult to apply and seems to maintain some degree of orderly organization operation. Theoretically, it seldom is the most efficient, but is justified on the basis that it supplies a solution to a complex problem of keeping the organization viable under the current conditions with the people available.

In addition, the compromise and control technique sets up and carries out policy pertaining to the problems under study by the adaptive adjustment. Frequently the managers act with relatively little information about problems external but indirectly affecting them, but their efforts are almost always to optimize this relationship. The more common forms are to utilize resources better in the outgoing operations, to seek stability of the organization, or to use the organization for additional work by utilizing its latent capacities.

This technique is carried out by the managers, but a change in organization structure is usually not called for in the case of stability maintenance whereas a change is required in the case of the adaptive adjustment. This follows primarily because basic policies are altered in the adaptive situation and these changes necessitate transforming the organization itself.

## ORGANIZATIONAL CONFLICTS

We are concerned in information management with organization bringing about an integration of efforts. This proper mixture and timing of efforts are sometimes thought of as being achieved through a rational and mechanical process, i.e., the specialists handling different portions of the total work are integrated simply by initiating an adequate "chain of command." Seldom, if ever, however, is this the case. Organizational integration is not accomplished by edict or by an automatic process. The functional specialists commonly hold different viewpoints which lead to conflicts about what action to take.

These conflicts must be resolved, if effective integration is to be realized. The resolution can come about in many different ways. Individual integrators and committees may be designated to facilitate collaboration among the various department heads. Scheduling of work and routine controls are also employed. The office manager, both in official and unofficial channels, is also an important means for much of this integrating activity. In any event, the beliefs, emotions, and concepts of the integration seekers are important for we now realize that interpersonal skills are required to achieve organization integration. The environment and human relationships among the members should be such that they are frank and forthright about their views and positions as they work together. Conflicts must be brought into the open, not suppressed or avoided. Also, a climate of trust among the parties should prevail.

Some conflicts involve problems which have many possible solutions. Interests may be divergent, but ingenuity helps find an answer that minimizes these differences. Many items of information may bear on the makeup of a new information system. Various managers may favor different alternatives, but the final outcome may be a compromise derived by complete sharing of available information including the value given to the different selection criteria. Implicit in this approach is agreement on fundamental objectives.

A specific and common type of conflict arises when each of two managers has an interest in an issue and a gain by one means a loss for the other. Bargaining is usually resorted to in which concessions are alternately made to discover and explore any common goal wherein agreement can be reached. Attempts are made to discover information about the aspirations and desires of the other party while at the same time withholding this same information about yourself.

## INFORMAL ORGANIZATION

The term *informal organization* has won popular usage and commonly designates a structure which is loosely organized, ill-defined, and spontaneous. Membership is gained sometimes without real knowledge of it. The exact nature of the relationships among members is unspecified and frequently the precise goals are not spelled out. They may, in fact, be more emotional than rational, more social than economic. Informal relationships can be quite complex, often difficult to explain, and commonly exert a powerful influence upon job satisfaction and productivity. The informal organization always exists to some degree whenever group activity is present. It is a normal state of affairs and arises as people associate with one another. The experienced manager knows he cannot abolish the informal organization like he can cancel the formal. Having created the latter he can do away with it if he so desires. But he did not create the informal and he holds no power to abolish it, even though he may so desire.

Informal organization gives emphasis to people and their relationships. It can be thought of as being attached to a person and is personal in its characteristics. Power in the informal organization is either given willingly by group members or it is earned. It is neither delegated nor does it follow a chain of command in the sense that these concepts are used in formal organization. Subject to the sentiments of people, it normally is not as stable as formal authority, is of a subjective nature, and typically cuts across organizational lines into various units. It is not subjected to controlling in the way that formal organization is.

Figure 27–1 shows a chart of an informal organization. Sometimes the term *interpersonal chart* is used. It is common to superimpose upon the formal organization chart lines to indicate the interactions of employees based on with whom an employee checks when the employee is other than his supervisor, with whom does he spend most of his time, or with whom does he confide and "talk things over." The chart of Figure 27–1 is developed from actions known to management members number 23 and

35. Notice that these contacts are outside formally prescribed channels of authority.

Why do informal groups arise and persist? Because they perform functions which the group members want and get due to the informal group's presence. For example, they supply social satisfaction—give a member recognition and an opportunity to relate to others. He may look to the informal group gathering to meet his friends, exchange experiences, and have coffee with them. These agreeable activities help make his work pleasant and something to look forward to. On the other hand, the manager must see to it that the fulfilling of these social satisfactions does

FIGURE 27-1. Informal Interactions of Manager 23 Are Indicated by Dotted Lines A, B, and C, Those of Manager 35 by D, E, and F.

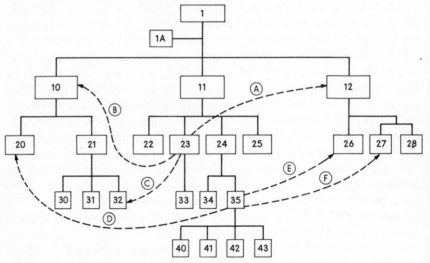

not lead members from the objectives of the organization. The informal organization should satisfy and supplement the major goals set forth.

Another contribution of informal organization is the exercise of social control both within and without the group. In other words, the behavior of the members is influenced and regulated by the informal organization. The young woman wearing a dress or suit not acceptable to the informal group will be subjected to comments and suggestions that sooner or later will convince her that the particular dress or suit is not an accepted style in the group. As a result, she stops wearing it to work. The overall effect is toward conformity as conceived by the informal members. Some management experts point out that this conformity can be carried to undesirable extremes whereby the informal leader may manipulate a group toward selfish or undesirable goals and bring about unnecessary conflict using the group for his own selfish purposes. In addition, the experts state that the conformity tendency is caused by informal groups, not by formal organization as commonly assumed.

A third major contribution of the informal organization is the continuation of cultural values deemed important by the members. This resolves into maintaining the status quo. Change is viewed as a threat to cultural values. This means that managers contemplating change should understand and take into account the informal groups for they will be a force with which to reckon.

## INFORMAL ORGANIZATION ADVANTAGES

The advantages of informal organization are many. We will note four important benefits, the first of which is that informal organization helps to share the load of the formal organization. A formal supervisor enjoying the support of the informal groups can operate highly successfully with loose supervision. The group is working with him, close checks are not required, and an effective cooperation is evident. Also, the informal organization tends to make a better manager out of a formal manager. He knows his plans must be correct and complete or the informal group will "tear him apart." Likewise, any changes, modifications in controlling, for example, will be well prepared before implementation. A third advantage is the satisfaction provided the employee groups. Security, a sense of belonging, and activity in affairs that concern a member are provided. Lastly, there is the oustanding benefit of improved communication. Informal organization members are without peer in gathering information they want to know and in distributing it. The "grapevine" is hard to beat. However, they may not always get the complete story and their information may not always be completely factual, but they do assist in answering the communication requirements. Also they provide an outlet for the employee with frustration and misunderstanding. He can talk with a person who will "hear him out."[1]

## INFORMAL LEADERS

Informal leaders arise for many reasons such as seniority, responsive personality, friendship, work location, and age. Informal groups usually overlap and one person may belong to several different groups. He may be the real leader in one, and a subleader or simply a member in others. The group typically looks to one leader on matters dealing with certain problems and subjects and to another leader for other interest or problem areas. That is, for each area, there usually is one primary leader who

---

[1] Communication is more fully discussed in chapter 32, p. 744.

stands above all the rest. A significant consideration is the esteem in which each informal leader is held. It should be added that the informal organization is an excellent training ground for future formal leaders to develop, but not necessarily future formal managers. In some instances the informal leader makes a poor formal manager because he shuns formal responsibility, lacks a broad comprehension of the formal job's makeup, or is overcautious.

## ORGANIZATIONAL DYSFUNCTIONS

Dysfunctions are the characteristics or conditions of the formal organization that cause or permit unintended behavior to take place. They emit from the formal organization and are a part of it. Hence, they differ from the condition of the informal organization which exists not from within but in addition to the formal organization. The behavior steming from dysfunctions can be desirable or undesirable depending upon the stated objectives. Quite often a dysfunction results in an improvement in efficiency, aids necessary socializing on the job, or assists hidden cultural likes. In such cases the effect of the dysfunction is usually considered advantageous even though it was not planned for and came into being somewhat by chance.

Specification of the type of processing to be followed and the hierarchy of decision makers with the defined limitations on decision making of each are probably the more representative of dysfunctions. An employee brings ideas, practices, and personalized efforts to his job. He tends to influence to some degree how the work is handled, i.e., processed, and his own contribution may not meet exactly the specifications, yet the work is completed entirely satisfactorily. In the case of decision making, it is extremely difficult and laborious to define each type of formal authority for each type of situation. Some gaps usually exist or unusual or new situations are encountered for which no formal authority is defined. Yet the decision must be reached and the group efforts moved ahead.

It also follows that some dysfunctions bring about behavior that is not in the best interests of the group's unity of effort. Included are lack of fixed responsibility, misinterpretation of the specific duties to be performed, and the unwarranted assumption that job instructions are updated and complete.

## THE HUMAN ELEMENT INFLUENCE

What we have been stating is that the power behind any organization structure is the personnel of that structure. For an activity to be performed, a responsibility to be assumed, and an authority to be exercised, the presence of human beings is required. We must never lose sight of the human element of any organizational structure for it is people that make organization—formal or informal—important.

Psychologically, the fact of individual differences is well established. What one person seeks, another abhors. The aims of one may differ widely from those of another. The capacity of creative work of "A" might be unusual, while that of "B" is such that he can think of a new idea only after extended and considerable effort. Likewise, the intellectual curiosity of one person might be concentrated upon mathematics, while that of another is very broad, covering many major subjects.

The various functions to be performed differ in any organizational structure so that there are many functions to be performed by many different types of persons. This condition is not paradoxical, as might first be expected. Rather, it is extremely fortunate, for it makes it possible to match a person of certain likes, capacities, and curiosities with the particular function which requires those particular characteristics. And to some extent it is the cause of informal organization coming into existence.

We strive to place the right person in the right job for this supplies enormous motivating power. The assigned job should meet the candidate's current capacities and interests. Proper placement makes for overall harmony within the organization and there is less adjusting to be done. Also, it provides for high efficiency because a person does his best when he is engaged in activities that fit fully his individual characteristics. Furthermore, there is the advantage of a better social order. The employee feels that he is doing the things which he believes are worthwhile and that he is contributing to society according to his individual ability.

## KEY MANAGERIAL DIFFERENTIALS

The differences among people manifest themselves in managerial personnel in a number of ways. Their differences in ways of thinking and working are reflected in organization primarily by (1) the formality of the structure adopted, (2) the interpersonal organization that exists, (3) the time-orientedness of the organization members, and (4) the goal-orientedness of the organization members. These can be a mixture of both formal and informal organizational efforts.

The formality of the structure adopted encompasses such considerations as the formal tasks of each unit, the levels of management, controls practiced, the importance given to cost, and the system of rewards granted for the accomplishment of desired goals. This formality of structures frequently differs somewhat for each major section of the entire structure and reflects the wishes of top managers.

Managers differ in the way they deal with their colleagues, their superiors, and their subordinates. The manager's interpersonal orientation is therefore of prime consideration in organization. For example, the manager in one part of an organization may be detailed-minded, watch costs very closely, and instill this type of thinking by his subordinates. In contrast, the manager of another unit may give most of his attention to developing and maintaining good relationships with his comanagers. The formal organization seldom spells out what interpersonal action a manager is to take. What he does in this area is highly personal and depends mainly on his subjective feelings and the people with whom he is working.

Among some managers, time-orientedness is a dominant characteristic and is the strong thread in their cloth of managerial actions. The effective use of time, meeting schedules, and placing time limits on projects are followed by such managers. And by custom and environment some managers are more time-minded than others. The management member faced with the immediate daily problem of processing a large quantity of orders views time and its use in a different light than the systems and procedures manager who is researching a new approach in handling a large segment of the paper work processing.

There is also a significant managerial differential with respect to goal-orientedness. We discussed early in this chapter the different goals among managers as well as the different interpretation of the same goal by them. What we are saying now is that goal identification and adhesiveness account for a major amount of the different behaviors among managers. This is a major source of conflict between the information manager and the other managers of an enterprise. In his eagerness to help, the information manager frequently assumes what information services will best assist the other managers in their work, but the other managers may fail to comprehend what the information services are and in what ways they can be of assistance to the information manager.

## THE NECESSITY OF FORMAL ORGANIZATION

There can be little doubt that informal organization is a natural outgrowth of organization as such and that informal organization meets important needs of members that the formal organization does not. Formal organization, however, is a basic requirement of management. There must be some well-defined and inclusive foundation by which the efforts of many human beings can be blended together effectively toward a common goal. And the basis should be orderly to avoid needless waste and to operate effectively. You cannot have all members totally independent and actively pursuing goals and performing activities their respective emotions, subjective desires, and personal wishes dictate. This would make for a very difficult situation—something like "all fleas and no dog."

The question arises, "How can the formal and the informal organizations be brought to an acceptable compatible state?" Mutual understanding, adjusting, spotting conflicts, and immediately working toward their resolution are possible avenues. But the approach of striving to relate the organization goals with those of the individual employee seems to offer the greatest practical helpfulness. To the degree that these goals are compatible, the employee attains personal satisfaction in achieving the organization's goal. The personal requirements vary among individuals and, fortunately, the organization requires different kinds of jobs and relationships so that it appears feasible to attain satisfactory combinations of individual needs and jobs. In addition, many managers feel that the answer lies in decreasing the dependency and submissiveness of the employee by providing him with greater responsibility and a larger scope of job. The need is for "bigger" jobs and less specialized and narrow small jobs. Also, required is greater recognition of the fact that organizing provides a facility through which employees join together to support efforts of truly competent leaders and for more productive efforts benefiting others as well as themselves.

## SIMPLICITY IS EFFECTIVE

The best all-around organization structure features simplicity in its makeup. Simplicity can be defined as "that delightful perfection between too much and too little." A complex structure is almost certain to make difficulties for a manager. Likewise, an organization structure that excludes necessary functions or stifles wanted informal arrangements is a serious handicap to the success of the enterprise.

The known rules of nature are comparatively simple; the natural way to perform a task, to relate one's work to that of another, or to accomplish a common goal, is to do it the simple way; it is against natural instincts to follow a complex and involved manner. The true concept of a particular function—what is to be done, when, and how—is best understood by people when they are informed in simple language and in a direct manner and are permitted and expected to decide some matters about the job's content and performance by themselves.

Efforts to make an organization structure seem profound by adding complex relationships and using involved theoretical concepts make for confusion. Efficient managers work with things that are simple; they understand them better; and they know that simplicity brings the best results.

It is appropriate to quote from a statement attributed to Sir Henry Deterding of the Shell Oil Company, who said:

There is a master key to success with which no man can fail. Its name is simplicity, simplicity I mean in the sense of reducing to the simplest possible terms every problem that besets us. Almost every man can succeed if only he will simplify everything in his life. That has been my working theory for forty years. As a very young man I stumbled upon this fundamental truth that everything that is complicated is wrong. Simplicity rules everything worth while. Whenever I have met a problem which after taking thought I could not reduce to simplicity, I have left it alone.

If more managers would follow this suggestion, our managerial efforts would certainly improve.

## CHALLENGE OF ORGANIZATION

A major challenge of organization is to integrate fully the work being done by the people of the various units into a cooperative and coordinated whole. This sounds fairly simple, but acquiring it in actual practice is a different story. People are not entirely unpredictable, yet they certainly cannot be considered the same as machines. Based on available knowledge, the intricacies of the human mind are far more difficult to understand than the chemical reaction of several compounds. But we should strive to understand and to use human resources for mutual benefits.

Another and perhaps eternal challenge is to develop a favorable organizational environment in which people are stimulated and permitted to grow. Environment is among the strongest influences to which an employee is exposed. Every organization provides environmental stimuli that affect its members, and likewise the members affect the organization. Favorable surroundings conducive to the development of a way of life, operating under the arrangement devised by organizing, must be provided. Among other things, this means the existence and operation of a healthy informal organization. The competency of an employee must not be curbed due to improper organizational relationships. In the best of organizing work, there is spirit, an attitude of mind, a belief in people and what they can accomplish. A solid organization structure is not built on form or body alone.

Finally, in the work of organizing, there is the challenge of utilizing all available resources, especially people, to their utmost. The tendency is to create new authorities, new units, and to go out and get "new faces." Adequate regard should be paid the tried and true. It is not always wise to discard the traditional for something new, mainly because it is new. Good organizing requires concentration on fundamentals. From a practical viewpoint, a manager must use in the best possible manner what is available to him. At the same time, changes and newness cannot and should not be avoided, for progress demands and is a part of something different.

## QUESTIONS

1. In your opinion is it better to think of organization in terms of groups of people or as individuals banded together to achieve a common goal? Justify your viewpoint.

2. Carefully define each of the following:
   a) Informal organization.
   b) Technical proficiency of an organization.
   c) Interpersonal organization.
   d) Organizational dysfunction.
3. Do you agree with this statement: "Organization objectives are the basis for effective organizing. There's no other really satisfactory means to evaluate the effectiveness of an organization." Why?
4. In what specific ways do you feel considering organization as a system will contribute to our knowledge of organizing?
5. Discuss in some detail a major beneficial contribution of informal organization.
6. Discuss the subject of stability maintenance as an important dynamic of organization.
7. Relate an example from your experience demonstrating that change in the behavior of a group is easier to accomplish than the behavior of individuals separately within the group.
8. What is meant by the managerial differential of time-orientedness and of what importance is it in organization?
9. In your opinion is formal organization really required in office management? Why? Informal organization? Why?
10. What is your understanding of organizational conflicts, and suggest what measures a manager might take to resolve them.
11. Explain Figure 27–1 in your own words.
12. Elaborate on the statement: "Human beings tend to prefer a status quo with internal arrangements and to blame most organizational malfunctioning on outside causes."

## CASE PROBLEMS

### Case 27–1. Read Company

Philip Randolph quit when corrective action of the type he believed mandatory was not taken by his superior, Edmund Jennings. Trouble had been brewing for some time, but two days ago it came to the boiling point. Mr. Randolph, supervisor of the cost department, must deal with the supervisor of the data-processing department, Milton Kirkman. The two—Randolph and Kirkman—don't get along too well. As long as they are not together, all is well, but anything might happen when they must work effectively with each other. Their common superior, Mr. Jennings, has known this for some time. He had hoped that with time, the problem might resolve itself.

The incident that triggered a disturbance took place when Mr. Randolph brought some work to Mr. Kirkman's department to be processed. There were some questions about a new format that Mr. Randolph requested be followed. Mr. Kirkman indicated it would mean extra work and expense for which he would charge Mr. Randolph's department. Further, Mr. Kirkman stated the data would not be any more valid or useful than in the format they had always followed. Differences of opinion became stronger. An argument ensued. Tempers flared and

Mr. Kirkman let out a blast of derogatory comments about Mr. Randolph, his mannerisms, and his processing ability that could be heard all over the department. Mr. Randolph complained to Mr. Jennings who immediately summoned Mr. Kirkman to his office. "Phil has told me what's happened. I want you to apologize now to him." Although still distraught, Mr. Kirkman said he was sorry, let bygones be bygones, but he honestly was convinced that Randolph knows little about data processing and what is worse, doesn't want to learn. He then left and Mr. Randolph remained in the office.

RANDOLPH: That man is impossible. I'm not working with him anymore. His people don't like him either and I don't blame them.

JENNINGS: You shouldn't talk that way. You really don't know. Nothing to that effect has come to me. Kirkman knows data processing and that's why he's here. Besides, I have no one to put in his place. Now you go back to your desk and give it another try. We're behind in our cost work, so let's get going.

RANDOLPH: I'm telling you—either he goes or I go. Put him somewhere else, just so I don't have to be around him.

JENNINGS: Kirkman is staying. I need him.

Mr. Randolph left the premises of Read Company and went home. Today, two days after the incident, the personnel manager showed Mr. Jennings a letter he has received from Mr. Randolph. In it, Mr. Randolph states that his employment was unjustly terminated. He was subjected to abusive language and to practices by company management personnel, all with the intent to get him out of the company's employ. He asks full severance pay of three months.

## Questions:

1. What is the problem?
2. In your opinion, what conditions have led to this problem?
3. What action do you recommend Mr. Jennings take? Justify your answer.

### Case 27–2.    Gleason Manufacturing Company

Clarence Cross, age 37, an industrial engineer, came to the Gleason Manufacturing Company about two years ago. He was assigned to the industrial engineering department of the manufacturing division. His work record showed him to be a highly competent and qualified man, and the company felt very fortunate in acquiring his services. During the first few months with the company, he handled several projects admirably well; and when the office requested an engineer to assist in some office work measurement, Mr. Cross was given the assignment. Soon he became extremely interested in office work and the possibilities it offered for improvement. He worked diligently and established many standards. However, many of the office employees thought Mr. Cross too aggressive and too much for himself. They did not trust him believing he would eliminate many of their jobs if he could.

Nearly a year ago, the office manager who reports to the vice president of finance quit to move south on account of his wife's health. The dynamic qualities and eagerness of Mr. Cross, together with his competency, suggested to the company's executive vice president that Mr. Cross was the man for the office manager's job. He so advised the vice president of finance who offered the office manager's job to Cross who accepted.

He was elated at the prospect. Within his first two months on the new job, he submitted a new coordinated plan for office operations which would save the company a considerable sum. Reluctantly, the office supervisors approved the plan. Mr. Cross had interviews with the vice president of finance and the vice president of sales. He stressed how his proposal would improve the office work processing and reduce the costs of his department. He also indicated that for too long the office has been considered as a secondary department and should be at a higher level in the company's organization. He hoped to achieve this objective for his department.

After six months of trying to make headway with the office improvement program, Mr. Cross began to feel he was getting nowhere. His superior, the vice president of finance, kept giving him special work to do, which work Mr. Cross classified as strictly "busy" work and of no real importance. One job was an investigation of the reception service; another, of the trend in the number of items included on a typical order received by the company. Also, at the suggestion of the executive vice president of the company, Mr. Cross visited several large offices using computers and also spent several days each with two different computer manufacturers. Reporting back to the executive vice president on the results of these visits, Mr. Cross felt that the executive vice president had little interest in the visits and would rather not hear about them.

Things continued about the same for the next four months. Mr. Cross kept busy on special assignments which he believed were whims of the company's top executives. He felt that he was achieving nothing. He arranged an interview with his superior and challenged the situation. He received a vague response. Thinking over the situation for several days, Mr. Cross decided to quit and tendered his resignation.

## Questions:

1. Should the company accept the resignation of Mr. Cross? Why?
2. What do you think the real problem is in this case? Explain.
3. What action should be taken, and by whom? Discuss.

### Case 27–3. Toole-Heedsman Corporation

The operations of the Toole-Heedsman Corporation are worldwide, with plants and offices located in the United States, South America, Europe, Asia, and northern Africa. Mr. Robert M. Fitzgerald, director of systems, procedures, and office machines, has two assistants, one for systems and procedures, and one for office machines. Mr. Fitzgerald finds that he must spend much of his time away from the corporation's main office in New York and quite often it happens that one of his assistants is out of town the same time Mr. Fitzgerald is absent. Under the circumstances, Mr. Fitzgerald has followed the general practice of delegating much work of a semiexecutive nature to his private secretary, Mrs. Irene Best, who has been with the company for seventeen years, the last five with Mr. Fitzgerald and before that, eight years with Mr. Fitzgerald's predecessor.

Officially Mrs. Best has no recognized line authority and issues orders only in the name of Mr. Fitzgerald. It is the opinion of the personnel manager that Mrs. Best is not fitted by training or personality for promotion to any other job in the office. Actually, she has become a fixture in the office, becoming well-nigh indispensable to her superior, Mr. Fitzgerald. She has knowledge of the policies, traditions, and routines of the various departments of the company.

Long experience has made Mrs. Best expert in keeping "in the clear" and in avoiding responsibility, and thus in many instances she is heartily disliked by junior executives, who resent her arbitrary assumption of authority but who, nevertheless, are reluctant to register a complaint with their superior or Mr. Fitzgerald because of the recognized dependence of the latter upon Mrs. Best to assume the burden of routine administration.

As a result, Mrs. Best has come to occupy a position of authority out of all proportion to her direct responsibility, and to some exerts an irritating influence detrimental to the morale of many office employees.

## Questions:

1. What are the chief weaknesses of the organization situation described above? What advantages?
2. What suggestion would you make to improve the situation?
3. How would you go about getting top managers to accept your suggestions?

# chapter 28

# Dynamics of office organizing

The men who stir the world most are not always
those who lift it most. To lift a little is better than
to stir much.
—*Arthur E. Morgan*

ORGANIZING is a vibrant, living activity. Change takes place whether or
not it is planned because organizing is what it is. Work demands change,
relationships and interactions of employees change, and the views of top
managers change. The astute management member not only recognizes
this, but he strives to utilize the inevitable changes to update his organization and thus employ the best possible work groupings, personnel, and
relationships in keeping with current demands.

Too often, an existent organization expands or contracts without any
genuine direction or guidance by the managers. New functions and new
personnel are added and the organization just grows, or in contrast,
functions are combined, peculiar organization relationships established,
and personnel placed on jobs requiring but a small portion of their
capacities. Or a needed organizational adjustment may be postponed
indefinitely—the outmoded organization being permitted to give rise to
difficult managerial problems. More precisely, this failure to recognize
organization dynamics and utilize them constructively leads to these
undesirable conditions:

1. The functions become disproportionate in their relationship to each
   other when judged by the relative importance of each function to
   the objectives of the enterprise.

2. Important functions are neglected, or they are subordinated to other functions; either condition makes it difficult to carry out the requisite activities.
3. New functions of a planning nature which might greatly strengthen the organization are ignored.
4. Capable men are confined to mediocre jobs.
5. Authority relationships become blurred; differences arise over who is supposed to decide what.
6. The necessary coordination among the major functions is decreased, since the personnel for each major function tend to stress their individual activity exclusively.

## MANAGEMENT AND ORGANIZATION CHANGE

As pointed out in chapter 25, the organization used is primarily the result of managers' attitudes and thoughts in this area of management. Especially is this true of top managers, for in most cases, they cast the die and decide, sometimes arbitrarily, what the organization pattern will be and when and where changes in it will be made. True, top managers are influenced by their subordinates regarding what changes in the existent structure should be made. But in most cases, organizational suggestions initiated by subordinates are conditioned by them in order to insure approval by the top managers. The location, timing, and extent of any organizational modification is regulated ultimately by the top managers.

Fortunately, the growing practice among enterprises of updating and improving the organization at regular intervals is being recognized as advantageous. For example, in some companies, this task is assigned to a manager within the organization. He works closely with the other management members, discussing possible organizational improvements with the managers who would be affected by such changes, and encouraging them to offer their ideas and participate in developing needed organizational improvements. Having an individual to head up the activity of possible organizational changes is an effective way to insure that attention will be given this important work. Some enterprises have even established a special organization unit for the sole purpose of studying and recommending organization changes and improvements. They report excellent results for these "organization evaluation" units.

## ORGANIZATION CONTINUITY

The continuity of an organization is conditioned chiefly by (1) the work—both its flow and its type—and (2) the time element. A relatively stable organization usually results when the flow of work is steady. Under this condition, modifications in organization are likely to be minor and infrequent. The line as well as the staff functions are usually well defined and known. On the other hand, when demand for the products or services is irregular, the predominant idea is usually to meet current requirements; and generally, the organization is of a line type, with relatively few staff functions. It tends to be a "nothing or all" existence.

Under the consideration of type of work, assume that office A handles the same work day in and day out and that office B handles a certain type of work X for a part of a month, work Y for another part of a month, and work Z for still another part of a month. The structural organization of office A will probably differ from that of office B, and the personnel must be attuned to changes periodically as a normal state of affairs. Office A probably will emphasize staff elements. Office B, on the other hand, will tend toward a line type of organization in which most employees can perform several activities with equal skill.

The time element also affects organization continuity. A structure set up temporarily to accomplish an emergency task might be far different from one set up to exist over a long period of time. Organizations having little continuity are usually very simple. An office group to handle registrations for a one-day convention might well be organized quite differently than a group organized to handle tax registrations. Or consider the example of a crowd of people organized to put out a fire in the neighborhood. They probably will be organized far differently from the firemen of the local fire department. The crowd of people will probably organize so that every member does something physical to put out the fire. It is unlikely that there would be any staff advisory members. Speed of action would be paramount and at the conclusion of the fire, the group would be dissolved. In contrast, the local fire department probably utilizes not only direct fire fighters but also a trained staff of experts in carrying out the task of fire fighting. Through time, the fire department has developed an efficient, highly coordinated organizational structure. And it is permanent —it is not dismantled after each fire-fighting experience.

## NEED FOR ORGANIZATIONAL BALANCE

Organizing, to be effective, must represent a balance among the various activities in relation to their real worth and contribution. An office is not all billing, all tabulating, all procedures analyzing, all storing and retrieving, or all anything else. It is a proper balance and blending among the many activities believed essential. The effective organizer thinks in these terms, yet he recognizes that organization dynamics has a significant effect upon the maintenance of this balance.

Normal changes within an organization take place in different areas and to different degrees. This results from current popular interest, research and development, and personal managerial intent. To illustrate, the records retention unit spurts in size due to a strong swing in managerial thinking on its importance; or systems and procedures develops into a central activity of those concerned with paper work processing, and organizational units within which this type of work is performed are expanded and given greater authority.

The result of these localized changes may tend to make the entire organization unbalanced. In some instances, the strengthened unit needed just that to place it in proper balance with the other organizational units. But frequently, the strengthening does not stop at the point of balance; it continues until a state of imbalance among the units is again present.

The meaning of organizational balance is subject to a great many interpretations. Good organizing maintains the relative importance of the various functions. Too frequently, however, managers continue to improve what is already relatively effective. Bettering the weak areas would be more helpful from the viewpoint of the entire organization. An important part of the problem is not to place all strong managers of the enterprise in one or a few organizational units. Success begets success. Commonly, the strong manager tends to attract trainees with the greatest managerial potential, and the more proficient manager tends to develop good managers under him.

In analyzing an office organization, it may be found that a certain activity such as electronic data processing appears grossly overemphasized relative to its importance in view of all the other office activities. Further study may reveal that the past experience and work of the office manager was in the area now seemingly too large or being given too much emphasis. Why is this? Because there is a human tendency by managers to emphasize and manage well those activities in which they are most interested and experienced. If the office manager "knows" electronic data processing, this work will tend to be organized and managed well. On the other hand, if he knows very little about office personnel research, this activity may be somewhat neglected and not developed to its required relative importance.

## IMBALANCE ILLUSTRATION

Let us discuss briefly an example of imbalance and see what was done about it. The illustration concerns a billing department, the original organization of which is shown by Figure 28–1. The department consists of four units—posting, typing, filing, and adjusting. The number of employees in each unit is indicated in the chart. Of the total of 93 employees reporting to the departmental manager, 60 or nearly 65 percent are in the posting unit, about 11 percent in typing, 20 percent in filing, and 4 percent in adjusting. While the relative work volumes may require this huge majority devoted to posting, nevertheless the organization unit for this work appears too big in relation to the other units of the department. By subsequent investigation and analysis it was disclosed that the efficiency of posting work was quite low. Common complaints included records missing and errors in posting. In defense of this poor condition, the supervisor stated that she could not properly supervise the huge number of posting employees and that there wasn't time to install an adequate plan of inspection. In the typing unit, six specialized job positions were found among the nine typists. Each performed her specialized or particular duties. Seniority played an important role in who gets what typing job position. This arrangement had evolved gradually over several years. Absence of a typist usually necessitated reassigning of personnel.

FIGURE 28–1. Original Organization of a Billing Department.

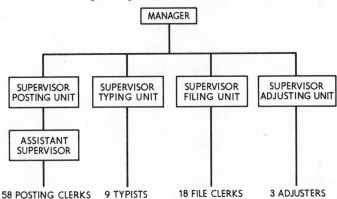

In the filing unit, there appeared to be little control. Material is not charged out and misfiling of records is numerous. As a result excessive search-time to locate missing records exists. About every week some filing personnel quit and replacements are hired. The filing supervisor states that 14 of her 18 clerks, or nearly 80 percent, have been with the company less than 6 months. She blames the trouble on the filing system used and the low pay for filing personnel. The four employees making up the adjusting unit are experienced and their work is entirely satisfactory. Absences, however, create difficulties as there is little flexibility in meeting fluctuating work volumes.

To improve this situation, various possible changes were discussed with the supervisors who were given much opportunity to recommend what should be done. The operative employees were also interviewed and requested to make suggestions for improvement. From all these ideas, several alternative plans of action were drawn up and presented to a billing council consisting of the manager, the four supervisors, the assistant supervisor of posting, and an employee from each of the four units.

The employees of each unit selected their representative to the council. After three council meetings, a plan of action was selected and implemented.

Figure 28–2 shows the revised organization. The posting unit was divided into four groups of 13 posting clerks each. These four groups are more manageable, serve as parallel competitive units, and encourage improved supervision. The former supervisor of adjusting became the new supervisor of posting. The former supervisor of posting became the assistant to the posting supervisor, a staff position dealing with the work of

FIGURE 28–2. Revised Organization of a Billing Department.

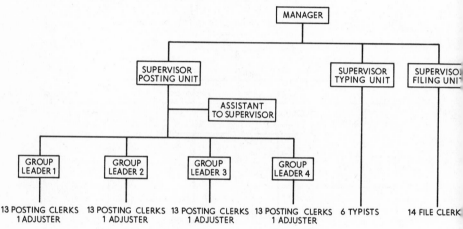

establishing work measurement, standards, and a quality program for posting work. The former assistant supervisor of posting was made one of the group leaders. The other three leaders were selected from the posting clerks. The former adjusting unit was eliminated and the three adjusters transferred to posting, one each to each group. The fourth adjuster needed was selected from the posting clerks.

With elimination of the unnecessary specialization in typing along with unnecessary work and certain typing practices, it was estimated that the typing could be handled by six typists. Flexibility among the typists was regained; two grades of typist were established: Typist I and Typist II. Unauthorized personnel were forbidden to remove material from the files. A charge-out system was installed and a records retention program started. Pay of the file clerks was increased 10 percent. Facts indicated that the filing work could be handled with 14 file clerks.

Comparing "the before and after" organization picture, the revised organization features much better balance among the required activities, supervision can be effective, and personnel are assigned to better defined jobs which contribute to improved departmental efforts. In addition, manpower needs are reduced from 93 to 84 persons, or about 10 percent. At an annual salary of $5,000 per person, the savings equal $45,000 a year.

## MAJOR INFLUENCES BRINGING ORGANIZATION CHANGE

There are many factors which bring about change in an organization. To exhaust a list of causes is beyond our purpose here. But four major influences will be discussed in detail because they represent important considerations in organization dynamics. These four influences are (1) the process and machines used, (2) the relationships followed, (3) the degree of centralization practiced, and (4) the personnel employed.

## PROCESS AND MACHINES USED

As indicated in chapter 25, the process quite often determines the main components of the organization structure. In the handling of a purchase order, for example, receiving, costing, billing, and mailing may contribute the main components. However, research and concentrated efforts for improvement may evolve a different process for the handling of purchase orders. Information in a different form or time sequence may be adopted to reduce costs. It is also possible that some computer means or duplicating improvement might revolutionize the old process into one that is different and brand new. This, in turn, would mean organizational changes.

Closely allied with process changes are the machines used. Mechanization may use the identical process, but it may perform the work in such a manner and at such speed that changes in the organizational pattern are necessary. Certainly, when the office work is being accomplished largely by manual means and is changed to one of mechanical processing, organizational modifications are in order. Mechanization may eliminate certain functions and change others, resulting in the need for different people, at least in the sense of the displaced people being retrained for the new work, and new organizational relationships being established.

## THE RELATIONSHIPS FOLLOWED

There is an old saying that "authority clusters around the person willing to accept it." The employee of managerial competence, ambition, and desire for authority tends to acquire additional wanted authority. Hence, over a period, authority tends to be increased by such individuals; and as a result, organization relationships change, at first in practice, and ultimately formally, in keeping with conditions as they have developed.

In chapter 26, it was pointed out that for a small organization many functions are usually grouped into each organization unit, the total number of such units is small, a line type organization is used, and the number of relationships is relatively low. In contrast, when few functions are in each organization unit, the number of units is large, a line and staff type of organization is used, and the relationships are relatively high in number. In either of these cases when the relationships are altered, there is a necessity of change in the organization structure. There can, in fact, be an organization change caused by a modification in relationships only; a change in functions or in their grouping or in personnel is not necessary.

## THE DEGREE OF CENTRALIZATION PRACTICED

A key contributor to organization change is the movement either to or from centralization. As already stated the current trend is toward more

FIGURE 28–3. Recording Form to Simplify Inventory of Clerical Functions.

| CLERICAL FUNCTIONS INVENTORY | | | | | |
|---|---|---|---|---|---|
| COMPANY: | | INFORMATION BY: | | DATE: | |
| WORK GROUP | LOCATION AND DEPARTMENT | NUMBER OF EMPLOYEES | | MAJOR WORK PERFORMED | OFFICE MACHINES AND EQUIPMENT USED |
| | | SUPERVISORY | NON-SUPERV'Y | | |
| | | | | | |
| | | | | | |
| | | | | | |
| | | | | | |
| | | | | | |
| | | | | | |

and more centralization of office work. In and of itself this makes for organization changes. But the degree of centralization should not be determined by following blindly what others may be doing. The soundest approach is to make an objective study within the given enterprise. For this purpose, a four-step program can be followed:

*1. Determine the Major Centers of Office Work Activity.* Essentially this is an inventory showing, by centers, the name, location, number of employees, major work performed, quantities of work, and equipment utilized. From these data, it is possible to identify the areas offering the greatest potential for improvement. The use of a simple form such as that shown in Figure 28–3 is helpful in this recording work.

*2. Ascertain the Productive Efficiency of These Centers.* Find out if any relationship exists between the volume of work processed by a group and the work output per person in that group. In general, a high volume of available work per person is related to high individual productivity. This results partly from the fact that there must be a sufficient work volume to keep an employee busy throughout the work period. Figure 28–4 shows that for a given enterprise, the greater the number of billings processed, the higher the employee productivity or billings processed per employee. Each dot in the figure represents a district office of the company. In the case of two district offices, the number of billings processed is about 420, and the corresponding productivity per employee is 73 and 77, respectively. When the volume of work is higher, at 700 or 750, as in other district offices, the productivity jumps to 97. This suggests gains to be

FIGURE 28–4. Relationship between Average Productivity per Employee Performing Billing Processing and Number of Billings Processed for Each of 11 District Offices.

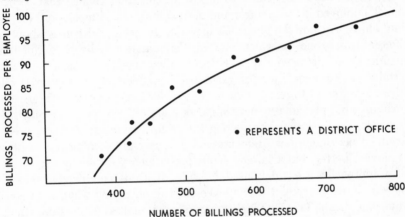

derived by centralizing all billing work; but before this conclusion can be reached, the analyst should conduct similar investigations for other clerical work performed in the district offices, such as credit and collections, and accounts receivable, to determine if a similar pattern emerges. From this range of information, the feasibility of consolidation can be demonstrated.

**3. Establish an Optimum Number of Major Office Work Centers.** We are trying to answer the questions: To what degree should the centralization be pursued? Do you collapse office work done in 11 district sales offices to six or three regional office service centers, or some number in between? In some cases, the optimum size can be determined for the data utilized in step 2 by noting the volume point at which definite plateauing takes place, that is, employee productivity remains constant regardless of the work volume. Using this optimum work volume as a base, the number of district offices can be determined. But this mathematical answer usually must be qualified by nonmeasurable factors, such as the potential office mechanization, the need of communication between the organizational units, the cost of conversion, employee training required, and the vulnerability and risk involved should the centralized units become incapacitated due to equipment breakdown, strikes, or disaster.

**4. Decide on the Location of the Major Office Work Centers.** Top managers normally make this decision, keeping in mind certain criteria among which are the present organization structure, the personnel involved, the availability and cost of labor, and the likely direction of the company's future growth and paper work requirements.

## THE PERSONNEL EMPLOYED

Of all the influences contributing to organization change that of personnel employed is the greatest and most significant. It merits full discussion which will now be given. Change due to personnel comes about in different ways one of which is that the manager believes a different organizational arrangement will prove advantageous. It is a fact that certain types of people tend to work together effectively as a group, while others never seem to reach the level of expected cooperation. The reasons are many; but presumably most important are differences in personalities, capacities, and relationships among the group's members. Various predetermined personnel measurements and devices can be employed to place employees better, but trial-and-error, probationary, or temporary placement approaches are widely used. Nothing, it seems, completely takes the place of actually trying the employee out and observing what is achieved from this trial. This shuffling of personnel makes for organizational changes and is done in the interests not only of employee social satisfaction but also for production efficiency.

Another reason for change in organization personnel is that with time employees change. They acquire new knowledge, new skills, new interests, and new attitudes. This is inevitable; in fact, it is promoted by managers in management development programs and many efforts of motivation. But it is perhaps more important that people change because it is a natural evolutionary process which takes place as a person increases in age, participates in more experiences, and reflects on life and its meaning. An office job satisfactory to a young woman of 20 probably will not satisfy her when she reaches 26. She will seek a change, and the alert manager will recognize this and do something about it. Later, at age 35, it could well be that no job in industry will satisfy her, as her interests and desires are now centered on work in connection with her own family. The point here is that no person remains static. Some change more rapidly than others, but change they do. Managers, in their organizing work, should take these personnel changes into account; and this means the organization structure will be dynamic.

There is also the reason that sooner or later, all offices have the problem of employee replacement due to the normal state of affairs of some employees leaving the office or the employee requirements of the office changing as the office work either expands or contracts. A basic need of every office is to supply and to maintain a satisfactory working force. To do this, likely candidates must be located and those best qualified selected and hired. This suggests practicing good human relations in making organizational change.

## HUMAN RELATIONS AND ORGANIZATIONAL CHANGE

It is the responsibility of a manager to update his organization so that it is effective and helps in the accomplishment of desired goals. The assigning, transferring, promoting, and demoting of personnel are included in this responsibility. Usually these efforts bring about a period of joy, disappointment, and confusion from the occupants of the affected personnel. Hence, the implementation of needed organizational change involves issues of human relations.

Obtaining full employee cooperation and acceptance of reorganization can be complex. People resent being pushed around, ignored, and losing status. And they like to know and to have their associates know why they were promoted or given more responsibility and authority. The top manager in charge should make it known that improvements are sought and that accomplishing these improvements probably will require organization change. All management members who probably will be affected by these changes should be kept fully informed of the progress of possible reorganization plans and their suggestions should be solicited. Likewise steps should be taken to make certain that nonmanagers are aware of the improvements sought and that their ideas on what to do are welcomed. Unfortunately many reorganizations are handled confidentially and human relations are slighted. What is forgotten is that employees always find out some information about the changes from various sources including the grapevine and normally know more about the situation than they are credited with having. It is far better for the manager in charge to give others the facts, outline the tentative decisions, and welcome suggestions. Handling an organization change effectively is a test of real leadership.

A reduction in the work force is one of the serious problems faced. If at all possible this should be handled by either transferring the excess employees to another unit or permitting the normal attrition rate to operate without replacing any employee who leaves the company. In some instances it may be necessary to terminate employment, and when this is done, efforts by the company to assist the employees in getting relocated should be followed. Reassigning the older office employee with limited skill and experience may pose special problems. However, there are ways to handle such situations. The older person may be transferred to a needed staff job where she has something to offer and has an interest in serving. A displaced supervisor with long tenure may prove to be a very satisfactory training instructor and fill a need until retirement several years hence. Sometimes the work can be split logically with the former employee continuing to perform in those areas where she is competent, the remainder of the duties being reassigned to a new employee. Each situation has its own individual considerations which challenge the reorganizer's managerial creativity and practice of decent human relations.

## PLANNING AND ORGANIZATION CHANGE

The astute manager will look ahead and try to determine what future organization changes probably will take place. The planning efforts regarding how the data processing will be handled, probable changes in company policy, and the future value to be placed on information work are but a few sources which can be used to forecast the probable future office organization of an enterprise. It should be emphasized that all these data are predictive and therefore possess uncertainty. We are dealing with probabilities. There is no positive assurance that the events will take place in the future.

Future office goals are sought and, using these as a basis, the office organization of the future is projected. In turn, the type of personnel—supervisory, technical, and profession—which will be needed to achieve these future goals can be estimated. Decisions are then made regarding how these personnel requirements differ from the present requirements with respect to qualifications such as education, skill, attitude, and cooperativeness. This comparison between present and future requirements reveals the gap that must be filled. This will take into account present positions that will be terminated as well as new positions that will be created. From this information helpful actions can be planned. For example, the need for developmental programs by present employees can be ascertained. And the number and identity of present employees who will not be needed in the future can be approximated. From all this, specific actions to promote an orderly transition to the future office organization and to utilize best the available office personnel can be decided.

Figure 28–5 shows an evaluation organization chart to assist in identifying probable future as well as excess personnel. The chart refers to a stated future period. At that time, for example, the information manager is expected to have a staff assistant, a new department, A, will be in existence, and the assistant manager of Department C will be excess.

FIGURE 28–5. Organization to Identify Probable Future and Excess Personnel for a Stated Future Period.

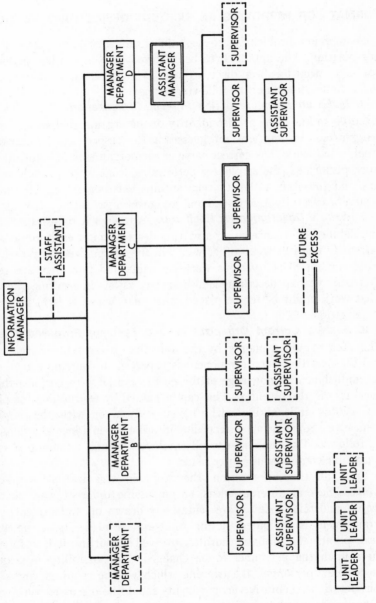

Other predicted changes in the organization can be observed from the chart.

## FORMAT FOR IMPROVING AN EXISTENT OFFICE ORGANIZATION

A common problem is to seek improvements in an existent office organization. The approach to be followed here is similar, in some respects, to what has been discussed above, but significant differences exist to warrant inclusion of the following format:

*1. Make an Inventory of the Present Organization.* It is absolutely essential to know the precise identity of the organization structure being reorganized. Assumptions and guesses in this respect lead to unnecessary trouble and work. The correct name of each organizational unit, the exact work performed, the employees performing what work in each unit, the line and the staff authority relationships existing among all the units should be carefully ascertained and set down in writing.

*2. Write a Description for Each Job.* Although it requires much time and detailed effort, preparing a written description of each job is usually extremely helpful. In no other way will the reorganizer fully realize the exact content of the various work segments and how they are related. Preparing written descriptions also greatly assists in securing clues as to what work might better be placed other than where it is in the present organization.

*3. Analyze Current Organization, and Evaluate Proposed Changes.* This step is guided mainly by the objectives of the entire organization and the part that each component is expected to contribute to the goal accomplishment. Knowledge of the people available to perform the various tasks is also essential. This can be gained by researching the personnel records and talking with the supervisors or with the employees themselves. Some means of recording information in a logical order should be followed. Data common to all employees should be obtained so that reasonable comparisons can be made.

From all this information, the proposed organization is gradually evolved. Several different ideas, encompassing different work divisions, people, and relationships, are tentatively drawn up. Subsequently, each arrangement is evaluated, noting what appear to be its strong and its weak points, the probable hurdles involved in putting it into force, the effect upon the personnel to be changed, the possibility of acquiring needed new personnel, the training which will be required, and similar considerations. Tentative arrangements should be discussed with various management members and affected personnel to gain their appraisals and exchange reactions regarding the advantages and disadvantages to be incurred and the consensus regarding what should be done. Based on the results of this overall investigation, the decision is made as to the makeup of the reorganization to be used.

**4. Determine the Phases or Steps to Be Taken from the Present to the Proposed Organization.** It may be deemed wise to institute the reorganization at once. In situations where an extremely inefficient or costly organizational structure exists, it may be best to implement the change without delay. However, in many cases, the gradual shifting from the present to the ultimate organization takes place in several phases or steps. Normally, this makes for greater acceptance by the employees, who will go along with a small change but will balk if the modification is too large or believed radical from their viewpoint. Individual situations may govern the timing of the change. For example, the retirement or resignation of a key executive may signal the most opportune time to adopt change. However, regardless of the reason, in each instance the plan of what is to be done and by whom should be worked out in advance. To reorganize without adequate predetermination and study usually leads to poor results.

Figure 28–6 illustrates the phases of reorganization that might be followed by a company whose present office organization is like that shown by the top diagram. Note that seven managerial chiefs report to the office manager. It is desired to reduce the number of chiefs reporting directly to the office manager, to install and use a computer, and to consolidate relative functions in order to get a more tightly knit and effective organization structure.

The first phase in this reorganization is shown by the middle illustration of Figure 28–6. Procedures and research has been given the subfunctions of work simplification and the newly created standards section. Under the new unit of physical office facilities is placed office layout and office purchasing. The correspondence and reports unit now includes filing along with reception, mail, and communicative services consolidated into one subunit. The computer unit is added and initially will process data in connection with billing and payroll. Accounts payable remains a separate unit, as does duplicating; the head of each reports directly to the office manager.

The second and final phase consists of adding systems to the procedures and research unit and transferring this enlarged unit to the computer section. Work simplification with standards and a manuals unit under it report directly to the office manager. Duplicating is transferred and becomes a subunit under correspondence and reports, while accounts payable is placed under the computer organizational unit.

**5. Take Necessary Reorganization Action.** The last step is to put the reorganization into action. Once it is decided what changes to make and a time schedule established, definite action should be taken. To hesitate or display indecisiveness can hamper the entire reorganization. A positive and fair viewpoint generally assists in getting satisfactory results.

It is important to give the reorganization time to prove itself. Time is required for people to adjust to new assignments, become familiar with

FIGURE 28–6. Phase Charts Are Commonly Used in Reorganization. The present organization is illustrated by the top chart. The first phase of changes to be made is shown by the middle chart. Subsequently, the organization of the middle chart is changed to that shown by the bottom phase chart.

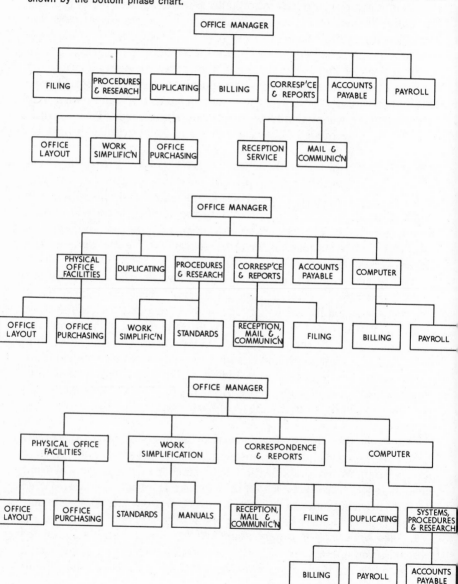

new authority relationships, and utilize new formal channels of communication. All managers should be thoroughly indoctrinated in the reorganization, be able to answer questions concerning it, publicize its advantages, and counsel any employee in need of such help. Successful reorganization plans always include these important follow-up features.

Specific attention should be called to the fact that the previous list does not include copying the organization of another enterprise in a similar business. Organizing is highly personalized and should be tailor-made for the specific objectives, type of work, and people of a given enterprise. Needs and circumstances vary. Basic guides are available for the construction of an effective organization and should be used in keeping with the basic requirements. The work is similar to the architect designing a building. The best architect does not copy an existing building. He employs basic guides of building and engineering and creates a structure that meets the specific and personal needs of his client.

## QUESTIONS

1. What are the major influences which bring about organization change? Select one you feel is important and discuss it.
2. Relate several examples of the time element affecting organizational continuity.
3. Comment fully on this statement: "The old adage of keeping an organization in balance is so much academic nonsense. Activities are never in balance; some are always more important than others. Hence, it is perfectly natural and nothing to worry about to have organizations that are not in balance. It is a natural state of affairs."
4. Carefully identify each of the following:
    *a*) Major centers of office work activity.
    *b*) Phasing in reorganization.
    *c*) Imbalance of an organization.
    *d*) Organization continuity.
5. Give an example from your experience or reading where an organization has ignored organization dynamics with the result that important functions are being neglected or are subordinate to other functions of lesser value.
6. Explain the meaning of Figure 28–6 in your own words.
7. Suggest an alternative to the organization change followed by the example illustrated in Figures 28–1 and 28–2.
8. Do you agree with this statement: "For a given enterprise, personnel changes over a period, but the organization remains fundamentally the same. If more managers kept this basic truth in mind, there would be less organizational problems." Why?
9. Discuss how a change in personnel brings about a change in organization.
10. Discuss the handling of personnel where the organization change involves a reduction in the work force.
11. Enumerate some specific planning activities you recommend in connection with organization change.

12. Explain how establishing an optimum number of major office work centers tends to result in organization centralization.

## CASE PROBLEMS

### Case 28–1.    Raut-Wyatt, Inc.

Mark Mattix gave his employer, Raut-Wyatt, Inc., two weeks notice to take the position, vice president in charge of EDP, with the corporation's chief competitor, Arnold Products Company. Mr. Mattix enjoys a reputation for great competency and is a recognized leader in his type of work. With him went considerable knowledge of operations, cost, plans, and problems of Raut-Wyatt, Inc.

Mr. Mattix keeps in touch informally with Sam Neylan, a Raut-Wyatt executive, in charge of programming. They meet about twice a month or whenever Mr. Mattix is in town at a local club where Mr. Mattix has retained his membership. Their meetings may be termed secret, but the fact that they get together is known by the top managers of Raut-Wyatt, Inc.

During the past seven months, two programmers and one computer operator of Raut-Wyatt, Inc. have switched over to Arnold Products Company. They stated they had better offers and left after giving three to four weeks notice. Neither the president or the personnel director of Raut-Wyatt, Inc. have disclosed any tangible evidence that these three former employees were influenced by Mark Mattix to join Arnold Products Company. But the president feels strongly that Mark Mattix is the one behind the changes.

Three weeks ago, Sam Neylan started his vacation. When the vacation ended, he announced his new position as assistant to Mr. Maddix with Arnold Products Company. He was assuming his new job in four weeks. The president of Raut-Wyatt, Inc. was alarmed at the drain of hard-to-get personnel. He resolved to stop it. Summoning Mr. Neylan to his office he stated directly that he did not want to lose him.

PRESIDENT: What do we have to do to keep you?

NEYLAN: Nothing, I am just leaving that's all.

PRESIDENT: Well, why are you planning to leave us?

NEYLAN: I am not planning to leave, I am leaving. I prefer not to discuss the matter.

PRESIDENT: I see. I am sure you know, Mr. Neylan, that we all think very highly of you. Your record with us is outstanding.

NEYLAN: Thank you, sir.

PRESIDENT: Mark's been after you hasn't he?

NEYLAN: I really would prefer not to discuss the matter.

PRESIDENT: Sure he has. You can tell me. We can give you everything he can and more. You think it over, and we'll talk about it again tomorrow.

NEYLAN: As I said, I'd rather not discuss the matter, sir.

## Questions:

1. What factors do you suspect led to the current situation faced by Raut-Wyatt, Inc.?

2. Comment on the action of Mr. Mark Maddix.
3. What action do you recommend the president take? Why?

## Case 28–2. Express Cartage Company

Some 20 years ago, this company started with one truck and one driver, who is now president of a thriving cartage business. Initially, Mr. Tom Flanagan, nicknamed "Gabby" by all his close friends, had his wife, Angela, prepare all the paper work in connection with the business. As the business grew, he hired Phideas Plummer, then aged 43 years, as a bookkeeper, and soon, there were a junior bookkeeper reporting to Phideas and a sales manager with two salesmen reporting to Mr. Flanagan. A little later, August Wagner served as an assistant to Mr. Flanagan in the operations department, which had grown to a fleet totaling six trucks and drivers.

About five years ago, it became apparent that something would have to be done about Phideas Plummer, who, although quite proficient at keeping books, was indeed a poor manager. At this time, Phideas had the title "office manager," with two bookkeepers and a file clerk reporting to him. He seemed to have become very irritable, was curt with the employees, and seldom was able to supply Mr. Flanagan with information requested. Since he had been with the company for 15 years and knew the business, there was reluctance to let him go. Accordingly, one of the bookkeepers, Mrs. Myrtle Ashenbrenner, aged 48 years, was made the office manager and given two girls, one who would take care of billings and the other to do the filing. Mr. Plummer continued to handle bookkeeping, including accounts receivable, and had one helper.

About six months ago, further changes appeared imperative. Phideas Plummer was getting more cantankerous and just did not seem to know the meaning of co-operation with the other employees. However, his three people, an accounts receivable accountant and two general accountants, voiced no difficulty with him. Myrtle Ashenbrenner, now with the company 11 years, failed to show any aggressiveness in managing the office. She seemed content to run only her unit, consisting of herself, handling credit matters, a billing clerk, and a filing clerk. It was quite obvious that she and Phideas Plummer did not get along, even though there was no evidence of discord between them. The company now had a very competent sales manager, Peter Ferreti, who had a secretary, a file clerk, and three salesmen reporting to him. "Gabby" Flanagan was very well pleased with the work of Mr. Ferreti; and in talking over the problem of having a better office manager, they agreed that Miss Eileen Fogarty, currently private secretary to Mr. Flanagan, should be given this job. Miss Fogarty is a very reliable employee; all of her six years with the company have been as Mr. Flanagan's private secretary. Her present age is 29 years. When offered the new job, Miss Fogarty was not too enthusiastic but stated if it was what Mr. Flanagan wanted, she would accept it.

At that time, the office unit consisted of a telephone switchboard operator, two stenographers who also did filing work, a watchman, and a purchasing clerk who bought items up to $300; over this amount, the purchasing was done by Mr. Flanagan. The operations unit, still headed by August Wagner, had a file clerk and 16 drivers and trucks.

Mr. Flanagan is today still dissatisfied with the operation of the office. He does not know what to do about it although he has given some thought to it. He has asked you for assistance.

## Questions:

1. What are your reactions to the changes made in the organization of this company?
2. Draw a chart of the current organization.
3. In your opinion, what are the major problems requiring managerial attention?
4. What recommendations would you give Mr. Flanagan? Substantiate your suggestions.

# PART VIII

# ACTUATING

In the opinion of many, actuating is of foremost importance in office management. Today's office manager has the challenge of inspiring his fellow employees to use their highest attainable skills and capacities in work they are genuinely interested in doing.

Actuating includes the creating and the continuing of the desire by each employee to achieve work goals willingly and enthusiastically. It can be thought of as the ability to get others to do the work you want done because they want to do it.

The following five chapters are devoted to office managerial actuating, "Challenge of actuating," "Office supervision," "Developing office employees," "Effective actuating practices," and "Office salary administration."

chapter **29**

# Challenge of actuating

There is no problem of human nature which is insoluble.

—*Ralph J. Bunche*

It is people who make or break the management of any office. All other resources such as materials, machines, and buildings can be readily replaced; they can even be insured against loss. But capable and loyal human beings cannot be readily replaced, nor can their loss be adequately insured. Efforts to develop and maintain competent and cooperative human beings must be made and this means that human motives must be understood and actions taken according to that understanding.

Most employees want and will respond favorably to help. They want to develop, to perform greater service, to acquire status, and to contribute importantly. This means that in many respects a manager is really a helper of employees. His task is to help his followers do their best. His challenge is to get employees to do more for him than they will for others. This means that knowledge of people's behavior and skill in influencing them are extremely important attributes of the manager. Work is to be accomplished effectively, but this can be done and at the same time make the employee's work life happier and his work more meaningful and satisfying.

## HISTORICAL DEVELOPMENTS OF VIEWPOINTS TOWARD EMPLOYEES

Our viewpoint toward employees was not always as it exists today. Actually, we have progressed through several stages. At one time, an employee was considered in the same light as a commodity—something to be bought on the open market, and of a fairly uniform quality. Later, the so-called machinery conception of labor became prominent; the employee was considered a producing unit and his value measured in terms of the goods produced. After years of struggle and unhappiness, a new concept of employer-employee relationships gradually evolved. It was that an employee is a human being and that his welfare is important; hence, the employer should encourage and supply various welfare services deemed desirable. A paternal attitude toward the employee developed. This represented an improvement over the employee's previous status, but it was not the answer to satisfactory employer-employee relations. Many employees were suspicious of these welfare efforts and resented being the children of a paternalistic policy. Since the period of around 1915–20, the concept that an employee is a human entity and must be treated as such has gained headway. This means that consideration for an employee's psychological makeup and recognition and utilization of his desires, attitudes, interests, and motives are as important as attention to his physical efforts, perhaps even more so.

As thinking along this human-entity line progressed, the basis for a great many current practices developed, including the idea that individuals vary in their personal aptitudes and interests, that no two people respond identically to the same opportunity, that different jobs require different abilities, that the emotional makeup of the employee is important, and that the prevailing spirit or feeling of the work force affects its productivity. A "mutuality of interests" between employer and employee is being recognized. This means that both have an interest in the well-being of the enterprise and that the relationship between employer and employee should be a harmonious working together toward their common objectives, which are compatible over the long-run period of time.

## CONTEMPORARY MOTIVATION

It is now generally accepted that the most successful motivation is self-direction by the employee. The urge or desire should come from within the individual, not from someone else in the form of an outside force. This means that successful motivation usually requires providing work and a climate within which it is performed that permits the employee to act in a manner that is satisfying. Our knowledge of motivating is increasing daily, but there still remain many unknowns in this fascinating subject area. Agreement is usually voiced with the statement that every employee has a motivation response and this response can be fostered and utilized by managers creating opportunities, removing obstacles, providing guidance, and encouraging growth. The implementation or taking of actions, however, rests with the employee.

Figure 29–1 lists some basic concepts to remember in dealing with people. These concepts can be utilized in motivating employees, the application depending upon the particular circumstances in the individual case.

Self-direction by an employee is likely to take place most effectively when it is implemented to satisfy his need or want which is particularly strong at a given time or period. Logically then the managerial challenge is to find out what these wants are and either satisfy them through the

FIGURE 29–1. In Dealing with People, Remember These Concepts.

1. People like to help others. Ask for their opinions.
2. People like to feel important and needed. Acknowledge their contribution and recognize their help occasionally in front of others.
3. People like to be encouraged. Help them see the successful accomplishment of their aims and ambitions.
4. People like good listeners. Let people talk about their accomplishments and disappointments. Give the other fellow a real hearing.
5. People like to be brought into the picture when talking about yourself. Give your conversation a "you" angle. "You will find this of special interest because. . . ."
6. People like a word of praise whenever merited.
7. People like a choice, if possible. Let a person decide for himself; help him reach conclusions, but do not make decisions for him.
8. People like to avoid embarrassment and being "boxed in a corner." Give a person an "out" and a chance to save face.
9. People like people who keep well groomed. Keep your body clean, clothes neat. This is a subtle way of saying to others, "I care about your opinion of me."
10. People like their image to be accepted. Strive to sense what this image is and let them know that you understand their picture of themselves.

work and its accomplishment or supply reasonable explanations why they cannot be fulfilled.

## WANTS OF EMPLOYEES

The important wants of employees are now believed to be known. Actually they form a hierarchy consisting of five levels from basic psychological drives at the bottom to the highest experience of the human spirit at the apex. Starting at the bottom, *the survival or physiological needs* include the need for adequate food, clothing, shelter, rest, and activity. What constitutes adequacy will differ among people and likewise the degree of motivation to acquire satisfactions of these needs will vary. When these needs are taken care of, they cease to motivate behavior, and new and higher needs emerge. Next in the hierarchy are *safety needs* which include protection from physical danger, economic security, philosophic and orderly explanation of the surroundings in which he lives.

Next is *social needs*. Togetherness, belonging to a group, and acquiring acceptance become major goals. In this stage the typical employee wants to know that what he is doing is worthwhile and has merit, that he expects, at least in part, to satisfy these needs by having an opportunity to demonstrate his talent, acquire prestige, and gain recognition. The fourth level is *esteem needs*, both self-esteem and the esteem of others. Self-esteem is represented by the desire for competence, achievement, and freedom of thought. Esteem by others includes status, prestige, and reputation. Obviously, the fulfillment of these esteem needs are important behavior determinants. Last, and at the top of the hierarchy of wants are *self-realization needs*. This entails the fulfillment of a person's highest potential, to become everything that one is capable of becoming. Satisfaction of this need can take many different forms such as managing a department, advancing a business theory, writing, or being an excellent swimmer. Fulfillment of capacity is the underlying characteristic of this want.

Knowing these wants, the next step is to set operations in action in order to satisfy them. Here is where the real skill of motivating enters. Employees' wants are not identical for each group or for each member of a group. Furthermore, the wants do not remain constant; they vary from day to day. The reasons for these conditions are numerous and can be quite complex. On the following pages we will discuss some of the more important influences.

**BASIC VALUES**

Actuating efforts are conditioned by the fundamental beliefs that the individual possesses. In some instances, these beliefs can be changed but usually this is a long-run effect. The immediate practical viewpoint is to start with present basic values and gauge the extent to which they are affecting current behavior. An employee's belief about office work, for example, is an important consideration in motivating efforts. Does he view it as a vital service, a real contribution to his fellow employees, his company, and to society? If he does, there is opportunity for satisfying his social, esteem, and even self-realization wants from the work situation. In contrast, if office work is looked upon as a boring, something-to-do activity the chances for obtaining genuine wants satisfaction from performing it are indeed minute.

Of probably more significance is what the employee thinks of himself. Concentrating his thoughts on his strengths rather than his weaknesses has a favorable motivating effect. Also, this viewpoint assists in setting goals he is able to reach rather than those he feels he ought to reach. This assumes two fundamentals that the employee (1) has solid strengths, often unidentified and unused, and (2) has meaningful personal goals. Research appears to confirm that these fundamentals exist in the great majority of cases. This being true, it follows that if the employee can see he has something to gain or a want satisfied from his work, he will be successful and satisfied throughout his work life.

It needs to be added, however, that in some cases ability and interest are acquired as a result of discipline which requires an employee to perform certain work. Actually, the employee may be unaware of his like for the given type of work until it is suggested that he try it. Subsequently, he knows the work and gains proficiency in it, and he may well find the work quite satisfying. This experience is fairly common among employees who don't honestly know what type of work they really like or whether they could perform it satisfactorily.

## EXPERIENCE AND MOTIVATION

There is little doubt that experience plays a major role in what motivational tool is effective and what one is not. The person with much experience has found out what to change and when. He has probably become expert in adjusting to various conditions and accountabilities. And he has coped with economic and social structures, difficulties, and opportunities.

This is not to say that those with little experience cannot be influenced by or cannot use motivation effectively. Such persons may be quite eager to compete and possess great confidence in their performance. Further, they may enjoy a high promotion rate. All such criteria do not dictate managerial motivational practices, but they contribute to what motivation is used and how successfully it is applied. Among other things, success is influenced by widely different backgrounds and experiences plus a variety of conditions that serve to either impress or depress a person's efforts. Experiences of a variety of sorts, both positive and negative, affect motivation.

## LEADERSHIP

Vital in supplying a motivating environment is leadership. People prefer to be with a successful leader. Being a part of victorious accomplishments, following a man who has demonstrated an ability to get things done, and having firsthand experience in observing successful management in action are in and of themselves highly motivating to an employee. Members of a group receive strong stimuli from effective leadership; and in turn, a strong leader acquires his position, in part, because of his ability to motivate members of his group.

What is leadership? It has been defined in a number of different ways; but for our purposes here, we can consider that leadership implies a threefold meaning:

**1. Skill to Direct—to Show the Way.** A leader possesses the ability to guide people—to point out the proper means for attainment. This leadership characteristic usually means that the leader is out in front leading, not in back pushing. While not directly applicable, the concept can be illustrated by considering a piece of ordinary wrapping twine. When the front end of the twine is directed and guided along desired paths, the rest of the piece of twine will follow. In contrast, when the twine is pushed, it follows no predetermined path and flounders in an aimless direction.

**2. Ability to Win Cooperation and Loyalty.** A leader is able to get people to act jointly and to work toward a common goal. All efforts of the group are knit together and concentrated into one large force toward the attainment of the objective. This unity of operation is accomplished by strong and enthusiastic feelings, so that each member has a deep sense of obligation to the leader.

**3. Courage to Carry On until the Assigned Task Is Accomplished.** A leader is dauntless and ever confident that the task to be done will be completely accomplished. He has implicit faith in the success of his actions and gives a feeling of confidence and positiveness to all associated with him.

People like to be led by a dynamic leader. They like to be led by a person who clearly envisages the goal, who knows how to achieve that goal, and who goes out after it. Once the decision is made as to what the goals are and what people must do to achieve them, leadership at all levels of the organization plays a dominant role in seeing that they are accomplished.

## BUILDING PEOPLE

Material achievement is a long-time measurement, almost a standard, of success. In most instances, the information manager's performance is not evaluated by building people. Recognition of scholarship, artistic ability, and genius is subordinated to "practical results." Under the prevailing conditions it is easy to see why a manager devotes the little time he usually does to developing employees. Yet this building of people is a cardinal activity in motivational efforts.

Recognition of this basic activity will cause a manager to encourage actively the growth and progress of his promising employees. Competently using the tools and techniques for measuring the ability and the accomplishing of definite tasks are commendable, but of far greater significance is the formulation of an acceptable and effective underlying philosophy about the enterprise, the work, and the people doing it.

Answers to such questions as these are needed: Is the attitude toward the enterprise and its products or services highly enthusiastic? What are the mental and physical capabilities of each individual employee? Where does he want to be in five years? Ten years? Twenty years? What will it take to get him there and does he know this?

The management member must view sincerely the building of people as a principal responsibility and work at it, otherwise the job will not be done. Assigning employees to special projects or to short tours of duty and observing how they perform these tasks represents an effective approach. Also, promoting as rapidly as abilities permit should be followed. Further, it brings good results to hire outside people whose ideas, initiative, and ambition demonstrate that these qualities are recognized no matter where they are found. In addition, employees with limitations should be identified and kept from becoming obstacles to the advancement of others who are qualified. There are many ways of doing this, for example, limit the assignment of the nonpromising employee, encourage lateral movements or transfers, and transfer certain work to a new unit and appoint the promising employee as the head of it.

## ACTION AND REACTION

There is a fundamental principle in the science of physics that states that every action is followed by a reaction. Transferring this to the field of human behavior and with certain qualifications we can say that every motivating action directed to an employee is followed by a reaction by him and the group to which he belongs. Motivating a person is not a one-way stimuli. There is also a reaction to the stimuli. And different reactions to the same stimuli can exist among different employees.

The implications here are quite clear. Motivation efforts must be selected and applied carefully. What is quite appropriate in one case may not work out satisfactorily in another. Further, in a given case the state of human relations affairs existing among employees is probably the result of previous actions, i.e., what now exists are the reactions to previous actions. Motivating has a continuity about it and the motivator is responsible for what acceptance or rejection his motivating efforts receive.

Further, any evaluation of motivating should be from a long-range viewpoint. Overnight results are not conclusive. In all probability a high current level of motivation is the result of efforts over a considerable period of time during which employees' reactions have been favorable. Likewise, if the current level is unfavorable, this condition is a composite of many reactions either to disliked motivating efforts or no motivating efforts at all.

It is a fact of life that in the long run what one gives in human relations he tends to receive. The ability to provide human satisfactions out of work output and work relationships is predicated upon what is given or provided to bring about the desired result. Needed understanding, environment, and mutual trust are essential. Irritation and antagonism do not make for either a pleasant or a productive work place. An employer or an employee following practices which irritate the other, even though he has a perfect legal right to do so, cannot expect admiration and friendliness in return. And it is difficult to see how a pleasant work atmosphere will be acquired if either party persists in being obnoxious to the other, as he interprets it. You make your own bed in human relations. Cries of anguish because those whom you antagonize strike back fall on deaf ears. It reflects the situation of action and reaction.

## ATTITUDE TOWARD WORK

When you get down to it, the most important influence upon motivating and for that matter success of an enterprise is the attitude of employees toward their work. Almost everyone wants a job, but not everyone

FIGURE 29–2. An Honest Answer of "Yes," to Each of These Questions Indicates a Favorable Attitude toward Work.

1. Do you offer to take over some of the work when absence of a fellow employee means that someone must help?
2. Do you feel it is a privilege and an opportunity to work for the company and the people with whom you are?
3. Do you seek additional work and responsibility to increase your value to the company?
4. Do you accept discipline realizing it is honest criticism and a necessity for most work?
5. Do you review your own work and try to achieve excellence?
6. Do you find genuine satisfaction in your work?
7. Do you willingly help other employees wherever you can?
8. Do you feel you are being paid fairly for what you do?
9. Do you inspire those around you to sound work attitudes?
10. Do you believe that you have been and will be advanced as rapidly as you really deserve?

wants to work. As used here, work entails the responsibility for thinking and planning in the interest of the enterprise. It goes beyond the minimum requirements of the job. For an employee, work includes figuring out better ways to perform his job, seeing the relationship of his work to that of others, and accomplishing more than the tasks set before him each day.

Figure 29–2 lists some selected questions to check your everyday attitudes. An answer of "Yes" to each question suggests a favorable work attitude.

Thinking success on his job and for his employer are essential. Basic to this attitude is that a good and needed product or service is being supplied; employees take pride in their work excellence; and the enterprise is financially solvent and well managed, having adequate reserves as well as funds for its growth. An employee who thinks of his company's success as directly related to his own reflects this positive thinking.

Work is an opportunity to provide a product or service of value to others. This is the attitude toward work that should prevail. But each man must acquire this viewpoint for himself. No one can give it to him; it must come from within. And with this personal experience or discovery comes the truth that the secret to successful work lies not only in performing what we like, but also in learning to like what we have to do. Our work attitude, which is controlling, is formed by our thinking; it results entirely from facilities of which we can be master. From the proper attitude of work, a glowing sense of accomplishment and usefulness arises.

## OFFICE TRADE UNIONS

Trade unions for office employees are another important consideration in actuating work. When they exist, managers are required to bargain with the authorized representatives concerning "wages and other conditions of employment." This process which might be called "collective cooperation" is used whereby employers and representatives of employees arrive at agreements covering compensation and the conditions under which employees will work. This includes a broad spectrum of policies covering such subjects as wages, discharge, discipline, and transfer which are incorporated into a mutually agreed upon labor contract. Subsequently, decisions utilizing these policies are made by management members but are frequently subject to question by and explanation to the union, via an established grievance procedure. In essence, the union wants to be consulted and to present its views in matters affecting its members during the decision-making process so that the decision reached will be in keeping with its views. The ultimate decision, however, is made by a management member; but from the practical viewpoint, the decision must be acceptable to the representatives of the employees in order to be entirely effective.

## ORGANIZING WHITE-COLLAR EMPLOYEES

During the late 1960's there was an increase in the unionization of white-collar employees. The Teamsters; Retail, Wholesale, and Department Store Union; Auto Workers; Office and Professional Employees

Union; Insurance Workers; and Newspaper Guild are among the most active labor organizations in the white-collar area. Opinions differ regarding what the future trend might be.

An analysis of the situation in a number of offices indicates that the major managerial reasons that appear to have encouraged unionism are as follows. First, is the office employee's beliefs and feelings about the company such as whether he is treated with respect and with fairness. Note that this is based on beliefs and feelings—it is what the employee thinks, it may or may not be a fact. Wages are important, but commonly not the real reason. Wages are usually corrected to eliminate inequities, but only infrequently does this cause interest in the union to disappear. Second, top management members are unaware of what is bothering most office employees. There is insufficient communication whereby the employees can be heard or get their story across. Complaints and beliefs about poor ventilation, for example, or favoritism in assigning overtime or lack of a seniority system are typical of statements about which employees may have strong feelings but to which top management pays little or no attention, taking the position that it is all complaining which will exist as long as someone will listen to it. This leads to the third and last point which is that supervisors can and will provide a realistic account of employee opinions regarding their work and its environment. In reality, the supervisor is frequently unable to provide such information. He commonly is intimately involved with day-to-day operations and loses his objectivity in attempting to evaluate the morale of his unit. Further, although a management member, the supervisor may not really feel that he is. He doesn't participate in many managerial decisions. For the most part he is given orders and procedures to follow and is expected to carry them out effectively. Little has been done to instill any great loyalty by him to the management group. Furthermore, reporting poor morale in his department may reflect unfavorably upon him.

## CHARACTERISTICS OF CONTRACTS

Most labor contracts contain clauses covering such matters as recognition of the union, union status, union security, salaries, hours of work, seniority, employment procedures, transfers and dismissals, grievance procedures, penalties, maternity leaves, and severance pay. A discussion of several of these subjects follows.

*1. Union Recognition Clause.* A "recognition of the union" clause points out that the union named in the contract is fully recognized by the employer; frequently, it also states what jobs and what employees are covered by the contract. Sometimes, a statement is included to the effect that the union will not accept into membership those employees in the excluded groups.

**2. Status of Union.** Union status concerns the relationship of members of the union with the company. In general, there are three kinds of union status:

*1. Union shop.* Nonunion members may be hired; but after a certain period, they must, as a requirement of employment, become union members.

*2. "Maintenance of membership" shop.* All employees are not required to join the union, but all present union members must retain membership during the time the contract is in force.

*3. Exclusive bargaining shop.* The union is recognized as the exclusive bargaining agent for all employees, but no employee is compelled to join it or to remain a member.[1]

**3. Wage Rates.** Clauses on wage rates frequently include the recognition of job classifications and wage rates for each class. Minimum rates only might be stated. Uniform adjustments, either in amount or in percentage, may be provided; and the effective date of such adjustments may be included.

The following is a typical contractual statement pertaining to wages.

SECTION 2. The wage schedules as set forth in this schedule, attached hereto as Exhibit B and made a part hereof, shall apply and be in effect as of July 1, 1967, and shall remain in effect for the life of this agreement.

SECTION 3. Overtime compensation and deductible time lost shall be computed by dividing the monthly salary by one hundred seventy-three and one third ($173\frac{1}{3}$) to arrive at an hourly rate to be used for such computations.

**4. Layoffs and Seniority.** While most unions favor the governing of layoffs and rehires on seniority, they will grant a statement to the effect that seniority shall govern when the employee involved has the ability to do the work under question. Questions arising in connection with seniority are sometimes clarified by the practice of preclassifying employees either by occupation or by departments or divisions. In this way, employees making up a fairly comparable group are associated together.

To illustrate:

SECTION 3. A reduction in working forces resulting in demotions and layoffs will normally be on a departmental seniority basis except for stenographers and filing clerks, who will be on a company-wide basis.

**5. Penalty Clauses.** Penalty provisions provide punishment for members who violate parts of the contract. Penalties might be in the form of reductions in pay, temporary or permanent layoffs, or less severe disciplinary measures, depending upon the nature of the violation.

---

[1] The Labor Management Relations Act of 1947 outlawed in interstate commerce (1) the closed shop—in which the employer agrees to hire only union members, and all employees must continue their good standing in the union during their terms of employment and (2) the preferential shop—in which preference in hiring and in layoff is given union members.

## LABOR MANAGEMENT RELATIONS ACT OF 1947

A long list of labor laws make up the legal background upon which current management-union cooperation is administered. But for our purpose, the provisions of the Labor Management Relations Act of 1947, commonly referred to as the Taft-Hartley Act, and the Landrum-Griffin Act of 1959 can be considered as making up the current labor legislation. There are also important state labor laws. We are omitting them, however, in order to keep this discussion a reasonable length. The Landrum-Griffin Act of 1959, among other things, permitted employees to file with the government complaints about the acts of their union leaders. Most of the complaints to date have dealt with questions pertaining to voting by union members in union affairs, and the misuse of the dues by union officers.

By the Labor Management Relations Act of 1947, a National Labor Relations Board (NLRB) was established with the power to hear testimony, render decisions, and decide the appropriate unit for purposes of collective bargaining. The board serves mainly in a judiciary capacity. Three important provisions of this law will be discussed as follows:

1. *Unfair Labor Practices.* These are prohibited. By an employer they consist of (1) interfering with or restraining employees from forming or joining a labor union, (2) dominating or influencing a labor organization, (3) discriminating in the hiring or in the conditions of employment of any employee because he is a member of a union, (4) terminating employment or discriminating against any employee for any charge made or testimony given under this law, and (5) refusing to bargain collectively with representatives of his employees.

Unfair labor practices by unions or their agents include (1) coercing or restraining employees in connection with their joining a union, (2) charging "excessive or discriminatory" union initiation fees (the meaning of "excessive or discriminatory" is determined by the labor board in cases where there is an authorized union shop contract), (3) refusing to bargain collectively with the employer, (4) participating in jurisdictional strikes, and (5) practicing "featherbedding," i.e., making the employer pay for services not performed.

Charges of unfair labor practices on the part of either employer or union are investigated, complaints issued, and prosecution carried on before the National Labor Relations Board by the general counsel, who has exclusive authority to prosecute unfair labor practices. He is appointed by the President of the United States and has general supervision over all attorneys employed by the board, except trial examiners and legal assistants to board members.

Basing its decision on the preponderance of evidence and testimony, the board decides whether any defendant named in the complaint is guilty of an unfair labor practice. If he is not guilty, the findings are stated, and an order is issued dismissing the complaint. If he is guilty, the board states its findings and causes a cease and desist order, prohibiting the continuation of the unfair practice, to be served on the guilty party. For enforcement of its orders, the board has the power to petition the Circuit Court of Appeals with jursidiction where the unfair labor practice occurred.

**2. Strike Controls.** A 60 days' notice must be given the other party before the normal termination of a labor contract. The Federal Mediation and Conciliation Service must be notified at least 30 days after the 60-day notice if no agreement is reached. This provision is, of course, intended to help settle the differences of opinion. Lockouts and strikes are prohibited during the notice period. There is no compulsory arbitration or court injunction right against a legitimate noncritical strike, i.e., one not threatening "national health and safety" or affecting an entire industry.

In contrast, threatening lockouts or strikes affecting "national health and safety" or an entire industry may be delayed 80 days by the President in this manner: A board of inquiry may be appointed to determine the facts involved in the dispute. A report stating these facts, along with each party's statement of its position, is filed with the Federal Mediation and Conciliation Service, and the contents are made known to the public. In addition, the President at this time may, through the Attorney General, seek a court injunction against the lockout or strike. If the injunction is issued, there follows a period of 60 days in which to bring about a settlement. If this is not reached, the National Labor Relations Board holds, within the ensuing 15 days, a company-by-company election on each employer's last offer of settlement and certifies same within five days to the Attorney General, who then moves to dissolve the injunction. Then, the President submits a comprehensive report of the proceedings to Congress, along with any recommendation which he deems fitting and proper for appropriate action.

**3. Checks on Unions.** The law provides that a union may seek an election under NLRB supervision or file an unfair labor practice charge with the board. For such action, the union must previously file (1) pertinent union information and (2) noncommunist affidavits by each officer of the union.

The pertinent union information is filed annually with the Secretary of Labor. The report must include name, title, compensation, and allowances for each of the union's three principal officers and for any other officer or agent of the union if the aggregate compensation and allowances of any one of these persons exceeded $5,000 for the preceding year. The report must also include the manner of election or appointment of these officers or agents; the amount of initiation fees and regular dues; a statement showing the procedure followed for such things as qualifications for union membership, levying of assessments, authorization for bargaining demands, for strikes, for disbursement of union funds, and for the basis for expulsion of members; and a report showing receipts and expenditures for the fiscal year and total assets and liabilities at the end of the fiscal year. All union members have a right to a copy of their union's financial report.

The affidavits by union officers can be filed either contemporaneously with a union action privileged by the act or within the preceding 12-month period. The affidavit is a sworn written statement signifying that the union officer is not a member or affiliate of the Communist Party and does not believe in, belong to, or support any organization believing in or teaching the overthrow of the United States government by force or by illegal or unconstitutional methods.


## ADDITIONAL IMPORTANT PROVISIONS

There are other provisions of the Labor Management Relations Act of 1947 that merit mentioning. Listing them for convenience they include:

1. Union shop agreements must be in accordance with the prevailing state law and are void in states that forbid them.

2. An employee or a group of employees can petition that the union's authorization to enter into a union shop contract be withdrawn; such a petition must contain the signatures of 30 percent of the employees represented by the union. However, only one election on union security can be held each year.

3. In instances of authorized union shop contracts, the failure of a member to pay union dues and initiation fee is the only cause for loss of good standing with the union for which an employer can be forced to discharge an employee.

4. Union dues checkoff is allowed only with the employee's written consent.

5. If the majority of professional employees desire a union, they can be represented, if they wish, by a union other than that representing the production workers.

6. The individual employee can present grievances directly to his supervisor, provided the union representative is informed and given an opportunity to be present. Settlement of the grievance can be made if such settlement is not contrary to any terms of the existing union contract.

7. Unions as well as employers can sue and be sued for violations of contract under this act. Judgments against unions must be collected from them, not from the individual employees.

8. Efforts to resolve differences by interpretation of the labor contract and mutual agreement are encouraged, but if unsuccessful, differences can

be handled by (*a*) *mediation*—a third party, or mediator, relays opinions to each party in order to reach an agreement, (*b*) *conciliation*—similar to mediation except the third party, or conciliator, is aggressive in trying to reach a settlement, but he has no legal power to compel acceptance, and (*c*) *arbitration*—whereby parties agree to submit the case to an impartial umpire, or arbitrator, whose findings will be accepted as final.[2]

## OBSERVATIONS ABOUT MANAGEMENT-LABOR RELATIONS

It is well to note that there are actually *three, not two,* interested parties in a labor contract: (1) the employees, represented by the union; (2) the owners, represented by managerial personnel; and (3) the consumers, or general public. The negotiators are usually only the managers and the union representatives, but the agreements they reach should be consistent with the public interest. Disagreements resulting in strikes or shutdowns obviously affect public interest.

Another observation is that managers desire freedom to meet their responsibilities and resent restrictions which curtail the performance of their job. Traditionally, managers want no restrictions on their right to hire, fire, discipline, and maintain order and efficiency. On the other hand, unions feel that one of their main functions concerns the welfare of their members. They are interested in all matters which involve the employee; conditions of employment, they reason, are of vital concern to them.

In addition, managerial goals are commonly unknown to unions and, likewise, the goals of unions are a mystery to managers. Identifying the goals of each may reveal that they can exist in harmony. The goals of managers usually include (1) an equitable income for the owners, (2) a reasonable income for contingencies, expansion, and improvements, (3) a good reputation for products and services, (4) a reputation as a good place to work, and (5) a favorable attitude by the public. Among the union's chief aims are (1) security of employment, (2) wages consistent with a decent standard of living and commensurate with the quality and quantity of work output, (3) consultation and opportunity for suggestions in shaping policies, (4) employee recognition and status for work well done, and (5) good working conditions.

Furthermore, it seems clear that application of the best minds is necessary to find the superior means of bettering management-union relations. Office managers need to take the offensive and acquire an enlightened view of their role in collective bargaining. They should find out the real reasons behind the union demands. Perhaps this is a part of

---

[2] Arbitration, as discussed here, applies to reaching a contract agreement and is not the common type of arbitration which deals with the interpretation and application of existing contracts to specific disputes.

envisioning the whole meaning of unions and their relationship to the total actuating efforts of a manager.

## RESEARCH IN ACTUATING OFFICE EMPLOYEES

Information managers commonly do not tap the ultimate of what an employee is capable of doing. The main reason is because our knowledge of actuating, its makeup, and the various entities that affect it are not known completely. Much more needs to be known about actuating and how to apply it.

It is hoped that research will supply the answer. Good research starts with basic factual knowledge about each employee. Included are records of what motivating techniques were used and the results obtained from each. Also included is information on what rigidities and obstacles seem to exist and detract from accomplishing maximum motivation. In order to codify relationships, evaluation of results is essential. Adequate and complete personnel records are necessary. Standardized personnel forms are helpful, but they should be reviewed in terms of what is essential for the particular program. Among the more common records are: personnel history of the employee; employee's application form; physical examination findings; results of selection tests; identification record; data on training; merit ratings; seniority ratings; safety record; first-aid record; record of attendance, warnings, and demerits; salary and earnings; and termination.

In addition, a personnel record folder on each employee is very helpful. This folder consists of a collection of all personnel records pertaining to the employee; it gives the complete story on that employee and makes this information available for instant reference. Normally, it contains the records listed above; but in some cases, either more or less records may be retained.

## SUGGESTIONS FOR EFFECTIVE MOTIVATING

Certain general guides which, in many offices, have proved successful in motivating employees will now be given. To some extent, these are a review of what has already been stated; but in the following form, they can prove helpful and convenient.

*1. Believe in Yourself and in Other People.* Effective motivating starts with a genuine belief both in yourself as a management member and in the people under your direction. A manager must sincerely believe that he can motivate and must want to motivate his employees. Belief in employees means thinking and promoting the idea that they can plan better, exercise authority better, and do their work better, and giving them the opportunity to do so.

**2. Set a Good Example.** The management member should demonstrate by his actions the kind of effort he would like his employees to exert. Performance on the part of the leader, his attitude, and his work habits tend to set a pattern which employees copy. Important in this consideration is to keep busy—everyone, including the supervisor, should have enough meaningful work to do, otherwise dissatisfaction usually develops.

**3. Place Employees in Proper Jobs.** Employees normally will give their best efforts in work they like and feel competent to perform. Finding the field of endeavor best suited for each individual employee's capacity and interest, as well as following up to insure that each member is on the best job for which he is currently adapted, will assist in stimulating the employee's best efforts.

**4. Stress Participation.** Rare indeed is the person motivated to unusual achievement without some participation in the planning, discussion, and decision making of the activity in which he is going to take a part. Actually, this can be viewed as a basis for practicing delegation of authority.[3] An employee wants to say something about conditions that affect him. Employees want to be asked their opinions about factors involving their work. They appreciate an audience. By such means, the employee gains the feeling that his employer has an interest in, and cares about, those working for him.

**5. Keep Employees Informed.** It is a natural human tendency to want to know what is going on, why this or that operation is important, and what changes are being considered—in short, to be kept informed. This adds to an employee's sense of belonging and of being an integral part of the organizational structure. Employees want to feel they are valued members of the team. Communicating effectively with people is essential in motivating them.

**6. Give Adequate Incentive and Reward.** This can and does take many different forms including the amount of wages, the granting of special privileges, the conferring of titles, and the instilling of competition between departments or among employees. Comparable pay for comparable work is what employees want, and salaries that are in line with those of other enterprises in the area are expected. They may be less interested in the amount of their pay than in the relationship of their pay to that of other employees. Individual recognition, awarding of honors, and seniority are common means of granting special privileges.

**7. Recognize Achievements of Employees.** Most employees want to feel useful; they want their efforts to be appreciated. In short, they want recognition. Credit where credit is due and a sincere expression of satisfaction from the employer for a job well done are effective motivating means. Holding periodic talks in private with each employee affords

---

[3] See chapter 26.

recognition, permits the employee to voice his feelings about aspects of his job, and helps establish a better employer-employee understanding.

**8. Develop Group Spirit.** Motivation is assisted by making employees feel they are a part of the group and are needed on the team. In this respect, various employee recreational activities can be used to good advantage. The group spirit among an interested and participating number of employees is also fostered by giving them certain facts and an objective, then letting them, as a team, come up with a recommended course of action.

**9. Give Information about the Job Itself.** To be motivated effectively, each employee must believe his work is wholesome and important. The relationship of his assignment to the entire office and to the aims of the company should be clearly brought out. It is helpful to point out why the particular equipment and machines are supplied so that an attitude of pride in performing work well and in being a part of the enterprise is developed.

**10. Provide an Opportunity for Job Security.** Almost every employee is concerned about having steady work. Job security is the main reason for demanding restrictions on the type of work that an employee can perform. Also, adequate financial support for old age or to take care of illness or accidents is an important security want of the employee. Providing a wanted security can have a stimulating effect upon the employee.

**11. Employ Fear Judiciously.** Fear is a negative force; but when properly used, it can serve as a very strong motivator. The apprehension of not wanting certain happenings to take place can cause a person to exert unusually strong efforts in the direction away from the unwanted event.

**12. Exercise Strong Leadership.** All normal persons are motivated by competent leaders. The typical employee wants a leader who knows what he is doing, can speak authoritatively, never makes promises he cannot keep, builds confidence, and takes prompt disciplinary action whenever necessary.

## QUESTIONS

1. Discuss the influence of an employee's basic values in the actuating efforts of a manager.
2. What is your interpretation of "building people" and how would you do this as an office manager?
3. To demonstrate a concept of dealing with people, refer to Figure 29–1, and give an example of bringing the other person into the picture when talking about yourself.
4. What is meant by each of the following?
   a) Self-realization needs.
   b) Paternalistic attitude toward employees.

  *c*) Union shop.
  *d*) Unfair labor practice.
5. Referring to Figure 29–2, to which of these questions is your answer "No"? For each such question, what might you do to justify a "Yes" answer?
6. How important do you feel the actuating of office employees really is? Elaborate on your answer.
7. Is the work of the office manager changed by the existence of a union in his office? Explain.
8. In a unionized office, should an office employee take his work problems to his supervisor, the union steward, or a member of the personnel department? Justify your answer.
9. Discuss the provisions of the current national labor laws on what is commonly referred to as "checks on unions."
10. What area of motivating employees do you feel warrants considerable research over the next five years? What types of additional information would you like discovered?
11. Of the twelve means of motivating employees given in this chapter, which five, in your opinion, are probably the most effective for most cases? Why?
12. In company RST, the office employees are nonunion, and the factory employees are members of a union. Recently, as a result of collective bargaining, a 4 percent increase in wages was given factory employees. At the same time, a like increase was given office employees.
  *a*) Do you feel the office employees are justified in accepting this increase?
  *b*) How can the managers of the company justify the increase to office employees?
  *c*) Should the office employees join the union?
  Give reasons for your answers.

## CASE PROBLEMS

### Case 29–1.  Melville-Tobey Company

Henry Langley, a cost clerk, has been on jury duty for the past 12 days. He expects the case to close not later than Thursday which will mark his 13th day of jury duty. However, the case continued through Friday afternoon after which the jury was "locked up" to render a verdict on the important case. On Monday afternoon, the jury reached a verdict. On the next day, Tuesday, Henry Langley returned to work. During the noon hour, he discussed his jury experience with coemployees who seemed quite interested. Two days following (Thursday) was payday and Henry Langley received his paycheck from his supervisor, Mr. Thomas Johnson. A few minutes after looking at it, Mr. Langley complained to Mr. Johnson that the amount of the check was incorrect. There was no pay for Saturday.

MR. JOHNSON: Of course not. You were on jury duty and the company pays you straight time less juror's fees for each day served on a jury. But this applies to regular workdays or those on which the employee is scheduled to work. Last Saturday is not such a day.

MR. LANGLEY: That's not my understanding. You called me last Thursday evening and told me it was my turn to work Saturday which is an overtime day. I said I'd be glad to work that day and believed I'd finish the jury duty by Friday afternoon. But I did not get away till Monday afternoon.

MR. JOHNSON: You did not work Saturday so you do not get any pay. Saturday is not a regular workday—it's in the contract. And besides you received jury fees for Saturday.

MR. LANGLEY: But I've lost money through no fault of my own. Saturday is an overtime day.

MR. JOHNSON: I'll talk with Mr. Matthews in Industrial Relations and see what he says.

MR. LANGLEY: All right. I want my money. I'm going to talk with Mr. Hawkins [the business agent of the union].

Subsequently, Mr. Matthews related to both Mr. Johnson and Mr. Langley that Mr. Langley was not entitled to company pay for Saturday which was a day on which overtime was scheduled. It is not a regular workday and company pay of straight time less juror's fees does not apply. The company's obligations were fulfilled when Mr. Langley was called and he did not appear for work on Saturday.

Mr. Langley talked with Mr. Hawkins who stated, "The jury pay clause is to reimburse an employee for lost time while he is on jury duty. Mr. Langley lost pay because he was unable to take advantage of the overtime offer; he did not refuse to work on Saturday for any personal reason. He was performing important civic duty and should not be penalized."

## Questions:

1. In your opinion, what is the problem and how should it be resolved? Why?
2. What are the important factors leading to this problem?
3. How can a similar problem be avoided in the future?

### Case 29–2.    Howe Products Company

The supervisor of the card-punching and tabulating department, Edward Pierce, went to his superior, office manager Byron Duffel, and inquired if there was danger in letting a company romance continue. He explained that one of the women employees in his department was apparently quite interested in a Mr. Daniel Schloesser, an executive in the systems and procedures department. It probably had been going on for six to eight months and everyone in card punching and tabulating seemed to know about it.

DUFFEL: Who is the girl?

PIERCE: Agnes Cushman.

DUFFEL: She's a very good worker, if it is the one I'm thinking about. She has long black hair, short, rather stocky, big brown eyes?

PIERCE: Yes, that's Agnes.

DUFFEL: Well, this Schloesser man must be 40–45 years old. I would guess Agnes at about 25 years.

PIERCE: I believe the records show she is 28 years of age.

DUFFEL: I don't know too much about Schloesser—whether he's married or has been married.

PIERCE: I've heard very little about him. Nothing about a wife or family of his. Do you think I ought to do anything?

DUFFEL: I guess it's their own private affair.

PIERCE: Yes, I guess it is. Yet, on the other hand, he's coming over and talking to her quite a bit. And she gets far more telephone calls now, but I don't know if they are from Schloesser or not. Some of the other girls are making kidding remarks to Agnes and she doesn't seem to be taking them too well.

## Questions:

1. What should Mr. Duffel say to Mr. Pierce? Why?
2. What action, if any, should Mr. Pierce take? Mr. Duffel?
3. In general, what do you feel should be done about company romances? Why?

### Case 29–3.   Kubera Company

Edmund DuBarry is a cost clerk, has been with the company two years, and performs satisfactory work. Several months ago he purchased for his home a stereo set and a quantity of long-play records. Soon after that he developed the habit of humming and whistling at his work. His sounds were somewhat lacking in artfulness, but Edmund apparently derived much satisfaction from his efforts for he continued with them off and on throughout the entire day. Fellow cost clerks working near Edmund made no complaints, but to his supervisor, Harvey Olsen, "the sounds" were very disturbing. At first, he had hoped that Edmund would "stop the music" after a week or so of such goings on. But the practice persisted.

Finally, Mr. Olsen spoke privately to Edmund and requested that he stop his humming and whistling during working hours as they were distracting, in bad taste, and not in keeping with a well-run office. Edmund complied and was quiet for several days. Then he again started humming and whistling while on the job. After a couple hours of this, Mr. Olsen walked to Edmund's desk and in front of the entire department shouted to Edmund, "Stop it." Edmund did. Then after several seconds, Edmund stated softly, "None of the boys here in the department have complained. All of us are doing our work. The trouble is supervisors don't want to adjust to individual employee differences, but employees are expected to adjust to individual manager differences." Mr. Olsen told Edmund to keep quiet and get to work. Edmund said nothing.

## Questions:

1. Is there a problem here? Discuss.
2. What do you believe would have happened had Mr. Olsen said nothing to Edmund DuBarry?
3. What should Edmund do now? Mr. Olsen? Justify your views.

chapter **30**

# Office supervision

> If you wish your merit to be known, acknowledge
> that of other people.
>
> —*Oriental Proverb*

THE OFFICE supervisor is a key figure in the managerial work of actuating. Almost every plan, policy, and decision originated at the top of the organization structure must filter down through the supervisory level. Because of his strategic location both to influence and to implement the many actuating techniques, the supervisor is extremely influential in motivating employees, in developing them, and in building teams which carry out specific duties.

An organization unit is what it is largely because of the supervisor's influence. Actually, many problems are reduced to simple tasks when supervisors are competent and get complete cooperation from their employees. The accomplishment of satisfactory office production and the establishment of a favorable work climate depend in large measure upon the quality of offce supervision. The supervisor is charged with seeing that the work in his unit is performed within a reasonable time and at a reasonable cost. He is the ultimate regulator of what is accomplished.

## THE SUPERVISOR'S STATUS

The supervisor is at the critical focal point about which the top managers' wishes are distributed and the operative employees' desires are concentrated. He is the point of contact between management members

708

and nonmanagement members. To many employees, the supervisor represents management.

Usually, a supervisor is thought of as being below the executive level. The supervisor's work is similar to that of the executive; but the scope of the work, the matters on which decisions must be made, and the general overall executive work are not as broad in the case of the supervisor as in the case of the executive. For convenience, a "supervisor" can be defined as *a management member working at an organizational level where personal oversight of tasks assigned to small groups is assumed in order to assure satisfactory performance.*

## THE WORK OF THE SUPERVISOR

Actually the supervisor's work, in great measure, consists of getting work performed properly by others. This is the heart of supervisory success. A person who insists upon doing everything himself never makes a satisfactory supervisor. Most failures in supervision are in getting things done through people. It is not always the employee's fault, although this is the common explanation.

It is possible to classify the work of the supervisor in a variety of ways. Since the supervisor is a management member, the following outline appears logical and helpful.

Under planning, the supervisor has such activities as:

1. Participating in the formulation of establishing objectives for his unit.
2. Understanding and knowing the work to be done.
3. Knowing and interpreting company policies to the employee.
4. Keeping up with new developments.
5. Improving current methods being followed.

Controlling encompasses the following work by the supervisor:

1. Following stated practices and procedures.
2. Utilizing standards established for the work.
3. Evaluating work output in terms of cost.
4. Checking accuracy and quantity of work.
5. Minimizing peak work loads.

Organizing efforts by the supervisor include:

1. Delegating work to others.
2. Allocating the work among members of the unit.
3. Placing similar work in the same unit.
4. Establishing proper authority relationships among members of a unit.
5. Keeping employee-work relationships up to date.

The supervisor's managerial actuating efforts deal with:

1. Informing employees of changes.
2. Evaluating and disciplining employees.
3. Developing understudies.
4. Securing teamwork and harmony among employees.
5. Increasing the value of employees.

## KNOWLEDGE AND SKILL OF THE SUPERVISOR

To perform his work effectively, the supervisor must have certain knowledge and must be able to do skillfully certain activities. Knowledge requirements of the supervisor vary from one office to another, but the ability to perform certain activities skillfully is fairly constant regardless of the office and its type of work.

The basic knowledge needs are:

*1. Technical Knowledge.* This includes knowledge of systems, procedures, materials, office forms, equipment, and the manner in which results are used. Much of this knowledge might be acquired while one is serving in a nonsupervisory capacity. The supervisor should know enough about the detail work that is done to provide the necessary leadership to those performing the tasks and to plan and control their work so that orderly and reasonable rates of accomplishment are realized.

*2. Knowledge of Responsibilities.* This includes comprehension of the company's policies, rules, and regulations; of the extent of the supervisor's authority and responsibility; and of matters on which he can make final decisions. An acquaintance with basic information about organization, management, collective bargaining, communication, budgeting, and any area of direct or indirect concern in the particular supervisory job appears to be a minimum requirement.

Basic needs concerning what the supervisor's skills are:

*1. Skill in Teaching.* Whether a supervisor gives specific instructions on a particular task or makes assignments in fairly broad terms, it is necessary that he pass along his knowledge to others and develop them. This, in turn, calls for skill in teaching and is a prime means for making supervision more effective. Generally, an employee is more satisfied, has greater interest, and will be more industrious when informed clearly what work is wanted and how it is to be performed. This means that the supervisor should have skill in instructing, so that a well-trained work force is available.

*2. Skill in Methods Improvement.* Better utilization of materials, machines, and manpower is the constant aim of progressive managers. Some methods of performing work are inherited, others are hastily thrown together, while still others are copied from similar operations. All can be improved. Skill in analyzing, supplemented by ingenuity, usually results in improved ways of performing work.

**3. Skill in Human Relations.** This sometimes suffers as a result of the pressure and volume of day-to-day work. Working with and getting along with people are vital to the supervisor. This emphasizes the important areas of understanding the behavior and attitudes of individual employees and of recognizing and using basic human relations. Further discussion of human relations and supervision follows.

## THE SUPERVISOR AND HUMAN RELATIONS

The modern office supervisor must use human relations in his work, in fact, many feel he must be an expert in understanding and in dealing with employees. Material facts, basic information, and technical knowledge are necessary, but the daily challenge to most supervisors lies not in these areas, but in stimulating his group members to perform the maximum quantity and quality of work and making it possible for them to achieve contentment and satisfaction for these work efforts.

The ability to treat the employee as a human being, to gain mutual respect and understanding, to have his trust, and to win his utmost cooperation without any command or coercion are among the essential qualities that characterize the truly successful supervisor. Yet the supervisor should not become too friendly or intimate and thus risk the loss of his members' respect and confidence. The amount of friendliness and intimacy is an artistic determination and will differ somewhat for different situations. Always the supervisor must be objective, find out and review both sides of problems or disputes, refrain from jumping to conclusions, and solve the issue fairly without playing favorites. He should keep promises made to any member of his group or explain to the member's satisfaction why such agreements are invalid. He should be approachable, listen to their work or personal problem, assist in determining what should be done, and help, wherever feasible, in achieving a favorable solution.

Impartiality by the supervisor in his human relations is extremely important. Characterized as being fair is a cardinal quality to be developed by a supervisor. It can overshadow possible weaknesses that he may have. Trying to understand the employee's point of view, giving straight answers to employee's questions, keeping records of work performed by every member, and disciplining, yet still retaining the employee's sincere respect, are indications that a supervisor practices fairness in dealing with his group members. Five simple human relations practices for office supervisors are shown in Figure 30–1. Sincere application of these practices brings surprisingly helpful results.

FIGURE 30–1. Human Relations Practices for Supervisors.

1. Judge each member of a group by his good qualities. Work is achieved by positive attitudes, not by stressing lack of abilities and skills.

2. Make every personal contact helpful and constructive. Take the viewpoint that you are trying to assist every member of your group achieve the ultimate of his potential.

3. Get your group members to participate in your plans. Modify plans to strengthen them and to uncover and eliminate objections; and adopt the plan that will achieve the predetermined goal most effectively and serve the interests and desires of the group to a maximum.

4. Eliminate opposition of interests among your group. Find out the common motives. Strive toward group unity and effective teamwork.

5. Give instructions clearly. Be certain the basic idea is identified and transferred to the recipient of the instruction. Do not take anything for granted. Provide sufficient details.

## ADVANCEMENT TO SUPERVISOR'S JOB

Today, there are plenty of supervisory opportunities for those who have prepared themselves, are qualified, and have a good work or experience background. Supervisors are appointed because something needs to be accomplished and the appointee appears to be a person who can get the accomplishment performed in a better than average way and takes pride in performing it. From what has been stated, the supervisory prospect must have knowledge of people and of how to get work accomplished through them. And he possesses the ability to carry out a leadership role. In addition, he needs to have (1) knowledge of the enterprise and (2) knowledge of self. The supervisor makes decisions and performs in a work environment conditioned by the enterprise, yet with consideration of the human values and needs of his people. Information on the policies, beliefs, traditions, and operation conditions of the enterprise are helpful to the supervisor in the performance of his work.

The person ready for supervisory responsibility has studied himself; he knows his strengths and weaknesses. He builds on his strengths, and tries to overcome his weaknesses. He strives to improve personality traits that admittedly need some mending, and studies to keep abreast of latest developments in his chosen field. He sets goals realistically, plans carefully, and works to get what he wants. He willingly assumes responsibility, makes choices, utilizes his education and experience as best he can, tries, and accepts his failures as well as his successes.

## SELECTION OF OFFICE SUPERVISORS

Selection of office supervisors can be considered the beginning of effective supervision. The employee having the longest service, the highest production volume, or the longest no-tardiness and no-absenteeism record is not necessarily the best selection for a supervisory job. Much of the work the supervisor is called upon to perform differs from that of the operative employee.

The first step in the selection of office supervision is to determine the background and characteristics needed for the supervisory jobs. Such information can be used to set the minimum employment qualifications and standards. Preparation of such information should take into account the realities of the specific condition.

The actual task of selection is assisted by the use of any one or all of the following: (1) appraisals of the candidates, (2) written tests, (3) interviews, and (4) evaluation of experience and training. The first, or appraisal of candidates, can take many different forms, including inquiry of the candidate's present superior, talking with those acquainted with the candidate's work performance, and discussing with friends the candidate's activities in clubs and other groups outside the office.

Written tests are increasing in usage, but they probably do not yet qualify as a common means for office supervisory selection. Tests are designed to measure work, personality, and technical factors. They provide a means to screen initially a large number of candidates, and they stress objective evidence instead of someone's opinion and judgment. However, considerable criticism has been leveled against tests in which it is pointed out that they concentrate on selected areas rather than the "entire man," that some candidates are practically certain not to reveal their true ability by written word, and that the candidates answer test questions for a prescribed situation in one way, yet for the same situation perform in a different way under actual working conditions.

As pointed out in chapter 25, interviewing is perhaps the most common means of selection, and this statement includes supervisory selection. The face-to-face meeting, the opportunity to clarify ambiguous written statements, and the flexibility to shape the interview to the individual case make for the wide use and popularity of the interview method.

Finally, the evaluation of experience and training provides a practical element to the selection method followed. A detailed investigation of the candidate's work history is sometimes undertaken. Thus, elements which might be overlooked in the other selection approaches are brought into the program. Knowledge of the enterprise and technical competence are illustrative of these elements.

## AUTHORITY OF SUPERVISOR

In a relatively small enterprise, the general manager, who in many cases is also the owner, has supervisory authority over each employee. The general manager makes the decisions that concern job requirements, keeps the employee informed about changes and the progress of the business. With growth of the company and the resultant spreading of the gap between top management and nonmanagement members, it is generally agreed that supervisors must narrow the gap and conduct many of the needed managerial relations with employees.

The size and complexity of the enterprise, as well as the viewpoint toward employees, tend to modify the supervisor's formal authority. Unfortunately, in many offices, it is not precisely stated what the office supervisor is expected to do. The former concept of the supervisor "running his unit," with complete authority to hire, fire, change work sequence, make improvements, and handle operations in any way believed satisfactory, no longer exists in most offices. The common state of affairs is a somewhat indefinite arrangement which has evolved over the years and is due, in part, to the very nature of the job—the fact that the work of supervision is so varied, the scope so large, and the activities involved so numerous. Part of the present status can be said to have been brought about by the use of staff members to assist and to render advice to the supervisor in carrying out his work. In some cases, it is believed that the work of office supervising has become so complex that expert help to the supervisor is an absolute necessity. In contrast, others are of the opinion that staff helpers usurp authority and take over activities which constitute the fundamental duties of the supervisor. For example, in many offices, the supervisor does not interview and select new employees, but he does have a voice in the final hiring. Further, the use of participation to give members of the group the opportunity to express themselves on matters of mutual interest; the stress on communication, sharing information, and keeping everyone fully informed; and the higher educational level of the typical office group today have modified not only the relationships between the supervisor and the individual members but also the makeup of the supervisory job itself.

The office supervisor is expected to utilize his employees' capacities and interests effectively. He assigns employees definite work, points out certain goals, and gets them to want to perform accurately and do a satisfactory volume of work. In addition, he is called upon to review and evaluate the work performance of his employees, and to answer questions concerning the methods in action to accomplish the work. Various means can be used by the supervisor, depending mainly upon the type of employee, the work situation, and the kind of office work.

## RELATIONSHIPS WITH SUPERIORS AND WITH PEERS

Relationships are especially important to the supervisor. His destiny is controlled largely by other people. Much of what he achieves comes as a result of their approval. We have already pointed out the relationship between supervisor and subordinate. There remains the relationship between supervisor and (1) superiors and (2) peers.

With reference to the first, the supervisor is expected to implement a specific portion of a plan at the operative level. To do this, he is given instructions, receives specialized assistance from various staff members, attends indoctrination meetings, and communicates with his superiors. In these relationships, the astute supervisor discovers that certain practices assist him appreciably. He finds that he must have *a firm belief in the essentiality of supervisory work.* He must realize that his efforts to help manage the office work are fundamental to the success of the enterprise. He should reveal this belief by viewing enthusiastically his opportunity to contribute to the success of the office. Also, with experience it is found that it is wise to *focus appeals to superior's greatest interests.* Normally these are improved service, lower costs of operation, and increased net income. The office supervisor who knows how his unit will help achieve these goals will capture the attention and support of his superiors. Actually, with some concentrated thinking, it is not difficult to do this, but some showmanship in presenting the idea is helpful.

Further, the office supervisor learns to *expect some resistance to suggestions and new ideas.* Some top and middle managers favor a sort of "do not disturb things, let them be as they are" attitude. Especially is this true if there are no complaints and things are running quite smoothly. The feeling of "Why take a chance?" may prevail. In addition, it is well to *act in a manner that justifies recognition as a member of management.* Too frequently, recognition of office supervisors as management members is lip service only, the recognition is by decree only. Nothing tangible is done to make supervisors a part of management or to make them feel that they are. To overcome this condition, supervisors can offer, as a group, means for obtaining certain goals of top management by their (the supervisors') efforts. Suggestions along this line are offered by Figure 30–2.

With reference to peers, it is axiomatic that within any given enterprise an office supervisor should have good relationships with the other office supervisors. To achieve this status, most of the points just stated under supervisor-superior relationships apply here. In addition, each supervisor should know where he "fits into the organization picture" of the enterprise. Such information will help to clarify the relationship of any one supervisor. It is also essential that each supervisor knows the work for which he is responsible, from what supervisor or department the work comes to his department, and to what supervisor (or department) he sends it. Close cooperation among these supervisors, related by work flow, should be maintained. Further, practices and decisions found effective by one supervisor should be shared with other supervisors not only to keep

FIGURE 30-2. The Supervisor in Management.

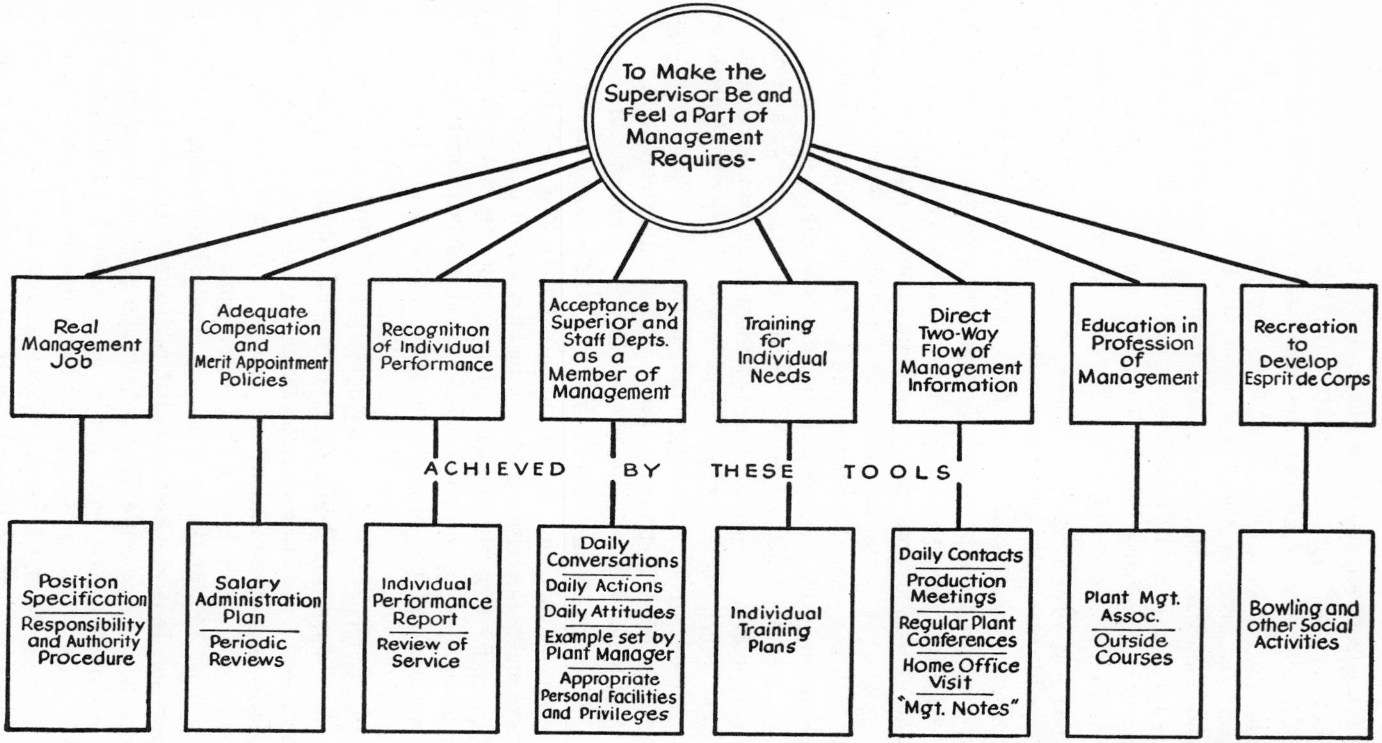

To Make the Supervisor Be and Feel a Part of Management Requires—

| Real Management Job | Adequate Compensation and Merit Appointment Policies | Recognition of Individual Performance | Acceptance by Superior and Staff Depts. as a Member of Management | Training for Individual Needs | Direct Two-Way Flow of Management Information | Education in Profession of Management | Recreation to Develop Esprit de Corps |

ACHIEVED BY THESE TOOLS

| Position Specification Responsibility and Authority Procedure | Salary Administration Plan — Periodic Reviews | Individual Performance Report — Review of Service | Daily Conversations — Daily Actions — Daily Attitudes — Example set by Plant Manager — Appropriate Personal facilities and Privileges | Individual Training Plans | Daily Contacts — Production Meetings — Regular Plant Conferences — Home Office Visit — "Mgt. Notes" | Plant Mgt. Assoc. — Outside Courses | Bowling and other Social Activities |

Courtesy: Armstrong Cork Company, Lancaster, Pa.

them informed, but also to propagate the successful means which are proving helpful.

## SUPERVISORY TRAINING

Strictly speaking, any educational activity designed to prepare the candidate for supervisory work or to improve the supervisor in carrying out his duties successfully can be termed "supervisory training." The field is quite broad and deals with many, yet related, subjects. Supervisory training is not confined to learning to perform a set of movements more efficiently but includes the development of attitudes, control of emotions, and the broadening of one's views. Keeping the supervisor fully informed constitutes one of the biggest challenges in supervisory training. Conditions are constantly changing; new developments are taking place; and in most cases, the supervisor finds himself confronted with new personnel, new attitudes, and new problems.

Excellent work in supervisory training is being accomplished by the members of the Training Within Industry Foundation, a nonprofit organization which advocates gaining maximum results from employed people through better supervision. Years of intensive research and many office tryouts with groups of supervisors have helped develop highly successful training programs for supervisors. Among the more important for normal office use are:

**1. Job Instruction.** The *JI* course consists of five two-hour sessions and is intended to give skill in instructing. It is especially helpful where there is work involving long break-in periods, numerous errors, or difficulty in getting the information work out on time. To illustrate the content, the course consists of four main parts: (*a*) preparing the employee, (*b*) presenting the operation, (*c*) trying out the performance, and (*d*) following up on performance.

**2. Job Relations.** Known as the *JR* course, this also consists of five two-hour sessions. It helps provide skill in leadership and is recommended where there are too many misunderstandings among employees and complaints are numerous in the human relations area.

**3. Job Methods.** This *JM* program likewise is five two-hour sessions. It gives skill in improving methods through practice sessions and on-the-job coaching. This program is effective in finding better methods of accomplishing office work.

**4. Job Economics Training.** Known as the *JET* course, this requires five 1½-hour sessions and presents the basic principles upon which the U.S. economy operates.

**5. Discussion Leading.** This *DL* course of four three-hour sessions is designed to give skill in getting participation in meetings and in discussing thoroughly matters of common interest.

**6. Program Development.** The *PD* course is intended for the instruction of one person in a company who has responsibility for designing and conducting training programs in his company or some unit thereof. The normal time required for this course is five days, dispersed among two or three weeks, to permit specific application of program material to the trainee's company.

In addition, the following means of supervisory training are helpful and widely used:

1. Company supervisory schools in which organized classes in problems of supervision are studied.

2. Individual study of the various available materials on the theory and practice of supervisory work.

3. Conferences and seminars that afford discussions with supervisors of other departments, group training, and an opportunity to talk over problems of mutual interest.

4. Dramatized meetings in which supervisors act out their problems, this acting-out to be followed by discussions and comments to bring out possible improvements in the handling of problems.

5. Observation of and talks with employees to gain a better insight into their jobs and their attitudes.

6. Interviews with top management members to gain advice and suggestions regarding what supervisory action might be taken under various circumstances.

7. Involvement in an actual situation, handling the work of supervision with a "learn by doing" technique. Usually, some background data are desirable before using this means of obtaining information.

## EFFECTIVE TIME-USE BY THE SUPERVISOR

Basic to supervisory success is the wise use of time on the job. To this end, the office supervisor can concentrate on essentials—the really important tasks. The best supervisors perform key tasks only and do not let themselves get involved in endless details. Unnecessary work is quickly identified as such and abolished. Also, for most supervisors, the completion of a task once it is started makes for efficient time utilization. Tasks not quite finished are the vexation of many supervisors. Staying with a job until it is finished and not giving in to interruptions are key habits to be followed. In addition, the budgeting of one's time is a time-saver. The time-minded supervisor decides what tasks he has to perform, estimates the time for each, and schedules these time periods through his workday. This approach helps utilize time more effectively and establishes goals that are achieved during the day, thus providing a sense of satisfaction. Furthermore, the office supervisor should acquire speed in reading and become more selective in what is read. Few adults receive reading training beyond the elementary school level. Many people read at this pace, which is a serious detriment to their efficiency in time utilization. By practice and accelerated reading courses increases up to 75 percent in reading efficiency can be attained.

With better utilization of time, a proper balance among the various facets of the supervisory work should be attained. An equitable appraisal of all the various supervisory tasks must be made and compared with established levels of satisfactory performance. For example, data on cost, quantity of work achieved, quality of work, number of grievances, number tardy, number absent, and labor turnover rates are helpful. Trends in these data are significant. Also, changes in some factors may help predict future changes in others—frequently before either the difficulty or the favorable accomplishment is revealed by standard operating reports.

## COACHING AND COUNSELING

The office supervisor has frequent occasion to use coaching and counseling. Information and inspiration are stressed by coaching. The particular data needed for a given situation are supplied and the unique capacities of members of a group are both stimulated and integrated by a coach. Emphasis is on "setting up the plays," but permitting the employee to carry them out as best he can. The supervisor must have the respect of the employee, understand how he feels, and possess an ability to use analogies and demonstrations. In contrast, counseling emphasizes leading a person to self-insight and improvement by means of carefully selected questions and suggestions along with skillful listening. To get the person to see what he can do to improve his accomplishments is the goal of counseling. It can be viewed as a suggestive and supportive technique to instill self-motivation in the person being counseled. The role of the counselor is to help the employee help himself to become independent in his own right and to build confidence in himself. The amount of direction and assistance given depends upon the individual being counseled. Both coaching and counseling emphasize a person-to-person individualized relationship.

To be able to use coaching and counseling successfully it is first necessary to make clear what you want the employee to do and to be sure that he knows it too. This supplies the needed orientation and something toward which he can measure his progress. Second, be sensitive to capabilities, behavior, and likes of the employee. Some excel in physical pursuits, others rank high in mental endeavors. Some are "detailists," other comprehend mainly broad generalities. Find out these individual differences and be guided by them in coaching and counseling. In brief, know your employee. Next, stress the immediate future. Concentrate on the present job. Reach agreement on what is to be done for the next day, next week, or next month at most. It is easy to make commitments for three or four years ahead and then gradually forget about them. Fourth, stay with specific, concrete examples. Talk about actual happenings. Discuss actual incidents and their effect upon his work and standing. Lastly, use constructive criticism. Tie in with his work and bring out ways which would make for improvement. Stress the potential gains and the feasibility of his achieving them.

## OFFICE SUPERVISOR'S CHECK LIST

It is helpful for the office supervisor to take stock of himself periodically. Figure 30–3 offers the opportunity to do so. There is no scoring

FIGURE 30–3. Check List for Supervisor's Self-Appraisal.

|  | *Yes* | *No* |
|---|---|---|
| 1. Do I have a sense of time-consciousness? | | |
| 2. Do I approach decision making free from preconceived notions and prejudices? | | |
| 3. Do I decide and seldom worry about decisions already made? | | |
| 4. Do I plan my work so that each member of my group is fully occupied? | | |
| 5. Do I employ periodic meetings or interviews with employees to keep communication channels open to share information and issue instructions? | | |
| 6. Do I give time to my members to talk over problems that are bothering them? | | |
| 7. Do I listen attentively so that people tend to open up to me? | | |
| 8. Do I have a reasonable knowledge of what each of the other departments of the enterprise does? | | |
| 9. Do I set a good example by meeting deadlines, respecting opinions of others, and displaying enthusiasm for the work to be done? | | |
| 10. Do I maintain reasonable and fair quality and quantity standards? | | |
| 11. Do I know the best way to motivate each of my key people? | | |
| 12. Do my people know where they fall short and what they can do to improve? | | |
| 13. Do I take criticism and correction and view them as opportunities to improve? | | |
| 14. Do I analyze reverses and see ways to prevent them from recurring? | | |
| 15. Do I recognize and reward exceptional contributions? | | |
| 16. Do I treat each member of the group as I would like to be treated? | | |

system, but an insight into strengths and weaknesses and a spur to improve future performance are provided. The top supervisor can honestly answer, "Yes," to each of the questions.

## SUPERVISING FEMALE EMPLOYEES

Since the majority of office employees are female, the subject of supervising female employees is important. In many respects, what has been stated about supervision applies equally to female and to male employee. Certain additional suggestions, however, may prove beneficial. A cardinal point is to give very careful consideration to women's work assignments. They do many things extremely well, but usually are outstanding on work requiring manual dexterity, caring, and mediating functions. That is, women are more likely to do better in work where patience, interest in human beings, and human needs are considerations. But women, like men, should be encouraged to do what they can do or what they can learn to do. It is also helpful to treat each female employee as an individual. Many women feel that their problems are different—even though other women have the same problems. Let them stand as individuals, in fact, encourage this viewpoint which usually meets with favorable response.

Pay correspondingly greater attention to the workplace of women employees. Women want "a nice place to work," including a clean, attractive area with good decor. They are actively aware of their surroundings. An opportunity for socializing, conversing with others, and allowance for family obligations are also desirable. Furthermore, exercise authority, but don't be a tyrant. Women office employees expect authority to be used and they won't rebel against it. What they won't tolerate is tyranny. Finally, recognize certain facts about the psychology of women. They tend *to show* their emotions more readily than men, probably because it is more culturally acceptable in our society. Moods in women differ and change throughout the day. With ten women employees there can be ten different moods at one time. These moods vary or multiply during the day. Frequently, female supervisors are more rigid than male supervisors would be. This is because there is a tendency for women supervisors to act as they think men would act under the same situation. The answer here is to point out that the best supervisor is both firm and considerate. Fairness must be a part of all supervisory efforts. Also recognize that all supervisors must earn the respect and confidence of his or her subordinates. It is inevitable that the work group will test the new supervisor.

## SECURING EFFECTIVE SUPERVISION

Much material is available concerning how to be an efficient supervisor. Some of it is quite idealistic and contains many platitudes. The subject is broad, but the following ten points are included in order to indicate, in general, the type of activity which is recommended.

1. *Treat All Workers Alike—Show No Favoritism.* The successful supervisor operates objectively; his personal likes and dislikes are not permitted to influence his work.

2. *Practice Participative Management.* Talk things over with the employees and give them an opportunity to suggest the best way to accomplish a task. Such a practice makes for strong group identity and a sense

of belonging and recognizes the fact that no one has a monopoly on good ideas.

**3. Enforce All rules and Regulations Promptly.** Usually, nothing is gained by delaying action in cases where violations are involved. In fact, delay might be interpreted as a lack of decisiveness and an inability to cope with the situation.

**4. Keep Your Instructions Simple.** Repeat them frequently to the new employee. Acquire a patient, helpful attitude particularly in working with the employee who is not yet fully familiar with all the job requirements.

**5. Insist Upon and Stress the Need for Each Employee to Give a Full Day's Work for a Full Day's Pay.** Satisfactory work outputs are the chief responsibility of every supervisor.

**6. Watch Waste—Material Loss and Time Loss.** Guarding against waste of all types will add significantly to the work output.

**7. Keep Fully Informed on Company Policies and Their Interpretation.** It is the supervisor's responsibility to interpret company policies to the employees.

**8. Secure Employees' Opinions Regarding Supervision.** By means of attitude surveys, spot interviews, casual conversations, and discussion groups, find out what is bothering the employees and what "gripes" are developing. Adequate and correct information at the right time and place may avoid much needless trouble.

**9. Develop Capable Assistants.** Good management requires that qualified replacements be available to maintain the supervisory force at a satisfactory number and caliber. Failure to develop an understudy jeopardizes the supervisor's chances for promotion.

**10. Inform Top and Middle Management Members What Supervisory Action Is Taking Place and Why.** This merits attention because supervision is not only vital to the enterprise, but it requires the complete backing by top and middle management members.

**QUESTIONS**

1. Elaborate on the statement: "An office supervisor needs knowledge of (1) the enterprise, and (2) himself.

2. As you see it, is the office supervisor a key figure in information management? Justify your viewpoint.

3. Discuss the work of an office supervisor in what might be considered a typical office.

4. Discuss the subject of the supervisor and human relations.

5. Justify your viewpoint toward this quotation: "With more and more specialists and expert staff people being used in the modern office organizational structure, the importance and status of the office supervisor has decreased. He is not as important as formerly. In many cases, he decides virtually nothing, his superiors telling him what to do."

6. What is counseling? Relate for what purposes, and how it can be used effectively by an office supervisor.
7. What means can an office supervisor use in order to make better use of her time?
8. Make several specific suggestions usually effective for improving the relationship between a supervisor and his superiors.
9. Draw up a program for the recruitment and selection of office supervisors for a large office. Assume candidates will be recruited from both within and outside the enterprise.
10. Identify each of the following:
    *a*) Supervisor.
    *b*) Knowledge of responsibilities by an office supervisor.
    *c*) *JM* course for supervisory training.
    *d*) Coaching.
11. Figure 30–1 lists five human relations practices for office supervisors. Which one do you feel is most important? Justify your selection.
12. Discuss several considerations to keep in mind in supervising female employees.

## CASE PROBLEMS

### Case 30–1.  Veerkamp Company

Miss Virginia Foster, a systems analyst, lived beyond her financial means. A competent employee, Miss Foster has been with Veerkamp Company for nearly two years. She gets along well with all employees, dresses in good taste, and lives alone in her own apartment. Her salary appears ample to justify her economic level of living. Trouble is apparently her compulsive buying habits. During the past year or so, she has been embroiled in disputes with her creditors. Several have brought their problems to the company to assist in paying the debts. Others have turned over the account to collection agencies which badger the company for help in making the collections.

The personnel manager through Mr. Shepard, head of the systems department, has warned Miss Foster that her creditors are becoming a terrible nuisance and urged her to clear up her debts. Mr. Shepard has offered to help formulate a workable budget for her, or to help in planning her financial matters, but to date these offers have been to no avail. Mr. Shepard insists that she is intelligent and personally cannot understand why she owes so many different people.

Day before yesterday a crisis occurred. One creditor garnished her pay. The company immediately discharged Miss Foster stating it wanted no part of wage garnishments and had experienced enough harassments from Miss Foster's creditors without any sign of her paying past debts. The company has spent much time answering telephone calls and letters from Miss Foster's creditors. Miss Foster is apparently a poor credit risk. The company wants employees who can handle their personal affairs. When an employee is troubled by financial matters, she cannot devote her full effort to her job.

Miss Foster claimed employment termination was too harsh, one garnishee and you're out. She continued, "The company does not know that this creditor is acting unfairly and is trying to put something over on me. I am not going to pay him and intend to fight the claim—alone, if necessary. I have been told my work here at Veerkamp is satisfactory. What I do with my money is my own business."

## Questions:

1. Is there a problem here?
2. As Mr. Shepard, what action would you now take? Why?

## Case 30–2. Moyer Manufacturing Company

After considerable thought and talking it over with other management members, office manager Maurice Stetler decided to terminate the employment of Elmer Pick who in Stetler's opinion is not the type of employee wanted by the company. Employed three years ago as a programmer in the computer group, Elmer demonstrated little initiative, was careless about his appearance, and was not thorough in his work. When hired, he was what Stetler describes as a marginal recruit. More important, however, as a reason for his dismissal was Elmer's poor job attitude. Especially during the past year, Elmer showed lack of interest in his work and repeatedly gave silly reasons why certain programs could not be constructed when all the time they are being designed and implemented.

Elmer Pick was given his discharge notice. He went to his supervisor to protest, but was surprised to find that his supervisor, Jerome Carroll, was also given his dismissal notice. Jerome curtly told Elmer that he (Jerome) didn't want to hear any gripes. Said Jerome, "I've put up with you too long, Elmer, and now it has cost me my job." Jerome requested and received an interview with Maurice Stetler. Jerome pleaded for anther chance, stating that no warnings of company dissatisfaction had been given him. He had erred in trying to run his unit with incompetent people but this was all the personnel department sent him. He would change this, however, if given another opportunity. Maurice Stetler stated he would reconsider the entire matter, but frankly as of now, he believed the termination should be carried out.

Later the same day, Elmer Pick called at Mr. Stetler's office and requested reinstatement of his job. "I need the work badly," he explained. "I've been here for a spell and certainly seniority means something around here." Mr. Stetler answered, "All facts have been considered. Primarily, it is your poor job attitude. But your personal record will read "resigned voluntarily." Elmer thanked him and added, "Let me ask you something. What is poor job attitude? I'm a member, or I was, of a poorly run department. The fact that you are letting Mr. Carroll go is proof of that. If a guy is in an atmosphere of poor supervision, how do you expect him to be a 'Willing Willie' especially to all the half-baked and wild ideas they bring you. Now that you are getting rid of Mr. Carroll, things should be better. Your charges against me are vague, Mr. Stetler. You have no records or witnesses to prove I didn't do the work or had any wrong view toward it. And, as I say, I want to keep my job. I need it."

## Questions:

1. Discuss what are probably the major factors leading to the situation as presented in this case?
2. What further action do you recommend be taken by Jerome Carroll? By Elmer Pick?
3. As Maurice Stetler, what would you do? Why?

### Case 30–3. Peerless Products, Inc.

In the accounting department are 14 employees who—Edgar Crawford, the supervisor, believes—make a very effective team. One employee, Bernard Oakton, aged 30 years, married, with three children, started a tax service company last year. He assisted a number of people to prepare their income tax returns and made several hundred dollars extra. As a result of this work, he secured the part-time job of keeping the books for two small businesses. By working several evenings and weekends, he was able to do this work. Although it was confining, he did not mind, as he could use the extra money; and he thought that with some luck, the business might develop into an independent accounting firm of his own.

Oakton has never said anything about this outside work to Edgar Crawford, who nevertheless knows about it through friends and the grapevine. There is no company policy pertaining to such matters, and Crawford has said nothing to Oakton about the outside work. But he has observed that Oakton looks tired, even the first thing in the morning, and for the past six weeks has been absent quite often from his regular job. About two weeks ago, he heard that Oakton had hired a part-time helper to assist him on these outside assignments.

Last week, Oakton was absent for a day and a half. When he reported for work at noon, Edgar Crawford requested that he come to his office and fired him.

BERNARD OAKTON: This is the rawest deal I ever heard of. I wasn't here because my wife is ill. I wanted to explain this to Marcey [the telephone switchboard operator]; but while holding the line, I was cut off.

EDGAR CRAWFORD: Yes? Well I'll tell you something. I do not believe you.

OAKTON: Well, now I. . . .

CRAWFORD: You're trying to misrepresent your absence, which is another reason why you deserve to be fired. And if you were cut off on the switchboard, why didn't you call back to offer your explanation? You know as well as I do that company rules require notification from anyone who is not going to report for work on a regular workday.

OAKTON: Sure, I know that. But the phone call has nothing to do with it. You're sore because of my outside business.

CRAWFORD: I did not say that.

OAKTON: It's what you're thinking, all right. I know. But let me ask you this, Mr. Crawford. You've known about my outside work and never said anything. So what gave you the right to get tough about it all of a sudden and terminate my employment?

## Questions:

1. What do you believe Bernard Oakton should do now? Why?
2. What should Edgar Crawford do? Why?
3. Could the circumstances that led to this problem have been eliminated? Explain, showing how and why.

# chapter 31

# Developing office employees

> Every man has within himself a continent of un-
> discovered character. Happy is he who proves the
> Columbus of his soul.
>
> —*Goethe*

THE PLANNED development of employees is vital in managerial actuating and has grown tremendously during the past several decades. Employee development takes place everyday in most enterprises. Employees acquire their development either by means of planned and well-administered programs or by a hit-or-miss manner which includes learning by mistakes, by trial and error, and by absorption. Since developing is vital and goes on continually, progressive managers have set up definite development programs so that proper direction and control can be given to make the employees more satisfied and their work contribution more useful to the enterprise.

## FUNDAMENTALS OF DEVELOPING

Most employees are developing most of the time through the acquisition of additional knowledge and skill. This is a perfectly natural process. The sources include personal performance, behavior of other employees, hearing, observing, and imitating. These means are commonly referred to as "experience." Development from these sources places a strong emphasis on what is practical and is conditioned extensively by experiment and accident. As such, it is neither an efficient means nor necessarily applicable to the employee's job.

Intentional efforts to teach someone can be far more effective, provided the efforts are properly managed. Beginning with what the trainee now knows and can perform, it is possible to determine what the trainee must know and be able to do in order to perform successfully particular work assignments. The differential between what is now known and what is needed constitutes the gap which training seeks to fill. This gap is reduced gradually, because learning is a gradual process. An employee learns bit by bit, not all at once. Knowing the gap to be filled and considering the gradual doses which can be absorbed by the trainee and in what sequence, the formal training operation can be set in motion. Usually, tie-ins or association of new concepts with knowledge or skills already possessed by the trainee proves effective in training work.

There exist today many different schools of thought about the means of developmental efforts. And new proven techniques about training are appearing from time to time and being added to those already available. Certain types of training are superior for certain types of training needs. In other words, the instructors of today have many training tools at their command and an important portion of their job is to select the best training means to be used under given circumstances. In this selection, the objective should be foremost in the decision of what form of training to provide. Fundamentally, all instruction should (1) proceed from the known to the unknown, (2) go from the simple to the complex, and (3) follow the order of "prepare, present, and apply."

## OBJECTIVES OF EMPLOYEE TRAINING

Future plans of the office, anticipated increases in personnel, and changes in methods are direct and basic sources for determining the objectives of an employee training program. The specific goals will depend upon the particular needs of the situation. They may include better creativeness, methods improvement, or human relations. The training need may be quite specific such as to gain proficiency in the operating of an electronic accounting machine and to know and apply satisfactorily the policies covering the writing of accounts receivables.

Developmental efforts are of two major types (1) job-oriented and (2) self-development. The former helps the individual to improve that which he is paid to do; the latter, is directed toward individual improvement usually on his own time and for the most part to serve his own fulfillment. Both are important not only to the manager in that they assist in accomplishing objectives, but also to the individual because they increase his personal satisfaction. The developmental objective of every manager should be to devise a plan which not only will contribute to and make possible an effective and harmonious work force, but also accomplish assigned work goals and provide full opportunity for each individual to develop himself to the maximum of his potential.

More specifically, each employee should have complete knowledge of what constitutes his job and what its relationship is to other jobs in the organization. This should not be left to chance. Planned efforts in the form of a training program should be utilized to get job content information to each employee. Improved relations are a certainty when the employee understands completely what his job is, the relationship of his work to other work in the department, and, in time, that of his department to the entire organization structure.

Up-to-date knowledge of operating policies and procedures is another important and common objective in office training. Information on personnel practices should be made known to all. Likewise, the general scope of desired public relations and the quality of paper work required are among the types of information which should be a part of every employee's knowledge.

Each member should have knowledge of the best known methods of doing his work. This is fundamental, but typically there are always a few who lack this essential knowledge or do not use it if they do know it. The best methods are needed to attain a satisfactory efficiency in work output.

Also, recognition or advancement should be extended when training is completed satisfactorily. This may take the form of improved status, public recognition, increased earnings, or promotion. It is a mistake for an enterprise to develop an employee for a better job or to improve or add to his knowledge and skill without subsequently offering him a job on which he can use the newly acquired ability, either in the present or at some future date, within or outside the enterprise.

## THE INDIVIDUAL AND DEVELOPMENTAL EFFORTS

The individual being developed is the key figure in all developmental efforts. His personal interest in and capacity for being developed are of prime importance. Economic or social gains may motivate him, but a stimulus must be present. Necessarily, people start from where they are in any training effort, and they are most likely to want to learn when they see what is taught is helpful to them. An indication of the capacity for developing can be gleaned from the use of tests and a study of a candidate's past education, experience, and accomplishment. While not conclusive, such indexes are helpful.

Furthermore, it should be pointed out that for satisfactory developmental achievement, the trainee must be in a receptive mood, emotionally settled, and free from worries, personal troubles, and anxieties. Also, it must be recognized that the trainee must learn for himself; he must

FIGURE 31–1. Some Key Points in Learning.

1. A person learns best what he likes best.
2. A person learns by doing; watching or listening is insufficient.
3. A person remembers longer if he understands the *why* of the knowledge.
4. A person tries harder for rewards than he does to avoid punishments.
5. A person learns fastest when the teaching makes it easier for the learner to learn.

subject himself to the learning process. The instructor's role is primarily one of guidance and stimulation.

Figure 31–1 lists some key points in learning. Keeping these simple truths in mind will assist anyone who is helping others to develop.

## HUMAN OBSOLESCENCE

With the rapid and fundamental changs taking place in the information area has come a condition known as human obsolescence. Now grown to significant proportion, it is commonly discussed in connection with developmental efforts, the thought being that such efforts offer a possible answer to the obsolescence dilemma. It appears fitting, therefore, that a brief discussion of human obsolescence be included here.

During the past several decades, office jobs have changed drastically, entirely new methods of work performance have been introduced, and brand new types of work have become commonplace. The trend toward more and more change seems destined to continue. With all this dynamics, the office employee finds that he can become obsolescent similar to a plumbing fixture, a road, or an automobile. To a person with more than one half of his life to live, this can be tragic. Yet, as the more experienced realize, most things have little certainty. The challenge is to make sure this peril does not overtake you. What can be done?

First, fully and sincerely recognize that all things change—some more than others. This recognition must be more than a positive nod of the head, it must be accepted as a basic fact of life. To mediate, in part, these inevitable changes, it is necessary to keep flexible and maintain a constant vigilance against solidifying your ways of doing things. Contemporary success frequently breeds contentment and a dislike to vary, even in the slightest, what we are doing.

The fresh viewpoint, however, is necessary even though somewhat repugnant. To acquire this openmindedness takes cultivation. There is a better way. Are we going to know about it or will it overtake us by surprise? Readiness to learn and to improve necessitate a willingness to read, to listen, and to think.

New ideas and new ways of doing things never seek us out. They must be pursued. Being a part of training programs and adopting a definite plan for keeping abreast of things force us to search for new concepts and new developments which will affect our jobs and our life. In other words, a specific combat against obsolescence appears necessary in this day and age.

There are also what might be termed the physical aspects of human obsolescence. Nervous tension, for example, reduces our ability to plan, decide, and exercise judgment. And it appears that the human being slows down and requires preventive maintenance. Periods of relaxation are mandatory and warning signs that a person's health standards are not up to par should be heeded.

Human obsolescence is not confined to the over 45 group. It can happen to a man within five years after his university graduation. Human beings can and do become obsolete. Effective measures against this happening exist and should be applied. Participation in developmental programs is a major part of the answer.

## ADVANTAGES OF TRAINING

One who really manages makes use of training to help him manage. To the management member, training assists in improving his planning, controlling, organizing, and actuating. For example, creating effective plans, maintaining proper standards of quality, building a satisfactory organization structure, delegating authority, and stimulating employees are all assisted by effective training.

In addition, the responsibility of supervision is lessened. Training does not eliminate the need for good supervision but it reduces the requirement for detailed and constant supervision. A well-trained office employee is self-reliant in his work, because he knows what to do and how to do it. Under such conditions, close supervision is ordinarily not mandatory.

Also, the best available methods of performing the work can be standardized and made available to all employees. High levels of performance become the rule rather than the exception. The advantages of past knowledge and experience can be retained.

Furthermore, office employees, well trained, will usually show a greater increase in, and a higher quality of, work output than will an untrained group. Employees do a more intelligent job and make fewer mistakes when they possess the know-how, have an understanding of their jobs and of the interdependence of one job and another, and know the *why* of the company's policies and procedures. And it is important to note that morale can be boosted effectively *after* the employee knows what to do.

On the other hand, these advantages are not obtained without a price. Certain difficulties and possible losses are incurred and should be recognized in any training program. First of all, regular office work is likely to be interrupted or delayed by time spent in training. The output of the trainee might be temporarily reduced. Also, training might foster dependence upon others for solutions to challenges which the employee should think through for himself. Self-reliance and capacity for new ideas might be stifled. Furthermore, competent training leaders are difficult to obtain. When mediocre instruction is utilized, not only may the results of the training be below what is expected, but they may actually prove harmful.

## TYPES OF TRAINING

Training can be classified in many ways. One useful classification is training for present jobs and training for future jobs. Another is training for any or all of the following: job knowledge, job skills, and attitudes. Still another is training for basic information, for personal development, and for specific production in definite work application. A useful list showing the range and types of training may be outlined as follows:

*1. Preemployment Training.*  This deals with the type and amount of instruction needed by inexperienced employees prior to their entering the office. This training is generally provided by educational institutions outside the enterprise, such as high schools, universities, business colleges, night schools, and correspondence courses. Preemployment training is generally broader and more fundamental than the other types of training. It is intended to provide basic skills. Likewise, it sometimes is of a theoretical nature, in contrast to the practical aspect of the other types; it seeks to provide an intellectual background and to develop the art of thinking and reasoning.

*2. Induction Training.*  The objective of induction training is to provide the new employee with the information necessary for a complete knowledge and understanding of practices and procedures of the enterprise. Included in this aspect of training are welcoming the new employee to the company, explaining the office rules and regulations, acquainting him with employee's benefits, informing him of the company's policies and operations, and telling him what is expected of him as an employee. The new office employee's impression of the company is frequently formed during the first several hours at the new job. Introductions should be made to the new employee's department head, fellow employees, and those supervisors with whom he will be associated. If it is possible, an introduction to one of the officers is also helpful, as this gives the new employee a feeling of worth and helps him to visualize the extent of the company. Experience shows it is a good idea to give the employee some job which he can do without too much instruction and then leave him by himself. This gives the new employee a chance to digest some of the new surroundings. Follow this up with contacts about every hour or so throughout the rest of the day. Encourage the new employee to ask questions.

**3. On-the-Job Training.** This type of training aims to give the employee the necessary skill required for a specific job. The job can be either that of the present or some future assignment. In some cases, the job is of a higher grade than the employee's present one; in other words, the employee is being prepared for promotion. The makeup of on-the-job training takes many different forms, including lectures in specific subjects, practice on new machines, job rotation—including all jobs of a certain group, special assignments of a temporary nature, understudying a junior executive, special courses, reading assignments, and special workshops by professional associations. On-the-job training stresses just that

FIGURE 31–2. Types of Training Given to Various Classifications of Employees

| Classification of Employee | Type of Training | Training Required |
|---|---|---|
| New | Induction | To give information relative to the job and to the policies and practices of the company. |
| | On-the-job | Specific training in the important details of the employee's job. To help the employee acquire the necessary knowledge and skill. |
| Seasoned | On-the-job | To instruct in changes in procedures, routines, policies, and new equipment. Also, to prepare for jobs of higher grade (promotion). |
| Transferred | Induction | To give information relative to new duties and work environment. |
| | On-the-job | Specific training in the important details of the new job. To help the employee acquire the necessary knowledge and skill. |
| Supervisor | Supervisory | To give information relative to the theory and practical application of supervisory techniques. |

—on the job—but some of the training may be acquired, in part, outside the enterprise. The entire program, however, should be carefully coordinated.

**4. Supervisory Training.** One of the most important types of training in any enterprise is supervisory training. Training of supervisors is vital because of their essentiality in management. Special courses in supervisory training have been designed, and many of these are generally considered effective. Discussion of supervisory training is included in the chapter on office supervision (chapter 30).

Figure 31–2 indicates the type of training which is given to employees of different classifications or circumstances. For example, the new employee is given induction training and on-the-job training. The former provides information relative to his new job and to the policies and practices of the company; the latter includes specific training to help him acquire necessary skill.

## MAKEUP OF TRAINING PROGRAM

Every training program includes trainees, an instructor, a training period, and training material. We now turn our attention to these areas.

The proper selection of trainees is of major importance if permanent, gainful results are to be obtained. A trainee should be trained for the kind of job he likes and is fitted to perform. In this respect, training is closely related to the selection of personnel. Evidence is quite conclusive that careful screening of candidates for training raises the effectiveness of the training work.

In the case of supervisory training, it is best to include all supervisors and those considered for promotion to such posts. Excluding some employees on the basis that they do not need the training or that they are already doing their work satisfactorily is a poor policy. Even outstanding supervisors profit from well-managed training programs, and their presence assists in many ways the less competent supervisors in attendance.

The instructor is a key figure in an effective training program; he contributes immeasurably to its success. Qualified instructors may be obtained from inside or outside the company; however, many office employees are not good instructors. The efficient employee does not necessarily have the ability to teach. Instructors need many qualifications besides knowing how to do the work. A good teacher has the skill to instruct and is tolerant, understanding, and patient. Also important is an appreciation for the value of the training work in relation to the enterprise and an understanding of what the employee goes through in order to acquire the skill and knowledge which the program is designed to achieve.

The length of the training period depends upon the skill to be acquired, the trainee's learning capacity, and the training media used. For example, a simple indoctrination program for clerks may require an hour a day over a period of a week, while a course in computer programming may be given two hours a week for 15 weeks. The use of effective visual material usually helps to reduce the training time. Some training directors claim that effective visualization reduces the teaching time by upward of 35 percent. Also, certain means of training such as programmed instruction, which is of a visual nature, is reputed to save up to 70 percent of training time.

To maintain interest and to secure maximum accomplishment, no single session should last longer than two hours. One hour is even better. The best practice is to pay employees for training time if the course relates in any way to their work. Many states have laws or rulings affecting training time; and in addition, certain federal laws are applicable. Controversial issues are likely to appear if the employee does any productive work during the training time, if the training is outside regular working hours, or if the training work is intended to train the employee for a new or additional skill. It is advisable to check federal and prevailing state laws to help determine whether trainee or company time should be used.

There is always the need for training material. A text or some written material is usually desirable as a basis for instruction, review, and reference. For most subjects, a satisfactory book can be selected; but in instances where the course content is of a special nature, it may be well to prepare material for this specific use. A complete outline of the entire course should be made with the main topics included under each meeting or session. When a text is used, the parts to be covered must be clearly indicated; and assignments which require some preparatory time should be made for every meeting. This helps to keep the program on schedule, points the meeting toward definite subjects, and usually assists in the progress and satisfaction of the trainee.

## AVAILABLE TRAINING MEANS

The means of training to be followed are paramount in every office training program. A number of different means are available. For convenience, we will confine this discussion to the following 12 different means, listed alphabetically: computer assisted instruction, conferences, demonstrations, guided experience, in-basket technique, incident process, job rotation, lectures, problem solving, programmed instruction, role playing, and understudy method. Choice of office training means depends upon many factors, including the objectives of the training, the number of trainees, the preferences of the instructor, the type of material to be covered, the cost, the time allotted, and the wishes of the trainees.

Computer assisted instruction (CAI) is one of the newer means of instruction. The trainee takes a course by means of a computerized teaching machine. Instructions, questions, and guidance are stored in the computer and presented to the trainee by means of a typewriterlike communications terminal linked to the computer. A number of trainees can hook into the course at the same time. After giving an identification number to verify trainee and course, the first question is written out by the computer on a continuous paper form of the terminal unit. In a course on statistics, for example, the first question might be, "How is the arithmetic average calculated? Type answer." If you answer, "By determining the number in the series appearing most frequently," the computer will answer immediately, "That answer is incorrect. The arithmetical average is not determined by the frequency of a number in the series but by averaging mathematically. Will you answer again?" Prompted by the hint, you now type the answer, "Add the numbers of the series and divide this sum by the quantity of numbers in the series." To this the computer will answer, "Correct," then proceed to the next question. To date, CAI appears to work best in conjunction with a human teacher who can answer questions and conduct periodic seminars. Computer trainees retain more material than conventional trainees and in a test of a statistics course needed only 13 hours to complete what requires 45 hours in an ordinary classroom.

The conference method permits trainees to express themselves orally and to exchange thoughts, and enables the instructor to judge the trainee's understanding of the subject material. The conference method is especially popular in supervisory training. Trainees are encouraged to express themselves freely. A group of about 20 participants is the ideal size for best results from the conference method. Demonstrations provide forceful presentation of how the job is done. This means stresses learning by eye rather than by ear and is especially helpful for jobs where physical skills are vital. The guided experience method utilizes evaluation of the trainee to reveal his weaknesses; then, the causes of these weaknesses are decided, and experience to remedy them is planned. Extreme care is taken to select the proper work assignments so that the trainee's shortcomings are ultimately removed. The assignments vary and include such things as writing reports, serving on committees, solving specific problems, performing research work, and working on normal day-to-day tasks. The guided experience method can be considered a highly personalized, informal type of training.

The in-basket technique realistically simulates actual office conditions. Actually it is in the nature of a business game. From two to about fifteen play the game which ordinarily takes two hours—one hour actual playing time and one hour of discussion among the players following conclusion of the game. Each trainee or player sits at a desk on which there is an "in" and an "out" basket, paper, and pencil. Instructions are given by the instructor indicating, for example, that you have certain helpers and you are leaving on your three-week vacation tomorrow. Identical packets of papers are then placed in the "in" baskets of all players. These papers require your office managerial attention. A typical packet may contain three letters, five memos, a telegram, two reports, and four telephone messages. Each trainee studies the materials and writes what he believes is the most appropriate action, clips the material to the original paper, and places it in his "out" basket. Figure 31–3 shows a representative paper with answer written at the bottom. The in-basket technique is reasonable in cost, highly practical, and can include an almost unlimited number of potential problems and situations.

The incident process emphasizes careful questions asking to obtain pertinent facts upon which to reach decisions or solve problems. An incident or problem situation is presented to the group by the discussion leader. The incident is described in several sentences. The leader has all the background facts about the problem, but he gives out facts only as participants ask for them. The technique stresses participation, stimulates thinking, develops insight, and promotes teamwork. It is especially effective for problem solving and supervisory training.

Job rotation, sometimes referred to as the "merry-go-round" basis, rotates trainees among different organizational units, thus providing the trainees with overall knowledge of the company's operations and the work done by each unit, and the opportunity to participate in the affairs of the

FIGURE 31-3. Typical Paper from an "In-Basket" Training Session. The top portion poses the problem, the bottom portion is the respondent's answer.

June 17, 196–

To: William Danzek

From: Horace Goulet

Subject: Edith Davis

I understand through informal sources that Edith Davis is dissatisfied with her salary and is looking for another job. To the best of my knowledge she does not have any other job offer at this time. You know, of course, that she is one of the best girls we have had on the job of filing computer data runs and she is extremely capable and efficient in her work. I believe she would be hard to replace especially at her present salary. Within the next few days, I would like to discuss with you a salary increase for Miss Davis even though regular salary reviews are not scheduled at this time.

6/18
Horace.

O.K. to get together on this next Thursday at 3 P.M. Please review our entire work history with Edith Davis and find out if present salary is real cause for dissatisfaction. Also check Personnel to see if any likely applicants for this filing job are on file.
W. D.

various units. This method assists the individual to think in terms of universal managerial principles rather than the immediate activities at hand. Lectures are effective for initially explaining information to trainees. They should be carefully prepared, reinforced by the use of charts, sketches, and models, and presented by a qualified speaker. The means of problem solving is effective when the problems are well selected and bring out considerations pertinent to the work at hand. In short, solving the problems should meet specific development needs, such as an ability to analyze and relate given facts, to determine the problem to be solved, to read and to substantiate the recommended actions to be taken. Unless a developmental need is met, this method of training may be inadequate, time-consuming, and ineffective.

Programmed instruction is self-instruction and utilizes a systematic method of presenting information to the trainee. Presented one step or frame at a time, the material can be easily understood and absorbed. The increasing difficulty between two subsequent frames is narrow so that advancement is gradual but continuous and complex material is encountered only by the trainee prepared for it. The trainee advances at his own individual pace and learns at the speed most convenient for him. For each frame, he is required to select an answer from several alternatives and checks his answer with the approved reply. Thus immediate feedback is provided. He proceeds only after knowing the correct response to the question of the immediate frame. Programmed instruction incorporates sound instructional principles in that the trainee is actively participating in the teaching-learning process, the material is presented to lead each trainee into making the correct response, uniformity and consistency of instruction are possible, and the trainee advances gradually from the simple to the complex aspects of the material. Various research studies reveal the effectiveness of programmed instruction. To illustrate, in imparting knowledge of how to operate a modern office machine, training time required 31 percent less time with the trainees retaining 53 percent more knowledge compared to that obtained with conventional methods. Furthermore, programmed instruction permits training on a decentralized basis, is suited for individual training—a group is not needed, and the instructor can concentrate on special problems of training; he need not spend the majority of his time on routine training work.

Role playing narrows the gap between talking about what should be done and actually doing it. For training purposes, the playing out of a typical problem situation can be quite effective. It is especially helpful in situations involving employee relations. The method permits the trainees to participate, to gain an insight into their own behavior, and to look at the problem from many different viewpoints. By means of the understudy method, the trainee works as an assistant or helper to his teacher, thus acquiring familiarity with the work and practices of his teacher, who normally is an employee at the same or higher organizational level as the trainee. Experience with dynamic events and acquaintance with the atmosphere and position in which the trainee will eventually perform are acquired. On major issues, the trainee may be required to submit complete data affecting the issue along with his recommendations for action. In this way, thinking is stimulated, and the accepting of responsibility is encouraged. The understudy method is commonly used in supervisory training.

Regarding these various means, a current practice, growing steadily, is to use a variety of training means to add spice to learning. The change of pace keeps trainees motivated and minimizes boredom. Of course, the

739. Developing office employees

selected means must fit the particular requirement, but current thinking is to vary the overall pattern of instruction.

## COST OF TRAINING

Training costs money. Many analyses of its cost are unrealistic, in that comparisons are made between the expenditures of "no training"—actually a misleading term—and those of a formal training program. The fact is that training costs are tangible and intangible. Erroneously, the latter group is commonly ignored in the cost of training.

Under tangible training costs are training materials, nonproductive time of trainee, and nonproductive time of employee instructor, or fee charged, if an outsider. Under the intangible classification are such things as a longer time for the trainee to attain a reasonable level of production, loss of employees seeking better job opportunities, time of experienced employees asked to "show me how to do this" by the trainee, loss due to work spoilage and errors, practicing of poor work methods, and improper work viewpoints and attitudes being permitted to develop and spread.

Training is a necessity in modern management, and reasonable expenditures for it should be made. The amount depends upon the needs and the aims of the office. However, costs should be kept under control. Management members should have some idea of what is being acomplished for the expenditures being made. This brings up the question of training effectiveness.

## EFFECTIVENESS OF TRAINING

From the managerial viewpoint, it is an excellent idea to measure the effectiveness of training efforts. The evaluation, however, must be in terms of a particular training problem. This problem may be expressed in the form of questions, such as:

1. Has the training increased production?
2. Has there been a decrease in the number of errors?
3. Has there been a reduction in labor turnover?
4. Has there been a reduction in absenteeism, requests for transfers, and number of grievances?
5. Has the attitude, work environment, and enthusiasm of the office work force improved?

It is usually best to measure effectiveness by departments or by some homogeneous group, for the problems of measurement become quite complex when the entire office is considered. It is advisable to make comparisons between office groups as units. A good procedure is to use as a control one group which is characterized by little or no formal training, by training of a particular type, or by a different method of training. Special care should be exercised to see that the groups compared are reasonably similar with respect to such factors as age, sex, and time of week, month, or year.

Evaluating the results of training is not, however, a simple matter. Many companies make little effort to evaluate training results as such, or they are satisfied with general overall indications of the training's worth. It is difficult to determine what factors contribute to employee development.

It is possible to overdo training to the point that the efforts and costs in its behalf exceed the highest estimates of benefits within a reasonable period. Developmental efforts should be carefully managed, not engaged in simply because "it is the thing to do." It is a continuous, not an "off and on," activity. It can start on a small scale and subsequently increase as the benefits become known and the needs and progress of the enterprise dictate.

Every enterprise trains its employees, formally or informally. If effective efforts are being exerted in training, the attainment of full manpower potential is enhanced and benefits both to the individual and to the enterprise are being won. To these ends, keep these facts in mind: (1) office training is desirable and necessary, (2) office training must be carefully selected to fit the specific need of the enterprise, (3) the questions of *what* training should be conducted, and *when, where,* and *how,* require answering, (4) the needs of the office as shown by job analysis, prevalence of errors, low work output, employees' attitudes, and supervisory effectiveness indicate where training is needed, (5) office training should be preceded by careful selection of trainees, and (6) the training of office supervisors is vital.

## QUESTIONS

1. Discuss the objectives of employee training.
2. Figure 31–1 lists key points in learning. Which of these key points are emphasized in the training means of the in-basket technique? Role playing? The incident process? Elaborate on your answers.
3. Justify the viewpoint that developing an employee is a vital actuating force in management.
4. Do you agree with this statement: "All known training means have an element of artificiality in them. Of necessity they must operate under an assumed arrangement. This leads to the fundamental principle that actual practice—learning by doing—is the superior teaching process. There is no satisfactory substitute for experience which emphasizes application of the employee's knowledge to the task that confronts him at the particular time." Justify the position you take.

5. What means of training have you personally found to be most effective? How do you justify this means as being the most effective?

6. A new employee has just completed a two-week indoctrination training program given by a bank. The training director of the bank has rated the new employee as unsatisfactory, basing his opinion on the training results. Should the new employee be placed on the job, asked to repeat the training, or dropped from the payroll? Explain your answer.

7. Discuss programmed instruction as a means of office developing, indicating whether you favor its use, along with your reasons why.

8. What are some important personal attributes that should be present for developmental efforts to prove most helpful to an individual?

9. Discuss the justification for using developmental programs to cope with the problem of human obsolescence.

10. Carefully identify each of the following:
    *a)* Job rotation.
    *b)* Computer assisted instruction.
    *c)* Induction training.
    *d)* Intangible costs of training.

11. Using Figure 31–1 as a guide, relate a learning experience that bears out the validity of several key points listed.

12. While office training may be highly desirable, it also has some disadvantages. Briefly relate several of these disadvantages.

## CASE PROBLEMS

### Case 31–1. Carrier-Wirth Company

Homer Davis believes that a development program for the 15 office supervisors should be reinstituted at Carrier-Wirth Company. As the newly appointed office manager, he is not impressed with the present office operations in general and feels that regularly scheduled supervisory meetings and training sessions will help, but not answer all of the current shortcomings.

After a recent announcement suggesting the office supervisory development program, Mr. Davis talked informally with each of his office supervisors. Somewhat to his surprise, but not entirely in the case of some supervisors, he found a lack of enthusiasm for his program. However, a few supervisors expressed favorable interest beyond what was expected. Typical of the reactions obtained are:

1. "Yes, I go along with it. Might help. Certainly can't do any harm."

2. "I don't really know. The ones we have had offered good material and I thought were well presented. But for the most part the topics were what we already know. It was the same old stuff all over again."

3. "The past programs have been interesting, but not very practical. There has been nothing I can use directly in my day-to-day work."

4. "Yes, I say have them, but get an outside consultant to handle the sessions. New approach, new ideas, new faces are what we need."

5. "I think I'd get more by taking a course at the local university in an evening class."
6. "Frankly, I feel such meetings are a waste of good time. Nothing is ever settled. Just a bunch of words, and more words."
7. "We never get to the real issues which remain covered and never brought into the open. You know it as well as I do that the old timers won't open up. Each session is a nice friendly get-together. Go ahead and have the sessions but don't expect much from them."

Approval for the development program must be obtained from Mr. Clarence E. Tate, president of the company. He must approve the required appropriations and the use of company time during which training sessions have been held in the past. Mr. Davis can keep the appropriations down using company personnel and he has in mind to hold 12 sessions on Tuesdays from 10:50 to 11:50 A.M. which is probably the most convenient time for all the supervisors to get together. Mr. Tate likes to relate all proposed expenditures to forecasted results. He thinks in terms of the company's return on its investment.

Mr. Davis is aware that Mr. John Almen, Jr., the factory manager and close ally of Mr. Tate, is dead set against any development program for factory foremen. In Mr. Almen's opinion, such meetings are an excellent medium for wasting time, are too theoretical, and raise issues that should not be raised. He advocates having the foremen work for an effective superintendent of production from whom a foreman can learn how to be an effective foreman. In Mr. Almen's opinion there is no substitute for experience for developing a good foreman.

## Questions:

1. What alternatives are available to Mr. Davis?
2. What is your reaction to the viewpoints of Mr. Tate? Mr. Almen, Jr.?
3. What should Mr. Davis do? Why?

### Case 31–2. Mitchell Company

Martha Cole is an excellent typist and has been with Mitchell Company for three years. The office employees total 12 people and work in an informal, pleasant, and friendly environment. The bookkeeper announces her resignation effective in six weeks. She is getting married and will move from the city. Martha is asked whether she would like to do the bookkeeping work which would give her more pay. She replies that she would, but has very little knowledge of bookkeeping. The sales manager, who manages the office, then explains that the company will enroll her in a school, pay her tuition, and she can learn bookkeeping. The class meets evenings twice a week and starts in two weeks. Martha is elated at the opportunity.

Martha enrolls at the school and is also shown key points of the bookkeeping work by the bookkeeper before she leaves. After a month of being on the bookkeeping job, it appears to those around Martha that she is having some difficulty mastering the new work. But Martha does not complain and does not ask any coworkers for assistance. On Wednesday morning of the following week, Martha is absent. In a telephone call by her at about 10:00 A.M. she explains that she has quit her job. When asked why, she replies, "To accept another position." A telephone call to the school reveals that she has been absent from classes for the past two weeks.

## Questions:

1. Discuss some plausible explanations for Martha's behavior.
2. What might the company do to avoid reoccurrence of situations such as indicated by this case?
3. What action do you recommend the company take? Why?

# chapter 32

# Effective actuating
# practices

Every individual has a place to fill in the world, and is important in some respect, whether he chooses to be or not.

—*Nathaniel Hawthorne*

A GREAT many actuating practices are available to the alert manager. In this chapter we discuss the more salient practices that can be followed. The selection of the practice and its application in a given case reflect the managerial art of its user. Over a period, most managers will probably use to some extent most of the practices included in this chapter.

## COMMUNICATION

High on the list of effective actuating practices is communication. Employees want to know what is going on and especially to be informed about achievements, problems, or changes that affect them. The normal tendency is to underrate the importance of communication. An aggressive and sincere communicative effort will do wonders toward achieving a cooperative, confident, and enthusiastic working force. An informed employee is usually a good employee. Employees like to be told firsthand about new policies and why they are being adopted, and they feel that they have a right to know about changes to be made in existing conditions.

Likewise, top managers like other management members to communicate—to tell them what is going on and what is on their minds. Also, supervisors are eager to hear from the members of their work group. Both the good and the bad news are wanted. This bottom-up flow of communication is essential for decision making and as a check on how things are progressing.

Most difficulties of communication can be classified under the headings of either telling too little or assuming complete understanding of communication. Both of these habits tend to detract from our communication effectiveness. Managers should take the initiative and supply full information to employees. Dependence upon "word of mouth," or believing that "everybody knows that—it's common information," leads to incomplete and frequently incorrect information. The employee is eager to know any news in which he is involved. He wants to be informed, not coddled. Any information that will help him do a better job ranks high in his preference.

Tell an employee something you want him to understand, and the chances are 12 to 1 he will not fully understand you. Why is this? Because many believe that the act of writing or telling another certain information completely fulfills their job of communicating. However, to communicate effectively requires definite skills and knowledge. Included among these criteria are the following:

**1. Communication Is Two Way.** One tells, informs, or requests; the other listens, asks, or interprets. Without listenership, the communication just does not exist. As Thoreau put it: "It takes two to speak the truth—one to speak, the other to hear it." Listening is an art and requires effort. For best results, involve the listener as soon as possible. Asking leading questions such as the following are effective: "How do you feel about . . . ?" "Well, what do you think—will it work?" "Now, what other information can I give you?"

**2. Think Before You Write or Talk.** Some people are so intent on communicating that they start to write or talk before evaluating the situation and organizing their thoughts. As a result, they confuse the reader or listener. Before communicating, it is a good idea to decide: (1) Why do you want to say anything? (2) What do you want to say? (3) What is the objective in saying this? and (4) What do you know about the receiver or listener?

**3. Use Effective Words—Focus Words and Mutually Known Words.** Focus words help to spot the key points in a communication. The listener or reader is assisted by phrases such as: "Our goal is to. . . ." or "To summarize, . . . ." These expressions aid in drawing inferences and value judgments. The use of mutually known words is essential. To describe the wage structure as "lucrative" reduces real communication if the receiver does not know the meaning of the word.

**4. Practice Empathy.** Communication is assisted by the sender placing himself in the position of the receiver and judging the message from the receiver's point of view. This guide helps win acceptance by the receiver and emphasizes his interests, goals, and fears by giving the receiver what he wants to hear or read.

**5. Create a Follow-up.** The recipient should be given the feeling that he can return with questions or ask clarification on any part he fails to understand. Offering assistance and closing with expressions such as: "Call me if any questions arise," or "Let's get together again next Monday noon and . . . ," are usually effective in this respect.

## COMMUNICATION MEDIA

Normally, the formal lines of communication should be employed. These are the same connecting links as "lines of authority," discussed in chapter 26. Organization shows relationships, and these relationships are made meaningful by exercise of both authority and communication. In fact, authority to put decisions into action necessitates communication. As pointed out in previous chapters, the traditional office grapevine is effective as a dispenser of information. It can never be completely eliminated, people and communication being what they are. The wise manager recognizes this and uses the grapevine as an auxiliary, but is exceedingly careful that accurate, complete, and timely messages are conveyed through the normal channels so that half-truths and incomplete information are not spread by the grapevine.

Many communication media are available. The selection depends chiefly upon the type of information and the type of employees to be reached. Figure 32–1 suggests the features and the organizational level for six selected media.

FIGURE 32–1. Media Available for Communication Purposes.

| Medium | Features | Organizational Level for Which Effective |
|---|---|---|
| Conversation | Man-to-man, forthright personal relationship | All organizational levels |
| Letters | Excellent for statistical data and where permanent record is desired | Top managerial and supervisory levels |
| Pamphlets and booklets | Suitable for large volume of material | All organizational levels |
| House organs | Adequate coverage satisfactory for reminders and announcements | All organizational levels |
| Motion pictures, radio, and television | Dramatize presentation; helpful in training, relating company history, and special achievements | All organizational levels |
| Speeches | Impressive for special events and celebrations | Top managerial and supervisory levels |

## SUGGESTION SYSTEMS

A suggestion system is a means by which employees can submit their ideas to a manager and, if these ideas are adopted, receive an award, usually consisting of an amount of cash. Generally, the suggestions concern ways to save time, to reduce waste, to improve quality, or to simplify practices and procedures. A suggestion system can be a strong employee motivator because the employees are given the opportunity to say somethings, to feel that the company is "their company," to think of constructive ideas, and to contribute to the progress and betterment of the enterprise.

In addition, the economic gains can be quite large. Financial gains are made by the company as well as by the successful suggester. But these gains should not be stressed to the exclusion of the others mentioned. A suggestion system is far more than a mechanism for the buying of useful ideas.

Each and every suggestion should be answered promptly with reasons for decisions reached. Replies can be by individual letters or personal interviews; it is not a good practice to post lists on the bulletin board. Replies to turndowns, i.e., those suggestions receiving no award, must contain the reasons why such action is taken. This practice is recommended because it lets the employee know that his suggestion was evaluated and reveals whether the judging committee understood his idea. Furthermore, explaining why his idea was not worthy of an award, helps him to become more knowledgeable about what is acceptable and stimulates further thinking along what might be award-winning ideas. The award must be worthwhile and must offer some inducement to the employee. Many companies have found that $10 is a minimum figure to use and that maximum awards based on 10 percent of the savings for the first year are satisfactory.

Suggestion systems have a tendency to become dormant; for this reason, they must be continually promoted. Showmanship, publicity stunts, and promotions can be used to keep the program alive. Devices which have proved successful include the following: attractive suggestion forms; appealing and well-located suggestion boxes bearing the sign "Have you deposited your suggestion here today?"; attention-getting posters; reminders in payroll envelopes; and notices in company papers.

The suggester's identity is unknown to the investigator in most systems. This anonymity is obtained by means of a numbering and coupon arrangement on the suggestion form. The suggester retains a numbered coupon which corresponds to the number of the suggestion. Under this arrangement, impartiality on the part of the investigators is promoted. In contrast, some systems require the suggester's signature, a practice which affords close contact with the suggester.

Suggestion stimulators can be directed to all employees in order to encourage their participation in the suggestion systems. Letters and announcements can be used; or more direct and definite means may be utilized, such as the manager asking: "What can you suggest to save time in the filing department?" Employees then start thinking of ways to improve that department. This practice appears to bring usable results, but it involves a serious disadvantage. It directs attention to fields foreign to the employee. A suggestion system is supposed to enable the employee to take advantage of the things he already knows but which have not as yet been used to full advantage. Directing his attention to new fields, therefore, might mean a loss of excellent ideas stemming from his intimate on-the-job knowledge.

## PARTICIPATION

An emphasis in current management is to have people work as mutually helpful members rather than as single competitive individuals. "Democratic supervisorship" rather than "authoritarian direction" is loudly advocated. Also, giving employees some voice in matters that affect them is heralded as a key principle to follow in efforts of motivating. In the fabric of all these suggested concepts is a common thread. It is participation, i.e., permission granted the other member, either manager or non-manager, to have a part in the activity whether it is planning, decision making, or communicating.

Among the major justifications for practicing participation is that it helps win enthusiastic acceptance of proposed actions. People tend to accept their own ideas and will strive to prove them correct once they are put into effect. Obstacles will be overcome by the suggestor, in part, to demonstrate the wisdom of his suggestion. More than this, it is probably true in most cases that the best answer to a perplexing situation is evolved, that is, best in the sense that it is superior for the particular person or group to follow. Participation tends to tailor make the answer. Further, participation aids in the development of employees. Having them become familiar with the problem and evolve what is the most satisfactory way of handling it provides practical experience in issues of management.

However, participation should be used very carefully. It should be encouraged in those subjects which are within the employee's province or knowledge. He should be given ample explanation of the situation or acquire knowledge about it in an acceptable way and made to feel that his suggestions and opinions are welcomed. It is extremely frustrating and "demotivating" to request participation by an employee who knows little or nothing about the subject at hand. Furthermore, the management member in charge of the activity should not step away from his charge and duty to manage. The final decision is forthcoming from him.

## GIVING INSTRUCTIONS AND ORDERS

The competent practitioner of actuating tells an employee to do what needs to be done and wins the employee over in the process. Employees require direction. Giving instructions and orders in such a way that the recipient can carry them out without further help is one of the distinguishing marks of an effective manager.

Begin with something the recipient already knows and which is fairly simple. Such an approach makes it easy to understand and places the instruction or order in a context or background with which he is familiar. The human being comprehends quickest when starting from the known and going to the unknown. The familiar is firmly established. To illustrate, in explaining a new procedure, it might be worded this way: "It's like the charge-out control of storing and retrieving. Just as only authorized personnel use the files, this procedure will control copying and have authorized personnel only use the copying machines. For obtaining copies of a document, the copy-control form is. . . ." Just as we should go from the known to the unknown so we should also proceed from the simple to the complex. Studies clearly show that starting with the comprehensible, then leading to the more difficult, is the effective format. To do otherwise, risks the possibility of losing your receiver at the very outset.

The receiver should become emotionally involved in the understanding of the instruction or order, if this is feasible. Effective ways to accomplish this is by using appropriate visuals and encouraging the use of questions. Most everyone enjoys watching things happen—the clever TV commercial is evidence of this. And what we enjoy we tend to remember. Hence, effective visuals to demonstrate by the eye as well as the ear what the message is about are usually effective. The display need not be elaborate. A group of data, a chart, or a sample will suffice. But the proper timing of its appearance is vital. Using visuals to provide a solid impact, a climax to a series of events, or the answer to a verbally described complex difficulty are usually effective. In addition, the asking of questions should be encouraged for this is an excellent means of determining whether the instruction or order is fully comprehended and, in fact, whether essential parts have been inadvertently omitted. Questions serve as the necessary feedback; they indicate how well the message is going over. If the recipient has no questions, it may be advisable to reverse the situation and ask him questions to make sure complete understanding exists.

Generally speaking, positively expressed instructions and orders are comprehended more readily and completely than are those expressed negatively. People prefer to know what they can do, not what they can't do. Keeping it positive is more constructive and direct. So to minimize misunderstandings, keep your instructions and orders positive. Further, it is advisable to practice the familiar follow-up of management in order to evaluate the results being accomplished. A conference or visit now and then may suffice or, in the case of a long project, short written progress reports may be requested. What a management member doesn't do is to look over the subordinate's shoulder and criticize his every move. Give him room to operate on his own and, when you find he's doing a good job, sincerely express your satisfaction and encourage him to continue his excellent efforts. This will not only boost his self-confidence, but will assist in developing him and promoting the continuance of satisfactory work.

## USE OF SILENCE AND SELL

Silence and sell are extremely important tools in achieving actuating under certain circumstances. Frequently it is not what we say or write, but rather what we don't say that carries the real punch. Silence is powerful and when well timed it has no equal. Lack of any comment on an issue before a discussion group has a significance even though no one said anything. Considerable skill is required to know when maintaining silence is better than saying something. Restraint requires courage and is an art in itself.

Most managers refrain from the word *sell*, believing it has a repugnant meaning to many people. Yet in the sense that selling is the effort to get others to view certain things as we view them, all managers are salesmen and the efforts are honorable, if not basic and essential. A manager tries to persuade another person to desire, accept, or acquire the concept, idea, program, or whatever he is presenting. The decisive action is that of the person being involved, not the manager. His biggest job is to know when to keep silent.

One skilled in the use of persuasion trys to "move" a person instead of attempting to "stop" him. If we sell people anything, they like to be told what they can do, not what they can't do. Usually this can be accomplished by adding the reasons why such a request is being made. For example, effective is, "If you put large index cards in the tray under the table, they will not get mixed with the punched schedule cards and nobody will disturb or get them out of sequence." In contrast, "Don't leave large index cards on the table; they don't belong there," fails to move the employee.

Silence and sell are helpful in acquiring mutual understanding. In the final analysis, it is the meaning, not the words, and the desired reaction, not the technique, that the manager is after. If we seek to be understood we discover that silence is golden and sell is essential.

## PROMOTIONS, ABSENTEEISM, AND TARDINESS

Promotions are effective motivating actions in that they afford satisfaction to the average individual in his desire to develop, to advance, and to improve his status. Most companies have the policy of promoting from among their present employees whenever possible. This requires keeping a sharp eye open for the discovery of promotable personnel—those people who demonstrate a desire to advance by qualifying for a better and more responsible job. Quite a few managers, however, feel that some of the vacancies for better jobs should be filled by candidates from outside the enterprise. By this means, it is contended, new ideas, new attitudes, and different methods of operation are brought in which tend to foster an active, healthy condition.

The initiative for promotion work belongs with the manager. Without prodding, the manager should see that worthy people are promoted. The knowledge of whom to advance is gained through records covering each employee's merit, competence, and length of service. Actually, promotion implies two-way action. It calls for action by the managers—to open up avenues along which employees can advance; and it calls for action by employees—to qualify themselves for advancement.

The failure of an employee to report on the job when scheduled to work is one of the difficult personnel problems with which the average office manager must cope. Absenteeism disrupts the smooth flow of work; either the work stops completely, or extra work is forced upon another employee. There is no single cure for absenteeism. It is an individual problem and the correction must suit the particular case. Records revealing who is absent, how long, how often, and why give information on where to concentrate corrective efforts.

Among the actuating means used to reduce absenteeism are pointing out to employees the importance of being on the job, talking with each absentee upon return and thoroughly discussing the cause and explanation offered, checking to see if the right person is on the right job, maintaining a continued health program, allowing a definite number of days off per year, requiring absentees to make up time, and showing some outward thanks and appreciation to those employees who are always on the job.

Bad timekeeping on the part of employees indicates a disrespect for others and a lack of dependability. Tardiness is contagious. When one or two continue to come into the office late, the idea gets in the minds of other employees that such behavior has managerial approval. Being early is as much a habit as being late. The hour at which work starts has little influence on the problem. The tendency to procrastinate must be corrected and the importance of keeping time obligations stressed.

An effective motivating means consists of creating a strong employee interest in promptness. Supervisors should set good examples and always be on time themselves. They should also keep reminding the employees about the importance of being on time. In many instances, the employee simply fails to allow himself sufficient time to get ready for work. Dependence upon hairline transportation connections and failure to allow extra time for travel under bad weather conditions are common causes. The means of correction here are self-evident.

In many offices, a tardy employee is required to report first to the office manager or to the timekeeper, where an explanation is given verbally for the tardiness and a form filled out indicating the reason why. The idea of going through a "lot of red tape" helps discourage tardiness. The imposition of a penalty, such as making up time lost or doing the least desirable work, proves effective. However, before using such a plan, it should meet the approval of the employees, who should agree to "go along with it." One company uses a unique plan which brings surprisingly good results. An employee's name is selected at random from the payroll list; and promptly at starting time, the employee is called on the telephone. If he answers, indicating presence and promptness on the job, he receives a reward of $20.

## EMPLOYEE ECONOMIC SECURITY

Various arrangements are now available to help provide a measure of economic security to employees. These arrangements have a motivating influence and are beneficial in that they assist in supplying economic aid in case of sickness or old age. Also, at the time of death some help is given dependents of the deceased employee. These economic security measures have been brought about through the efforts of companies and employees and the influence of state and federal laws, among which are unemployment insurance regulations, workmen's compensation laws, and social security regulations. The form, purpose, and content of these various plans vary considerably and require special study for complete understanding.

The discussion here will be confined to three arrangements, including:

*1. Hospitalization Plans.*    These plans are a form of insurance which pays a portion of hospital expenses resulting from all nonoccupational illnesses or accidents suffered by the employee. Premiums are usually paid by the employee, although in some instances the company contributes toward the plan. Under a typical plan, costs might be $20 per month for an unmarried employee for semiprivate accommodations. The amount of cost varies with such factors as the number of employees in the plan, their sex and age, and the benefits provided.

*2. Pension Plans.*    These provide regular payments to an employee retired from service. The great majority of large enterprises now have such plans. They make it possible not only to give needed relief and to grant rewards for long service but also to retire older employees, thus permitting the employment of younger persons as replacements. This helps keep the work force alive and vibrant, and the existence of a retirement pension plan makes for high morale and attracts better employees.

The cost of a pension plan can be paid by either the company or the employees, or both. The amount of retirement pay generally provided is about 50 percent of the average rate for the five-year period preceding retirement. The trend is toward a reduction in the waiting period for eligibility and the elimination of high age requirements of participants for pensions. Programs under which the employee contributes are also becoming more common. The plan should be based on a sound actuarial basis. It is usually advisable to employ the services of specialists in this field.

**3. Group Insurance Plans.** Protection for individual employees as members of a group is provided by group insurance plans. Usually, employees are eligible only after a stipulated period of service and in an amount relative to their earnings. The company or the employees may pay the full cost of the plan, or the cost may be assumed jointly. Employees are usually able to secure protection at a cost below that of individually purchased insurance of the same protection. The exact nature of the policy varies with different plans; the basis of all is straight life insurance coverage, but this frequently is supplemented with other benefits.

## EMPLOYEES' RECREATIONAL ACTIVITIES

Recreational activities have actuating influence, but they also help provide a balance between work and play. A well-rounded program of recreational activities is important because it improves employer-employee relations, increases efficiency, and makes for healthy, satisfied employees. Such activities may include the following: archery, baseball, softball, basketball, tennis, horseback riding, golf, bowling, horseshoe pitching, swimming, hiking, band, glee club, photography club, and amateur shows.

The participation of management members in recreational activities should consist of a readiness to furnish advice, to offer suggestions, and to lend assistance *upon request*. Managers should not attempt to force inclusion of certain activities or to run the program. Any semblance of paternalism should be avoided.

In guiding the development of the program, the following approach is usually helpful:

1. Measure the adequacy of the activity to find out the total number of employees who can participate.

2. Examine each existing activity to see if it is attracting a capacity number of employees.

3. Investigate public and private recreational facilities to determine how and when they can be used.

4. Find out what is included in programs of other companies.

5. Publicize the existence of the activities so that all employees who can and want to participate may do so.

## PERFORMANCE APPRAISAL

A keystone of actuating is that employees are clear as to what is expected of them and how they are to be judged. The typical employee wants to know how he is doing. Also, it is motivating to him to know that his employer has an interest in his accomplishments, is willing to give praise when deserved, and is interested to point out his shortcomings when existent, so that he can improve himself.

Performance appraisal is a two-way understanding between the employee and his supervisor involving the setting of objectives for the employee to develop himself and the means for achieving these objectives. Performance appraisal can be viewed as an inventory of the most valuable asset of the enterprise—its employees. Such efforts are essential to effective management; they constitute an important tool of managerial actuating and provide information helpful in many ways. Among the important uses of merit rating are:

1. To assist in developing the supervisor's critical evaluation of the employee's worth.

2. To provide a record of the progress of new employees or those in training.

3. To indicate areas where training is needed.

4. To let the employee know what management members think of his performance.

5. To uncover employees of unusual abilities along specific lines.

6. To guide personnel work in promoting, demoting, or transferring an employee.

7. To justify increases in wages within the established job range.

## PERFORMANCE APPRAISAL PLANS

Performance appraisal is accomplished by rating the employee on a number of predetermined factors. These factors are considered to be directly associated with, as well as indicative of, the employee's performance on the job. They should be carefully selected and include only those factors necessary to give adequate data. Usually, six to eight factors are sufficient, as the use of too many might lead to carelessness in rating, and too few might distort the ratings. Information which is available elsewhere, such as attendance, punctuality, and length-of-service data, should not be included in the performance appraisal form. In each case, however, the factors selected are considered to be applicable to the employee, not to the job requirements.

There are four basic types of performance appraisal plans: (1) employee comparison, (2) man-to-man basis, (3) check lists, and (4) charts. The first is an elementary form of ranking in which a comparison of the relative performance of employees is determined. Normally, the employees under a given supervisor or in one department are ranked, from the most satisfactory at the top of the list to the least satisfactory at the bottom of the list. The ranking can be by separate traits or on an overall basis.

In the man-to-man type, the employee is rated by comparing him to another employee believed to exemplify the highest rating of the particular factor being considered. Sometimes, a rating scale, established by the highest, middle, and lowest exemplary employees, respectively, is used. Thus, on the quality of dependability, for example, employee A is compared with each of the three employees included in the rating scale and is then given a rating it is believed he deserves. The man-to-man basis is not widely used in offices because it is rather complex and time-consuming. Difficulty is encountered in selecting the employees to use in the rating scale, and wide variations in the characteristics of those selected appear common.

Check lists consist of a series of statements or questions dealing with the employee's performance. Frequently, the statements have different values or weights which are unknown to the respondent. Questions which can be answered either "Yes" or "No," or by "It applies to this employee" or "It does not apply to this employee," are used. The following illustrates a portion of a check list:

| *Item* | *Scale Value** |
|---|---|
| 1. He works at a slow but steady pace | 5 |
| 2. He is usually ahead of his work schedule | 3 |
| 3. He gets along with fellow employees | 8 |
| 4. He makes few mistakes in his work | 10 |
| 5. He asks for considerable time off | 7 |
| 6. He usually thinks of the company first | 4 |

\* Not included in form supplied to rater.

Charts are probably the most common type of performance appraisal used in an office. This is because they are easy to use, readily understood, and accepted by both the raters and the ratees. The chart type consists of a list of selected traits, each accompanied by a scale indicating different degrees of the trait. The rater indicates on each scale the extent to which the employee displays that respective trait in his work. For guidance to

FIGURE 32-2. An Effective Performance Appraisal Chart.

**BLUE CROSS - BLUE SHIELD PLANS**
CHICAGO

**PERFORMANCE RATING**

NAME:_____

DEPARTMENT:_____

DATE of RATING:_____

JOB CLASSIFICATION:_____

| | | | | | |
|---|---|---|---|---|---|
| **JOB KNOWLEDGE** | How Well Does This Employee Understand The Requirements Of Job To Which Assigned: | | | | |
| | Thoroughly understands all aspects of job. | More than adequate knowledge of job. | Has sufficient knowledge to do job. | Insufficient knowledge of some phases. | Continually needs instruction. |
| **QUALITY OF WORK** | How Accurate, Neat And Complete Is The Work: | | | | |
| | Consistently neat, accurate and thorough. | Careful worker seldom needs correction. | Work is acceptable. | Occasionally Careless —needs checking. | Inaccurate and careless. |
| **CO-OPERATION** | Does This Employee Work Harmoniously And Effectively With Co-Workers And Supervision: | | | | |
| | Exceptionally willing and successful as a team worker. | Usually tactful and offers to assist others. | Gets along well enough, no problem. | Cooperation must be solicited, seldom volunteers. | Tends to be a troublemaker. |
| **RESPON-SIBILITY** | How Does This Employee Accept All The Responsibilities Of The Job: | | | | |
| | Accepts all responsibilities fully and meets Emergencies. | Conscientiously tries to fulfill job responsibilities. | Accepts but does not seek responsibility. | Does some assigned tasks reluctantly. | Indifferent—avoids responsibilities. |
| **INITIA-TIVE** | How Well Does This Employee Begin An Assignment Without Direction And Recognize The Best Way Of Doing It: | | | | |
| | Self starter: makes practical suggestions. | Proceeds on assigned work voluntarily and readily accepts suggestions. | Does regular work without prompting. | Relies on others: needs help getting started. | Must usually be told exactly what to do. |
| **QUANTITY OF WORK** | How Much Satisfactory Work Is Consistently Turned Out By This Employee: | | | | |
| | Maintains unusually high out-put. | Usually does more than expected. | Does sufficient amount of work. | Inclined to be slow. | Inadequate turn-out of work. |
| **DEPEND-ABILITY** | How Faithful Is This Employee In Reporting To Work And Staying On The Job: | | | | |
| | Places company interests ahead of personal conveniences. | Punctual and does not waste company time. | Generally on the job as needed. | Some abuses — occasionally needs to be admonished. | Chronic abuses of working schedules. |

COMMENTS:_____

_____

_____

Rated By:_____    Discussed With Employee: By_____

Is any action being taken to help this employee improve his performance?  ☐ No  ☐ Yes—Specify_____

_____

RB–9-7-59

Dept. Manager_____

(See Reverse Side For Instructions in Rating)

*Courtesy: Blue Cross-Blue Shield Plans, Chicago*

the rater, short descriptions for various degrees are usually provided. Figure 32–2 shows a performance appraisal chart.

## ADMINISTRATION OF PERFORMANCE APPRAISAL

Performance appraisal is formally made about twice a year. The supervisor normally is charged with the responsibility of appraising employees. Sometimes, assistance is given by his superior or by a member of the personnel department; and in some instances, several superiors who are in intimate contact with the employee rate him, in order that more than one judgment of his performnance will be available. In most cases, the supervisor knows or should know most about the performance of the employee in his division or unit. Actually, no competent supervisor depends upon an appraising form or waits for a given time of the year to appraise his employee. It is a continuous job. Formal and periodic performance appraisal helps codify results and insures that some orderly appraisal is taking place.

An interview between the employee and the management representative affords an opportunity for a forthright discussion on the employee's performance. Each factor of the performance appraisal can be discussed in a constructive and factual manner. Recognition of the employee as an individual can be increased and employee goodwill can be enhanced. The interview can be highly objective, because preplanning and concentration upon specific topics are feasible.

Employee self-appraisal is another helpful technique. When office employees are fully informed in advance of the purpose, operation, and application of performance appraisal, they make remarkably accurate self-appraisals. There is some tendency, however, for the better employees to underrate themselves, and the problem employees may overrate themselves. Employee self-appraisal helps to give the *how* and *why* of performance appraisal to the employee. He knows what is expected of him and uncovers areas in which improvements can be made. Self-analysis encourages self-development. Self-appraisals can be recorded on special forms provided for this purpose. They supplement the regular ratings determined by management-designated raters.

Since judgment and subjective factors are so important in performance appraising it is advisable to supply a training program for appraisers in order to help secure intelligent and well-considered appraisals. Training helps to implement the plan properly and constructively. The appraiser must understand the purpose of the form and what method to follow. Competent appraising work is a key area of satisfactory performance appraisal. Also, it is important to provide retraining periodically, so that new developments in performance-appraising work and future plans can be brought to the attention of the appraisers. A retraining program also aids in reviewing the principles of good appraising with each appraiser before each appraising period.

Review by a management panel is highly successful in many companies. Funneling all appraisals within an enterprise through one body makes for better control and greater uniformity of ratings. Employees who are qualified for promotions, transfers, training, and salary increases are readily identified. Likewise, those requiring remedial action are identified, and proper measures can be taken. The major considerations that

FIGURE 32–3. These Considerations Are of Greatest Significance in Administering a Performance Appraisal Program.

1. Top management backing for performance appraisal is essential to its success.
2. Performance appraisal should serve primarily to motivate employees, to inventory personnel, and to improve the working force.
3. The appraisal form should include only those traits that cannot be measured objectively by standard personnel records.
4. Only those traits of greatest importance to an employee's progress should be utilized; usually, eight to ten traits are adequate.
5. To expedite comparisons and the appraising work, rate all employees on one trait, then all on the second trait, and so forth.
6. Normally, and in keeping with statistical probability, of the appraisals for many on a single trait, a few will be low, a few will be high, and the greatest number, perhaps 60 percent, will be average.
7. Each trait should be a single one, not compound; should be defined objectively, not subjectively; and should be in terms of work performed on the job.
8. Appraisals should be based on observations of definite and concrete actions.
9. Appraisals of an employee should be discussed with him in private by the appraiser.
10. Periodic training and retraining of appraisers are essential for success of a performance appraisal program.

warrant attention in administering performance appraisal are shown in Figure 32–3.

## ADDITIONAL CONSIDERATIONS OF PERFORMANCE APPRAISAL

The questions of what traits should be included in a performance appraisal, what is the accepted definition of each, should all traits have equal value, and can prejudice of the rater be overcome have given rise to the practice of concentrating on performance itself and forgetting the personality traits. But simply to ask questions about performance begs the issue. To ask, "How effectively does the employee overcome problems?" elicits the answer, "He displays much common sense in overcoming problems." The answer is still trait-oriented.

Goal achievement offers improvement. Here the focus is on measurable accomplishment, and the assumption is that at any given time an employee should be working toward a quantifiable goal that is in harmony with the objectives of the enterprise. A difficulty with this approach is the measurement of what is accomplished, but this can be approximated; more serious is the timing. Goals of an employee are not neatly scheduled at 6- and 12-month intervals as is performance appraisal. Some goals require one week, some three months, others one year or more. It would seem that the appraisal should be phased with the time of the goal accomplishment. However, this makes for an uneven pattern of appraisal reportings, and involves some administrative hurdles. It might be that a day-to-day, or a week-to-week basis, would be superior for establishing a climate of understanding, a will to work, team spirit, and rapport—the ultimate of motivating.

Typically, a great deal of importance is attached to the interview during which time the employee's appraisal is carefully discussed with him. Certainly this is a period when frank discussion should take place about the employee's accomplishments and potentials. Too often, however, it is personality oriented. It becomes a heart-to-heart talk about the man himself, not what he has done or hopes to do. And there may be no specific agenda followed. Whatever comes to mind is talked about instead of a systematic summarization of just what the employee has accomplished, how he can continue to develop, and what improvements he can make. Also, the employee may not be given full opportunity to express himself. The best appraisal interview is a mutual and friendly back-and-forth conversation. When it consists primarily of the employee being told what he has been doing right and wrong, the chances are high that the employee does not agree with every statement made to him.

## SAFE WORK PLACE

Providing a safe place in which to work is another major activity of actuating. Accidents can and do happen to office employees. Severe falls and injuries result from slipping on highly polished floors and running on stairways by women in high-heeled shoes. Reclining too far back in a chair can result in the occupant's being thrown with considerable force; and serious, sometimes permanent, injuries have been suffered by office employees in this way.

There is a cause for every accident. It is some defect or lack of action which must be corrected in order to prevent a recurrence of the accident. Falling down a stairway is not a cause; it is a result—an accident.

Some writers have classified the causes of accidents under three headings: mechanical, physiological, and psychological. These terms are self-explanatory. Under mechanical causes, for example, are classified such things as improper lighting, unguarded machines, and technical defects in

equipment. Physiological causes include bad eyesight and age of employees; psychological causes cover such things as the employee's tendency to
take unnecessary chances, carelessness, horseplay, and temporary emotional and mental disturbances. These causes are interrelated and must be
attacked jointly in most practical activities designed to reduce accidents.
Figure 32–4 illustrates practices that frequently result in accidents.

FIGURE 32–4. The Practices Illustrated Commonly Result in Accidents. These pictures
were especially posed for accident prevention promotional work.

*Courtesy: "GM Folks," General Motors Corp., Detroit*

It is a well-known fact that accidents are expensive. The loss might be
in money, skill, time, human suffering, work output, or interruption in the
flow of work. The hidden or incidental costs of accidents are much greater
than the measurable direct costs. Such things as the cost of hiring and
training new employees, the interference with production, and the loss of
goodwill are sizable expenses not generally thought of in connection with
the costs of accidents. The ratio of hidden to direct costs of accidents may
be as high as 4 to 1, which means that total accident costs are far greater
than most people realize.

## ACCIDENT PREVENTION

Experience and records show that accidents can be reduced; in fact,
most can be prevented entirely. The best course of action for preventing
accidents depends upon the circumstances in each particular case. Some
advocate the so-called triple E program, which consists of engineering,

education, and enforcement. That is, the first step is to engineer all equipment and machines with safety guards, cutoff switches, and other devices to make them as safe as is technically possible. Next, education for all employees is provided, to instill work habits and practices for winning high safety achievements. Last, enforcement insures that safety regulations are carried out.

This means that the initiative rests with the manager, but he must win the cooperation of the employee to make office safety really effective. Aggressive managerial action is required. Merely supplying a safe working place is insufficient. The manager must also see to it that safety measures are recognized and enforced; but what is more important, he must accomplish this with enthusiastic approval and encouragement by the nonmanagement members.

## INITIAL SAFETY STEPS TO BE TAKEN

Hazards causing accidents must be identified before they can be eliminated. The main types of office accidents have to do with slipping, tripping, handling materials, being hit by falling objects, and striking against objects. Assistance in locating hazards to eliminate is provided by a check list such as that shown in Figure 32–5.

With factual data as a background, steps can be taken to incorporate needed safety actions into a program. Usually included are the following:

*1. Educate Employees to Possible Dangers.* Each employee should be made thoroughly aware of all the possible dangers of his job. All the details that make for safety should be carefully explained. These efforts can be planned and made a regular part of the job process and the training work. Thus, the correct way of doing the job, which is also the safe way, becomes habitual.

*2. Provide Safe Work Areas.* Supplying all the necessary provisions for safe working places and equipment for employees is paramount. Office floors should be covered with nonslippery material; adequate lighting should be provided; desks and chairs should be free of sharp edges.

*3. Promote First-aid Service.* Insistence upon first-aid treatment for minor injuries means little if adequate facilities are not available. When these facilities are provided, managers show that they wish all injured employees to receive treatment promptly.

*4. Make Safety Clothing Available.* The use of special clothing designed to protect employees from injuries should also be included. Plastic aprons, for example, should be available to employees working around large quantities of ink, glue, and cleaning solutions.

*5. Maintain Good Housekeeping Practices.* The habits of orderliness and cleanliness contribute to good office safety because they help to set good examples for employees and to keep the office personnel safety-

FIGURE 32–5. Portion of a Form Designed to Assist in Determining Safety Hazards.

OFFICE SAFETY INSPECTION DATA

Carefully inspect the office, and for each question, check whether a hazard exists. If "Yes," briefly note the important details.

| QUESTION | DOES HAZARD EXIST? | | COMMENTS (GIVE LOCATION AND DETAILS.) |
|---|---|---|---|
| | Yes | No | |
| 1. Are aisles obstructed?................... | | | |
| 2. Do pencil sharpeners project over desk or table?........................................ | | | |
| 3. Are file drawers kept closed when not in use?.............................. | | | |
| 4. Are machines properly guarded?......... | | | |
| 5. Are glass desk tops broken?............. | | | |
| 6. Are there any sharp metal projections on any equipment?...................... | | | |
| 7. Is electrical wiring concealed?........... | | | |
| 8. Are office accessories insecurely placed?.. | | | |
| 9. Are papers and waste properly disposed of?.......................... | | | |
| 10. Are facilities for smokers adequate....... | | | |
| 11. Are materials stacked on desks or cabinets?................................ | | | |
| 12. Are extension cords used extensively?.... | | | |
| 13. Are floors too highly polished?........... | | | |
| 14. Is carpeting loose or worn?.............. | | | |

minded. Stairways should be kept clear of all loose subjects; aisles should be marked for traffic lanes; an adequate number of wastepaper baskets should be furnished; and regular cleanup service should be provided.

## OFFICE SAFETY RECORDS

Adequate records should be kept of all accidents. It is important to know what accidents happened, where, when, the types of injuries incurred, and the conditions which caused them. By studying such data, a manager is able to take intelligent corrective action and knows where to stress safety efforts.

There are two widely used and accepted indexes in safety statistics: (1) the frequency rate and (2) the severity rate. The former measures the occurrences of accidents; the latter measures the seriousness of accidents. The frequency rate is calculated by the formula:

$$\text{Frequency rate} = \frac{\text{Number of disabling injuries} \times 1,000,000}{\text{Total number of man-hours worked}}$$

Disabling injuries include death, permanent total disability, permanent partial disability, and temporary total disability (the injured is unable to return to his job within 24 hours after the start of the shift during which he was injured). The formula for calculating the severity rate is:

$$\text{Severity rate} = \frac{\text{Time charged (in days)} \times 1{,}000{,}000}{\text{Total number of man-hours worked}}$$

The time charged for an accident is taken from a table of values to indicate differentials among various types of accidents. For example, an accident resulting in death or in permanent disability is charged at the rate of 6,000 days for each case.

## OFFICE SAFETY PERSONNEL

Department heads are the key personnel in office accident prevention work. In many respects, the success of the entire safety program depends upon the supervisors. It is promoted by the cooperation of the department heads, and they can do more than anyone else toward keeping the employees safety-minded. Furthermore, supervisors can correct unsafe conditions, they can see that safety rules are followed, that first aid is provided in case of accident, and that proper reports are filled out.

Usually there is a recognized head of safety work. He may be a member of the personnel department or head a separate department, which includes safety work in the factory and office. The safety director may not spend all his time in safety, but generally he devotes a certain amount of time regularly to the program.

The use of a safety committee with rotating membership is recommended. A five-member committee, with membership rotating bimonthly, usually works out very well. The system of replacements should be such that not more than two new members are added at any one time, thus insuring that the remaining three members are familiar with the work of the committee. The work of this group is advisory. It submits suggestions for the reduction of accidents within the office. Frequently, the safety committee may also:

1. Sponsor accident prevention contests.
2. Review safety suggestions made by the employees.
3. Make regular safety inspections of the office.
4. Suggest additions and changes in safety rules.
5. Post safety materials on the bulletin boards.
6. Maintain the first-aid equipment.

## PROMOTING SAFETY CONSCIOUSNESS

The mental attitude of the employee toward safety is exceedingly important in accident prevention work. There is a great deal of truth in the saying: "The best safety device in all the world is located an inch or two above the eyebrows." The employee who "thinks safety" and who has developed a safety consciousness "from the ears up" has gone a long way toward preventing accidents.

All efforts designed to keep safety on the employee's mind and to keep accident prevention a live subject in the office will help substantially in the safety program. Although it may seem strange, it is a common occurrence for people to be careless. Safety-mindedness requires alert-mindedness. Safety work is a continuous process, requiring constant reminders to the employee to work safely, to avoid taking chances, and to keep safety foremost in his thoughts. The task is not an easy one, but persistence and steadfastness of purpose will achieve good results.

Safety rules should be explained, and the reasons for their rigid enforcement given to the employees. The entire safety program can be seriously handicapped if there is any letdown in either the education or the enforcement of safety rules. Quite often, having the rules in writing is helpful.

Also, employees should be informed of safety fundamentals. This can take various forms, including articles in company papers, talks at meetings, informal suggestions to employees, movies, and safety instruction cards. This latter medium provides the employee with pertinent suggestions about safety and serves as a series of timely reminders, helping to keep safety on the minds of the employees. Figure 32–6 shows several examples of safety instruction cards.

Pictures, posters, and cartoon sketches can also be used to arouse the employee's interest in safety. It is usually best to have this material specific in nature, telling the employee what to do under particular conditions. Giving the employee general safety cautions and slogans is probably of limited value. It is usually well to supplement this type of safety promotion with intensive individual follow-up. The bulletin boards used should be located in areas that are frequently seen, accessible, and in full view.

Lastly, safety contests are helpful. They stress the competitive spirit and usually rely upon the employee's desire to excel. An award in the form of a plaque, banner, special pin, or money may be given the individual, group, or department having the best safety record for a given period. A reversal of this technique can also be used, and it is generally effective. In this case, a booby prize is given the unit having the poorest safety record, with the requirement that this "award" be displayed promi-

FIGURE 32–6. Safety Instruction Cards.

## Butter side down . . .

*Cheerful thought for the day: Every year enough people to populate a city the size of Gloucester, Mass., are killed by falls. NOT TO MENTION INJURIES BY THE MILLIONS...*

Minor, serious, even fatal injuries are caused in offices by . . .

. . . falls from chairs and boxes

. . . falls from ladders

...f a l l s d o w n-s t a i r s, a n d e v e n upstairs

. . . falls over phone and lamp cords

. . . falls over desk drawers left open

. . . falls from tripping or sliding on things which don't belong on the floor

And of course no lady will, and no gentle-man should, lean way back in an office chair.

SAFETY INSTRUCTION CARD **No. 807**

National Safety Council     PRINTED IN U S A.

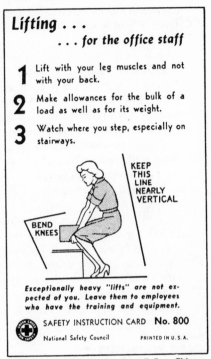

## Lifting . . .
### . . . for the office staff

**1** Lift with your leg muscles and not with your back.

**2** Make allowances for the bulk of a load as well as for its weight.

**3** Watch where you step, especially on stairways.

KEEP THIS LINE NEARLY VERTICAL

BEND KNEES

*Exceptionally heavy "lifts" are not ex-pected of you. Leave them to employees who have the training and equipment.*

SAFETY INSTRUCTION CARD **No. 800**

National Safety Council     PRINTED IN U. S. A.

*Courtesy: National Safety Council, Inc., Chicago*

nently. This approach appeals to the employee's pride and to his desire to escape any designation which makes him look ridiculous. Like all promo-tional plans, safety contests must be publicized and made acceptable to the employees.

## QUESTIONS

1. What are some key considerations a manager should keep in mind when giving instructions and orders?
2. As an office manager, outline the general policies and handling of absenteeism that you would follow. Justify your views.
3. Indicate what medium of communication you would recommend for each of the following, along with your reasons for its use:
   a) Announcing that the company has just puchased another company, the office work of which will be merged into the office of the purchasing com-pany.
   b) Giving employees the data on the company's contribution to the employees' pension fund for the year just ending.
   c) Advising the discontinuance of operations at Plant C in Big Ridge, Michigan.

4. Discuss the advantages and the disadvantages of the use of participation by employees and by management members in practicing management.
5. Draft a performance appraisal chart that to you seems satisfactory for a "systems analyst." Justify your recommended chart.
6. As you see it, what are the five most important considerations in administering a performance appraisal program? Why?
7. Do you favor the use of periodic self-appraisals by employees? Why?
8. Six months ago, Company XYZ established a suggestion system, which unfortunately has proved to be very ineffective. You are asked to investigate the system and make recommendations for improvements. Describe your approach and what you would do to fulfill this assignment.
9. What is the meaning of each of the following:
   *a*) Two-way communication.
   *b*) Group insurance plans.
   *c*) Severity rate.
   *d*) Psychological causes of accidents.
10. Describe what in your opinion the general content of the interview should be that is held during the time the employee's appraisal is discussed with him.
11. Explain the meaning of the statement: "Perhaps the key factor in any office safety program is to develop safety consciousness among all employees."
12. Assume you have just been appointed safety head in an office employing 150 people. What steps would you take to initiate an effective safety program?

## CASE PROBLEMS

### Case 32–1. Morse and Marx, Inc.

Wanda Hutchinson requested a transfer to another department "to get out of the duplicating department" where she has been employed for the last three years. In talking with the company's director of personnel, Miss Hutchinson stated that she would never get above the job level she was now on because the duplicating department seemed to be a graveyard insofar as advancement was concerned. She indicated that her supervisor, Natalie Walker, appraises her work and she has received small salary increases every six months, the same as all the other employees in the department. Miss Hutchinson added that all are given increases. The girls exchange salary information among themselves. There is a performance appraisal ritual, but it seems to be simply a justification for the pay increase.

The director of personnel assured Miss Hutchinson she was probably doing satisfactory work and the company was recognizing her work accomplishments. However, he promised to investigate the situation further with Mrs. Walker. Subsequently, during an interview, Mrs. Walker stated that Wanda Hutchinson was an average worker and did not appear to offer any outstanding value to the company. She was somewhat careless about her personal appearance and suggestions for improvement had brought little change. Wanda was given wage increases because her performance appraisal justified it. Further, help was difficult to get and while Wanda had shortcomings she did come to work regularly and provided a willing pair of hands.

It was well known by the director of personnel that the vice president of finance of the company favored elimination of the present performance appraisal efforts. He suggested replacing it with individual work goals for each employee. How well the accomplishment of this individual work goal was achieved, would determine the employee's rating. In his opinion, the current appraisal program is a source of needless disputes and misunderstandings. The director of personnel encounters differences of opinion about the present performance appraisal, but he doesn't believe it is a major problem. Under the present program, the factors being used include (1) value to the company—future potential developmental power, (2) initiative and adaptability—thinking constructively and ability to meet changing conditions, (3) personal appearance—cleanliness and neatness, and (4) attendance—amount of excessive absenteeism and tardiness.

The supervisor appraises each of his employees once every six months. The appraisal is discussed with the employee. All appraisals are then turned over to the director of personnel where they are reviewed and the recommended action is noted and, if possible, implemented.

## Questions:

1. Is there a problem here? Justify your viewpoint.
2. What further action would you take as Miss Hutchinson? Mrs. Walker?
3. What recommendations to the company management do you feel are in order? Why?

### Case 32–2. Lanthier Company

One of the biggest events for employees of Lanthier Company, located in a small town in Pennsylvania, is the company's annual picnic. The food is lavish, many contests are scheduled, and good music is furnished by a local band. Traditionally, the local government sets aside a picturesque portion of the local park for the picnic.

The managers of the company have decided unanimously to eliminate the picnic entirely. Influencing the decision is that the affair gets out of hand. Last year, several outsiders crashed the picnic and made nuisances of themselves. Heated debates and bad feelings develop from the athletic contests and subsequently seem to appear in the various work areas. One outsider who competed in one of the sponsored ball games, broke his thumb while attempting to steal second base. Efforts to collect medical expense and for loss of working time by this injured person are pending with the company. Also, a number of complaints about unequal distribution of the free food at the picnic caused further ill feelings.

Announcement of the picnic termination was received with disappointment. Spokesmen for the employees stated the decision was a mistake and should be reconsidered. The picnic has become a traditional event anticipated and enjoyed by the employees. Nothing can replace it. If any changes are made they should be better planning and controlling of the picnic.

The managers pointed out that the picnic was really a gratuity of the company and was granted at the discretion of the management. Contrary to expectations for

768     *Office management and control*

better understanding and relationships, the picnic appeared to give rise to unnecessary difficulties. Further, the company did not want to be exposed to legal liability arising from the annual picnic.

## Questions:

1. Do you feel the managers of Lanthier Company took the proper action? Why?
2. What alternatives were open to the company?
3. What recommendations would you make to the company's management? Why?

## Case 32–3. Bellows Company

Not much attention was paid to office safety by the office manager because, in his opinion, there were too many more important things demanding his time. True, there have been very few serious accidents in the office of Bellows Company during the past several years. However, three days ago, an employee in the filing department pulled out the top drawer of a five-drawer file and before she realized it, the entire file cabinet tipped and fell on her. She suffered an arm injury in trying to prevent the file from falling and a broken ankle when her foot was caught under the file. She required hospitalization and latest word is that she will be away from work for at least three weeks.

The office manager deeply regretted this accident happening in his office. He believed some safety measures probably were in order so he wrote a personal letter to each office employee, explaining that an accident had occurred, the company's strong desire to maintain a safe office, and each office employee's responsibility to exercise care to avoid possible accidents in the future. In addition, he urged each office supervisor to cooperate fully in helping to keep the office a safe place in which to work. He also posted several notices on the office bulletin board suggesting, "Be careful. Office accidents do happen. Do not take chances. Help avoid serious injury to yourself." For the most part, these efforts were well received, but some of the employees argued that the office manager was splurging and wanted to look pious in light of the accident that occurred in the filing department.

Yesterday, a fire started in the duplicating division of the company's office. Two employees suffered minor burns in extinguishing the flame, and some damage was done to a desk and to carpeting. An investigation revealed that the cause was carelessness on the part of an employee, who had placed a lighted cigarette on the edge of his desk. The lighted cigarette had fallen into a wastebasket filled with papers, and the fire had started.

## Questions:

1. What are your reactions to the handling of the situation by the office manager after the accident in the filing department? Explain.
2. What action do you recommend that the office manager now take? Why?

# chapter 33

# Office salary administration

The optimist proclaims that we live in the best of all possible worlds; and the pessimist fears this is true.
— *James Branch Cabell*

COMPENSATION is another important area of actuating. Man does not work for money alone, but for what he can do with the money he receives. Indirectly money satisfies many of his wants. His need for food and shelter, for example, can be satisfied if he has the money to purchase them. And possession of wealth is commonly associated with status and influence. Monetary reward for accomplishing work is therefore a fundamental consideration in actuating and helps get work accomplished that otherwise might not be accomplished.

## ADMINISTRATION OF COMPENSATION

There are a myriad of influences affecting office salary administration. At any given time some factors are tending to push salaries up while others are having the directly opposite effect. And these respective forces are of varying degrees. The subject of compensating can become quite complicated. To simplify our discussion, we will identify three considerations which are normally of major significance in the office area. These include (1) salary surveys, (2) salary differentials, and (3) salary patterns.

Salary surveys are conducted to find out what enterprises are paying so that you can keep your salaries competitive and in line. Great care must be taken to make certain that valid comparisons are being made. As pointed out previously, one of the greatest sources of error involves identical job titles, with wide differences in job content. Likewise, what is actually being produced may differ. For example, in company A an accounting machine operator may be paid $95 a week and perform 20 transactions an hour whereas in company B an accounting machine operator is paid $95 a week and performs 16 transactions an hour. Is a comparison between the two $95-a-week salaries truly meaningful? Salary surveys are helpful but not conclusive. Frequently they are performed by a trade association, a professional society, an organization of manufacturers, or similar enterprises. Each participating company receives a copy of the results, which are coded to mask the sources.

Salary differentials exist and are justifiable because job requirements differ. Work that requires higher knowledge and skill normally commands a higher salary than work requiring lower knowledge and skill. That salary differentials should exist is generally accepted; the real question is, "What differential is fair and just?" In addition, wage differentials exist between different geographical areas. Office salaries in San Francisco, for example, are higher than those in Memphis. Furthermore, office salaries for the same type of office work can vary within San Francisco. A typist for an import-export firm may receive less salary than a typist in a San Francisco bank.

Salary patterns tend to be formulated by the leading enterprise or enterprises in an area and in many instances these patterns are adopted by other enterprises in the area. This follow-the-leader practice can be extremely rigid or somewhat flexible, in which case the leader enterprise can have an influence, but its policies and practices may not be adopted in totality. Leader or pilot enterprises, however usually in some degree affect salary administration actions and constitute an influence with which to reckon.

## APPROACHES USED

The guideline method of determining compensation is one of the newer techniques and is winning favor as a realistic and fairly simple approach. Job evaluation, or some adaptation of it, is used by many information managers to provide proper wage differentials among office salaries and to be competitive salarywise. Also, most office salary administration programs include consideration of how well the incumbent is doing the particular job, regard for the amount paid for "fringe benefits," and recognition of certain social and economic influences. Each of these will be discussed. We will start with the guideline method.

## THE GUIDELINE METHOD

A combination of direct job pricing, ranking, and grading techniques features the guideline method. It emphasizes and reflects the relative job prices as interpreted by the labor market. In the final analysis the pice of the position on the market is considered the ruling factor. Job rates change due to the forces of supply and demand and a realistic wage administration must take this into account.

To implement, a guideline wage scale of salary ranges or grades is constructed. This serves as a common scale for all positions to be evaluated. A minimum, midpoint, and maximum are established for each salary

FIGURE 33–1. A Salary Scale for Use with the Guideline Method of Salary Administration.

| Salary Grade | Minimum | Midpoint | Maximum |
|---|---|---|---|
| 1 | $ 3,550 | $ 4,200 | $ 4,850 |
| 2 | 4,050 | 4,800 | 5,550 |
| 3 | 4,600 | 5,500 | 6,400 |
| 4 | 5,250 | 6,400 | 7,550 |
| 5 | 6,150 | 7,600 | 9,050 |
| 6 | 7,450 | 9,300 | 11,150 |
| 7 | 8,800 | 11,800 | 14,800 |
| 8 | 10,800 | 15,400 | 20,000 |

grade. Usually this begins with a number of key jobs which are the universal positions easily identified in the marketplace through salary surveys. In essence, this illustrates the direct pricing feature of the method. A relatively large number of these key jobs increase the accuracy of the salary scale. Their selection and comparison are basic to the overall success of the guideline.

Figure 33–1 shows the data for eight salary grades. Usually a spread of about 30 to 35 percent exists in the lower grades, and increases gradually to about 60 to 65 percent in the higher grades. As indicated in Figure 33–1, the spread for grade 1 is $3,550 to $4,850, or 15 percent on either side of the midpoint value of $4,200. In contrast, the spread for grade 8 is $10,800 to $20,000, or 30 percent on either side of the midpoint value of $15,400. In addition, the differential between midpoints of each successive pair of grades increases as the higher grades are reached. Further, a "salary price" can exist in two or more grades thereby giving needed flexibility. For example, $5,400 can exist in grades 2, 3, and 4.

After data for the key jobs and the guideline scale are established, the evaluation process takes place. The average salary for each key job is matched with the nearest midpoint on the scale. From this can be seen the relationship among key jobs as guided by the salaries being paid in the external market. To this are added and compared the salaries being paid by the company for key jobs that are similar in makeup. If inequities appear within the internal salary schedule, the manager can study such cases and decide which ones, if any, should be adjusted. Likewise, the remaining jobs for which no similar outside comparability exists are evaluated using a ranking or comparing technique, based on the evaluator's judgment and using as a guide the key jobs or other jobs that have already been assigned grades. The finished array of jobs is carefully reviewed both from the entirety viewpoint and from that of salaries for jobs within a department or other organizational unit. Inequities existing can be corrected as a result of this study.

The guideline method gives basic advantages. First, it is inclusive and eliminates the need to have several salary structures to satisfy geographical differentials. And it is objective. Data are based on facts as revealed by what is being paid for different jobs in the marketplace. Not only spotting the inequity, but doing something about it is emphasized by the guideline method. Further, the maintainence cost is low—expensive individual evaluations are kept at a minimum. The entire method is quite simple.

## JOB EVALUATION

The concept of the job and its relative worth are considered in job evaluating, which can be formally defined as follows: *Job evaluation is the determination of the relative value of each individual job in an enterprise and is arrived at by means of a systematic procedure using jobs or selected job factors for comparison or measurement.* There are four main methods of carrying out job evaluation work, including (1) ranking, (2) classification, (3) factor comparison, and (4) point.

**1. Ranking Method.** The jobs within an enterprise can be arranged according to their relative difficulty. A ranking of the jobs is thus obtained; and in this manner, the relative importance of each one is established. The job at the top of the list has the highest value, and the job at the bottom of the list has the lowest value. The usual procedure is (1) to rank the jobs in an individual department and (2) to combine all departmental rankings into one composite ranking.

Figure 33–2 illustrates the results which might be obtained from this method. For example, the job of accounting clerk I was considered of greater value than the job of purchasing clerk, while the job of office boy was ranked lowest in the office. If the weekly salary of the top job is set at $145 and that of the lowest job at $70, then the rank order of the

FIGURE 33–2. Array of Jobs according to Ranking Method.

| Rank Number | Name of Job | Earnings per Week* |
|---|---|---|
| 1 | Accounting clerk I | $145 |
| 2 | Purchasing clerk | 140 |
| 3 | Traffic clerk I | 135 |
| 4 | Cashier | 130 |
| 5 | Accounting clerk II | 125 |
| 6 | Traffic clerk II | 120 |
| 7 | Cost clerk | 115 |
| 8 | Tabulating-machine operator | 110 |
| 9 | General bookkeeper | 105 |
| 10 | Correspondent | 100 |
| 11 | Stenographer | 95 |
| 12 | Switchboard operator | 90 |
| 13 | Typist I | 85 |
| 14 | File clerk | 80 |
| 15 | Typist II | 75 |
| 16 | Office boy | 70 |

\* In uniform variation from top to bottom.

intermediate jobs, assuming a straight-line or uniform variation, is shown in the last column in the illustration.

**2. Classification Method.** Under this method, a predetermined number of job classes or groups are established, and the jobs are assigned to these classifications. For example, the job classes, from highest to lowest, might include:

Class A.  Executive
    Office manager
    Office departmental supervisor
Class B.  Skilled
    Purchasing clerk
    Traffic clerk
    Cashier
Class C.  Limited skilled
    Tabulating-machine operator
    Stenographer
    Switchboard operator
Class D.  Unskilled
    File clerk
    Office boy

In this method, the jobs within each grade frequently must be graded further to show more adequately the existing relationships. To do this, the ranking method, previously described, can be employed.

**3. Factor Comparison Method.** Jobs can also be evaluated according to predetermined factors which have been established as a measure of ranking. Customarily, a key-job comparison scale is established and used for this purpose. Job factors are listed across the top and the dollars per week or salary-rating schedule in the left column. The scale provides the means for applying *salary rates* to job relatives as needed.

Assume four job factors: education, experience, responsibility, and working conditions. On each of these factors, each key job is ranked. Generally, eight to ten jobs are considered key jobs, selected on the basis of the jobs requiring widely different amounts of the job factors being utilized. To illustrate, for the accounting clerk I job, the rating values given for each of the job factors might be:

| | |
|---|---:|
| Education | $ 43.00 |
| Experience | 35.00 |
| Responsibility | 53.00 |
| Working conditions | 14.00 |
| Total | $145.00 |

In other words, from the key-job comparison scale, it is possible to determine what portion of the present salary of a job is being paid for each factor.

This scale is the measuring device for evaluating all other jobs in the company. Other jobs are fitted into this scale, with the key-job evaluations being used as guides. To illustrate, consider the job of tabulating-machine operator. The evaluator would first read the job analysis sheet for this job. Then, concentrating his attention on the factor of education, he judges where under the education column the job of tabulating-machine operator seems to fit. He might decide that this job requires a little more education than a certain key job but less than another key job. Hence, he would evaluate tabulating-machine operator between the two considered key jobs. In similar manner, the job is evaluated according to the other job factors, and the other jobs in the company are evaluated in a similar manner.

**4. Point Method.** In this method, job factors are selected, and each is assigned a maximum number of points or credits. The selection of job factors is qualified by the following: that each job factor (1) exists in all the jobs to be evaluated, (2) varies in amount in the different jobs to be evaluated, and (3) is mutually exclusive of other job factors. The maximum point value assigned to each factor is determined by its relative importance. This is governed primarily by the judgment and experience of the analyst. Normally, from eight to fourteen factors are used. Those most common include skill, experience, education, responsibilities, working conditions, effort, and supervisory requirements.

Each selected job factor is defined in clear and simple language. The degree or intensity of each selected factor is broken down, and points are

FIGURE 33–3. Illustrating the Different Levels of Responsibility for Loss and the Number of Points Assigned to Each Level.

| 4. Responsibility for Loss | | |
|---|---|---|
| Level | LEVEL DEFINITION | Points |
| A | Nature of work involves negligible opportunity for loss. Normal or reasonable care required and all work is verified or proved by repeating entire operation. | 3 |
| B | Nature of work is such that more than normal or reasonable care is required to prevent loss. However, work is checked by proving against totals or some standard rather than by repetition of operation. | 15 |
| C | Nature of work involves moderate but constant opportunity for error, limited only by daily or subsequent spot check or examination. Great care should be exercised to prevent loss. Potential serious loss from errors in transcription or computation. | 27 |
| D | Good judgment must be exercised regularly to prevent loss. Work is of such nature that complete and correct performance is hard to control, reliance being placed on the individual. Work subject to general supervision and occasional review. | 38 |
| E | Work of such a nature that commitments are made which may involve the entire bank. Work is frequently released without any check being made or is checked only by individual doing the work. A high degree of financial responsibility is involved. | 50 |

*Courtesy: J. D. Moore Organization, Ann Arbor, Mich.*

assigned for each level of the factor. Figure 33–3 shows these data for the factor "responsibility for loss," which has been given five levels, *A* through *E*, ranging in value from a low of 3 to a maximum of 50 points. Figure 33–4 illustrates 11 job factors selected for use in the evaluation of clerical and supervisory jobs. In this case, the data showing the level and the points of rating, along with pertinent comments for the job of junior accountant, are indicated for each factor. Note that under factor 4, responsibility for loss, the rating level of *B* is valued at 15 points, which was arrived at by referring to the guide shown by Figure 33–3.

FIGURE 33–4. Job Factors, Ratings, and Comments for the Job of Junior Accountant.

CODE ........................................................................................ SALARY GRADE ........ VI ........................

JOB TITLE ......... JUNIOR ACCOUNTANT .........................................................................

## CLERICAL AND SUPERVISORY EVALUATION

| | NO. | FACTOR | RATING LEVEL | PTS. | JOB REQUIREMENT |
|---|---|---|---|---|---|
| SKILL | 1 | Essential Knowledge | D | 84 | Requires a knowledge of advanced accounting methods and procedures and a working knowledge of company financial policies. |
| | 2 | Experience and Training | G | 73 | Normally requires 3 to 5 years' training and experience, including 2 years' accounting training plus 3 years' company experience as an Accounting Clerk. |
| | 3 | Analytical Requirements | C | 27 | Requires analysis of figures and data which vary in content but follow general patterns of application |
| RESPONSIBILITY | 4 | Responsibility For Loss | B | 15 | Requires more than normal care to prevent loss due to miscalculations. However, work is usually checked against totals. |
| | 5 | Confidential Information | B | 6 | Involves preparation and use of limited confidential matters in the Accounting Department. |
| | 6 | Contacts Public and Internal | B | 28 | Involves routine contacts with persons where detailed subject matter must be presented satisfactorily. |
| | 7 | Individual Initiative | B | 12 | Involves initiative in planning details of own work. |
| EFFORT | 8 | Mental Effort | C | 15 | Requires moderate mental effort to solve problems of accounting. |
| | 9 | Physical Effort | A | 6 | Involves light physical effort with intermittent standing and sitting at comfortable intervals. |
| | 10 | Work Conditions | A | 0 | Working conditions are excellent. |
| | 11 | Supervisory Requirements | FX | 18 | Involves immediate leadership over Accounting Clerks and Typists. |
| | | | | | |
| | | TOTAL POINTS | | 284 | |

*Courtesy: J. D. Moore Organization, Ann Arbor, Mich.*

## PRICING THE JOB

The ultimate aim of job evaluation is to determine the job price or rate of pay. Jobs of high evaluation should command high rates of pay; in general, the higher the evaluation, the higher the pay. The immediate problem is to determine what the rate of pay should be when the evaluation is a known amount. The job prices to be established must be consistent (1) externally (rates within the enterprise are in line with the rates paid outside the enterprise) and (2) internally (rates within the enterprise are directly associated within the evaluations).

External consistency is accomplished by securing the current wage rates in the area from salary surveys conducted by enterprises specializing in this type of work or from local governmental offices. Sometimes, to supplement available information, a thorough salary survey must be made. It is also well to remember that accurate job descriptions and productivity data add greatly to the usefulness of salary survey results.

Internal consistency is determined by comparing the job evaluations with the rates paid. In some cases, this can be done by a simple comparison of columnar data. Very often, however, a graphic representation helps to visualize this comparison, especially when the point system of evalua-

FIGURE 33–5. Scatter Diagram Showing Relationship between Wage Rates and Evaluation Measurements.

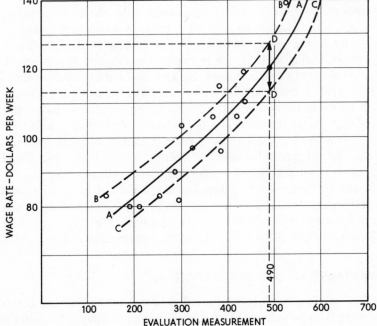

tion has been used. Commonly employed is a chart or scatter diagram in which existent wage rates are plotted on the vertical axis and evaluations on the horizontal axis. A curve showing consistent relationships between rates and evaluations can then be drawn on the chart. The deviations of actual rates from this curve can readily be spotted, and jobs overpaid or underpaid with respect to their evaluation can be quickly observed.

Figure 33-5 (p. 777) shows by diagram the relationship between wage rates and evaluations. The plotted points are indicated by the small circles. Curve *AA* has been drawn in and represents what is considered to be a consistent relationship between rates and evaluations. Curves *BB* and *CC* have been drawn in for reasons discussed in the paragraphs that follow.

## JOB PRICE RANGE

From a practical viewpoint, the office manager is interested in more than a job price for each job. What he really wants is (1) *a price range for each job,* not a single price for each job; and (2) *a price range to cover a group of jobs,* not just one job. A price range provides flexibility and makes for a better salary plan. Furthermore, when a group of jobs are within one price range, the entire task of wage determination is simplified.

Referring again to Figure 33-5, a wage range has been indicated by the two curves *BB* and *CC* drawn on the chart. Observe that in the figure the vertical spread between these two curves is a *constant amount.* Some advocate that a *constant percentage* change from the center line be used to establish the outside large lines, a practice which makes the spread greater for higher priced jobs since the percentage is of a larger amount. The job of traffic clerk II, for example, evaluated at 490 points, has a range from $113 to $127 per week, indicated by ordinate *DD* on the chart.

To provide a group of jobs within one price range, it is customary to group jobs into classes so that all jobs in the same class have the same price range. In other words, jobs of the same worth are put into the same class. The number of job classes depends primarily upon the total number of jobs, and the spread between the highest and the lowest job. Usually, a total of six to ten job classes is sufficient in most offices.

As already discussed, the classification method of job evaluation automatically puts the jobs into various classes. On the other hand, when any of the other methods of job evaluation are used, the alignment of jobs is arbitrarily divided into different numbers and levels or classes.

## ADVANTAGES OF JOB EVALUATION

Office salary administration is aided by job evaluation because it (1) shows the relative value of office jobs within a company, (2) assists in the evaluating of new office jobs, (3) helps obtain a satisfactory wage level for all office jobs within the company, (4) helps to eliminate salary inequalities by putting office jobs having similar requirements in the same salary range, and (5) affords factual data for the settling of salary disputes. It is imperative, however, that the work of determining job content, grades, and price ranges be kept up to date by regular, periodic checkups. The content of many jobs changes in the normal course of events; and this, in turn, frequently changes the relative values of the jobs. Likewise, changes in the general wage levels appear to be the usual rather than the exceptional happenings.

## HOW WELL THE INCUMBENT IS DOING HIS JOB

Up to this point we have confined our discussion to what the job price range is or, in other words, what salary range is paid for its performance. We will now consider an equally important concept in office salary administration, namely, how well the incumbent is doing his job. For this purpose, performance appraisal, discussed in chapter 32, is commonly used. In some programs, performance appraisal tempered with seniority is followed. The justification for this approach is that the employee who has been on the job for a long period tends to perform the work better or at least knows more about how it should be performed. This viewpoint, however, is open to question, but in offices where it is followed, it is usually popular and brings quite satisfactory results.

Bonus arrangements are employed by some companies to demonstrate approval of satisfactory office work accomplishments. Usually the payments of bonuses commemorate special occasions, such as Christmas, a birthday, or an employment anniversary. These payments commonly amount to sizable sums—perhaps an extra month's pay or, in some cases, as much as 20 percent of a year's salary. They are given to share the results of profitable operations, to recognize outstanding service, to continue a traditional custom, or to improve employee morale.

Financial incentive plans are another means of recognizing how well the incumbent is doing. These plans provide for total compensation based to some extent on the amount of work accomplished instead of strictly on the basis of time spent at work. Generally speaking, financial incentive plans are not common in offices, but their use is growing. The more common incentive office work includes transcribing, card punching, order processing, and billing.

## FUNDAMENTALS OF OFFICE INCENTIVE PLANS

There are two fundamental concepts in practically all office incentive plans: (1) a base or standard amount of work output and (2) the amount of wage payment which will be given for production below standard, at standard, or above standard. The first concept, the base amount of work output, can be determined by any of the work measurement, time-use techniques discussed in chapter 20. Customarily, this standard amount of work is expressed as 100 percent. The amount of work which is established as standard is extremely important, for it is commonly, but not always, the point at which the incentive pay begins. The second concept, or pattern of the amount of wage payment, varies with the incentive plan. Most plans guarantee base rates up to standard; a few do not. Some divide the excess above standard equally between employee and employer, while others share the overflow according to various percentages.

The same general type of plan can be used for a group as for a single employee. The group can be used when the nature of the work is such that its segregation among individual employees is very difficult or costly. The group incentive pay is figured first, then divided among the members according to either the individual base wage rates, the number of hours worked by each member, the individual gross base pay, or on some other agreed basis.

Incentive wage plans should be tailor-made to suit the particular work and to achieve the particular objectives desired from the plan. The following guides are helpful:

1. Incentive plans should have the backing of the top managers.

2. The best incentive plan is usually the simple plan. It should be thoroughly understood by all concerned.

3. There should be a close relationship between reward (incentive pay) and results (contribution).

4. An incentive based on the individual employee is generally better than one based on a group.

5. The work output should increase as well as the amount of salaries.

6. The base or standard production amounts should be carefully determined—preferably by measured time analyses.

7. The number of temporary standards should be held to a minimum. When standards are temporary, this fact should be known to all concerned.

8. The incentive wage should be neither guaranteed nor limited. In most instances, the base wage should be guaranteed.

9. The standards should be reviewed for possible revision whenever any change is made in the material, machine, or method used.

10. If indirect production employees, such as messenger boys, receptionists, and telephone operators, are included in the plan, they should be affiliated on some measurable basis, such as the maintenance of an acceptable ratio between the total indirect man-hours to the total direct man-hours, or the total indirect man-hours to total work output. This tends to keep the indirect man-hours under control.

## FRINGE BENEFITS

Another major area of modern office salary administration is fringe benefits. These include (1) legally required benefits—social security, unemployment, workmen's compensation requirements, (2) pay *away* from the job—paid leaves, vacations, and holidays, (3) pay *on* the job for time off—employee meetings, overtime pay, and shift premium pay, and (4) special benefits—service awards, meal allowances, relocation expenses, and tuition aid. Various estimates point to an average of about 34 percent of total base payroll costs constituting expense for fringe benefits. The trend in the amount of fringe benefits has been steadily upward during the last decade and wage experts predict fringe benefits will continue to increase.

Many office employees give considerable weight to the fringe benefits included in a job. The dollar "take home" pay is adjusted in view of the fringe benefits received; and it is common to find an office employee preferring to work for a particular concern where the dollar salaries are average or even low, but the numerous fringe benefits provided make for an attractive total remuneration.

A big need in the fringe benefits area is for employers to explain and publicize their benefit programs. Too frequently complicated mathematical formulas and legal phraseology are communicated in response to simple employee questions. As a rule, employees want simple answers, not problems. They want to know their benefit position. What is available to an employee and his dependents if and when an emergency arises is what he wants to know. The wise office manager tells him in language that he can understand.

## SOCIAL AND ECONOMIC INFLUENCES

Last of the major areas of office salary administration discussed here is social and economic influences. A number of factors could be discussed under this heading, but the discussion here will be limited to (1) career influence and (2) the supply of and demand for office jobs. Career influence is made up of what an employee is looking forward to when he accepts a job and the influence of this ambition on his work. The pay for a job may be too low, in terms of what the job requires; but because of career influence, the employee willingly forgoes the higher and appropriate pay in order to get ultimately to a job he wants. The case of a young law graduate in a law office illustrates this point. On the other hand, the career influence may cause a job to be rated too highly by the employee, based on the actual job requirements. The job might be of the dead-end type and offer no usable training or advancement beyond a well-known level. In this case, sufficient salary must be paid to secure and hold the proper type of employee.

Salary rates are affected by the condition of supply and demand. Some of these economic factors are highly dynamic; they change within short periods of time and exert a "push and pull" effect on salary rates. As a matter of practical consideration, recognition must be given to significant changes in the supply and demand for employees of specific skills. As stated earlier, direct recognition of current price levels of jobs is a feature of the guideline method. From the practical point of view, current conditions may make it necessary to start a new employee at a figure higher than the stipulated starting wage. In some instances, the figure may be outside the applicable job range. This state of affairs may be temporary, but if it persists, it is well to revalue the job and possibly change its classification, thus giving reality to the salary administrative plan. This does not mean that established salary ranges should be ignored, but that it is normal to find some deviation for some jobs. Also the need for adjusting all job ranges, up or down, may be required. All these modifications stem from the influence of supply and demand for employees of specific office skills; such changes can neither be ignored nor eliminated.

**Questions:**

1. Would you say that job evaluation is scientific in its determination of the value of a job? Why?
2. As an office manager, would you favor the use of bonus payments as a part of your salary administration program? Justify your viewpoint.
3. Which method of job evaluation do you consider the simplest? The most accurate? The easiest for employees to understand? Substantiate your answers.
4. Discuss (a) what is meant by the guideline method in salary administration, and (b) how this method is employed.
5. Would you say that the current conditions of supply and demand upon salary rates are taken into account by the job evaluation method of salary determination? Justify your viewpoint.
6. Explain Figure 33–5 in your own words.
7. In your opinion should an information manager rank compensation as a very important medium for actuating, an average medium, or a very poor medium? Give reasons for your answer.
8. Define each of the following:
   a) Salary differentials.
   b) Job evaluation.
   c) Factor comparison method.
   d) Price range for a group of jobs.
9. Discuss the importance you feel the office employee places upon fringe benefits. Justify your viewpoint.

10. For an office employing 750 employees, can the wage rates be externally, but not internally, consistent? Internally, but not externally, consistent? Elaborate upon your answers.
11. What steps do you feel might be taken to make an office employee more aware of the fringe benefits he is receiving?
12. Do you believe we should have more or less office incentive plans in American industries? Why? Is your answer from the viewpoint of a manger or a nonmanager? Does the viewpoint make any difference?

## CASE PROBLEMS

### Case 33–1. Starr Products Company

Orville Drake, information manager, is trying to hire a qualified person for an opening of cost accountant B. He has been seeking such a person for nearly two weeks. To date, the only apparently qualified applicant, Mr. Lee Gillis, wants $10,000 a year. He says he will not accept a job for less. His credentials are satisfactory, his background is good, and during an interview, he impressed Mr. Drake as being desirable to add to the accounting group. Mr. Gillis expressed a desire to join Starr Products Company.

There are currently eight employees in the accounting department including the chief accountant, three general accountants, a cost accountant A, two cost accountants B, and a tax expert. The filling of the present opening for a cost accountant B will make a total of three accountants of that classification. The present salary range for cost accountant B is $675 to $775 a month. Periodically, Mr. Drake checks the company's salary ranges with those paid by other companies in the general area. His last study, conducted six weeks ago, showed his company's salary rates for office jobs are in line with others in the area. The salary range for cost accountant A is $725 to $850 a month. In Mr. Drake's opinion candidate Gillis is not qualified for the A classification of cost accountant job.

Questions:

1. Name the major alternatives available to Mr. Drake.
2. What action should Mr. Drake take? Why?
3. Discuss the implications of this problem upon the office salary structure of the company.

### Case 33–2. Forsythe Company

Arthur Kadell was being paid $625 a month. He joined the company three and one-half years ago, was promoted to his present job on which he has received two pay increases. Due to the installation of a computer and changes in work content, Arthur Kadell's job will no longer be necessary. His supervisor told him not to worry, that he would be transferred to another job. Meanwhile, he will continue on his present job for approximately the next two months while the changeover is being made.

Some seven weeks later, Mr. Kadell is informed that he will be transferred to another department and job which will pay him $540 a month, and he will retain his full seniority and company benefits. Mr. Kadell protests, claiming he should continue to receive his present rate of pay. He reasons that the company offer gives him a cut in pay through no fault of his own; he has a good work record with the company, and prior to now, nothing has been said about his having to take less pay. He adds, "Had I known this, I would have started looking outside for something else the minute I found out my job was to be eliminated."

## Questions:

1. What further action do you feel Arthur Kadell should take? Why?
2. What should the company do? Why?

# INDEXES·

# Index to cases

# Subject index

Computers—*Cont.*
  digital, 214–15, 222
  displacement versus replacement of man-
    power by, 204
  employment problems avoided by, 196
  error reduction function, 196
  factory use of, 195
  feasibility of automation, 205–6
  first generation, 222, 248
  FORTRAN, 225
  fourth generation, 248–49
  future in uses of, 277–78
  glossary of terms, 219, 222–23; *see also
    specific term*
  hardware, 215, 222, 252
  hybrid digital-analog, 214–15
  illustrations of uses of, 194–95
  importance of, 194
  information interchange, 236–37
  information retrieval and storage, 312
  information supplying function, 195
  input data media, 227
  input unit, 239–40
  integrated circuitry, 248
  integration with company operations,
    201–3
  judgment of, 225
  language of, 226–27
  location of, 202
  machine readers, 229–30
  magnetic ink characters, 237–38
  magnetic tape, 235–36
    ledger record, 236–37
  managerial aspects of, 194 ff
  manpower displacement by, problem of,
    203
  mass memory hardware, 207
  Math-Matic, 225
  memory unit, 239–40, 241–43
  microscopic monolithic integrated cir-
    cuits, 248–49
  multiplication process, 219
  numerical codes, 232
  octal notation, 232
  office management and, 194 ff
  office use of, 194–95
  on-line, 206
  on-line real-time, 206
  organization for use of, 202–3, 582–89
    centralization of, 589–92
  output data media, 227
  output unit, 239–40
  page readers, 228–30
  perforated paper tapes, 234
  permutation code, 236
  physical office requirements for, 208
  planning activities as affected by, 199–
    201

Computers—*Cont.*
  preprogrammed packages, 225
  printed material on paper, 228–30
  problem solving uses of, 195
  processing unit, 239–40, 243–44
  program, 219, 224–25
  program flow chart, 216–18, 220
  program interrupt, 207
  programming, 215, 219, 224–25
  punched cards used in, 232, 234
  punched holes, code for, 233
  random access, 206, 223
  reading machine for, 228–30
  real-time process scheduling, 206–7
  reasons for use of, 195–96
  reduction of monotonous tasks by, 204–5
  responsibility of managers as affected by,
    198
  room space for, 434
  routine jobs, elimination of, 194–95
  savings effected by, 196
  second generation, 223, 248
  significance of, 194
  size, shrinking of, 248
  social aspects of, 204–5
  software, 215, 223, 252
  speed, increase of, 248
  storage units, 239–40, 241–43
  stored programs, 225
  strategic areas, use in, 250
  suggestions for users of, 208–9
  system design, 216–18
  system of, 214, 239
  technical considerations, 214 ff
  technological aspects of, 214 ff
  terms used in connection with, 207, 219,
    222–23; *see also specific term*
  third generation, 223, 248
  throughput, 207, 240
  training requirements, 205
  transistors, 248
  transmission of data into, 228–30
  trend toward greater usage of, 154
  typewritten material on paper, 228–30
  types of, 214–15
  Unicode, 225
  vacuum tubes, 248
Conceptualizing work to be done, 23 ff
Conference of American Small Business Organizations, 10
Conference call service, 295
Conference room
  colors for, 455
  layout of, 439–40
Conferences, 735–36
Confucius, 418
Console controlling unit, 239–40, 244–45
Contact copying, 372–73

Job evaluation; *see* Salary administration
Job Instruction (JI), 717
Job Methods (JM), 717
Job Relations (JR), 717
Job rotation, 735, 737
Job specialization, 600–601
Job statement; *see* Job description
Job titles; *see* Job description
John Hancock Center in Chicago, 392–93
Judgment myth, 490

## L

Labor contracts
  characteristics of, 696–97
  layoffs, 697
  penalty clauses, 697
  seniority, 697
  status of union, 697
  three interested parties in, 701
  union recognition clause, 696
  wage rates, 697
Labor Management Relations Act of 1947, 698, 700–701
  checks on unions, 699–700
  outlawing of closed and preferential shops, 697 n
  strike controls, 699
  unfair labor practices, 698–99
Labor relations
  arbitration, 701
  conciliation, 701
  goals of manager and union, 701
  mediation, 701
  office trade unions, 695
Labor unions; *see* Unions
Landrum-Griffin Act of 1959, 698
Landscaping of office space, 425–27
Laser beams, 253
Lateral files, 324–26
Layout; *see* Office space planning
Leadership
  defined, 692
  motivational force, 691
Leases
  data communication facilities, 253
  defined, 402
  information machines, 152
  office location, 401–2
  private telephone lines, 297
Lectures, 735, 737
Left- and right-hand work simplification charts, 85–91
  symbols for, 88
Letters; *see also* Reports
  automatic typing machines, 136–38
  business, 121
  coordination among personnel in writing of, 132–33
  cost analysis of, 131

Letters—*Cont.*
  designing of, 124–25
  dictating machines, use of, 139–40
  duplication process for production of, 138–39
  effective short memorandum, 123
  essential elements for writing of, 124
  firm-but-fair approach, 124–25
  form, 123–24
  form paragraphs, 123–24
  format of, 121
  function of, 120
  guide furnished by company, 133–34
  importance of, 120
  management of, 130–34
  meaningful writing of, 124
  office manual, use of, 134
  persuasive approach, 125
  reply at bottom type, 131, 371
  sell approach, 124
  speed, 121–23
  standards to measure quantity and quality of, 133
  types of, 120–24
  typewriting of, 135–36
  well-planned printed form to expedite written information transmission, 122
  window type, 138–39
  writing of; *see* Writing
Levinson, Harry, 597
Library, 222
Lighting, 446–53, 457
  adequacy of, 447
  advantages of, 447
  amount of, 448
  basic designs of system of, 452–53
  brightness of, 448–49
  color in relationship to, 457
  concepts of, 448–50
  design of systems of, 452–53
  diffusion of, 448–50
  direct, 452
  expenditures for, 450–51
  filament bulbs, 451
  fixtures for, arrangement of, 453
  floating-panel luminaires, 453
  fluorescent bulbs, 451
  general, 451
  general diffuse, 452
  glare, 450
  indirect, 452
  investment in, 450–51
  maintenance of, 451
  natural bulbs, 451
  office building, 395, 399
  quantity of, 448
  recommended values of, 448
  semi-direct, 452

Punched-card machines—*Cont.*
  gang punch, 167
  importance of, 163
  interpreter, 167
  multiplying punch, 167–68
  optical scanning punch, 168
  printing from punched cards, 167
  punching machine, 165
  reproducer, 167
  samples of work prepared by, 169
  significance of, 163
  sorter, 165–66
  special types, 167–68
  tabulator, 165, 169
  uses made of, 163, 165, 168–69
    key considerations in, 169
  verifier, 167–68
Punched cards; *see also* Punched-card machines
  computer use of, 232, 234
  source data automation, 180–81
Punching machine, 165–66

## Q

Quality control
  approaches to, 513–17
  decision regarding, 513–14
  implementing program of, 512
  improper, results of, 512
  100 per cent inspection method, 513–14
    shortcuts in, 514
  problem of, 511–12
  program to follow, 512
  review of present systems and procedures, 512–13
  sample checking, 513, 515
  spot checking, 513, 515
  statistical methods, 513, 515–18
  tally sheet for recording errors, 513
Quantitative measurement approach, 17–18
Quantity control
  availability of knowledge and information, 520
  backlog of work, 525
  centralization in organization, 523
  constructive nature of, 520–21
  coordination of efforts, 520
  cycling, use of, 523–24
  dispatching, 525–26, 529–32
  efforts of, 520–21
  evaluation of, 521
  flying squadron units, 522
  importance of, 519
  means employed in, 521–32
  mobile units, 522
  nature of, 519–20
  objectives of, 520
  orderly work flow, 525–32
  overtime work, 522

Quantity control—*Cont.*
  part-time help, employment of, 521–22
  routing, 525–26
  scheduling, 525–29
  service bureaus, use of, 521–23
  standards, use of, 521
Questionnaires; *see* Charts *and* Checklists

## R

Radio-telephone service, 296
Ramp metering, 269–70
Random access, 206, 223, 251
Reading data, 11, 13
Reading machines, 228–30
Real time computation, 223
Real-time output, 223
Real-time process scheduling, 206–7
Reception room
  colors for, 455
  space, 439
Receptionist, function of, 439
Reciprocating files, 324, 326–27
Recording data, 11, 13
Records; *see also* Forms
  active use, 354
  data, synonymous with, 4
  defined, 99–100
  disposition of, 355
  elimination of, 354
  function of, 99
  inventory of, 355–56
  life cycle of, 354
  life of, 356–58
  safety, 762–63
  storage of, 354; *see also* Records retention
  survey of, 355–56
Records management, 25, 311 ff; *see also* Copying; Storing and retrieving information; *and* Supplies
Records retention
  active and inactive materials, 361–62
  advantages of, 354–55
  defined, 354
  entire-unit transfers, 361
  fiberboard drawer storage, 358
  helpful records, 357
  important records, 357–58
  indexing system, 358
  individual method of transfer, 361
  nonessential records, 357
  objective of, 355
  periods for, determination of, 356–58
  program of, 360
  storage area for, 358–59
  transfer records, 359–62
  types of records for, 356–57
  vital records, 358

Scheduling—*Cont.*
common practice in, 526
defined, 526
folders, 526–27
means of, 526–29
operation cards, 528–29
quantity control through, 525–26
short-interval, 527
time insert cards, 528
visible index cards, 527–29
Scientific approach, 15, 17
SDA (source data automation), 178
Second generation computers, 223, 248
Secondary colors, 456
Segregating data, 11 n
Semi-direct lighting, 452
Semi-indirect lighting, 452
Sequencing, 223
Serial arrangement of work, for organizing, 601–4
Service bureaus
functions served by, 523
nature of, 522–23
part-time help obtained through, 521–22
services offered by, 523
use of services of, 521–23
Service staff authority, 632–34
Severity rate of accidents, 762–63
Shelton, Fred E., Jr., 540
Shingle-strip accounting, 114
Silence and sell, use as actuating practice, 750
Simplicity
defined, 659
effectiveness in organization, 659–60
Simplification of work; *see* Work simplification
Single print accounting machine, 157
Site; *see* Office location
Software of computers, 215, 223, 252
Sohl, William I., 420 n
Sorter machine, 165–66
Sorting data, 11, 13
Sorting machines, 379
Sound conditioning, 446, 459–61
acoustic treatment, 461
characteristics of sound, 460
noise, effects of, 459–60
Source data automation (SDA)
advantage of, 180
analyses required for, 182
analysis of pertinent information, 184
applications of, 183–84
common language link, 180–81
common language media, 180–81
concept of, 178
modification of, 179
cost considerations, 183
definition of, 178–79

Source data automation—*Cont.*
director to head activity in, 183–84
distinguishing features of, 182–83
economic considerations, 183
edge-punched card, 180, 182
effectiveness of, 183
evolution of, 179–80
flexibility of, 182–83
flexowriter automatic writing machine, 182, 185
gathering of pertinent information, 184
guides in application of, 184
installation of, 184
inventory control, use in, 185
machine-oriented, 182
manufacturing applications of, 187–91
Numerical Control (NC), 188–91
office illustrations of, 184–87
original data, 182
perforated tape, 180–81
program for, 183–84
public utility bills, 187
punched cards, 180–81
recommendations, making of, 184
review of areas for study, 183
Source Record Punch, 187–89
symbolic control, 188–91
systems-oriented, 182
target dates, establishment of, 184
top management approval, 183
turn-around documents, 187
types of machines available for, 179
U.S. Steel Corporation introduction of, 179
Source Record Punch, 187–89
Space; *see* Office space
Space planning; *see* Office space planning
Space satellites, 253
Span of authority, 626–28
Special reports, 125–26
Speed letters, 121–23
SQC (Statistical quality control), 513, 515
Staff authority, 631–34
advisory, 632–33
control, 634
functional, 633
service, 633–34
Standard costs, 544
Standard sized envelopes, 285
Standard time data, 495, 499–500
Standards
accepted rule or regulation, 480
Administrative Management Society, 483
advantages of, 482–83
American Standards Association, Inc., 483–84
associated, 481
change in, reasons for, 480
conditions, 479

*This book has been set in 10½ point Old Style
#7, leaded 1½ points, and 9 point Old Style #7,
leaded 2 points. Part numbers and titles and
chapter numbers and titles are in Helvetica and
Helvetica Bold. The size of the type page is 27
by 45½ picas.*